The Prose Literature
of the Gaelic Revival,
1881–1921

The Prose Literature of the Gaelic Revival, 1881–1921

Ideology and Innovation

Philip O'Leary

The Pennsylvania State University Press
University Park, Pennsylvania

This publication was assisted by a grant from the Trustees of Boston College.

Library of Congress Cataloging-in-Publication Data

O'Leary, Philip, 1948–
    The prose literature of the Gaelic revival, 1881–1921 : ideology and innovation / Philip O'Leary.

        p.   cm.
    Includes bibliographical references and index.
    ISBN 0-271-01063-0 (cloth : alk. paper)—ISBN
0-271-02596-4 (paper : alk. paper)
        1. Irish prose literature—20th century—History and criticism.
        2. Irish prose literature—19th century—History and criticism.
        3. Ireland—History—Autonomy and independence movements.
        4. Ireland—Civilization—20th century.   5. Ireland
    —Civilization—19th century.   6. Nationalism—Ireland—History.
        7. Ireland—Historiography.   8. Ireland in literature.
        9. Civilization, Celtic.   I. Title.
    PB1336.043   1994
    828'.808099415—dc20   92-47013
                                                                 CIP

Published by The Pennsylvania State University Press,
Barbara Building, Suite C, University Park, PA 16802-1003

It is the policy of The Pennsylvania State University Press to use acid-free paper for the first printing of all clothbound books. Publications on uncoated stock satisfy the minimum requirements of American National Standard for Information Sciences—Permanence of Paper for Printed Library Materials, ANSI Z39.48–1984.

For my parents

Contents

Acknowledgments

In the many years spent on this project, I have incurred debts of gratitude on both sides of the Atlantic. In Ireland, I would like to single out for thanks Brian Ó Cuív and Proinsias Mac Cana of the Dublin Institute for Advanced Studies; Margaret Kelleher of the Mater Dei Institute (and Boston College); Seán Ó Coileáin and Cornelius Buttimer of the Department of Modern Irish, University College Cork; Gearóid Denvir and Nollaig Mac Congáil of the Department of Modern Irish and Gearóid Ó Tuathaigh of the Department of History, University College Galway. In addition I must offer heartfelt gratitude to the staff of the National Library of Ireland for their unfailing professionalism and courtesy.

In the United States, I would first like to thank my colleagues in the Irish Studies Program at Boston College, especially Adele Dalsimer, and also Charles Dunn, John Koch, John Carey, and most especially John V. Kelleher of the Department of Celtic Languages and Literatures at Harvard University as well as the regular participants in Harvard's Celtic seminars and annual Celtic colloquium. Of this group I must single out Kenneth Nilsen and William Mahon for special thanks. In addition, Daniel Reddy offered invaluable computer assistance. On a more personal note, my parents have provided a lifetime of support, and Joyce Flynn's contributions have been too varied and valuable to even try to acknowledge.

Introduction

Many of the leading writers of the Gaelic Revival never read a book in the Irish language in their formative years. Some had not even imagined that such a thing was possible. Looking back on the language movement and his own involvement in it, one of the most prolific pioneers of modern Gaelic prose, "Beirt Fhear" (Séamus Ó Dubhghaill) recalled: "I myself never laid eyes on a book in Irish until I was twenty years old [i.e., 1875]."[1] The fault was not his. Shán Ó Cuív provides a concise sketch of the cultural milieu that produced An tAthair Peadar Ua Laoghaire (Father Peter O'Leary), the man he pronounced "the greatest writer of Irish prose that has ever lived":

1. Séamus Ó Dubhghaill, "Gluaiseacht na Gaedhilge / A Tosach agus a Fás" (The Irish Language Movement / Its beginning and its growth), *Misneach*, 18 December 1920. "Níor leagas féin súil ar leabhar Gaedhilge go rabhas fiche bliadhain d'aois." Surveying the linguistic / literary situation of 1882, the year the bilingual journal *Irisleabhar na Gaedhilge / The Gaelic Journal* was founded, Tadhg Ó Donnchadha wrote in 1909: "If there were fifty people in all of Ireland at that time who could read and write Irish in the native script, I'd say that that would be the total number." (Má bhí leathchéad duine i nÉirinn go léir an uair sin go raibh léigheadh agus sgríobhadh na Gaedhilge aca sa chló ghaedhlach, déarfainn gurbh é an t-iomlán é.) See Ó Donnchadha, "Réamhrádh" (Preface), *Index to "Irisleabhar na Gaedhilge," 1882–1909*, vii.

The nineteenth century . . . was the blackest that the language
has ever known. Literary Irish in the nineteenth century probably touched the lowest level ever reached since the language was
first written. Up to the middle of the century Irish was spoken
by the majority of the population, but it was little cultivated as a
written language. There was certainly an oral literary culture,
the remnants of which survive to the present day, but of written
Irish, in either prose or verse, there was very little indeed. . . .
Thus, while books in other languages were being printed by the
million, Irish had to be content with a few hundred copies of a
few books.[2]

The causes of this literary destitution lie in the turbulent disjunctions
of Irish colonial history. A coherent cultural evolution had little chance
against the incessant and savage religious and ethnic warfare of the seventeenth century, the penal legislation of the eighteenth century that
attempted to degrade the Gaelic-speaking Roman Catholic Irish to illiterate penury, or the Famine and subsequent almost instinctive emigration of the nineteenth century that accelerated an already marked linguistic shift toward English.[3] Writing as a witness and victim of that
violence and oppression, the poet Dáibhidh Ó Bruadair (c. 1625–98)
lamented:

After the death of the poets, whose riches were poems
    and wit;
Woe unto him who hath seen the fate that hath come
    upon us;
Their books, now unheeded in corners, lie
    mouldering, covered with dust,

2. Shán Ó Cuív, "Canon O'Leary's Part in the Making of Irish Prose," *Weekly Freeman, National Press and Irish Agriculturist (WF)*, 7 December 1918. Máirtín Ó Cadhain was
in full agreement, writing, "There is not a period in the history of Ireland that I find
sadder and more shameful than the 19th century." (Níl tréimhse i stair na hÉireann is mó
is díol bróin agus náire liom ná an 19ú céad.) See Ó Cadhain, "Conradh na Gaeilge agus
an Litríocht" (The Gaelic League and literature), in *The Gaelic League Idea*, ed. Seán Ó
Tuama (Cork: Mercier, 1972), 52.
3. See Garret Fitzgerald, "Estimates for Baronies of Minimum Level of Irish-Speaking
amongst Successive Decenniel Cohorts: 1771–1781 to 1861–1871," *Proceedings of the Royal
Irish Academy* 84, C, 3 (1984); and Seán de Fréine, *The Great Silence* (Dublin: Foilseacháin
Náisiúnta Teoranta, 1965).

> While of their mystical treasures no whit is possessed
> by their sons.[4]

The impact of these social upheavals on Ó Bruadair and his fellow poets was chronicled in their own work, and has been discussed by many
scholars, most memorably Daniel Corkery in *The Hidden Ireland* (1925).
But while the immemorial Gaelic system of poetic patronage and the
extensive training and consequent intricate technical mastery it made
possible were irrevocably doomed after the fall of Limerick to Williamite forces in 1691, a simpler but still sophisticated lyric verse continued to be composed, recited, written, and sung in quantity right into
our own century by poets like Aodhagán Ó Rathaille (c. 1670–1726),
Eoghan Ruadh Ó Súilleabháin (1748–84), Brian Merriman (c. 1749–
1805), Antoine Ó Reachtabhra (Raftery) (c. 1748–1835), Tomás Ruadh
Ó Súilleabháin (c. 1795–1848), and Colm de Bhailís, who lived to see
his poems published by the Gaelic League in 1904 before dying in 1906
at the age of 110.

Prose, however, was a different story. Of oral folktales there was and
would remain an extraordinary wealth, but more extensive and sophisticated literary efforts demanded an educated readership, and the aristo-
crats and clerics who had provided such an audience since the time
when the Irish epic was the first vernacular prose literature in Europe
north of the Alps were at this time scattered across the Continent, while
their humbler compatriots could only maintain contact with the native
tradition through poetry, folklore, the odd manuscript, or the work of
the often itinerant teachers of the so-called hedge schools. Moreover, as
Cathal Ó hÁinle has stressed in his essay "An tÚrscéal nár Tháinig"
(The novel that didn't come), at precisely the time the new technology
of print was revolutionizing the prose literatures of other European languages, Irish was denied access to the press, except for a few devotional
works, grammars, and a dictionary, many the work of Franciscan exiles
in Louvain.[5]

This loss was compounded by the intriguing and promising developments in what Gaelic prose was being written in the seventeenth and

---

4. "D'Aithle na bhFileadh n-Uasal" (Gone Are All the Noble Poets), in *Duanaire
Dháibhidh Uí Bhruadair / The Poems of David Ó Bruadair*, ed. and trans. John C. Mac
Erlean, S.J. (London: Irish Texts Society, 1917), 3: 4–5. The translation here is that of
Mac Erlean. "D'aithle na bhfileadh dár ionnmhus éigsi is iul / is mairg do chonnairc an
chinneamhain d'éirigh dúinn / a leabhair ag tuitim i leimhe 's i léithe i gcúil / sag macaibh
na droinge gan siolla dá séadaibh rún."

5. See Cathal Ó hÁinle, "An tÚrscéal nár Tháinig," in *Promhadh Pinn* (Testing the
pen) (Má Nuad: An Sagart, 1978), 96.

eighteenth centuries. In particular, the kind of romantic tale popular in
late medieval Ireland was, as Maighréad Nic Philibín and Alan Bruford[6]
as well as Ó hÁinle have detailed, showing distinct signs of following
the general European pattern and thus may well have evolved into a
genuine Gaelic novel. Most important, while all of these tales remained
fabulous, there was some movement toward greater credibilty, if not
realism in any meaningful sense. In addition we find in works like
Tóruigheacht Gruaidhe Griansholus (The Pursuit of Gruaidh Griansholus)
and *Eachtra na gCuradh* (The adventure of the champions) that deal with
Cú Chulainn and the ancient heroes, a self-reflexive awareness of the
native literary tradition that could border on and even cross into burlesque of the romantic conventions, as it does in *Siabhradh Mhic na Mí-
ochomhairle* (The delusion of the son of ill-counsel). Moreover, several
of these works, notably *Eachtra Áodh Mhic Goireachtaidh* (The adventure
of Áodh Mac Goireachtaidh) and *Stair Éamuinn Uí Chléirigh* (The history of Éamonn Ó Cléirigh) show a keen awareness of contemporary
political, social, and linguistic realities, a characteristic they share with
the seventeenth-century *Pairlement Chloinne Tomáis* (The parliament of
Clan Thomas), a savagely unjust satirical picture of the foul habits and
treacheries of Irish agricultural "churls" and their benefactor, Oliver
Cromwell.[7] *Stair Éamuinn Uí Chléirigh*, written by Seaghán Ó Neachtain (1655–1729), is of special interest, since it was edited by an important Revival figure, Eoghan Ó Neachtain, and published in the period
covered by this study. Seaghán Ó Neachtain's story deals with the
theme of temperance, satirizes those Irish willing to exchange fluency in
their own language for broken English, and even, albeit briefly, introduces the city of Dublin—a hostile place!—into Gaelic literature.[8] It was

---

6. See Maighréad Nic Philibín, *Na Caisidigh agus a gCuid Filidheachta* (The Cassidys
and their poetry) (Baile Átha Cliath: Oifig an tSoláthair, 1938), esp. 14; and Alan
Bruford, *Gaelic Folktales and Medieval Romances* (Dublin: Folklore of Ireland Society,
1969).

7. The tale actually consists of two separate "books," written perhaps fifty years apart.
The tale's editor, N. J. A. Williams dates "Book I" to "the early years of the seventeenth
century, and probably no later than ca. 1615," and "Book II" to "some fifty or so years"
later. See *Pairlement Chloinne Tomáis*, ed. N. J. A. Williams (Dublin: Dublin Institute for
Advanced Studies, 1981), xxi and xxxv. For an idea of the tone of the satire, see pp. 46–7,
lines 1438–86 (English text, p. 102).

8. *Stair Éamuinn Uí Chléire do réir Sheáin Uí Neachtain* (The history of Éamonn Ó
Cléire according to Seán Ó Neachtain), ed. Eoghan Ó Neachtain (Baile Átha Cliath:
M. H. Mac an Ghuill agus a Mhac, 1918), 5–11, 30–31, 49–51. Excerpts from the work
appeared in *The United Irishman* (*UI*) as early as 16 and 30 August 1902. Although unat-
tributed, these could very well have been prepared by Eoghan Ó Neachtain as well.

to be a long time before this kind of innovative energy would be seen again in Gaelic prose.

That prose did not, of course, disappear altogether in the nineteenth century. As has been noted, oral composition continued to flourish, and there was an impressive amount of scribal activity, a clear notion of whose extent and nature, for a single county, can be gained from Breandán Ó Conchúir's nearly 400-page catalogue and discussion, *Scríobhaithe Chorcaí 1700–1850* (Cork scribes 1700–1850). Much of this work was relatively predictable and repetitive—there were, for example, any number of copies of Geoffrey Keating's seventeenth-century history of Ireland, *Forus Feasa ar Éirinn* (A survey of Irish history), as well as genealogies, devotional material, and collections of poetry—but there were also medical and grammatical texts, copies of earlier literary tales, and even translations.[9] Furthermore, as An tAthair Pádraig Ó Fiannachta has illustrated in "Litríocht an Lae (1800–1850)" (The literature of the day, 1800–1850), there was also a not insignificant output of original prose throughout the early and mid-nineteenth century. While the range of this material was rather narrow—much of it was ecclesiastical and the majority of that homiletic—there were as well short commentaries and scribal notes on manuscripts, the philosophical reflections of Aodh Mac Domhnaill, the diary of Amhlaoibh Ó Súilleabháin (Humphrey O'Sullivan), and some letters, like those written home from Utica, New York by the poet Pádraig Phiarais Condún.[10] In addition, there were the devotional works and translations of Archbishop MacHale that will be discussed below in Chapter 6.

Mention of the nationalist and native-speaking MacHale brings us to a consideration of movements for the preservation and revival of the Irish language as a spoken and literary medium. MacHale was not only the patron of Canon Ulick Bourke, a man whom one prominent contemporary called "the Father of the Irish Language Movement,"[11] but was also credited by An tAthair Peadar Ua Laoghaire with enlisting him in the cause when he criticized the young seminarian for ignoring

---

9. See Breandán Ó Conchúir, *Scríobhaithe Chorcaí, 1700–1850* (Baile Átha Cliath: An Clóchomhar, 1982), 233–45.

10. See Pádraig Ó Fiannachta, "Litríocht an Lae (1800–1850)," in *Léas ar Ár Litríocht* (Light on our literature) (Má Nuad: An Sagart, 1974), 102–16. See also M. A. G. Ó Tuathaigh, "An Chléir Chaitliceach, an Léann Dúchais agus an Cultúr in Éirinn, c. 1750–c. 1850" (The Catholic clergy, the native learning, and culture in Ireland, c. 1750–1850) in *Léann na Cléire* (The learning of the clergy), *Léachtaí Cholm Cille* 16 (1986): 110–39.

11. See Proinsias Ó Maolmhuaidh, *Uilleog de Búrca: Athair na hAthbheochana* (Ulick Bourke: The father of the revival) (Baile Átha Cliath: Foilseacháin Náisiúnta Teoranta, 1981), 11. The speaker was Michael Logan, editor of *An Gaodhal*.

his own country's literature in a prize-winning essay at Maynooth.[12] Of course, interest in the Irish language was not new with MacHale. The Ossianic fervor had, for example, inspired considerable curiosity about genuine Gaelic literature in the eighteenth century and led to the 1789 publication of Charlotte Brooke's *Reliques of Irish Poetry*, an event one scholar has said "marks the enfranchisement of the language from the bar which had so long rested upon it."[13] The motive for such interest was, however, almost entirely antiquarian, and remained so through the various "Celtic" societies of the nineteenth century, affecting even native speakers of the language. Peadar Ua Laoghaire wrote of the discouraging influence on his own young self of the implicit defeatism of scholars like Eugene O'Curry:

> If they were so certain, with Irish as alive as it was then, that it was dying and that, no matter how brilliant they were, they had no way to save it from death, what would they say were they alive at this time if they saw how Irish has gone from more than half the island! If they felt they had no way to check the decline at that time, what would they say to the person who imagined that anyone would be able to check the decline now![14]

Fortunately, not all had surrendered. Philip Baron and Richard d'Alton were two active revivalists before their time, Baron opening a short-lived Gaelic school in County Waterford and publishing an equally short-lived weekly journal, *Antient Ireland* in 1835; and d'Alton publishing the paper *An Fíor-Éirionach* in Tipperary in 1862.[15] MacHale himself promoted the use of Irish in the schools and churches of his diocese, and attempted through translation to provide modern reading matter in the language. He was assisted in this work by his secretary, the scholarly Canon Bourke, whose *Easy Lessons or Self-Instruction in*

12. See Peadar Ua Laoghaire, *Mo Sgéal Féin* (My own story) (Baile Átha Cliath: Brún agus Ó Nualláin, n.d.), 104–5.

13. E. W. Lynam, quoted by Ó hÁinle, "An tÚrscéal," in *Promhadh Pinn*, 96.

14. Ua Laoghaire, *Mo Sgéal Féin*, 102. "Má bhíodar súd chomh deimhnightheach, agus an Ghaeluinn chómh beó agus a bhí sí an uair sin, go raibh sí ag dul chun báis agus ná raibh aon bhreith acu féin, d'á fheabhas éirim aigne a bhí acu, ar í choimeád ó bhás, cad déarfaidís dá mbéidís beó an uair seo agus go bhfeicfidís conus mar atá an Ghaeluinn imthighthe a' breis agus leath an oileáin! Má thuigeadar súd ná raibh aon bhreith acu féin ar an meathalughadh do chosg an uair sin, cad déarfaidís leis an t-é a mheasfadh go mbéadh aon bhreith ag aoinne ar an meathalughadh do chosg anois!"

15. For a survey of the work of these men and their predecessors and successors in the language movement, see Desmond Ryan, *The Sword of Light, from the Four Masters to Douglas Hyde, 1636–1938* (London: A. Barker, 1939).

Irish was serialized in *The Nation* from 1858 to 1862 and published sep-
arately in 1863. Bourke was also a pioneer of Gaelic journalism, assisting James Ronayne with the publication of the *Keltic Journal and Educator* in the city of Manchester in 1868.[16] With the failure of this periodical
after only seven numbers, Bourke in 1870 founded the *Tuam News and
Western Advertiser*, whose "Gaelic Department" under the editorship of
John Glynn was the most important forum for new writing in Irish in
the 1870s.

With a weekly column in a provincial newspaper the main literary
voice of the language, one of the goals of the new Society for the Preservation of the Irish Language was more than ambitious. Among the
six objectives of the SPIL listed in a circular issued in 1877, the year
after its foundation, was "to encourage the production of a Modern
Irish Literature—original or translated." The circular continued: "in addition to the foregoing, the Society hopes to be in a position to publish
a Journal partly in the Irish tongue, for the cultivation of the language
and literature of Ireland."[17] The SPIL made a start with the edition and
publication of modern versions of stories like *Tóruigheacht Dhiarmada
agus Ghráinne* (The pursuit of Diarmaid and Gráinne), *Oidheadh
Chlainne Lir* (The death of the children of Lir), and *Macghníomhartha
Fhinn* (The boyhood deeds of Fionn), but the creation of a modern
magazine in Irish would have to wait until after the 1878 secession of
more activist members of the organization like Bourke, Thomas
O'Neill Russell, Douglas Hyde, and David Comyn, and their formation of the Gaelic Union (Aondacht na Gaedhilge).

In the meantime, in October 1881 the first true magazine devoted to
the modern Irish language was published on Pacific Avenue in
Brooklyn, New York, by Michael Logan, an emigrant from Milltown,
Co. Galway, who may well have been a pupil in one of MacHale's
schools.[18] The editorial policy of *An Gaodhal* (The Gael) was spelled out
on its masthead beginning with the issue for February 1882: "The Gael,
a Monthly Journal devoted to the Preservation and Cultivation of the
Irish Language and the Autonomy of the Irish Nation" (Leabhar-aithris
Miosamhail tabhartha chum an Teanga Ghaedhilge a chosnadh agus a

16. The contents of this journal are discussed in some detail by Ó Maolmhuaidh in
Uilleog de Búrca, 96–99.
17. See Máirín Ní Mhuiríosa, *Réamhchonraitheoirí: Nótaí ar Chuid de na Daoine a Bhí
Gníomhach i nGluaiseacht na Gaeilge idir 1876 agus 1893* (Pre-Leaguers: Notes on some of
the people who were active in the Irish Language Movement between 1876 and 1893)
(Baile Átha Cliath: Clódhanna Teóranta, 1968), 6.
18. See Fionnuala Uí Fhlannagáin, *Mícheál Ó Lócháin agus An Gaodhal* (Michael Logan
and An Gaodhal) (Baile Átha Cliath: An Clóchomhar, 1990), 11.

shaorthughadh, agus chum Fein–riaghla Cinidh na hEireann). As Fionnuala Uí Fhlannagáin notes in her recent monograph *Mícheál Ó Lócháin agus An Gaodhal* (Michael Logan and An Gaodhal), the significance of Logan's bilingual paper has been consistently undervalued if not ignored. *An Gaodhal* was not merely a pioneering venture; it also, as we shall see, regularly published material of genuine interest and importance throughout the entire period up to Logan's death in January 1899.

Still, it was hardly possible for a single man, operating in his spare time from his own house at his own expense, to spearhead a linguistic and literary revival some three thousand miles away. The Gaelic movement needed a Gaelic magazine in Ireland itself, and it got it with the publication of *Irisleabhar na Gaedhilge / The Gaelic Journal* under the editorship of David Comyn in November 1882. The *Irisleabhar*, which after initial irregularities ran as a monthly until 1909, was again bilingual, but it was a heftier and far more scholarly enterprise than *An Gaodhal*. For example, in its first edition it commenced serialization of Canon Bourke's Gaelic biography of MacHale and Father John O'Carroll's "Dramatic Scenes in Irish," and was later to publish folktales, literary texts, historical studies, original poetry, fiction, and drama, and articles on topics both academic and controversial. With both *An Gaodhal* and the *Irisleabhar* appearing regularly, Gaelic journalism had established a credible base, and soon the foundation by Hyde, Eoin Mac Néill, and others of the populist and popular Gaelic League (Connradh na Gaedhilge) in 1893 created a demand for a bilingual newspaper more accessible in focus (and price) than the *Irisleabhar*. The need was met by Bernard Doyle's *Fáinne an Lae* (The dawning of the day) in 1898 and by the league's own official organ, *An Claidheamh Soluis* (The sword of light) the following year.[19] Other Gaelic journals of varying interest and longevity were to follow and will be examined below. At about the same time, the league in 1897 founded its annual cultural festival, the Oireachtas, whose literary competitions would quickly attract entries from a growing number of aspiring Gaelic authors. To make these literary efforts available to the readership emerging from its own classes across the country, the league began to publish original creative work as well as educational booklets like Father O'Growney's *Simple Lessons in Irish* or its series of propaganda pamphlets in English. By 1899 the organization felt it necessary to coordinate these activities under the aegis of a Publications Committee, and by 1908 had established its own press, An Cló–Chumann (later Clódhanna Teoranta), to deal with the

---

19. *An Claidheamh Soluis* absorbed *Fáinne an Lae* in 1900. The league had already assumed responsibility for *Irisleabhar na Gaedhilge* in 1893.

growing number of circulars, pamphlets, and books of all kinds. Indeed, as early as 1900, less than two decades after *An Gaodhal* had first appeared in Brooklyn, *An Claidheamh Soluis* could boast:

> The Oireachtas has demonstrated two things. The first is that the national language movement has taken a firm grip on national public opinion. The second is that a living literature in the Irish language has again become not merely a possibility, but a reality—that in song, in speech, and in writing, the national tongue has once more asserted itself a power and a growing power in the land.[20]

It wasn't quite that easy. A literature suppressed and largely oral for two centuries could not simply be resumed by an act of patriotic will. There was a tradition to be restored and the process by which that restoration would be achieved was at the heart of the most important, acrimonious, and lengthy debate of our period, extending from the 1880s through the first decades of this century. The practical focus of this controversy was on whether the new prose of the Revival should attempt to pick up where the tradition had been ruptured in the seventeenth century or whether it should accept the fact of discontinuity and root itself in the spoken language as it had evolved for two hundred years. Proponents of the former position argued that it was foolish to start over from debased peasant dialects when the language had a magnificent literary history and eminently suitable prose models. This minority opinion was given forceful expression by one "Maelduin" in 1901:

> It is true that modern Irish is different from the Irish of the 10th century; but we have a standard of classic, modern Irish in the writings of nearly all the Irish authors of the 16th and 17th centuries which is about as perfect as could be desired. We have the works of Keating, O'Donnell, O'Malloy, Bedel, Dunleavy and a host of others, and some who lived later, and why should we not adhere to the standard they have given us?[21]

The vast majority of Gaelic scholars, and more important, writers, felt they had the answer to this question, as they committed themselves to the contemporary spoken language, "the speech of the people" (cai-

---

20. "The Oireachtas," editorial, *An Claidheamh Soluis* (*ACS*), 2 June 1900.
21. "Maelduin," "Are We To Have One Irish Language?" letter, *UI*, 6 July 1901.

nnt na ndaoine), on the principle advanced by Father Patrick Dinneen in
1911:

> Keating has been in the clay for almost 300 years—God's bless-
> ing on his soul. He was a fine writer, and it would be worth-
> while for students to study his language. But the grumblers
> abusing and reproaching contemporary writers because they
> don't imitate the old language and the old spelling in his
> books—God save us from the likes of them![22]

Ua Laoghaire was less restrained in his opinion of Keating:

> How I detest Keating's big words! I tell you, with all due respect
> to him Keating is a fraud. His Irish is *not* true Irish. It was not
> the living Irish of his time. A single particle of the true *raciness* of
> the language is not to be found in him.[23]

This informal alliance for *cainnt na ndaoine* took shape early. Logan, for
example, was a consistent advocate of the literary use of the spoken
language, writing in a review of the folk collection *Siamsa an Geimhre*
(Winter pastimes) in 1892: "What will give the book its greatest value in
the eyes of Irish Scholars is the stories are told in the living Irish tongue
as it is spoken in the field and by the fireside today in Connacht."[24]
Irisleabhar na Gaedhilge also advanced the cause of *cainnt na ndaoine*, especially after John Fleming succeeded Comyn as editor in 1884, and under
the subsequent direction of Father O'Growney (1892–94), Eoin Mac
Néill (1894–99) and their successors Seosamh Laoide (J. J. Lloyd)
(1899–1902) and Tadhg Ó Donnchadha (1902–9). *Fáinne an Lae*, where
Mac Néill was again Gaelic editor, followed suit, as did *An Claidheamh
Soluis* from its inception, and through several changes of title, under

---

22. Patrick Dinneen (Pádraig Ua Duinnín), "Saothrughadh na Teangan" (The cultivation of the language), *Guth na Bliadhna* 8, no. 4 (Autumn 1911): 388–89. "Tá an Céitin-
neach san úir le trí chéad bliadhain nach mór; beannacht Dé le n-a anam; budh mhaith an
scríobhnóir é agus b'fhiú do mhacaibh léighinn stuidéar do dhéanamh ar a chainnt. Acht
lucht an ghuairneáin ag bearradh agus ag imdheargadh scríobhnóiridhe an lae indiu toisc
ná deinid aithris ar an tseanchainnt agus ar an tseanlitriughadh atá ina leabhraibh. Go
saoraidh Dia sinn ar a leithéididhe!"
23. Peadar Ua Laoghaire, letter to Séamus Ó Dubhghaill, 31 January 1900, quoted by
Pádraig Ó Fiannachta in "Ag Cogarnaíl le Cara: An tAthair Peadar mar a Nochtann
Litreacha Áirithe dá Chuid Dúinn é" (Conspiring with a friend: An tAthair Peadar as he is
revealed to us in certain of his letters), *Irisleabhar Mhá Nuad* (*IMN*) (1991): 117. Emphasis
in original.
24. Michael Logan, "New Gaelic Books," *An Gaodhal* 9, no. 5 (November 1892): 224.

Mac Néill (1899–1901), Eoghan Ó Neachtain (1901–3), Patrick Pearse (1903–9), Seán Mac Giollarnáth (1909–17), and Piaras Béaslaí (1917–21). In addition, the Gaelic originals in the bilingual folk collections by Hyde that in their Hiberno-English dialect translations had such an effect on Yeats, Lady Gregory, and Synge, were all recorded as Hyde heard them told.

It was, however, in An tAthair Peadar Ua Laoghaire that *cainnt na ndaoine* found its most tireless and compelling champion. In essays and letters for more than two decades Ua Laoghaire led the fight against what he contemptuously dubbed " 'Noble' Irish" ("Gaedhluinn 'Uasal' "),[25] returning again and again to a single simple tenet: "It is not by any means possible to write proper Irish unless it is written in the way it exists in the mouths of the people who speak it."[26] Opposition on this point was quite simply unacceptable:

> Let the scholars say what they want, the speech of the people will triumph in the end. To build up a literature without laying its foundations on the actual living speech of the people is like building your house commencing at the chimney! It won't be easy to convince the Dublin people of that truth. But if they won't accept it, it will have to be forced on them as food is forced on turkeys. The food will do them good even if it is forced on them against their will.[27]

More important, however, than his logic was the prolific example of his own work, especially that of *Séadna*, the first major prose work of the Revival and one An tAthair Peadar himself boasted contained nothing but the purest and most authentic West Cork *cainnt na ndaoine*.[28]

25. Peadar Ua Laoghaire, "Gaedhluinn 'Uasal,' " *An Crann*, no. 4 (Feast of St. Adhamhnán, 1917): 3.

26. Peadar Ua Laoghaire, "Éist le Fuaim na h-Abhan a's Gheabhaidh Tú Breac" (Listen to the sound of the river and you will get a trout), in *Sgothbhualadh* (Light threshing) (Baile Átha Cliath: Brún agus Ó Nóláin, n.d.), 29. This piece was originally published in *The Leader*, 27 June 1903. "Ní féidir Gaeluinn cheart do sgrí' i n-aon chor mura sgrítear í sa chuma 'na bhfuil sí i mbeulaibh na ndaoine atá 'há labhairt."

27. Peadar Ua Laoghaire, letter to Séamus Ó Dubhghaill, 17 September 1900, quoted by Ó Fiannachta in "Ag Cogarnaíl le Cara," *IMN* (1991): 114. "Abradh na scoláirí a rogha rud, is í caint na ndaoine a bhéarfaidh bua sa deire. . . . Ba dheacair an fhírinne sin a chur ina luí ar mhuintir Bh'l'áth Cliath. Ach nuair ná glacfidís í caithfar í chur siar orthu mar a cuirtear an bia ar na turcaithe. Déanfaidh an bia maitheas dóibh bíodh gur dá n-ainneoin a curtar siar orthu é." The sentence "To build . . . chimney" is in English in the original.

28. Ua Laoghaire wrote to Mac Néill, then editor of *Irisleabhar na Gaedhilge* where

Expertly rendered colloquial speech like that of Ua Laoghaire and many of his followers and contemporaries could be assigned such a specific geographic provenance by those familiar with the dialects of the language. And therein lay a source of concern for many like Mac Néill who worried that instead of developing again into a genuinely national language, Irish might degenerate into a variety of increasingly distinct patois, each with its own literary proponents and masters. The long lack of written standardization had allowed the language to split into three major dialects in Munster, Connacht, and Ulster, each with a web of local variants. In the early years of the Revival a touchy pride characterized the writers of each dialect and even subdialect, so that contributions to the various journals were often specifically labeled according to province, county, or even townland of origin. For a while it looked as if the enormous prestige of Ua Laoghaire and the fact that so many of the early prose writers were also from Munster might make of his particular Irish a kind of unofficial standard. But the rise of talented writers in the other provinces soon rendered the question of Munster's linguistic expansionism moot, in the process establishing a thoroughgoing regionalism as the keynote of the new Gaelic literature. While as time went on regional loyalties even led to the creation of separate journals for each Irish-speaking province, the centralizing influence of the league, its Oireachtas, and its official publications did mean that even the most dedicated local chauvinist remained aware that his brand of Irish was only an offshoot of a single national language. Nonetheless, the provincial suspicions and jealousies originating in dialect variation remained unresolved and could and did flare up throughout our period.

Rooting a modern European literature in a rural language split into three distinct dialects and lacking a recent written tradition created other fundamental problems of authorial intention and audience. Put simply, the writers were coming forward; the readers weren't. Some of these issues were never properly addressed in our period. Writers usually wrote what they felt they should or could, often with the goal of providing the language with types of literature or even whole genres it had long if not always lacked. As sales figures from league records make clear, not much thought seems to have been given to who would read some of these works. For example, in the period from 1 March to

---

Séadna was being serialized: "There is not a single word in *Séadna* except for the word I heard from 'Peg' or from her mother or from my own mother. As I progress with the story, the speech comes to my memory." (Ní bhfuil focal air bith i "Séadhna" acht focal a chloiseas ó "Peg" nó ó n-a máthair, nó ó m' mháthair féin. Fébh mar théighim air aghaidh leis an sgeul tighean an chaint chun mo chuimhne.) See the Eoin Mac Néill papers, National Library of Ireland, MS. 10,879.

31 December 1908, while the first and most basic book of O'Growney's instructional series sold 5,645 copies, the more difficult fifth book sold but 90. Little pamphlets containing single simple folktales could sell as many as 4,206 copies, while a more scholarly anthology of folk material was bought by only 44 people. An original comic story set in the country attracted 3,106 buyers, while of four plays, the best-seller was bought by 145 and the worst by 13. A solitary reader bought the translation of a Greek hero tale from a German original.[29] As we shall see in Chapter 1, there was a general consensus at the time that Gaelic literature would be an enobling as well as nationalizing force, but little "market research" or even commonsense reflection seems to have been brought to bear on who might be enobled by reading it.

On the other hand, those best able to appreciate the polished use of the language, the rural native speakers, were overwhelmingly illiterate in Irish, a fact accepted without question or complaint by an tAthair Peadar in a letter to Séamus Ó Dubhghaill in 1900:

> You are perfectly right. It *is* easier to write Irish dialogue than *continuous* Irish prose. The reason is not far to seek. Irish has *lived* for the past two or three centuries, only in the people's mouths and in the utterances of the poets. . . . It is speech addressed by a *speaker* to a *listener*, not by a writer to the general public. A writer of Irish has really, as yet, *no general public to address himself to*.[30]

Paradoxically, however, the needs of this potential (and literal) audience were to some extent at least thought through, understood, and accepted by their neighbors of literary bent. As we shall see in Chapter 2, Gaeltacht writers like Ua Laoghaire, Pádraig Ó Siochfhradha ("An Seabhac"), and Séamus Ó Dubhghaill believed that the ideal "readership" for their work would be illiterate native speakers to whom it would be read aloud. Such an audience was, however, neither passive nor pre-

29. See "Liosta de leabhra a díoladh ó Mhárta 1adh, 1908—Nodlaig 31adh, 1908 do réir Mhuintir Mhac an Ghuill" (A list of books that were sold from 1 March 1908 to 31 December 1908 according to the Gill Company) in the Fionán Mac Coluim papers, National Library of Ireland, MS. 24,405. It is interesting to note that a book of translations from Latin to Irish by Tomás Ua Nualláin was turned down by the Publications Committee because of concern about its marketability. See the mimeographed report of the 20 April 1910 meeting of Coisde na gClobhann [sic] in the Fionán Mac Coluim papers, National Library of Ireland, MS. 24,405.

30. Peadar Ua Laoghaire, letter to Séamus Ó Dubhghaill, 31 January 1900, quoted by Ó Fiannachta in "Ag Cogarnaíl le Cara," *IMN* (1991): 117. Emphasis in original.

dictable, and as Pearse astutely pointed out, both empathy and tact
were essential for anyone who wished to reach it:

> The old Irish speakers like to hear Irish being read. Let "reading
> groups" be established in these places. But listen. The native
> speakers must be approached carefully. Some of them think that
> what they themselves have is without flaw or fault. If they hear
> the dialect of another province, they usually say that it is a cu-
> rious speech. . . . There are other native speakers, and they
> firmly believe that nothing wrong whatsoever is ever put in
> books, and that what they themselves have is rubbish.[31]

While many if not most Gaelic writers of the Revival never seem to
have paid more than lip service to the illiterate native speaker and while
the more sophisticated and aesthetically committed among them knew
that it would be a betrayal of their art as well as an absurdly artificial if
not downright condescending gesture to act the country storyteller, the
appeal of a linguistically competent audience was powerful enough to
attract even so urbane a revivalist as William P. Ryan, who in a 1903
review urged the reading aloud to country folk of a new historical adventure novel on the grounds that "book-shelves are all very well, but
firesides are alive."[32]

In reality a man like Ryan must, of course, have felt far more at
home among his bookshelves, the contents of which would have baffled and even scandalized the average native speaker. Indeed the central
ideological issue that will form the subject of this study hinges on just
what kind of books in Irish a Gael would welcome or tolerate on those
shelves. Often misleading, labels are perversely difficult to affix to individual revivalists, who quite simply will not stay put in predictable
ideological categories, but instead shift positions and alliances with
blithe disregard for the hobgoblins of foolish, sometimes it seems any,
consistency. Nevertheless, to facilitate discussion I have with some care
chosen the terms "nativist" and "progressive" to identify ideological
tendencies and stances. These terms are, however, with very few ex-

31. "Buidhne Léighte" (Reading groups), editorial, *ACS*, 12 December 1903. "Is maith
leis na sean-Ghaedhilgeóirí Gaedhilg chloisint dá léigheadh. Cuirtar 'buidhne léighte' ar
bun ins na háite seo. Acht cogar. Caithfar breith go bog ar na Gaedhilgeóirí. Ceapann
cuid aca go bhfuil a bhfuil aca féin gan bhéim gan locht. Má chloiseann siad canamhaint
chúige eile, is gnáthach leó a rádh gur aisteach an chainnt í sin. . . . Tá Gaedhilgeóirí eile
ann, agus creidid go daingean nach cuirtar rud ar domhan ins na leabhra acht an rud atá i
gceart, agus nach bhfuil aca féin acht dríodar."
32. "Irish Mountain Magic," review of *An Gioblachán* by Tomás Ó hAodha, *ACS*, 22
August 1903.

ceptions all but useless for the classification of people. Father Henebry may have been an almost unswerving nativist, and Pádraic Ó Conaire may have rarely failed to take the progressive line, but even they can surprise, and for the bulk of their colleagues personal labels are as often as not meaningless. Thus when I say that a particular person at a particular time on a particular issue is a "nativist" or a "progressive," I mean that he or she is expressing a nativist or progressive position on that issue at that time. And when I refer to more intellectually consistent revivalists like Henebry, Ó Conaire, or Pearse as "nativists" or "progressives," I only mean that their general tendency, however strong, is in that direction. Examples of their deviation from full orthodoxy should make this point and my practice clear.

What then constituted Gaelic nativism and progressivism? First of all, the terms are here used solely in the context of the issues discussed in this book. In no way are they meant to imply any allegiance to political, social, or economic philosophies or ideologies beyond that context. This caveat is doubtless most relevant with regard to the term "progressive." A person could espouse "progressive" views on individual issues within the Revival while remaining conservative and even reactionary on other questions. Such was the case, as we will see, with several clerical revivalists like An tAthair Peadar, Father Dinneen, and An tAthair Cathaoir Ó Braonáin. Similarly, a Gaelic nativist need by no means have been either a xenophobe or a strict traditionalist in his approach to other issues. The examples of Fathers Henebry and O'Reilly will be illustrative here. Still, with regard to the central questions of the Revival, the nativist position was essentialist and (pre)determinist, asserting that the answers had already been found in Ireland and had only to be rediscovered and properly understood in the light of the existing Gaelic tradition. Their focus was thus inward, *siar* in the dual sense of the Irish word, back to a real, imagined, or invented past where that tradition was most vibrant, and to the West, where it had maintained itself most tenaciously.[33] Gaelic progressivism, on the other hand, accepted the reality of cultural discontinuity and believed that the emergent Gaelic nation would have to literally move forward, advanc-

33. Edward Said's comments on anti-imperialist "nativism" are suggestive here: "It is the first principle of imperialism that there is a clear-cut and absolute hierarchical distinction between ruler and ruled. Nativism, alas, reinforces the distinction by revaluating the weaker or subservient partner. And it has often led to compelling but often demagogic assertions about a native past, history or actuality that seems to stand free not only of the colonizer but of worldly time itself." See Said, *Nationalism, Colonialism and Literature: Yeats and Decolonization* (Field Day Pamphlet 15) (Derry: Field Day Theatre Company, 1988), 14–15.

ing both toward the future and toward the wider world from which it had so long been artificially isolated by British colonialism. In the process, not only would that nation have to draw on and adapt elements from its own tradition, but would also have to assimilate from any appropriate source all that that tradition lacked. Even when nativist and progressive thinking seemed to converge, there could be profound differences of perspective and focus. For example, progressivism had a genuine interest in and willingness to learn from any culture in contemporary Europe and even farther afield. Nativism could also appeal to the Continent; but if so, what was being invoked was almost without fail a specifically and safely Roman Catholic historical past as a contrast to modern Protestant (or godless) England and Anglo–Ireland, a virtual reflex of traditional Irish political alliances with Catholic powers against the English crown.

The period to be covered in this study will extend from Logan's initial publication of *An Gaodhal* in 1881 to the Easter Rising of 1916, a watershed event that drew many of its leaders from the Gaelic movement and which left that movement irrevocably altered in its aftermath. Chapter 8 will trace developments in that post-Rising period, ending with the signing of the Anglo–Irish Treaty of December 1921. After the treaty, Irish interest was fixated on its ratification or rejection and the ensuing civil war. When the fighting ended in April 1923, an independent Irish state had come into existence, creating an entirely new situation for Gaelic literature. The basic approach throughout will be documentary. Like their far better known comrades in the independence movement or the Anglo–Irish literary "renaissance," the Gaelic revivalists were dealing with enormous issues at a time of rapid national resurgence. Working directly with and in a threatened national language to which others often appealed only for its emblematic or symbolic value, they at times experienced those issues closer to the bone than their counterparts in other causes. However, while mention of the Gaelic Revival is a commonplace in Irish cultural studies, little has been said in any detail about the questions that inspired, defined, troubled, and even split the language movement. There is no mystery here. Much of the most significant and fascinating source material for the period is not only in the Irish language, but lies in the files of old and not infrequently obscure Gaelic newspapers and periodicals, as well as in books, booklets, and pamphlets of very limited press runs and long out of print. Since there is little chance the average student of modern Irish literature or history, even should he or she know Irish, will ferret through all this material, I have quoted from it extensively, drawing on the widest possible range of sources and thus allowing both the original revivalists a fair hearing on their own terms and the modern scholar a chance to form his or her own opinions independent of my interpretive paraphrasing or summary. In addition, I have used the notes not only to give further references to important confirmatory or illustrative material, but also, in the interest of accuracy and simple justice, to allow dissenting voices from the period to have their say.

All citations from Irish originals in the text, except in a very few instances duly noted, are my own English translations, kept as literal as is feasible. The original Irish text is, however, always provided. Short Irish phrases are often incorporated in parentheses in the text itself; longer passages are in the notes. Since contemporary controversies over orthography were both important in themselves and often reflected dialect usages, I have, apart from silently emending obvious typographical errors and inserting an "h" in place of the Irish *ponc* or dot above a letter as indication of lenition, left all Irish passages as I found them. Where I have used and referred in the notes to texts reprinted in the standardized orthography, I have always gone back to check the original for the spelling used in quotations. With regard to Irish personal names, I have tried to balance accuracy and consistency, favoring the former. Once again, personal names are left in the form those who bore them seem to have preferred and have not been standardized. The anglicized form of names is given on first usage where writers regularly used both the Gaelic and Anglicized versions of their names, and in the case of those writers like Hyde, Pearse, Dinneen, and W. P. Ryan far better known under the Anglicized form, that is what is used throughout. On another point consistency was a bit harder to achieve. Pseudonyms have a long history in the Gaelic tradition, and the Oireachtas regulations requiring competitors to submit entries anonymously reinforced the custom. For some writers such pseudonyms were merely temporary expedients, while others assumed a succession of different names for different or unknown reasons. For still others, however, the nom de plume became a true persona, far more familiar than the given name. Indeed in some cases it is impossible to ascertain the identity behind the alias. Using the standard Gaelic reference works as well as my own research, I have identified many but by no means all of these pseudonyms. The given name of those using them will be provided when they are first mentioned, and thereafter will be the form used. In a few instances, however, where a pseudonym became universally accepted, it will frequently be used in alternation with the author's real name. And, since there were no fewer than three important writers in our period named Pádraig Ó Séaghdha, and since all three conveniently used pseudonyms, these will be availed of when there is any chance of confusion.

In general, translation of pseudonyms leads to absurdity and so will be avoided. Some place names will appear in the text in their Gaelic form, in particular those in the Gaeltacht (plural, Gaeltachtaí) or Irish-speaking area. Places of publication will be those given on title pages, so that one will find Baile Átha Cliath (Dublin), Corcaigh (Cork), Gaillimh (Galway), Má Nuad (Maynooth) and Cill Áirne (Killarney). Titles of books and journals will always be given in the original with English translation added at first occurrence.

A final question of nomenclature remains to be settled. Some people have told me that the term "Gael" sounds condescending. Nothing could be further from my intention. I do on occasion use "revivalist," but find it both too formal and curiously evocative of Burke and Hare. "Language enthusiast," on the other hand, is condescending. "Gaels" is what with pride they called themselves and thus seems most appropriate for regular use here. "Gaelic" is more problematic. I fully accept the prior claim of writing in Irish to the title "Irish literature," but to so use it for a more general audience could only cause confusion, and the circumlocution "literature written in Irish" soon becomes tiresome. Therefore, in the interest of clarity and concision, though with some discomfort, I have regularly referred to that literature here as "Gaelic."

1

The Nation's Tongue, the Nation's Soul

"In Communion with the Past of Our Race": Nativism

"I'd build a wall around Ireland! A wall thirty cubits high, the same as Tibet . . . a wall of brass around it. I wouldn't let in an idea. Not an idea, mind you—from the outside world." The speaker here is, startlingly, the aggressively cosmopolitan Pádraic Ó Conaire, and the wall he wished to erect was one of words, the words of the Irish language, "Ireland's only sure and safe frontier."[1] While Ó Conaire saw his wall as a temporary defensework behind which Gaelic culture could regroup in preparation for resuming an active role in contemporary European civilization, other language revivalists envisioned it as a permanent feature of the Irish intellectual landscape, one designed to keep the country safely quarantined from what they regarded as the pernicious moral atmosphere of the new century. Developing the image of the language as a "protective wall" (falla cosanta) in a 1914 sermon in Cork

---

1. Quoted by Negley Farson in *The Way of the Transgressor* (London: Victor Gollancz, 1935), 533.

City, An tAthair Peadar Ua Laoghaire proclaimed: "There is enmity between the Irish language and infidelity. They cannot keep house together. If Irish is inside, infidelity must remain outside."[2] And this defensive metaphor recurs again and again in the jeremiads of many proponents of the Revival. Thus in the Gaelic League propaganda pamphlet, *Ireland's Defence—Her Language*, Father Patrick F. Kavanagh argued: "There is no stronger rampart behind which nationality can entrench itself than a native language. Erect, then, the defence around your nationality which your foreign enemy has so long striven to destroy."[3] Father Peter Yorke was more extreme: "He believed that if a wall of brass, as Dean Swift said, was built one thousand feet high around Ireland it would be for the benefit of her people. He believed that if they could tow Ireland out into the Atlantic and free it entirely from English and Continental influences that such a measure would not be too much to restore to Ireland her diminishing nationality."[4]

Unfortunately, the proponents of this view are all too often seen as representative of the Gaelic movement as a whole and then caricatured as either harmless provincial buffoons or dangerous cultural chauvinists, the sort of yahoos who badgered Yeats, persecuted Synge, and disgusted Joyce. Yet in their own time these revivalists were an influential, articulate, and often colorfully disparate lot, united by what Terence Brown has termed a "vision of national fragility"[5] and by what will here be called their nativism, their belief that the primary function of the Irish language and its embryonic modern literature was to nurture and protect what they perceived as indigenous Irish values against the threats of foreign, particularly English, contamination.

Layman and cleric, native speaker and learner, provincial and Dubliner, these writers frequently and at times bitterly argued over a wide range of issues. But if they couldn't agree on what they liked, they were entirely sure of what they feared and despised: "the cheap smartness, the glare, the coarse materialism and sensuality of the modern world."[6] Similar lurid denunciations of contemporary "values" were a

2. "Sgéal Ióib agus Sgéal na hÉireann" (The story of Job and the story of Ireland), *An Síoladóir* (The sower) 1, no. 5 (July 1921): 1–2. The sermon was originally delivered on 21 January 1914. Tá namhdas idir an nGaeluinn agus díchreideamh. Ní féidir dóibh aontigheas a dhéanamh. Má bhíon an Ghaeluinn istigh ní foláir do'n díchreideamh fanmhaint amuich.

3. *Ireland's Defence—Her Language* (Dublin: Gaelic League, [1902?]), 10.

4. "The Turning of the Tide / Lecture by Rev. P. C. Yorke, San Francisco' " *ACS*, 16 September 1899. The Maynooth-educated Father Yorke was a close friend of Father O'Growney.

5. *Ireland: A Social and Cultural History, 1922 to the Present* (Ithaca: Cornell University Press, 1985), 62. Brown specifically refers to this vision as "an ideological weapon."

6. "The London Gaelic League / Fine Address by Fr. Moloney," *ACS*, 13 October 1900.

commonplace in Gaelic League lectures, especially those by priests, in
the first decade of this century. Thus in 1904 the lexicographer Father
Patrick Dinneen presented the Keating Branch of the league with a so-
bering challenge: "This country is, to a large extent, still untainted by
the teaching of the positivist, the materialist, the hedonist, which pervades English literature whether serious or trivial. . . . It will be difficult to prevent that literature from planting the seeds of social disorder
and moral degeneracy amongst even our still untainted population."[7]

English literature was, of course, only the most obvious expression
of the English spirit, a spirit dissected in 1900 by Father John M. O'
Reilly in a lecture to the Maynooth Union later published as *The
Threatening Metempsychosis of a Nation*: "It is a fleshly spirit, bent towards earth; a mind unmannerly, vulgar, insolent, bigoted; a mind
whose belly is its God . . . a mind to which pride, and lust, and mam-
mon are the matter-of-course aims of life . . . a mind where every
absurd device, from grossest Darwinism to most preposterous spiritual-
ism, is resorted to, and hoped in, to choke the voice of eternity in the
conscience."[8] For O'Reilly, the only sure defense against this wretched
worldview was the Irish language, presumably the preferred language
of "the voice of eternity in the conscience" at least when addressing
Irish people, for it was "a language unpolluted with the very names of
monstrosities of sin which are among the commonplaces of life in English-speaking countries."[9] A similar view was expressed by an Irish
priest familiar with conditions in one such country, the Reverend Dr.
Shahan of the Catholic University of America, who saw Irish as "a
balm for this suffering society of ours; a salt for the corruption and
crass materialism of our age; a refreshing breeze for the wearied and
disgusted heart of the modern world."[10]

There was, obviously, little doubt about either the source or nature
of the threat, but what precisely was to be sheltered behind this linguistic rampart? Here the nativists often differed sharply with both Gaelic
progressives and with each other in their emphases and approaches, but
all agreed that the challenge was to be met on three broad fronts: religious, cultural, and literary. For many clerical revivalists the religious
element was predictably of prime importance. Despite its sincere commitment to nonsectarianism and the visibility and official prominence
of Protestants like Douglas Hyde, Seosamh Laoide, Feardorcha Ó Conaill ("Conall Cearnach"), or Ernest Joynt, the Gaelic League was an

7. *Lectures on the Irish Language Movement* (Dublin: M. H. Gill and Son, 1904), 9–10.
8. "The English Mind in Ireland," *FL*, 30 June 1900.
9. "English Mind," *FL*, 30 June 1900.
10. Rev. Dr. Shahan, "Let Us Save the Language," *FL*, 11 March 1899.

overwhelmingly Catholic organization.[11] Moreover, from the days of Archbishop Mac Hale there were many who saw the language itself as inextricably linked with a uniquely Irish version of the Roman Catholic faith.[12] A forceful, though by no means idiosyncratic, expression of this view can be found in an 1899 lecture to Maynooth's Columban League by Father Patrick Forde: "God made the Irish heart a kingdom all fair and rich and wide, and the Irish heart threw open its portals to God and to Mary the Mother of God, and they entered in and took possession of it and reigned in it through all the ages. . . . And, therefore, has the high sainthood of Ireland entered in and taken possession of the language of Ireland, and therefore is that language one long profession of faith and hope and love, one glad song of praise to God."[13] Father Forde would no doubt have been gratified had he seen the circular issued five years later by this same Columban League, proclaiming: "When we remember that in the past our religion and language grew up side by side, and that the spirit of one became inseparably bound up with that of the other, we cannot help concluding that in the future also, the one must go hand in hand with the other, if we would have Irish Ireland also a thoroughly Catholic Ireland."[14]

11. The implications of this fact have been examined by Tom Garvin in "Priests and Patriots: Irish Separatism and Fear of the Modern, 1890–1914," *Irish Historical Studies* 25, no. 97 (May 1986): 67–81. Garvin writes: "Because clerical ideology contained such a strong element of siege mentality, the language appeared to offer a barrier against secularism" (74).

12. See Tomás Mac Aoidh, "Leon Tréada Iúda: An tArdeaspag Seán Mac Héil 1791–1881" (The Lion of the Flock of Judea: Archbishop John MacHale, 1791–1881), in *Leon an Iarthair: Aistí ar Sheán Mac Héil (The lion of the west: Essays on John MacHale)*, ed. Áine Ní Cheannain (Baile Átha Cliath: An Clóchomhar, 1983), 15–24, esp. 22–23.

13. "The Revival of the Irish Language," *ACS*, 12 January 1901. Forde's lecture was later published by the league as a propaganda pamphlet. The prevalence of this identification of the Irish language with the Roman Catholic faith could, however, create difficulties for the league, which was officially nonsectarian. Commenting on Forde's address, an anonymous contributor to *ACS* attempted to downplay its explicit, indeed triumphant, sectarianism:

> We are sure that there is nothing either in the manner or matter of what Father Forde says which would give offence to any Protestant, yet this argument is not one which the Gaelic League either could or would put forward; as an organisation the League is non-sectarian, even though the vast majority of its members are Catholics. It may seem strange, therefore, that the League should have issued a pamphlet containing this view, but if it be remembered that it was originally written for and read before an exclusively Catholic Society and that it is a broadminded and brilliant exposition of the *rationale* of the movement, it will be apparent that it was better to issue it in its original form.

See "Reviews," *ACS*, 3 August 1901. Eoin Mac Néill was editor of *ACS* at this time and may well have been the author of this review.

14. "Carraig," "A Circular from the Columban League," *ACS*, 3 December 1904.

Nor was this identification limited to clerics only marginally involved with the language movement. Some of the most prolific and influential Gaelic writers of the Revival were priests, and all of them agreed that Irish was, in the words of Father John O'Reilly, "the Trusty Vehicle of the Faith of the Gael."[15] Thus in an early essay in *The Irish Ecclesiastical Review*, Father Eugene O'Growney identified Irish literature as "the most Catholic literature in the world" and argued that "even if Irish were to perish as a spoken language, it would remain valuable from the pure literature point of view, and still more valuable from a Catholic standpoint."[16] Indeed, the numerous eulogies preached over O'Growney during his long funeral procession from Los Angeles to Maynooth were marked by a heavy emphasis on his devotion to the language as a safeguard of Irish Catholicism.[17] For example, in his address at Cobh An tAthair Peadar Ua Laoghaire saw O'Growney's work for the language, as we know he saw his own, as essentially a continuation of his ministry for the protection and propagation of the faith, calling Irish "the best thing we have, after the Faith, the strongest shield for the Faith except for the grace of God itself."[18] Father Richard Henebry expressed the idea in characteristically tendentious fashion in a speech at Maynooth, following a warning against the wiles of "the progeny of vile Luther and of grasping Calvin" with an exhortation to build the surest defense against them: "It is obvious that every little bit of work we do to help Irish benefits our Faith."[19] An even more sweeping analysis of the threat to the faith posed by the English language was provided by An tAthair Cathaoir Ó Braonáin in his 1913 pamphlet *Béarla Sacsan agus an Creideamh i nÉirinn* (The English language and the

15. *The Trusty Vehicle of the Faith of the Gael* (Dublin: Gaelic League, 1902).
16. "The National Language," in *Leabhar an Athar Eoghan / The O'Growney Memorial Volume*, ed. Agnes O'Farrelly (Dublin: M. H. Gill and Son, 1904), 231–36. The essay was originally published in the *Irish Ecclesiastical Review* in November 1890.
17. Several of these tributes are collected in *Leabhar an Athar Eoghan*.
18. Quoted in *Leabhar an Athar Eoghan*, 52. Ua Laoghaire called Irish "an rud is feár a bhí againn i ndiaigh an chreidimh, an sgiath cosanta is treise a bhí againn ar an gcreideamh lasmuich de ghrásta Dé féin." See also the report of a 1908 lecture by An tAthair Peadar to the seminarians at Maynooth in "Faith and Language," *ACS*, 10 October 1908. Ua Laoghaire is reported to have said: "The intelligence which the Creator had given them involved the responsibility that they should work for the language of this country, because the religion of this country depended on the work they would do for the language."
19. "Agallamh Tionscnaimh Cumainn" (Inaugural address to a society) in *Scríbhne Risteird de hIndeberg .i. Sagart dona Déisibh* (The writings of Richard Henebry: A priest from the Decies), ed. Seán Ó Cuirrín (Baile Átha Cliath: Brún agus Nualán, n.d.), 114. Having warned against "sliocht Lúther ghránda agus Chailbhin chraosaigh," Henebry said: "Is so-fheicsithe go dtéid i sochar dár gcreideamh gach mion-bhlódh saothair dá ndeinmíd ag cabhrughadh leis an nGaedhilg."

faith in Ireland): "English is the language of infidelity. It is infidels who for the most part speak English. It is infidels who for the most part compose literature in English. Infidels have most of the power in the English-speaking world." His conclusion was inescapable: "The sooner we discard English and revive our own language, the better off the Faith will be in Ireland."[20]

Given this identification of tongue with creed, there was logic in Father Dinneen's aggressive attempts to advance the interests and extend the influence of Catholic priests and bishops in the movement. Ever suspicious of anticlericalism on all sides, he was, for example, angered by *An Claidheamh Soluis's* muted criticism of the hierarchy's indifference to the language in their 1903 Lenten pastorals, and outraged by the league's official stance in a 1905–6 dispute over coeducational language classes between the local parish priest and the officers of the Portarlington (Co. Kildare) branch, among them "Cú Uladh" (Peadar Mac Fhionnlaoich). He must have found particularly offensive the tone and implications of the laypeople's defence of their position:

> The laity must have a right to live in Ireland as well as the clergy. Let us give their due to the clergy and reverence and high respect in their own sphere. But we have to advance our own work and the work of the country, and if some people don't like that, so be it. If we cannot run an Irish class without being under the control of the clergy, how could we run the work of the country in matters more weighty, for example, making laws, enforcing laws, and the like? Many things were yielded to in this country when the oppression of the Penal Laws was in effect that would not be yielded to in freer times.[21]

20. (Baile Átha Cliath: M. H. Mac Guill agus a Mhac, 1913), 15–16. "Teanga an ain-chreidimh is eadh an Béarla. Lucht an ain-chreidimh is eadh is mó a labhrann an Béarla. Lucht an ain-chreidimh is mó a cheapann litridheacht i mBéarla. Ag lucht an ain-chreidimh is eadh is mó atá comhacht i saoghal an Bhéarla. . . . An túisce caithfimíd Béarla Sacsan uainn agus ár dteanga féin d'aithbheodhchaint is amhlaidh a b'fhearr do'n chreideamh i nÉirinn."

21. *Sgéal Ruaidhrí Uí Mhórdha / Autobiography of the Ruairi O'More Branch of the Gaelic League, Portarlington* (Dublin: An Cló-Chumann, 1906), iv. "Is éigin do thuataíbh teacht i dtír in Éirinn chomh maith le cléirchibh. Tugamaois a gceart féin do'n chléir agus urraim agus áird-mheas in a n-áit féin. Acht caithidhmid ar n-obair féin agus obair na tíre do chur ar aghaidh, agus mura dtaithneann sé le daoinibh éigin bíodh aca. Mura féidir linn rang Gaedhilge do stiúradh acht sinn bheith faoi smacht ag an gcléir goidé mar thiocfadh linn obair na tíre do stiúradh i néidhthibh níos troime, cuir i gcás ag ceapadh dlíghthe, ag cur dlíghthe i bhfeidhm, agus a leithéidí eile. Is iomdha rud do géilleadh dó 'sa' tír so nuair bhí géirleanamhaint na ndlíghthe pianamhail ann nach ngéillfidhe dó in aimsearaibh níos

Anger became rage when the league took on, and defeated, the bishops on the issue of Irish as a compulsory subject for matriculation at the new National University, and he was finally and irrevocably alienated from the league when the Keating Branch of which he himself was president sided with Father O'Hickey in his long and losing battle with the Maynooth authorities concerning his language activism with regard to the University issue. Yet despite frustrations of this sort, intensified by his sincere conviction that the Catholic clergy were by right the proper leaders of the overwhelmingly Catholic native-speaking population—*cainnt na ndaoine* here being given a sectarian component that was also advanced by Ua Laoghaire and that must have shaken more progressive champions of the living speech of the Gaeltacht—Dinneen did not, as has been claimed elsewhere, advocate the creation of an explicitly and exclusively Catholic Gaelic League. His most extensive comment on the issue, his essay "The Gaelic League and Non-Sectarianism," could not be clearer:

> The League, if its constitution be rightly understood, finds certain religious beliefs existing, finds certain forms of Christianity established; its business is not to interfere with these beliefs, not to seek to undermine these forms of Christianity. It has its own work to do, its platform is wide enough for the different denominations of Christianity; it would itself narrow that platform if it endeavoured in the slightest degree to interfere with the religious tenets of its members or of those outside its body. Its attitude must be one of neutrality on questions of religion and on questions closely connected with religion.[22]

---

saoire." See also William P. Ryan, *The Pope's Green Island* (Boston: Small, Maynard, n.d.), 102–15. Dinneen's clericalism and his "fear of liberal Catholicism" were consistently opposed by Ryan in his paper *The Irish Peasant*. For a witty summary of Ryan's side of the debate, see *The Pope's Green Island*, 122–92. For a reading more sympathetic to Dinneen, see Proinsias Ó Conluain and Donncha Ó Céileachair, *An Duinníneach: An tAthair Pádraig Ó Duinnín, A Shaol, a Shaothar, agus an Ré inar Mhair Sé* (Dinneen: Father Patrick Dinneen, his life, his work, and the period in which he lived) (Baile Átha Cliath: Sáirséal agus Dill, 1958), 163–97, 216–22.

22. *The Irish Rosary: A Monthly Magazine Conducted by the Dominican Fathers* 11, no. 1 (January 1907): 9–10. It need hardly be said that he could have been more sensitive to the convictions and feelings of those Jews involved in the language movement. This must be the work Ryan refers to as "a magazine published by the Dominicans" that was the source for his assertion that Dinneen believed "it might be necessary to establish a strictly Catholic Gaelic League" (*Pope's Green Island*, 126). It is specifically cited by John Hutchinson in *The Dynamics of Cultural Nationalism* (249 n. 50), where he says that in it "Dinneen even mooted a separate Catholic Gaelic League." If so, it was a very muted mooting.

While a willingness to enlist and subordinate the language to the cause of the faith was predictably most explicit amongst clerical revivalists, it was shared in various usually more muted forms by many leading lay writers, not all of them nativists. For example, in his essay "Teanga Bheannuighthe Ár Sean is Ár Sinnsir" ("The Blessed Language of Our Ancestors") Breandán Ó Raghallaigh argued: "One does not find the same spirit of simple piety in any other language, least of all in English. . . . We have great reason to fear that if English is to be the sole medium of expressing our thoughts, the rejection of our olden tongue in favour of the speech of the conqueror will be most prejudicial to the intense religious spirit which is so especially characteristic of our people."[23] On the other hand, Henry Morris was as categorical as any clergyman when in April 1898 he pronounced Irish "pre-eminently the language of prayer and devotion" and asserted that "I don't think then that any Irish Catholic can deny that there rests with him a moral obligation to assist in preserving the Irish language, seeing that its loss is a danger and a menace to the religion he professes."[24] The young Pearse could also be downright strident on this issue, as he was in a 1901 lecture to the Catholic Commerical Club:

> What he talked about was the War Between Two Civilizations. One of them is a civilization concerned with spirit, mind, intellect, good manners, and piety. That is the civilization of the Gaels. The other is a civilization of the body, worldy force, the strength and power of money, and the comfort of life. That is the civilization of the English. . . . The native language is the barrier and the firm protective wall against the onslaught of the enemies of our nationality and our civilization.[25]

23. *Irish Rosary* 10, no. 5 (May 1906): 407. This lengthy essay commenced serialization in November 1905. Because it was published in both Irish and English, I have used Ó Raghallaigh's own less than literal English version in the text. "Níl an spiorad naomhtha simplidhe sin i n-aon teanga eile agus dar ndóigh, níl sé sa Bheurla. . . . Is mór is eagal liomsa má chailltear an Ghaedhilg agus má gheibheann an Beurla réim agus gradam ar fad i nÉirinn nach fada uainn an lá 'na mbeidh a mhalairt sgéil aguinn."

24. "The Loss of the Irish Language and Its Influence on the Catholic Religion in Ireland," *FL*, 2 April 1898.

25. "Le h-Aghaidh na Gaedhilgeóiridhe" (For the Irish speakers), *Weekly Freeman, National Press and Irish Agriculturist* (*WF*), 2 March 1901. This piece was a report of Pearse's address. "Budh é rud ar a dtrácht sé, .i. Cogadh Idir Dhá Shibhialtachtaibh. Ceann aca is é sibhialtacht bhaineas leis an spiorad, an intinn, an intleacht, an deighbheus agus an chráibhtheacht, sin é sibhialtacht na nGaedheal; agus ceann eile sibhialtacht an cholainn, bríghe an tsaoghail, neirt agus cumais an airgid, agus seasgaireachta na beatha; sin é sibhialtas na Sacsanach. . . . 'Sí an teanga dhúthchasach fál agus balla daingean díona agus cumhdaigh i n-aghaidh ruathair námhad ár náisiúntachta agus ár sibhialtachta."

Even later, after occasional disputes with Church authorities over their treatment of Irish[26] and despite the obvious restrictions imposed on him by his editorship of the league's official organ, he more than once proposed the language as an ally of the faith. For example, in an editorial urging a new initiative to encourage Gaeltacht parents not to speak English in the home, he attempted to enlist the aid of the clergy: "A crusade preached for twelve months from the altars of the Irish-speaking districts would kill the habit of speaking English to children. The killing of that habit would mean the saving of the life of the Irish language. There are some who hold that it would also mean the saving of Ireland to the Church."[27] A similar approach was taken by Tadhg Ó Donnchadha ("Tórna") in his review of Ó Braonáin's *Béarla Sacsan agus an Creideamh i nÉirinn*. Having summarized the author's argument, Ó Donnchadha commented: "Isn't that a terrible story, and who among us would deny that every word of it is true?"[28] Even the sea-divided Gaels of America shared such concerns. For example, in 1912 the Springfield Massachusetts Feis offered a prize for a "Gaelic essay" on the theme "Are Catholic institutions in Ireland which ignore Irish serving the best interests of Catholicity?"[29]

Some of this doubt about the future viability of Irish Catholicism must have been self-consciously rhetorical. To be blunt, the institutional Church doesn't seem to have been in much danger in turn-of-the-century Ireland. What was, however, being relentlessly undermined was the elusive quality that made Irish Catholicism or Irish anything else recognizably Irish, that is, the very ethos that identified Irish culture as a distinct entity. Ireland would remain Catholic, but would she remain Irish? Of course for the revivalists "Irish" and "Gaelic" were synonomous terms, and here the logic of the language movement, expressed in its most ideologically coherent and consistent form by the

26. For example, he forthrightly opposed the hierarchy on the issue of making Irish compulsory for matriculation in the new National University, and defended Father Michael O'Hickey on his dismissal from his post at Maynooth as the result of this controversy. His *ACS* editorials on these episodes have been collected by Séamas Ó Buachalla in *A Significant Irish Educationalist: The Educational Writings of P. H. Pearse* (Dublin: Mercier, 1980), 202–42. See also Donnchadh Ó Súilleabháin, *An Piarsach agus Conradh na Gaeilge* (Pearse and the Gaelic League) (Baile Átha Cliath: Clódhanna Teoranta, 1981), 116–61; and Ruth Dudley Edwards, *Patrick Pearse: The Triumph of Failure* (London: Victor Gollancz, 1977), 74–78.

27. "Wanted—A New Crusade," editorial, *ACS*, 13 October 1906.

28. "Ceilteachus / 'Béarla Sacsan agus an Creideamh i nÉirinn,' " *ACS*, 15 November 1913. "Nach uathbhásach an scéal é sin, agus cia againn a déarfadh ná go bhfuil an fhírinne insan uile fhocal de?"

29. "Feiseanna in America," *ACS*, 24 August 1912.

nativists, was irrefutable. Gaelic culture could not be divorced from the Gaelic language, which language constituted the only effective safeguard for a threatened national identity. Thus in *Ireland's Defence—Her Language*, Father Patrick F. Kavanagh rather surprisingly downplayed the idea that the language was the medium of a particular creed and instead stressed its potential to unify Irish people of all faiths in opposition to the incessant foreign assault against what he loosely termed their "nationality": "There is no stronger rampart behind which nationality can entrench itself than the native language. . . . Now it is, I say again, as a barrier the strongest that can be erected against the anglicisation of Ireland which to my mind is the chief advantage to be derived from the Irish language movement" (10–11).

While Kavanagh's vagueness about just what constituted this "nationality" was widely shared, there was agreement that it was both ancient and unique. Speaking to a branch of the league in December 1899, Father Patrick Forde proclaimed: "Gaels we all are, and therefore our only possible perfection consists in the development of the Gaelic nature we have inherited from our forefathers. . . . Our forefathers are our best models and patterns; they alone can show us what our common Gaelic nature can and ought to be. We must copy their greatness and their goodness; trustworthy are they of affectionate and reverent imitation."[30] Such imitation would not, however, be easy, as "Cara na nUghdar" (William P. Ryan) made clear in his 1914 acknowledgment that "the 'Gaelic mind' is not the same thing from age to age. No one fully understands the Gaelic mind."[31] Éamonn Ó Donnchadha offered a downright intimidating picture of the challenges facing the would-be "proper Gael" (Gaedheal ceart) in his 1911 essay on "Dia agus Éire" (God and Ireland): "It is difficult for a Gael to be a proper Gael now. . . . The Gael who wishes to be a Gael in earnest must protect himself against the folly of this age and conduct himself like a person who would enter eagerly into the heritage of his ancestors and who would eagerly shed his heart's blood so that that heritage would remain, entirely undiminished, with his decendants forever."[32]

30. "The Revival of the Irish Language," *ACS*, 11 October 1900.

31. "Filidheacht agus Fíordhacht" (Poetry and truth), *ACS*, 12 September 1914. Ryan stated "nach é an rud céadna 'an aigne Gaodhlach' ó aois go haois. Níl eolas ag éinne ar an aigne Gaodhlach ar fad." The progressive Ryan wrote this essay as one in a series he contributed to *ACS* during a lengthy debate on Gaelic poetry that he undertook with the more conservative and traditional Tadhg Ó Donnchadha.

32. *ACS*, 1 July 1911. "Is deacair do Ghaedheal bheith 'n-a Ghaedheal cheart anois. . . . An Gaedheal gur mhian leis bheith 'n-a Ghaedheal i ndáiríribh ní fuláir dó é féin a chosaint ar bhaois na haoise seo agus é féin d'iomchar mar le duine do gheobhadh le fonn i

On a less stirring note, "An Seabhac" (Pádraig Ó Siochfradha) emphasized the value of prosaic discussion and debate as well as metaphoric martyrdom in the revival of this ineffable Gaelicism: "As for the Gaelic mind, it is hard to say what it is. We often see a native Irish speaker insisting that the Gaelic mind is this or that, and another native Irish speaker contradicting him altogether and saying he is entirely wrong. They should settle the matter amongst themselves, and there's no way to do so but the old way, 'Learning comes from work'; lack of learning is responsible for a disagreement of that kind."[33] Ironically, as Breandán Ó Conaire has illustrated with copious and often hilarious examples in his Myles na Gaeilge,[34] this apotheosis of Gaelicism could, in its more ill-defined manifestations, unintentionally anticipate the later parody of Myles na gCopaleen in An Béal Bocht (The poor mouth): "The wide world is watching Gleann Áireamh now and saying that there isn't a place in Ireland more Gaelic, that the Gaelic spirit is stronger here than anywhere else, that everyone in the Glen, old and young, has great regard for the Gaelic."[35]

Yet however foggy their definition of this ethos, all revivalists, progressive and nativist alike, insisted that "Gaelachas" was only fully accessible through the Irish language. Thus Father Forde posed the rhetorical question: "Who will speak to us about our forefathers, about what they thought and what they did, about what they felt and what they sought for, about their high and holy ideas and their grand heroic ways, which, believe me, are our best ways too? Where is the voice in the wilderness to tell us of our fathers?" Unlike his prose style, his answer was clear and simple: that voice, "heard across the gulf of time,

---

n-oighreacht a shinsear agus a thabharfadh fuil a chroidhe d'fhonn as go bhfanfadh an t-oighreachas sain ag a shliocht go deo gan a luigheadughadh badh lugha do dhul dó."

33. "An Ghaedhilg ag Dul Síos Fánaidh an Chnuic" (Irish going downhill), ACS, 11 March 1911. "Maidir leis an aigne Ghaedhealaigh, is deacair a rádh céard é. Is minic achímíd Gaedhilgeoir ó dhúthchas agá áiteamh orainn gur seo nó siúd í an aigne Ghaedhealach agus Gaedhilgeoir ó dhúthchas eile ag gabháil na choinnibh ar fad agus ag rádh nach eadh ná cor ar bith. Níor mhisde dhóibh an sgéal a réidhteach eatorra féin agus níl aon slíghe chuige ach an tsean-slíghe 'as an obair thigh an fhoghluim'; easbaidh fhoghluma 'seadh is cionntach le haighneas de'n tsórt sin."

34. Myles na Gaeilge: Lámhleabhar ar Shaothar Gaeilge Bhrian Ó Nualláin (The Irish Language Myles: A handbook on the Irish language work of Brian O'Nolan) (Baile Átha Cliath: An Clóchomhar, 1986).

35. Peadar Ó Dubhda ("Cúchulainn"), "Gleann Áireamh," ACS, 21 September 1912. Ó Dubhda was here reporting on a speech delivered by Pádraig Mac Duibh. "Tá an domhan mór ag amharc ar Ghleann Áireamh anois agus a ráidhte nach bhfuil áite ar bith i nÉirinn níos Gaedhealaighe ná é, go bhfuil an spiorad Gaedhealach níos láidhre anseo ná i n-áit ar bith eilig, go bhfuil céist mhór ag gach uile duine ins a' Ghleann, aosta is óg, ins an Ghaedhilc."

down through all the centuries" was "the old language itself, the God-given outlet of the warm throbbing Irish heart and the restless fiery Irish soul, that tongue whereby the lightning genius of the Gael flashed in upon the souls of men."[36] Father O'Reilly was equally categorical if less flamboyant: "Ireland's history, literature, legend, song, story, superstition, saga—all those outlets of the nation's mind which would give her true character to the world—all those are simply illegible without the Irish language."[37] The archnativist Father Henebry used this tenet as the basis for a concise apologia for the entire language revival movement: "We wish to revive Irish. This Irish was the old time tongue of our fathers, moulded by them through immemorial use to fit all the wards, crevices, and chinks of the Gaelic mind. From such long and intimate contact with the Irish soul it must breathe for us the veritable spirit of our forefathers."[38]

As has been noted, the fundamental cogency of this argument was and is unassailable, and it thus provided one of the few ideas on which the league's progressives and nativists could agree. Moreover, while the progressives generally avoided the rhetorical excesses of the nativists as well as their occasionally zestful xenophobia, they were compelled by both the logic of revivalist orthodoxy and by a practical appreciation of the actual contemporary state of the language to share what Frank O'Connor called "the backward look," a potentially oppressive awareness of and attachment to a golden past as a principal source of cultural integrity and validity. For example, Pearse, who as editor of *An Claidheamh Soluis* consistently urged Gaelic writers to confront the new century and to lead Ireland out of the Anglicized backwaters and into the European mainstream, acknowledged that, before they could advance with confidence on the future, Gaels had to reestablish "communion with the past of our race."[39] Indeed, even if we allow for the hyperbole inspired by national holidays, Pearse's pious sentiments on St. Patrick's Day 1905 could, excepting the optimism, have been expressed by Father Henebry: "All this symbolizes the fact that Ireland is resolutely turning her face back to the old paths, that the ideals and traditions and culture for which Patrick stands are still the ideals, traditions, and culture of the Gael."[40] The most thoughtful attempt to incorporate "the backward look" into a progressive philosophy for the Revival was

36. "The Revival of the Irish Language," *ACS*, 11 August 1900. This piece originally appeared in the *San Francisco Leader*.
37. "The English Mind in Ireland," *FL*, 14 July 1900.
38. "Best Method of Learning Irish," *ACS*, 5 July 1902.
39. "What Is a National Language?" editorial, *ACS*, 28 January 1905.
40. "The National Holiday," editorial, *ACS*, 25 March 1905.

that of George Moonan, who in a 1904 lecture to the League's Central Branch on "The Spirit of the Gaelic League" somewhat disingenuously claimed:

> One never hears a Gaelic Leaguer of any standing speak of the 'Dear Old Tongue' or the 'Grand Old Tongue.' . . . If they use any similar phrase, it is 'Ar dTeanga Fein'—'Our Own Tongue'! It is as the living Irish tongue they think of it, the language of Bridget and Columcille, certainly; but just as much so the national language of Ireland at the present day, the surest bulwark of her national existence, the truest exponent of her national soul, the keenest incentive to national effort in any form.[41]

Yet despite the attempts of progressives like Pearse and Moonan to secure the past and turn without undue delay toward the wider world of the future, the nativists managed to a significant degree to impose their somewhat claustrophobic notion of *Gaelachas* on the Revival as a whole; all too often their legitimate insistence that that tradition be protected degenerated into a campaign of sterile preservationism. Nowhere was the impact of this ultimately defeatist perspective more evident than in the startling imagery used by Douglas Hyde in his address to the inaugural meeting of the league's Central Branch in 1911: "Just as Yellowstone Park, the national reservation in America, contains all the noble fauna which have disappeared elsewhere, so does our national reservation of the Irish-speaking districts contain for us the invaluable life and traditions of the past."[42] Moreover, the idea was neither a passing nor a personal quirk; when he repeated it in a 1914 Belfast address, he was supported by Tadhg Ó Donnchadha, although Ó Donnchadha did advise that the proposal would require some considerable "preliminary study" (stuidéar roimh ré): "It is a good thing to establish 'Reservations' in the Gaeltacht. But before they are established it would be proper to study the question closely. Let us keep in mind that the reservations are a part of Ireland; and that perhaps the people of those areas might not want a change of system or a change of laws, or anything that would provide an excuse for foreign fops to look down on them."[43]

41. *ACS*, 19 November 1904.
42. "What An Craoibhin Did Say," *ACS*, 26 October 1912.
43. "Deascán Díoghluma / Óráid an Chraoibhín" (Miscellany: An Craoibhín's speech), *ACS*, 31 October 1914. "Is maith an nídh é 'Reservations' a chur ar bun sa Ghaedhealtacht. Acht sara gcuirtear ar bun iad, badh cheart stuidéar cruinn a dhéanamh ar an gceist. Bíodh a fhios againn gur cuid d'Éirinn na reservations; agus b'fhéidir nár mhian le muinntir na gceanntar soin, malairt córach, ná malairt dlíghthe, ná éinnidh a thabhar-

From its foundation in 1893 the Gaelic League had made the creation of a modern literature in Irish a central goal of its agenda, but in the eyes of most revivalists—Pearse and Pádraic Ó Conaire were notable though by no means solitary exceptions here—the aesthetic was to be consistently subordinated to the mundane and ideological throughout, indeed well past, the early years of the Revival. Apart from its strictly educational value, there was a general consensus that the new literature could serve two main functions. In the long run, as the language returned to widespread use, it would offer a uniquely Irish vision of the contemporary world rooted in an unbroken continuity with the nation's cultural heritage. In the short term, it could provide a wholesome substitute, particularly in the *Gaeltachtaí*, for the English-language reading matter that was perceived as flooding and corrupting the country. Of course, concern about the sort of cultural exports reaching Ireland from England was by no means limited to Gaelic or even Catholic circles in the early years of this century. Yeats, for one, lamented the effect of such material on his personal Ireland of the spirit.[44] But Catholics were the most vocal and active in their concern, creating in 1899 the Catholic Truth Society of Ireland to combat amoral and immoral literature, a social problem to which in the following year the Irish bishops devoted their Lenten pastorals. Not surprisingly, these developments were widely applauded by revivalists. For example, *Fáinne an Lae* published in full the text of the CTS's inaugural address to the clergy and laity of Ireland along with a warm editorial welcome and an appeal for support "from all Irish men and women desirous of preserving the purity of our people and those national characteristics which it is our duty

fadh leathscéal do bhoicíní gallda chun féachaint síos ortha." Ó Donnchadha's concerns have proved prophetic. In a detailed recent study of the state of Irish in independent Ireland, Reg Hindley has written: "The small size of the Gaeltachtai causes a 'fishbowl effect' or 'native reservation syndrome,' as native speakers perceive that they are being visited as museum pieces or historical survivals by urban people who find them quaint. . . . The diminutive pockets of survival are fascinating as such . . . but the inhabitants do not in general feel flattered by the attention, do not want to be treated as 'different.' " See Hindley, *The Death of the Irish Language: A Qualified Obituary* (London: Routledge, 1990), 188.

44. For example, in an address to the league's Central Branch, Yeats blasted "the English music hall and all the complex vulgarities of a life which was essentially decadent, the life of a very vulgar commercialism," and rhapsodized in terms Fathers O'Reilly, Forde, and Henebry would have applauded: "The civilisation that existed in the Irish language, which they could spread if they could spread the Irish language, was an old and better civilisation which had been reeling under the shocks given to it by modern vulgarity everywhere, an old and better civilisation which it was their duty to preserve until the deluge had gone by." See "Central Branch Sgoruidheacht [Entertainment] / Address by Mr. W. B. Yeats," *ACS*, 27 October 1900.

to foster and preserve."[45] The conjunction of purity and threatened "national characteristics" is, of course, revealing. Moreover, Gaelic periodicals and platforms echoed with vitriolic denunciations of "the coloured abominations of the English press,"[46] "the paganising flood of nauseous books, papers, and magazines, which are doing more harm to our people than Cromwell's troopers could do,"[47] "the full sewerage from the *cloaca maxima* of Anglicisation."[48] At times such frenzied condemnations could become far more offensive to modern sensibilities than the literature that provoked them, as when Father Francis McEnerney drew laughter and applause with these lines from a speech in the Antient Concert Rooms in 1900: "If they were to take away all the spirit of the Irish race by cutting away their language and traditions, and put them swimming in the stream of dirty literature coming into the country every day for two or three generations, they would be like the little effeminate corner boys of the English cities who would run away from the sight of a Boer, aye, even of a black."[49]

However regrettably phrased, such an emphasis on the role of the Irish language and its traditions as a defense against the debilitating effects of decadent foreign literatures and worldviews was central to the nativist position and shared by many other less ideologically rigid revivalists. Indeed, it is probably fair to say that most Gaels supported both bishops and county councillors when they denounced immoral publications, and welcomed the Catholic Truth Society and new Catholic periodicals like the *Irish Messenger of the Sacred Heart*, the *Irish Catholic*, and the *Irish Rosary* (all of which first appeared between 1885 and 1900), the *Catholic Bulletin* (founded in 1911 and later edited by the Gaelic writer Seán Ua Ceallaigh, league president from 1919 to 1923), and the Gaelic version of the *Messenger, Timthiridh Chroidhe Neamhtha Íosa* (first published in 1911).[50] Yet they also invariably pointed out that many of those most distressed by questionable literature were overlooking the most potent protection against it, the Irish language and its new modern literature. The Gaelic position, to be reiterated regularly in

45. See "A Crusade vs. Imported Literature," *FL*, 9 December 1899.

46. "Notes," *ACS*, 16 September 1899.

47. Tomás A. Mac Gearailt, O.F.M., letter, *ACS*, 22 February 1908. Father Mac Gearailt was the treasurer of the league's Galway branch.

48. "Beirt" "An Sgiath Cosanta" (The protective shield), *ACS*, 8 November 1913.

49. "The Public Meeting," *FL*, 26 May 1900. The meeting was held to advocate the teaching of Irish in all Irish schools.

50. See Garvin, "Priests and Patriots," 70–71; Brown, *Ireland*, 50–57; and Margaret O'Callaghan, "Language, Nationality and Cultural Identity in the Irish Free State, 1922–7: the *Irish Statesman* and the *Catholic Bulletin* Reappraised," *Irish Historical Studies* 24, no. 94 (November 1984): 226–45.

succeeding years, was given forthright expression in an 1898 *Fáinne an Lae* editorial: "To expel the poison we must use the natural antidote. The cultivation of the native speech, giving to the people a literature pure and simple, sane and strong, will be the surest bulwark here as elsewhere against this debasing, denationalising influence."[51] Father Kavanagh offered similar advice in *Ireland's Defence—Her Language*: "Debased and debasing English ideals, the rank and poisonous growths of diseased minds and corrupt hearts will not take root and flourish in the pure atmosphere created by the diffusion of Gaelic literature throughout our land" (10). Offering his readers in the *Catholic Bulletin* the choice of "A Gaelicised or a Socialised Ireland—Which?" Michael J. Phelan, S.J., lamented a lost opportunity in a welter of mixed metaphors: "Had we erected a Catholic library and established a branch of the Gaelic League in every parish; with these two engines alone, worked with all the motor force that fiery zeal in a holy cause can generate, we would have placed an angel sentinel with a flaming sword at the entrance to every avenue that leads to Ireland's heart; and the slush of Anglicised filth now flowing over and engulfing us would be sternly met by a wall of brass."[52] Apparently in timely and propitious circumstances such preventative action could be of instantaneous and near miraculous efficacy. For instance, Craobh Locha Reamhar reported to the Central Branch in 1902 that in their area "the novelette and the half-penny comic have retreated at the advance of O'Growney."[53]

The necessity for combating debasing literature was, in theory, another issue that could unite progressives and nativists. The catch was, however, how to reach consensus on just what made a work debasing. Condemnation of the English gutter press and trashy popular fiction was easy enough, but beyond that there were differences of opinion so profound that they can serve as the most reliable touchstone to distinguish progressive from nativist. Products of their time, place, and late Victorian schooling, all Revival intellectuals believed that literature had a high moral function. Thus Mícheál Breathnach, who lined up with the progressives on a range of important issues, could warn: "Don't be satisfied with trivial, foolish talk, with unpleasant stories—with authors without interest in or respect for the brightest and most beautiful things in the great world. Avoid the writer from whom one does not get clean, pure teaching and healthy, sound knowledge for the mind."[54] But

51. "The Remedy Against Debasing Literature," editorial, *FL*, 12 March 1898.
52. *Catholic Bulletin and Book Review* 3, no. 11 (November 1913): 774.
53. "Notes," *ACS*, 15 February 1902.
54. "Lean Lorg na Laochra" (Follow the path of the heroes), in *Sgríbhinní Mhíchíl*

for the nativist, such wholesome intellectual sustenance was rare to the point of nonexistence in virtually all contemporary writing on controversial or even serious topics. For example, as we will see, in 1908 An tAthair Peadar Ua Laoghaire pronounced English fiction in toto "poisonous" and in 1917 even launched a successful campaign to have Pádraic Ó Conaire's 1906 story collection *Nóra Mharcuis Bhig* and his 1910 novel *Deoraidheacht* (Exile) removed from the syllabus of the National University on the grounds of sensuality and perversity, the latter title being replaced with his own *Séadna*.[55] Father Henebry, repulsed among other things by the "dreary wastes of love-making in modern literature,"[56] proclaimed: "The resuscitation of the Irish language is not merely a protest against English and Englishism. It is of far deeper significance, for it opposes itself squarely to the modern European spirit, whether that finds expression in current thought (as it is called), in philosophy, in ethics, or in aesthetics."[57]

Others agreed that degrading literature was not defined exclusively by the depiction of sexual behavior. However reactionary at times, Henebry, Dinneen, O'Reilly, and many who shared their moral philosophy took ideas seriously. Thus in a 1908 *An Claidheamh Soluis* leader on "Droch-Litridheacht Ghallda" (Evil foreign literature), we read "Now we have another kind of foreign 'literature' . . . the books being published by the Rationalist Press in London. Copies of these are available for 6d. apiece, for example the book Darwin wrote on 'The Descent of Man.'"[58] And in "Cad is 'Darwinism' ann?" ("What is 'Darwinism'?"), one "Tighearnach'" having discussed evolutionary theory with an imposing vocabulary of neologisms, concluded by pronounc-

---

Bhreathnaigh maille le n-a Bheathaidh (The writings of Mícheál Breathnach, along with his life), ed. Tomás Mac Domhnaill (Baile Átha Cliath: M. H. Mac Guill agus a Mhac, 1913), 42. "Ná bí sásta le cainnt shuaraigh sheafóidigh, le sgéalta mí-thaithneamhacha—le ughdair gan suim gan meas ar na neithibh is gile agus is áilne san saoghal mór. Seachain an sgríbhneóir nach bhfuil teagasg glan glé agus eólas sláinteamhail folláin do'n aigne le fágháil uaidh."

55. Tomás de Bhaldraithe, "Conspóid faoi Phádraic Ó Conaire," in *Pádraic Ó Conaire: Clocha ar a Charn* (Pádraic Ó Conaire: Stones on his cairn), ed. Tomás de Bhaldraithe (Baile Átha Cliath: An Clóchomhar, 1982), 101–6. Ó Conaire's work was ably (and courageously) defended by Hyde.

56. "Revival Irish," *The Leader*, 9 January 1909.

57. "Revival Irish," *The Leader*, 16 January 1909.

58. See "Droch-Litridheacht Ghallda," *ACS*, 4 July 1908. " 'Nois tá cineál eile 'litridheacht' ghallda againn. . . . 'Siad na leabhra atá 'ghá gcur amach ó'n gCló-Chumann Fáthmhar (nó Rationalist Press) i Lonndain. Ta cóipeannaibh dhíobh so le fágháil ar 6d. an ceann, cuir i gcás an leabhar a sgríobh Darbhuin ar 'Bhunughdar Cholonn Daoine' (nó 'Descent of Man')."

ing Darwin's ideas obsolete as a result of the rediscovery of the work of Father Gregor Mendel.[59]

Like Henebry, Pádraig Ó Siochfhradha found the entire contemporary European ethos as expressed in the literature not only obsessed with the sordid, but also antagonistic to the very spirit of the Irish language. Arguing that Gaelic works modeled on the writings of authors like Zola—and here he could only have had the fiction of Pádraic Ó Conaire in mind—had failed, "An Seabhac" urged his fellow Irish language authors to create "a literature that will be truly Gaelic" (litridheacht bhéas fíor-Ghaedhealach), taking as their exemplars the stories "Gaels created out of their own spirit when they had no knowledge of or contact with any storytelling but their own."[60] The reasons for and results of seeking such homely inspiration will be the subject of Chapter 2.

Unfortunately, the activities of some of the nativists were not limited to the creation of a salubrious Gaelic alternative to literary corruption from abroad. Through their support of the Vigilance Committee movement[61] some revivalists joined in the effort to ensure that Irish readers would remain securely ignorant of any literature deemed inappropriate. As early as 1900, the author of "Tír-Chonaill Notes," in An Claidheamh Soluis, had proposed the formation of such groups, urging Catholic priests to follow the lead of some Belfast ministers in policing bookshops and news agencies: "There would be little difficulty in making a change for the better if a vigilance committee of the Catholic clergy would take the matter in hands, visit the Catholic news-shops, and—as the Protestant clergymen did—demand the removal of the obnoxious papers."[62]

In October 1911 a group of Limerick people, among them some local Gaelic figures, did take matters in hand, forming a vigilance committee and seizing and burning a shipment of English Sunday papers. Some revivalists applauded the action, as did "An Leipreachán," the author of the regular "In the Gaelic World" column of the Weekly Freeman: "The

59. ACS, 12 September 1908.

60. Pádraig Ó Siochfhradha, "Sgríobhthar Finn-Sgéalta Dhúinn" (Let romantic tales be written for us), ACS, 11 December 1909. "An Seabhac" praised the stories "do cheap Gaedhil as a meon féin amach nuair nach raibh aon eolas ná aon chaidreamh aca ar aon sgéalaidheacht ach ar a gcuid féin."

61. For commentary on the roots and long-term influence of the Vigilance Committee movement, see Brown, Ireland, 54–61; Garvin, "Priests and Patriots," 67–81; and Michael Adams, Censorship: The Irish Experience (University: University of Alabama Press, 1968), especially 13–21.

62. ACS, 22 September 1900. The idea was a persistent one. See "G.," letter, ACS, 25 July 1908.

Irish language movement stands to gain by the campaign which is now being carried on so energetically throughout the country against the importation of objectionable newspapers and periodicals into Ireland."[63] One religious, An Bráthair Bearchán, went farther, proclaiming the Limerick people national heroes: "It is the people of Limerick who long ago fought most fiercely and tenaciously against the foreigners in the time of Cromwell and in the time of William of Orange, and great credit is due their descendants today for being in the vanguard to fight the new foreign foe, evil literature."[64] Moreover, there were those who felt that revivalists owed active support if not actual service to the vigilance movement. Writing in the following year in *The Literature Crusade in Ireland*, a booklet he dedicated to the Limerick Vigilance Committee as "the first on the Roll of Honour," Father Thomas A. Murphy first appealed to Revival orthodoxy that "we are reaping now the fruits of all that is summed up in the one word—Anglicisation," and then went on to recruit new "crusaders" from amongst the Gaels: "Seeing that, *as a matter of fact*, most of the objectionable publications come from England, it is equally logical that Irish-Irelanders should throw themselves heart and soul into the new work, and thereby check the greatest anglicising influence in the country. If the people continue to read little or nothing but English publications, the Irish Revival will be *saothar i n-aistear*—labour in vain."[65]

Yet to their credit most Gaels continued to believe that the problem was one to be confronted on a more intellectual and constructive level, agreeing with Father Michael Phelan that "the place to deal effectively with evil literature is not in the street but in the Gaelic classes."[66] And while their concern about decadent literature was intense and their support for campaigns to enlighten readers as to its dangers consistent, they never compromised their own perception of the problem and its

63. "An Leipreachán," "In the Gaelic World / Notes on the Language Movement," *WF*, 11 November 1911.

64. "Droich-Litridheacht Ghallda" (Bad foreign literature), *Catholic Bulletin and Book Review* 2, no. 3 (March 1912): 144. The first part of this essay, which included a swipe at Darwin and Huxley, had been published the previous month. Brother Bearchán claimed that booksellers throughout Ireland had been reasoned with in vain before the Limerick committee acted. " 'Siad muinntear Luimnighe do dhein an troid ba dhéine is ba bhuaine fad ó i n-aghaidh Gall i n-aimsir Chrombhail is i n-aimsir Liam Bhuidhe, agus is mór an chreideamhaint atá ag dul dá sliocht indiu toisc bheith ar thosach chum troda leis an nuadh-namhaid Gallda, an droich-litridheacht so."

65. (Limerick: Munster, 1912), 30–31. Murphy also wrote that "the whole movement will be misunderstood and attacked, and for this reason it may be well to state here . . . that the crusade is directed not against the liberty of the press, but against its license" (2).

66. "Gaelicised or Socialised Ireland," *Catholic Bulletin* 3, no. 11 (November 1913): 774.

solution: "The cheap, putrid literature of England gets no support among those who have taken up the serious study of the Irish language, and of national history, trade, and resources."[67] It should not, therefore, be surprising that the institutional Gaelic movement dissociated itself from the proceedings in Limerick. *An Claidheamh Soluis* at first made no editorial comment on the burning, simply quoting verbatim the account of the incident in the *Limerick Leader* and the vigilance committee's rationale for its actions.[68] But after considering the implications of such free-lance censorship, the league's official organ spoke out the following month in an editorial whose title, "Vigilance Committees on the Wrong Track," left no doubt about the stand to be taken. While sympathetic with the motives of the Limerick committee and convinced that "burning is much too good for the Sunday papers," Seán Mac Giollarnáth affirmed in this editorial the league's long-held position: "We have no unbounded faith in the methods of those who, of late, are loud in their denunciations of English newspapers, but who do nothing to give the people a taste for better things."[69] Lest there be any uncertainty about just what the best of those better things was, Mac Giollarnáth spelt it out in a later editorial comment on a Cork meeting to protest immoral literature: "None of the speakers appears to have hit on the true remedy, viz., the spread of the Irish language and literature through the length and breadth of the land."[70] Revivalists were particularly frustrated by the ongoing failure of the Catholic Truth Society to realize the logic of this position, a frustration they did not hesitate to express in print.[71]

Not surprisingly the most prominent Gaelic progressives, Ó Conaire and Pearse, were always willing to take the offensive against what they saw as nativist philistinism masquerading as moral fervor, both before

67. "Wanted—Gumption," editorial, *ACS*, 6 April 1912. See also "Droch-Litridheacht Ghallda," *ACS*, 4 July 1908.

68. See "Limerick Burns English Papers," *ACS*, 4 November 1911; and "English Publications," *ACS*, 25 November 1911.

69. *ACS*, 9 December 1911.

70. "English Immoral Literature," *ACS*, 13 January 1912. The *ACS* position was consistent through time. See "Sop i n-Ionad Sguaibe," *ACS*, 20 June 1914.

71. See, for example, "Catholics and Galldachas," *ACS*, 23 October 1915; An tAthair Tomás de Bhall, "An Chléir, an Creideamh, agus an Ghaedhealg" (The clergy, the faith, and the Irish language), *ACS*, 2 September 1916; and Ó Donnchadha, "Cúrsaí an tSaoghail" (The world's affairs), *ACS*, 21 October 1916. On the other hand, in a 1915 letter to *ACS*, Mary Butler defended the CTS with reference to a speech delivered in Irish to its annual meeting by Agnes O'Farrelly and plans for "an exclusive Irish section" to form part of future annual meetings. See Mary Butler, letter, *ACS*, 30 October 1915. Clearly the commitment of the CTS to the language was merely token.

and after the vigilance movement became active. Extolling the modern Russian writers in 1908, Ó Conaire articulated what could be seen as an apologia for his own artistic vision and method:

> In Russia, a country that was dependent on folktales and folk songs until a hundred years ago, a group of distinguished writers arose—a group that drew back from no question that was of interest. Some of them began digging deeply in search of the truth, for they were in earnest. They had faith and they were not satisfied with the lying fables that were put before them. When they came up out of the hole in which they were searching, they had a filthy, smeared thing with the shape of a human being, and they cried out at the top of their lungs: Here is the human! Here is the man! Here is the truth! But they weren't paid much attention at first. It was thought that the filthy, smeared thing was too ugly to be a man. But those authors, Gogol and those who preceded him, were not fearful or timid. They vowed and they swore that they had found the truth, and Turgenev and many others came after them to prove that they were right—that the good and the noble existed within the filth and ugliness of that form that they had found.[72]

Writing in 1912 in his short-lived political weekly *An Barr Buadh*, Pearse created his own fable to attack what he saw as the vigilance fanatics' obsession with such filth and ugliness, real and imagined. His

72. Pádraic Ó Conaire, "Sean-Litridheacht na nGaedheal agus Nuadh-Litridheacht na hEorpa curtha i gcomh-mheas le n-a chéile 'fhéachaint cia aca is fearr mar cheap agus mar sholúid nuadh-litridheacht do sgríbhneoiríbh na Gaedhilge" (The ancient literature of Ireland and the modern literature of Europe, compared to see which would be better as a mold and model for Gaelic writers of a new literature) in *Aistí Phádraic Uí Chonaire* (The essays of Pádraic Ó Conaire), ed. Gearóid Denvir (Indreabhán: Cló Chois Fharraige, 1978), 47. This essay won a first prize at the 1908 Oireachtas and was serialized in *ACS* commencing on 12 December 1908. "Sa Rúis, tír a bhí taobh le na sean-sgéaltaibh agus le na seanamhránaibh go dtí le céad bliadhain, d'éirigh dream ughdar oirdhearc suas—dream nár tharraing siar ó aon cheist i n-ar cuireadh suim. Chuaidh cuid aca ag rómhar go doimhin i dtalamh ar lorg na Fírinne, mar bhíodar i ndáríribh. Bhí creideamh aca agus ní rabhadar sásta leis na finn-sgéaltaibh bréagacha a bhí curtha os a gcomhair. Nuair a thángadar aníos as an bpoll 'n-a rabhadar ag cuartughadh bhí rud salach smeartha a raibh dealbh duine air aca agus ghlaoidheadar amach i n-árd a ngotha: Seo é an duine! Seo é an fear! Seo í an fhírinne! Ach ní mórán aírd a bhí ortha ar dtús. Do ceapadh go raibh an rud salach smeartha ró-ghránda le bheith 'n-a fhear. . . . Ach ní raibh na hughdair úd, Gogol agus an dream a tháinig roimhe, go faitcheach scáthmhar. Do mhionnuigh agus mhóidigh siad go raibh an fhírinne fáighte acu, agus tháinig Tourgéníbh agus mórán eile 'n-a ndiaidh le cruthughadh go raibh an ceart aca—go raibh an mhaith agus an uaisleacht taobh istigh de shalachar agus de ghrándacht an deilbh úd a bhí fáighte aca."

protagonist is "Fear Meathta" (A degenerate man) who spends his life ferreting out and publicizing the literary corruption he sees everywhere he looks. The piece concludes:

> He continued in that way until his mind and the minds of his friends were so corrupted that they could not think or speak of anything but rottenness and filth and the very foulest things.
> And when that man died at the end of his life, he was damned and sent to Hell.[73]

As has been noted, Pearse and Ó Conaire were not alone in their distaste for the excesses of the vigilance mentality, and it may here be instructive to compare the generally enlightened approach of the institutional Gaelic movement as given voice by *An Claidheamh Soluis* with that taken by the other two principal Irish-Ireland weeklies, Arthur Griffith's *Sinn Féin* and D. P. Moran's *The Leader*. Griffith was fully in sympathy with the goals of the vigilance movement, writing in *Sinn Féin* on 11 November 1911: "We are glad that a movement is about to stem the poisoned flood that is pouring into the country, and its promoters will need and deserve all the support they can get."[74] And while the Limerick burnings brought second thoughts, he seems to have felt that it would be a tactical mistake to criticize the campaign after it had been set in motion: "Since the crusade has been entered upon, however crude its methods, we desire its success." Nevertheless, he took pains to underscore "the obvious remedy . . . the revival of the Irish language," for "it is evident that if modern English literature is essentially decadent, the English language is an impossible medium to fight decadence." His editorial concluded: "The movement, it is evident, cannot be permanently founded on a policy of compelling newsagents not to sell objectionable papers. It must be based on a policy of inducing people not to buy them. Unless that ground is taken soon the evil it attempts to grapple with will not be overcome."[75] Griffith's ideas continued to evolve, and two years later the editorial stance of *Sinn Féin* on this question was indistinguishable from that of *An Claidheamh Soluis*:

---

73. "An Fear Meathta," in *Collected Works of Pádraic H. Pearse: Scríbhinní* (Writings), 265. The fable originally appeared in *An Barr Buadh* in 1912. "Do lean de an fear sin gur truailligheadh a intinn-sean agus intinn a cháirde chomh mór sin nár fhéadadar cuimhniughadh ná labhairt ar aon ní acht ar an lobhthacht agus ar an salachar agus ar gach ní dhá bhréine. Agus an uair do fuair an fear sin bás i ndeireadh a shaoghail do damhnuigheadh agus do cuireadh chum Ifrinn é."
74. "Immoral Literature," *SF*, 11 November 1911.
75. "The English Mind in Ireland," *SF*, 13 January 1912. Griffith was here commenting on Murphy's *The Literature Crusade in Ireland*.

"To attempt to successfully fight the imposition of decadent English tastes and ideas on Ireland without reviving the Irish language is as sensible as Mrs. Partington's attempt to keep out the Atlantic with her broom. When our Vigilance Committees, as well as exhorting the people against evil English literature, exhort them to have their children instructed in the Irish language that they may have a native literature to read, they will have a logical objective."[76]

A regular contributor at the time, "Mr. Must" shared none of Griffith's initial ambivalent tolerance of the campaign's "crude" methods. In an article published two months after the burnings, he warned that the vigilance movement had spread "with almost dangerous rapidity," and that while "the ultimate object of the various vigilance committees is all that can be desired, not only by every Irishman, but by every clean-minded man and woman of whatever nationality," Sinn Féiners should keep in mind that "a movement of this nature . . . requires care and generalship to guide it safely over one or two very perilous rocks." He then went on to discuss two such perils, one practical and one ethical. First, he drew attention to the simple fact that people tend to become fascinated by that which they are denied by force, and second, anticipating Pearse's allegory in *An Barr Buadh*, he cautioned that "men engaged on the committee are apt to become fanatics in spite of themselves, and in their praiseworthy efforts to strike at the root of the evil, to find evil where none is intended." Curiously, while stressing that "it is essential that these two dangers be avoided if the movement is to have any permanent effect for good," he made no mention whatsoever of the role the Irish language could play in the campaign.[77]

On the other hand, the paper's regular Gaelic columnist, "Dubh Dorcha" (Seán Ó Caomhánaigh), was forthright in his condemnation of what he saw as the vigilance campaign's attempt to manipulate if not hijack the language movement, a concern that may not have been all that far-fetched considering the thousand-member-strong contingent from the vigilance association that marched in the 1913 Language Procession in Dublin.[78] Commenting on this procession, Ó Caomhánaigh wrote:

76. "How to Counter Evil Literature," *SF*, 8 February 1913. See also T. Kelly, "The Vigilance Campaign," *SF*, 29 March 1913.

77. "Mr. Must," "Swaggering Saxons," *SF*, 2 December 1911. The rest of the column is devoted to a discussion of ways to deal with the prostitution associated with the English garrison in Dublin.

78. See John Hutchinson, *The Dynamics of Cultural Nationalism: The Gaelic Revival and the Creation of the Irish Nation State* (London: Allen and Unwin, 1987), 195.

A great mistake was made at the big Dublin meeting, that is, making any reference whatsoever to evil literature from abroad. I don't know what that has to do with the cause of our language. Why don't those who are so zealous against it start Irish language groups? . . . Let those who are troubled by this literature join the Gaelic League and I am certain that this cursed stuff from abroad won't make them so anxious. The sooner the League ignores things of this sort that are none of its concern, the better off it will be.[79]

There is, incidentally, no slight irony in the fact that Ó Caomhánaigh was later to earn the distinction of being the only Gaelic author to fall afoul of Free State censorship with his 1927 novel *Fánaí* (Wanderer). Shortly after its publication, some individual priests as well as the Catholic Truth Society found the book's treatment of sexual attraction and its depiction of an attempted rape even more startling than its setting on the Minnesota–North Dakota border. As a result of their written protests to the publisher, the newly established government agency An Gúm, the first edition of the novel was withdrawn from circulation shortly after its publication pending the author's revision of offending passages. It is, however, worth noting that while Ó Caomhánaigh accepted some of the suggested excisions of his would-be censor, Dublin's archdiocesan examiner Father Michael Murphy, he rejected others and was supported in his dissent by An Gúm itself, which then re-released the book in its revised (i.e., partially censored) form.[80]

Concerning the whole issue of vigilance and censorship, the views of D. P. Moran and his colleagues and correspondents at *The Leader* demand special attention. Due perhaps to the not unrelated facts that Moran was a very vocal personality in the Irish-Ireland movement for a very long time (he edited *The Leader* for thirty-six years), that he saw

79. "Aiste na Connartha" (The condition of the league), *SF*, 29 March 1913. "An chruinniugh mhór Átha Cliath deineadh an-dhearmhad, sé sin, aon tagairt do dheunamh don dhroichlitridheacht so tar lear. Ní feas dom cad é an bhaint atá ag san le cúis ar dteangan. Iad so atá chómh dícheallach 'n-a haghaidh cad fáth ná tosnuighid buidheanta Gaedhilge? . . . An drong go bhfuil an litridheacht so ag cur buaidhrimh ortha tagaidís i gConnradh na Gaedhilge agus táim cinnte ná cuirfidh an rud malluighthe seo ón imigcéin aon charabuaic ortha. Dá luaithe scaoileann an Chonnradh tháirse nidhthe don tsaghas so ná baineann léithe is feárrde í é."

80. For a detailed discussion of this whole episode, including a full list of the offending passages identified by Father Murphy, Ó Caomhánaigh's response to them, and An Gúm's final editorial decision concerning them, see Tadhg Ó Dúshláine, "Scéal Úirscéil: *Fánaí*, Seán Óg Ó Caomhánaigh, 1927" (The story of a novel: *Wanderer*, Seán Óg Ó Caomhánaigh, 1927), in *Litríocht na Gaeltachta, Léachtaí Cholm Cille* 19 (1989): 93–128.

himself as *a* if not *the* obvious conscience of that movement, and that he expressed his acerbic opinions in a vigorous and memorable prose style and exclusively in the English language, his attitudes on a wide range of issues have often been accepted as paradigmatic of those of revivalists in general. For example, John Hutchinson can call him "the dynamo" and "the major figure" of the "politico-cultural revival,"[81] and in an unreliable amalgam of insight and wishful thinking, D. George Boyce can assert that "Moran had the unpleasant knack of stating clearly and unequivocally the direction in which the Gaelic movement was heading."[82] Such intellectual shortcuts, while on occasion convenient can lead the unwary astray. For example, while Terence Brown in his *Ireland: A Social and Cultural History, 1922 to the Present* explicitly denies any monolithic, much less institutional, Gaelic support for the later Censorship of Publications Act, his disclaimer, with its focus on Moran, is so perfunctory and half-hearted that it seems to resurrect the indictment just dismissed. Brown writes:

> In writings of this kind the cultural exclusivism of the Irish-Ireland movement helped create a climate of opinion in which authors whose work might encounter moral disapproval could also be suspected of a lack of national authenticity or will. . . . In this way the thinking of the Irish Ireland movement must be associated with the conservative climate in which the Censorship Bill of 1929 was enacted and put to work, even where, in individual cases, supporters of the movement may not have espoused the cause of censorship at all or as vigorously as did D.P. Moran in his *Leader* editorials (58).

While there can be little doubt that the reduced and somewhat rudderless Gaelic movement did become more conservative and philistine after the birth of the Free State—indeed after the Rising if not even earlier—Brown's appeal to Moran, his chronologically vague reference to some undifferentiated orthodoxy called "the thinking of the Irish Ireland movement," his invocation of just plain vague "climates," "conservative" and "of opinion," and his recourse to the subjunctive mood are less than fair to those individual revivalists who for a variety of often complex reasons stood up to the vigilance movement that was eventually to midwife the censorship act.

None of the above is, however, intended to deny that Moran was a

81. See Hutchinson, *Dynamics*, 168–78. It is worth noting that Hutchinson gives no indication that he knows Irish.

82. *Nationalism in Ireland* (Baltimore: Johns Hopkins University Press, 1982), 243.

major figure or that he and his *Leader* columnists indulged in almost
rabid demagogery in their support for the vigilance campaign. Moran
himself took the lead in an October 1911 editorial piece praising the
Limerick committee for "giving a lead to tame Ireland, and particularly
dirty Dublin."[83] Two weeks later, "T.J.F." lauded "the splendid and
inspiring lead which Limerick has given to all Ireland,"[84] and the following month "Avis" congratulated the city, for "once again its inhabitants are gallantly opposing the invader."[85] One "Sarsfield" (the usual
pen name of the levelheaded and tolerant P. S. Ua hÉigeartaigh
[O'Hegarty], but here likely to be a Limerick man invoking a local
hero) was rhapsodic over the burnings: "They have crushed the wealthy
reptile Press, laughed at morbid 'intellectuals,' lovers of license and advocates of filth."[86] His hope was that the movement would spread
through the convening of a "vigilance congress": "For the Vigilance
Committees to stop when half-way would be folly. Let them go forward and perfect their work."[87] According to one "Oscar," such future
projects should include "disinfecting the picture shows."[88] Par-
enthetically, a Censorship of Films Act was passed by the Free State
Dáil (Parliament) in 1923, six years before the law regulating printed
matter. But not even Moran could make one of his columnists toe a
party line. Father Dinneen, who regularly lined up with the nativists
and was a regular contributor to *The Leader* after his falling out with the
league, was in the end far closer to Mac Giollarnáth than to Moran in
his attitude to the vigilance committees. Thus in two pieces on the English papers that appeared in *The Leader* in the same month as the burnings, he made no comment whatsoever on the Limerick situation, and
argued the orthodox position that the best defense against bad books
was to ignore them and to read good ones, particularly good ones in
Irish.[89] And in that high-minded if unrealistic exhortation, rather than in
the fulminations of Moran, one hears the true voice of the Revival.

In retrospect, the vigilance movement, even when unified in 1911
under the Dominican Order's umbrella organization, the Irish Vigilance

83. "Current Affairs," *The Leader*, 14 October 1911.
84. "The Corrupt Imported Press," *The Leader*, 28 October 1911.
85. "Limerick City and Its Citizens," *The Leader*, 11 November 1911.
86. "Legislation and Indecent Literature," *The Leader*, 9 March 1912.
87. "Sarsfield," "A Vigilance Congress—Why and When?" *The Leader*, 1 June 1912.
88. "Disinfecting the Picture Shows," *The Leader*, 9 December 1912.
89. See Dinneen, "Léightheoireacht an Domhnaigh" (Sunday reading), *The Leader*, 4
November 1911; and "Leabhair agus Léightheoireacht" (Books and reading), *The Leader*,
11 November 1911. Miraculously, to judge from Shán Ó Cuív's bibliography, An tAthair Peadar Ua Laoghaire wrote nothing about the burnings. See Ó Cuív, "Materials for a
Bibliography of the Very Reverend Peter Canon O'Leary, 1839–1920," supplement to
Celtica 2, no. 2 (1954).

Association, proved to be no major threat to the free flow of ideas at this time, in part, no doubt, because the political and military turmoil of the succeeding years made the English weeklies seem among the least of the nation's problems. But in such an ideologically charged atmosphere, it required both intellectual integrity and moral courage to maintain the moderate and principled stand taken by the leaders of the Gaelic movement, including those like Dinneen with strong religious and denominational convictions and clear nativist tendencies. Patrick Pearse's 1915 call for an Ireland "not free merely, but Gaelic as well; not Gaelic merely, but free as well" was here as elsewhere more than a rhetorical flourish.

Of course even the most committed nativist saw Gaelic literature as more than a mere medium for pure, noble, and prophylactic propaganda. Those holding nativist views were, from the beginning, among the most active creators of the new literature as well as among its most thoughtful and at times vociferous critics, often reserving their sharpest attacks for fellow nativists whom they saw as deviating from the straight and narrow path of orthodox *Gaelachas*. The most significant literary debate in the early years of the Revival, that between advocates of *cainnt na ndaoine* and those favoring the "classical" Irish of the seventeenth century, is frequently regarded as a battle between progressive forces attempting to forge a modern literature through a modern language, and reactionaries quixotically attempting to resurrect the lost glories of a severed literary tradition. In effect, while progressives like Pearse, Eoin Mac Néill, and Ó Conaire did play a prominent and influential role in the victory of *cainnt na ndaoine*, the acknowledged leaders on both sides of the debate were nativists, who, despite major tactical differences, shared a vision of the new literature as the vehicle for the expression of an indigenous Irish ethos firmly rooted in Gaelic tradition and uncorrupted by foreign influences. Thus, the greatest champion and practitioner of *cainnt na ndaoine*, An tAthair Peadar Ua Laoghaire, could defend his commitment to the spoken contemporary language in terms of its continuity with the past, not its literary merits or potential: "Our national minds, and our national speech, have been interdependent during all the ages and generations of the past. No nation can break with its past without disaster. Those who understand that fact are bound to strain every nerve to prevent the language of the nation from disappearing. We are bound to speak Irish, and to teach Irish, and to write Irish."[90]

Progressives like Pearse and Mac Néill could hardly dissent from

---

90. Quoted by Séamus Ó Dubhghaill in "An tAthair Peadar Ó Laoghaire and Classical Irish," letter, *ACS*, 16 December 1911.

such sentiments, but they did point out that *cainnt na ndaoine* was just that, the *speech* of the people, the raw material of literature which it was the writer's duty to fashion for the expression of a personal aesthetic vision. Furthermore, as we will see in Chapter 2, the progressives insisted that an acceptance of the language of the Irish-speaking peasantry should not restrict the Gaelic writer to the worldview of that peasantry. As Pearse wrote in 1906: "Those who would build up a great national art—an art capable of expressing the soul of the whole nation, peasant and non-peasant—must do even as we propose to do with regard to the language: they must take what the peasants have to give them and develop it."[91] Moreover, according to both Pearse and Mac Néill, that was precisely what the best of the nativist practitioners of *cainnt na ndaoine* were doing, often despite their own occasional protestations that they were only attempting to reproduce the living speech of the Gaeltacht faithfully. Indeed, in the final analysis it was their ideological ends rather than their linguistic means that divided progressives and nativists in their approach to and use of *cainnt na ndaoine*. Mac Néill and Pearse may well have sympathized with the 1902 assertion of Séamus Ó Dubhghaill that "the only Irish worth anything is the Irish of the countryside."[92] They would, however, have found absurd his 1913 definition of literature: "I don't care what thoughts are in a person's mind, be they high or low, smooth or rough, bitter or sweet. If he puts those thoughts in pure Irish I say his work is true literature and I praise it."[93]

In some ways writers who urged the adoption of "classical" Irish as the medium of Revival literature were more philosophically consistent with the general nativist position. For those like Thomas O'Neill Russell, Richard Henebry, and John M. O'Reilly, much of the "Revival Irish" allegedly based on *cainnt na ndaoine* was, with its Anglicisms, corruptions, and neologisms, another and more insidious instance of foreign contamination of the native tradition. This position was represented at its most extreme by Thomas O'Neill Russell, who offered the editor of *Fáinne an Lae* the following advice in the paper's very first issue: "Pay no attention to any kind of Irish for which examples are not to be found in the writings of learned people of the 16th and 17th and

---

91. "Traditionalism," editorial, *ACS*, 9 June 1906.

92. Letter, *ACS*, 8 March 1902. "Ní fiú faic aon Ghaedhilg acht Gaedhilg na tuaithe." Pearse did, however, engage in a spirited controversy with Diarmuid Ua Cruadhlaoich in *Sinn Féin* in the summer of 1911.

93. "Cad Is Litridheacht Ann?" (What is literature?), *ACS*, 22 November 1913. "Is cuma liom-sa cad iad na smaointe a bhíonn istigh i n-aigne an duine, bídís árd nó íseal, mín nó garbh, searbh nó mílis. Má chuireann sé na smaointe úd i nglan-Ghaedhilg deirim-se gur fíor-litridheacht a shaothar, agus molaim-se é."

18th centuries."[94] Although both O'Reilly and Henebry were to stir up lengthy and acerbic controversies due to the aggressive and often personal manner with which they argued—one is tempted to say promulgated—their positions in *The Native Speaker Examined Home* and "Revival Irish" respectively, the two were actually slightly less unyielding than was Russell. Thus O'Reilly always emphasized the central importance of the contemporary native speaker for the maintenance and survival of Irish,[95] while simultaneously rejecting the dialect Irish such a person of necessity spoke as the basis for the new literature: "The spoken language of any people, and so of the Irish, is the merest fustian and fag-ends compared with its literary counterpart. But even if it were the very purity of diction, it could not serve as a model for writing, because of its countless varieties. Even if the varieties were not there, folk language could never be made adequate for the million million themes that must be handled nowadays in writing."[96] And if he was so critical of the fluent Irish of the native speaker, for the acquired "Revival Irish" of many Gaelic literary figures O'Reilly had unmitigated contempt: "The reflection most apt to come first and remain to the last is that 'Revival Irish' is something to guard against with all our vigilance, and that it is hard to know where one is secure of Revival Irish" (77). In place of this "folk fustian," he offered as inspiration and model the entire corpus of Irish literature extending to the eighteenth century, "the genuine language of Erin's mind, or, to speak more accurately . . . the language of Erin when Erin had a mind" (87), and urged those working to create a new Irish literature: "Stay at home and work at your books. Read, read, and never tire, and let it be the literature" (188).

Henebry was willing to allow *cainnt na ndaoine* a more active, though still strictly subordinate, role in the creation of the new literature: "The spoken language must be the basis of our restored written style but cannot become the literary language, because such can never be."[97] In his view a handful of works by native speakers—a handful that at times seems to have consisted exclusively of the writings of An tAthair Pea-

94. Letter, *FL*, 8 January 1898. "Ná cuir aon tsuim i n-aon chineál Gaedhilge nach faghthar somplaidhe uirthi i sgríbhnibh daoine foghlamtha na seiseadh, na seachtmhadh, agus na hochtmhadh aoise déag." See also his "How the Irish Language Has Been Distorted," *WF*, 12 December 1903.

95. See, for example, O'Reilly, "Books in Irish," *SF*, 4 March 1911.

96. Father John M. O'Reilly, *The Native Speaker Examined Home: Two Stalking Fallacies Anatomized* (Dublin: Sealy, Bryers and Walker, 1909), 86–87.

97. "The Want of an Irish Dictionary / Views of the Reverend Professor Henebry," *FL*, 12 February 1898.

dar—could see valid service as primers to prepare readers for the study
of the more sophisticated texts from the past that would serve as the
true inspiration of the new literature. For contemporary Irish writing
not the work of native speakers or not imbued with what he termed
"the Irish philosophy, the Irish outlook, the Irish *Weltanschauung*,"[98] in
other words for the vast bulk of what was being produced in the early
years of the Revival, he had only scorn: "And besides such literature is
not in continuity with any Irish literature that ever went before it, nor
in agreement with the idiom of those who still speak Irish to-day, and
hence it cannot be called Irish at all. And so is all Revival Irish."[99] Indeed in his famous series of articles on "Revival Irish" in *The Leader* in
1908–9, he lambasted virtually all of the new Gaelic writers for both
their intellectual and aesthetic exoticism and their deficient command of
the language, frequently dissecting their work line by line or word by
word and at times accompanying his dismemberment with what he saw
as a proper reconstruction of what the authors *should* have written in
"classical" or even Middle Irish![100] Herein lay the fatal flaw in the O'
Reilly–Henebry literary program: strict adherence to its principles made
the writing of acceptably "correct" Irish all but impossible for anyone
in the twentieth century. Contemporary critics were quick to point out
that for all their Gaelic erudition, both men chose to write their most
important and extended work in English, apparently unwilling to trust
their own mastery of the language they claimed to be trying to save.[101]
Nor did their opponents fail to exploit this inconsistency, as when
Séamus Ó Dubhghaill all but taunted Henebry in a 1908 letter to *An
Claidheamh Soluis*: "If Father Henebry were to set about writing a book,
there is no danger there would be any provincialism in his speech. But

98. "Revival Irish," *The Leader*, 9 January 1909.

99. "Revival Irish," *The Leader*, 5 December 1908.

100. See, for example, his discussion and reconstruction of the preface to Séamus Ó
Dubhghaill's *Cathair Conroí agus Sgéalta Eile* in "Revival Irish," *The Leader*, 14 November
1908. In an *ACS* editorial response to Henebry's series, Pearse told of the results of an
experiment he conducted with Henebry's "Irish translation" of Ó Dubhghaill's preface:
"We have just read it to five native speakers in succession—two of them young lads
recently come to Dublin from Western homes in which no English is ever spoken. The
passage, in Dr. Henebry's version, was unintelligible to them, one and all. They could
only dimly guess at its general drift. Some sentences they could not even guess at re-
motely. They were as Greek to them." See "Is Irish a Living Language?" editorial, *ACS*,
21 November 1908.

101. For criticism of O'Reilly, see Liam Ua Domhnaill, " 'The Vile Irish
Speaker' / Father O'Reilly Examined," review of *The Irish Speaker Examined Home*, *ACS*,
2 October 1909; for criticism of Henebry, see "Is Irish a Living Language?," editorial,
ACS, 21 November 1908; and Micheál Ó Máille, "Revival Criticism," letter, *ACS*, 12
December 1908.

see here, I'll wager that 'Tadhg Gabha' will be better understood down in the Decies than any book from the hand of Father Richard."[102] Father O'Reilly's response to such criticisms, despite its aggressive assertiveness, was woefully lame, as he argued that given the state of the modern language, he himself would have been reduced to recourse to some kind of "Revival Irish" entirely incapable of conveying the intellectual subtlety of his thesis: "For Revival Irish, remarkable as it is in many ways else, seems to abhor thought as nature does a vacuum, and avoids ideas so strenuously in itself, as to give clear hint that it is not prepared to afford them a good reception from another. A book with ideas in it would be, by the very fact, not Irish; for ideas would take words to convey them, and words too, most likely, which we have never heard in our village, nor ever come across in the idioms of the Handbook, or in the writings of Canon O'Leary."[103]

Losing causes are, of course, easy to patronize, and all too often the nativists have been perfunctorily dismissed as provincials, puritans, or pedants, people whose arguments were either irrelevant to begin with or were soon rendered so by the literary successes of more adventurous and gifted authors. Moreover, this assessment has a venerable if unreliable history. Their Anglo-Irish literary contemporaries frequently ridiculed Gaelic revivalists as provincial and reactionary, a half-truth whose injustice has been compounded by the fact that few scholars of Anglo-Irish literature have taken the effort to go behind the stereotype and, even more unfairly, by the fact that a distortion of the nativist stance has been uncritically accepted as representative of the Gaelic movement as a whole. For example, in 1907 J. M. Synge lashed out at revivalists whom he saw as leading instigators of the attack on his *Playboy of the Western World*: "Was there ever a sight so piteous as an old and respectable people setting up the ideals of Fee-Gee because, with their eyes glued on John Bull's navel, they dare not be Europeans for fear the

---

102. Séamus Ó Dubhghaill, "Fearg gan Chúis" (Anger without cause), letter, *ACS*, 19 December 1908. Henebry was himself a native speaker from the Decies. "Dá gcuirfeadh an tAthair de hEinebre chun leabhair a sgrí' níor bhaoghail go mbeadh aon chúigeachas ag baint le na chuid cainte. Acht féach, cuirfead-sa geall leis gur fearr a thuigfar 'Tadhg Gabha' theas ins na Déisibh ná aon leabhar ó láimh an Athar Riseárd." On the other hand, in essays in *Comhar* in 1961 and 1962, Flann Mac an tSaoir argued that Henebry has long been misrepresented and caricatured. See Mac an tSaoir, "An Dr. Risteárd de Hindeberg," *Comhar* 20, no. 11 (November 1961)–21, no. 1 (January 1962).

103. "Why Not Write Something in Irish?," *SF*, 4 February 1911. It is worth noting that, unlike Henebry, O'Reilly did not invariably exempt An tAthair Peadar from his criticism of "fustian" and Revival Irish.

huckster across the street might call them English."[104] In 1903 Yeats included among the three kinds of philistinism Irish artists had to combat, "the hatred of ideas of the more ignorant sort of Gaelic propagandist, who would have nothing said or thought that is not in country Gaelic."[105] For Joyce, the Gaelic Revival was personified by Dedalus's well-meaning but willfully provincial friend Davin and, more ominously, by the old man John Alphonsus Mulrennan meets in the West of Ireland:

> Old man had red eyes and short pipe. Old man spoke Irish. Mulrennan spoke English. Mulrennan spoke to him about universe and stars. Old man sat, listened, spoke, spat. Then said:
> —Ah, there must be terrible queer creatures at the latter end of the world.
> I fear him. I fear his redrimmed horny eyes. It is with him I must struggle all through this night till day come, till he or I lie dead, gripping him by the sinewy throat till. . . . Till what? Till he yield to me? No. I mean him no harm.[106]

Yet perhaps more typical of the attitude of Anglo-Irish writers to the Revival was the utter condescension of "John Eglinton" (William Kirkpatrick Magee). Speaking of an elderly bumpkin named "Ar dTeanga Fein" ("Our Own Language"), Eglinton pontificated:

> While his European contemporaries have lived and grown to what they are amid the stress of epoch-making ideas and movements, have enjoyed ceaseless intercourse with one another, been partners in the same enterprises, and made common cause against the foes of intellectual and spiritual liberty, he fell, at the very dawn of what we call the modern movement, out of any share in the titanic struggle of the new ideas, and living out his life in solitude and far from towns, with all their iniquities and revolutions, indulged his dreamy inclinations, sharing the kindly life of simple peasants.[107]

104. "Can We Go Back into Our Mother's Womb?: A Letter to the Gaelic League by a Hedge Schoolmaster" in Synge, *Collected Works*, ed. Alan Price (London: Oxford University Press, 1966), 2:400.

105. W. B. Yeats, "An Irish National Theatre" in *Uncollected Prose*, ed. John P. Frayne and Colton Johnson (London: MacMillan, 1975), 2:307.

106. James Joyce, *A Portrait of the Artist as a Young Man* (New York: Viking, 1964), 251–52.

107. "John Eglinton," "The Grand Old Tongue" in *Anglo-Irish Essays* (New York: John

Given their impressive achievement in a world language, it is hardly surprising that the Anglo-Irish writers made their charges stick. It is also impossible to deny that there was some basis for their criticism. Much of the influence of the nativists *was* baneful. They were, for example, responsible to some extent for both the sectarianism and the self-imposed censorship that Pádraic Ó Conaire and others saw stifling Gaelic literature in the years surrounding the birth of Saorstát Éireann (the Irish Free State)[108] and that would eventually lead to the Censorship of Publications Act. Perhaps even more important, they encouraged what Piaras Béaslaí called "the great faults of Irish literature, the things which most retarded their development—insularity and conservatism"[109] —and thereby fostered what in the same post-independence years became an obsession with a narrowly defined and moribund *Gaelachas* of the kind lampooned by Myles na gCopaleen in *An Béal Bocht*.[110]

On the other hand, it is unfair to condemn writers like Ua Laoghaire, Ó Dubhghaill, Henebry, and O'Reilly for the effects distortions and even caricatures of their ideas were to have in circumstances radically different from those that engendered them. When the nativists entered the field, the Gaelic tradition was both threatened and despised, and their efforts in restoring, interpreting, and expressing Henebry's "Irish *Weltanschauung*" were invaluable in preserving for the language and its new literature a sense of its own past. With this contribution and with the personal integrity, dedication, and ability of its adherents, nativism earned the hearing it will be accorded in this study as well as the right

---

Lane, 1918), 31. The anonymous *ACS* review of Eglinton's book praised the literary quality of his work while charging that he was incapable of writing objectively about Ireland and in particular about the Irish language, for "his mind is under the control of that preconception, that is, that disease he himself calls 'Anglo-Irishness.' " (Tá a aigne fé smacht ag an mbuntuairim sin .i. an galar úd ar a dtugann sé féin "GallÉireannachas.") See "An GallÉireannach" (The Anglo-Irishman), review of *Anglo-Irish Essays* by "John Eglinton," *ACS*, 22 December 1917, 3–4.

108. See, for example, "Páistí Scoile: Bhfuil Siad ag Milleadh Nualitridheacht na Gaedhilge?" (Schoolchildren: Are they destroying modern literature in Irish?), "Scríobhnóirí agus a gCuid Oibre: An Easba Misnigh Atá Orra?" (Writers and their work: Is the problem a lack of courage?), and "Lucht Peann faoin Saorstát" (Writers under the Free State), in *Aistí Uí Chonaire*, 80–81, 165–68, 177–79. The first essay was originally published in *ACS*, 17 February 1917; the second in *Old Ireland*, 28 February 1920; and the third in the *Free State*, 8 April 1922.

109. Shán Ó Cuív, "The Gaelic World / Notes on the Language Movement," *WF*, 15 December 1917. Ó Cuív was reporting on a lecture Béaslaí delivered in which he paid a judicious and balanced tribute to Henebry.

110. See Brown, *Ireland*, 13–79; Margaret O'Callaghan, "Language, Nationality, and Cultural Identity," 226–45; and Breandán Ó Conaire, *Myles na Gaeilge*, especially chapter 2, "An Gael agus Gnéithe den Ghaelachas" (The Gael and aspects of Gaelicism).

to be judged on its own terms, on the degree to which it fulfilled what
Father Henebry proclaimed to be its mission:

> Ours is to teach our distracted people to look to themselves for
> their deliverance, to help them to acquire a reflex national con-
> sciousness; to strengthen, to intensify it; to roll back the pall of
> ignorance and show them the barter they are unthinkingly mak-
> ing; to foster and encourage the race pride begotten of knowl-
> edge, that whereas now they cringe and crave for shame of their
> blood, there may not be found then a Gael of all the Gaels of the
> world who would not say: "Scotus sum"—"I am a Gael, and I
> accept all the responsibility."[111]

"Forlorn Isolation?": Progressivism

If the nativists have suffered the injustice of condescension on the basis
of a perversion of their actual and legitimate positions, an even greater
wrong has been inflicted on the progressives, who have often been dismissed for their supposed adherence to caricatured ideas they not only
never held, but actively and at times courageously opposed. Particularly
unfair to the progressives was Synge's sarcastic indictment that revivalists in general were attempting to insulate themselves from the challenges of contemporary European culture, for no single issue more
sharply distinguishes progressivism from nativism than the eager openness to literary and intellectual innovations from the Continent.

Writing in the heat of the debate over the place of Irish in the new
National University, Pearse confronted the issue head-on: "Gaels are
not 'obscurantists' nor 'provincialists' nor 'medievalists.' There is no
learning, however exalted, no thoughts, however profound, no knowledge, however mysterious, that we don't wish to see explored and explained in the new university."[112] And Pearse was by no means alone in

111. "The Want of an Irish Dictionary," *FL*, 12 February 1898.
112. "An tÁrd-Léigheann" (Higher learning), editorial, *ACS*, 22 May 1909. "Ní 'obscurantists' ná 'provincialists' ná 'Medievalists' Gaedhil. Níl aon léigheann dá áirde, níl
aon smaointe dá dhoimhne, níl aon eolas dá dhiamhaire, nár mhian linn dá sgrúdughadh
agus dá míniughadh san Iolsgoil nuaidh." "Medievalism," properly understood, was no
nativist vice in Pearse's mind. In thanking Hyde for his Sgoil Éanna lecture on the Catholic heritage of Oxford and Cambridge, he claimed of his Gaelic colleagues: "Their ideal
was an Irish university as Irish as Oxford and Cambridge were English. They must build
up a new Clonmacnoise in Ireland, and the new Clonmacnoise must be as national as the

his resentment of this imputation of parochialism. While Agnes O'Far-relly (Úna Ní Fhaircheallaigh) attacked "a vague something called 'cos-mopolitanism'" in a 1900 lecture later published as a pamphlet under the title *The Reign of Humbug*, her main target was clearly mindless West-Britonism, not a genuine openness to the wider world, a healthy attitude she saw as the natural result of the Revival's efforts to ground Ireland in her own indigenous Gaelic culture. Indeed, she proposed what can be regarded as the progressives' definition of sound and proper cosmopolitanism: "It means that, having fulfilled our duties to ourselves and to the land where God has thrown our destinies, we are ready to stretch the hand of friendship to all men. It means that having developed the individualism that is our birthright we are ready to give and take in the mutual action of nations."[113]

In 1904 Mary Butler (Máire de Buitléir) tried to put the league's "cos-mopolitan" critics on the defensive: "Ireland is resuming her place in Europe and in the entire civilised world. This is one of the results of the 'retrograde' Gaelic League which our friends the enemy warned us was 'to put back the hands of the clock,' and 'cut us off from all modern thought and progress.'"[114] George Moonan dealt with the issue more dispassionately in his paper "The Spirit of the Gaelic League," read to the Central Branch this same year: "The spirit of the Gaelic League is also a progressive spirit. . . . It does not hope or work to re-establish in the twentieth century, crudely and arbitrarily, irrespective of altered circumstances, the traditions of Pagan Ireland, the glories of early Christian Ireland, or even the conditions of eighteenth century Ireland. It recognises clearly that a nation must progress or stagnate. Its ideal is not to make Ireland a Western Thibet."[115] Éamonn Ó Néill took the offensive, claiming that revivalists were at least as cultured and up-to-date as their English-speaking "cosmopolitan" contemporaries: "The Gaelic Leaguer loves his Shakespeare and his Sophocles and his Goethe, and sometimes his Ibsen too, but he has grasped the principles of life in addition. He may not have travelled much, or been long at school or

old Clonmacnoise, yet, like the old Clonmacnoise, as broad as the human thought and culture of its day." See "I nDún Éanna" (In Enda's stronghold), *ACS*, 6 November 1909.

113. (Dublin: Gaelic League, 1901), 2. Similarly, in his very first editorial in *The Leader*, D. P. Moran, tempered his emphasis on the need to "re-establish a real Irish identity" and his admonition that "imitation is not assimilation" with a warning against cultural solips-ism: "We have no sympathy with the country that endeavours to bind itself round with a wall of brass, and refuses to learn from other nations or to assimilate from foreign sources anything that may suit its own constitution." See *The Leader*, 1 September 1900.

114. "The Oireachtas Industrial Exhibition," *ACS*, 20 August 1904.

115. *ACS*, 19 November 1904.

college, but he is a more cultured man."[116] The achievement of such culture required work, as one "Feargus" made clear in a 25 July 1914 *An Claidheamh Soluis* editorial entitled "Ireland, Europe and Literature," in which he set all serious Gaelic litterateurs a demanding program involving "French, German, and other study, very laborious for long stages," in preparation for a rigorous course of essential reading: "Individualities like Goethe and Balzac (to mention very different types) demand years of attention to begin with. Wide and varied is the ground to be gone over before one is ready for the seekers and teachers of our own day, like Euchen, Bergson, Maurice Barres, to take a few examples. Croce and others in Italy cannot be neglected; Russia has a hundred literary interests; Spain has a notable literary life and so on."

As we well know, not all Gaelic Leaguers shared the confident liberalism of Moonan and Pearse or the fashionable literary taste of Ó Néill and "Feargus," but if they chose to go public with opinions rooted in philistine reaction, they could expect to be challenged by their more enlightened colleagues. Thus in 1907 Pearse used the occasion of a letter from Éamonn Ceannt attacking *The Playboy of the Western World*, to issue a ringing affirmation of the progressive view that the Revival should be a vital force for cultural liberation into pluralism: "The Gaelic Leaguer who confines himself to Irish—if there be any such—*does not* appreciate the full extent of the present-day literary movement, nor would the Gaelic Leaguer confining himself to Irish *and* English, nor even the Gaelic Leaguer who might superadd a little French and German."[117] Moreover, Pearse, who was himself familiar with both French and German, put these principles into practice by having these two languages as well as Italian and Spanish taught through the Direct Method at his Sgoil Éanna (St. Enda's School). Writing in the school's prospectus, Pearse stated: "Under this system it is hoped that every pupil who passes through St. Enda's will, at the end of his course, have obtained a good oral and literary knowledge of at least three modern languages."[118] Other Gaels took a similar pride in being polyglot. For

116. "An Interesting Meeting," *ACS*, 9 November 1901. This literary meeting at 9 Merrion Row was called by Lady Gregory and attended by Yeats.

117. "About Plays and Play-Acting," editorial, *ACS*, 13 April 1907. Father John O'Reilly took a similar position: "The man who sets up a pretence to Irish while ignorant of Latin and Greek, is a fool positive. It were all the better if he also knew Spanish and German." See *The Native Speaker Examined Home*, 83–84. Of course, it would hardly be surprising for a priest at that time to have known Latin or, to a lesser extent, Greek. Dinneen, for example, published *Aistí ar Litridheacht Ghréigise is Laidne* (Essays on Greek and Latin literature) in 1929.

118. "Bilingualism in Practice," *ACS*, 28 August 1909.

example, commenting on a journey to a commemorative ceremony at Fontenoy, Mary Hayden and Henry Morris were upset at "the monoglot character of their fellow travellers," presumably Irish nationalists unaffiliated with the language movement.[119] Indirect tribute was paid to the linguistic abilities of many revivalists by An tAthair Tomás Ó Ceallaigh when in a 1907 reference to members of the League of St. Columba at Maynooth, he acknowledged that "unlike so many patrons of the Gaelic movement they claim, perhaps no extensive acquaintance with the languages of Europe."[120]

We are, obviously, a good ways from Joyce's Irish-speaking wrestling opponent of the red-rimmed eyes here, and Pearse's reference to Continental languages hints at perhaps the progressives' most creative and fruitful corollary to the Revival dogma that Ireland's key to an intellectually vital future lay in an authentic understanding of her past. For the progressives, historic Ireland was not a misty if magnificent realm of saints, scholars, and heroes, but a vibrant culture fully in the European mainstream. For the nativist the salient feature of the past often seems to have been an almost invulnerable glory, as they put their emphasis on Ireland as a proselytizing, not assimilative, culture. Thus in the aptly titled 1914 American anthology *The Glories of Ireland*, Dinneen could boast: "I claim, moreover, that when circumstances were favorable, no people have shown a more adventurous spirit or a more chivalrous devotion in the advancement and spread of learning . . . and from the fifth to the ninth century Ireland led the nations of Europe in learning and deserved the title of the 'Island of Saints and Scholars.'"[121] For the progressive, on the other hand, the most valuable lesson from the past was the need for a confident openness to the wider world. As early as 1898 *Fáinne an Lae* editorialized: "When Ireland was truly Irish, not only did we influence the entire civilisation of Europe, but hospitality was given here to the literature of the Continent, and Irishmen were, indeed, in contact with every stream of European thought. So nationalism led to the widest and best cosmopolitanism."[122]

---

119. "Jottings," *ACS*, 14 September 1907.
120. "The Maynooth Sermons," review of *Seanmóirí Mhuighe Nuadhad*, vols. 1 and 2, *ACS*, 28 September 1907.
121. "Irish Love of Learning" in *The Glories of Ireland*, ed. Joseph Dunn and P. J. Lennox (Washington, D.C.: Phoenix, 1914), 38.
122. "Nationalism vs. Cosmopolitanism," editorial, *FL*, 1 October 1898. The Anglo-Irish litterateur George Sigerson held a similarly high opinion of the ancient Irish as "the most progressive people in Europe": "Their minds flew high and far. Because of their seeing Intellect, they recognised, but looked over and beyond, those boundaries of race and region which fettered others. Because they were alert, ready of resource, quick of

This same note had of course been sounded by Douglas Hyde in his 1892 address to the National Literary Society entitled "The Necessity for De-Anglicising Ireland." However, Hyde's emphasis was on what had gone wrong since: "If we take a bird's-eye view of our Ireland to-day, and compare it with what it used to be, we must be struck by the extraordinary fact that the nation which was once, as everyone admits, one of the most classically learned and cultured nations in Europe is now one of the least so."[123] Hyde's explanation became instant and un-wavering Gaelic orthodoxy, as is evident from the views of one "Fios Fátha" eight years later: "I have heard people contend that a more gen-eral use of the Irish language would result in isolating Ireland from the civilised world. The truth is that Ireland never was isolated from the world till she adopted the English language; never was so free to the world, never so cosmopolitan, yet never so Irish as in the days when her gentry and her men of letters spoke their native tongue."[124]

Pearse agreed in an early editorial blast at the pseudosophistication of foes of the Revival: "We fear that in Ireland, 'cosmopolitanism'. . . is only another word for Anglicisation, and that the 'world' of which 'we' are citizens is that portion of the British Empire which—we speak met-aphorically—lies between Westminster and Fleet Street." Then, having dealt with the enemy, he challenged his fellow Gaels with their own past, asking: "Do you seriously contend that we should be wise to cut ourselves adrift from the great world of European thought? . . . Were we then completely aloof from European thought when we were Irish, and are we more in touch with it now that we are more than half English?"[125]

Although the question was clearly rhetorical, not all seemed to see the self-evident answer, and several years later Pearse felt compelled to restate the obvious in an open letter to the Trinity professor and Irish M.P. Thomas Kettle, reminding him that "to be European one must be

---

wit, they were tolerant of old and hospitable to new ideas—which so many resentfully resist or reluctantly admit." See "The Adventurous Intellectuality of Ancient Ireland," *St. Stephen's: A Record of University Life* 2, no. 10 (February 1906): 216–21.

123. In *1000 Years of Irish Prose: The Literary Revival*, ed. Vivian Mercier and David H. Greene (New York: Grosset and Dunlap, 1961), 79.

124. "Initiative," *ACS*, 21 April 1900.

125. "Gleó na gCath" (The tumult of the battles), *ACS*, 22 August 1903. Pearse's scorn for the provincialism of the press was anticipated by William P. Ryan: "At the moment whole tracts of English-speaking Ireland are to a most extraordinary degree 'cut off from the world'; they know no more of deep and significant things in the life of Europe than it suits the British and Anglo-Irish Press to tell. . . . There are great forces beyond the ken of 'Reuter' and many importances outside the pale of the Press Association." See *Lessons from Modern Language Movements* (Dublin: Gaelic League, 1902), 2.

Irish and to be Irish one must be an Irish-speaker."[126] George Moonan developed this point, stressing that Anglicization was a provincializing as well as de-nationalizing force, a process that not only deprived the Irish of their own culture, but also blocked them from encountering that of Europe. Of the Gaelic League he wrote: "It has always pointed out that we were more closely in touch with the civilised world when we had our national language in full vitality, that with the growth of the English language in Ireland the gross bulk of England came between us and the rest of the world, and that at present it shuts our voice off from civilisation and shuts us off from all its lessons of art and literature and science, except what filters through and is contaminated by England itself."[127] "Fear Taistil" who contributed a series of travel essays in Irish to An Claidheamh Soluis in 1910, chose more dramatic imagery to make the same point: "The Gaels have been a race imprisoned by the gods for many years. The great sea around us on every side; the English to our east like a great iron wall . . . and because of this wall being between the Gaels and the outside world, we have had, until recently, to get all the knowledge we needed about that world from the English or in Anglicized ways."[128]

It must, of course, have been well-nigh irresistible to believe that England, along with all its other enormities, was also the cause of "the squalid provincialism of life in Ireland,"[129] her being "hardly known in art or literature."[130] From all sides, nativist and progressive alike, abuse

126. *The Letters of P. H. Pearse*, ed. Séamas Ó Buachalla (Gerrards Cross: Colin Smythe, 1980), 426. Pearse stated "nach Eorpach go hÉireannach agus nach Éireannach go Gaedhilgeoir." He added that Kettle himself would understand "that there were many new things in the New Europe that were old things in ancient Ireland" (gur iomdha rud nuadh san Nua-Eoraip gur sean-rudaidhe iad sa tSean-Éirinn). This open letter was originally published in *An Barr Buadh* on 25 May 1912.

127. "The Spirit of the Gaelic League," *ACS*, 19 November 1904. Moonan's views were echoed by the editor of the London journal *Inis Fáil* five years later: "The truth is, one of the best arguments in favour of the Gaelic League is that it will make Irish men and women, not merely good citizens of Ireland, but good citizens of the world. . . . As we have grown more English in speech, we have grown less thoughtful, less joyous, less imaginative." See "Irish and Culture," *Inis Fáil: A Magazine for the Irish in London* (November 1909), 2.

128. "Thall 's i bhFus ar fud na hEorpa" (Here and there throughout Europe), *ACS*, 15 January 1910. "Cinneadh a bhí i gcarcair ag na déithibh le na ciantaibh 'seadh na Gaedhil. An mhuir mhór 'n-a dtimcheall ar gach taobh; na Sasanaigh ar an taobh thoir díbh mar bheadh árd-bhalla iarainn ann. . . . Agus mar gheall ar an árd-bhalla seo a bheith idir na Gaedhil agus an saoghal mór, b'éiginn dúinn go dtí le goirid, an t-eólas a bhí uainn ar an saoghal úd fhághail ó na Sasanaighibh nó ar shlighthibh Ghallda."

129. "Nationalism vs. Cosmopolitanism," *FL*, 1 October 1898.

130. "Resurgent Nationalities," *ACS*, 1 May 1909.

was heaped on the mindless materialism, the cultural stagnation, and most damningly, the boorish insularity of the ruling power and its Irish imitators.[131] Thus F. A. Fahy warned the members of the London Branch of the league against "the latter-day British worship of mere size, of convention, of the superficial in art and literature, and the hopeless British insensibility to ideas in the wider world—the Continent, Ireland, Scandinavia."[132] Pádraic Ó Conaire traced what he saw as England's literary mediocrity to the nation's materialism and "commercialism," both fueled by wealth stolen from the colonies.[133] William P. Ryan saw England as "curiously ignorant of the main and secondary currents of modern European literature,"[134] and found frankly ludicrous "the assumption that the cultivation of English will keep us in touch with world culture," asking "if the general Englishman is a very happy embodiment of 'world-culture'?" His own exultant answer was "The gods may laugh at the bare suggestion."[135] Father Henebry agreed, telling a St. Patrick's Day audience in Denver that "to know only English was to be trapped in the prison of ignorance. It was nowadays the only European tongue in which it was impossible to be educated."[136] Such criticism of England as a decadent and ultimately second-rate and declining culture, influence from which would benumb the Irish mind, achieved concise and memorable expression in a league branch's circular soliciting funds for the annual language appeal: "Pinero has described England as, intellectually, the suburb of Europe. In that sense Ireland has been, and still is to a great extent, a suburb of a suburb."[137]

There was, however, no small element of (self?) deception in Gaelic

131. In his 1906 editorial "The Seoinín," Pearse stated his position succinctly: "The fight against Seoininism is not a fight against refinement and culture. It is a fight against vulgarity, not in favour of it" (ACS, 15 September 1906).

132. Quoted in "London Notes," ACS, 19 April 1902.

133. "Sean-litridheacht na nGaedheal agus Nuadh-litridheacht na hEorpa," in Aistí Phádraic Uí Chonaire, 49.

134. Lessons from Modern Language Movements, 23.

135. "London Notes," ACS, 3 August 1901. These unsigned notes, a regular feature in ACS at this time, are obviously the work of Ryan. Lord Ashbourne (Liam Mac Giolla Bhríde / William Gibson) also stressed this point in an address to the London Branch of the league in 1913: "What the Irish wanted was to be in touch with the world . . . to know what was going on outside their own country, and the best way to do that was that they should be Irish—that, instead of speaking a language that tended to isolate them they should speak only their own native tongue." See "The London Inaugural Meeting / Denunciation of 'John Bull,' " ACS, 11 October 1913.

136. "Gleó na gCath," ACS, 2 May 1903. Henebry's comments are paraphrased rather than quoted verbatim in this report.

137. "Thoughts," ACS, 7 April 1906. The appeal was from Dublin's liberal Craobh na gCúig gCúigí.

discussions of English literary culture. Doubtless many of the nativists, like many Irish conservatives unconnected with the language revival, were genuinely shocked by some intellectual and artistic developments in the neighboring island. Fathers O'Reilly, Yorke, and Ó Braonáin were by no means alone in their belief that "English is the language of revolt, of proud, successful rebellion against religious authority . . . the tongue of private judgment . . . the tongue of passive and aggressive unbelief, to some extent of professed and triumphant immorality."[138] Yet paradoxically, the frightening ability of this language to expand and assimilate was often seen as a further indication of a vacuum at its spiritual core. The best-known expression of this idea came from the Anglo-Irish writer George Moore during his brief period as self-proclaimed savior of the Irish language. Addressing a meeting of supporters of the Irish Literary Theatre in February 1900, Moore declared: "From universal use and journalism, the English language in fifty years will be as corrupt as the Latin of the eighth century, as unfit for literary usage, and will become, in my opinion, a sort of volapuk, strictly limited to commercial letters and journalism."[139]

An Claidheamh Soluis endorsed this appealing notion without reservation: "English language literature has come and gone again, and it left that language bruised and worn-out after it. Now it is nothing but twaddle-talk."[140] From this perspective, the wonder was that Anglicization could hold any appeal for the Irish, a puzzle given memorable expression by Mac Néill in a 4 August 1900 *An Claidheamh Soluis* editorial entitled "Conquered": "Our fathers held English civilisation at a spear's length when it was fresh, young, heart-whole and healthy. Shall we embrace it now when it is wrinkled, with painted face, false teeth, fake hair, heart-rotten, diseased, a slave to gain and to coarse enjoyment?"

Father Patrick Kavanagh also drew on metaphors of morbidity to describe a civilization to which he would not even concede past glory, writing of England that it was "a nation never really great or good even in its best days, and which is now descending to the lowest grade amongst civilised peoples—poor in wit, poor in literature, and feeble in

---

138. Rev. J. M. O'Reilly, *The Trusty Vehicle of the Faith of the Gael* (Dublin: Irish Book, 1902), 17.

139. "Literature and the Irish Language," in *Ideals in Ireland*, ed. Lady Gregory (London: Unicorn, 1901), 49. See also the republication of a Moore letter to the *Times* of London as "Mr. George Moore on the Language," *FL*, 28 July 1900.

140. "Sgéalta Thairis" (Resolved issues), *ACS*, 21 September 1901. "Tá litridheacht an Bhéarla tagtha agus imighthe arís, agus d'fhág sí an teanga soin brúidhte caithte 'n-a diaidh. Ní'l ann anois ach twaddle-talk."

arms—a decaying and decadent nation whose apparent greatness is but the swelling of putrefaction."[141]

Yet when Gaels turned to a more specific discussion of the "poor" literature of that putrid society, they often seemed uneasy and evasive at best, and less than fully honest at worst. There were three chief Gaelic responses to English literature. The first, suggested in the discussion of the vigilance committees above, was to make no distinction whatsoever between trashy periodicals, popular fiction, and serious art, leaving the impression that all English literature was worthless. Thus in an 1899 editorial response to Alfred Webb, who had suggested that Gaelic Leaguers should not allow the study of Irish to cut them off from English culture, *An Claidheamh Soluis* commented: "He would next throw open to them the wide field of English literature with all its suggestive and demoralising novels and magazines, its 'penny dreadfuls,' its jingo barrack-room ballads, and its rule Britannia music hall songs."[142] Peadar Mac Fhionnlaoich claimed to have arrived at an identical position through distressful personal experience. Stuck in a hotel in a Scottish provincial town and seeking something to pass the time, he turned to a selection of English novels:

> I attempt to read one or two of them. But no, it won't work. I haven't got through two pages when I meet with a reference to one or more of the shining virtues of the Anglo-Saxon race, or their great ruling qualities, or their predestination in this world or the next, or the glories of the flag, or the all-nipotence of the fleet or some other well-seasoned note which I might have stood in the days of my innocent youth. Or is it a reference to the great "English-speaking race" or the progress of the English language in the world or the virtues of English femininity?

Overwhelmed by "the arrogance, the bounce, the self-laudation, and the obtrusive foreignism of English literature," Mac Fhionnlaoich concluded with a pronouncement and a vow: "The novels are all bad, no man shall catch me opening an English novel again."[143] If possible, Pea-

141. *Ireland's Defence—Her Language*, 10.
142. "Notes," *ACS*, 16 September 1899.
143. "P. T. MacG.," "Nothing to Read," *ACS*, 10 August 1901, Duilleachán an Oireachtais (Oireachtas supplement). Mac Fhionnlaoich treats American (and Australian) literatures in English as the virtual footnotes they seem to have been in the minds of revivalists. Having leafed through a pile of American magazines like the *Atlantic Monthly* and *Scribner's*, he wrote: "They too are English, and, like our own West-British literature, are but a weak imitation of the original article. Indeed your Yankee is the true original

dar Ua Laoghaire was even more sweeping in the denunciation posed by his essay "Is the English language poisonous?":

> Look over the whole range of English fiction. . . . No change. No new thought. Not a single new idea. All the talk we hear about "plot" and "art" and "originality," save the mark! is only talk about some new jingle rung on the very same three strings! In order to ring those new jingles, all the lowest and most degrading of human passions are searched for and exhibited to the mind of the reader. Then, and here is the point which answers the above question: the most polished refinement and diction is used for the purpose of covering, but not hiding, the vilest matter. That refined diction is poisonous language. It is rotten language, as rotten as anything which is corrupt. It is unwholesome. It ruins the mental health of those who read those English "navvils" [novels], just as rotten food would ruin their bodily health. The minds which feed on those "navvils" become injured in every way. Their faith becomes weakened. So does their patriotism, if they have got any patriotism at all.[144]

The second Gaelic response to English literature seems more reasonable in its acknowledgment that not all English writing was at the level

West Briton, following slavishly and without need the ways of the Saxon." Translation can provide a rough indication of Gaelic interest in the literatures of languages they knew. For our entire period I am only aware of a handful of American poems, the most ambitious being the 1917 Oireachtas Prize–winning translation of Longfellow's "Evangeline" by Mícheál Ó Cuileanáin; Bret Harte's "Plain Language from Truthful James," in *An t-Európach* (vol. 1, no. 5, May 1900); a Gaelic "Oncal Remus" by Aodh Beag Mac Fhinn (*ACS*, 27 January 1912); and Tomás Ó hEidhne's rendering of Hawthorne's "The Great Stone Face" as "An tEudan Mór Cloch" that won a 1916 Oireachtas Prize and commenced serialization in *ACS* on 18 November 1916. Anglo-Scottish fared little better, orthodoxy insisting that the proper tongue for Scotland was Scots Gaelic. Scottish writers who wrote in English were ignored in the Gaelic journals, with the exception of passing references to Scott or "Fiona Macleod" (William Sharp) and a few translations like Seán Tóibín's versions of stories by Neil Munro like "The Lost Pibroch" and "The Secret of the Heather Ale," serialized in *ACS* commencing on 18 April and 3 October 1914 respectively.

144. *The Leader*, 7 November 1908. Ua Laoghaire was participating in a debate initiated by one "P.F." who in a *Leader* article on 24 October 1908 entitled "Mission of the Irish Race" had called English "poisonous to Faith and Patriotism." He was answered on 31 October by "Imaal" who wrote that he was not interested in whether English literature was "unwholesome" ("that may be, or may not"); what he wanted to know was "how can a language—any language—be unwholesome or poisonous, and why, in particular, is the English language so?" The lengthy response of "P.F." himself to this question was published a fortnight after Ua Laoghaire's (21 November).

of the Sunday papers and Marie Corelli. But the distinction, once made, was then pronounced irrelevant. There may well have been some good English literature, but not much, and what there was didn't seem to find its way into Ireland. Lecturing his membership in 1901, the president of the London Branch of the league, Francis A. Fahy declaimed:

> The Irish youth and maiden leave school. What is the literature they read?—those of them who do read, and those are few. . . . It is English literature; not English literature of the better type; not Shakespeare or Tennyson or Dickens or Thackeray. Not at all. Our book shops and newspaper shops tell the tale. It is *Answers* and *Tit-Bits* and *Comic Cuts* and *Ally Sloper* and *Home Chat* and *Scraps*—the veriest gutter garbage of England.[145]

Similarly, the London journal *Guth na nGaedheal* (*The Voice of the Gaels*) included among its "Facts for Irish Men and Women" in March 1908, the statement that "English civilisation in Ireland does not mean Shakespeare and Meredith, and the sixpenny reviews. It means the Sunday papers, and the betting tipsters, and the music hall song" (3). "Sliabh Bladhma" offered a more sophisticated version of this view of English literary culture in 1911:

> In London—or rather the many Londons—there are, of course, high-minded and cultured elements, but the other elements ranging from the crude and the semi-literate to other things a little better, outnumber them to an overwhelming degree. . . . The general English fiction of to-day is multitudinous, chaotic, ephemeral. Not the hundredth part of it is literature in any sense. A fraction of it has sincerity and touches of greatness, the rest is mere manufacture for different "markets."[146]

Eight years earlier William P. Ryan, himself resident in London, had written of the sorry plight of those capable of producing or even appreciating that great and sincere fraction:

> The unhappiest people I have met have been a few Britons with a genuine instinct for pure literature, and they were unhappy because, while born to be literary or nothing, they knew the

145. *The Irish Language Movement* (London: Gaelic League, n.d.), 10.
146. "The Fate of Our Authors," *ACS*, 11 November 1911. Shane Leslie, on the other hand, stressed the fact that while there were "great English masters" the debased taste of Anglicized Ireland ensured that "the only literature that has poured upon Irish shores in unlimited tonnage and garbage has always been of the penny dreadful or shilling-shocker variety." See "Mr. Shane Leslie on the Gaelic Movement," *ACS*, 13 January 1912.

weary ordeal that was before them ere an unliterary land would either listen to or attempt to understand them. . . . They realised that they were aliens to their age, strangely and ironically situated in a land where real literary art is misunderstood, and where most of the stuff that passes for criticism of literary art is either ignorant or dishonest.[147]

Ryan must have known better, but it was his ideology doing the talking here. Several Gaels were, however, able to avoid this blind spot and adopt the third approach, assessing English literature with some genuine openness. Thus in an address to the Wexford Branch of the league in 1909, Father Martin O'Ryan railed against "floods of bad and immoral literature coming into our country from England," but drew a sharp and positive distinction between this trash and "good English literature . . . good English poets and novelists whom it was good to read."[148] "Maire" had some reservations about English literary influences, but stressed that young Gaelic authors "have much to learn from English."[149] And Liam Ua Domhnaill was downright fed up with those who thought to advance the revival of Irish by denigrating the English language and its literature:

I regret to say that Leaguers have a bad habit of constantly criticizing the English language. They tell you in dead earnest that English is a language that a beggar (called John Bull) gathered while traveling the world. They say that rags that every other language discarded trail limply from English! The talk of such people is nonsense. . . . The world knows—and not the English world alone—that English is an entirely fine language. It suits the English beautifully and some of its good literature suits every race under the sun.[150]

147. "I mBaile 's i gCéin" (At home and abroad), *ACS*, 3 October 1903.
148. "In Loch gCarmain" (In Wexford), *ACS*, 30 October 1909.
149. "A Word of Encouragement," *ACS*, 18 December 1909.
150. "I mBaile Átha Cliath" (In Dublin), *ACS*, 8 February 1908. "Is oth linn a rádh go bhfuil de dhroch-nós ag Connrathóiribh a bheith ag síor-lochtughadh an Bhéarla. Deirid go lom-dáiríribh leat gur teanga é an Béarla do chruinnigh bacach (ris a ráidhtear Seaghán Buidhe) le linn do an domhan a thaisteal. Deirid go bhfuil na ciortacha do chaith gach aon teanga eile dhi ar sileadh go liobarsach leis an Sacs-Bhéarla! Ní'l i n-a gcainnt siúd ach ráiméis. . . . Is eol do'n tsaoghal—agus ní'l don tsaoghal Sasanach amháin—gur breágh go léir an teanga é an Béarla. Oireann sé go háluinn do Shacsaibh agus oireann cuid dá dheagh-litridheacht do gach aon chineadh fá'n ngréin." Six years earlier, Muiris Ó Dubhda had issued a similar appeal to the movement in "Seachain an Fuath" (Avoid hatred), pointing out the absurdity of "many people I have met who will not listen to English

This position could, of course, be pushed too far, and when in 1905 Louis H. Victory published in *The Leader* a virtual paean to English literature as "the refined gold of the whole world's literary form," he instigated a lively controversy that lasted several weeks.[151]

What is most significant about even favorable comments on English literature is, however, that they remained just that, vague and passing comments. Given their educational background and cultural milieu, all Gaels of a literary bent must have read and enjoyed a good deal of English writing, and at times they gave honest, even startling, expression to that fact, particularly in the years before the orthodox stand on this question had fully evolved. For example, in an August 1886 "Plea for the Irish Language" in the *Dublin University Review*, Douglas Hyde ("An Craoibhín Aoibhinn"), raising a hypothesis he almost simultaneously rejected, could write: "If by ceasing to speak Irish our peasantry could learn to appreciate Shakespeare and Milton, to study Wordsworth or Tennyson, then I would certainly say adieu to it" (670). In an 1899 address in Tuam, County Galway, J. P. Gannon of the *Tuam Herald* overlooked the obvious native role model, Cú Chulainn, and instead urged Gaelic Leaguers to keep before them "the example of the hero of that superb poem of Robert Browning's, who, in quest of a high ideal, a noble enterprise, rode alone into a barren land, although, for aught he knew, destruction awaited him at the end of his journey."[152] More revealingly, Father Patrick Forde invoked the great names of English literature to validate for both his audience and no doubt himself the intellectual and artistic stature of the Gaelic literary tradition: "What note from the Celtic lyre reached the ear of Spenser in his Kilcolman retreat, what gentle breathings Shakespeare heard in London, where the oldest bards were found when the Irish Chieftains visited the court of Elizabeth, what sweet music Tennyson learned from the old Celtic legends and reproduced in his 'Idylls of the King?'"[153] Such Tennysonian delights in Gaelic guise were even proposed as valid fare for Oireachtas

---

music, although it is fine music" (iomdha duine do casadh orm nach n-éisteochadh le ceol Sasanach, bíodh gur ceol maith é). See *ACS*, 24 May 1902.

151. "The Irish Scorn of English Literature," *The Leader*, 7 October 1905. Victory described himself as an Irish-Irelander. For the flavor of the debate he inspired, see "Imaal," "Irish Ireland, Literature, and Scorn," *The Leader*, 4 November 1905; and the contributions of "Fionnbarr" (28 October and 25 November 1905); and of "C." (28 October 1905).

152. "Connradh na Gaedhilge / Tuam," *ACS*, 23 December 1899. The poem must be "Childe Roland to the Dark Tower Came."

153. "The Revival of the Irish Language," *ACS*, 15 September 1900. See also Rev. Dr. Shahan, "Let Us Save the Language," *FL*, 8 April 1899.

entertainment when Tadhg Ó Donnchadha's translation of "The Voyage of Maeldune" set to music by Robert Dwyer was scheduled for performance in 1903, until the protest of Father Joseph Callahan caused its cancellation and replacement by native airs.[154]

However suggestive, these occasional references to English writers indicate no more than a predictable familiarity, not the sort of close study that would be essential if the new literature in Irish was to open itself to constructive influences from England.[155] But what of those revivalists who claimed such literary study as their special provenance? While this problem would not have troubled those like Henebry, O' Reilly, Mac Fhionnlaoich, and Ua Laoghaire who denied the very possibility of any inspiration from that source, it should have been a challenge for progressives like Pearse, Ó Conaire, or Ryan. If it was, they dodged it. Although we occasionally find in their work a more up-to-date awareness of contemporary literary developments, their references to English literature are on the whole no more detailed and profound than those we have already noted.

Pearse is an especially interesting case, since a caricatured version of his attitude to English culture has gained some currency among scholars of Anglo-Irish, particularly students of James Joyce. In his biography of Joyce, Richard Ellmann, with reference to Frank Budgen, tells of how Joyce dropped his study of Irish "because Patrick Pearse, the instructor,

154. See Douglas Hyde, Mise agus an Connradh (Myself and the league) (Baile Átha Cliath: Oifig an tSoláthair, 1937), 116–17.

155. One influence all were agreed on resisting was the introduction of English stylistic conventions, grammatical constructions, and unnecessary loanwords into Irish. The views of Henebry on this subject have already been cited. Mac Néill was of the same opinion, urging writers to be on their guard since "it will require a vigorous effort in the Irish writers of the future to keep clear of the influences of English literature in the style both of their prose and of their verse." See "Comhairle" (Advice) ACS, 18 November 1899. See also Séamus Ó Dubhghaill, "Caint agus Litridheacht," ACS, 25 October 1913; and the response of Aongus Ó Duibhne, "Múchta le Béarla" (Smothered with English), ACS, 8 November 1913. Such appropriate and justified vigilance could, however, become counterproductive, as when a Leader critic insisted the first Gaelic novel, Dinneen's Cormac Ua Conaill not be judged by "a false Anglicising standard" with regard to "plot and construction and knowledge of human nature" and worried that young Gaelic writers might get the idea that they "should keep before their minds for imitation the impossible 'plots,' the unnatural 'human nature,' and the morbid sensationalism of our present-day English writers of fiction." See "F.P.," review of Cormac Ua Conaill, The Leader, 25 May 1901. Responding to "F. P.," "Mac Ríogh Éireann" pointed out that the book was simply a novel "in the ordinary sense of the word, be it Irish, French, German, Russian, or English." See "Mac Ríogh Éireann," letter, ACS, 1 June 1900. Of course, when Dinneen set to work, the language had neither the word nor the thing, and he did indeed borrow heavily from the foreign literary tradition he knew best.

found it necessary to exalt Irish by denigrating English."[156] While, like the young Joyce, the young Pearse could take—or be goaded into— extreme and even risible positions, there is nothing of any significance in his voluminous writings that would confirm this image of him as a literary bigot. On the contrary, we know that he explicitly condemned ignorant denunciation of the English language and its culture:

> As an instance of the sort of "argument" on behalf of the language movement which we would deprecate, we may refer to the indiscriminate abuse of English as "an unmelodious jargon," "a mere conglomeration of other tongues," "a worn-out garment," and so on, which we frequently hear. Such "arguments" may or may not be tenable, but they are irrelevant. The English language is not *our* language: in stating that fact we have stated our whole case against it.[157]

Moreover, we have evidence of his interest in English writers from both first-person accounts and the academic record he established as a secondary school headmaster. For example, in her memoir *The Home Life of Padraig Pearse*, his sister Mary Brigid tells of his lifelong fascination with Shakespeare and recalls how he organized the occasional production of scenes from Shakespearean plays at Sgoil Éanna.[158] The histo-

156. *James Joyce* (New York: Oxford University Press, 1965), 62. Ellmann cites Budgen's *Further Recollections of James Joyce* (1955). After researching Pearse for his play to celebrate the Pearse centennial, Criostóir O'Flynn rejected this reading of the Pearse-Joyce interaction. In his *A Man Called Pearse*, the protagonist tells his family that "this Joyce fellow," a young man "a bit self-opinionated, a bit aggressive even in his ignorance," has been telling people he dropped his Irish class because of the teacher's disparagement of English. When his father wonders whether Joyce found Irish too difficult, O'Flynn's Pearse disagrees and says "I'm very disappointed at losing him." Two reasons suggested in the play for Joyce's decision are his unwillingness to be taught by a graduate of the Christian Brothers or by a man only "a year or two older than himself." (Pearse was actually three years older than Joyce.) At any rate, O'Flynn's hypothetical reconstruction seems to me no less convincing than that of Budgen / Ellmann. See Criostóir O'Flynn, *A Man Called Pearse: A Play in Three Acts* (Dublin: Foilseacháin Náisiúnta Teoranta, 1980), 44–45.

157. "The Case for Irish," editorial, *ACS*, 21 January 1905. His views on this issue coincided with those of Trinity College's Stephen Gwynn. See his comment on Gwynn's essay in the December 1904 issue of *Dana* in "The Gael and English Literature," *ACS*, 17 December 1904.

158. *The Home Life of Padraig Pearse, as Told by Himself, His Family and Friends*, ed. Mary Brigid Pearse (Dublin: Mercier, 1979), 46–48. This book was first published in 1934. See also *An Macaomh* 2, no. 2 (May 1913): 49. It is also worth noting that Pearse published a brief excerpt from Hamlet's "To be or not to be" soliloquy, in the Irish

rian Desmond Ryan, a student at the school, wrote that while Pearse was "antagonistic" to Anglo-Irish literature, an antagonism to be explored in Chapter 5, "his knowledge of the work of Irish men and women was as appreciative and as exact as his knowledge of English literature itself. . . . Next to the *Tain Bo Chuailgne* . . . his favourite author was Shakespeare, innumerable editions of whom had an honoured place on his bookshelves."[159] Nor was his interest limited to this one towering figure. In a review of Mícheál Breathnach's Irish translation of Charles Kickham's *Knockagow*, he noted in passing that he had heard "persistently" "the call of Puritan England" as well as that of Gaelic Ireland, and could "feel a kinship on the one hand with An tAthair Peadar Ua Laoghaire and on the other with, say, William Makepeace Thackerary."[160] Elsewhere he calls Tennyson's "The Charge of the Light Brigade" "splendid."[161] Furthermore, as Ryan makes clear, he shared his knowledge and enthusiasms with his pupils: "Long before his students had reached the higher classes, Pearse had introduced them to the classics of English and Irish literature."[162] Unfortunately, however, he did not provide his fellow Gaelic writers such an introduction, an educational task that would have been particularly valuable if undertaken from the comparative perspective he could have brought to it.

If Pearse offers us little more than scattered, generally positive references to English literature, Ó Conaire and William P. Ryan, both of whom spent a good part of their lives in London, developed a more coherent view of what they believed to be the central lesson to be learned from it. For both, English literature had a rich past, but was seemingly moribund. Ó Conaire could, for example, extol the Elizabethans as "that noble people who gave to their nation drama and poetry that have never been surpassed,"[163] but argue that the glory days were over because most contemporary English writers lacked the nerve to challenge the mercenary values of their society. And even when he lists that handful of exceptions "whose fame will live forever" (a mair-

translation of Feargus Ó Nualláin, in his school magazine *An Macaomh*. See "Shacspeare do Tháinig go hÉirinn" (The Shakespeare who came to Ireland), *An Macaomh* 2, no. 3 [sic] (Christmas 1910): 49.

159. Desmond Ryan, *The Man Called Pearse* (Dublin: Maunsel and Company, 1919), 19.

160. "Literature, Translations, and 'Cnoc na nGabha,' " review of *Cnoc na nGabha* by Mícheál Breathnach, *ACS*, 27 October 1906.

161. Pearse, "Gaelic Prose Literature," in *Three Lectures on Gaelic Topics* (Dublin: M. H. Gill and Son, 1898), 19.

162. Ryan, *Man Called Pearse*, 84.

163. "An Fhírinne agus an Bhréag sa Litridheacht," in *Aistí Uí Chonaire*, 198. This essay originally appeared in *FL*, 12 May 1923.

fidh a gclú go deo)—"Hardy and Meredith, Conrad, and perhaps (b'fhéidir) Galsworthy"—he never moves much beyond listing their names.[164] Indeed, in the only extended essay he wrote on an English writer, "Conrad agus Smaointe faoi Litridheacht" (Conrad and thoughts about literature), his principal point is that the work of Conrad (and others) proves that great art can be created in a writer's second language, an important and useful idea in the context of the Revival, but not one that tells us much about Conrad or his influence on Ó Conaire.[165]

Ryan, with his regular forum in the "London Notes" and later "I mBaile 's i gCéin" (At home and abroad) columns of An Claidheamh Soluis, returned again and again to his basic theme that "English literature is deteriorating, and the outer peoples, to put it bluntly, are not likely to trouble their heads about a language whose thought and tone will be distinctly inferior."[166] For him, London was a place "where literature had become for the most part another form of 'mafficking'";[167] where that literature itself was "in the main superficial, sensational, material, utterly lacking style, insight, or a sense of the spiritual";[168] and where the critical discussion of that literature—by writers like Ryan himself—was but another sign of "an inferior or 'unoriginal' age," since "a people, with any freshness of mind, and determined to be themselves, have nothing to do with, nothing to learn from, such criticism (so-called)."[169] It is worth noting in passing that in his reservations about literary criticism, Ryan was responding to Dinneen's call for the development of a critical vocabulary in Irish. Nowhere do we find more neatly confounded our preconceptions about who would end up on what side of an issue in the early Revival! But what exactly was Ryan condemning and what excepting? We do learn the odd detail, for example that he respected Lionel Johnson and thought H. G. Wells was "a London novelist of a sensational order."[170] But beyond that we are left with that same sense of evasion, the feeling that either ideological orthodoxy or tactical strategy in face of the imperial language and its

164. "An Fhírinne agus an Bhreag" in Aistí Uí Chonaire, 201. His taste could be surprising; he was quite taken with The Admirable Crichton. See "Na Coinghilí a Stiúirigheann Sgríobhnóireacht Dráma," in Aistí Uí Chonaire, 73–74. This essay originally commenced serialization in the ACS Oireachtas supplement for 19 August 1911.

165. "Conrad agus Smaointe faoi Litridheacht," in Aistí Uí Chonaire, 212–15. This essay originally appeared in FL, 30 August 1924.

166. "London Notes," ACS, 26 October 1901.

167. "London Notes," ACS, 18 October 1902.

168. "London Notes," ACS, 2 November 1901.

169. "London Notes," ACS, 25 October 1902.

170. For Johnson, see "London Notes," ACS, 18 October 1902; for Wells, "London Notes," ACS, 26 October 1901.

widely known and assimilative culture prohibited the Gaelic intellectual from discussing a subject about which he must have had something to say.

In this light the forthrightness of Father Dinneen is both refreshing and impressive. As we have already observed, Dinneen's literary tastes were not only conservative but often Catholic in a strictly confessional sense, and he could be critical of what he saw as "the positivist, the materialist, the hedonist" strain in the English ethos as voiced through its literature. But unlike other revivalists who read that literature, he was not only willing to admit that he did so, but also to acknowledge that he often enjoyed and learned from it. And he was willing to share his reflections, positive and negative, on individual writers in some detail. His interest was of long standing. As a student in the 1880s, at a time when his primary academic interest was mathematics, he had won first-class honors in English at the Royal University, where one of his professors was Gerard Manley Hopkins. He was later to present English literature as one of his principal subjects for the M.A. and to teach it at University College, Dublin.[171] His special favorites seem to have been poets like Donne, Milton, Dryden, and Pope, his knowledge of whom was so extensive that William P. Ryan wrote in *The Pope's Green Island* that "it has been said that if every extant edition of Pope's poems were lost or burned he could re-write them all from memory" (122). Indeed, quotations from English poets from Donne to Tennyson are even cited for illustrative purposes in his Irish-English dictionary of 1904.[172] Moreover, as early as 1903 he had translated Dickens's *A Christmas Carol* into Irish as *Duan na Nodlag*, the only major translation of an English work into Irish in this period with the exception of Tadhg Ó Murchadha's incomplete *Eachtra Robinson Crúsó* (1909) and the adaptation of an English play by Mrs. E. R. Dix.[173] His respect and affection for the author of his original are evident in his "Preface" to *Duan na*

171. For this summary of Dinneen's interest in English literature, I am indebted to Proinsais Ó Conluain and Donncha Ó Céileachair, *An Duinníneach*, 84–92, 98–100. Ó Conluain and Ó Céileachair even record that as a teacher at St. Stanislaus College in 1882, Dinneen spoke in school debates against the revival of Irish (99–100).

172. For examples, see Ó Conluain and Ó Céileachair, *An Duinníneach*, 98–99.

173. Mrs. Dix's *Cruadh-Chás na mBaitsiléirí, nó Is Éigeantach do Dhuine Agaibh Pósadh* (The bachelors' dilemma, or One of you must marry) won an Oireachtas Prize in 1916 and was produced at the Irish Theatre on Hardwicke Street in December of that year. See "Gaelic Plays at the Irish Name [*sic*]," *ACS*, 9 December 1916. In addition, an Irish version of Antony's funeral oration from *Julius Caesar* appeared in the very first number of *An t-Európach* in June 1899. The fact that there were so few translations from English literature is more striking in light of the amount of such material produced after the founding in 1926 of An Gúm, the new Irish government's Irish-language publishing venture. See Chapter 6.

Nodlag: "Keen satire and melting pathos, well known characteristics of Dickens, are fairly represented in this piece, and these qualities are calculated to commend him to Irish readers. Besides, the sympathy with the poor and outcast, with which this story abounds, will ensure it a welcome in many an Irish home."[174]

Dinneen was later to use his weekly column in *The Leader* to discuss English literature on a regular basis, devoting essays not only to Dickens, but also to Shelley, Newman, Alfred Austin, Belloc, Byron, Crabbe, and Thackeray. At times, his perspective and tone are familiar, as when he writes in "Filidheacht Bhéarla an Lae Indiu" (Contemporary poetry in English) that "every poetry that is being composed at present on the face of the earth is bad poetry—except for poetry in Irish," and continues: "English language poetry will improve with time. But that improvement will not come until the mind of the people is purified and until they have more respect for the law of God and the rights of their neighbor."[175] Nevertheless, insight generally takes precedence over ideology, certainly over propaganda, in these pieces. For example, in his column on Thackeray, he sees the novelist in what we might now call a colonial context, stressing his identity as an outsider in English society due to his birth in Calcutta, and writing, "I don't think he had any special fondness for England or for the English."[176] Although the connection is never made explicit, one wonders whether Dinneen saw the overall success of Thackeray's *Irish Sketchbook* as rooted in some sort of psychic empathy between the "English" novelist from the colonies and the colonized nation about which he was writing. In a June 1913 column occasioned by the death of the poet laureate Alfred Austin, Dinneen maintained a discreet silence on the work of the deceased laureate, but paid tribute to the genius of some of his predecessors, and defended the institution itself as easily worth the small cost it entailed.[177] In a

174. Patrick Dinneen, Preface to *Duan na Nodlag / A Christmas Carol in Prose le Seárlas Dicens, aistrighthe ó'n mBéarla mBunadhasach leis an Athar Pádraig Ua Duinnín* (A Christmas Carol in prose by Charles Dickens, translated from the original English by Father Patrick Dinneen) (Baile Átha Cliath: M. H. Gill agus a Mhac, 1903), 3. Dinneen credited the idea for the work to "my friend, Mr. H.J. Gill."

175. *The Leader*, 20 July 1912. "Drochfhilidheacht is eadh gach filidheacht atá dá ceapadh ar dhruim an domhain fá láthair—acht filidheacht na Gaedhilge. . . . Tiocfaidh feabhas ar fhilidheacht an Bhéarla leis an aimsir. Acht ní thiocfaidh an feabhas soin go nglanfar aigne na ndaoine agus go mbeidh breis measa aca ar dlighe Dé agus ar cheart a gcomharsan."

176. "Úrscéaluidhe Éachtach" (An extraordinary novelist), *The Leader*, 29 April 1911. "Ní dóigh liom go raibh aon chion fá leith ar Shasana na ar na Sasanaigh aige."

177. "Áirdéigseacht na Breataine Mór" (The Poet Laureateship of Great Britain), *The Leader*, 14 June 1913.

January 1916 piece on poetry and social conscience, he praised George Crabbe for his sympathetic focus on real people, particularly the poor, writing: "And therefore his poetic work is more lasting than the work of those who dealt with the birds of the air or the heavenly clouds, paying no attention to humanity or human beings."[178] A similar interest in people and their common humanity characterizes many of Dinneen's *Leader* essays at this time—among them one on the status of African-Americans in the United States[179]—a further reminder if one were needed that the defining terms of this study, "nativist" and "progressive" apply to intellectual and emotional tendencies far more reliably than they do to complex living people and their often contradictory enthusiasms and commitments.

Dinneen's columns on English literature are, of course, most interesting just because they are sui generis in the context of the Revival. Those writers with whose nativist perspective he often found himself in agreement had little interest in or use for such literature, while of those holding progressive views, virtually all, as we have seen, maintained at best a suspect silence on cultural developments in England. Indeed, it was the progressives who took the lead in pressing the artistic indictment against the traditional foe, no doubt taking delight in the delicious irony that their charge was not that England was too sophisticated or intellectually daring, but rather that the imperial center was stagnant and dull. Far from decrying foreign influence, the progressives were here rejecting the attempt of what they saw as a particularly unimaginative foreign country to deny them access to a more stimulating world. In effect, the progressives wanted to run toward, not away, from Europe. In 1910 the challenge was spelled out with a rather cautious cosmopolitanism by "Fear Taistil": "Wouldn't it be better for us to occasionally follow the example of the French or the Germans or the Italians—if it is necessary to follow the example of any race—rather than to be always and forever trailing after John Bull?"[180] Máire Ní Chinnéide felt no such ambivalence. When her lecture advising Gaels to read French literature,

178. "An Cine Daonna agus na Filidhe" (The human race and the poets), *The Leader*, 8 January 1916. "Agus dá bhrígh sin is buaine a shaothar filidheachta ná saothar lucht tráchta ar éanlaith an aeir, agus ar néalltaibh nime is gan toradh aca ar dhaonnaidheacht ná ar dhaonnaidhibh."

179. Patrick Dinneen, "An Cine Gorm sna Státaibh Aontuighthe" (The black race in the United States), *The Leader*, 18 February 1911.

180. "Thall 's i bhFus ar fud na hEorpa," *ACS*, 15 January 1910. "Nárbh fhearr dhúinn sompla an Fhranncaigh agus an Ghearmánaigh agus an Iodálaigh a ghlacadh ar uairibh—má's éigin sompla aon chinnidh a ghlacadh—ná bheith i gcomhnaidhe gcomhnaidhe ar leirg Sheagháin Bhuidhe?"

specifically the work of Anatole France, was criticized by several priests fearful of French "immorality," she rejected their reservations out of hand, and turned the tables with an imputation of West British provincialism: "I don't think there is a better way to fight against this excessive power of the English language than for us to know another language and especially another literature."[181]

Predictably, a major source of Continental interest for revivalists was the progress of other national-language movements. In 1902 the league published as one of its propaganda pamphlets William P. Ryan's *Lessons from Modern Language Movements*, a survey of organizations and activities throughout Europe. Furthermore, leaving aside revival efforts in the other five Celtic languages—efforts that received extensive coverage and that will be discussed in Chapter 6—we find in the Gaelic press reports in various degrees of detail on language issues in Belgium, Bohemia, Poland, the Ukraine, Hungary, Malta, the Orkneys, Finland, Serbo-Croatia, Denmark, Greece, Holland, Provence, the Channel Islands, Rumania, Norway, Portugal, Catalonia, and Switzerland. Among non-European languages that attracted attention were Esperanto, Quebec French, Hebrew, Yiddish, Japanese, "Egyptian," Afrikaans, Guarani (Paraguay), Nahuatl (Mexico), Chippewa, and Sioux.

Yet however interesting—and surprising—some of these reports and commentaries may be, they do not of themselves validate the European credentials of the revivalists. Instead we must ask whether a serious attempt was made to understand and appreciate the cultures of the Continent. The evidence here is somewhat mixed. One of the braver experiments in establishing such cultural contact was the appropriately named though short-lived Trinity College magazine *An tEurópach*, whose introductory editorial proclaimed: "If things were as they should be, there would be no need to seek permission or to make excuses for this paper. . . . There is an invitation and a welcome here for the inhabitant of every country and for the speaker of every language in Europe. The purpose of this paper is to give a forum to anyone able to write his thoughts in any European language now spoken."[182] Although *An tEu-*

181. Letter, *ACS*, 9 April 1910. "Is dóigh liom . . . ná fuil caoi is fearr chum troda i gcoinnibh na ro-chomhachta so an Bhéarla ná eolas do bheith againn ar theangain eile agus go mór-mhór ar litridheacht eile."

182. Editorial, *An tEurópach* 1, no. 1 (June 1899): 1. "Dá mbeadh ceart le fághail níor ghadh cead ná leithsgéul do ghabháil i dtaoibh an pháipéir so. . . . Atá cuireadh agus fáilte annso roimh áithreachaibh gach tíre, agus fear labhartha gach teangaidh 'san Euróip; agus is é fáth an pháipéir so, ionad a thabhairt do gach uile dhuine fhéudfas a smuainte do sgríobhadh i n-aon teanga Európach d'á bhfuil d'á labhairt faoi láthair." The paper did, actually, ban English, "not from hatred of it" (ní le fuath roimhe), but because Trinity

rópach did attract contributions in Spanish, Dutch, German, and trans-literated Japanese, the creation of a polyglot literary journal was more than a bit premature for the Irish speakers of 1900. For a while at least the Gaels would have to be the students rather than the teachers of Europe.

Needless to say, the nativists were concerned about the sort of lessons that might be learned there, although even the most committed of them showed some degree of openness to the Continent. Dinneen was, for example, honest in his admission that Irish was totally lacking in a critical vocabulary for the mature, much less scholarly, discussion of literature, and was willing to tap foreign sources for help in the creation of such a technical language.[183] Father Henebry, the most forceful champion of native models and values for the new literature, was also a genuine polyglot who felt young Irish scholars could benefit greatly by studying, as had he, in Germany, where they would be exposed to "the results of the understanding of the cleverest men in the world."[184] Nonetheless, the overwhelming impression that emerges from a reading of even the most worldly of the nativists is that foreign cleverness, particularly that of amoral and areligious modern Europe, was always to some extent dangerous. An tAthair Peadar was a prolific translator, but none of his adaptations was from the work of a Continental author later than Cervantes.

Some of the aggressiveness with which the nativists attacked what they perceived as European decadence must have been due to their angry awareness that, with the exception of the odd column or letter, on the issue of foreign inspiration for the new literature the progressives held sway in the Gaelic press, particularly in *An Claidheamh Soluis* under the editorship of Pearse.[185] While Pearse's views on the development

---

already had in *T.C.D.* a paper to serve English speakers. The editor of *An tEurópach* was "Conall Cearnach" (Feardorcha Ó Conaill).

183. See Dinneen, "Literary Criticism in Irish," *ACS*, 1 November 1902.

184. "Do Theagosc Gach Foghlama as Gaedhilg," in *Scríbhne Risteird de Hindeberg*, 73. Henebry spoke of "toradh tuigsiona na bhfear ba chlisde ar domhain." Henebry's linguistic accomplishments were assessed, perhaps generously, by his friend Séamus Ó hEochaidh ("An Fear Mór"): "He knew Irish, Breton, and Welsh, English and German, Latin and Greek and French and Sanscrit, and I don't know but that there were others." (Do bhí Gaedhealg, Bretonais, Breathnais aige, Beurla agus Gearmáinis, Laidean agus Gréigis agus Fraingcis agus Sanscrit, agus ní fheadar ná raibh a thuilleadh aige dhíobh.) See "An Fear Mór," "Portláirge agus na Déise," *ACS*, 4 August 1917.

185. Pearse was appointed editor of *ACS* on 2 March 1903. He intended to resign when he founded Sgoil Éanna in 1908, but was prevailed upon by the league's Executive Committee to take a leave of absence for a few months instead. The leave covered the months of July, August, and September 1908, during which time Seán Mac Éinrigh served as

of literature in Irish have already been studied in detail by Raymond Porter and Frank O'Brien,[186] some of his more important critical statements must be again examined here: as editor of the league's official weekly organ for six critical years, years in which he published an imposing number of thoughtful and provocative editorials, leaders, and reviews in two languages, he was the point man for the progressives in the formulation and promulgation of an aesthetic philosophy for the Revival. Central to that philosophy was a vision of Ireland reclaiming her legitimate and traditional place as a full member of the contemporary European cultural community. Thus in his 26 May 1906 editorial "About Literature," a piece in which he rejected the folktale as a model for the new Gaelic prose, he wrote:

> Irish literature gave models to Europe. Is it not high time that it should give models to Ireland? . . . We must get into touch also with our contemporaries—in France, in Russia, in Norway, in Finland, in Bohemia, in Hungary, wherever, in short, vital literature is being produced on the face of the globe. . . . We would have our literature modern not only in the sense of freely borrowing every modern form which it does not possess and which it is capable of assimilating, but also in texture, tone, and outlook.

The previous year he had given some idea of the practical direction such assimilation might take. Arguing that "the characteristic literary type of the present day is the short story," he urged his fellows to turn to the writers of France, Belgium, Russia, and Norway, and specifically to Camille Lemonnier and Maxim Gorky, for inspiration.[187] A fortnight later, he chided Gaelic writers for their excessive preoccupation with rural themes, stating: "It is . . . in the highest degree necessary that modern Irish should be applied to the discussion of every religious and

---

acting editor. In November 1909 Pearse gave up the position for good, Seán Mac Giollarnáth being appointed his successor on 9 November 1909. See Donnchadh Ó Súilleabháin, *An Piarsach agus Conradh na Gaeilge*, 74–101, 116, 126, 157; and Pearse's own comments on his leave in "Partly Personal," *ACS*, 3 October 1908.

186. For Porter, see "Language and Literature in Revival Ireland: The Views of P. H. Pearse," in *Modern Irish Literature: Essays in Honor of William York Tindall*, ed. Raymond J. Porter and James Brophy (New York: Iona College Press, 1972), 195–214; and *P. H. Pearse* (New York: Twayne, 1973), 46–57. For O'Brien, see *Filíocht Ghaeilge na Linne Seo* (Contemporary poetry in Irish) (Baile Átha Cliath: An Clóchomhar, 1968), 17–48.

187. "Recent Booklets," *ACS*, 10 July 1905. Pearse stated that all unsigned material in *ACS* during his editorship was from his pen. See his letter to Tomás Ó Flannghaile of 30 September 1905 in *Letters*, 98.

secular subject, that its outlook should be broadened, its culture widened and deepened . . . that it should strengthen itself by drinking deep draughts of its own past, and that it should assimilate some of the thought and culture of other tongues and peoples."[188]

Pearse's leading ally in the campaign to create a twentieth-century literature in Irish was Pádraic Ó Conaire. Widely read in contemporary literature and one of what Stephen McKenna called "the European kind,"[189] Ó Conaire illustrated his commitment to literary internationalism best through his fiction, but he did also write several important critical essays, most notably "Sean-litridheacht na nGaedheal agus Nuadh-litridheacht na hEorpa" (The ancient literature of Ireland and the modern literature of Europe) (1908), "Na Coinghilí a Stiúirigheann Sgríobhnóireacht Dráma" (The conditions that govern the writing of drama) (1911), and "An Fhírinne agus an Bhréag sa Litridheacht" (Truth and falsehood in literature) (1923). Ó Conaire arrived at his mature literary philosophy early in his career, and his ideas show little if any change over time. That philosophy is given its most extensive development and expression in his 1923 essay, where, having referred to writers like Hardy, Conrad, Chekhov, Lagerloff, France, and Hamsun, he affirms a central tenet of the progressive attitude: "Gaelic writers would be better for studying their work. Our literature would be better. The truth would benefit as well."[190]

The courageous and sustained literary campaign of Pearse and Ó Conaire has deservedly attracted a good deal of scholarly attention in Gaelic circles, but here again it should be emphasized that theirs was not a lonely crusade. Many less celebrated revivalists shared a willingness, even at times an eagerness, to learn from their European contemporaries.[191] In a 24 February 1906 letter to *An Claidheamh Soluis*, Henry Morris, whose nativist view of Irish as "pre-eminently the language of

188. "Irish Prose," *ACS*, 21 October 1905.
189. Letter to Edmund Curtis, 1924 or 1925, in *Journals and Letters of Stephen MacKenna*, ed. E. M. Dodds (London: Constable, 1936), 218.
190. "An Fhírinne agus an Bhréag sa Litridheacht," in *Aistí Uí Chonaire*, 201. "B'fheárrde sgríobhnóirí na Gaedhilge staidéar dhéanamh ar a saothar siúd. B'fheárrde ár litridheacht é. B'fheárrde an fhírinne é mar an gcéadna."
191. It is surprising to find that even Gearóid Denvir has underestimated this fact, writing in "Pádraic Ó Conaire agus Éire a Linne" (Pádraic Ó Conaire and the Ireland of his time): "Apart from the exceptional person like Ó Conaire himself and W.P. Ryan, those involved with the Irish language at the beginning of this century showed little intellectual curiosity." (Cés móite de chorrdhuine eisceachtúil, ar nós Uí Chonaire féin agus Liam P. Uí Riain, is beag fiosracht intleachtúil a bhain le lucht na Gaeilge ag tús na haoise seo.) See *Pádraic Ó Conaire: Léachtaí Cuimhneacháin* (Pádraic Ó Conaire: Commemorative lectures), ed. Denvir (Indreabhán: Cló Chonamara, 1983), 34.

faith and devotion," was noted above, wrote: "Is Ireland to be a western China and equally unprogressive? Decidedly not. Wherever the progress of learning, or the thing called 'civilisation' brings out anything new which is really good, and which fills a 'want,' let us have it, and the sooner, the better." In the same year, one "J.J.M.," writing on "Modern Irish Literature," argued:

> A perfect literature would be cosmopolitan, if not in expression at any rate in character. And as our aim and ambition should be to make our modern Gaelic literature a perfect literature, we should try to convey or translate into Gaelic the best of each foreign literature. With a mastery of our ancient writers, and the knowledge of the best work of foreign schools, our countrymen should develop a literature such as Gaelic would have become if foreign intrigue and political subterfuge had not brought their usual ruin and wreckage.[192]

Discussing translation in 1908, Liam Ua Domhnaill, who regularly used his "I mBaile Átha Cliath" (In Dublin) column to broaden the perspective of his colleagues, wrote: "Today every race is linked to the other races. They preserve what of their own is good, and they attempt to share fully in what good things their neighbors have."[193] In June 1909, Eibhlín Nic Niocaill asserted: "We are moderns, steeped in the modern literature of other nations; we cannot be satisfied with the literary forms that were in vogue centuries ago. The story, the novel, the drama of modern life, these are what we demand, and what our authors ambition to produce."[194] Six months later, "Maire" offered "A Word of Encouragement," an essay directed to young Gaelic writers: "For the treatment of modern ideas and problems they must go to foreign literature. . . . Our literature knows not the men or movements of the modern world. For mere knowledge, if for nothing else, our young authors must go to the modern literature of Europe." Among specific models he suggested for the aspiring writer to study were Goethe, Meredith, and Ibsen.[195]

As bold as their embrace of Europe was the progressives' willingness

---

192. *ACS*, 29 December 1906.
193. *ACS*, 8 February 1908. "Indiu tá baint ag gach cineadh leis na cineadhachaibh eile. Coinnighid aca féin a bhfuil de mhaitheas aca féin agus tugaid iarracht ar bheith go rannpháirteach ina bhfuil de mhaitheas agá gcomhursanaibh."
194. "Some Thoughts about the Future of Irish Literature," *ACS*, 12 June 1909.
195. *ACS*, 18 December 1909. This is most unlikely to have been the famous "Máire," the novelist and short-story writer Séamus Ó Grianna (1891–1969).

to confront the nativists on their own ground. For many of those wary of foreign contamination of the emerging Gaelic literature, the safest models lay in the Gaelic past, in a time when the language was a widespread literary medium. For these revivalists, the seventeenth-century historian Seathrún Céitinn (Geoffrey Keating) provided the standard for "modern" Irish prose, while the eighteenth-century poets of what Daniel Corkery would later call "the Hidden Ireland" were the surest guides to native versecraft. Yet far from being awed by these illustrious dead, some progressives were quick to enlist them in their own cause; as "Maire" wrote in "A Word of Encouragement," "It is a mistake to think that the writers of our old literature were free from the influence of Continental literature." Piaras Béaslaí, a scholarly poet who believed "an Irish literature must grow out of an Irish-speaking life,"[196] and whose own taste in Gaelic verse was quite conservative,[197] was aggressive in rescuing both Keating and Brian Merriman from the clutches of cultural xenophobes. Believing that "the 'Keating' fetish helped to cripple all attempts to write Irish prose in the nineteenth century . . . and even at the present day, a new school has arisen which seeks to fetter Irish literature with the archaic and obsolete,"[198] Béaslaí set the record straight in a 1910 lecture at Coláiste na Mumhan (the Munster College): "Keating was unmistakably under foreign influence. The praisers of the past have made a fashion of praising him, forgetting that he was in his time an innovator, a revolutionary . . . Profoundly versed in our older Irish culture, but at the same time in touch with Latin culture, he widened the Gaelic horizon."[199]

196. "Literature and the Gaedhealtacht," letter, *SF*, 16 March 1912. Béaslaí took pains to avoid saying that only the native speaker could produce true Irish literature, but given the linguistic situation in Ireland at the time this essentially nativist conclusion must have seemed to many inescapable. For example, of his own work in Irish he wrote: "I know the process of mind by which I produce what my critics are good enough to call 'Irish literature.' It is a necessary process, but it is not one that makes for vital, vigorous literature, with its roots in life." Béaslaí solved the dilemma with an act of faith in a cosmopolitan, Irish-speaking future: "For my part, I believe that the future of Irish literature depends upon the generation now in the cradle or yet unborn. Produce a healthy, vigorous, Irish-speaking life, in contact with modern thought, and our literature may be trusted to look after itself."

197. Béaslaí was an active member of Árd-Chúirt na hÉigse (originally Árd-Chúirt Shochaide na Suadh) from its foundation in 1903. The Árd-Chúirt was a group of poet-scholars dedicated to the preservation of a distinctive Gaelic poetic. They met regularly at feiseanna or at the Oireachtas to discuss that poetic and to adapt the native meters, rhyme schemes, and verse ornamentation to contemporary subjects and themes.

198. "Language and Literature," letter, *SF*, 30 March 1912.

199. "Irish Literature / Lectures by Mr. Piaras Béaslaí," *ACS*, 17 September 1910. Béaslaí was still within the bounds of orthodoxy here—but only just, for Keating's Latin-

Béaslaí saw Brian Merriman as an authentic literary radical, arguing that "the 'Court' occupied a unique position in Irish literature. Its author broke away from all the trammels of convention in metre, style, subject, and treatment, and the result, from the artistic point of view, was a striking triumph."[200] And in his introduction to Risteárd Ó Foghludha's edition of *Cúirt an Mheadhon Oidhche* (*The Midnight Court*), he underscored Merriman's cosmopolitanism, in the process linking him with what a nativist would have found most disturbing intellectual company: "It is curious to find him so closely in contact with the most advanced ideas of the latter half of the eighteenth century . . . One feels that Merriman's entrance into the homes of the gentry must have brought him into contact with men who had read Voltaire and Rousseau."[201] When we consider that at least some of the revivalists who exalted the hunted priest Keating may have been motivated as much by dread of the modern world as by appreciation of elegant prose, we can better understand the force of the challenge in Béaslaí's words and in Eoin Mac Néill's deliberately contentious 1908 essay "Tréigidh Bhur dTrom-Shuan" (Abandon your deep sleep), a blast at the lethargy and intellectual and artistic timidity of many Gaelic writers: "Irish writers must begin again where Ceitinn left off. They must resume the task of conquest. They must come out from their village walls and face the world."[202] Despite their nativist colleagues, the progressives claimed

---

ism was widely acknowledged and admired. What was new here was his unreserved openness to the oft-dreaded "foreign influence." Of course, the influences he had in mind were principally thematic, and he would doubtless have agreed with the anonymous reviewer of Father John Mac Erlean's edition of Keating's poems, *Dánta, Amhráin is Caointe Sheathrúin Céitinn* (Poems, songs and laments of Geoffrey Keating), who, having asserted that "like many of the Irish poets of the 17th and 18th centuries, Keating was well versed in contemporary English literature," went on to argue that Keating's practice as a poet "ought surely to be the last word on this question of verse form, that our best native poets knew the English form well and rejected it completely." See "Publications," *ACS*, 15 September 1900.

200. "An Leipreachán," "In the Gaelic World / Notes on the Language Movement," *WF*, 22 January 1910. This column provides a report on a meeting of the literary discussion group Cumann Oisín at which Béaslaí defended Ó Foghludha's edition of *Cúirt an Mheadhon Oidhche* against Seán Ua Ceallaigh's charge of immorality.

201. Piaras Béaslaí, "Merriman's Secret: An Interpretation," in Brian Merriman, *Cúirt an Mheadhon Oidhche*, ed. Risteárd Ó Foghludha (Dublin: Hodges and Figgis, 1912), 16. Béaslaí conceded that other Gaelic poets of the time showed no such knowledge of Continental developments, but attributed their ignorance to lack of opportunity rather than willful provincialism.

202. *IG* 18, no. 1 (January 1908): 16.

that such a willingness to confront the modern world could be rooted in the most authentic Gaelic tradition.

As has been shown, the literary world to be faced by Gaels was not that of London. Even the progressives for the most part accepted Edward Martyn's dictum at the Galway Feis of 1899: "Let us take our foreign influences from the Continent, but none from England."[203] French literature was offered as a generally accessible source of contemporary literary models, although some critics did not hesitate to point out the dangers of France's notorious infidelity and anticlericism.[204] Among the league's prominent Francophiles were Pearse, Ó Conaire, Éamonn Ó Néill,[205] Mícheál Breathnach,[206] Cathaoir Ó Braonáin (author of Béarla Sacsan agus an Creideamh i nÉirinn),[207] and especially Máire Ní Chinnéide, whose lecture on Anatole France stirred considerable controversy on its publication in An Claidheamh Soluis in 1910.[208] Unbowed, Ní Chinnéide published another essay on the same author in An

---

203. "Galway Feis / A Successful Gathering," FL, 23 September 1899. Martyn's statement appears in a letter read aloud at the Feis.

204. Reports on anti-Catholic activity in France appeared frequently in ACS. See, for example, the piece by "Diarmuid Donn," "Ain-Chreideamh sa bhFrainnc" (Atheism in France), 23 July 1904. The activities of Zola were of particular interest to some literary Gaels. His brief death notice in ACS states: "Zola was among the most famous writers not only in France but on the European continent. . . . It is said that he was a foulmouthed writer and that he hated the Catholic Faith." (Bhí Zóla ar na hughdaraibh ba mhó céim ní hé amháin sa bhFrainnc acht 'san Roinn Eórpa. . . . Deirtear gur dhrochbhéalach an fear é mar sgríbhneoir agus go dtug sé fuath do'n Chreideamh Chatoilceach.) See "Cúrsaidhe an tSaoghail," ACS, 4 October 1902. As we have seen, "An Seabhac" specifically cited Zola's work as the kind of literature Ireland should avoid. See "Sgríobhthar Finn-Sgéalta Dhúinn," ACS, 11 December 1909. The evil specter of Zola was also invoked by Tadhg Ó Donnchadha in a piece praising the Bretons for using their language as a barrier against French infidelity. See "Scéala ón mBriotáin" (News from Brittany), ACS, 14 October 1916.

205. On 7 January 1903, he read "translations of Legends from the French of Daudet" to the Central Branch of the league, where they were "much appreciated." See ACS, 17 January 1903.

206. See, for example, his comments on French literature in "Lean Lorg na Laochra" (Follow the path of the heroes), in Sgríbhinní Mhíchíl Bhreathnaigh, 49. Breathnach, who spent a considerable amount of time in a sanatorium in Switzerland, spoke French and was well read in French literature.

207. See, for example, his long essay on the poet Pierre Jean de Beranger, serialized in IG from March to June of 1908.

208. "Anatole France: Príomh-Sgéaluidhe na Frainnce Indiu" (Anatole France: The prime storyteller of France today), ACS, 26 February and 5 March 1910. Letters from priests critical of Ní Chinnéide's enthusiasm for France appeared in ACS on 26 March and 16 April 1910. In the latter, An tAthair Seán Ó Gormáin suggested Gaelic Francophiles read René Bazin and other orthodox Catholic writers.

Claidheamh Soluis in 1913,[209] and one on Alphonse Daudet the following year.[210] Ní Chinnéide made her literary standards clear at the very start of her 1910 lecture: "But if France is supreme in many ways, in no area does she excel more than in literary matters."[211] Of the other major literatures of Western Europe the Gaels had surprisingly little to say, apart from passing references to or a few translations from German literature by Tadhg Ó Donnchadha, William P. Ryan, Béaslaí, Nic Niocaill, or "Maire."

However, when we move out of the shadow of the major literatures, we find a heightened awareness among the Gaels. Their interest in literary developments in the other Celtic languages will be discussed in detail in Chapter 6, but they also moved well beyond linguistic kinship to a sense of communion and solidarity with long ignored or suppressed cultures rediscovering their creativity throughout Europe. Pearse, Ó Conaire, and William P. Ryan were the leading Irish apostles of this literary brotherhood of the unjustly neglected. Thus, writing in 1908, Ó Conaire stated:

> Considering this question, a person may find it strange when he notices that it is the new races or the races who have just begun to cultivate their literature and their languages of late, or who have begun to revive their old literature, who are most given to this constant digging. Perhaps they have the most courage, for courage is needed for this work, but it doesn't matter why since they are going about it with zeal. Look at the new literature of Russia and Norway and Finland and you will be in no doubt about the truth of what has been said concerning the literature of these new races.[212]

209. "Anatole France agus Sprid na Frainnce" (Anatole France and the spirit of France), *ACS*, 27 December 1913. "Má tá barr ag an bhFrainnc 'n-a lán slighe, níl éinnidh is mó 'na bhfuil an buadh aici ná i gcúrsaíbh litridheachta."

210. "Alphonse Daudet agus Cuid dá Shaothar" (Alphonse Daudet and some of his work), *ACS*, 31 January 1914.

211. "Anatole France," *ACS*, 26 February 1910.

212. Pádraic Ó Conaire, "Sean-Litridheacht na nGaedheal," in *Aistí Uí Chonaire*, 47. "Is ait le duine, ag cur na ceiste seo thrí chéile dhó, nuair a thugann sé faoi deara gurab iad na nuadh-chineadhcha nó na cinidheacha a thosuigh ar a gcuid litridheachta agus a gcuid teangan a shaothrughadh go mall sa ló, nó a thosuigh ar a sean-litridheacht a bheodhadh, is mó atá tugtha don síor-romhar seo. B'fhéidir gurab iad ba mhó misneach, mar teastuigheann misneach i gcomhair na hoibre seo, ach is cuma cia an fáth, is fíor gurab iad is dúthrachtaighe 'n-a héadan. Féach ar nuadh-litridheacht na Rúise agus Chríoch Lochlann agus Thír na Finne agus ní bheidh aon amhras ort nach bhfuil an ceart sa méid adubhradh faoi litridheacht na gcineadh nuadh seo."

This essay is full of the names of writers from these various cultures, writers with whose work Ó Conaire himself was familiar and comfortable.[213]

Pearse offered his own literary litany to fellow Gaels in his first year as editor of *An Claidheamh Soluis*: "What does Ireland know of Maeterlinck, Ibsen, Bjornson, Tolstoi, Gorki, Jokai? . . . How far are we being influenced by the young literatures of Russia, Finland, Norway, Hungary, Brittany, Provence?"[214] Two years later he included Belgium, a country he knew well from his trips there to study bilingual education, Russia, and Norway with France as "the four 'livest' countries in the matter of pure literature of the present day."[215] A shorter list of literary exemplars was offered by *Fáinne an Lae* to inspire Yeats to join the Gaelic cause: "Mr. Yeats, who might do for us what Kollar, with his patriotic poems . . . did for the Czech movement, who might do for us what the burning strophes of Alexander Petofi did for Magyar, has taken up Irish as a serious study, and has already, we are informed, made considerable progress therein."[216]

Was there more than name-dropping involved in such cultural roll calls? Unfortunately, with regard to writers in less widely spoken languages, such skepticism is inescapable. None of the revivalists knew Magyar, Finnish, or Czech, and while there were, of course, some contemporary English translations as well as French and German versions of the work of authors like Kollar and Jokai, none of the references by the Gaels goes beyond a mere conjuring up of rather exotic names and exemplary contributions to the revival movements of their respective nations.[217] In an essay on literary developments in the Ukraine, Cathal Ua Seanáin simultaneously exemplified this tendency to litany, ex-

213. For instance, Seán Mac Giollarnáth recalled the eagerness with which Ó Conaire read translations of the new European literature when he was living in London. See Mac Giollarnáth's contribution in *Pádraic Ó Conaire: Clocha ar a Charn*, ed. de Bhaldraithe, 68.

214. "Gleó na gCath," *ACS*, 22 August 1903. In a January 1907 editorial, Pearse wrote of the Irish-speaking child: "We have only to educate him and we set him free to strive with the Alcuins and the Fearghals and the Ceitinns, with the Ibsens and the Tolstois and the Jokais." See "The Fire in the West," editorial, *ACS*, 12 January 1907. Peadar Ó Maicín accepted the validity of Pearse's goal, although he was obviously less optimistic concerning the time frame involved, writing of Gaeltacht Irish that it was "just that kind of Irish we will want to see spread over the English-speaking part of Ireland before we can hope to see Irish grow and strike out new roots and make the name and fame of an Irish Jokai or an Irish Turgenev." See Ó Maicín, "The Simplified Spelling and Other Matters," *SF*, 27 May 1911.

215. "Recent Booklets," *ACS*, 7 October 1905.

216. "Notes," *FL*, 27 August 1898.

217. Understandably, Ryan's *Lessons from Modern Language Movements* provides a rather exhaustive (and exhausting) example of this tendency.

plained if not justified its roots in linguistic insularity, and blamed that insularity for the most part on Anglicization. Writing of the poet Tarás Shevchénko, he acknowldged: "It is still not possible to read his works except in Ukranian, Russian, and German. His fame did not reach Great Britain until recently and there is no need to say that not even his name is yet known in Ireland because the Irish are dependent on the English language."[218]

On the other hand, when we turn to the literatures of Russia and Scandinavia, particularly Norway, we find a considerably more informed awareness among the Gaels, although again that awareness, like that of their Anglo-Irish counterparts, was based almost exclusively on translation. For example, in his evidence to the Intermediate Education Commission in 1900, Hyde called "the revelation of the Russian temperament" by writers like Pushkin, Turgenev, Dostoyevsky, and Tolstoy "perhaps the chief event of nineteenth century literature."[219] Both Pearse and Ó Conaire felt it was an event that could and should have a profound and liberating effect on writing in Irish. Thus in his 1906 editorial "Literature, Life, and the Oireachtas Competitions," in which he proclaimed the demise of the traditional novel and prophesied that "the evangels of the future will go forth in the form of light, crisp, arresting short stories," Pearse concluded: "Gorki rather than Dickens suggests the style."[220] As is evident from his own fiction, Ó Conaire was an even more enthusiastic student of the modern Russian masters.[221] In particular, he extolled their courage, integrity, and tenacity: "With zealous heart and sincere will they set out in search of the truth, and not

218. "Náisiún Beag agus a Theanga" (A small nation and its language), *ACS*, 25 September 1915. "Ní féidir go fóill a leabhra do léigheadh acht san Úcráinis, san Rúisis agus san Ghearmánais. Níor shroich a cháil an Bhreatain Mhór go dtí le goirid agus ní gádh a rádh nach bhfuil a ainm féin ar eolas i nÉirinn go seadh de bhrígh go bhfuil Gaedhil taobh leis an mBéarla."

219. "Irish in Intermediate Education: Memorandum Put in by Douglas Hyde LL.D. to Supplement His Evidence," *ACS*, 20 January 1900.

220. *ACS*, 2 June 1906. With this praise of Gogol, Pearse was unintentionally guilty of cultural and linguistic heterodoxy, for as Cathal Ua Seanáin pointed out in his 1915 piece on Ukranian literature, Gogol wrote in Russian rather than in the language of his homeland and therefore "although Gogol described in a fine and precise way the old life of the Ukraine, his country gains not the slightest credit as a result" (gidh gur chuir Gogol síos go breágh agus go beacht ar shean-shaoghal na hÚcráine níl oiread is dadadh de chreideamhaint ag dul d'á thír dá bharr). See "Náisiún Beag agus a Theanga," *ACS*, 25 September 1915. Gogol was, however, to make an impact on later Gaelic writing as a source of inspiration for Tomás Ó Criomhthainn in writing *An t-Oileánach* (*The Islandman*) (1929).

221. See, for example, Áine Ní Chnáimhín, *Pádraic Ó Conaire* (Baile Átha Cliath: Oifig an tSoláthair, 1947), 25–26.

only did they find that deceptive queen, but they put life (borradh) into the literature of their country so that that literature is the freshest and sweetest and most vigorous to be found on the surface of the earth today."[222]

Interest in the Scandinavian literary revival was as widespread among the Gaelic progressives as it was among the Anglo-Irish writers on whom Ibsen had made such an impact. Indeed, no doubt with the Anglo-Irish as well as the Gaelic movement in mind, the committed progressive William P. Ryan, having argued that "our own writers are the better for the study of their Scandinavian brethren," could admit, "I am getting just a little bit weary of the blessed word Scandinavia."[223] If so, his weariness was not generally shared. Once again Pearse and Ó Conaire took the lead in focusing the Revival's attention on creative activity to the north, Ó Conaire, for example, writing of the Norwegians: "And that is a small race that has left the trace of its intellect not only on the literature of the world, but also on the modes of thought of every race. Isn't it possible to do what was done in that country yesterday, tomorrow in the country that first taught it to write?"[224] This notion that in turning to Scandinavia Ireland was in some sense merely calling in a long-standing literary debt was expressed more picturesquely by one "R. O'K." in 1906: "If Skald in the old days once swore brotherhood with File, perhaps in these modern days an Irish File may still learn some lessons from the study of a brother-poet's labours in the Norway of to-day."[225] And one Gael at least could have done such learning in a Scandinavian language. From 1907 to 1921 the appropriately surnamed Gearóid Ó Lochlainn made his living as an actor in Copenhagen, from which city he sent regular, personal accounts of lit-

---

222. "Sean-Litridheacht na nGaedheal," in Aistí Uí Chonaire, 48. "Le díograis chroidhe agus le dísle deoin' chromadar ar an bhfírinne a lorg, agus ní hé amháin go dtángadar ar an ríoghain mhealltaigh úd, ach chuireadar borradh i litridheacht a dtíre i dtreo go bhfuil an litridheacht sin ar an litridheacht is úire agus is cumhartha agus is mó brigh dá bhfuil le fágháil ar dhruim an domhain indiu." The young Daniel Corkery also urged his fellow Gaels to study the Russians. See "Russian Models for Irish Literature," The Leader, 27 May 1916.

223. "I mBaile 's i gCéin," ACS, 24 October 1903.

224. Pádraic Ó Conaire, "Sean-Litridheacht na nGaedheal," in Aistí Uí Chonaire, 48. "Agus sin cineadh beag a bhfuil rian a inntleachta fágtha, ní amháin ar litridheacht an domhain acht ar mhodhthaibh smaointe gach cinidh. An rud a rinneadh indé 'san tír úd nach féidir a dhéanamh i mbárach sa tír eile úd a chéad-mhúin an scríbhneoireacht di?"

225. "Ireland and Norway," ACS, 21 July 1906. See also "Sliabh Bladhma," "Ireland and Iceland," the Irish Nation and Peasant, 25 September 1909. The latter offers a brief survey of Icelandic literary developments and their lessons for Irish. "Lasairfhiona" discussed political parallels between the two countries in "Ireland and Iceland: Latter Day Lessons" in the Irish Nation and Peasant, 9 October 1909.

erary developments in Scandinavia, as well as translations of Norwegian folktales.[226]

Ó Lochlainn was later to play a leading role in the history of Gaelic theatre, as actor, director, playwright, and manager of An Comhar Drámuidheachta, the company responsible for the production of Gaelic plays in the Abbey Theatre after its sponsorship as the National Theatre under Saorstát Éireann. And reference to the theater brings us to a consideration of what was, along with the translations that will be the subject of Chapter 6, the principal concrete result of Gaelic literary cosmopolitanism. Here we move beyond name–dropping or even the profound influence of foreign models on the work of isolated and exceptional Gaelic authors like Pearse or Ó Conaire. Drama was not an indigenous Irish genre, though virtually all Gaelic writers, even the nativists with the possible exception of Henebry,[227] felt it should be developed in the new literature. As we will see in the discussion of Gaelic relations with the Anglo–Irish movement in Chapter 5, some of those with nativist tendencies suggested that adequate traditional models for a truly Irish drama could be found in the medieval Ossianic dialogues or in the histrionic narrative style of the Gaeltacht seanchaí (storyteller). However most revivalists saw drama as an area in which foreign aid could be sought without apology. Thus Dinneen defended his use of the neologism dráma against the charge that a native speaker would not understand it, by arguing that as things stood, an Irish-speaking monoglot would have no idea at all of what drama was no matter what it was called: "Now I think one who knows only Irish cannot have an adequate idea of what the term 'drama' implies. Our ideas of it come to us from English, French, etc., and the classical languages."[228] What is again of particular interest here is that the search for theatrical models did not stop on Abbey Street or in the West End. For example, "An Irish Pressman," having lamented the ineptitude of Gaelic theater in 1906, argued in An Claidheamh Soluis: "Owing to the unhealthy condition of our national life at present we are obliged to be insular in many things, but I

226. See, for example, his "Ó'n Mór-Roinn Thoir-Thuaidh" (From the northeast of the Continent), ACS, 28 September 1912; and "Aisteoireacht 'san Íslinn" (Acting in Iceland), ACS, 5 October 1912. He also contributed reports to the London journal An t-Éireannach and, under the pen-name "Lochlannach," translations of three Norwegian folktales from Asbjornsen and Moe to Sinn Féin. See "Éire agus an Saoghal Eorpach" (Ireland and the European world), An t-Éireannach, no. 19 (January 1912): 3; and "Seanscéalta Lochlannach" (Norwegian folktales), SF, 30 July–1 October 1910.

227. See Diarmuid Breathnach and Máire Ní Mhurchú, 1882–1982: Beathaisnéis a Dó (1882–1982: Biography two) (Baile Átha Cliath: An Clóchomhar, 1990), 35.

228. "Iasacht Focal san nGaedhilg" (The borrowing of words into Irish), IG 16, no. 7 (March 1906): 97.

submit that in this matter of creation of an Irish stage extreme insularity will retard instead of serve the cause. The English stage of the present day can safely be ignored, but to adopt the same policy with regard to the drama of all other countries would be extremely foolish."[229]

Many revivalists saw the French stage as the most promising model for the new Irish drama, for as Máire Ní Chinnéide claimed, "in the drama there has not for years been any comparison between France and any other country—not only with regard to the writing of dramas, but with regard to their production as well."[230] One "S.," in his essay "A National Theatre," suggested a grandiose scheme to be managed by the Gaelic League: "What we want now in Ireland is a Conservatoire and a Comédie Française, a school of acting and a national theatre."[231] Padraic Colum, one of the Anglo-Irish playwrights most respected by the Gaels, likewise suggested French models of the sort that Lady Gregory adapted for the Abbey players: "It might be well if some of our Gaelic writers who are working for the stage would study Molière."[232] In the wake of the *Playboy* riots, "Liúdaidhe Óg" won a contest in *Irisleabhar na Gaedhilge* with an essay on acting in which he advised Gaelic dramatists to study foreign plays, particularly those of Classical Greece and France.[233] In addition, there were, as we will see in a later chapter, several Irish translations of French plays, whose production provided lessons in stagecraft for Gaelic playwrights and actors and livelier and more sophisticated entertainment for urban audiences tired of the standard rural kitchen comedies.

Turning to the revivalists' other favorite sources of potential literary inspiration, we find that while Ó Conaire included Chekhov among the modern giants in his 1923 essay "An Fhírinne agus an Bhréag sa Litridheacht,"[234] and while in 1913 *An Claidheamh Soluis* reprinted an article from its Scottish Gaelic counterpart *Guth na Bliadhna* urging the Gaels of both Scotland and Ireland to study the Moscow stage,[235] Russian drama had no discernible influence on Gaelic playwrights. The situation

---

229. Letter, *ACS*, 7 July 1906.

230. "Anatole France," *ACS*, 26 February 1910. "San dráma, níl éan-chomórtas idir an Fhrainnc agus éin tír eile le bliadhantaibh— ní amháin ins na drámannaibh do sgríobhadh, acht ins an léiriughadh leis."

231. *ACS*, 2 March 1907.

232. "Some Notes on Dramatic Method," *ACS*, 27 August 1910. A year later Colum again urged those interested in Gaelic theater to look abroad for dramatic models, this time to the marionette theater, particularly that of Italy and Sicily. See "A Marionette Theatre for Gaelic Plays," *ACS*, 5 August 1911.

233. "Aistigheacht," *IG* 17, no. 18 (March 1907): 292.

234. In *Aistí Uí Chonaire*, 201.

235. R. Erskine, "Gaelic Drama in Albain," *ACS*, 13 September 1913.

was somewhat different with regard to Scandinavia, where drama was, of course, at the heart of the literary revival. Bjornson and Ibsen were frequently invoked by Gaelic progressives like Éamonn Ua Tuathail, who wrote: "It is Ibsen and his fellow writers who were responsible for the revival of literary drama in Europe."[236] Interestingly, however, few Gaelic critics seem to have been aware that both Bjornson and Ibsen stood pointedly apart from the language movement in their homeland, declining to write their plays in the *Landsmál* that was the focus of Norwegian revivalists.[237] Indeed the Anglo-Irish playwright Padraic Colum took a certain glee in pointing out this ignorance when he defended himself against a *Sinn Féin* critic who contrasted his linguistic patriotism unfavorably with that of Ibsen:

> Now that the pencil is in my hand I may as well bring your impressions of Ibsen into line with reality. . . . You imply that Ibsen wrote in a language which is to Norway what Irish is to Ireland. In Norway there are two literary languages—the "Landsmaal," derived from ancient Norse, a local and popular language, and a literary language known to the whole of Scandinavia—Norway, Sweden, and Denmark. I might make a point by describing this language as Danish. It is sufficient that Ibsen did not write in the language peculiar to Norway—the "Landsmaal."[238]

The greatest contribution the Scandinavian theater would make to Gaelic drama would come through its formative influence on Gearóid Ó Lochlainn, who spent the years from 1907 to 1921 acting both on the stage and in movies with the Nordisk Film Company in Denmark.

236. "Drámanna Dúinn Féin" (Dramas for ourselves), *ACS*, 29 November 1913. "Is é Ibsen agus a chomh-sgríobhnóirí ba chionntach le aithbheodhughadh an dráma liteardha i nEuroip." See also the profiles of Bjornson, Ibsen, Grieg, and Sars in Louise Kenny's series, "Men Who Re-Made Norway," *SF*, 13 November–4 December 1909.

237. For example, Louise Kenny blurred the linguistic issue by stating that "from a boy Bjornson had set himself to the Norsking of the root-Danish language used in his own land," and by emphasizing that Ibsen's "mixed Norwegian, Danish, German, and Scottish blood" meant "in such a nature as his the natural jarring cross-currents were never dumb nor untroubled." For her views on Bjornson, see *SF*, 13 November 1909; for those on Ibsen, *SF*, 20 November 1909. On the other hand, Ibsen's decision not to write in the *Landsmál* was discussed somewhat negatively by an anonymous contributor to *ACS* in "An Dá Theanga san Orbhuaidh," *ACS*, 3 January 1914; and Bjornson's much more directly by "Ross Faly" in "The Evolution of the Gaelic Struggle," *SF*, 6 July 1912. Incidentally, "Ross Faly" (as "Ros Fáilghe") translated a few Scandinavian stories. See Chapter 6.

238. "Muskerryism—A Reply to 'X,'" *SF*, 23 July 1910.

From Copenhagen, Ó Lochlainn monitored developments at home while keeping the achievements and example of the Scandinavians before his Gaelic comrades: "Think of the renowned people Denmark and Norway have given the world—Ibsen, Hans C. Andersen, Bjornson, Selma Lagerloff, Niels Finsen, August Strindberg, and others who won fame and honor throughout the whole world for the excellence of their intellect and spirit." Ó Lochlainn ranged even farther afield, introducing Irish readers to the history of the Icelandic stage and the work of Mathias Jochumson, Indridí Einarsson, and Jóhann Sigurjónsson, and urging the Irish capital to follow the example of Reykjavík in establishing a resident national theatre.[239]

Needless to say other revivalists of theatrical bent shared Ó Lochlainn's enthusiasm for developments in newly emergent or reviving cultures. Once again, however, without some command of the various languages or access to translations (into English) of plays from them, the primary impact of theatrical news from these countries was inspirational rather than literary or practical. Thus in an 1899 editorial note attacking the Irish Literary Theatre for its claim to be a "national" theater, An Claidheamh Soluis described in some detail what it saw as the truly national drama movements of Hungary and Bohemia, exclaiming sarcastically: "How Kisfaludy, Szechyeni, Kossuth, and Paul Nagy would have laughed to scorn and torn to tatters, the idea of a Magyar drama in the hated German speech."[240] Two years later, William P. Ryan, in a plea for a permanent national theater in the Irish language, recalled the example of the Czechs, who had expended 235,000 pounds on the construction of a national playhouse and its rebuilding after a fire. Ryan concluded his appeal: "Have our 'cosmopolitans' learned nothing from the Continent?"[241] Indeed, in the preface to a collection of his own plays, Ryan turned again for inspirational support to the successes of theatrical movements in emergent cultures: "Countries in Europe—from Denmark to Hungary—succeeded magnificently with national dramas a century or two ago. . . . It is clear that Ireland will have to progress like Denmark and Hungary."[242] Pádraig Ó Síor-

239. "Aisteoireacht 'san Íslinn," ACS, 5 October 1912. "Cuimhnighthear ar na daoinibh mór-chlúiteacha do bhronn an Danmarc, an Orbhuaidhe, agus an tSuain ar an saoghal—Ibsen, Hans C. Andersen, Bjornson, Selma Lagerloff, Niels Finsen, August Strindberg, agus daoine eile nach iad do bhuaidh cáil agus clú ar fuaid an domhain le feabhas a n-intleachta agus a meoin." Éamonn Ua Tuathail also referred to developments in Iceland in "Drámanna Dúinn Féin," ACS, 29 November 1913.
240. "Notes," ACS, 6 May 1899.
241. "London Notes," ACS, 26 October 1901.
242. "Drámanna Náisiúnta" (National dramas), Preface to Plays for the People (Dublin: M. H. Gill and Son, 1904), vi. "D'éirigh ádh mór le tírthibh 'san Eúróp—ó'n Danmarg

dáin added German-speaking Alsace-Lorraine to the list of theatrically active regions from which the Gaels could learn:

> The growth and development of the Alsatian Theatre tends to show that with a little of it [money] a National Theatre can be established. We must first have the fixed idea of the great good a National Theatre can do; we must, secondly, turn our thoughts from the English play; and, lastly, we must get actors, playwrights, and the patriotic play-going public to co-operate, and never cease until a National Theatre is established—the National Theatre of Ireland.[243]

In passing we should also note that many revivalists shared the general Irish enthusiasm for the new medium of film, although they were also aware of its potential dangers as a force for Anglicization:

> What work the Gaelic League could do for the language if it cinematographed the everyday life of the Irish-speaking districts, the feiseanna, the language procession, the Irish colleges at work, and arranged moving-picture plays of Irish-Ireland as it should be! It is not too late for something of the kind to be set on foot by the League, and there is money as well as propaganda in it. . . . It is a pity that, as Wesley said, we should persist in leaving the Devil all the good music, and thinking it piety.[244]

"Seán Óg" Ó Caomhánaigh was in full agreement, writing in a lengthy feature piece in *An Claideamh Soluis* in February 1913: "The movie theatre is amongst us, and it is no passing thing; it is here to stay. Will we Gaels make use of it to help our movement? Now is the time. The movie theatre can be a fine agent for Anglicization or for Gaelicization. Will we attempt it in time?"[245] Ó Caomhánaigh appreciated the educational potential of the movies with their ability to disseminate to people

go dtí an Ungáir—as drámannaibh náisiúnta aois nó dhá aois ó shin. . . . Is léir go gcaithfidh Éire dul ar aghaidh mar an Danmarg agus an Ungáir."

243. "A National Theatre on the Rhine," *SF*, 2 January 1909.

244. "Irish-Ireland and the Cinematograph," *SF*, 16 March 1912.

245. "An Scáine agus an Ghaedhilg," (The film and the Irish language), *ACS*, 8 February 1913. "Tá an Peictiúrlann 'n-ár measc agus ní haon rud duthain é; cómhnochaidh sé. An mbainfeam-ne, Gaedhil, aon áis as chun cabhartha ár ngluaiseachta? Anois an t-am. Ara mhaith Gallduighthe nó Gaedhealuighthe 'seadh an Peictiúrlann. An sanntócham é i dtráth?" Four months later, he returned to this subject in *SF*, complaining that nobody seemed to have paid any attention to his *ACS* piece. See "Seán Óg," "An Scáine agus an Ghaedhlig," *SF*, 21 June 1913.

of all classes and educational backgrounds "knowledge . . . about the ways, manners, and customs of people in foreign countries, about their beautiful sights etc., and even about events of just the other day, public meetings, races, fires, deaths, games, etc. Everything before the eyes just as it happened."[246] However, he also had a keen commercial sense, proposing as subjects for early Gaelic films such stirring material as *Táin Bó Cúailnge*, the story of Diarmaid and Gráinne, and two very different novels of the Revival, Ua Laoghaire's *Séadna* and Ó Conaire's *Deoraidheacht.*[247] "Seán Óg" was himself excited by the screen version of *Les Misérables*, an enthusiasm shared by the Gaels of Belfast when the film reached their city.[248] Of course, at this same time readers of Irish were getting a firsthand, inside look at the new medium through the reports that Ó Lochlainn was sending from Copenhagen to *An Claidheamh Soluis* and to the London League monthly *An t-Éireannach.*[249]

All Gaelic Leaguers and all revivalists accepted as dogma the league motto "Tír gan Teanga, Tír gan Anam" (A nation without a language is a nation without a soul), but as should be clear from this chapter, there was no such agreement on practical details and definitions with regard to either of these two ineffable and indispensable ideals. In his first year as editor of *An Claidheamh Soluis*, Pearse challenged both his fellow Gaels and critics of the Revival with the question: "Is it possible to conceive an Irish-Ireland more forlornly isolated from the thought of its age, from the great world outside the ken of London newspaperdom, than is this vulgar, half-illiterate Anglo-Ireland?"[250] It was a question that the leaders of the Anglo-Irish movement were also posing, and one of the greatest tragedies occasioned by the souring of relations between the two major forces in the broader cultural renaissance was

246. "Catharach Nuadh" (A new urbanite), *SF*, 9 March 1912. He saw the movies providing "eolas . . . ar shlighthibh, bheusaibh, nósaibh daoine i dtíorthaibh coigcríocha, ar a radharcaibh áilne etc., agus fiú amháin ar theagmhasaibh an lae fé dheireadh, cruinnighthe puiblidhe, ráiseanna, teintidhe, diobháidhteacha, cluichidhe, etc. Gach nidh fé leith na súl díreach mar thárla."

247. "An Scáine," *ACS*, 8 February 1913.

248. "Fear na Feirsde," "Sgéala na Feirsde" (News from Belfast), *ACS*, 22 February 1913. Gaelic enthusiasm could, however, be tempered for reasons other than the purely linguistic. Thus in a 1916 note praising the work of the Irish Film Company, *ACS* commented: "The pictures are in sharp contrast with many of the unwholesome foreign productions which deal with questionable stories depicted in anything but a wholesome way." See "Sgéalta don Sgáil" (Stories for the screen), *ACS*, 14 October 1916. The work of the Irish Film Company was not in Irish.

249. See, for example, "Beo-Phictiúirí" (Moving pictures), *An t-Éireannach*, no. 23 (May 1912): 1–2. In this piece, Ó Lochlainn summarized and commented on an American film he had seen in Odense.

250. "Gleó na gCath," *ACS*, 22 August 1903.

the loss of this potential alliance of enlightened Irish artists from both linguistic traditions. This stillborn attempt at literary cooperation will be discussed in detail in Chapter 5. Here it is both sufficient and essential to note that the extreme nativists who did so much to wreck the initiative did not speak as the sole representative voice of the Gaelic movement. That movement's progressives saw the challenge of the Revival as the restoration to Ireland of her true past, a restoration that would involve her resumption of active intercourse with the Europe she had so long ignored under the yoke of English cultural imperialism. In a recent review of works by Canetti and Borges, the contemporary Gaelic poet Gabriel Rosenstock has decried what he sees as the persistent insularity of writing in Irish, concluding with the admonition: "If we understood that the sparse spiritual provision that is nourishing us is a fairly new phenomenon in the history of the nation, there is still a good chance that we won't be swallowed up our own arseholes."[251] No doubt couched somewhat differently, his concern could just as well have been expressed eighty or more years ago by Pearse, Ó Conaire, Béaslaí, Ryan, Ní Chinnéide, or Nic Niocaill, all of whom, in their utter rejection of unthinking provincialism, tried to save their cause and their comrades from the dire fate of Rosenstock's warning.

251. Review of *The Conscience of Words* by Elias Canetti and *Seven Nights* by Jorge Luis Borges, *Comhar* 45, no. 9 (September 1986): 34. "Dá dtuigfimís gur feiniméan cuibheasach nua é i stair an chine an lón cúng anama atá ár gcothú tá seans maith fós nach slogfar suas ár dtiarpa féin sinn."

2

Seanchuidhthe, *Séadna*, Sheehan, and the Zeitgeist: Folklore, Folklife, and the New Prose

Taking the offensive in his response to Henebry's extended diatribe against his story "Íosagán" (Little Jesus) as a prime specimen of "Revival Irish," Patrick Pearse wrote in 1909: " 'Íosagán' has been described by an able but eccentric critic as a standard of revolt, but my critic must pardon me if I say that the standard is not the standard of impressionism. It is the standard of definite art form as opposed to the folk form. I may or may not be a good standard bearer, but at any rate the standard is raised and the writers of Irish are flocking to it."[1] Yet however enlightened, Pearse's flock of literary rebels was never partic-

1. "By Way of Comment," *An Macaomh* 1, no. 2 (December 1909): 18. Henebry's attack on Pearse, part of his "Revival Irish" series, appeared in *The Leader*, 30 January; 6, 13, and 20 February 1909. Of the opening passage of "Íosagán," Henebry wrote: "The extract is of very high value as affording a sample to beginners of that which must be shunned in thought, in feeling, in outlook, in expression, in word, punctuation, everything" (30 January 1909).

ularly large, and the adherents of the folk form more than held their own in Gaelic fiction through most of this century. Indeed, a subsequent generation of Gaelic writers seems to have taken to heart the 1927 editorial dictum of the folklore journal *Béaloideas* that any contemporary Irish literature worthy of the name had to have "its roots planted and fixed in the literature and folklore of the Irish language" (a préamhacha bunuithe, greamaithe i leitríocht agus i mbéaloideas na Gaedhilge).[2]

Of course Pearse's reservations were not directed toward folklore itself. From the very beginning of the Gaelic movement, language revivalists had committed themselves enthusiastically to the collection and publication of Irish folklore, with Gaelic League founder and president Douglas Hyde playing a particularly prominent role from the publication of his *Leabhar Sgeuluidheachta* (Book of storytelling) in 1889 to his death sixty years later.[3] Few if any Gaels would have disagreed with the views of Pádruig Ó Laoghaire in the preface to the first volume of his *Sgeuluidheacht Chúige Mumhan* (Munster storytelling) in 1895:

> When I heard many stories when I was young, I said that if they were collected and published it would benefit many, especially those who had never heard them. I knew they were valuable, for they reveal to us the mind and the intellect of the Gael more clearly and distinctly perhaps than anything else we now have left, and anything that sheds light on their customs should interest us. Even if they are fragments and at times corrupted fragments, they are nonetheless a rich inheritance.[4]

2. "Ó'n bhFear Eagair" (From the editor), *Béaloideas* 1, no. 1 (June 1927): 3. Of course, Pearse's battle against a blind obsession with folk standards continued to be waged by later members of his progressive flock not only through genuine creative effort, but also through satire, as in Myles na gCopaleen's *An Béal Bocht*, and through critical polemic, as in Máirtín Ó Cadhain's 1950 lecture on folklore and the folklore establishment. See "An Chré" (The clay), "An Chré Mharbh" (The dead clay), and "An Chré Bheo" (The living clay) and the letters Ó Cadhain's views provoked in *Ó Cadhain i bhFeasta* (Ó Cadhain in *Feasta*), ed. Seán Ó Laighin (Baile Átha Cliath: Clódhanna Teoranta, 1990), 129–81.

3. For an overview of Hyde's literary career including his work as a collector, editor, and translator of folklore, see Mary Helen Thuente's entry in the *Macmillan Dictionary of Irish Literature*, ed. Robert Hogan (London: Macmillan, 1979), 302–6.

4. "Roimh-Rádh" (Preface), *Sgeuluidheacht Chúige Mumhan* (Baile Átha Cliath: Pádruig Ó Briain, 1895), iii. "Ag clos mórán sgeul dom agus mé go han-óg adubhairt féin dá mbaileóchaidhe iad, agus iad do chlóbhualadh go dtairbheóchadh sé d'á lán—dóibh seo go háirithe ná cuala iad. B'fiosach mé go rabhadar luachmhar, óir taisbeánaid dúinn intinn agus intleacht na nGaodhal níos soiléire solusmhaire, b'fhéidir, ná aonnidh eile atá fágtha

Ó Laoghaire's call for collection and publication was to be echoed repeatedly by nativists and progressives alike in editorials, essays, and letters in the Gaelic press in the first decades of this century.

Moreover, Gaelic support for the preservation of folklore was not merely theoretical or emotional. Local feiseanna all over Ireland and in London offered prizes for both the collection and performance of folk material. Many names later prominent as sources of Gaelic lore first appear in the prize lists of such festivals. For example, Micheál Mhag Ruaidhrí was recognized at the 1898 Galway Feis for "a collection of unpublished Irish songs,"[5] an honor he reciprocated by offering a prize at a 1902 Mayo feis "for the young girl who would best tell a folktale" (do'n chailín óg do b'fhearr a d'innseóchadh sean-sgéal).[6] The excitement even the prospect of such recognition could generate among local "active carriers of tradition" is evident in "An Seabhac's" account of the reaction of a Corca Dhuibhne seanchaí to the news that league organizer Tomás Bán Ua Concheanainn was to visit Dingle: "Micí na gCloch was like one possessed on that day, standing on the steps in front of the great door of the church, his powerful voice ringing out in triumph at the promise of the resurgence of the Gaedheal."[7]

---

anois againn, agus aonrud soillsigheas ar a nósaibh-san is cóir dúinn bheith suimeamhail ann. Má's blúireacha iad féin agus blúireacha truaillighthe, ar uairibh, is oighreacht saidhbir iad i n-a dhiaidh san." For an appreciation of Ó Laoghaire's work as a folklorist, see Seán Ó Súilleabháin, "Pádraig Ó Laoghaire," *Béaloideas* 3, no. 5 (December 1932):409–12.

5. "The Galway Feis/List of Awards," *FL*, 10 September 1898.

6. Mícheál Ó Tiománaidhe, "An Dealg" (The brooch), *ACS*, 12 July 1902. Ó Tiománaidhe was himself an active collector of folklore. For a brief account of his activities, see Diarmuid Breathnach and Máire Ní Mhurchú, *1882–1982: Beathaisnéis A hAon* (1882–1982: Biography one) (Baile Átha Cliath: An Clóchomhar, 1986), 107–8.

7. Pádraig Ó Siochfhradha, "Notes on Some of Jeremiah Curtin's Storytellers," *Béaloideas* 12, nos. 1–2 (June–December 1942): 155. As Peadar Ó hAnnracháin makes clear in *Fé Bhrat an Chonnartha* (Under the banner of the league), his account of his own career as a league organizer, traveling teachers, organizers, and other league officials like Ua Concheanainn did indeed seek out and pay unwonted tribute to people like "Micí na gCloch." Throughout *Fé Bhrat* Ó hAnnracháin notes that he collected songs and stories whenever time permitted. See "Béaloideas" (Folklore), in *Fé Bhrat an Chonnartha* (Baile Átha Cliath: Oifig an tSoláthair, 1944), 356–59. Of one old man he met at Feis na Mumhan in Cork City, Ó hAnnracháin wrote (520):

I'm very pleased that I was listening to him, for when I became acquainted with him I heard a good amount about the region in which I was raised that I hadn't heard before, and I got verses and stories from him that were not to be found at that time in the place where he had learned them.

(Is maith liom go mór go rabhas ag éisteacht leis mar nuair a fuaras aithne air d'airigheas cuid mhaith i dtaobh an cheanntair 'nar tógadh mé nár airigheas cheana, agus

Obviously the annual national Oireachtas could and did have a far greater impact in fostering this work. From the very first gathering in 1897, prizes were offered for the collection of folklore, with the emphasis always on unpublished material.[8] While the competitions became increasingly diverse and specific over the years,[9] they never lost their initial popularity and ability to attract entries. Thus in 1900 Hyde, in his capacity as judge, reported to Oireachtas officials:

> I have great pleasure in announcing to the Committee that the competitions in folk-story and folk-song were again most successful; and as excellent as the results of last year were, this year surpassed them. The contributions sent in filled over 700 pages of MS., many of them folio pages, closely written. About half of these contained folk stories, of which there were 25. . . . Several of the stories were quite new, and will be a valuable acquisition to the national folk-lore.[10]

This acquisition was to be shared with the nation through the publication of prize winners in periodicals and full-length collections, the first of which, containing winners of the 1900 competitions, was ambitiously announced by the league's Publication Committee in October of that year:

> It is the intention of the committee to include in these annual volumes of folklore all the unpublished folklore of value that

---

fuaras ranna agus scéalta uaidh ná raibh le fagh*á*il an uair chéadna san áit 'nar fhoghlamuigh seisean iad.)

8. League collectors were, however, sufficiently sophisticated to recognize that some of the material recited by their informants was of literary origin. For example, the adjudicators' report on the folk-song competition of the 1901 Oireachtas commented:

The great difficulty of an adjudication is to know how far these folk-songs have been written down this year from the lips of living people, and how far they have been copied out of manuscripts made during the last fifty years. . . . For instance none of Eoghan Ruadh's poems came last year, but this year a great many of them, and if it is true that these poems in their elaborate metres and rather hyperbolic language still live upon the lips of the people in such perfection, we can only think of it as a marvel not to be paralleled in any other country in western Europe.

See *Imtheachta an Oireachtais 1901* (The proceedings of the Oireachtas, 1901), ed. Tadhg Ó Donnchadha (Baile Átha Cliath: Connradh na Gaedhilge, 1903), 1:156. See also the comments of Seosamh Laoide in his notes to some of the tales in *Cruach Chonaill* (Baile Átha Cliath; Connradh na Gaedhilge, 1909), 117–19.

9. See the lists in Donncha Ó Súilleabháin, *Scéal an Oireachtais 1897–1924* (The story of the Oireachtas, 1897–1924) (Baile Átha Cliath: An Clóchomhar, 1984), 168–71.

10. See *Imtheachta an Oireachtais 1900* (Baile Átha Cliath: Connradh na Gaedhilge, 1902), 1:86.

comes into its hands over the years, as it believes that the only adequate means of preserving the vast mass of oral literature still extant is to get it into print as soon as possible. In six or seven years there will thus be in print what will probably be the most extensive published collection of National folklore of which any country can boast. The successful carrying out of this project will mean the saving for all time of the existing body of Irish folklore, which is now threatened with extinction. Secretaries of Feiseanna and others who may have folklore collections in their hands are invited to forward them to the committee for publication purposes.[11]

Unfortunately the very success of the Oireachtas competitions over the years put the realization of this goal beyond the means of the league. For example, the publication of prizewinners from the 1901 Oireachtas would eventually involve four volumes, the last of which did not appear until 1910.[12] Nevertheless, although the Oireachtas was never able to share in print all of the folk treasures it unearthed, it did provide early recognition as well as an introduction to a nationwide audience for many of the figures, informant and collector alike, who would later play leading roles in the preservation of traditional lore. Thus Micheál Mhag Ruaidhrí was a consistent winner;[13] Amhlaoibh Ó Luínse, a hefty volume of whose tales was published by the Folklore Commission in 1971, was honored in 1903;[14] Seán Ó Cadhla took prizes in 1899 and 1902;[15] and William Shortall in 1903, 1904, and 1906.[16] Pearse's "Bríghid na nAmhrán" ("Brigid of the Songs"), in which the

11. "The Book of the Third Oireachtas," *ACS*, 27 October 1900. In the inaugural edition of *Béaloideas* in 1927, Ó Duilearga praised the work of the league and in particular of the Oireachtas in preserving folklore, but added: "It is with regret that we have to state that the greater part of these collections have been irretrievably lost. During the troublous years, 1916–1921, much valuable material was, to our own knowledge, destroyed." See "Ó'n bhFear Eagair," *Béaloideas* 1, no. 1 (June 1927): 4.

12. The volumes, all edited by Laoide, were *Fionn agus Lorcán* (1903), *Madra na nOcht gCos* (The eight-legged dog) (1907), *Éan an Cheoil Bhinn* (The bird of the sweet music (1908), and *An tÉinín Órdha* (The little golden bird) (1910).

13. See Ó Súilleabháin, *Scéal an Oireachtais*, 168–71, for the years 1899, 1903, 1904, 1905, and 1906.

14. *Seanchas Amhlaoibh Í Luínse* (The folklore of Amhlaoibh Ó Luínse), collected by Seán Ó Cróinín, ed. Donncha Ó Cróinín (Baile Átha Cliath: Comhairle Bhéaloideas Éireann, 1980).

15. In both instances, Ó Cadhla split the second prize. In 1902, his co-winner was Ernest Joynt, one of the leading Protestant members of the league.

16. Shortall won his prizes for stories he collected from Mhag Ruaidhrí. See Ó Súilleabháin, *Scéal*, 169–70.

hardships of a grueling trek to perform at the Oireachtas in Dublin cause the death of an elderly Conamara *sean-nós* singer at the very moment of her triumph, provides a vivid if unconvincingly romantic depiction of the fascination the national festival inspired in culturally aware native speakers.[17]

Of course tales others than those submitted to the Oireachtas also appeared regularly in *An Gaodhal*, *Irisleabhar na Gaedhilge*, *Fáinne an Lae*, and *An Claidheamh Soluis*,[18] while folk material was a prime focus of the Munster-based monthly *An Lóchrann* (The lantern) from its inception in 1907.[19] Indeed, the *Irisleabhar* had published a folktale, an Irish translation of one of the Grimm stories, as early as 1883, proclaiming: "It being the province of the *Gaelic Journal* to occupy itself with everything related to the Irish language and literature, it would ill become it to neglect that department of antiquities and archaeology still existing to a certain extent among the mass of our people, and well denominated folklore."[20] On a more ambitious level the league published, in addition to the Oireachtas anthologies, a significant number of folklore collections, among them volumes edited by scholars like Seosamh Laoide, Eoghan Ó Neachtain, Seán Ó Cadhla, and Séamus Ó Searcaigh. Indeed in its first thirty years as a publisher the league actually produced twice as many volumes of folklore (31) as it did instructional books (16). By way of comparison, 38 songbooks and only 24 volumes of original fiction were issued in this period.[21] It is, however, interesting to note that sales did not keep pace with production, with *An Claidheamh Soluis* commenting in 1911 that "the sale of folk tales . . . was not good," most folk collections averaging annual sales in the 200–300 range, while Pearse's *Íosagán agus Sgéalta Eile* sold 979 copies in

17. *Collected Works of Pádraic H. Pearse: Scríbhinní*, 93–98.

18. Some tales appeared as the result of research in the library rather than in the field. Thus in 1915 Éamonn Ó Tuathail published in *ACS* two anecdotes that had been written down in 1847 by the Meath poet Aodh Mac Domhnaill for the Belfast antiquarian Robert MacAdam. See Éamonn Ó Tuathail, "Tiomsughadh Sgéalta" (A collection of stories), *ACS*, 10 July 1915.

19. In its opening editorial, *An Lóchrann* claimed it was "a journal catering particularly for Éire Óg [Young Ireland]," but that "at the same time we intend making the paper interesting to persons of all ages and especially to members of the Gaelic League and sympathisers with the Irish-Ireland Movement." See "Our Mission," *An Lóchrann* 1, no. 1 (March 1907): 3. When the first number of the "new" *Lóchrann* appeared in April 1916 this same claim to be directed to a young audience was made again. There is, however, no real internal indication that the paper was directed specifically to such a readership.

20. "Clann Conchobhair," "Folklore [Introductory]," *IG* 1, no. 7 (May 1883): 205.

21. Máirín Nic Eoin, *An Litríocht Réigiúnach* (Regional literature) (Baile Átha Cliath: An Clóchomhar, 1982), 27.

1910 alone (three years after it first appeared) and Pádraic Ó Conaire's *Deoraidheacht* "close on 300" in only four months of the same year.[22]

On the whole such folk collections were, then, a labor of love, and that labor was generally done with admirable thoroughness in difficult conditions. There was, first of all, an acute shortage of workers with sufficient Irish to record tales accurately from oral narration, and a regular lament of those so qualified was that time did not allow them to collect even a fraction of what they discovered. For example, Peadar Mac Fhionnlaoich tells of an evening spent with the Donegal *seanchaí* Proinnsias Chonaill Ruaidh: "I said that I hoped to hear folktales or poems or songs. Proinnsias said that there was a time when he had plenty of things of that sort, but that he was getting old and losing many of them. I objected, and at last he gave a slight cough to clear his throat and began a Fenian tale that he called 'Cormac Mac Airt.' I didn't write it down because I didn't have the available time that evening."[23] And of course when there was time the snail's pace and sheer drudgery of longhand transcription often seriously distorted the performance of a tale: "Mrs. Twomey, who has splendid Irish, at first related this story

22. "70,000 Irish Books Sold," *ACS*, 26 August 1911. On the other hand, as has been noted, two little booklets each containing a single tale from Ó Laoghaire's *Sgeuluidheacht Chúige Mumhan* had been very popular; *Rí na mBréag* (The king of the lies) sold 4206 copies in the final ten months of 1908. Similarly, the seven booklets composing Henry Morris's series *Greann na Gaedhilge* (The humor of the Irish language), a collection of comic anecdotes with clear folk roots, sold a total of 5256 copies in this same period. Seosamh Laoide's longer and more demanding *Measgán Músgraidhe* (Muskerry miscellany) attracted but 44 purchasers. These figures are from a mimeographed sheet headed "Liosta de leabhra a díoladh ó Mhárta 1adh, 1908—Nodlaig 31adh, 1908 do réir Mhuintir Mhac an Ghuill" (A list of books that were sold between 1 March 1908 and 31 December 1908, according to the Gill Company), in the Fionán Mac Coluim Papers, National Library of Ireland, MS. 24,405.

23. Peadar Mac Fhionnlaoich, "Thall 's i bhFus i dTír Chonaill" (Here and there in Donegal), *ACS*, 26 April 1902. "Dubhairt mise go raibh mé ag súil le sean-sgéaltaibh a chluinsint nó dánta nó amhráin. Dubhairt Proinnsias go raibh lá ann agus bhí go leor neithe de'n chineál sin aige-sean acht go raibh sé ag éirigh sean anois agus go raibh sé ag cailleadh cuid mhór aca. Chuir mise sárughadh isteach, agus 'sa' deireadh leig sé mionchasacht as ag glanadh a sgornaigh agus thoisigh ar sgéal Fiannuidheachta ar a dtug sé 'Cormac Mac Airt.' Char sgríobh mé síos é mar nach raibh faill agam an tráthnóna sin." In his autobiography *Mise* (Myself), Colm Ó Gaora tells of a more awkward problem he encountered in his dealings with informants as an underpaid league organizer: "The tradition bearers used to expect some offering from the collector—something for which they can't be blamed. . . . They didn't understand . . . that this collecting of folklore was work for the nation." (Bhíodh súil ag na seanchuidhthe le síneadh láimhe éicínt—rud nár mhilleán ortha—ó'n mbailightheóir. . . . Ní thuigidís . . . go mb'obair náisiúnta bailiughadh seo an bhéaloidis.) See *Mise*, eagrán nua (Baile Átha Cliath: Oifig an tSoláthair, 1969), 83–84.

in a very fluent, racy, conversational style, but afterwards, when she had to wait on the pencil of the scribe, this completely disappeared, and the narration took the above form."[24] It was doubtless a desire to re-create such performances for non-Gaeltacht readers as well as a simplistic obsession with verisimilitude that inspired so many rural writers of the early Revival, among them An tAthair Peadar in *Séadna*, to frame their invented narratives in the carefully detailed context of a traditional storytelling session presided over by a genuine *seanchaí*.

Yet despite all the frustrations of collection in the field, conscientious folklorists like Sean Ó Cadhla, Aodhmáin Mac Gríogóir,[25] and Seosamh Laoide persevered, questioning their informants as tales were told and reading to them the completed transcriptions for correction or revision. Such collaborative sessions with the *seanchaí* Tadhg Ó Conchubhair were recalled by Ó Cadhla in his brief preface to *Eachtra Fhinn Mhic Cumhaill le Seachrán na Sál gCam* (The adventure of Fionn Mac Cumhaill with the Wanderer with the Crooked Heels): "It's many a pleasant, sunny and warm afternoon we spent by a stone wall during this past summer, writing them down; and as we wrote a bit, we would always stop for a while then to talk of the warriors and the heroes of Ireland."[26]

---

24. "An Gobán Saor," *IG* 12, no. 142 (July 1902): 98. Some Gaels did consider the possibility of applying modern, even state-of-the-art, methods to the traditional material. In 1905 P. J. O'Sullivan was hyperbolic in his projection of what league collectors could accomplish with a knowledge of shorthand: "Our present organisers furnished with a knowledge of Irish shorthand could in twelve months collect almost every scrap of folklore, etc., on the lips of Irish speakers." See "Irish Shorthand," *ACS*, 2 December 1905. In 1909 "An Stocaire" chided his fellow Gaels for their reluctance to avail themselves of promising new technology: "Listen, what do the Irish-language people in Dublin have against recording machines that they won't buy one or two for the organizers so that they could be gathering songs and music as they travel the country." (Cogar, cad é an doicheall atá ag muinntir na Gaedhilge i mBaile Átha Cliath roimh an gcóir aithris nach ligfeadh dóibh ceann nó dá cheann do cheannach dos na timthiribh chum go mbeidís ag bailiughadh amhrán agus ceol rompa ag taisdeal na tíre dhóibh?) Actually, "An Stocaire" was thinking of such recordings as educational aids rather than as a means of preserving lore. See "An Stocaire," letter, *ACS*, 7 August 1909. Two weeks later, Seán Ó Ciarghusa ("Marbhán") wrote in response to "An Stocaire," saying that he had done some such recording, but was having trouble getting the necessary equipment (letter, *ACS*, 21 August 1909). Gaels seem to have embraced the new technology with enthusiasm when it was available to them. As early as 1903, an Oireachtas Committee had disqualified the performance of one Mr. Judge in the "Unpublished Airs" competition "for refusing to play his airs into the Gramaphone." On his protest, the adjudicators' decision was upheld. See "The Oireachtas Committee," *ACS*, 20 June 1903.

25. In his *Fréamhacha na h-Éireann* (The roots of Ireland) (Baile Átha Cliath: Maunsel, 1906), Mac Gríogóir collected eight stories from Inis Meán in the Aran Islands, identifying the name and residence of each of his informants.

26. Ed. Seosamh Laoide (Baile Átha Cliath: Connradh na Gaedhilge, 1906), 2.

Speaking of his work with Mhag Ruaidhrí in revising stories originally collected by Pearse, Laoide explained how the business side of such sessions worked: "I reread them in the presence of the storyteller, and any word that displeased him was changed so that only the words that he himself chose were allowed in."[27]

This concern for accuracy was also commonly if not universally reflected in the provision of source and provenance for published tales, although one does occasionally find a collector reporting that he got a story "from an old man who was visiting in our house the other night" (ó sheanduine a bhí ag sgoruidheacht 'nár dtigh-ne an oidhche fá dheireadh).[28] Yet even the most meticulous collectors were not above deviating from full literal fidelity, despite the editorial advice in one of the very first issues of Fáinne an Lae: "Take down the stories exactly as the people say them. That is the best and safest way."[29] One problem, perhaps insuperable at the time, concerned the satisfactory transcription of dialect differences. In a note accompanying a Cork folktale, the collector explains that "I was often of two minds while writing down this story about the spelling of words. Most of it follows the pronunciation . . . 'A small amount is tasty' with regard to emendation as with regard to everything else."[30] More extreme was the suggested approach of "T.D.F.G." in his 1914 review of Scéaluidhe Éireann (Ireland's storyteller), a collection compiled by "An Connachtach Céasta." "T.D.F.G."

27. "Réamhrádh" to Éan an Cheoil Bhinn (Baile Átha Cliath: Connradh na Gaedhilge, 1908), v. "Do aithléigheas-sa os comhair an sgéalaidhe iad, agus cibé focal nár thaithin leis do hathruigheadh é sa gcaoi nár leigeadh isteach acht na focail ba rogha leis féin." While this method would obviously allow Mhag Ruaidhrí to fashion a more polished tale than he would be capable of in traditional performance, it would also enable him to correct inaccuracies in transcription. See also further comments by Laoide on his work with Mhag Ruaidhrí in his prefaces to Lúb na Caillighe agus Sgéalta Eile (The craftiness of the hag and other stories) (Baile Átha Cliath: Connradh na Gaedhilge, 1913), vi; and Triúr Clainne na Bard Scolóige: Sean-Sgéal ó Thír Amhalgadha (The three children of the country poet: An old story from Tirawley) (Baile Átha Cliath: Connradh na Gaedhilge, 1914), v.

28. "Cú Chulainn" (Peadar Ó Dubhdha?), "An Croiceann agus a Luach" (The skin and its value), ACS, 5 January 1901.

29. "Seanchus" [a sort of notes and queries column], FL, 19 February 1898. Likewise, in a 1908 lecture to the Ard-Chraobh urging all leaguers to become amateur collectors of folklore, Eoin Mac Néill stressed that "the main thing for them to do in the first instance was to collect the evidence with fidelity, not to build up conclusions and explanations." See "Preserve the Traditions!" ACS, 17 October 1908.

30. D.P., "An Fear Mór agus an Fear Beag" (The big man and the little man), FL, 28 May 1898. The storyteller was Cáit Ní Shúilleabháin. "Bhíos i gcás idir dhá chomhairle go minic ag sgríobhadh an sgéil thuas dam, um litriughadh na bhfocal. Tá an chuid is mó dhe de réir labhartha. . . . 'Bíonn blas ar an mbeagán' de leasuigheacht mar le gach rud eile."

was more than willing to emend to their "legitimate" forms what he regarded as "excrescences" and "amputations" in the colloquial dialects.[31] Another problem, this one ultimately ideological, was resolved by the relatively regular substitution of Irish words and phrases for the frequent Anglicisms of native-speaking informants. In his 1913 preface to *Maighdean an tSoluis agus Sgéalta Eile* (The maiden of light and other stories), Henry Morris ("Fearghus Mac Róigh") could write: "I inserted six or seven words of pure Irish in place of English words in the stories, and there is indeed a good amount of English in some of them, something that does not please me at all."[32]

Of course even greater liberties were taken with the many tales re-created, rather than recorded, from the narration of an informant. Perhaps the most popular examples of such re-creations were the brief tales eventually published by Peadar Ua Laoghaire as *Ag Séideadh agus ag Ithe* (Breathing hard and eating) and *Ár nDóithin Araon* (Enough for both of us) in 1917 and 1919 respectively. While Ua Laoghaire was quite specific about the sources of many of these anecdotes (which he also claimed were "positive fact"),[33] he acknowledged that he had heard them in his youth decades before, and a few characteristic authorial intrusions in which he addresses the reader directly make clear that the tales as we have them are entirely the work of An tAthair Peadar himself.[34] But if Ua Laoghaire allowed himself considerable freedom in the re-creation of folk material, he was less tolerant of what he perceived as invalid variants offered by others. Thus in 1898 he angrily criticized the editor of *Fáinne an Lae* for publishing what he felt was an anticlerical tale involving Eoghan Ruadh Ó Súilleabháin, and offered in its place the innocuous "correct" version (fíor an sgéil).[35] Fortunately Ua Laoghaire's attitude toward "unacceptable" aspects of folk tradition did not generally prevail, and *Fáinne an Lae* and other journals occasionally publish tales revealing unedifying and disturbing facets of the folk

31. "Scéaluidhe Éireann," *SF*, 14 March 1914.

32. "An Díon-Bhrollach" (Preface) to *Maighdean an tSoluis agus Sgéalta Eile* (Dundalk: Dundalgan, 1913), 5. "Chuireas isteach sé nó seacht d'fhoclaibh ghlan-Ghaedhilge i n-ionad focla Béarla agus tá méid breagh d'fhoclaibh Béarla ionnta go seadh, rud nach dtaitheann liom ar chor ar bith." Compare the comments of Laoide in his "Brollach" to *Cruach Chonaill*, where he states that he replaced English words with "pride" (uaill) not "apology" (taithleachas).

33. See the comments from a 1917 letter by Ua Laoghaire in Risteárd Pléimeann's preface to *Ár nDóithin Araon* (Baile Átha Cliath: Brún agus Ó Nóláin, n.d.), iii–v.

34. See, for example, his nationalistic asides on 26 and 43 of *Ár nDóithin Araon*.

35. "Fíor an Sgéil" (The truth of the matter), *FL*, 9 April 1898. The offending story, "An tSlighe 'n-a bhFuair Eoghan an tairgead" (How Eoghan got the money) by Muiris Ó Dubhdha, appeared in *FL*, 26 March 1898.

imagination, such as the tale in which a man cuts out the tongue of his loquacious wife and later drowns her,[36] or the one in which a miserly father plots, unsuccessfully, to drown his septuplets to save money.[37]

If Gaels were united in their appreciation of the value of Irish folklore, they were also unanimous concerning the major source of that value, the rich linguistic resources of the tales and songs. Repeatedly, reviews of folk collections stress the beauty of the language, often virtually ignoring the narrative or imaginative qualities of the stories. An extreme example is provided by a June 1894 editorial comment by Father O'Growney in *Irisleabhar na Gaedhilge*: "Some people are anxious to know why we publish folk-stories. It is not so much for their value as folk-lore, as for the number of old words, not to be found in dictionaries, which they contain."[38] A more sweeping claim for the linguistic value of folklore was offered by Séamus Ó Searcaigh in a review of Micheál Mhag Ruaidhrí's *Mac Mic Iasgaire Bhuidhe Luimnighe* (The son of the son of the ugly Limerick fisherman): "If I were to be asked where the best Irish being spoken today is to be found, I would without doubt say that it will be found in the folktales and songs in books or still on the tongues of old people in the west, south, and north of Ireland."[39]

36. Risteárd Ó Séaghdha, "Teanga Mhná, Ní Stadann go Bráth" (A woman's tongue, it never stops), *FL*, 13 May 1899.

37. "Sliabh Díle," "An Móirsheisear Easpog" (The seven bishops), *FL*, 12 August 1899. On the other hand, "T.D.F.G." did feel that "exceptional matter" such as "gruesome" incidents "crudely done" should be omitted from tales aimed at a student readership, the precise audience he seemed to see as the ideal one for such "little gems" of folk material. See T.D.F.G., "Scéaluidhe Éireann," *SF*, 14 March 1914.

38. *IG* 5, no. 3 (1 June 1894): 33.

39. "Ó Chúige Uladh" (From the Province of Ulster), *ACS*, 20 November 1909. "Dá gcuirtí ceist orm cá bhfuil an Ghaedhilg is fearr dá bhfuil dá labhairt nó dá sgríobhadh indiu le fágháil, déarfainn gan amhras go bhfuighfear í ins na sean-sgéaltaibh agus ins na hamhránaibh atá i leabhraibh nó atá ar theangaidh seandaoine go fóill thiar, theas, agus thuaidh i n-Éirinn." See also the comments of "Tír-Fhiachrach" (Seaghán P. Mac Éinrigh) on this same collection of Mhag Ruaidhrí's stories: "His stories are a perfect mine of beautiful Irish idioms, and his vocabulary is so extensive, and he uses so many words which have perished in other districts that natives of the latter have suspected him of coining the words himself." See "A Gleaning from a Famous Literary District," *ACS*, 13 November 1909. To assist learners in placing such linguistic survivals and idiosyncrasies in their proper regional context, tales were frequently classified according to dialect (as "Gaedhilg na hÁrainn," etc.), a practice that one "Tadhg na hAille" rejected as creating the impression that there was no coherent modern Irish, merely a scattering of local patois. See his letter to the editor of *FL* for 6 May 1899. Conceding that "Tadhg" had a valid point, the editor responded that he was responsible for the dialect labels "for the sake of the learners of Irish . . . lest they take every spelling and every form they see in them as standard practices" (ar son lucht foghlumtha na Gaedhilge . . . ar eagla go nglacfadaois gach litriughadh agus gach foirm do chífidís ionnta mar ghnásaibh choitceann).

Indeed, even as committed a folklorist as Seosamh Laoide could offer an almost apologetic linguistic justification for its publication: "Some, indeed, have so poor an opinion nowadays of folklore that they do not care to have too much energy devoted to its publication, although the study of it is undoubtedly the very best means of learning the spoken tongue."[40]

This unanimity concerning the linguistic value of folklore did not, however, by any means extend to a consensus concerning its literary worth, either inherent or potential as a model for the prose fiction of the early Revival. In fact, as Pearse's defense of "Íosagán" makes clear, the role of folklore in the development of Gaelic creative prose was to become one of the major battlegrounds in the war between nativism and progressivism. To many nativists, with their dread of foreign contamination of the new literature, folktales seemed to offer safely indigenous models to link the increasingly Anglicized present with the pristine Gaelic past. Thus Henebry could say of the stories collected by Father Michael Sheehan: "They present a richness of idiom, a plenitude of grammatical forms and a wealth of vocabulary that mark them as the natural and untainted continuation of the last literature in our great books."[41] And of course the main thrust of his "Revival Irish" series in *The Leader* during 1908–9 was that this cultural continuity was under assault from Anglicized writers who through ignorance deviated from those indigenous standards whose sole if flawed contemporary guarantors were the native-speaking peasantry, particularly the *seanchaithe*. Moreover, for Henebry such a deviation was not simply a literary lapse, but an apocalyptic act of national apostasy: "The effort to revive Irish is not merely a contention of Irish vs. English, but it is a veritable Battle of the Standards. It is not alone then a question of the vernacular and literary use of Irish as opposed to English, but it means, in addition, the Irish philosophy, the Irish outlook, the Irish *Weltanschauung*

40. Letter, *ACS*, 15 July 1905. In his preface to *Measgán Músgraighe*, Laoide acknowledged that the tales were an uneven lot, but emphasized that "folktales have one advantage over every other story, however excellent: the language in them is always beautiful, particularly if they are gotten from storytellers entirely unfamiliar with English." (Tá aon bhuaidh amháin ag na sean-sgéaltaibh ar gach aon sgéal eile, dá fheabhas é .i. bíonn an chainnt ar áilleacht i gcómhnuidhe ionnta, go háirithe má gheibhtear iad ó sgéalaidhthibh nach raibh puinn taithighe aca ar Bhéarla.) See "Brollach" to *Measgán Músgraighe: Cnuasach Beag Sgéalaidheachta* (A Muskerry miscellany: A little storytelling collection) (Baile Átha Cliath: Connradh na Gaedhilge, 1907), ix. For a survey of Laoide's extensive activities as a folklorist, see Ciarán Bairéad, "Seosamh Laoide," *Béaloideas* 15, nos. 1–2 (June–December 1945): 127–40.

41. Richard Henebry, letter to Michael Sheehan, in Sheehan, Preface to *Gile na mBláth* (Dublin: M. H. Gill and Son, 1912), vii.

vs. the world. In the coming struggle, the Irish stand to win or lose tremendously along the whole line."[42]

Father Patrick Dinneen was more concerned with the future capabilities than the past glories of the folk tradition, writing in 1902: "In the beginning of this century, if we wish to bring new prose to maturity, it only remains for us to wed high, noble thoughts to the clearness and harmony that we have inherited for generations, and which are to be found abundantly in the stories our ancestors cherished for ages."[43] This is, of course, precisely the method that Peadar Ua Laoghaire claimed to have followed in *Séadna* and that he recommended to Laoide as early as 1895: "Look around you. You will see some little anecdote somewhere here or there that you can spin out fine and smooth and easy to make a vivid, enjoyable story."[44]

Apparently "An Seabhac" felt that Gaelic writers were losing sight of this sound approach: in a previously cited lengthy front-page piece in *An Claidheamh Soluis* for 11 December 1909, he faulted efforts to Europeanize Gaelic literature and urged his fellow authors to turn again for inspiration to "the old stories the old folks have and the old stories in the old books and the old stories that have been retold for us in modern Irish—those are all stories the Gaels created out of their own spirit when they had no knowledge of or contact with any storytelling but their own."[45] Others would go farther, as did the anonymous author of

42. "Revival Irish," *The Leader*, 9 January 1909.

43. *Prós Gaedhealach* (*Irish Prose*) (Dublin: Society for the Preservation of the Irish Language, 1902), 100. This essay was published with Dinneen's own facing English translation, which has been used in the text. "Níl uainn féin i dtosach na haoise seo chun nuadh-phrós d'abaidhiughadh acht smuainte árda, neamh-choitchiana do shnaidhmeadh leis an soiléireacht is leis an bhinneas atá le sinsearaibh mar dhúthchas againn, agus atá le fagháil go flúirseach ins na sgéaltaibh do chleachtadar ár n-aithreacha ós na ciantaibh." See also the comments of the anonymous *Freeman's Journal* correspondent in "The Oireachtas," 28 April 1898.

44. Letter to Seosamh Laoide, 17 December 1895, quoted by Liam Mac Mathúna, "Réamhrá" (Foreword) to Peadar Ua Laoghaire, *Séadna* (Baile Átha Cliath: Carbad, 1987), xix. "Feuch ad thímcheall. Chídfir sgéilín beag éigin thíos nó thuas, thall nó abhus, go bhféadfair é shníomh amach go breágh bog réidh, agus sgeul bríoghmhar suairc do dhéanamh ass."

45. "An Seabhac," "Sgríobhthar Finn-Sgéalta Dhúinn," *ACS*, 11 December 1909. "An Seabhac" recommended "na sein-sgéalta atá ag na sean-daoinibh agus na sein-sgéalta atá insna sein-leabhraibh agus na sein-sgéalta do h-aith-innseadh dúinn i nGaedhilg na haimsire seo—sgéalta iad san go léir do cheap Gaedhil as a meon féin nuair nach raibh aon eolas ná aon chaidreamh aca ar aon sgéalaidheacht acht ar a gcuid féin." The "old stories" referred to here include both modern folk- and folk-inspired tales like Ua Laoghaire's *Séadna* and modernized versions of earlier Irish literature like Ua Laoghaire's *An Craos-Deamhan* and several by "An Seabhac" himself.

the "Le hAghaidh na nGaedhilgeóiridhe" (For the Irish speakers) column of the *Weekly Freeman* for 10 January 1903: "It is not fitting for an
Irishman to accuse the Gaeltachtaí of not having a developed literature."[46]
Séamus Ó Searcaigh agreed, and in his 1914 preface to *Cú na gCleas
agus Sgéalta Eile* (Cú of the Feats and other stories), asserted that the
kind of tales in this very book were not mere models from which literature could be developed, but were themselves aesthetically successful
creations: "There are people who say we have enough folktales in print
already, that we need literature from now on. But what is literature?
Are any of the stories in this book literature? If not, I don't know what
literature is."[47]

Other Gaels believed they knew full well what literature was or
should be, and questioned how a vitally contemporary prose relevant to
the concerns of a modern European society could evolve from the folktales of a rural peasantry. As we have seen, Pearse became the standard
bearer for these literary progressives, and his views will be discussed
below in some detail. But by no means did he stand alone. As early as
the first Oireachtas in May 1897, Alice Milligan wrote in a prizewinning essay on "How to Popularise the Irish Language": "The Irish peasantry have done nobly for the literature of their country in preserving
and treasuring this traditional literature; and the scholars of Ireland
have done and are still doing good service in collecting and publishing
these floating relics of the once ample verbal literature of the bards and

---

46. *WF*, 10 January 1903. "Ní iomchabhaigh an nídh é d'Éireannach cur i leith na
nGaedhealtachta nach bhfuil litridheacht foirfe acu."
47. "Réamh-Rádh" to *Cú na gCleas agus Sgéalta Eile*, collected by Íde Nic Néill and
Séamus Ó Searcaigh, ed. Séamus Ó Searcaigh (Dundalk: Dundalgan, 1922), iii–iv. "Tá
daoine ann adeir gur leor a bhfuil de shean-sgéaltaibh i cló againn cheana féin, gur litridheacht atá de dhíth orainn feasta. Acht cad is litridheacht ann? An litridheacht sgéal ar
bith de na sgéaltaibh atá sa leabhar seo? Murab eadh, níl a fhios agam cad is litridheacht
ann." Ó Searcaigh's foreword is dated 29 June 1915. In an essay on "Irish Folk-Lore—
What It Teaches," Henry Morris pointed out that Ó Searcaigh's dilemma could be resolved through a proper understanding of oral literature:

> The *seanachaide* has a literature—is master of an oral literature in his native tongue—a
> literature that is thoroughly his own. . . . He has lays and poems, and stories, and
> hymns, and proverbs, and he repeats these with an evident interest and pleasure that
> bespeaks a literary taste and culture. . . . This literature is not of the highest type, but
> as a proof that it is good and beneficial it affords himself and others intellectual
> delight and entertainment.

See "The Irish Folk-Lore—What It Teaches," *FL*, 16 December 1899. The piece originally appeared in the *New Ireland Review*. Morris was without doubt responding in this
piece to Trinity College Professor Robert Atkinson's famous dictum that "all folklore is
at bottom abominable," a slur that rankled for more than a decade. See, for example, the
comments of An tAthair Tomás Mac Gearailt to the National Literary Society in 1915 as
reported in *ACS*, 6 March 1915.

shanachies. But in the country now-a-days a hundred men will read the newspapers for one who will care to listen to the old legends."[48] Indeed, in 1899, an anonymous critic in *Fáinne an Lae* dared to question An tAthair Peadar's methods in *Séadna*: "It is impossible not to regret the incongruity that follows from the mingling of fiction with folk-lore."[49]

48. "Geal na Gréine" (Alice Milligan), "How to Popularise the Irish Language," *Imtheachta an Oireachtais/Full Report of the Proceedings at the Oireachtas or Irish Literary Festival Held in the Round Room, Rotunda, Dublin, on May 17th, 1897. Including the Prize Pieces, Now Published for the First Time* (Dublin: Gaelic League, 1897), 91.

49. "Séadna," *FL*, 18 March 1899. Both contemporary and subsequent critics seem to have found Ua Laoghaire's approach equally problematic, as is evident in their attempts to fit *Séadna* into one of the conventional literary genres. Norah Meade said that Ua Laoghaire could not be called a "novelist . . . according to the English definition of the term" and that "his work comes more accurately under the class known by the name of *Novelle* in German, for which English has no better equivalent than Tale." See Meade, "The Contemporary Irish National Movement in Literature," *WF*, 12 March 1910. One "Bard Briosc" agreed that *Séadna* was not "a novel as the term is at present understood (ní úrsgéal é de réir mar tuigtear an focal fé láthair), but was vague as to what it then was, calling it "a sort of book to itself" (sórt leabhair fé leith). See "Bard Briosc," "Sean-Scéaltaí agus Litridheacht" (Folktales and literature), *National Student* 2, no. 7 (March 1912): 34. Aodh de Blácam called the book "a sort of folk-novel" (*Gaelic Literature Surveyed* [Dublin: Talbot, 1929], 379). Seán Ó Tuama, who in 1955 saw *Séadna* as "a literary genre unto itself" ("genre" litríochta ann féin) ("*Cré na Cille* agus *Séadna*," *Comhar* 14, no. 2 [February 1955]: 8), has since come to agree with this classification, calling Ua Laoghaire's work a "folknovel" (úrscéal tuaithe). See "Úrscéalta agus Faisnéisí Beatha na Gaeilge: Na Buaicphointí" (Irish language novels and biographical accounts: The highpoints), *Scríobh* 5 (1981): 148. J. E. Caerwyn Williams and Máirín Ní Mhuiríosa place the emphasis on the folk rather than the novelistic aspect of *Séadna*: "*Séadna* is not a truly creative work; rather, it is fundamentally a picture of the life the author himself knew in his youth with, woven through it, a folktale about a man who sold his soul to the devil." (Ní saothar fíorchruthaitheach é *Séadna*; séard atá ann go bunúsach ná pictiúr den saol ab eol don údar féin le linn a óige agus scéal béaloidis fite tríd faoi dhuine a dhíol a anam leis an diabhal.) See *Traidisiún Liteartha na nGael* (The Gaelic literary tradition) (Baile Átha Cliath: An Clóchomhar, 1979), 362. A sharp dissent from this condescending view of *Séadna* is that of Pádraig A. Breatnach, who has argued that critics have denied the book a fair reading through their insistence on judging it as a failed novel rather than seeing it as the successful *Sage* it actually is: "It is now clear that An tAthair Peadar was not writing in the novelistic tradition, but rather was working within a tradition far closer to his own experience and more suited to his talent and goal. That is the tradition of the *Sage*." (Is soiléir anois ná raibh an tAthair Peadar ag scríobh laistigh de thraidisiún na húrscéalaíochta, ach gurbh amhlaidh a bhí sé ag obair laistigh de thraidisiún ba ghiorra dá thaithí agus ab oiriúnaí dá scil agus dá chuspóir go mór ná é. Is é sin traidisiún an *Sage*.) See Breatnach, "*Séadna*: Saothar Ealaíne" (*Séadna*: A work of art), *Studia Hibernica* 9 (1969): 112. See also the comments of Liam Mac Mathúna in the "Réamhrá" to his 1987 edition of *Séadna*, xlvii–xlviii. But by far the most challenging revision of traditional readings of *Séadna* is that proposed by Alan Titley, who rejects the standard view of the work as "for long the rural novel *par excellence* that showed us a strong Irish-speaking community in which piety and folklore were dominant" (an t-úrscéal tuaithe *par excellence* ar feadh i bhfad a nocht pobal láidir Gaeilge dúinn a raibh an chráifeacht agus an bhéaloideas in airde

Other Gaels were considerably more forthcoming and explicit in their reservations about such a mingling. Thus, commenting on the Oireachtas collection *Trí Sgeulta* (*Three Stories*) in his "London Notes" column, William P. Ryan wrote:

> In a deal of such lore we find a certain strength and richness, and a sure and easy power over language is suggested, but in the end it is acutely disappointing that there are not more of the finer qualities of literature. . . . We ask in the end if the Irish wealth of folk-lore, interesting and appealing in so many ways, has not been in others a great misfortune. . . . The old way of telling, turning, and saying things was enough—a fatal notion in literature. Yes, Irish folk-lore was a fine thing in its way, but native writers who will follow their own bent will be a refreshing blessing, a joy for ever.[50]

Two leading Gaels who often lined up on opposite sides of the ideological divide between nativism and progressivism were in agreement on this point, and both expressed their views with pointed clarity. Father John O'Reilly, who himself in 1905 edited and published a long folktale, *Curadh Glas an Eolais* (The green hero of knowledge),[51] dismissed the native-speaking folk out of hand as a source of literary inspiration:

> Modern life has never existed among the folk whose proper vernacular is the Irish language; and so, its ideas and its mode of presenting them have never yet taken a really Gaelic shape. In as far, therefore, as modern life has touched the folk at all, it is not

---

láin ann). Instead, noting the wide range of possible readings that Ua Laoghaire's work invites, he concludes: "*Séadna* is a modern, experimental, self-referential novel whose principal theme involves timeless human concerns with regard to good and evil" (úrscéal nua-aimseartha turgnamhach féinthagarthach is ea *Séadna* arb iad cúraimí síoraí an duine maidir leis an maith is leis an olc a phríomhthéama), a book "always ahead of every slave that came after it and of every follower of fashion that has never yet overtaken it" (i gcónaí chun tosaigh ar gach mogha a tháinig ina dhiaidh agus ar gach sodairín ar shála an fhaisin nár tháinig suas leis fós). For Titley's discussion, see his *An tÚrscéal Gaeilge* (*The novel in Irish*) (Baile Átha Cliath: An Clóchomhar, 1991), 150, 534–38, 572–74.

50. *ACS*, 27 September 1902.

51. An tAthair Seaghán Maolmhuire Ó Raghallaigh, *Curadh Glas an Eolais* (Baile Átha Cliath: Muintir na Leabhar Gaedhilge, 1905). He got the story from Tomás "Tommuny" Bhid, and later used this publication in an unsuccessful attempt to establish his credentials for the chair of Irish at University College, Galway. See Breathnach and Ní Mhurchú, *Beathaisnéis a hAon*, 95.

through Irish, but through English it has touched them. But it can scarcely be said to have touched them at all, and so, the value of their assistance to a man who would treat a modern subject in Irish would be exactly *nil*, and worse, waste of time and vexation of spirit.[52]

Similarly, Eoin Mac Néill sparked no slight outrage when in a 1908 *Irisleabhar na Gaedhilge* piece he directed his exasperation toward some of those literary Gaels who were attempting just such an approach, charging them with, among other things, "stupid incapacity": "Credit is actually claimed in proportion to the fidelity with which writers have acted the part of literary gramaphones with chimney-corner records. They even wall themselves up in villages, and sedulously avoid adopting anything from the foreigners in the villages outside. . . . It is the most artificial humbug imaginable."[53] Among those siding with Mac Néill in the subsequent controversy was Máire Ní Chinnéide: "But let us not bother with trying to imitate the folktales of the people or to write fine pseudo-Fenian tales. We have enough of those kinds of things already, some of them in print and some in the mouths of the people, and they'll do the job for us for a long while to come."[54] Her view was echoed several years later by an *An Claidheamh Soluis* correspondent commenting on a proposal to launch a new Gaelic magazine: "I'll support it if money is needed, but I will do so on one condition: that FOLKTALES are not allowed into the magazine, or at least no more than a page's worth for the children!"[55] And of course Pádraic Ó Conaire, the most successful practitioner of these progressive principles, was at this time publishing his most important and influential works of fiction in

52. O'Reilly, *The Native Speaker Examined Home*, 28.

53. "Tréigidh Bhur dTrom-Shuan," *IG* 18, no. 1 (January 1908): 15. Needless to say, Mac Néill was by no means opposed to the collection and publication of folklore proper, for in this same year he appealed to all members of the league "to write down faithfully and accurately, without addition, omission, or alteration an account of every detail of peculiar local custom and observance and every local tradition that they met." See "Preserve the Traditions!" *ACS*, 17 October 1908.

54. "Nuadh-Litridheacht na nGaodhal agus Cionnus is Fearr í Chur chum Cinn" (Modern Irish literature and how best to advance it), *IG* 19, no. 1 (January 1909): 616. "Acht ná bacaimís le bheith ag iarraidh aithris a dhéanamh ar shean-sgéaltaibh na ndaoine, nó ar 'sgéalta breaghtha bréige fiannuigheachta' do sgríobhadh. Tá an oiread dá leithéid siúd ann cheana féin, cuid aca i gcló agus cuid aca i mbéalaibh na ndaoine, agus déanfaidh an gnó dúinn go ceann i bhfad."

55. "Maolmachta," letter, *ACS*, 4 December 1915. "Bhéarfaidh mé cuidiughadh leis má tá airgead ag teastáil acht bhéarfad é ar aon choingheall amháin .i. nach leigfear SEAN-SCÉALAIDHEACHT san Irisleabhar nó ar a laighead gan acht leathanach amháin de a bheith ann i gcóir na bpáistí!"

an attempt "to free ourselves from the false Gaelicism that has sprouted
in our own time"[56] and "to cut the cord of the past that was around the
writer's neck . . . to break with the old styles of writing that have come
down to us, and to put the new literature on a level with every other
modern literature throughout Europe."[57]

It was, however, Pearse who, as editor of *An Claidheamh Soluis*, most
comprehensively and cogently developed and defended the progressive
position. His views were, however, by no means static or simplistic.
Writing in the Royal University magazine *St. Stephen's* in 1901, he
could sound very much the orthodox nativist:

> "If you have a story to tell," a man who was gathering folktales
> used to say once, "tell it to me as your grandmother would." I

56. "Clónna. Brostaigí, a Lucht na bPeann!" (Publications. Hurry up, writers!), in
Iriseoireacht Uí Chonaire (Ó Conaire's journalism), ed. An tSr. Eibhlín Ní Chionnaith
(Béal an Daingin: Cló Iar-Chonnachta, 1989), 93. This essay originally appeared in the
Shamrock and Irish Emerald, 20 November 1920. "muid féin a sgaoileadh ó shlabhraibh an
Ghaelachais bréige chuir géaga i n-áirde len-ár linn féin."

57. "Lucht Leabhar agus Lucht Peann: Cén Donas Atá Ortha?" (Readers and writers:
What is wrong with them?) in *Aistí Uí Chonaire*, 162. Ó Conaire was praising Pearse for
his attempt "gad na seanaimsire bhí ar sgórnach na sgríobhnóirí a ghearradh . . . na sean-
nósa sgríobhtha tháinic anuas chugainn a bhriseadh, agus an nuadhlitridheacht chur ar aon
chothrom le gach nuadhlitridheacht eile ar fud na hEorpa." This essay originally appeared
in *Old Ireland*, 21 February 1920. That Ó Conaire was supportive of the collection and
publication of genuine folklore is evident from his advice to Free State teachers enrolled in
summer programs in the Gaeltacht:

> But as for the person with the right attitude for learning Irish, it's not the lectures
> that he will hear in the Colleges during the months that he spends in the Gaeltacht
> that will benefit him most, but rather the amount of rural folklore he will pick up
> during his visit.

> (Acht an té a bhfuil an fuadar ceart faoi chun Gaedhilge d'fhoghluim, ní hiad na
> léigheachtaí a chloisfeas sé sna Coláisdibh is mó a rachas chun tairbhe dhó le linn na
> míosa a chaithfeas sé san nGaedhealtacht ach an méid de bhéaloideas na tuatha a
> phiocfas sé suas le linn a chuairte.)

See "Dualgas an Oide. Obair Mhór" (The duty of the teacher. Important work) in
Iriseoireacht Uí Chonaire, 190 (originally published in the *Connacht Sentinel*, 9 August
1927). See also his 1919 praise for the journals *An Lóchrann* and *An Stoc* (*Iriseoireacht Uí
Chonaire*, 77–78).

More important, Ó Conaire could, on occasion, write a story like "An Cochall Draoidheachta" (The magic hood) (*UI*, 1–29 April 1905) with a strong folk flavor, or, more
subtly, could weave folk motifs into his fiction, as he does in the 1904 story "Páidín
Mháire," where he alludes to the belief that the Ó Conaola family of which Páidín is a
member is related to seals. The reference renders even starker the contrast between the
natural freedom and dignity of Páidín's life as a fisherman and the degradation of his later
incarceration in a poor house. See "Páidín Mháire," in *Nóra Mharcuis Bhig agus Sgéalta Eile*
(Nóra Mharcuis Bhig and other stories) (Baile Átha Cliath: Connradh na Gaedhilge,
1909), 38–51.

give the same advice to every Irish speaker who wants to write
Irish. . . . Your grandmother was a marvellous woman. . . .
Follow her style at first and everything else will come by de-
grees, just as castles are built.[58]

Nor did he shed this attitude (or metaphor) immediately. In an editorial
on the Oireachtas, he lauded "the old learning" (an sean-léigheann) and
proclaimed: "We intend to build the castle of the new learning. For that
purpose we must first dig until we strike the bedrock of the old learning. Then we will begin to raise the walls of the castle."[59] A year later
he returned to this theme in another Oireachtas editorial, entitled
"Sean-Scéalaidheacht" (The telling of folktales): "We must never forget
that we who are involved in this Irish-language work are obliged to
preserve the stories and pastimes of the people who came before us.
When we have taken down the stories, it will be possible to rework
them and to develop them. On these old stories modern Irish literature
must be modeled and built."[60]

Yet at this very time Pearse was in other pieces expressing reservations about the value of the folktale as a literary model. For example, in
his October 1904 review of Micheál Ó Máille's *Eochaidh Mac Ríogh
'nÉirinn* (Eochaidh, the son of a king in Ireland), he rather evasively
commented: "We have elsewhere discussed the advisability of retaining
the archaic spirit and form in modern literary work."[61] The "elsewhere"
here referred to must be his review of *Séadna* the previous month. After
lauding Ua Laoghaire's work by emphasizing its stylistic verve and
originality rather than its folk origins, Pearse wrote: "In thought, and
speech, and form, 'Séadna' is so entirely original and characteristic, so
much the product of An tAthair Peadar's individuality, that it is, in the
highest sense, a creation. We have here, indeed, the everyday speech

58. "Litridheacht Nua-Dhéanta" (Contemporary literature), *St. Stephen's: A Record of
University Life* 1, no. 1 (1 June 1901): 10. "'Má tá sgéal le n-innsint agat,' adeireadh fear a
bhí ag cnuasughadh sean-sgéalta uair amháin, 'innis dom é mar d'innseochadh do shean-
mháthair.' Bheirim-se an chomhairle chéadna do gach uile Ghaedhilgeoir ar mhaith leis
Gaedhilg a scríobhadh. . . . B'iongantach an bhean í do shean-mháthair. . . . Lean dá nós-
san i dtosach, agus tiocfaidh gach uile rud eile i ndiaidh a chéile, mar thógtar na caisleáin."
59. "An Sean-Léigheann," editorial, *ACS*, 23 July 1904. "Táimíd chun caisleán an
nua-léighinn a thógaint. Chuige sin, is éigin dúinn rómhar chun go sroisfeam bun-char-
raigh an tsean-léighinn ar dtúis. Annsoin tosnuigheam ar bhallaí an chaisleáin a thógaint."
60. *ACS*, 27 May 1905. "Badh chóir dhúinn gan a dhearmad choidhche go bhfuil
d'fhiachaibh orainn san obair seo na Gaedhilge na scéalta is an caitheamh aimsire a bhíodh
ag na daoinibh a tháinig romhainn a shábháil. Nuair a bheidh na scéalta thíos againn,
féadfar iad a dheisiughadh is féadfar cur leo ansin. Ar na sean-scéaltaibh seo is eadh caithfear nuadh-litridheacht na Gaedhilge a cheapadh is a thógáil."
61. "Irish Storytelling," *ACS*, 15 October 1904.

and beliefs of the folk, and yet we have something entirely different from the folk-tale. The folk-tale is an evolution; 'Séadna,' like all works of art, is a creation."[62] In a March 1903 review of *An Buaiceas* (The Wick) by "Conán Maol," Pearse had already developed the distinction between conscious artistic creation and the faithful transcription of folk motifs in the folk idiom:

> "Conán Maol" is one of the few who have fashioned for themselves a distinctive style in Irish. Hosts of our writers can give us admirable photographic reproductions of Irish dialogue. That is good, but it is not the best thing. It is literature only in the limited sense in which a verbatim report of a parliamentary debate is literature. The language may be sinewy and idiomatic, the thought virile and racy, there may even be occasional gleams of imagination. But all that does not constitute literature. Style and form are essential. The true literary artist is like a painter as compared with a photographer. The one gives us back what he sees transformed into something radiant and gracious by the impression of his own personality, the other produces a mere mechanical copy."[63]

By 1906 Pearse had thought through what made works of art "entirely different" from folktales, and he developed his ideas in four editorials, one in Irish, three in English, in May and June of that year. In "Folklore and the Zeitgeist," a piece he himself regarded as "a glorification of the folktale,"[64] he called Irish folkore "as fair and noble an inheritance as was ever bequeathed a race by its past," and urged the preservation of every "precious scrap of lore."[65] However, the following week he made clear that folklore was "a beautiful and gracious thing only in its own time and place," and that that time and place was not the twentieth-century Irish Ireland striving to develop a genuinely contemporary prose:

> This week we lay down the proposition that a living modern literature *cannot* (and if it could, should not) be built up on the folktale. . . . In point of form the folktale is bound by a convention, which (by the way) is not a distinctively Irish convention but rather a distinctively folk convention, —that is to say, a con-

---

62. "'Séadna' and the Future of Irish Prose," *ACS*, 24 September 1904.
63. Review of *An Buaiceas*, *ACS*, 14 March 1903.
64. "About Literature," editorial, *ACS*, 26 May 1906.
65. "Folklore and the Zeitgeist," editorial, *ACS*, 19 May 1906.

vention which, in essentials, obtains amongst the folk universally. . . . Why impose the folk attitude of mind, the folk convention of form on the makers of a literature?[66]

A week later, in "Literature, Life, and the Oireachtas Competitions,"
he challenged Gaelic writers to think originally and to create from their
own experience, rejecting "a standard in prose which takes the gossip
by a country fireside or in a village taproom as the high-water level of
both its thought and its style."[67]

Pearse's criticism here was sharply focused; as we have noted, many
of his contemporaries did appeal to the authority of the fireside *seanchaí*
or the taproom wit, frequently placing their tales in the mouth of some
such traditional narrator. Indeed, it is often well-nigh impossible, in
the absence of specific comment or explicit attribution, to distinguish
authentic folktales from "original" material in the folk mode by early
writers such as "An Tais Dubh," "Taisdeal na Tíre" or "Níosairde."
How, for example, are we to classify narratives like "An Fear Gortach
agus an Táilliúr" (The miser and the tailor), "An Cipín Draoidheachta"

66. "About Literature," *ACS*, 26 May 1906. Ironically his conclusion here had no
doubt been arrived at from a study of the tales collected by the league itself. In a review of
Oireachtas stories in 1903, he had written: "And now the folklore competitions at the
Oireachtas bid fair to save our tales from whatever part of the country they may come,
and thus throw light upon the vexed question of how far the folklore of the country may
be looked upon as an Aryan heritage common to all, or how far it is the product of local
circumstance. . . . It is as yet premature to discuss these interesting topics." See "A Book
of Irish Folk-Tales," review of *Imtheachta an Oireachtais, 1901*, vol. 2, *ACS*, 1 August
1903. Clearly he felt that the time for the discussion, indeed the resolution, of such questions had come a scant three years later, thus justifying his claim in this same review that
"if the Gaelic League had done nothing else, its action in this respect alone would have
entitled it to the gratitude of folklorists and scientists over the world."

67. Editorial, *ACS*, 2 June 1906. In his serialized novel *An Bhóinn agus an Bhóchna* (The
Boyne and the sea), William P. Ryan has his protagonist say of the Western peasants:
"Their stories, their thoughts, are but remnants. As long as it is thought that those are the
genuine 'Gaels,' neither they nor ourselves will be able to progress. It would be as well
for you to insist that sickness is health." (A gcuid sgéalta, a gcuid smaointe, níl ionta ach
iarsma. Cho fada agus a cheaptar gurab iad súd "na Gaedhil" amach 's amach ní féidir leo
ná linne dul ar aghaidh. Bheadh sé cho maith dhuit bheith ag déanamh amach gurab í an
bhreoiteacht an tsláinte.) The person being addressed is the novel's AE figure; he echoes
Pearse's view that the culture of the West is more generic-peasant than specifically Irish
and claims that Ireland will never develop an authentic contemporary Gaelicism "as long
as we think that Gaelicism is equivalent to odds and ends of stories, proverbs, and superstitions" (cho fada agus a cheapaimíd gurbh ionann "Gaodhalachas" agus draobhaoil
sgéaluidheachta, sean-fhocla, agus piseoga). See "Cara na nUghdar" (Ryan), *An Bhóinn
agus an Bhóchna*, *ACS*, 20 November 1915.

(The magic stick), or "Tomáisín na hOrdóige" (Tom Thumb).[68] Similarly, in Laoide's 1907 folk anthology *Measgán Músgraighe* (A Muskerry miscellany), a collection in which Laoide himself notes the origin of each selection, the reader is hard put to define the differences between actual folktales, retellings of traditional stories, and works created by writers like Conchubhar Ó Deasmhumhna, a 1900 Oireachtas Prize–winner as a collector, "from his own ingenuity" (as a stuaim féin).[69]

And for some Gaels this was as it should be, for who could better set standards and judge the new literature than those who had preserved the old from which it would have to evolve? Thus, reviewing *Prátaí Mhichíl Thaidhg* (The potatoes of Micheál Thaidhg) in 1904, Micheál Ó Máille ("Diarmuid Donn"), the author of *Eochaidh Mac Ríogh 'n-Éirinn*, wrote: "If one wants to evaluate a book in Irish, there's one way for him to do it easily. Let him get the book and read some of it out loud in front of Irish speakers."[70] Other writers shared this view that their ideal audience as well as their only legitimate critics would be native-speaking country folk, many illiterate. The most influential of them was of course Peadar Ua Laoghaire, who laid down an unequivocal test of literary success in 1902: "If someone reads our Irish prose for that public [native-speaking peasants], and if our language goes home with full force and directness to the hearts and minds of that public, then we may

---

68. "An Tais Dubh," "An Fear Gortach agus an Táilliúir," *FL*, 19 February 1898; "Taisdeal na Tíre," "An Cipín Draoidheachta," *ACS*, 7 April 1900; "Níosairde," "Tomáisín na hOrdóige," *ACS*, 13–20 October 1900.

69. Indeed, it seems that the majority of tales in this particular collection fall into this grey area. See, for example, Laoide's comments on "Figheadóir an Ghleanna Chaim" (The weaver of Gleann Cam): "Donnchadh Ó Laoghaire wrote it. It is undoubtedly a folktale, but it's likely that Donnchadh told it in his own style." ("Donnchadh Ó Laoghaire . . . do sgríobh. Sean-sgéal is eadh é, gan amhras, acht is dócha gur innis Donnchadh ar a nós féin é.) Of "Sgríobhadh an Chorcáin" (The scraping of the pot), he tells us: "Mairghréad Ní Áilgheasa put a traditional narrative form [literally, "a thread of traditional lore"] on an original story—something new that happened in her district." (Mairghréad Ní Áilgheasa . . . do chuir snáithe sheanchais ar nua-sgéal—rud nua do thuit amach i n-a ceanntar féin.) More than one writer in the collection is referred to as putting this "thread of storytelling" (snáithe sheanchais, or snáithe sgéalaidheachta) on a folktale proper (sean-sgéal). Donnchadh Ó Laoghaire is also said to have put "a thread of history or synchronism" (snáithe chóimhghne) on another *sean-sgéal*. See "Bunadh na Sgéal" (The origin of the stories) in *Measgán Músgraighe*, 166–8. Incidentally, Ó Laoghaire like Ó Deasmhumhna was an Oireachtas Prize–winner for folklore collection.

70. "Prátaí Mhíchíl Thaidhg," *ACS*, 9 July 1904. "Má's maith le duine leabhar Gaedhilge a mheas, tá aon bhealach amháin a dtig leis sin a dhéanamh go réidh. Fághadh sé an leabhar agus léigheadh sé cuid de amach os comhair Gaedhilgeoirí." This critical standard persisted throughout our period. See, for example, the review by "Ultach" of Peadar Mac Fhionnlaoich's *Ciall na Sean-Ráidhte* (The meaning of the proverbs), a collection of brief stories illustrating Irish proverbs, in *ACS*, 8 August 1914.

feel certain that our work is a success. If our work fails to do that, it is a failure no matter how erudite it may be."[71] Séamus Ó Dubhghaill upheld the same standard more colorfully in 1913: "I swear that I would prefer to be able to say at the end of my life that the work of my pen drew a laugh from Taidhgín ricking turf on the bogland at Gearagh than that I set scholars and important people talking and grumbling from one end of the year to the next."[72]

One of those scholars did a great deal more than grumble. Father O'Reilly was infuriated by what he felt was often a disingenuously self-serving elevation of unlettered folk opinion to the status of literary criticism: "You can never be wrong; for, no matter what rubbish you write, and no matter how ever so much without spelling it you write it, you can always shout the 'mouths of the people' for your warrant, and anyone who cannot accept that password, is, of course, beneath being argued with."[73] Most "scholars" of the Gaelic literary world were less extravagant in the expression of their opinions, and many no doubt admired the rich and idiomatic Irish and appreciated the insight into a rural life they may never have experienced. Nonetheless, O'Reilly's sentiments must have struck a chord in the hearts and especially in the minds of more than a few "important people" as they attended cabin kitchen playlets like Ua Laoghaire's *Tadhg Saor* (Tadhg the carpenter) (1900) or *An Sprid* (The spirit) (1902); Hyde's *Casadh an tSúgáin* (The twisting of the rope) (1901), *An Tincéir agus an tSidheóg* (The tinker and the fairy), *An Pósadh* (The wedding) (both 1902), or *An Cleamhnas* (The match) (1905); "Domhnall na Gréine's" *Lá na nAmadán* (The day of the fools) (1901); Cathaoir Ó Braonáin's *An Cailín Deorach* (The tearful girl) (1901); Ó Dubhghaill's *Sgoláirí na Sgoile* (The scholars of the school) (1901), *An Táilliúir Cleasach* (The tricky tailor), *Dochtúireacht Nuadh* (New doctoring), *Eilís agus an Bhean Déirce* (Eilís and the beggar

71. *Irish Prose Composition* (Dublin: Muintir na Leabhar Gaedhilge, 1902), 17. In *Fé Bhrat an Chonnartha*, Peadar Ó hAnnracháin recalled Ua Laoghaire's reaction on hearing of the delight Ó hAnnracháin's native-speaking father took in having *Séadna* read to him: "There were almost tears of joy in the eyes of the person who was listening to me as I told my story. . . . When I had finished he put his hand on my shoulder and he said . . . 'That's praise as fine as *Séadna* ever got.'" (Is beag ná go raibh deora de dhruim áthais ar an té a bhí ag éisteacht liom agus mé ag nochtadh mo scéil dó. . . . Nuair a bhí sé críochnuighthe agam do leag sé a lámh ar mo ghualainn, agus ar seisean . . . "Tá sé sin chomh maith de mholadh agus fuair *Séadna* riamh.") See *Fé Bhrat*, 557–58.

72. Letter, *ACS*, 13 December 1913. "Fágaimse le huadhacht go mb'fhearr liomsa go mbeadh sé le rádh agam in earbaill mo shaoghail gur bhain saothar mo phinn gáire as Taidhgín, agus é ag cnochairt mhóna ar réidh an Ghaorthaidh ná dá gcuirfinn scoláirthí agus daoine móra ag cainnt agus ag cnáimhseáil ó cheann ceann de'n bhliadhain."

73. *Native Speaker*, 5.

woman), or *Ar Lorg Poitín* (Searching for Poitín) (all 1902); Dinneen's *An Tobar Draoidheachta* (The magic well) (1902); William P. Ryan's *An Mí-Ádh Mór* (The great misfortune) (1903) or *Grádh agus Gréithidhe* (Love and delph) (1904); Tomás Ó Ceallaigh's *Airgead na Croise Caoile / The Money of the Slender Cross* (1903); Tomás Ó hAodha's *Seaghán na Scuab* (Seán of the brushes) (1904); Séamus Ó Beirne's *An Dochtúir* (The doctor) (1904); Pádraic Ó Conaire's *An Droighneán Donn* (The blackthorn tree) (1906), *An Uadhacht* (The will) (1906), or *Bairbre Ruadh* (1908); Seán Ua Ceallaigh's *Seán Óg* (1908); Seán Ó Muirthile's *Pósadh an Iascaire* (The fisherman's wedding) (1914); or E. R. Dix's *An tSeift* (The ruse) (1915); and read rural tales in journals as well as Ua Laoghaire's books; Ó Dubhghaill's *Tadhg Gabha* (Tadhg the smith) (1900), *Prátaí Mhichíl Thaidhg* (1904), *Cléibhín Móna* (A creel of turf) (1907), and *Muinntear na Tuatha* (Country people) (1910); Henry Morris's *Greann na Gaedhilge* (The humor of the Irish language) (seven booklets, 1902–7); "Conán Maol's" *An Buaiceas* (1903); "Gruagach an Tobair's" *Annála na Tuatha* (Country annals) (1905–7); Peadar Mac Fhionnlaoich's *Ciall na Sean-Ráidhte* (The sense of the proverbs) (1915); and Seaghán Mac Meanman's *Sgéalta Goiride Geimhridh* (Short winter's tales) (1915).[74]

Once again Pearse took advantage of his editorial chair to lecture his fellow Gaels, venting his exasperation that "when you read the new stories and the plays, those we have, you would think that pride of place amongst modern Gaels went to cattle and chickens and potatoes." His challenge was direct: "Let us move away from the dungheap and

74. For a detailed summary and analysis of much of the work of these writers, see Aisling Ní Dhonnchadha, *An Gearrscéal sa Ghaeilge 1898–1940* (The short story in Irish, 1898–1940) (Baile Átha Cliath: An Clóchomhar, 1981), 9–48. It is, of course, important to keep in mind that "Conán Maol" was by no means merely a writer of rural tales. He played a pioneering role in many of the literary enterprises of the early Revival, writing history, plays, and a novel with a primarily urban setting. Pearse drew attention to his stylistic innovations, including his use of that Henebry bugbear the "explosive" opening, in his review of *An Buaiceas* in March 1903. Ní Dhonnchadha sees "Conán" as a transitional figure, writing of his stories (41):

The stories of "Conán Maol" were certainly an important advance, although they can't be called short stories in our current understanding of that term. They are short tales in a new style, stories that reveal competence, care, and imagination, and stories firmly rooted in the soil of folklore.

(Is cinnte gur chéim tábhachtach chun tosaigh a bhí i scéalta "Conán Maol" cé nach féidir gearrscéalta a thabhairt orthu de réir na tuisceana atá againn ar an bhfocal sin anois. Scéalta gairide nuachumtha ba ea iad, scéalta a léirigh cumas, cúram agus samhlaíocht agus scéalta a raibh a gcuid fréamhacha sáite go daingean in ithir an bhéaloidis.)

the turf-rick; let us throw off the barnyard muck."[75] Pearse received no doubt unexpected support from Father Dinneen, who for once turned his formidable sarcasm on his nativist allies:

There are authors who think there is nothing better than some simple question to write about in Irish. Some country hunt, or a single combat over a bit of tobacco, or the way some tinker attacked his son, or the drunkenness of some sooty smith, or the cabbage Domhnall Mhichil stole from his stepmother when his father was at the Mitchelstown Fair one fine day in May. Indeed I don't mind their talking of those things to the day they die if they enjoy it. It would give me joy to be watching them unloading books of that sort on the press every day of the week. Work is scarce, and it's a good thing to keep the poor printers busy.[76]

Nor were such criticisms limited to urban or urbanized Gaels. Taking part in a lively debate on the new literature in the pages of *Irisleabhar na Gaedhilge* in 1905, one "Ruaidhrí na Ruacán" boasted of his rural identity, but said he was fed up with writers "who think there is no higher achievement in Irish than an insipid account of the antics of Liam

75. "Nua-Litridheacht" (Modern literature), editorial, *ACS*, 19 May 1906. "Ag léigheamh na n-úr-sgéal agus na ndráma duit, an méid díobh atá againn, cheapfá gur do bheithidheachaibh agus do chearcaibh agus do fataibh bhí tús onóra ag dul i measg Gaedheal na haimsire seo. . . . Bogaimís amach ó'n carn aoiligh agus ó'n gcruaich móna; caithfimís uainn salchar na hothrainne."

76. "Leabhair Gaedhilge" (Gaelic books), *The Leader*, 6 September 1906. "Tá ughdair ann agus is dóigh leo ná fuil aon-nídh chomh maith le ceist éigin simplidhe chum trácht do scríobhadh air i nGaedhilg. Fiadhach éigin san dtuaith nó comhrac aoinfhir mar gheall ar bhlúire tabac nó an chuma gur ghabh tuincéar éigin ar a mhac nó meisceoireacht do thaithigh gabha dubh éigin nó an cabáiste do ghoid Domhnall Mhíchíl ó n-a leasmháthair an tan a bhí a athair ar aonach Bhaile Mhistéala lá buidhe Bealtaine díreach. Ambasa ní mór liomsa dhóibh bheith ag trácht ar na neithibh sin go lá a mbáis má thaithneann an cleas leo; is amhlaidh a chuirfeadh sé áthas orm bheith ag féachaint ortha ag scaoileadh leabhar den tsaghas sain ar an gclódh gach lá den tseachtmhain. Tá obair gann agus is maith an rud na clódóirithe bochta do choimeád ar siubhal." See also his "Saothrughadh na Teangan" (The cultivation of the language), *Guth na Bliadhna* 8, no. 4 (Autumn 1911): 380–89. It would be interesting to know how he reconciled this more sophisticated view of the scope of Gaelic literature with his 1907 belief that "the character . . . of the literature that receives the official sanction of the league should be such, that it be capable of penetrating into the most remote cabins in the Irish districts, and of being read at the humble firesides of these cabins without suspicion of offense." See "The Gaelic League and Non-Sectarianism," *Irish Rosary*, January 1907, 10. Another litany of rustic narrative cliches was offered by the league's chief organizer, Tomás Bán Ua Concheanainn, as early as 1899 in "Anonn agus Anall" (Hither and yon), *ACS*, 16 September 1899.

Mhuiris Dhiarmada or the small potatoes of Billí Sheáin Ghobnait or the best donkey in the district."[77]

Obviously, given the nature of Irish society, and particularly of Irish-speaking society, at the turn of the century, no one could argue that rural subjects and rural themes, many borrowed from or shared with folklore, were legitimate and even central concerns for the Gaelic writer. Moreover, the fact that that traditional society was then facing radical economic, linguistic, and cultural disruptions and changes could be seen as validating the conservatism, even the antiquarianism of many such writers, for whom Seaghán Mac Meanman, introducing his *Sgéalta Goiride Geimhridh*, may serve as the spokesman: "All of them deal with the life of Ireland and of the Irish, and from start to finish an attempt has been made to bring into the narrative the modes of thought, the customs, and the turns of speech of our grandfathers. These Gaelic elders who passed away unnoticed like springtime snow over the past twenty years had many, many customs and expressions that the half-foreign young don't have."[78] What bothered the more literary Gaelic critics was not, however, the raw material from which the ruralists built their fiction, but rather how raw many of them left it. Perhaps, given a creative ambition as restricted as that claimed by Séamus Ó Dubhghaill, there was little chance it could be otherwise: "What I wanted to do was to make an attempt to put before Irish-speaking people the manners and customs and way of life of the Gaels who lived when I was a boy."[79]

That Ó Dubhghaill succeeded in his goal and that that success exacted a literary price is evident from Seán Mac Giollarnáth's 1911 review of his *Muinntear na Tuatha*: "He likes to draw all the Irish he has

77. Letter, *IG* 14, no. 175 (April 1905): 775. His criticism is of writers "a mheasann ná fuil cúrsa ar bith is aoirde réim san nGaedhilg ná leamh-thrácht ar mhaingilíbh Liam Mhuiris Dhiarmada, nó ar sciolláin Bhillí Sheáin Ghobnait, nó ar an asal do b'fhearr sa cheanntar."

78. "Réamrádh do'n Ceud Chur Amach" (Foreword to the first edition), in *Sgéalta Goiride Geimhridh*, an dara chur amach (Dún Dealgan: Preas Dhún Dealgan, 1922), iii. (*Sgéalta* first appeared in 1915, but some of the stories had been previously published. For example, the longest of them, "Maghnus Mac Cormaic agus Cormac Mac Maghnuis," was serialized in *ACS* in 1911.) "Baineann an t-iomlán aca le saoghal na h-Éireann agus na n-Éireannach, a's ó thús go deireadh tá iaraidh tugtha na modha smuainte, na beusa, agus na cora cainte a bhíodh ag ár sean-aithreachaibh do tharraingt asteach ins an innsin. Na seanóiridhe Gaedhealacha seo a d'imigh go formhothuighthe mar sneachta earraigh le fiche bliadhain do bhí mórán mór nós agus abairteach aca nach bhfuil ag na sóisearaibh leath-Ghallda."

79. Letter, *ACS*, 8 July 1911. "'Sé bhí uaim ná iarracht a dhéanamh ar bhéasaibh, agus ar nósaibh, agus ar shlighe bheatha na nGaedheal a bhí suas agus mise i m'ghasúr a chur os comhair an phobuil Ghaedhilge."

into the story, anecdotes, nicknames, place names, and so forth. . . .
When an author is writing a story, he must stick to the story itself and
not pursue matters irrelevant to it."[80] This compulsion to chronicle even
the minutiae of folklife was, however, invariable and consistent in the
work of the Gaelic ruralists. *Muinntear na Tuatha* lovingly preserves a
range of country beliefs and practices,[81] while a reader is perhaps likely
to remember several of the stories in "Gruagach an Tobair's" *Annála na
Tuatha* less for their plot, characterization, or style, than for what they
tell about folk customs concerning gambling ("Mar Buaileadh Bob ar
an nGruagach"), wakes ("Ar Thórramh Sheana-Shéamuis"), or wed-
dings ("An Spiorad").[82] Certainly there can be little doubt that what
Myles na gCopaleen best remembered of the work of Seaghán Mac
Meanman were the multiple matchmakers of *Sgéalta Goiride Geimhridh*,
each heading off to do his job with the mandatory "five noggin bottle
in his pocket" (buidéal chúig naigín i n-a phóca).[83] Of course in keeping
with its length and its ultimate ambition "to define and reveal the characteristic nature of the Gaelic mind" (sain-aicne an aigneadh
Ghaodhalaigh do dhealbhadh agus do nochtadh [*definire et exhibere*]),[84]
Ua Laoghaire's *Séadna* is, among many other things, a virtual handbook of Irish folklore and folklife, with references to beliefs in the su-

80. "Saoghal na Malrach" (Boys' life), *ACS*, 25 February 1911. "Is maith leis gach a
bhfuil de Ghaedhilg aige, idir sgéalta beaga, leas-ainmneacha, ainmneacha áiteann agus
eile, do tharraing isteach sa sgéal. . . . Nuair a bhíos sgéal dhá sgríobhadh ag ughdar ní
mór dó leanamhaint do'n sgéal féin agus gan neithe nach mbaineann leis, is cuma céard
iad, do lorg." Sharper was the impatience of the anonymous *SF* reviewer: "We don't like
too much of the country and would prefer for the author to make an attempt to write of
the life of the city or life in general than to be always dealing with things with which we
are half exhausted." (Ní maith linn an iomarca den dtuaith, agus bfhearr linn an t-ughdar
a thabhairt iarrachta ar shaoghal na cathrach nó an saoghal i gcoitcheann ná bheith ag síor-
thrácht ar rudadhaibh go bhfuilimíd leath-chortha aca.) See "Clódhanna Nuadh" (New
publications), *SF*, 11 February 1911. Of course, Ó Dubhghaill did, as we will see, prepare
a series of urban dialogues in this very year.
    81. Séamus Ó Dubhghaill, *Muinntear na Tuatha* (Baile Átha Cliath: M. H. Gill agus a
Mhac, 1910). For example, he explains how farmers assessed a scytheman's ability (43);
discusses wake and funeral customs (62, 68, 79); and tells of people reading an American
paper (the Boston Catholic weekly *The Pilot*) sent them by an emigrant (71).
    82. "Gruagach an Tobair," *Annála na Tuatha* (Baile Átha Cliath: Connradh na Gae-
dhilge, 1905-7), "Mar Buaileadh Bob ar an nGruagach" (How "An Gruagach" was
tricked), part 1, 0[*sic*]-20; "An Tromluighe" (The nightmare), part 3, 1-13; "An Spioraid" (The spirit), part 3, 38-60. And of course many of "An Gruagach's" own notes to
the stories were offered to explicate such folk traditions and customs as well as to gloss
words or phrases.
    83. See, for example, Seaghán Mac Meanman, *Sgéalta Goiride Geimhridh*, 5, 12, 28-29.
    84. Peadar Ua Laoghaire, letter to Eoin Mac Néill, 20 March 1896, quoted by Mac
Mathúna, "Réamhrádh" to *Séadna*, xlii.

pernatural (11–12, 31, 91–92, 204–13), memorable pictures of matchmaking (84–85), of a country fair (*aonach*) (117–18), and of a wedding
and its subsequent dance (193–204); vignettes of folk history concerning
the Whiteboys (106–9) and tyrannical landlords (133–36), a bit of cooking lore (227) and a wealth of proverbial wisdom (175, 233, 239, 241,
243, 248, 249). Narrative flow is also threatened in these works by an
obsession with the accurate transcription of *cainnt na ndaoine,* particularly the much-prized idioms (*cora cainnte*) of an author's favored dialect. Indeed, one can occasionally get the feeling that the story, such as
it is, exists merely as a setting for these linguistic gems.

Paradoxically, the short stories of Pearse himself, when not read as
mere trial pieces to illustrate his critical principles,[85] have been either
praised or dismissed as attempts at just such naive realism. Thus in his
review of Pearse's first collection *Íosagán agus Sgéalta Eile* (Íosagán and
other stories) (1907), Pádraic Ó Domhnalláin wrote: "Isn't there many a
Brighdín and an Eoghainín of the Birds and perhaps an occasional Old
Matias?"[86] Another reviewer of the same volume shared Ó Domhnalláin's understanding of Pearse's intention, while taking a slightly
more jaundiced view of Gaeltacht youth: "The children the author
treats of are not the artificial little products of our modern town life.
They are the unspoiled children of the West, of his own Iar-Chonnacht.
Even in Iar-Chonnacht, the children of Pearse's tales would not be either typical or commonplace, but neither would they be impossible or
unreal."[87] Nor did time alter this perspective in any significant way.
Séamus Ó hAodha, whose bilingual *Pádraic Mac Piarais, Sgéaluidhe/*

85. For example, an early student of Pearse's fiction, Séamus Ó hAodha, wrote: "He
was not, I think, primarily interested in storytelling for its own sake; but he understood
that there was no better way of promoting an interest in the newer principles of the craft
than by producing a story written on those principles." See *Pádraic Mac Piarais, Sgéaluidhe / Patrick H. Pearse: Storyteller* (Dublin: Talbot, n.d.), 60. This view tends to exaggerate the importance of Pearse's fiction, as opposed to his criticism, in the development of
the new prose. Pearse himself praised "Conán Maol" as early as 1903 for using just the
sort of "explosive opening" that Henebry was to find so distastefully modern in "Íosagán," and in 1906 Ó Conaire's uncompromising "Nóra Mharcuis Bhig" won an
Oireachtas Prize and was serialized in *ACS.* It is, then, impossible to regard Pearse's
stories as essential to the cause of stylistic innovation and artistic freedom in Gaelic fiction. The "standard of revolt" had been raised, albeit quietly, before Pearse, as it would
have been without him, and was carried to the victory it has achieved by writers more
adventurous and gifted. If Pearse's stories are to claim more than passing attention, they
must do so on other grounds.

86. "Ó Chúige Chonnacht," *ACS,* 7 March 1908. "Nach iomdha sin Brighdín agus
Eoghainín na nÉan agus b'fhéidir corr-Shean-Mhaitias ann?"

87. E. Ua M. (Henry Morris?), "Children of the West: *Íosagán agus Scéalta Eile,*" *ACS,*
23 May 1908.

Patrick H. Pearse: Storyteller (1919) was the first critical study of Pearse's fiction, called attention to the monochromatically rosy nature of Pearse's literary palette, but never questioned that his intention was to provide a fundamentally realisitic portrait of Gaeltacht life: "He forgot that the land was cold and stony, that the mountainy man was poor to destitution, that the crop he was to reap was wretched. He thought only of the Beauty of the Irish World, the sweetness of its people, the purity of its children, the fairness of its landscape. . . . Yet it seems to me that his idealization concerns more the setting of the story than the characterization; it arises more from what is not told than from what is set down."[88]

No such reservations troubled Pearse's biographer Séamus Ó Searcaigh in his assessment of the fictional method shaping *Íosagán:* "The children of the Conamara Gaeltacht as Patrick Pearse saw them are in this book. The nobility of the guiltless child, the thoughts of the child around whom there is a spiritual world, the play of the youth who would never do a spiteful deed, the life of youth that hasn't been destroyed by the mean thoughts of the world—that is what we find in these stories."[89]

Moreover, even his two most vociferous contemporary critics, Fathers Dinneen and Henebry, seem to have accepted without question the notion that Pearse was trying, however ineptly, to offer a conventionally accurate depiction of the Gaeltacht. Dinneen was particularly contemptuous of what he saw as Pearse's linguistic and literary inadequacies as a convincing realist in his review of *Poll an Phíobaire* (The piper's cave), an adventure tale for boys set in Conamara: "I have tasted

---

88. *Pádraic Mac Piarais, Sgéaluidhe*, 62.

89. *Pádraig Mac Piarais* (Baile Átha Cliath: Oifig an tSoláthair, n.d.), 83. "Páistí Ghaedhealtacht Chonnacht mar chonaic Pádraig Mac Piarais iad atá sa leabhar. Uaisleacht an leinbh neamh-choirthigh, smaointe an tachráin a raibh saoghal spioradálta ina thimcheall, súgradh an ógánaigh nach ndéanfadh gníomh ar bith le holc, beatha na hóige nach raibh millte ag smaointe suaracha an tsaoghail a gheibhmid 'sna sgéalta atá ann." For other judgments on Pearse as rural realist, see "Darach," "Children of the Gaeltacht," review of Pearse's *An Mháthair*, *ACS*, 5 February 1916; Louis Le Roux, *Patrick H. Pearse*, trans. Desmond Ryan (Dublin: Talbot, 1932), 178–79; Desmond Ryan, *The Man Called Pearse* (Dublin: Maunsel, 1919), 52, 104; Cathaoir Ó Braonáin, "Poets of the Insurrection: Patrick H. Pearse," *Studies* 5 (September 1916): 348; Patrick Browne, Introduction to *Collected Works of Pádraic H. Pearse: Plays, Stories, Poems*, ix–xix; and Desmond Maguire, Introduction to *The Short Stories of Patrick Pearse* (Cork: Mercier, 1968), 7. Pearse did, of course, have considerable personal experience of the Conamara townland of Ros Muc (the "Ros na gCaorach" of his stories), where he maintained a cottage, and he naturally drew on that experience in his fiction. It was, for example, he who organized the entertainment that serves as the model for the one in "Na Bóithre." See Colm Ó Gaora, *Mise*, eagrán nua, 33–34. Ó Gaora also provides the sources for other incidents in the stories and claims that his own father was the model for Sean-Mhaitias.

Connemara butter before now: it has its defects . . . but in colour and taste it is natural. . . . It may at times be over-salted and over-dosed with the water of *bearlachas* but it is genuine mountain butter all the same and not clever margarine. I am afraid the storyette about the *Píobaire* smacks more like the margarine of the slums than pure mountain butter."[90] Henebry managed to express his sense of Pearse's artificiality in terms every bit as colorful and even more offensively personal: "If Irish literature is the talk of big, broad-chested men, this is the frivolous petulancy of latter-day English *genre* scribblers, and their utterance is as the mincing of the under-assistant floor-walker in a millinery shop."[91]

Later critics, removed from the enthusiasms and antagonisms of the Revival, have on the whole admired Pearse's critical contribution and granted his fiction a historical significance, while simultaneously agreeing with Dinneen that its precious artificiality entirely undermines its goal of capturing the "genuine" flavor of Conamara. For example, Risteárd Ó Glaisne stresses the sentimentality of Pearse's writing and states that that is "its greatest fault—the single great fault, but a disastrous fault."[92] Richard J. Loftus comments more extensively on Pearse's sentimentality, writing that his children are "forever prancing with 'bare feet upon the strand' or confessing their 'fault truly' or 'watching the wee ladybird fly away.' Pearse professed a belief in the child's inner life but . . . the point is generally drowned in excessive sentiment."[93] In his monograph on Pearse, Raymond Porter analyzes the fiction in perceptive detail, but his touchstone is again that of realism, with the greatest flaws marring the stories being "sentimentality and idealization of the Irish-speaking inhabitants of Connemara."[94] Applying the same criteria, Ruth Dudley Edwards finds some of Pearse's fiction downright embarrassing: "His prose often reached heights of absurdity when he fell to

---

90. "Poll an Phíobaire," *Irish People*, 5 May 1906. Dinneen also drew unnecessary and unjust attention to the story's "nauseous" title, a reference to the unintentional double entendre of the Irish word *poll*, "hole." In what Séamas Ó Buachalla calls his "literary testament," Pearse left instructions that the story be renamed "An Uaimh" (The cave). See Ó Buachalla, "Scríbhinní Liteartha an Phiarsaigh—Treoir do na Foinsí" (The literary writings of Pearse—A guide to the sources), in *Na Scríbhinní Liteartha le Pádraig Mac Piarais*, ed. Ó Buachalla (Baile Átha Cliath: Cló Mercier, 1979), 11.

91. "Revival Irish," *The Leader*, 6 February 1909.

92. *Ceannródaithe: Scríbhneoirí na Nua-Ré* (Pioneers: Writers of the modern period) (Baile Átha Cliath: Foilseacháin Náisiúnta Teo., 1974), 81. Ó Glaisne refers to sentimentality as "an locht is mó uirthi—an t-aon locht mór ach locht millteanach."

93. *Nationalism in Anglo-Irish Poetry* (Madison: University of Wisconsin Press, 1964), 127–28.

94. *P. H. Pearse*, 78.

describing his beloved 'kindly-faced, frieze-coated peasants.'"[95] More open and insightful, John Wilson Foster approaches a proper understanding of Pearse's intent, only to fall back on the standard reading, his failure to get in touch with "the real west": "In trying to recreate what he imagined as a simple and ageless Ireland still alive in the twentieth century west, he achieved merely a posed naivety."[96]

Recurrent in these critical dismissals is an emphasis on the one–dimensional nature of Pearse's Conamara. And it is undeniably true that in his stories Pearse seems oblivious to the reality of Gaeltacht life at the turn of the century. Yet such was by no means the case, as is clear from even a cursory reading of his editorial writing at this time. As a progressive and practicing educator, Pearse genuinely loved children, whatever language they spoke, and predictably idealization of Gaeltacht children features in some of his editorials. In a frequently cited piece, he rhapsodized: "Consider the Irish-speaking child. He is the fairest thing that springs up from the soil of Ireland—more beautiful than any flower . . . wiser than any seer."[97] Yet only three weeks later, we find him writing: "The gravest faults of Irish children, as we have known them, are a certain lack of veneration for the truth, and a certain thoughtlessness in their treatment of weaker or more sensitive companions, as well as of dumb animals, often amounting to positive cruelty."[98]

In other editorials, he shows a clear awareness of the harshness of Gaeltacht life and the effects of poverty and ignorance on those who live it. Thus in editorials in both Irish and English, he discussed the scourge of consumption in Conamara,[99] the economic stagnation in and consequent emigration from the West,[100] and perhaps most important as a corrective to the apparent apotheosis of native speakers in his fiction, the apostasy of those who willingly renounce their language and the traditions it enshrines.[101] It was no doubt with such "traitors" in mind

95. *Patrick Pearse*, 51.

96. *Fictions of the Irish Literary Revival: A Changeling Art* (Syracuse: Syracuse University Press, 1987), 305.

97. "The Irish-Speaking Child," editorial, *ACS*, 5 January 1907.

98. "The Formation of Character," editorial, *ACS*, 26 January 1907. Pearse also criticized Irish cruelty to animals in an Irish editorial, "Seanmóir Eile" (Another sermon), *ACS*, 19 January 1907.

99. "Saving Iar-Chonnachta," editorial, *ACS*, 22 February 1908. Pearse was here writing in enthusiastic support of the anticonsumption crusade of Dr. Séamus Ó Beirne, the progress of which was monitored closely by *ACS* under his editorship.

100. See, for example, "Capture the Gaeltacht," editorial, *ACS*, 7 March 1908.

101. See, for example, "The Irish-Speaking Districts," *ACS*, 29 September 1906; and "Wanted—A New Crusade," *ACS*, 13 October 1906. Pearse did, however, exempt the people of his beloved Ros Muc from this indictment.

that he wrote in 1907: "One may know Irish and still be a very sorry
Irishman or Irishwoman. Indeed, some of the meanest human beings
we have ever met have been Irish speakers."[102] While such criticism of
conditions or characteristics of Gaeltacht life is far outweighed by praise
of that life and its traditions in Pearse's columns in *An Claidheamh
Soluis*, not to mention his fiction, these few examples from among
many show that he was hardly blind to the darker facts of life in the
Gaeltacht. Had he wished, he could have presented a more "realistic"
picture of that life, as indeed he urged others to do. Successful or not,
his creation of an idealized Irish-speaking West was a fully conscious
aesthetic strategy.

As Frank O'Brien has discussed at length, a keystone of Pearse's literary philosophy was the Arnoldian principle that literature should be a
"criticism of life."[103] Applying this tenet in the parochial literary world
of the early Revival, Pearse used his influence, as we have seen, to
preach not only stylistic innovation, but also diversity and relevance of
subject matter and theme. Answering a correspondent who complained
that modern Gaelic literature spoke little of adult love, Pearse wrote in
1906: "Without doubt we do lack stories dealing with love. Or perhaps
we should say that we lack stories dealing with everyday modern life."[104]
The following week he expanded in English on precisely what aspects
of modern life were escaping criticism in the new literature:

> We should have the problems of to-day fearlessly dealt with in
> Irish: the loves and hates and desires and doubts of modern men
> and women. The drama of the land war; the tragedy of the em-
> igration-mania; the stress and poetry and comedy of the lan-
> guage movement; the pathos and vulgarity of Anglo-Ireland; the
> abounding interest of Irish politics; the relation of priest and peo-
> ple; the perplexing education riddle; the drink evil; the increase
> of lunacy; social problems such as (say) the loveless marriage: —
> these are matters which loom large in our daily lives, which bulk

102. "Éire Óg" (Young Ireland), editorial, *ACS*, 21 September 1907.

103. See O'Brien's discussion of "An Piarsach ina Léirmheastóir" (Pearse as critic),
Filíocht Ghaeilge na Linne Seo, 27–37. The considerable influence of Matthew Arnold on
Irish writers in both English and Irish is discussed by John V. Kelleher in "Matthew
Arnold and the Celtic Revival," in *Perspectives in Criticism*, ed. Harry Levin (Cambridge:
Harvard University Press, 1950), 197–221.

104. "Nua-Litridheacht" (Modern literature), *ACS*, 19 May 1906. "Gan amhras tá
scéalta ag baint leis an grá i n-easnamh orainn. Nó b'fhéidir linn a rá go bhfuil scéalta ag
baint le gnáth-shaoghal an lae indiu i n-easnamh orainn."

considerably in our conversation; but we find not the faintest echoes of them in Irish books that are being written.[105]

Of course, nowhere were the echoes fainter than in the fiction of Pearse himself, although this daunting inventory shows once again that the omission of such subjects from his fiction was the result of conscious choice and not willful ignorance.

Pearse the writer was not, however, untrue to the principles of Pearse the critic. Rather, his interpretation of the concept of literature as a "criticism of life" was broader than mere social realism, much less muckraking. In "Literature, Life, and the Oireachtas Competitions," he developed this broader and subtler notion:

> We do not mean that every piece of literature must be didactic in aim . . . neither do we suggest that every writer ought to take up the discussion of knotty problems, psychological, social, political and so forth. We simply put . . . the undoubted fact that every piece of literature . . . expresses the views of its creator on whatsoever may happen for the moment to be his theme. . . . It is, as far as it goes, the author's *view* of something, and it is in this sense a piece of criticism. It is a revelation of the artist's soul: a giving back again to others something as *he* saw it and felt it; *his* interpretation of a fragment of life.[106]

Herein lies the reconciliation between Pearse's theory of literature as "criticism of life" and his practice of presenting highly idealized, "uncritical" pictures of that life as lived in the Conamara Gaeltacht. In the fiction Pearse is offering us his interpretation of life in the Gaeltacht not as it was, but as it should and, to some extent, could be, and making use of this literally artificial model to point up the shortcomings of actual contemporary life in Gaelic and especially Anglicized Ireland. Pearse's belief in the power of such an ideal to illuminate present failings and to inspire change was lifelong and unwavering. As early as 1898 in an address entitled "The Intellectual Future of the Gael," he argued: "To those who would object that the sketch I have attempted to give of the intellectual future of our race is a mere ideal picture, I would reply that it is *intended* as an ideal picture. If you wish to accomplish anything great place an ideal before you, and endeavour to live up to that ideal." In this same address he emphasized the central role of literature in the creation of such inspirational standards: "That men

---

105. "About Literature," *ACS*, 26 May 1906.
106. *ACS*, 2 June 1906.

could be brought to realize that they are *Men*, not animals, —that they could be brought to realize that, though "of the earth, earthy," yet that there is a spark of divinity within them. And men *can* be brought to realize this by the propagation of a literature like that of the Gael."[107] His own creative writing represents his attempt to reveal to Irishmen and women their divine potential, in the process condemning by implicit contrast their "earthy" flaws.

It is, of course, in the stories themselves that we find the components of Pearse's utopia. Despite considerable differences in subject, mood, and tone between his two collections—the 1916 *An Mháthair agus Sgéalta Eile* (The mother and other stories) representing a significant artistic advance beyond *Íosagán*—the dominant qualities of his characters remain constant. Constant also is his omission of adult males from his fictional world. Children dominate the earlier collection and share the stage with women in the later. And once again, this exclusion is part of a conscious strategy. To write of men would of necessity have involved a direct confrontation with contemporary social and economic realities for whose discussion he lacked any coherent ideological framework until quite late in his life and which, more relevant here, he may have felt that he could deal with more appropriately as a journalist. In this sense, his exclusion of men from his Gaelic utopia provides further confirmation that his stories are not the work of a man out of touch with reality, but rather those of a writer deliberately seeking to preserve his personal vision and method from being overwhelmed by the sheer presence of that reality. Indeed, Pearse was if anything brutally aware of the grinding poverty of the Gaeltacht and its degrading effect on men struggling to raise families there: "The average Irish speaker in middle life is too impregnably ignorant, in many cases too ineradicably sordid ever to give his adhesion to a movement whose main appeal is intellectual and spiritual."[108]

And it is precisely to intellectual and spiritual values that Pearse's characters adhere in the stories: innocence, kindness, wisdom, generosity, piety, reverence for the truth, courage, self-sacrifice, and pride in and devotion to the Irish language and its traditions. The last three traits are of particular significance, for they were qualities that marked Pearse himself and that he felt were disappearing in an increasingly deracinated and mediocre Anglicized Ireland. Thus while Pearse the editor railed against the steady abandonment of Irish in the Gaeltacht, Pearse

107. In *Three Lectures on Gaelic Topics*, 57–58; 55.
108. "Na Sean-Ghaedhilgeoirí" (The Old Irish speakers), editorial, *ACS*, 10 October 1908.

the artist created characters who treasure their language and its ethos. Sean-Mhatias's delight in his mastery of the oral tradition is shared by a young audience eager to perpetuate it,[109] and a similar enthusiasm is evident in the young heroine of "Bairbre" when she recollects the performance of a local *seanchaí*.[110] In the title story of his second collection, a group of Conamara women almost reverently discuss their folk traditions both pagan and Christian, claiming that the song "Crónán na Banaltra" (Lullaby of the nursing mother) was sung by Mary to the Christ Child and had come down through time "from ancestor to ancestor . . . as the Fenian tales came down" (ó shinnsear go sinnsear . . . mar tháinig na sgéalta Fiannaidheachta).[111] In "Na Bóithre" ("The Roads"), the people of Ros na gCaorach flock to a traditional *fleadh* (festival) of which it has been announced "that there would be music and dancing and speeches in Irish; that there would be a piper from Carraroe there; that Brighíd Ní Mhainín would be there to sing "The County Mayo"; that Máirtín the Fisherman would tell a Fenian tale."[112] Young Cóilín in "An Bhean Chaointe" ("The Keening Woman") loves traditional storytelling and music, as befits the son of a *seanchaí*: "It was difficult not to listen to my father when he told a story like that by the hearth. He was an excellent storyteller."[113] Most striking of all, however, is the previously noted devotion to her culture of Brighíd Ní Mhainín, a performer at the *fleadh* of "Na Bóithre" whose story is told in "Brighíd na nAmhrán." For Pearse she embodies the tenacity of an unbroken Gaelic tradition, having, for example, learned "Conntae Mhuigheo" (County Mayo) from Raftery himself and preserving her songs for both present and future generations. Moreover, in Pearse's fiction if not in the facts he faced as an editor, those generations, represented here by the narrator of "Brighíd na nAmhrán," appreciate what is being entrusted to

109. "Íosagán," in *Íosagán agus Sgéalta Eile* (Baile Átha Cliath: Connradh na Gaedhilge, 1907), 11–12.

110. "Bairbre," in *Íosagán*, 60.

111. "An Mháthair," in *An Mháthair agus Sgéalta Eile* (Dundalk: Dundalgan, 1918), 6.

112. In *An Mháthair*, 16. It had been announced "go mbeadh ceol agus damhsa agus óráideacha Gaedhilge ann; go mbeadh píobaire ann ó'n gCeathramhadh Ruadh; go mbeadh Brighíd Ní Mhainín ann chum 'Conntae Mhuigheo' do thabhairt uaithi; go n-innseochadh Máirtín Iascaire sgéal fiannuidheachta."

113. In *An Mháthair*, 51. "Ba dheacair gan éisteacht lem' athair nuair d'innseadh sé sgéal mar sin cois teallaigh. Ba bhinn an sgéalaidhe é." Similarly, in *Poll an Phíobaire*, the boys' escapade is motivated by their interest in a local place-name tradition, while in Pearse's idyllic account of a day in Conamara, "Lá fá'n Tuaith" (A day in the country), he tells of his meeting with a young Gaeltacht boy fired with enthusiasm for Gaelic books and folk traditions. See *Ó Pheann an Phiarsaigh* (From Pearse's pen) (Baile Átha Cliath: Comhlucht Oideachais na hÉireann, n.d.), 36–40.

them: "I would be a rich man today if I had a shilling for every time I stood outside her door on my way home from school to listen to her songs."[114] And it is, of course, her passionate attachment to that tradition and pride in her mastery of it that give Brighíd herself the courage to make her fateful trek across Ireland to compete at the Oireachtas in Dublin.

Nor is the courage of Brighíd's act of faith, a courage rooted in her sense of belonging to a vital if threatened community, unique in Pearse's fiction. The "Keening Woman" travels even farther, walking to London to plead her case before Victoria herself. Consistently in stories like "Brighíd na nAmhrán," "An Bhean Chaointe," "An Mháthair," "An Gadaidhe" ("The Thief"), and "Bairbre," Pearse links such courage with an unquestioned sense of duty, an extraordinary capacity for endurance, and a serene acceptance of self-sacrifice, although even in the most idealized world it is hard to swallow the heroic action of a homemade Gaeltacht *doll* that throws itself to its destruction to save the life of the little girl who has spurned it for a fancy store-bought product!

Obviously all of these characters are too good to be true, but they were meant to be. Their embodiment of precisely those traits valued most highly by Pearse and in which he felt his contemporaries to be most deficient allows them to serve as ideal exemplars against which to measure the "real" Ireland in which he lived and wrote. Here one must, however, add a qualifying word about the most artistically satisfying of his stories, "An Dearg Daol" (The black chafer). As has been suggested, a strong note of melancholy runs through the stories of *An Mháthair*, but in only two of them is this sadness due to conscious and personal human evil. In "An Bhean Chaointe," the suffering is linked to English oppression, a source external to the Gaeltacht, but in "An Dearg Daol" the agent of malevolence is a Catholic priest, a, perhaps *the*, central figure in the local community. Indeed, in many ways "An Dearg Daol" offers a negative image of "Íosagán." In both stories a person has committed some undefined sin that puts him/her outside the institutional Church, the community's most important source of social as well as spiritual definition and cohesion. In both the community is in doubt as to how to deal with this person. However while the priest in "Íosagán" praises the self-evident virtue of Sean-Mhaitias and so quiets any misgivings the neighbors feel about him, the priest in "An Dearg Daol" inflames the community against a solitary and friendless

114. In *An Mháthair*, 29. "Do bheinn im' fhear shaidhbhir indiu dá mbeadh scilling agam i n-aghaidh gach uaire do sheasas taobh amuigh dá doras, ar mo bhealach abhaile ó'n scoil dom, ag éisteacht lena cuid amhrán."

woman and sets in motion the sequence of unnecessary cruelties that ends in her squalid death. The story was the author's personal favorite and may well indicate the direction his work would have taken had he survived. Desmond Ryan recounts that Pearse, "as if he had discovered a serious grievance," once expressed a "whimsical" regret that "none of my stories deal with turf."[115] Nonetheless, while "An Dearg Daol" is an intriguing anomaly in his fiction, certain elements remain constant, in particular the innocence of the young girl who refuses to heed the priest's curse on the woman, and the willingness to sacrifice self seen in the woman's own rescue of the girl and in the father's attempt, albeit late and futile, to help the ostracized "Dearg Daol."

Concerning nationalist constructions of the "people," Homi K. Bhaba has written:

> The people are not simply historical events or parts of a patriotic body politic. They are also a complex rhetorical strategy of social reference where the claim to be representative provokes a crisis within the process of signification and discursive address. We then have a contested cultural territory where the people must be thought in a double-time; the people are the rhetorical "objects" of a nationalist pedagogy, giving the discourse an authority that is based on the pre-given or constituted historical origin or event; the people are also the "subjects" of a process of signification that must erase any prior or originary presence of the nation-people to demonstrate the prodigious living principle of the people as that continuous process by which the national life is redeemed and signified as a repeating and reproductive process.[116]

Pearse, and to an even greater extent his critics, failed to elucidate just this distinction with regard to his own not terribly complex "narrative strategy." With a proper understanding of his fiction, however, as a conscious attempt to create a Gaelic utopia against which to measure the contemporary Ireland with which he was so utterly disillusioned, that strategy becomes clear, as does its direct if implicit relation to his political philosophy. As the years passed, Pearse came to base his radical nationalism on a sense of mystical identification with what he called

115. See Ryan, *The Man Called Pearse*, in *Collected Works of Pádraic H. Pearse: The Story of a Success and The Man Called Pearse*, 182–83; and Ryan, *Remembering Sion: A Chronicle of Storm and Quiet* (London: Arthur Barker, 1934), 187–88.

116. "DissemiNation: Time, Narrative, and the Margins of the Modern Nation," in *Nation and Narration*, ed. Homi K. Bhaba (London: Routledge, 1990), 297.

"The Sovereign People," of whom he wrote in "The Coming Revolution" (November 1913): "The people itself will perhaps be its own
Messiah, the people labouring, scourged, crowned with thorns, agoniz-
ing and dying, to rise again immortal and impassable. For peoples are
divine and are the only things that can properly be spoken of under
figures drawn from the divine epos. If we do not believe in the divinity
of our people we have had no business, or very little, all these years in
the Gaelic League."[117] In an essay entitled "The Sovereign People"
(March 1916), he expanded on this theme:

> It is, in fact, true that the repositories of the Irish tradition, as
> well the spiritual tradition of nationality as the kindred tradition
> of stubborn physical resistance to England, have been the great,
> splendid, faithful, common people—that dumb multitudinous
> thing which sorrowed during the penal night, which bled in '98,
> which starved in the Famine; and which is here still—what is left
> of it—unbought and unterrified.[118]

The Pearse-persona Mac Dara in the play *The Singer* claims to have had
his faith, religious and national, restored to him by "the people . . . the
dumb, suffering people; reviled and outcast, yet pure and splendid and
faithful," for "in them I saw, or seemed to see again, the Face of God."[119]
In "The Rebel," Pearse validates his own right to speak and fight for his
country through his identification with this sacred group:

> I am come of the seed of the people, the people
>   that sorrow,
> That have no treasure but hope,
> No riches laid up but a memory
> Of an Ancient glory . . .
> And because I am of the people, I understand
>   the people.

And the nature and fervor of that understanding admit no question:

117. In *Collected Works: Political Writings and Speeches*, 91–92.
118. In *Collected Works: Political Writings and Speeches*, 345. Nor was he alone in either
his ideology or his religious imagery here. Four years earlier, "X.L.P." (in "The Native
Speaker," *SF*, 2 March 1912) had offered the following contribution to the debate concerning the native speaker sparked by O'Reilly's views: "The native speaker of the Irish
language may possess every virtue under the heavens or he may possess all the vices. But
in addition to the virtues—or vices—he possesses one thing which none other of us
possess—the Apostolic Succession of the Irish Nation. He is the man with the pearl of
great price in his fist."
119. In *Collected Works: Plays, Stories, Poems*, 34.

I say to my people that they are holy,
   that they are august, despite their chains,
That they are greater than those that hold
   them, and stronger, and purer.[120]

It was not, however, the flesh-and-blood Irish people of Pearse's own or any other day, of whatever linguistic background, who were apotheosized here. Indeed, it is generally agreed that the rather introverted Pearse had little contact with and perhaps even less empathy with the great majority of the plain people of Ireland. Denis Gwynn, one of his pupils at Sgoil Éanna, recalled that "he scarcely ever met anyone who didn't belong to his own small circle of friends in the Gaelic League. He had no means of knowing what the ordinary Irishman and woman thought or cared about; all that he did know about them was, vaguely, that they did not share his own ideas."[121] Disgusted by the philistinism and materialism of contemporary Dublin, Pearse turned for solace to a new hidden Ireland, a potential Ireland more spiritual and thus more true to itself, in effect more real, than that in which he lived,[122] an Ireland that had but to be shown its divine nature to realize and repudiate its present and accidental flaws. In his stories Pearse constructed his myth of a Gaelic Ireland of extraordinary nobility, and, like others before him, he became his own best convert. Indeed, his bewitchment by his ideal Sovereign People mirrors his fascination and eventual identification with Cú Chulainn and ultimately with Christ, a development that will be discussed in Chapter 4. In *The Story of a Success*, a series of pieces about his experiment at Sgoil Éanna, he stated: "I have constantly found that to desire is to hope, to hope is to believe, and to believe is to accomplish."[123] So it was to be throughout his life.

Pinpointing what she sees as Pearse's major perceptual and conceptual failure, Ruth Dudley Edwards writes: "He wrote, acted, and died for a people that did not exist."[124] But this is, in Bhaba's terms, to place sole emphasis on his depiction of the "people" as "objects" for fictional re-creation, whereas Pearse himself was clearly more interested in his characters as salvific "subjects" who could "redeem" the life of the nation. On some level Pearse himself has to have known that, for in the

120. In *Collected Works: Plays, Stories, Poems*, 337–39.

121. "Patrick Pearse," *Dublin Review* 172 (March 1923): 93.

122. In his account of his educational experiment at Sgoil Éanna, Pearse wrote: "So does the spiritual always triumph over the actual for the spiritual, being the true actual, is stronger than the forms and bulks we call actual." See *The Story of a Success*, 51.

123. *The Story of a Success*, 49.

124. *Patrick Pearse*, 343.

stories we meet the people for whom he did offer his life, a people
rooted in his reading of national history, but entirely of his own creation. Pearse's fiction was of real aesthetic importance to the Revival as
a corrective to contemporaries' obsession with folk models for the new
prose. Yet in many ways their prime importance is not literary. In fact,
too cloyingly precious and, even as expressions of a utopian vision, too
simplistic for the modern taste, they are artistic failures. On the other
hand, as insights into the shaping of his mind, they are invaluable.
Pearse once wrote, "Everything that even pretends to be true begins
with a Credo."[125] His stories incarnate just such a creed. They are the
quiet acts of faith of a man who would make himself a political messiah.

Pearse's progressive ally, Pádraic Ó Conaire, has never been accused
of idealism, and in his rural stories and to a lesser extent in his plays, he
faced the obvious but ideologically unpalatable truth that human nature
is as complex, intriguing, and occasionally unedifying on the farm as in
the town, and that country life can be every bit as lonely and barren as
the urban existence he was among the first Gaelic authors to treat with
insight and honesty. Ó Conaire's almost unrelentingly bleak view of
the city will be discussed in detail in Chapter 7. Here it will be sufficient
to note that at times his picture of the debasing and soulless influences
of modern urban life would have both horrified and gratified many of
the rural nativists. Indeed, so stark is his portrayal of the city that even
as perceptive as writer as Seosamh Mac Grianna could mistakenly see
"Nóra Mharcuis Bhig" as rooted in a naive dichotomy between the
squalor of London and the innocence of Conamara.[126] But for Ó Conaire there was no pastoral Gaelic utopia where one could escape the
malaise of city life, and his boldness in introducing urban themes into
modern writing in Irish was matched by his courage in portraying the
failings and vices of rural, and particularly of Gaeltacht, society, a point
underscored by Liam Ó Briain as he recalled the thrill his generation
felt when they first read Ó Conaire's stories:

> Although Pearse began on his stories at exactly the same time,
> and although they are fine and beautiful, he didn't provide the
> same jolt out of the age of the traditional storytelling and into
> the twentieth century, into the bare, ugly reality of life as it was
> around the people of the Gaeltacht and the Galltacht, the jolt that

125. "The Murder Machine," in *Collected Works: Political Writings and Speeches*, 16.
126. "Pádraic Ó Conaire," in *Pádraic Ó Conaire agus Aistí Eile* (Pádraic Ó Conaire and
other essays), eagrán nua (Baile Átha Cliath: Oifig an tSoláthair, 1969), 12–13. The book
was originally published in 1936.

was necessary if our movement was to show any seriousness. It is not possible today to understand the courage it took to write something like "Nora Mharcuis Bhig" at that time.[127]

Contemporary insight into the sort of courage such artistic integrity demanded is provided by William P. Ryan's account of his showing the work of the still little-known Ó Conaire to "a judge of some authority":

> The judge was pained and in some measure indignant. Such things he said in effect, must be rigorously excluded from the books of the Gael. It was not romantic, nor flattering: in fact it was sometimes like a nightmare, and sometimes like other unpleasant things. . . . The judge used much further emphatic language, and declared that the young author ought to burn the book and create something pleasant. He plainly indicated that the book in question was an insult to Ireland.[128]

There was little that was pleasant, much less romantic, in Ó Conaire's Gaeltacht. None of his many urban exiles come to the city of their own free will; all are driven there by some radical deficiency in their home environment. The most obvious of these compelling circum-

---

127. Quoted in *Pádraic Ó Conaire: Clocha ar a Charn*, ed. de Bhaldraithe, 62. "Cé gur thosaigh an Piarsach ar a scéalta féin díreach an tráth céanna agus cé gur mhaith iad agus gur álainn, níor thug sé an croitheadh sin as ré na seanscéalaíochta isteach i réaltacht lom, ghránna an tsaoil mar a bhí thart timpeall ar lucht na Gaeltachta agus na Galltachta, a bhí ag teastáil san am, má bhí i ndán dár ngluaiseacht aon dáiríreacht a thaispeáint. Ní féidir a thuiscint inniu cén misneach mór ba ghá a bheith ag an té a scríobhfadh leithéid 'Nóra Mharcuis Bhig' an uair úd."

128. "I mBaile 's i gCéin," *ACS*, 3 October 1903. Actually, Ryan never identifies Ó Conaire as the subject of this essay, but he could be referring to no one else. This "judge" was not alone in his discomfort with the work of Ó Conaire. We have already seen that An tAthair Peadar campaigned successfully to have his work excluded from the Irish syllabus at the National University, and, according to Criostóir Mac Aonghusa, some native speakers had identical reservations:

> When some of his stories are read to the people of the Gaeltacht they show no interest in them at all other than to say "He's a dirty man." And remember that these people find no fault with the strong language of the folktales. The "strangeness" of Pádraic's stories explains their aversion to him.

> (Nuair léitear cuid dá chuid scéalta do mhuintir na Gaeltachta ní chuireann siad spéis ar bith iontu ach a rá: "Is salach an duine é." Agus cuimhnigh nach bhfuil aon locht ag na daoine sin ar chaint thréan na seanscéalta. "Coimhthíos" bheith i scéalta Phádraic a mhíníos an col a ghlacann siad leis.)

See Mac Aonghusa, "Pádraic Ó Conaire," *Comhar* 15, no. 12 (December 1956): 22.

stances is simple material poverty. In essays like "Ceisteanna a Bhaineas le Buanughadh na Gaedhilge 'san nGaedhealtacht" (Questions relating to the preservation of Irish in the Gaeltacht) or "An Ghaedhealtacht: Tuairisg an Choimisiúin" (The Gaeltacht: The commission's report), Ó Conaire discussed the grinding poverty of native speakers, describing them in their struggle even to feed their families as "constantly striving to do what can't be done" (ag síor-iarraidh an rud nach bhfuil iondhéanta a dhéanamh).[129] More important, in stories like "Páidín Mháire," he depicted the misery of Conamara peasants living with the ever-present specter of death in the dreaded poor house.[130]

Yet however grinding this material destitution, it was not for Ó Conaire the most painful deprivation for the sensitive spirit whether in the city or on the farm. With an honesty rare in its time and ideological climate, Ó Conaire confronted the social problems and human tragedies behind the rural myth, and more daringly behind the myth of the Gaeltacht. Thus greed, especially for land, is a central motive in several of his stories and plays. Indeed, it is the sole motive for the action in his 1906 play *An Uadhacht* (The will) and its 1907 fictional variant of the same title. In this curious dark comedy, the anticipated, if not longed for, death of a bedridden stepfather is of importance only because it will finally allow the publication and execution of his will and the disposal of his land.[131] More chilling examples of the perverting effect of such materialism on the profoundest emotional ties are found in Ó Conaire's depictions of the arranged marriage, a match rooted in land, cash, and dowry rather than in love. In two of his plays, *An Droighneán Donn* (The blackthorn tree) (1906)[132] and *Bairbre Ruadh* (1908),[133] preparation

---

129. "Ceisteanna a Bhaineas le Buanughadh na Gaedhilge 'san nGaedhealtacht," in *Aistí Uí Chonaire*, 54.

130. "Páidín Mháire," in *Nóra Mharcuis Bhig*, 42–43.

131. See Ó Conaire, *An Uadhacht*, in *Bairbre Rua agus Drámaí Eile* (Bairbre Rua and other plays), ed. Pádraig Ó Siadhail (Béal an Daingin: Cló Iar-Chonnachta, 1989), 34–50 (play) and 192–201 (story). Both were first published in *Inis Fáil*, the play from June to September 1906, the story from July to August 1907. There is no record of a first production of the play, although Ó Siadhail feels that it must have been produced in London while Ó Conaire was living there. See his "Réamhrá" to *Bairbre Rua agus Drámaí Eile*, 18, n. 7. However, in his *Conradh na Gaeilge i Londain, 1894–1917* (The Gaelic League in London, 1894–1917), Donncha Ó Súilleabháin mentions only publication of the play and says nothing of its performance. See Ó Súilleabháin, *Conradh na Gaeilge i Londain, 1894–1917* (Baile Átha Cliath: Conradh na Gaeilge, 1989), 100.

132. See Ó Conaire, *An Droighneán Donn*, in *Bairbre Rua agus Drámaí Eile*, 21–33. This play was first published in *ACS*, 15–29 July 1905, and first performed by a league branch in London on 24 February 1906.

133. See Ó Conaire, *Bairbre Rua*, in *Bairbre Rua agus Drámaí Eile*, 51–77. This play was

for such marriages is at the heart of the action, although in both the protagonists, a young man and a young woman respectively, manage to, quite literally, escape. But in his 1913 Oireachtas Prize–winning story "An Bhean a Ciapadh" (The woman who was tormented), the young bride is not so fortunate. Married to a well-off friend of her father's back from America, the woman is miserable from the start, and the marriage deteriorates further after her she loses her first child at birth and is told that to have another will imperil her health. Her older husband, fixated on producing an heir, turns to drink and on several occasions drunkenly forces himself on her. As the result of one of these marital rapes, she conceives and dies producing the all-important heir, in whom her husband takes belated and hypocritical solace for her loss. Ó Conaire's disgust with the arranged marriage finds clearest expression in the distraught woman's outburst at father and spouse: "You only wanted to get me a husband, and you didn't care at all what sort of man he was as long as he had a bit of money. All you wanted to do was sell me. There are men on whom God should not bestow daughters; there are other men and it is the greatest of sins that they get wives."[134]

Ó Conaire also faced up to the isolation of Gaeltacht life with its attendant ignorance and intolerance. For example, his hedge-school story "An Sgoláire Bocht" (The poor scholar) begins as a rather touching account of a young man's awakening to the significance of native learning under the tutelage of a wandering teacher. By story's end, however, the student has broken the heart and spirit of his master by burning a treasured manuscript on the order of a stupid parish priest fearful of Protestant proselytism through books in Irish, and has even begun to wonder whether all reading might be sinful.[135] This blind fear of the Church is if anything exceeded by the country people's fear of the opinion of their own neighbors, a fear that acts as a stultifying force for conformity. Dread of public opinion is treated comically in the

---

first published by the league as a booklet in 1908, and was probably first performed at the Oireachtas in that year. The heroine elopes with her brother's hired man, thus introducing an interesting class angle to the play. It is also worth noting that her sister willingly marries the older man she has rejected, apparently out of genuine attraction.

134. In *Síol Éabha: Sgéalta ó Láimh Phádraic Uí Chonaire* (The descendants of Eve: Stories from the hand of Pádraic Ó Conaire) (Baile Átha Cliath: Comhlacht Oideachais na hÉireann, n.d.), no pagination. "Ní raibh uait acht fear fhagháil dom, agus ba chuma leat sa mí-ádh mór cé'n sórt fir é acht beagán airgid bheith aige. Mé a dhíol—sin a raibh uait. Tá fir ann agus ní ceart go mbronnfadh Dia ingheanacha ortha; tá dream eile ann agus sé an peacadh mór é go bhfuighidís mná."

135. In *An Sgoláire Bocht agus Sgéalta Eile* (Baile Átha Cliath: Connradh na Gaedhilge, 1913), 1–35.

story "Rún an Fhir Mhóir" (The big man's secret) and in its dramatized version *A Chéad Bhean* (His first wife). In both works there is greater concern about the anticipated disgraceful arrest of the protagonist than about the murder he is believed to have committed: "If he had so great a need to kill his first wife, shouldn't he have done it in secret, without an uproar and without drawing this shame on himself and on his friends and relations?"[136] This theme achieves its most powerful tragic expression in "Nóra Mharcuis Bhig," in which Nóra's father feels more shame and humiliation than sadness and sympathy for the failure and exile of his two sons: "They had shamed him. The people were making fun of him. He was the laughingstock of the townland" (4).[137] When Nóra returns from London an apparent success, his primary reaction is not joy at having her home, but gratification over his personal vindication and enhanced social standing: "If his sons were no good, his daughter was splendid. She was an example to the whole parish" (13).[138] And when she finally gives in to temptation and gets drunk at a local fair, her father makes no attempt to understand much less help her, and is instead almost frantic to get her away from the neighbors' judgmental eyes as quickly as possible, a banishment whose end result even he must now appreciate: "If those are the habits you learned in England, it's there you'll have to practice them" (16).[139] For Ó Conaire the independent spirit often seems to have had little to choose between the degrading impersonality of the city and the all too personal degredation of the country. His comment on a somewhat different situation is particularly relevant to the sufferings of his Gaeltacht seekers in urban exile: "The person between two worlds is greatly to be pitied."[140]

Nevertheless, despite his almost unique awareness of rural shortcomings—or at least willingness to express that awareness—Ó Conaire did pay some tribute to orthodoxy by showing a positive side to country

---

136. In *Seacht mBuaidh an Éirghe-Amach* (Seven triumphs of the Rising) (Baile Átha Cliath: Sáirséal agus Dill, 1967), 166. "Má bhí gábhadh chomh mór sin aige a chéad bhean a mharbhughadh nár cheart dó é a dhéanamh 'gós íseal gan raic agus gan an náire seo tharraingt anuas air féin agus ar a cháirdibh gaoil." In this farcical tale, the missing supposed first wife is actually a rebel on the run he has helped to escape disguised in women's clothing.

137. "Bhí sé náirighthe aca. Bhí an pobal ag déanamh magaidh faoi. Bhí sé ina staicín aibhléise ag an mbaile."

138. "Má bhí a chlann mhac go dona bhí a inghean thar cionn. Bhí sí 'n-a sompla ag an bparáiste uile."

139. "Má's iad sin na béasa a d'fhoghluim tú i Sasana, is ann a chaithfeas tú a gcleachtadh."

140. "Beirt Bhan Misneamhail" (Two courageous women), in *Seacht mBuaidh an Éirghe-Amach*, 95. "Is truaigh Mhuire an té atá idir an dá shaoghail."

life almost entirely absent in his depiction of the city. There is a passion and honesty in his Gaeltacht people entirely lacking in the superficial and alienated characters who populate his cityscapes, a distinction he makes explicit in his Conamara sketch "An tSochraoid cois Tuinne" (The funeral by the sea) by contrasting the wild sincerity of mourners at a Gaeltacht burial with the sort of embarrassed repression that characterizes even so primary an emotion as grief among the "civilized."[141] On a less epic level, their willingness to experience and express genuine emotion makes country people capable of a warm consideration even for total strangers, as is evident in their maintenance of the wandering teacher in "An Sgoláire Bocht." Moreover, even their well-developed interest in the affairs of their neighbors can have a benign aspect. In "Fearfeasa agus an Fathach Fada" (Fearfeasa and the tall giant), Gaeltacht people are described as "inquisitive people, but well-mannered people as well" (daoine fiosracha ach daoine deagh-mhúinte).[142] In the previously noted "Rún an Fhir Mhóir," the involvement of his neighbors in the problems of the "Big Man" is largely motivated by a desire to help, and they identify themselves as "friends who came here for your good, friends who came here to help you, whatever crime you have committed."[143] And in the story version of An Uadhacht, though not in the play, Ó Conaire introduced a more encompassing notion of solidarity by making a rare concession to nationalist ideology and turning the cantankerous dying old man into a would-be language activist for whom the Gaelic League has come too late. As he listens from his bed to the speech of a league organizer, the man's last words are: "O Lord, if I were only young again."[144] It is, however, impossible to escape the conclusion that in his more serious and profound works Ó Conaire found the potential for group solidarity and support evident in these comic stories wholly inadequate compensation for the sensitive individual's loss of the freedom to develop in his or her own direction in response to personal emotional and spiritual imperatives.

A word must also be said here about Ó Conaire's attitude to both urban and rural life as it is revealed in various later sketches and essays,

---

141. In *Cubhar na dTonn* (The foam on the waves) (Baile Átha Cliath: Comhlacht Oideachais na hÉireann, n.d.), 6–7. This passage will be discussed again and quoted in full in the section on Ó Conaire's urban fiction in Chapter 7.

142. In *Fearfeasa Mac Feasa* (Baile Átha Cliath: Cló-Lucht an Tálbóidigh, Tta. i gComhar le hOifig an tSoláthair, 1930), 156.

143. In *Seacht mBuaidh*, 157. They call themselves "cáirde tháinic annseo ar mhaithe leat, cáirde tháinic annseo le cabhrughadh leat pé ar bith cé'n choir atá déanta agat."

144. "An Uadhacht," in *Bairbre Rua agus Drámaí Eile*, 201. "O! A Thiarna, dá mbeadh an óige agam arís."

for these have been widely anthologized in Ireland and have reached a wider audience without knowledge of Irish through translations published in paperback by Mercier Press.[145] In these late pieces, written after his return to Ireland in 1914 when he was eking out a precarious living as Gaelic Ireland's first full-time man of letters in centuries, the city appears only briefly as the stereotypical source of "sadness and anxiety and heartfelt sorrow" (an brón agus an imnidhe agus an doilgheas croidhe),[146] where people are "smothered" (mar a plúchtar daoine)[147] and whose attractions are "only airy toys compared to the joyful life you could have here with me in my old quarry, far from people and from the false civilization of this day and age."[148] Yet, as is evident in the passage just cited, even in these late sketches, often written with an eye on the shillings they would bring in and at times recycled without compunction under various titles, Ó Conaire never succumbed to the nativist myth of a rural Gaelic utopia he knew to be nonexistent.[149] Rather, his quite obviously inadequate, albeit lyrical and romantic, alternative to urban corruption and alienation was a vagabond life impossible for virtually all of his readers: "Come with me and your bruised heart will be lifted, your spirit expanded, your melancholy cured, and the pair of us will welcome the spring and the world's return to life."[150]

145. The Mercier collections are *Field and Fair* and *The Woman at the Window*, the latter containing some of Ó Conaire's finest work, including "Nóra Mharcuis Bhig." In 1982 Poolbeg Press published a volume of translations containing fifteen of Ó Conaire's best stories under the cumbersome title *Pádraic Ó Conaire: 15 Short Stories Translated from the Irish.*

146. "Cuireadh" (Invitation), in *An Crann Géagach: Aistí agus Scéilíní* (The branching tree: Essays and anecdotes) (Áth Cliath: Cló na gCoinneal, 1919), 11.

147. "Gracie," in *Béal an Uaignis* (The edge of loneliness) (Áth Cliath: Mártan Lester, Tta., 1921), 45.

148. "Amuigh faoi'n bhFásach" (Out in the wilderness), in *Béal an Uaignis*, 20. The city's attractions are only "bréagáin gaoithe i gcomórtas leis an saoghal suairc bheadh agad annseo liomsa 'mo sheanchoiléar i bhfad ó dhaoine agus ó shibhéaltacht bhréige na h-aoise."

149. Even in his glowing account of Conamara native speakers in the sketch "Cois Fharraige," his emphasis is on the toughness and integrity of a people locked in a ceaseless struggle with a harsh environment. See "Cois Fharraige," in *Seoigheach an Ghleanna* (Joyce of the glen) (Baile Átha Cliath: An Press Náisiúnta, n.d.), 77–81.

150. Ó Conaire, "Cuireadh," in *An Crann Géagach*, 11. "Tar liomsa go dtógfar do chroidhe brúighte, go mborruighthear do mheanma, go leighseóchar do ghalar dubhach, go bhfáiltighmid beirt roimh an earrach agus roimh athbheóchaint an tsaoghail." In "M'Fhile Caol Dubh" (My slender black-haired poet), the world-weary Dublin wife in love with the poet is enthralled by the paean to the open road delivered by Synge's tramp in *In the Shadow of the Glen*. See "M'File Caol Dubh," in *Seacht mBuaidh*, 192. For a discussion of the influence of the Romantics on Ó Conaire's depiction of nature and rural life, see An tSr. Éibhlín Ní Chionnaith, "An Rómánsachas i Scríbhneoireacht Uí

Unfortunately, few of their contemporaries seem to have been paying much attention to the stylistic and thematic experiments of Pearse and Ó Conaire. With the exception of Seán Ó Caomhánaigh's "Mallacht na Fola" (The curse of the blood), a story set in the mid-nineteenth century and recounting the intolerance inflicted on the mother of an illegitimate child, on the child himself, and even on the children of that child,[151] what social criticism we get is mild indeed, as when a farmer in *Muinntear na Tuatha* rejects the logic of a curate who has banned dancing in his parish.[152] And while we do find memorable characters, striking episodes, and authentic humor, too often we are left with mere country high jinks and generic bucolic.[153] More disturbing, the thematic range of the ruralists was equally constricted. In addition to their central underlying concern with presenting the Gaeltacht as a proud, resilient, and communal society, T. S. Eliot's "local organic community," their principal recurrent themes were the inherently superior cleverness of country Gaels over English or Anglicized officialdom, the comic absurdity of superstition, the cruelty of inflicting a foreign education on Irish-speaking children, and the physical and spiritual perils of emigration.

The first of these themes most frequently involves the legal system and its agents. Particularly popular was a courtroom scene in which the "ignorant" peasants play police, attorneys, and the judge himself for fools while securing their acquital from some unjust intrusion into their lives. Almost inevitably, the title "Fools" of the 1901 farce *Lá na nAmadán; nó, an t-Oifigeach agus Seaghán Bán* (The day of the fools; or, the officer and Seán Bán) were members of the Royal Irish Constabulary! The RIC are again humiliated in Séamus Ó Beirne's bilingual propaganda play *Obair!* (Work!) in which the only policeman with any sense quits the force.[154] Séamus Ó Dubhghaill, himself a civil servant,

Chonaire" (Romanticism in Ó Conaire's writing), *An tUltach* 68, no. 3 (March 1991): 6–9.

151. *SF*, 1–29 November 1913, esp. 1 and 22 November. However, even this story ends happily with the reunion of the wronged woman with her granddaughter and the latter's happy marriage (29 November 1913).

152. Ó Dubhghaill, *Muinntear na Tuatha*, 88–89.

153. See, for example, the contemporary criticism of Gaelic authors by "An Shiuineir" ("Chips/The Short Story in Gaelic," *SF*, 11 April 1914): "They have a gift of phrase, which to myself at least, appears beyond that of almost any writers in English or in French. . . . They seize curious types of character, and present them to us in a most vivid way. . . . But all or nearly all the stories fail utterly and finally in the one fatal fact that nothing happens in them."

154. Séamus Ó Beirne, *Obair!: A Bilingual Play in Four Scenes* (Baile Átha Cliath: M. H. Gill and Son, 1909).

was particularly taken with the comic possibilities of such encounters between Irish wit and British bureaucracy. For example, in both his story *Prátaí Mhíchíl Thaidhg* and his short play *Ar Lorg Poitín*, local men make a farce of the judicial process when tried for distilling *poitín*. In the former the joke hinges on a newly arrived officer's inability to distinguish home-brewed barm from *poitín*;[155] in the latter another English policeman new to the country is intentionally duped into prosecuting a man for possession of legally bought store whiskey.[156] In addition, Ó Dubhghaill underscored the willful ignorance of Irish culture behind such a mistake by having the officer fail to learn from the similar experience of one of his predecessors in the area, a man who had arrested as a Fenian band "muinntear na Brídeoige," a group of masked revelers celebrating in traditional fashion the feast of Saint Brigid.[157] The inability to sort out the most rudimentary facts of rural life is central to two stories of police ineptitude. In D. Ó Muimhneacháin's "true story" of the events that gave birth to the famous song "The Peeler and the Goat," a cowardly and drunken sergeant believes he has killed the agrarian rebel "Captain Moonlight" when in fact he has merely shot an evicted tenant's goat.[158] In Mícheál Ó Murchadha's "Paidí Bán agus an Saighdiúir" (Fair-haired Paddy and the soldier), a certain note of malice never entirely absent even from these farcical tales becomes more disturbing, as an English soldier whose dealings with Paidí are said to have been conducted "politely" (go béasach) on this their first meeting, is duped into holding what he believes to be a sheep on a rope only to find that it is in fact a ram that knocks him about. Thereafter the soldier is arrested, fined, and broken from the service for the theft of this beast. Throughout, the emphasis is on the man's gullibility. He gets what he deserves, and the whole episode is presented as a joke pure and simple.[159]

At other times, the joke is turned against the Irish themselves: in their

---

155. *Prátaí Mhíchíl Thaidhg* (Baile Átha Cliath: M. H. Mac Ghuill agus a Mhac, 1904), 7–10.

156. *Ar Lorg Poitín*, in *Cléibhín Móna* (A little basket of turf) (Baile Átha Cliath: M. H. Guill agus a Mhac, 1907), 30–36. See also the courtroom scene in "Conán Maol," "Míol Mara do Leag Cíos," in *An Buaiceas* (The wick), ed. Seosamh Laoide (Baile Átha Cliath: Connradh na Gaedhilge, 1903), 39–45.

157. *Ar Lorg Poitín*, 23. An equally farcical but less ethnically antagonistic treatment of the courtroom setting is found in "Greann na Cúirte" (The humor of the court) by "Pádraig na Léime" in which the comedy arises from the obstinate pettiness of the litigants and in which the judge seems very much at home in the rural community. Indeed, the only ethnic humor in this series of three anecdotes is directed at a cocky American and his slangy brand of American English. See "Greann na Cúirte," *ACS*, 9 November 1912.

158. "An Píléir agus an Gabhar" (The peeler and the goat), *ACS*, 9–16 January 1909.

159. *Banba* 1, no. 1 (December 1901): 13–14.

belief in otherworld beings and forces, some of the country characters are every bit as gullible as the officials elsewhere manipulated, and the authors depict their resulting discomfiture with surprising relish. One of the clearest distinctions between genuine folktales and rural stories modeled on them lies in the treatment of the supernatural. The folklore being collected at the time reflected a belief, either on the part of informants or on the part of those from whom they learned the tale, in a predictably varied cast of characters from the *sí* (Otherworld), some of them benign, some mischievous, some ominous, and a few even savage. In the original fiction by writers like "Gruagach an Tobair," "Conán Maol," Ó Dubhghaill, An tAthair Peadar, or "An Seabhac," such a belief in the Otherworld is almost invariably a sign of childish credulity, as it is, for example in "Conán Maol's" "Faitchíos Phádraig" (Patrick's fear)[160] or "Gruagach an Tobair's" "Peig Ní Luanaigh"[161]; or is fueled by alcohol, as in "Donnchadh na Breille agus An Sprid" (Donnchadh of the big lips and the spirit) by "Faill na mBó."[162] Repeatedly, even in *Séadna*, in which after all Satan himself plays a leading role, "miraculous" occurrences and supernatural "apparitions" are provided an entirely rational explanation, often to the discredit of the "visionary" in the eyes of the commonsensical and keen-witted neighbors who make up the vast majority of the rural population.[163] Indeed, it seems

160. *Banba* 2, no. 3 (17 March 1903): 140–41.
161. *Banba* 1, no. 3 (May 1902): 92–95.
162. *Banba* 2, no. 5 (May 1903): 191–93.
163. See, for example, Ua Laoghaire, *Séadna*, 62–63, 101–2, 151–61, 156–7. See also "Gruagach an Tobair," "An Spioraid," *Annála na Tuatha*, part 3, 55; Ó Dubhghaill, "Tadhg Óg," in *Cléibhín Móna*, 11; "An Seabhac," *An Baile Seo 'Gainne* (Our townland) (Baile Átha Cliath: Connradh na Gaedhilge, n.d.), 61–62 ("Liam na Giúise"); and 93–94 ("Doinnichín"). More newfangled meddling with the spirit world is ridiculed in one of the tales in the "Greann na Tuatha" (Country humor) series by "Pádraig na Léime," in which a man who boasts of his mastery of mesmerism is duped and made a laughingstock by his neighbors in Baile na gCat. See "Greann na Tuatha—I.," *ACS*, 15 February 1913. Note also that in Ó Conaire's 1918 dramatization of his story "Rún an Fhir Mhóir" as *A Chéad Bhean*, he turns his comic narrative into stage farce by having the protagonist terrify some gullible enemies by pretending to be his own ghost. See *A Chéad Bhean*, in *Bairbre Rua agus Drámaí Eile*, 189–90. An exception to this skeptical view of the Otherworld is found on occasion, most notably in the work of Seaghán Mac Meanman, especially *Sgéalta Goiride Geimhridh* where Mac Meanman draws an almost Yeatsian contrast between the traditional "strong faith in spiritual beings and in invisible activity" (creideamh láidir . . . i neachaibh spioradálta agus i ngníomhachas do-fhaicseana) and the contemporary "dull belief that doesn't extend half an inch beyond what our eyes see" (creideamhnas marbhánta nach síneann leath ordlach taobh thall d'amharc ár súl). See "Réamrádh do'n Cheud Chur Amach," *Sgéalta*, iii. In his "An Chreach Ghoidte" (The stolen herd), the appearance of a living man's spirit does indeed presage his tragic and

that here we have the explanation for the prevalence of this motif in the country stories. One of the many Gaelic reservations about Anglo-Irish writers from the esoteric Yeats and iconoclastic Synge to the lowbrow Seamas MacManus concerned their misappropriation of the "folk" and their misrepresentation of the peasant's religious worldview as fundamentally primitive and mystical. In these rural tales in Irish we are offered, in opposition to this vestigial paganism that so fascinated the Anglo-Irish, a public repudiation of superstition and a communal affirmation of wit, good sense, and rationally orthodox spirituality.[164]

Official lack of respect for that good sense and the culture that evolved from it is the focus of the third common theme of the ruralists, the injustice of imposing the English language and its ethos on Irish-speaking children, an injustice whose psychic repercussions on young minds denied more wholesome native inspiration was a seminal consideration in Henry Morris's 1899 essay "The Irish Folk-Lore—What It Teaches."[165] In a motif that later became de rigeur for Gaelic autobiographers and that was devastatingly parodied by Myles na gCopaleen in *An Béal Bocht*, rural writers detailed their scarifying experiences, particularly those on their first day, in the local national school. As early as "Conán Maol's" "Seaghán agus Micheál," a work that won an 1898 Oireachtas Prize for "a story about school life," the principal elements of the pattern were already in place: scorn for the Irish language and its culture; physical abuse by a cruel English-speaking master; the intellectual and personal deficiencies of that master, especially alcoholism; and

---

violent death; while in "Maghnus Mac Cormaic agus Cormac Mac Maghnuis," the snatching of children by folk from the *sí* is treated as a factual occurrence. However, even Mac Meanman has one story in which a man takes advantage of a young woman's belief in Samhain divination to win her hand. See *Sgéalta*, 28–40, 55–85, 1–13.

164. As is evident from *Séadna*, Christian supernaturalism was entirely acceptable. For example, just as Pearse introduced the youthful Jesus to lead old Maitias back to the faith in "Íosagán," "Ceann Fhaolaigh" has a boyish angel miraculously bring a priest to a dying man in "Má Rinne Mise Neamairt, Ní Theárn Dia Neamairt" (If I was neglectful, God wasn't) (*ACS*, 2 March 1907). In "Sgéal Fíor" (A true story), by Stephán Seoigheach, a priest is summoned to hear the confession of an apparently healthy lapsed Catholic, who dies shortly thereafter. The messenger turns out to have been the man's long-dead mother (*FL*, 10 February 1900). "An Cros" (The cross), an Oireachtas Prize–winning story from 1915 by Michael O'Connor, deals with the afterlife penance of a man who caused the death of his own son. See "An Cros," *WF*, 13 March 1915. Incidentally, this whole discussion should point up the superficiality of David Cairns's and Shaun Richards's view of the "essential literary function of the peasant" for "Irish-Irish" or "nationalist" (the terms are used indiscriminately) "intellectuals of the people-nation." See Cairns and Richards, *Writing Ireland: Colonialism, Nationalism and Culture* (Manchester: Manchester University Press, 1988), 71.

165. *FL*, 16 and 30 December 1899.

the arrogance toward both master and students of the educational inspector, the dreaded "cigire."[166]

While the rural writers on occasion explored the comic possibilities of
such classroom confrontations, they found nothing at all humorous in
the fourth and most significant of their principal concerns: emigration,
particularly the flight from the Gaeltacht. The dire reality was set forth
unflinchingly by Pearse in April 1903:

> The Emigration Terror is threatening the very existence of the
> language movement. We should despair, but that we cannot
> bring ourselves to believe that God does not care for this land.
> Recent statistics are appalling, stupifying, inexplicable. We are
> face to face with the tremendous fact that in spite of all the pro-
> pagandist work of the last decade the emigration fever is stron-
> ger, madder than ever in the veins of our people.[167]

As Pearse's distress makes plain, concern about the ongoing hemor-
rhage of emigration from the Gaeltacht was not limited to Gaeltacht
and other rural writers. Many urbanized Gaels were themselves emigrants, either to London or internally to Dublin, and wrote of the experience from closer to the bone. Pádraic Ó Conaire's father, for example, died soon after his arrival in the United States, and his "Nóra
Mharcuis Bhig" was, albeit misleadingly, subtitled "a true story dealing
with emigration" (fíor-sgéal a bhaineas leis an imirce) on its initial publication in An Claidheamh Soluis in January 1907. Indeed, it seems that
some Gaels at least read all of his urban fiction, including Deoraidheacht,
as in part antiemigration propaganda. In his defense of Deoraidheacht
against Peadar Ua Laoghaire's successful campaign to have the book
removed from the University College, Dublin syllabus, Hyde said that

---

166. "Conán Maol," "Seaghán agus Micheál," in An Buaiceas, 76–97. Actually, the
cigire of this story is, however intimidating, rather kind to the children, leading Pearse to
comment: "Truly a big, kindly heart has 'Conán': he is the first Gaelic Leaguer we have
known to write with sympathy of a school inspector" (review of An Buaiceas, ACS, 14
March 1903). See also "Conán Maol," "Ar Sgoil a' Chuais" (At the Cuas school), ACS,
14 December 1907; "Gruagach an Tobair," "Ar Thórramh Sheana-Shéamuis" (At the
wake of Old Séamus"), Annála na Tuatha, part 2, 8–10; and Ó Dubhghaill, "Tadhg Óg,"
in Cléibhín Móna, 11–13. To be fair, both "Conán Maol" and Ó Dubhghaill also write of
decent and even patriotic schoolmasters, "Conán" in "Tadhg a' tSiúnta," ACS, 21 December 1907; Ó Dubhghaill in Muinntear na Tuatha, 16–24. Ó Dubhghaill also offered an
idealized look at what Irish education should and could be in a series of schoolroom
sketches in Cléibhín Móna, 48–56. See also the essays by "Conán Maol," "Gruagach an
Tobair," Dinneen, and Ó Dubhghaill in Scoil Gaedhealach (A Gaelic school) (Baile Átha
Cliath: Connradh na Gaedhilge, 1903).

167. "Gleó na gCath," ACS, 25 April 1903.

if the book were understood properly it would be seen as a sermon against emigration from Ireland to urban failure and destitution.[168]

In response to this crisis, the league intensified its efforts, mounting one of its most extensive and sustained campaigns in the first decade of the century. Nor was the work merely propagandist. As the answers to the question set for a 1900 Oireachtas essay competition on the topic "Irish Emigration—Its Causes and Effects"[169] became increasingly obvious and insistent, the league sought immediate, concrete, and feasible solutions. For example, while leaguers and the league organ welcomed the Anti-Emigration Society on its foundation in 1903, one detects a hint of impatience in Pearse's comment that their plan for systematic research on the problem is a "businesslike program."[170] By no means were Gaelic activists afraid of what such research might reveal. For example, in 1905 the anonymous author of the "I bhFochair na nGaedheal" (With the Gaels) column in the *Weekly Freeman* took a hard and honest look at rural insanity as the result of isolation, loneliness, and lack of intellectual stimulation,[171] while in January 1916 *An Claidheamh Soluis* offered an unsentimental analysis of the entire question of rural depopulation shortly after British authorities prohibited emigration while the war was on. Taking advantage of this temporary and artificial suspension of the exodus, the league's paper addressed the intractable issues of celibacy and late marriage, the rising expectations of a more educated younger generation, and the stultifying isolation and loneliness of Irish rural life.[172]

Nor were the more intellectually adventurous of the Gaels afraid to face the potentially radical consequences of such an analysis. Thus in Máire Ní Chillín's 1902 story "Bainfheis Mherioca" (An American wedding), the author condemns the fatalism of her protagonist, who accepts his fiancée's emigration with the words "It can't be helped" (Níl neart air): "You're right, lad. . . . It cannot be helped as long as

168. See de Bhaldraithe, "An tAthair Peadar agus An Craoibhín: Conspóid faoi Phádraic Ó Conaire," in *Pádraic Ó Conaire: Clocha ar a Charn*, ed. de Bhaldraithe, 104.

169. See *Imtheachta an Oireachtais 1900*, 38–44, for the winning essay by "Domhan Thoir" (P. O'Sullivan).

170. "Gleó na gCath," *ACS*, 13 June 1903. The league in general was, however, strongly supportive of this organization. See "The Branches and the Anti-Emigration Society," *ACS*, 2 January 1904. It must, moreover, have been the publicity focused on emigration by this organization that caused the Gaelic movement, and in particular *ACS*, to devote such an extraordinary amount of attention to the problem throughout 1903.

171. "I bhFochair na nGaedheal," *WF*, 28 January 1905.

172. "An Saoghal Tuaithe" (Rural life), *ACS*, 8 January 1916. Less realistic at the time, but hardly surprising, was the nomination of the Gaelic League as the revitalizing savior of the Irish countryside.

the best land is closed up with nothing on it but the deer and the wild bird. It cannot be helped as long as the chains and the baseness of the slave are on our souls as they have been for 700 years. It cannot be helped, young men of Ireland, until our dear native land has its freedom again."[173] In the 1915 story "Giollaidheacht" (Servility) by "Maine" (Seán Mac Giollarnáth) in the short-lived nationalist weekly *Ná Bac Leis* (Don't bother with it), forty young Irishmen from Cavan decide to take a stand against rural hopelessness by driving cattle off a big farm they want for themselves, an act that leads to their arrest and inspires the following outburst from a previously pessimistic patriot: "That cattle raid is a better source of health for this country than the servility that has been killing us."[174] It was, in fact, through the antiemigration campaign that Pearse began to recognize the necessity for active and sustained state involvement in the eradication of poverty and the fostering of self-reliance, a recognition that would of course in time evolve into the more fully developed if idiosyncratic socialism that won the respect and trust of James Connolly. In his 1903 editorial "Imtheacht na nGaedheal" (The emigration of the Gaels), Pearse wrote: "But concerning the remedy of the Government. When one is as dependent as are we on the produce of the land, it would be proper to divide the land in such a way that every landholder in Ireland could derive a living from it. . . . But any person or group of people who undertake to rule a country is obliged to provide people a means of supporting themselves".[175]

Other leading Gaels also focused on equable land distribution as an antidote to emigration. For example, in a 1902 lecture to the London

173. "Ár dTeanga Féin/Bainfheis Mherioca" (Our own language/An American wedding), *UI*, 28 June 1902. The story commenced serialization on 14 June. "Is fíor dhuit, a bhuachaill. . . . Ní'l neart air chomh fad as bheidheas a roinnt is fearr don talmhuin dúnta suas gan dadaidh ann acht an fiadh agus an t-eun fian. Ní'l neart air chomh fad as bheidheas slabhraidhe is dubháilce an sclábhuidhe ar ar n-anamnaibh mar bhí le seacht gceud bliadhain. Ní'l neart air, a ógánaigh na h-Éireann go dtí go mbeidh saoirseacht ag ar dtír dhil dhúthchasaigh arís."

174. *Ná Bac Leis*, no. 1 (17 April 1915): 2–3. "Is fearr an t-ughdar sláinte do'n tír an táin bó soin ná an ghiollaidheacht atá ghár marbhú."

175. *ACS*, 11 April 1903. "Acht fá cheist leigheas an Riaghaltais. Duine ar bith atá i gcleitheamhnas toradh na talmhan chomh mór agus atámuid-ne badh cheart an talamh do roinnt i gcaoi is go bhféadfadh gach uile talamhaidhe i nÉirinn beatha a bhaint as. . . . Ach duine nó fuireann daoine a thiubhras fá thír a stiúradh, tá sé de riachtanas orra na daoine a chur ar shlighe chothuighthe." Of course, Pearse's political ideas took time to evolve, and he could in an another editorial two months later seem to see a potential solution in the moral suasion of Gaeltacht priests coupled with a "buy Irish" campaign to benefit the small native capitalist. See "Imtheacht na nGaedheal thar Lear" (The emigration of the Gaels overseas), editorial, *ACS*, 20 June 1903.

Branch, "Pádraic O'Conroy [i.e., Ó Conaire], in thoughtful and expressive Irish, boldly maintained the ideal of land nationalisation."[176]
"Conán Maol" prefaced his plan with a sharp criticism of the new class
of peasant proprietors on the make at the expense of the young, the
landless, and the urban workers: "It is said that when the farmers have
their own land the situation will change. I don't think so. Some of them
are little churls. They will grow arrogant." Astoundingly for one familiar with the countryside, "Conán" seems to have felt the farmers might
be persuaded to turn over some of their land voluntarily so that any
Irishman who so desired could have "grass for a cow . . . a nice clean,
snug house, and a good wage." Nevertheless, while he was apparently
unwilling to contemplate any kind of compulsory redistribution, his
essay ends with an implicit threat should the farmers persist in a selfishness that was contributing to the depopulation of the countryside: "It is
likely that if any farmer reads this piece, and if the shoe ["cap" in the
original] fits, he will feel contempt for me. First let him ponder well,
however, to see whether I am right. The townspeople are working for
Ireland singlehandedly. The farmer thinks he himself is Ireland, and
that the townspeople need only offer their money and their time for his
sake. It is time for him to wake up and hear the truth."[177] Some such
awareness of time running out may explain the otherwise miraculous
conversion to human decency of Manders, the villainous landlord in *Lá
an Chíosa* (Rent day), Labhras Ua Tuathail's 1903 drama of the land
war. Simultaneously impressed by his wife's moral suasion, his own
fear of being shot, and a new awareness of the woes of emigration,
Manders arranges for his tenants to buy their holdings for a fair price
over a reasonable time.[178] Still, whichever motive predominated in the

176. "London Notes," *ACS*, 27 December 1902.
177. "Cogarnaigh" (Whispers), *ACS*, 25 July 1903. "Deirtear nuair a bheidh a dtalamh
féin ag na feirmeoirí go mbeidh athrughadh sgéil againn. Ní dóich liom é. Bóidichíní is
eadh cuid aca soin. Beidh éirghe 'n-airde ortha." "Conán" wanted every Irish family to
have access to "féar bó . . . tigh deas, glan, cluthmhar, agus tuarastal maith," and chided
the property owners: "Is dócha má léigheann aon fheirmeoir an giota so, agus má oireann
an caipín dó go mbeidh seanabhlas aige orm. Machtnuigheadh sé go maith, ámh, ar dtúis,
féachaint an bhfuil an ceart agam. Tá muinntir na mbailtí móra ag obair ar son na hÉireann go leath-lámhach. Is dóich leis an bhfeirmeoir gurab é féin Éire, agus nach bhfuil ag
muinntir na mbailtí móra acht a gcuid airgid agus a gcuid aimsire do thabhairt ar a shon.
Is mithid dó dúiseacht agus an fhírinne do chlos."
178. *ACS*, 5 December 1903. Manders asks his agent: "Are you trying to get me shot
by the people?" (An bhfuil tú ag iarraidh na daoine mé 'chaitheamh le gunna?) and later
comments: "I've been thinking in my own mind for a while that it is time for the landlords of this country to make some attempt to put a stop to the people leaving the country in their thousands as they are." (Bhí mé 'smaoineadh in m'aigne le tamall go bhfuil sé

mix, this sort of conversion was a shaky foundation on which to erect a social or economic program.

Even shakier was the logic that led some activists to indict the emigrants themselves. In what now seems an extraordinary instance of blaming the victim, Pearse wrote in July 1903:

> We suggest that much might be done by directing well-aimed criticism—in certain cases even ridicule—against intending emigrants, both individually and collectively. There is a deal too much posing about many emigrants—too much mock pathetics. . . . Let us plainly tell the emigrant that he is a traitor to the Irish State, and, if he knew but all, a fool into the bargain. . . . We believe, moreover, that in a vast number of instances the emigrant, far from being a martyr, is a mere weakling and coward who emigrates mainly because he is too lazy or proud to do what he regards as "menial" work at home—on the far side of the Atlantic he is much less squeamish.[179]

This view was later repudiated by Pearse,[180] and it had always been rejected by many others, among them Seán Ua Ceallaigh, who wrote of anyone who understood the situation properly that "he would freely admit that the fault is not on the unfortunate exiles—they have no cure for or control over the constant draining."[181] Nevertheless the analysis

---

i n-am ag Tighearnaí Talmhan na tíre seo iarracht do dhéanamh le cosg do chur leis na daoinibh a bheith ag fágáil na tíre 'n-a míltibh, mar táid.) *Lá an Chíosa* was serialized in *ACS* from 24 October to 5 December 1903.

179. "Gleó na gCath," *ACS*, 18 July 1903. See also Pearse's comments the following week: "Turn the laugh against the thoughtless emigrant—put him in the same category with the *seoinín* and the Irish-speaker who teaches his children English of the 'They shave the sheeps twice in this counthry type'" ("The Anti-Emigration Campaign," *ACS*, 25 July 1903).

180. Only months later, in a discussion of the behavior of Irish-Americans home for a visit, Pearse wrote ("Gleó na gCath," *ACS*, 26 September 1903): "In their tones, and features, and general appearance, one might hear and see the joyful wish to impress their friends with a sense of their happiness. A desire both dangerous and natural. The whole question is one that must be treated with that tolerant tact and recognition of our common humanity which comes from deep and sympathetic natures, and which are a matter of right when dealing with the affairs of others."

181. "Dlúth-Mhuinnteardhas idir Fhíor-Ghaedhealaibh" (Firm friendship among true Gaels), *Banba* 2, no. 3 (17 March 1903): 147. "Adhmhochaidh sé go toilteannach nach ar na deóraidhibh mío-ádhmharacha atá an locht, —ná fuil leigheas ná neart aca ar an síorthrághadh." Others who objected to this charge included Seamus MacManus, who pointed out that many of the young left for America not from fear of hard or menial work, but rather from disgust with the sham bourgeois respectablity that caused such

did have some currency among revivalists active in the antiemigration campaign. For instance, Liverpool Gaelic Leaguers, who certainly should have known better, sponsored a 1903 feis competition, won by "Percy Beazley" (Piaras Béaslaí), for a speech on "'Shoneenism' or 'Emigration,'" the two topics apparently being seen as synonomous.[182] More significant, while Diarmuid Ó Laoghaire felt there was blame to spare for both farmers eager to convert arable land to tenantless grazing and workers lacking the frugal initiative of their ancestors, he placed primary responsibility for emigration on a failure of will in the rural and Irish-speaking communities, stressing that "the people thought it was a great pity to see a vigorous, strong man at home at all, but banished him abroad as soon as he was twenty years old. When the people grew accustomed to proceeding in that manner, there was no respect for anyone who stayed home."[183]

Creative writers took up these themes early, but their predominant perspective was simplistic and melodramatic. For the most part they did little but sketch dreadful monitory parables of the dangers facing the emigrant, particularly the Irish-speaking emigrant, in the ferment of the urban, usually American, melting pot. Thus in "Cailín Groidhe Gaedhealach" (A fine Irish girl) by "Pádraig na Léime" (Pádraig Ó Séaghdha), a mother counsels her daughter who has been bewitched by the "gold chains" (slabhraidhe buidhe) of returned Yanks: "How are things there with the rabble of every country in the world gathered there—

work to be stigmatized at home. He continued: "And if those of our people who have labour to sell . . . resolve to save themselves from indignities by flying to a country where slavishness, not being in the soul of the employer, is not expected of the employed, we upbraid them." See "The Likes of Us, and the Likes of Them," letter, *ACS*, 24 October 1903. See also the letter from Máire Bean Uí Cheallaigh published under the same title in *ACS*, 26 December 1903; and Micheál Ó Maoláin, "Imirce na nGaedheal," *ACS*, 3 October 1903. Ó Maoláin wrote: "Let no one think I'm in favor of emigration. Far from it. But it is not right for us to be criticizing people who are leaving Ireland, for the majority can't help it." (Ná bíodh éinne ag ceapadh go bhfuilim-se ar son imirce, is fada uaim é; acht níl sé ceart dúinn bheith ag cáineadh daoine atá ag imtheacht as Éirinn, mar níl aon neart ag a bhfurmhór air.)

182. "Liverpool Feis. Official Prize List," *ACS*, 5 December 1903.

183. "Imirce" (Emigration), in *Cogar Mogar* (Baile Átha Cliath: Muintir na Leabhar Gaedhilge, 1909), 23. All the essays in this collection had appeared previously in the *Munster News and Limerick and Clare Examiner*. "B'amhlaig a cheap na daoine gur mhór an truagh fear luath láidir fheiscint sa bhaile in aon chor, ach é ruagairt an loch amach chomh luath a's do bheadh sé fiche bliadhan de aois. Nuair a fuair na daoine tathaighe ar bheith ag gluaiseacht ar an gcuma san, ní bhíodh aon mheas ag aoinne fhanfadh sa bhaile." According to Séamus Ó Grianna, such an attitude was prevalent in the Rosses of Donegal at the turn of the century. See especially his *An Draoidín* (The midget) (Baile Átha Cliath: Oifig an tSoláthair, 1959).

most of them well prepared for the life facing them, and the poor Irishman trying to make a living among them all with no experience whatsoever of anything under the sky except for manual drudgery?"[184] The specific nature of the challenges facing those who left rural Ireland for the New World was spelled out again and again. To take just a few examples, in "Éadhmon de Búrc" by Máire Ní Chonaill, a well-off farmer's son emigrates, falls in with the wrong crowd, takes to drink, and ceases to practice his religion, though "without doubt he didn't lose his faith all at once, but when a person is amongst bad company, it is difficult to be good."[185] In "Sgeul Thomáis na Claise agus a Chuid Beurla" (The story of Tomás of Clash and his English) by "Mac Mic Mhairéid Ní Thaidhg," a young emigrant becomes rich in Boston and Los Angeles, but does so at the expense of his nationality, his language and, most important, his faith.[186]

184. *Banba* 2, no. 7 (June 1903): 242. "Cionnus tá an scéal ann indiu agus bruascar gach éin-tíre sa domhan bailighthe isteach ann—an chuid is mó aca leis gléasta go maith i gcomhair an tsaoghail tá rompa agus an t-Éireannach bocht ag iarraidh slighe beatha a dhéanamh amach eadartha so go léir gan taithighe ar bith aige ar aon nídhe fé'n spéir acht amháin an sclábhuigheacht."

185. "Éadhmon de Búrc (Scéal Nuadh-Dhéanta) [A modern story]," *Irish Rosary* 13, no. 11 (November 1909): 926. He later repents and urges his countrymen to stay home and build up their own land. "Gan dabht níor chaill sé a chuid chreidimh d'éan phreab, acht nuair tá duine imeasg droch-chómhluadar is deocair bheith go maith."

186. *FL*, 3–31 March 1900. In a letter to *ACS* from Seattle in September 1903, M. J. Henehan spoke of hard times for the Irish in America and provided three specific examples of Irish emigrants who had lost their faith. In his editorial response Pearse wrote: "Non-Catholic readers of 'An Claidheamh' will understand that we give insertion to our correspondent's remarks on the abandonment of their creed by so many Irish emigrants, merely because such abandonment almost certainly indicates a concurrent abandonment of Nationality. If an Englishman goes to Turkey and becomes a Mahometan it is reasonable to infer that he has doffed his English Nationality." ("The Legion of the Lost Ones," *ACS*, 12 September 1903). Whatever about his logic, Pearse's sensitivity to the feelings of non-Catholics would not have been universal amongst his colleagues. On the other hand, it is worth noting that in an essay in *The Republic*, a journal edited by the Protestant nationalist Bulmer Hobson, one "Domhnall Buidhe" also stresses the loss of their Catholicism as one of the greatest perils facing Irish emigrants. See "Na Deoruidhthe agus a dTír Dúthchais" (The exiles and their native land), *The Republic* 1, no. 4 (3 January 1907): 2. That this was seen as no mere convention of effective literary propaganda is evident from the comments of Father Michael Sheehan in an open letter to a Dublin meeting of the Anti-Emigration Society: "The few pennies they earn in America are of little good when they have lost their faith, corrupted their morals, given their sweat, and are afflicted with diseases and sickness as long as they live." (Is beag an mhaith na pighinneacha beaga a shaothruigheann siad i Meiriceá nuair atá a gcreideamh caillte aca agus nuair atá a mbéasa truaillighthe, agus a gcuid allus tugtha, agus galraí agus easláinte ag dul dóibh an fhad is mhairfeas siad.) See "Cosg a Chur leis an Imirce/Criunniughadh i mBaile Átha Cliath" (Stopping emigration/A meeting in Dublin), *ACS*, 8 August 1903.

Needless to say, apostasy does not usually bring such rewards, for success of any kind is rare in these stories. More typical is the fate of the young mother and her son in "Tadhg Ó Séaghdha" by "Carraig Eadhna." Destitute at Christmas in a big American city, they are assisted by the story's narrator, who goes on to hammer home the moral: "As I pondered the events of that night, it ran through my mind that perhaps there was an old couple in some cottage in Ireland expecting a little Christmas gift from Tadhg's mother and not knowing that the poor woman had far greater need of it herself. And also that it was not only Tadhg's mother that was in that situation but many other of the children of the Gael in this country, and it is to be feared Santa Claus won't come to them either."[187] Even more dire was the plight of the heroine of Máirtín Ó Ceallaigh's 1906 Oireachtas winner "Mustar an Bhodaigh" (The churl's arrogance), who emigrates to New York City, slaves in a stifling laundry, and dies in joyless poverty; meanwhile her fiancé, working in England to earn his passage money to join her, is mutilated in an industrial accident in a scene foreshadowing Ó Conaire's 1910 novel *Deoraidheacht*.[188] And downright horrific was Seán Ua Ceallaigh's "Éamonn Óg Ó Néill," a long Oireachtas winner from 1905 in which two young Irishwomen whom the heroine befriends on shipboard on her way to America are forced into prostitution by unscrupulous agents who meet them on their arrival. Máire Beag dies of shock on learning of their degradation, and the story ends with an antiemigration appeal.[189]

In this story, the uncle who brings Máire to Chicago is a Fenian exile who sees America as a land of freedom and opportunity for her and her politically active fiancé. But in later variants of this antiemigration genre, the Irish-American himself, particularly the "returned Yank" (*Poncán*), often becomes the experienced voice of antiemigration propaganda, preaching the gospel of the title character in *An Cneamhaire* (The knave), a 1902 novella by Agnes O'Farrelly: "America! My seven thousand curses on you, New World!"[190] In a gesture identical to that of "An

---

187. *Banba* 2, no. 4 (April 1903): 166–67. "Ag machtnamh dam ar chúrsaidhibh na hoidhche sin do rith sé am' aigneadh go mb'fhéidir go raibh sean-lánamha i mbothán éigint i nÉirinn agus go raibh a súil i n-áirde aca le síntiús beag Nodlag ó mháthair Thaidhg gan choinne aca gur mhó go mór gádh na mná boichte féin leis. Agus fós nár bh'í máthair Thaidhg amháin go raibh an scéal sin aici acht ag a lán eile de Chlainn na nGaedheal san tír seo agus is baoghalach ná geobhaidh Santa Claus chúca acht chomh beag."
188. *ACS*, 16–30 October 1909.
189. *ACS*, 2 March–13 April 1907.
190. (Baile Átha Cliath: An Cló-Chumann agus M. H. Gill agus a Mhac, n.d.), 9.

Cneamhaire," in Séamus Ó hArtagáin's "An Poncán Galánta Glic" (The
elegant clever Yank), a rich Irish-American buys a strong farm in Ireland to enable his niece to escape the poverty and unemployment he has
seen (although apparently not suffered!) in the United States, a land of
which he writes "this is not a place like the one you hear about in the
rumors sent home to you."[191] The male protagonist of Máire Ní
Cheallaigh's "Máire Ní Bhriain" literally brings this message home to
young potential emigrants by telling them of his own tragic experience
in the New World whose hardships claimed the life of his fiancée
Máire: "It's many a young man and young woman whose minds were
made up to go to America that Éamonn convinced to stay home when
he told them his own story and that of Máire Ní Bhriain—that what
she got from America was the length of her back of American soil as
her grave."[192] A similar message was delivered from the stage in one of
the most popular and widely performed Gaelic plays of the early Revival, Lorcán Ua Tuathail's 1907 An Deoraidhe: Dráma i n-aghaidh Imtheachda thar Sáile (The exile: a play against emigration). In this work it
is a returned aunt who makes available the resources for a young couple
to stay home, away from the real America of which they know nothing: "Don't be talking about poverty until you go to America. The
latest account published concerning poverty there says that there are
more poor people from Ireland in the poorhouses in America than from
every other country in the world put together!"[193]

191. ACS, 13 November 1909. "Ní háit é seo de réir na ráflaidhe a curtar chughaibh a
bhaile." See also O'Farrelly, An Cneamhaire, 36.
192. ACS, 21 March 1903. "Is iomdha fear óg agus cailín óg raibh a n-intinn déanta
suas aca dul do'n Oileán Úr, a chuir Éamonn 'na luighe orra fanacht ins an mbaile nuair
d'innsigheadh sé dóibh a sgéal féin agus sgéal Mháire Ní Bhriain, gurb' é a fuair sí do
bharr Mheriocá lán a droma do thalamh an Oileáin Úir bheith mar uaigh aici."
193. (Baile Átha Cliath: Connradh na Gaedhilge, 1906), 23. "Ná bí 'cainnt ar bhoc-
htanas, go dtéididh tú go Meiriocá. Deir an chunntas is deireannaighe atá puiblídhe i
dtaoibh bhochtanais ann go bhfuil níos mo daoine bochda as Éirinn ins na tighthibh déirce
i Meiriocá ná mar tá as uile thír eíle 'sa domhan, dá gcuirfidhe le chéile ar fad iad!" Over
the years both ACS and SF reported regularly on such poverty as well as publishing
accounts of chronic unemployment and the intimidating cost of living in the United
States. For example, Eoin Ó Cathail, writing from "Uisge-Glasda" in Michigan, drew on
his own experience of hardship to warn prospective emigrants against the harsh conditions and grinding hours of what jobs might be available to them in America, a land
whose climate also appalled him. See "Saoghal an Deoraidhthe" (The life of the exile),
ACS, 26 April 1902. See also "Depopulation Viewed from America," SF, 2 July 1910 (a
piece in which emigrants are called "our deserters" and their hardships their "punishment"); and "Litir Aniar" (A letter from the West), ACS, 21 March 1908. In addition, in
"Ó'n Domhan Thiar" (From the Western world), his weekly ACS column on American
affairs, Pádraig O hÉigeartaigh of Springfield, Massachusetts, often warned those con-

Positive images of Irish-Americans or depictions of Irish success in the United States are, as has been noted, rare. In "Sgéal Sheagháin na Claise" (The story of Seán of Clash) by "Mac Mic Mhairéid Ní Thaidhg," the protagonist becomes wealthy and is elected to Congress, accomplishments it is suggested he owes to his fidelity to the faith, homeland, and native language his apostate brother and so many other emigrants renounced.[194] But the only story I can think of in which the emigrants go to America for good reasons (to escape parental opposition to their marriage), achieve success with "a fine house and big pay" (teach breágh . . . pádh mór), and build a decent life for which they seem to have no regrets, is the 1905 "Séamus Crón" by "Finnéiges na Bóinne," otherwise a mere tale of rural rascality.[195] Similarly, I can only recall one story where a returned Irish-American becomes an active force for change in a Gaeltacht community instead of a mere pocketbook and mouthpiece for antiemigration propaganda. In Tadhg Ó Donnchadha's 1913 "Baile Abhfad Siar" (Wayback village), set in a post–Home Rule future, the Yank sets up a co-op to develop the local seaweed for medicine, thereby creating a prosperous Irish-speaking factory town to which its exiled youth come home.[196]

The vast majority of returned Americans in Gaelic literature have a lot more talk than initiative. At times their pomposity was treated satirically. For example, in "An Puncán agus an Ghealach Mhór" (The Yank and the big moon), a young woman after only a year or two in the States finds nothing right with Ireland, and when shown a lovely moon comments, "The moons you got here in Ireland, they ain't no good."[197] Again, in Seaghán Ó Cearbhaill's "An Corcaigheach a

---

templating emigration of just what challenges faced them on the other side. See, for example, "Ó'n Domhan Thiar," *ACS*, 1 August 1908. Australian problems could be even more exotic, as the title character of Micheál Ó Tiománaidhe's "Feidhlim Ó Neill (A Grádh agus a Chrádh) [His love and his misery]" discovered as he battled snakes, dingoes, and aboriginal peoples before returning home to raise an Irish-speaking family. See "Feidhlim Ó Néill," *Irish Rosary* 10, no. 2 (March 1907): 199–205. The story had commenced serialization the previous month.

194. *FL*, 24 March–7 April 1900. Incidentally, the author was himself an emigrant living in California, and provided an amusing account of efforts to preserve Irish folk culture in San Francisco and Oakland ("Talamh na Daraidhe") in "An Nós gur Bhuaidh Oscar Mac Oisín Cuid an Ghaisgidhigh ó Gholl Mac Móirne" (How Oscar the son of Oisín won the champion's portion from Goll Mac Móirne), *ACS*, 4–25 April 1903.

195. *UI*, 6 May–24 June 1905.

196. *Irish Weekly Independent*, 29 November 1913–3 January 1914. Needless to say, Gaels who were also advanced nationalists could be impressed by the political activism of some Irish Americans. See "Gaedhil Mheireacá" (The Irish of America), *Ná Bac Leis*, no. 11 (26 June 1915): 2.

197. *An Lóchrann* 1, no. 11 (November 1908): 2.

Chuaidh go Chicago" (The Corkman who went to Chicago), the returned blowhard who is so contemptuous of Ireland turns out to have
been a street-sweeper in America.[198] But more frequently, such boastful-
ness was seen as dangerous, as it was by the author of "I bhFochair na
nGaedheal" in 1904: "As has already been said, pride and bad conduct
send a big share of today's young people overseas. They're not over
there long until pretentiousness and vanity send them back entirely ru-
ined, without a word in their mouths but Yankee English. The ignorant Gael who comes home after spending a couple of years in America
is among the most dangerous enemies we have today. He is an enemy
of our faith, an enemy of our heritage and of our native land."[199]

Such pretensions were particularly threatening in the pages of the
"American letter," the bragging message home urging others to make
the passage. A letter of just this sort is, for example, at one point cursed
by the protagonist of An Deoraidhe;[200] implicit in her condemnation, as
in that of the anonymous author quoted above, is a perception of many
Irish-Americans, particularly "returned Yanks," as manipulatively dis-

198. *An Lóchrann* 3, no. 9 (October 1910): 4–5. He sees the error of his ways at story's
end.

199. *WF*, 30 July 1904. "Mar adubhradh cheana, taisbeach agus mí-iomchur a seolann
mór-chuid de dhaoinibh óga an lae 'ndiu thar sáile. Ní fada thall dóibh go dtreoruigheann
mór-chúis agus éirghe i n-áirde thar n-ais iad loithte glan gan focal 'na bpluic acht Béarla
na bPuncánach. An Gaedheal aineolach thagann abhaile tar éis cúpla bliadhan do chaitheamh i nAimeircé tá sé ar na náimhdibh is conntabhartaighe againn indiu. Námha d'ár
gcreideamh, namha d'ár nduthchas is d'ár nduthaigh is eadh é."

200. Ua Tuathail, *An Deoraidhe*, 23. The heroine of "Cailín Groidhe Gaedhealach," by
"Pádraig na Léime," issues a similar warning on her return to marriage and happiness in
Ireland. See *Banba* 2, no. 9 (December 1903): 279. Máire Ní Mhiach, the less fortunate
heroine of "An Cailín Gaedhealach i Sasana Nuadh" (The Gaelic girl in New England)
can only lament her decision to emigrate in a letter home shortly before her death. See
"Éire Óg i nEochaill," "An Cailín Gaedhealach i Sasana Nuadh," *ACS*, 9 May 1903.
Similarly, in "Duine de sna Míltibh" (One person of the thousands) by Micheál Ó Raghallaigh, who identified himself as living in New York, a dying emigrant admits in a final
message that he had lied in his previous letters home. See "Duine de sna Míltibh," *Banba*
1, no. 2 (17 March 1902)–1, no. 3 (May 1902). Gaelic activists felt that such honest
admissions of failure were all too rare, and criticism of the deceitful "American letter"
became a regular feature of antiemigration propaganda. For example, Pearse called such
letters "by far the most effective emigration agent that has ever come into play in Ireland"
("Gleó na gCath," *ACS*, 18 July 1903). "Pilib an Chleite" has one of the characters in his
dialogue "Seaghán agus Micheál ag Trácht ar Chúrsaíbh an tSaoghail" (Seán and Micheál
discussing current affairs) claim: "I would not believe a word from anyone in America
even if it were my own son." (Ní chreidfinn focal ó aonne i nAmericá dá mb'é mo mhac
féin é.) See *ACS*, 2 February 1901. See also the comments of An tAthair Peadar and
"Conán Maol" in "Cosg a Chur leis an Imirce," *ACS*, 8 August 1903; and those of
Diarmuid Ua Laoghaire, "Imirce," in *Cogar Mogar*, 23.

honest about their experiences abroad, as is, for example, "An Milli-
únaidhe" (The millionaire), the would-be bigamist of Peadar Mac
Fhionnlaoich's "Cuir Síoda ar Ghabhar is Beidh Sé 'na Ghabhar i
gCómhnuidhe" (Put silk on a goat and it will still be a goat).[201] Even
more insidious, the ultimate aim of much of this deceit is to lure others
to share their sorry exile in the New World. In such tales we can trace
the roots and early development of what we might label the "stage
American" or at least the "stage Poncán," a character whose principal
traits—ostentation, arrogance, and selfishness—were in place as early as
Séamus Ó Dubhghaill's description of the Poncán in a 1903 essay:
"There's another group, people who think a great deal of themselves,
but whom I don't have much respect for—the Puncáin—the Yankees.
They come over here to us after spending a couple of years over there,
they speak through their noses, and you would think with their hustle
that they owned all of America and that the sun rose out of America's
arse. Indeed it does not, and if it did I'm afraid the sun's face would be
none too clean."[202] Such a caricature was to dominate Gaelic depictions
of Irish-Americans for decades.[203]

201. In *Ciall na Sean-Ráidhte*, an dara chur amach (Baile Átha Cliath: Ó Cathail agus a
Bhuidhin, 1920), 24–25. The first edition of *Ciall* appeared in 1915; "Cuir Síoda" was
originally published in the "Seanchaidhe na Nodlag" (The Christmas storyteller), supplement to *ACS*, 20 December 1913.
202. "Óráid Shéamuis Uí Dhubhghaill sa Tuaith" (Séamus Ó Dubhghaill's speech in
the country), *ACS*, 25 July 1903. "Tá dream eile ann, daoine go bhfuil meas mór aca
ortha féin, ach ní mór é mo mheas-sa ortha—na puncánaigh—na Yankees. Buaileann siad
anall chughainn annso taréis bheith cúpla bliadhain thall, labharaid go caoch-shrónach,
agus badh dhóigh leat agus an fuadar a bhíonn fútha gur leo Ameiricá ar faid agus gur as
tóin Ameiricá éirigheann an ghrian—mhaise ní headh, agus dá mb'eadh tá eagla orm-sa
ná beadh aghaidh na gréine ro-ghlan." To be fair, he did acknowledge that he was acquainted with "educated and learned people from America" (daoine foghlamtha léigheannta ó Ameiricá), the proof of their civility and erudition being that they did not speak
"like a brood hen with a feather stuck in her beak" (ar nós mar a bheadh cearc guir agus
cleite sáithte 'n-a sróin). By the way, Ó Dubhghaill's crudeness drew sharp criticism in
Banba: "Some passages in his speech . . . are absolutely nauseating. He may think they
savour of humour: we assure him they do not. No self-respecting Irishman could listen to
such language at a public meeting" ("Untitled Notes," *Banba* 2, no. 8 [August 1903]:
266). These notes are in all likelihood the work of the journal's editor, Seán Ua Ceallaigh.
203. That Gaelic criticism was reserved almost exclusively for *Irish*-Americans is evident in the comments of "S. Mac G.," who, having duly noted "the returned emigrant's
flamboyant accounts of the Yankee's doings and abilities," argued: "It is a mistake to
judge Americans generally by the 'Dan the Dollar' types whom we meet and know. It is
equally wrong to suppose that all citizens of the States are braggart Uncle Sams" ("The
Importance of History in American Education," *ACS*, 30 October 1909). Father Henebry, whose own experience in Irish-America was not a happy one, was savage in his
dismissal of the cultural significance of the Irish diaspora: "The Irish there had contributed

In a letter written to be read aloud at a meeting of the Anti-Emigration Society in Dublin in 1903, An tAthair Peadar Ua Laoghaire blasted "stories coming from America" filled with "lying voices" (glórtha bréagacha) to entice the young from home, and continued: "It is a proverb that 'the hills far from us are green, but not grassy.' "[204] Readers of Gaelic fiction might well have objected that, judging from the rhapsodic descriptions of the Irish countryside and the consistent idealization of the proud character and communal life-style of the Irish-speaking peasantry in the work of Ua Laoghaire and his fellow ruralists, it would be hard to imagine that hills could be much greener. But there were dissenting voices. Taking the forensic offensive as usual, Father O'Reilly contrasted the situation of the language learner traveling in France or Spain with that of the student in the Gaeltacht:

> You will not have to be going to the remote and barbarous places, seeking out the poor and the illiterate. . . . You will not find the people *gauche*, and awkward. . . . They will not be going in for keeping a stupid silence, and waiting for you to do

nothing to civilisation because they were ashamed of the things they had brought over with them from Ireland. . . . They brought with them no history or tradition" ("What the Irish Have Lost/Striking Lecture by Doctor Henebry," *SF*, 5 March 1910). In Máire Ní Chillín's bilingual propaganda play *Mairghréad*, a pompous second-generation Irish-American wants to marry the play's young heroine and take her home to New York, to "the life yonder, the throbbing, full, pulsating life." When the parish priest objects on the grounds "You are an—American" and the man corrects him with "Irish-American, if you please," he is taken aback by the priest's scriptural response: "No one at all can serve two masters" (Ní féidir le neach ar bith seirbhís do dhéanadh do dhá thighearna). The young woman chooses, correctly, to stay in Ireland as a teacher in a Conamara school. See Máire Ní Chillín, *Mairghréad: A Topical Play for National Teachers in Two Scenes*, *SF*, 17 February–30 March 1912. For a discussion of this caricature as a dominant element in the work of a later Gaelic author, Séamus Ó Grianna, see Philip O'Leary, "Castles of Gold: America and Americans in the Fiction of Séamus Ó Grianna," *Éire/Ireland* 21, no. 2 (Summer 1986): 70–84. Indeed, it seems that O'Farrelly's antiemigration tale *An Cneamhaire* could have served as a model for some elements of Ó Grianna's best-known novel, the 1924 *Caisleáin Óir* (*Castles of Gold*). On the other hand, in his first novel Ó Grianna wrote of the American Irish: "These are the most loyal Gaels who ever lived. These are the children and the grandchildren of the people who were driven from their native land by hunger and by evil laws, and they never forgot Ireland." ('Siad seo na Gaedhil is dílse a tháinig ar an tsaoghal ariamh. 'Siad seo clann agus uaidh na ndaoine a ruaigeadh as a dtír dhúthchais le n-ocras agus le droch-dhlighthibh, agus ní thearn siad dearmad ariamh de Éirinn.) See Ó Grianna, *Castar na Daoine ar a Chéile 'sní Castar na Cnuic nó na Sléibhte* (People meet, but the hills and the mountains do not), *Irish Weekly and Ulster Examiner*, 4 September 1915.

204. See "Cosg a Chur leis an Imirce," *ACS*, 8 August 1903. "Is sean-fhocal é 'gur glas iad na cnuic i bhfad uainn, ach ní féarmhar.'"

the speaking, watching you the while with that imbecile look of suspicious curiosity. . . . You will not be obliged to put up in filthy hovels, and to lie down to sleep in still filthier beds. You will never have to task your brain for some plan to get people talking, nor for a subject which might, perhaps, suit their level and solicit their interest.[205]

As has been noted, even Pearse could write that "some of the meanest human beings we have ever met have been Irish speakers." Nor were the ruralists themselves entirely blind to the failings of Irish-speaking country folk, and if few of them were willing to create genuinely mean characters, all were close enough to country life to know of its occasional pettiness and worse. Thus "Gruagach an Tobair," whom Pearse called "an Irish realist"[206] and in whose work he detected a "slightly cynical strain,"[207] refers to past faction fights and the abduction of brides,[208] and present cardsharping,[209] drunkenness,[210] and lack of hygiene.[211] In "Conán Maol's" "Míol Mara do Leag Cíos" (A whale that lowered the rent) and "Bean an Leasa" (The woman of the fairy fort), there is some quite explicit violence.[212] Actual murder is committed in Seán Ó Dubhdha's "Má's Feall Fillfidh" (If it's treachery, it will return).[213] In *Muinntear na Tuatha*, Séamus Ó Dubhghaill introduces an authoritarian country priest whose edict against dancing contributes to the em-

205. *Native Speaker*, 71. See also O'Reilly, "The Native Speaker," *SF*, 28 January 1911. In the *SF* piece, O'Reilly charges the native speaker with linguistic apostasy and calls him "the immediate, indefatigable, and deadly destroyer of the language."

206. "An Irish Realist," review of *Annála na Tuatha*, part 2, by "Gruagach an Tobair," *ACS*, 15 December 1906.

207. "Recent Booklets," review of *Annála na Tuatha*, part 1, by "Gruagach an Tobair," *ACS*, 7 October 1905.

208. "Gruagach an Tobair," "An Spioraid," in *Annála na Tuatha*, part 3, pp. 39, 41. Séamus Mac an Bháird's *Troid Bhaile an Droichid* (The fight at Bridgetown) (Baile Átha Cliath: Connradh na Gaedhilge, 1907) is entirely concerned with faction fighting, while Mac Fhionnlaoich's playlet *Dochtúireacht Nuadh* (New doctoring) deals comically with a fight between two neighbors armed with blackthorn sticks. See *Dochtúireacht Nuadh* in *Miondrámanna* (Little plays) (Baile Átha Cliath: Connradh na Gaedhilge, 1902), 10–14. A factional vendetta is also threatened by the family of a woman whose arranged marriage has been foiled by the elopement of her would-be husband with his true love in Ó Conaire's *An Droighneán Donn*, a play set in the first years of the nineteenth century.

209. "Gruagach an Tobair," "Mar Buaileadh an Bob ar an nGruagach," in *Annála na Tuatha*, part 1, 016 [*sic*].

210. "An Spioraid," in *Annála na Tuatha*, part 3, pp. 51–60.

211. "An Spioraid," in *Annála na Tuatha*, part 3, pp. 49–50.

212. "Conán Maol," "Míol Mara do Leag Cíos," in *An Buaiceas*, 34–35; "Bean an Leasa" (The woman of the fairy fort), in *An Buaiceas*, 21–22.

213. *WF*, 7 December 1912. The story won a prize at the 1912 Oireachtas.

igration problem in his parish.[214] Along with the attempted bigamy noted above, Peadar Mac Fhionnlaoich depicts drunkeness and wife-beating,[215] a gang assault on a man to prevent his making a match,[216] and anticommunal niggardliness.[217] Greed is linked with dishonesty in Tomás Ó Ceallaigh's 1903 play *Airgead na Croise Caoile*, in which the miserly protagonist is outwitted by his neighbors.[218] A father's love of money threatens to destroy a family in Tomás Ó hAodha's 1909 play *An Scrabhadóir* (The miser), as he attempts, against the wishes of his wife, to arrange a loveless but profitable marriage between his daughter and an older man.[219] In "An Seabhac's" *An Baile Seo 'Gainne* (Our townland), a wife, driven past endurance by her ne'er-do-well husband, leaves him to go to America.[220] Indeed, even An tAthair Peadar could on occasion turn his sardonic eye on his beloved native speakers. There is no shortage of gossip, some of it quite malicious, in *Séadna* (69, 81–82, 111–12, 216), and his peasants are dishonestly greedy in their horse trading (130–32, 186–87) and potentially violent in their dealings with a neighbor they believe has defrauded them (121–22).[221] Yet never in the country stories do these brief references to personal failings evolve into a more profound analysis of the human condition in a rural setting. Whenever genuine conflict or tragedy threatens, the ruralists fall back, as does An tAthair Peadar in *Séadna*, on various folkloric dei ex machina to rescue a happy or at least humorous ending.

214. *Muinntear na Tuatha*, 88–89.

215. "Cuir Síoda ar Ghabhar is Beidh Sé 'na Ghabhar i gCómhnuidhe," in *Ciall*, 16–17.

216. "An Rud is Measa Leat ná Do Bhás b'Fhéidir gurab é Lár Do Leasa é" (Perhaps the thing you think worse than death is the very best thing for you), in *Ciall*, 41–42.

217. "Leig 'un an Bhodaigh Mé ach ná Leig an Bodach 'mo Chomhair" (Let me at the churl, but don't let him near me), in *Ciall*, 10–11.

218. *Airgead na Croise Caoile / The Money of the Slender Cross* (Dublin: M. H. Gill and Son, 1903).

219. (Baile Átha Cliath: Clódhanna Teo., 1909). At one point (37), the daughter suggests to the man she loves that they emigrate, but he says he could never leave Ireland. There is also cruelty to animals in this play (26).

220. "An Seabhac," "Callshaoth" (Strife), in *An Baile Seo 'Gainne*, 136–52.

221. Of his characters in *Séadna*, Ua Laoghaire wrote to Mac Néill in 1897 (12 February 1897, quoted in Mac Mathúna, "Réamhrádh" to *Séadna*, xxi):

There isn't one of the characters in the story (dramatis personae), man or woman, who doesn't have his or her own temperament or mind. There is worldly good and bad in every one of them, and there is spiritual good and bad, according to his or her resources, in every one of them as well.

(Níl aon duine de mhuintir an sgéil (*dramatis personae*), idir fhear agus bean, ná fuil a mheon agus a aigneadh féin, fé leith aige. Tá olc agus maith saoghalta i ngach duine dhíobh, agus tá olc agus maith spioradálta, do réir a acfainn féin, i ngach duine acu leis.)

If an obsession with folk material stood between the ruralists and an authentic exploration of Gaeltacht life at the turn of the century, their adherence to folk narrative formulae had an even more stultifying effect on the aesthetic potential of their work. As Máirín Nic Eoin has pointed out in *An Litríocht Réigiúnach*: "The worst thing about this link between folklore and literature is not that so much use was made of folkloric material but that the folkloric style so greatly influenced the style of modern literature in Irish" (36).[222] All of the narrative flaws that Nic Eoin traces in her study of later regional literature in Irish had taken root and flourished in the prose of the rural local colorists of our period: monotony of voice, redundancy of introductory detail,[223] episodic and disjointed structure, frequent appeals to improbable or supernatural solutions to plot difficulties, anticlimactic conclusions, and one-dimensional characterization. Pearse may have raised the standard in "Íosagán," but as he read the work of many of his contemporaries he must have realized that the narrative revolution in Gaelic prose fiction would be a lengthy and frustrating campaign.

While all too many writers seem to have done all too little thinking about the potentials and problems of the folk patterns and themes that inspired their work, some nevertheless did explore new approaches to traditional material. Such explorations could follow startlingly different routes. Nor were Pearse and Ó Conaire the sole pioneers in this venture. "An Seabhac" wrote of Gaeltacht life from the inside with a keen sense of irony, a detached if sympathetic objectivity, and a genuinely personal style, and Father Michael Sheehan experimented with the possibility of direct collaboration with the *seanchaí* to generate impeccably traditional assimilations of nontraditional material.

Sheehan's approach was at once both predictably mechanical and quirkily idiosyncratic. A linguist who collected folklore to illustrate the riches of Waterford Irish, Sheehan began his collaborations as early as

222. "An rud is measa faoin nasc seo idir an béaloideas agus an litríocht . . . ná ní hé gur baineadh an oiread sin usáide as ábhar an bhéaloidis ach go ndeachaigh stíl an bhéaloidis i bhfeidhm go mór ar stíl na nualitríochta Gaeilge."

223. It was, of course, in part for its omission of just such introductory detail, for its "explosive" opening, that Henebry attacked Pearse's "Íosagán." Actually, "Conán Maol" had already made use of such an opening in "Míol Mara do Leag Cíos" as early as 1898, an innovation for which Pearse praised him in words prophetically applicable to his own later "Íosagán" ("Reviews," *ACS*, 14 March 1903): "It is quite true that in point of form he breaks boldly away from Irish traditions. He does not commence with the genealogy of his hero, but plunges at once *in media res*. . . . That unquestionably is the modern short story style. . . . Genealogies are out of fashion, and one cannot always stick to the folk formula, 'Bhí fear ann fad ó agus is fad ó a bhí.'" [There was a man long ago and long ago it was].

1907 in *Cnó Coilleadh Craobhaighe: The Irish of the People* (A nut of the branching hazel wood). Conventionally identifying his sources for the book's tales, he writes of his conversational sketches (greasa cómhráidh): "Under this heading are included a number of pieces which were composed by native speakers under the direction of Pádraig Ó Cadhla or myself. We suggested the several themes and their treatment and exercised a censorship over the Irish with a view to excluding Anglicised turns of expression."[224]

Apparently satisfied with the result, he went on to apply his method on a grander scale in *Arthrach an Óir* (The golden vessel) in 1910: "Pádraig Ó Doghair from Ring gave me these stories. I helped him to compose them, but if I did, it's his speech and not mine that is in them. When we first composed them, we left them unwritten for a year so that there would not be any trace of my speech in them."[225] However, while all three stories in the book have ostensibly contemporary settings and while the second does involve the abuses of landlordism and agency, they are folk tales pure and simple, with their plodding introductions, conventional narrative patterns, supernatural interventions, and formulaic *cora cainte*.

Sheehan seems to have turned to some variant of this technique again in 1912 in the conventional wonder tale *Gile na mBláth* (The brightness of the flowers), although he was considerably less specific about the process that created this book: "I here thank Micheál Ó Cinnfhaolaidh

224. (Dublin: M. H. Gill and Son, 1907), 111. Such instructional dialogues in Gaeltacht settings were a regular feature in *FL* and *ACS* in the first decade of this century. The most famous was undoubtedly Séamus Ó Dubhghaill's "Beirt Fhear ó'n dTuaith" (Two men from the country), the series from which he took his pen name; it commenced serialization in *ACS* on 6 January 1900. In *Cnuasacht Trágha: From the Foreshore* (Dublin: M. H. Gill and Son, 1908), a collection that also includes both tales and dialogues, Sheehan identifies his sources (89), but says nothing of his own collaboration with them.

225. "Brollach" (Preface) to *Árthrach an Óir* (Dublin: M. H. Gill and Son, 1910), n.p. "Pádraig Ó Doghair ón Rinn tug dam na sceulta so. . . . Tugas-sa féin congnamh dhó ag á gceapadh, acht má tugas féin ní hí mo chaint-se acht a chainnt féin atá ionnta. Nuair do cheapamar ar dtús iad, do fhágamar gan scríobhadh iad go cionn bliadhna ionnus ná beadh aon rian de mo chuid-se cainnte orra." See also the discussion of his methods in the review of *Árthrach an Óir* by "Guaire":

Dr. Sheehan has in this book discovered a new way of using the native Irish speaker, that is, getting him to compose *original* stories. The reciter of *Sceulta Fiannaidheachta* [Fenian tales] was a treasure in himself, and a literary wonder, and his language was a well of Irish, but, as we are only too often told, *Sceulta Fiannaidheachta* won't do for the twentieth century—you must be up-to-date. Dr. Sheehan . . . simply won't have any but Irish Irish, and so when he wants an original Irish story he goes to Ring, helps a *sceulaidhe* there to construct a plot and then sits down and reports the *sceulaidhe* faithfully. ("A Suitable Text Book," *ACS*, 10 December 1910).

and Nóra Ní Chinnéide, who helped me to compose this tale. They put a great deal of effort into it from the very beginning."[226] He was even vaguer three years later concerning *Gabha na Coille* (The smith of the forest), a tale set on the Continent: "Although the mechanism of this story has been taken from a type of legend freely current in Alsace in olden days, the details as even a passing glance may reveal are from nearer home, and the language in sentence, phrase, and word, is an exact selection of the Irish of Ring."[227] At any rate, while Sheehan was critical of "those who would restrict literary effort in modern Irish to the expansion of native folklore," and acknowledged that "while preferring the simple narrative style, I should be slow to deny our language the freedom of choice of which other languages avail with such manifest advantage,"[228] his own creative work left Irish prose fiction just about where he found it. For this reason it is difficult to understand, much less accept, Peadar Ua Laoghaire's sharply negative assessment of his creative originality: "In his later books, he has, in an ever increasing degree, arranged and shaped the thought as well as the language, so that it is no longer the people's thought that he expresses in his stories but his own thought."[229]

Unlike Ua Laoghaire (in his role as critic rather than creative writer), Pádraig Ó Siochfhradha saw no reason why original insight or a developed personal prose style should of necessity distort a native speaker's depiction of his community. For "An Seabhac," folklore and folk speech were essential raw materials to be reshaped by the creative artist out of his own experience of Gaeltacht life. As early as 1910, he blasted the sterile obsession with mere *cainnt na ndaoine*: "We are destroyed with 'cainnt na ndaoine!' Bad Irish is bad Irish, and the people in the Decies and in Ballingeary and in Spiddal and in Dingle speak it as truly as do the people in Dublin. Good Irish is good Irish, and no one at all has it now except for those who know more than 'the people.'"[230] His

226. Preface to *Gile na mBláth*, viii. "Gabhaim buidheachas annso le Micheál Ó Cinnfhaolaidh agus le Nóra Ní Chinnéide tug congnamh dam ag ceapadh an scéil seo. Is iomdha anga do chuireadar ann ón uair do cuireadh tosach air."

227. Introduction to *Gabha na Coille* (Dublin: M. H. Gill and Son, 1915), v.

228. Introduction to *Gabha na Coille*, v.

229. "An tAthair Peadar and Dr. Sheehan," *The Leader*, 28 November 1912. One might, of course, wonder what was inherently wrong with expressing one's own thought, just as one might wonder whether An tAthair Peadar was unaware of just how distinctly personal his own folk-inspired work was. For a more positive assessment of Sheehan's work, with predictable emphasis on its linguistic importance, see the review of *Gile na mBláth* by "An Fear Mór" (Séamus Ó hEochaidh), Sheehan's colleague at Coláiste na Rinne, in *ACS*, 26 October 1912.

230. "An Seabhac," review of *An t-Éinín Órdha agus Sgéalta Eile*, ed. Seosamh Laoide,

views on appropriate subject matter and theme were equally forceful and independent, and he felt that the pseudotraditionalism of many writers in this regard had led them to patronize Gaeltacht folk by failing to challenge either their intellect or imagination. In his story "Moladh Beirte na Faille Móire" (The arbitration of Faill Mhór), his narrator describes fireside conversations in West Kerry: "It's many a subject we discuss. We are no more often discussing lobster pots and nets and potato ridges and the price of pigs, than discussing the Battle of Ventry or Táin Bó Cúalinge or Fionn Mac Cumhaill or John Redmond or Home Rule or Doomsday or some other great things of that sort."[231] For "An Seabhac" and his projected audience, the literary dungheap that offended Pearse's sensibilities had already been left behind.

As with the other ruralists, this projected audience is the key to understanding "An Seabhac," as he makes clear in his little blessing at the beginning of *An Baile Seo 'Gainne*: "A blessing with you, little book, and may the greatest joy that comes to you be to be read at the fireside by Old Diarmaid to Donncha Pheig and Liam na Giúise and to the Gad and to the rest of us."[232] Although at first glance "An Seabhac's" ambition here may seem identical with that of An tAthair Peadar or Séamus Ó Dubhghaill, the difference lies in the unassuming first-person-plural ending of that final prepositional pronoun in the original Irish. However they might reject the suggestion, many ruralists, including both Ua Laoghaire and Ó Dubhghaill, were, as writers with an ideological agenda, dealing with Gaeltacht life from the outside, and thus their manipulation of folk motifs and narrative patterns can seem forced and

---

ACS, 26 November 1910. "Táimíd marbh ag 'cainnt na ndaoine!' Droch-Ghaedhilg iseadh droch-Ghaedhilg agus tá sí ag na daoinibh i nDéisibh Mumhan agus i mBeul Átha an Ghaorthaidh agus insa Spidéal agus i nDaingean Uí Chúise chomh crónta a's mar atá ag na daoinibh i mBaile Átha Cliath. . . . Deagh-Ghaedhilg iseadh deagh-Ghaedhilg agus níl sí ag neach ar bith anois acht ag duine éigin go bhfuil níos mó eolais aige ná mar atá ag 'na daoine.'"

231. "An Seabhac," "Moladh Beirte na Faille Móire," *An Baile Seo 'Gainne*, 109. "Is iomaí scéal a bhíonn dá shuathadh againn. Ní minicí sinn ag trácht ar photaíbh gliomach agus líonta agus iomairí prátaí, agus an praghas a bhíonn ar mhucaibh, ná ag trácht ar Chath Fionntrá, nó Táin Bó Cúailnge, nó Fionn Mac Cumhaill no Seán Réamoinn, no Hóm Rúil, nó lá Philib an Chleite, nó rudaí móra iontacha éigin dá leithéidí." Of course, as we have seen, "An Seabhac" was a strict traditionalist with regard to literary form and felt there should be definite limits to the introduction of exotic subject matter and theme into Gaelic writing. All of the topics discussed around the fire here are, however erudite or timely, of Irish interest.

232. "An Seabhac," *An Baile Seo 'Gainne*, n.p. "Beannacht leat, a leabhráin, agus gurb é aoibhneas is mó bhéarfaidh ort bheith dod léamh ag Sean-Dhiarmaid cois tine do Dhonncha Pheig agus do Liam na Giúise agus don Ghad agus don chuid eile againn."

artificial.[233] Equally striking are the contrasting perpectives of "An Seabhac" and his fellow Corca Dhuibhne native "Seán Óg" Ó Caomhánaigh, who in late 1914 published in *An Claidheamh Soluis* a series
of stories under the general title "Daoine Greannmhara Greanmhara ar
M'Aitheantas sa Ghaedhealacht" (Witty, comical people I've known in
the Gaeltacht). In the initial installment of this series "Seán Óg" stated
that while he was writing factually from his own experience as a member of the Gaeltacht community, his ideal audience would consist of
sympathetic outsiders whom he could disabuse of their stage-Irish mis-
conceptions of rural life.[234] Ó Siochfhradha, on the other hand, wrote at
his best simultaneously from and for his own community. For this reason his recourse to those folk models with which both he and his neighbors were most familiar was a natural, indeed inevitable development.[235]
In fact, many of his plots, including several that appear with little apparent revision in *An Baile Seo 'Gainne*, were derived directly from
stories he heard at local *feiseanna*.[236]

Yet even when working with such folk material, "An Seabhac," unlike most of the rural local colorists, rarely lost the artist's command of
his materials and methods. Moreover he could, as Pádraig Ó Fiannachta
has illustrated, wring mature laughter and insight from the most stereotypical folktale situations: "It's not the tale per se, nor the plot, that is
praiseworthy, but the polish put on it by the incisiveness and the concision of the speech, the irony and the exaggeration of the style, and the

---

233. Obviously "An Seabhac" was well aware that the vast majority of his *readers*
would not be native speakers from Corca Dhuibhne, but they remained his ideal (and
literal) *audience*. In this context it is worth mentioning that Pádraic Ó Conaire singled out
the first installment of Ó Siochfhradha's *Jimín Mháire Thaidhg* in a review of *An Lóchrann*
in which he urged those financially able to send extra copies to the Gaeltacht: "Perhaps
there would be twenty people listening to someone reading this paper, especially now
with winter coming and the long nights upon us." (B'fhéidir go mbeadh fiche duine ag
éisteacht le duine ag léigheadh an pháipéir seo, mór-mhór anois ó tá an geimhreadh ag
teacht agus na h-oidhcheannta fada buailte linn.) See "An Lóchrann," in *Iriseoireacht Uí
Chonaire*, 77. This essay originally appeared in the *Freeman's Journal* for 18 October 1919.

234. *ACS*, 14 September 1914. Interestingly, "Seán Óg" praised the linguistic richness
of "An Seabhac's" *An Baile Seo 'Gainne*, but felt the stories in it, with the exception of
"Méinín," lacked substance. See Ó Caomhánaigh, "Dhá Leabhar Nuadha: Léirmheas"
(Two new books: A review), *SF*, 25 October 1913.

235. "An Seabhac" was, of course, a major figure in the collection and study of Irish
folklore for decades. He was, for example, editor of *An Lóchrann*, an expert on West
Kerry place-names as author of *Tríocha-Chéad Chorca Dhuibhne* (The baronies of Corca
Dhuibhne), a founding member of the Irish Folklore Commission, and a prolific contributor to its journal, *Béaloideas*. For a brief survey of some of his activities in these areas, see
the special commemorative issue of *Feasta* dedicated to him (vol. 36, no. 3, March 1983).

236. See Risteárd Ó Glaisne, *Ceannródaithe*, 206. Four such folktales that appeared in the
first edition of *An Baile Seo 'Gainne* in 1913 were, however, omitted from the various
later editions.

zest and the sport of the presentation."[237] When one adds the distinct, forceful, and consistent narrative voice of the best of the stories, it is hardly surprising that a contemporary critic could be both lavish in his praise and unrealistic in his expectations of "An Seabhac." Struck by the wit and willingness to confront, if only indirectly through satire, such rural social problems as loneliness, land greed that set children against parents, venal matchmaking, and loveless marriage, Tadhg Ó Ceallaigh sought more: "He is unerring in selecting his material, but he is wrong in refusing to play on more than one chord of human sympathies. To refuse ever to be serious is to forfeit greatness."[238] Had Ó Ceallaigh kept in mind that one chord was one more than most of Ó Siochfhradha's rural contemporaries managed to strike well, he might perhaps have been even more thankful for the insight and amusement "An Seabhac" provided.

Unfortunately, neither genuine seriousness nor satire was to play much of a role in Gaelic fiction after the creative energy of the early Revival burned itself out. What Aisling Ní Dhonnchadha has identified as the central literary question of the Revival—"Was the storytelling tradition to be a source of wealth for the writer or was it to be a convenient, ready-made mold that he could simply imitate?"—was answered by the triumph of those she labels "the conservers" (na caomhnóirí) over "the creators" (na cumadóirí).[239] For mixed motives of expediency and ideology, the folk-narrative standards against which Pearse had re-

---

237. "Scéalta an tSeabhaic" (The stories of "An Seabhac") in *Ár Scéalaíocht* (Our storytelling), *Léachtaí Cholm Cille* 14 (1983): 115. "Ní hé an scéal, mar scéal, nó plota an scéil atá le moladh . . . ach an mhaise a chuirtear air le gearradh agus le cóngar sa chaint, le híoróin agus áibhéil an stíl, agus le spleodar agus spórt sa chur i láthair." Alan Titley seems less taken with the humor of "An Seabhac," finding it superficially amusing rather than authentically comic. See Titley, *An tÚrscéal*, 112–13. See also Ní Dhonnchadha, *An Gearrscéal*, 128–38.

238. "A New Book," review of *An Baile Seo 'Gainne* by "An Seabhac," *ACS*, 2 August 1913. Unfortunately in his subsequent creative work, beginning as early as *Seáinín nó Eachtra Mic Mírialta* (Seáinín, or the adventure of the Unruly Son) (1915) and the better known *Jimín Mháire Thaidhg* (1919), "An Seabhac" seems to have fallen victim to Pádraic Ó Conaire's dread "tyranny of the schoolchild," substituting an innocuous anecdotal good humor for the satiric bite of the finest stories in *An Baile Seo 'Gainne*. It is, perhaps, significant that Ó Conaire's comments on *Jimín* mentioned above focused narrowly on "the plausibility and verisimilitude of the speech in it" (crot agus cosamhlacht na fírinne ar an gcanamhaint atá ann). See "An Lóchrann" in *Iriseoireacht Uí Chonaire*, 77.

239. *An Gearrscéal*, 9. "An raibh an traidisiún seanchais ina fhoinse saibhris aige [an scríbhneoir] nó an raibh sé ina mhúnla áisiúil réamhdhéanta ar a ndéanfadh sé lomaithris?" Indeed, Alan Titley (*An tÚrscéal*, 290) has gone so far as to claim that "this link between *caint na ndaoine*, folklore and the traditional life" was "the greatest curse on literature in Irish." (Is é an nasc seo idir caint na ndaoine, an béaloideas agus an seansaol an mhallacht is mó a bhí ar litríocht na Gaeilge.)

volted were to become, particularly for Gaeltacht writing, the orthodox
criteria of artistic achievement in an authentically native mode, the basis
of what Séamus Ó Grianna was in 1921 to call "*art* Gaedhealach."[240]
And a generation of Gaelic writers, of whom Ó Grianna himself was
the most prolific, were to rally to this standard, many of them to find
their ultimate recognition as footnotes to Myles na gCopaleen's *An Béal
Bocht*. Appropriately, we may leave the final critical judgment on the
folk-inspired efforts of the early revivalists to one of their own, a young
country girl in a sketch by An tAthair Tomás Ó Ceallaigh: "We will
accept the nonsense for the excellence of the Irish."[241]

240. ("Máire"), "*Art* na hAimsire Seo" (The art of this time), *Misneach*, 26 February
1921.
241. ("Íbh Máine"), "Céilidhe" (An evening visit), *ACS*, 5 January 1907. "Glacfamuid
leis an seafóid ar fheabhas na Gaedhilge." In a letter to *UI* ("All Ireland," 4 November
1905), Ó Ceallaigh was critical of the overemphasis on folklore or "the rehash of the
wonder tales" at the expense of Irish news and current affairs in Irish newspapers, writing: "The point has now been reached in the movement where thousands of our young
students are anxious to get out of the leading strings of these old wives' tales and to attack
serious, wholesome and interesting literature worthy of our education and of our age."

3

"The Dead Generations"
Irish History and Historical Fictions

What the battleaxe of the Dane, the sword of the Norman, the wile of the Saxon were unable to perform, we have accomplished ourselves. We have at last broken the continuity of Irish life, and just at the moment when the Celtic race is presumably about to largely recover possession of its own country, it finds itself deprived and stript of its Celtic characteristics, cut off from the past, yet scarcely in touch with the present. It has lost since the beginning of this century almost all that connected it with the era of Cuchullain and of Ossian, that connected it with the Christianisers of Europe, that connected it with Brian Boru and the heroes of Clontarf, with the O'Neills and O'Donnells, with Rory O'More, with the Wild Geese, and even to some extent with the men of '98.[1]

Thus Douglas Hyde lamented what he saw as nineteenth-century Ireland's simultaneous betrayal of her language and her history in

---

1. In *1000 Years of Irish Prose: The Literary Revival*, ed. Mercier and Greene, 84.

his seminal lecture "The Necessity for De-Anglicising Ireland." A central impulse in the program of the Gaelic movement he was soon to lead would be atonement for that betrayal by reestablishing those links with the dead generations, by restoring to Ireland her past.

Hyde's pessimism concerning Irish ignorance of the nation's history was widely shared among his fellow Gaelic intellectuals. In 1898 Gaelic League co-founder Eoin Mac Néill titled a *Fáinne an Lae* editorial "Ainbhios" (Ignorance), writing:

> The most knowledgeable authors say that there is no better way to keep the spirit of nationality alive in any race than by constantly recounting to them the deeds of their ancestors, and for them to have a good knowledge of the history of their native land. It's not like that with the people of Ireland. Irish history is not taught to them during their youth. They read accounts of the Armada and of the Battle of Waterloo, but they don't hear a word about the Battle of the Yellow Ford of about the deeds of King Dáithí. Some of them think that such things never happened at all. It's part of our ignorance.[2]

In 1901 "Níosairde" introduced a historical sketch of a Donegal hero of the '98 with an aggressive apologia: "There is no other people on the face of the earth that knows less of the traditions and history of their country and its important men and women than do the people of Ireland. The truth is bitter."[3]

Equally bitter was the persistence of this unpalatable truth, for such complaints continued to be voiced in the Gaelic press throughout the years before the creation of a native government in 1922. For example, in 1908 "Cill Cuiribh" wrote:

> It's rare that one finds a group of people uninterested in the history of their country, and who do not boast of and glory in the

2. *FL*, 2 July 1898. "Adeir na hughdair is eolaighe nach bhfuil slighe is fearr ann le spioraid náisiúntachta do choimeád beo i measg aon chinidh, ná síor-thrácht do dhéanamh leo ar ghníomharthaibh a sean agus a sinsear, agus eolas maith bheith aca ar stair a dtíre dhúthchais. Ní mar sin dalltha ag muintir na hÉireann. Ní múintear stair na hÉireann dóibh le linn a n-óige. Léighid trácht ar an Armada agus ar chath Bhatairliú acht ní airighid focal i dtaobh chatha Bhéil an Átha Bhuidhe ná i dtaobh ghníomhartha Ríogh Dháithí. Is dóigh le cuid aca nach raibh a leithéidí ann i n-aon chor. Cuid d'ár n-ainbhios is eadh é."

3. "Mánus Ó Domhnaill," *ACS*, 21 December 1901. "Ni'l daoine ar bith ar thalamh na cruinne go léir, bhfuil níos mó easbad eolais orra, i dtaobh seanchais agus staire a dtíre agus a cuid fear agus ban measamhla ná muinntir na hÉireann. Is searbh í an fhírinne."

traits and deeds of their ancestors. Long ago, when Ireland was respected and prosperous, people did not tire of recounting the fame of Ireland and spreading the great renown of the heroes and vigorous, strong warriors who were to be found throughout the country. Alas! It is no longer so, for the descendants of the Gaels know next to nothing about history.[4]

Indeed, in 1911 Mac Néill paid sarcastic tribute to the "mind-darkening education" provided by British authorities in Ireland, which was "of a set purpose to cut the Irish people off from their own past—to make them think that they were foundlings in the world, nobody's children—and thereby to destroy their self-respect and render them more easily handled like a set of broken paupers in a poorhouse."[5]

Clearly Mac Néill was here speaking as passionate activist rather than detached professional; he and his fellow revivalists saw Irish ignorance of Irish history as no mere academic deficiency. Rather, indifference to the national past undermined the very rationale of the movement to revive the national language, as Mac Néill emphasized in the same address: "To anyone who has not a feeling of Irish history and does not identify himself with Irish history, the learning of Irish is mere philology." Four years previously Pearse had made a similar charge more colorfully in an *An Claidheamh Soluis* editorial entitled "Irish History": "It is impossible, however, for the possessor of Irish fully to realise its importance or to grasp its significance without a familiarity with the facts and a knowledge of the course of Irish history. . . . The student who takes up Irish without a knowledge of Irish history loses the true meaning of the language: his study is but a cult: he may cherish the flower but he has torn it from its roots."[6] Many Gaels, moreover, shared Father Patrick F. Kavanagh's fear that without a sound knowledge of those historic roots, the Irish people might even fail to appreciate the enticements of that linguistic blossom. In his Gaelic League propaganda pamphlet *Ireland's Defence—Her Language*, Kavanagh wrote: "How can we expect people who know nothing of the history of their

4. Review of *Fiacha Mac Aodha Ua Broin* by Pádraig Mac Aodha, *ACS*, 10 October 1908. "Is annamh a fáightear dream daoine nach gcuireann suim i stair a dtíre agus nach ndéanfadh gaisge agus mórdháil fá thréithibh agus ghníomharthaibh a seanda. Fadó, nuair a bhí Éire fá mheas agus fá shéan, ní rabhthas tuirseach ach ag cur síos ar chliú na hÉireann, agus ag leathnughadh mór-cháile na bhfear dtréan agus na laoch luathmhara láidir a bhí go fairsing ar fud na tíre. Fairíor! ní amhlaidh atá an sgéal anois, mar is rí-bheag an t-eolas atá ag sliocht na nGaedheal ar stair."

5. "The Teaching of History in Irish Schools," *ACS*, "Seanchaidhe na Samhna" supplement, 28 October 1911.

6. *ACS*, 13 July 1907.

country to feel an interest in her language? How can we blame people for not being proud of the language of the country of which they know nothing or next to nothing?" (10).[7] If the answer to Kavanagh's question was plain, to Gaels like Éamonn Ó Donnchadha equally plain was the solution to the dilemma it posed: "The person who reads that history and understands it properly cannot help but be a loyal Gael, and a loyal Gael cannot help but give respect to the Irish language."[8]

However daunting, the course of action was, then, at least clear, and such forthright challenges called forth the best pragmatic energies of the early Gaelic League. In normal educational circumstances, the national schools would logically have provided universal instruction in national history. But as the Gaels were keenly and vocally aware, under English control the Irish "National" system—Pearse's dread "Murder Machine"[9]—had functioned since its inception in 1831 as an aggressively antinational force, suppressing a knowledge of both the Irish language and the Irish past. No single project consumed more of the league's time and resources than its relentless campaign to nationalize, Gaelicize, that educational establishment at all levels,[10] and one of the most important battles in their campaign was that for general and proper instruction in Irish history. For example, in 1903 the league's educational program included among its demands "the Introduction of Irish History into every school and college in Ireland."[11] Indeed, in 1915 *An Claidheamh Soluis* went so far as to state in an editorial that "the purpose of the Gaelic League is to make the Irish language, Irish literature and history the basis of Irish education and the sources of national inspiration."[12]

The struggle was, however, fraught with frustration, as Father Din-

---

7. Actually, in another essay Kavanagh strayed from league orthodoxy on this point by putting history ahead of the language: "I must say I look upon the teaching of Irish history to our young folk as even more important than that of the Irish language. I am strongly in favour of the latter, but the former I deem more important." See Kavanagh, "Beneficent or Maleficent?" *UI*, 6 January 1900.

8. "Ó Chúige Mumhan" (From the province of Munster), *ACS*, 26 June 1909. "An té léigheann an seanchas soin agus a thuigeann i gceart é, ní féidir dó gan bheith 'n-a Ghaedheal dílis, agus ní féidir do Ghaedheal dílis gan urraim a thabhairt do'n Ghaedhilg."

9. See "The Murder Machine," in *Collected Works: Political Writings and Speeches*, 5–50. The original pamphlet appeared in 1916. While it does not explicitly discuss the teaching of history in the "National" system, it does stress "the value of the national factor in education" with an invocation of illustrious names from the Irish past (39).

10. See Donncha Ó Súilleabháin, *Cath na Gaeilge sa Chóras Oideachais, 1893–1911* (The battle for Irish in the educational system, 1893–1911) (Baile Átha Cliath: Conradh na Gaeilge, 1988).

11. "An Educational Program," editorial, *ACS*, 7 November 1903.

12. "The Purpose of the Gaelic League," editorial, *ACS*, 10 July 1915. See also "Our Irish Schools," editorial, *ACS*, 21 August 1915.

neen acknowledged in a 1905 address to a sympathetic audience of patriotic teachers who had formed Cumann Gaedhealach na Múinteoirí Náisiúnta. Underscoring the anomalous place of national history in the classrooms of the nation, Dinneen proclaimed:

> Her story is one to inspire the young with aspirations after nobility and virtue: to breathe into their souls the spirit of the love of God, the love of truth and of country, to make them genuine Irishmen and not nondescript slaves. Then why, I ask, has the history of Erin been kept a sealed book from so many generations of Irish children, why is every mention of her name in the literature which they are spoon-fed introduced with apologies, why is she referred to with the finger placed on the lips, and in the language of doubt and suggestion?[13]

Nor was the situation to improve quickly or significantly, and despite the efforts of committed teachers like those of the Cumann Gaedhealach or members of religious teaching orders like the Christian Brothers, the league repeatedly felt compelled to criticize schools that simply ignored Irish history,[14] inspectors who, largely through ignorance of it, condoned its omission,[15] and teachers who presented it as "a footnote to English history,"[16] a subject "dragged at the tail of English history."[17]

While it waited, monitored, and exhorted, the league also characteristically took up the duty it saw the educational authorities by and large abdicating. In the first decade of this century formal lectures in Irish history were a regular feature on the schedule of many league branches, particularly those in urban areas like Dublin, Cork, or London.[18] Even a partial speakers' list reads like a who's who of contemporary Irish-Ireland: Mac Néill, Pearse, Dinneen, Cathal Brugha, Pádraic

---

13. *Native History in National Schools: A Lecture Delivered before Cumann Gaedhealach na Múinteoirí Náisiúnta at Their Rooms, 24 Upper O'Connell Street Dublin, February 4th, 1905* (Dublin: M. H. Gill and Son, 1905), 9–10.

14. See, for example, "Gleó na gCath," *ACS*, 4 June 1904; or, more than a decade later, "History Mar Dheadh [as It Were]," editorial, *ACS*, 25 November 1916.

15. See, for example, "Oideachas Dhá Theangthach" (Bilingual education), *ACS*, 7 August 1909.

16. "The Purpose of the Gaelic League," *ACS*, 10 July 1915.

17. "The Teaching of History," editorial, *ACS*, 16 October 1909. See also "Depressing Reports," editorial, *ACS*, 8 February 1913: "Irish History, lest the subject might suggest the idea of Irish nationality, is linked to the study of English literature."

18. For a summary of the London Branch's activities with regard to the study of Irish history, see Donncha Ó Súilleabháin, *Conradh na Gaeilge i Londain, 1894–1917*, 19–20, 47, 59, 63, 78, 84, 100, 151, 193, 195.

Ó Conaire,[19] William P. Ryan, "Conán Maol," Seosamh Laoide, Stephen Gwynn, George Moonan, Standish James O'Grady, Seán Ua Ceallaigh, Peadar Mac Fhionnlaoich, Arthur Griffith, P. S. O'Hegarty, Alice Stopford Green, Margaret Dobbs. Many of these lecturers were also pressed into service at the league's summer colleges, with Mac Néill particularly and predictably much in demand.[20] On a more ambitious level, the Central Branch in Dublin and the Cork and London branches all organized full lecture series in Irish history for the 1903–4 session. Noting the success of the Dublin initiative *An Claidheamh Soluis* urged other branches to follow the capital's lead:

> A series of history lectures on the same plan is not only within the legitimate work of a *craobh*, but it is a work that everyone should endeavour to undertake. The lectures need not be of an extremely erudite nature, but care should be taken to make them present history from the side of Ireland rather than from that of the Pale. The lectures will prove an interesting change from the study of the language, and will, at the same time, give point and meaning and increased interest to that study.[21]

The London Leaguers obviously needed no such guidelines as they listened to "Conán Maol" deliver the series of lectures of which Pearse stated: "Conán Maol has told the story of free Ireland more brilliantly than it has ever been told before whether in Irish or in English."[22]

19. Ó Conaire lectured to the London branch of the league on "the best way to teach Irish history from the Gaelic point of view." See "London Notes," *ACS*, 21 December 1901. Some twenty years later Ó Conaire himself wrote *Brian Óg* (1922–23), an adventure story set in 1690.

20. For example, in 1912 Séamus Ó Searcaigh suggested Mac Néill be jointly hired to visit all of the Gaelic summer colleges for a series of history lectures. See "Méadughadh Chúrsaí Léighinn na gColáistí nGaedhealach" (Expanding the curriculum of the Gaelic colleges), *ACS*, 18 May 1912. The proposal was never formalized, but Mac Néill's summers were always busy ones.

21. "Notes," *ACS*, 10 January 1903. Of the 1907–8 lecture series, the Central Branch's annual report (*Tuarasgabháil na Bliadhna, 1907–8*), said that "large audiences assembled weekly to listen to, and when occasion offered, to discuss the papers in Irish" (13–14). The report is in the Fionán Mac Coluim Papers, National Library of Ireland, MS. 24,401. On the other hand, sales of historical works were mixed. For the ten-month period 1 March–31 December 1908, the first volume of Ó Neachtain's *Stair-Cheachta* sold 1047 copies; Ua Ruaidhrí's novel *Bliadhain na bhFranncach*, 142; Ua Ceallaigh's biography *Brian Bóirmhe*, 438; and "Conán Maol's" *Éire*, just 80. See "Liosta de leabhra a díoladh," Fionán Mac Coluim Papers, National Library of Ireland, MS. 24,405.

22. "Recent Booklets," *ACS*, 7 October 1905. In addition to sponsoring its own historical lectures, the league and its press also advertised, reported on, and even reprinted

For those desiring a more active involvement in the educational process, the league through *An Claidheamh Soluis* suggested the organization of regular classes in Irish history: "An Irish History class is too rare in the branches: it will prove interesting and instructive to all. It will give a spirit to the work and will base the patriotic impulse on a sound foundation. Irish history is too little known at present; we look to the branches to promote it now."[23]

By 1903 both the Central Branch in Dublin and the London Branch had such programs in place, and the Londoners shared the main features of their course with the readers of *An Claidheamh Soluis*: "The general method adopted in the London League is this: The chapter for the evening is written in fairly simple Irish. Copies for the students are made from a cyclostyle, and these are to be read in the classes as texts. Questions on the various points will be asked and answered in Irish in the usual way, till the whole is fixed in the students' minds. The aim, of course, is to improve their Irish and give them Irish historical knowledge at the same time."[24] Such improvement was expected to continue through the summer months as various Gaelic colleges added Irish history to their curricula. To ensure an adequate supply of competent teachers if not of functioning cyclostyles, Irish history was also made an examination subject for those seeking league teaching certificates in both Dublin and London.[25] By 1915 the league seems to have been con-

---

significant addresses and essays on the study of Irish history by nonmembers. For example, in 1910 *ACS* published the texts of three lectures on historical teaching in Irish schools delivered by Professor Corcoran at University College, Dublin. See "History in Irish Schools," *ACS*, 19 November 1910; "History and Examination Systems," *ACS*, 26 November 1910; and "The Localisation of Irish History," *ACS*, 3 December 1910. Nor was the discussion limited to Ireland alone. See S. Mac G., "The Importance of History in American Education," *ACS*, 30 October 1909.

23. "A Word to the Branches," editorial, *ACS*, 21 September 1901. See also "Making Ready," editorial, *ACS*, 3 September 1904: "Are the branches doing all they should in the matter of Irish history? Our history should form an important portion of the curriculum of every branch, not alone for its own sake, but on account of its importance as a stimulus as regards everything Irish."

24. "Gaelic League of London," *ACS*, 10 January 1903. For some idea of the nature of the lectures and subsequent discussions, see "London Notes," *ACS* 24 January, 1903. *ACS* called the 1908 lecture series in Dublin "the nearest thing to University extension lectures on popular lines that Dublin has ever known ("In and Around Baile Átha Cliath," *ACS*, 23 May 1908).

25. For Dublin, see "Reports of Committees," *ACS*, "Duilleachán an Oireachtais," 23 May 1903; and "Sgoláireachta Chonnartha na Gaedhilge" (The Gaelic League scholarships), *ACS*, 11 September 1909. For London, see "Sasana—The Gaelic League of London," *ACS*, 19 September 1903.

fident enough of its own success in this enterprise to recommend that
all branches offer instruction in national history:

> Irish history should be taught and studied in all our *craobhacha*. It
> is not without definite purpose that the teaching of Irish history
> is practically excluded from the official education systems. . . .
> History gives enlightenment towards conviction and purpose re-
> garding the rights of the nation and the national path which the
> people should pursue. In the propagandist campaign which is
> soon to be set going in Corcaigh no branches should be estab-
> lished without definite provision being made for good and regu-
> lar teaching work.[26]

Less intellectually ambitious leaguers and those outside the organization were to be provided their history lessons in a less demanding form,
that of the tableaux vivants that were such popular features of league
entertainments in the early years of the century. Given the opportunities for colorful costumes and spectacular props offered by stirring
periods from the national past, it is hardly surprising that history, even
more than heroic literature, was the principal inspiration for the creators of the tableaux. These productions ranged from relatively modest
indoor stagings[27] to outdoor extravaganzas pulled on floats in the annual
Language Procession through the streets of Dublin. For example, of the
1908 floats that included Cormac Mac Airt, St. Brigid, Silken Thomas,
and Eoghan Ruadh Ó Néill,[28] *An Claidheamh Soluis* reported: "A striking feature of the procession was the Tableaux illustrating in a vivid and
realistic manner various periods of our country's story. . . . Each tableau was a thing of beauty in itself, the whole series not only produced
a fine artistic effect, but lent grace and dignity to the Procession. They
helped to recall stirring and eventful incidents in our history, they recalled the glories of the past, and conveyed a message of hope for the
future."[29] A rather more jaundiced view of the tableaux was offered by
an unlikely participant in one of them, a depiction of the marriage of
Strongbow and Aoife created by Sinéad Ní Fhlannagáin, the future
Mrs. de Valera, for a league St. Patrick's parade through Dublin. Ear-

26. "Gnó na Gaedhilge" (Irish language business), editorial, *ACS*, 25 September 1915.
27. See, for example, "Notes," *FL*, 4 February 1899; and Alice Milligan, letter, *FL*, 18
February 1899.
28. A detailed description of the ten tableaux can be found in "Sunday's Demonstra-
tion," *ACS*, 19 September 1908.
29. "Mór-Shiubhal na nGaedheal" (The great parade of the Gaels), editorial, *ACS*, 26
September 1908.

nán de Blaghd (Ernest Blythe) tells of the crowd's amusement as the actors struggled to maintain balance every time their horse-drawn stage jolted to a stop, and of his own futile attempts to keep warm in his heroic helmet, breastplate, and gaitered pink tights.[30] Nevertheless, even with the development of more substantial period theatricals in Irish, the tableaux seem to have remained populár. For instance, the league organized a series of them, "which will be presented very artistically and with historical truth," for production at the Abbey Theatre in February 1915.[31]

Mere enjoyment of flamboyant spectacle was, of course, no substitute for a sound understanding of native history. Patriotic pageantry might well spark interest, but only historical research and its scholarly and popular published results could satisfy it. At the turn of the century there had been precious little of either research or results available in Irish, a deficiency lamented by Donnchadh Pléimeann, one of the first to attempt its remedy in his biographical account of the scholar Eugene O'Curry:

> We are poor and wretched, lacking the history of our country in accessible books for us to read, where we could find without difficulty an account of everything concerning our country in the past. . . . Do we have any booklets in Irish giving an account of the life and times of Daniel O'Connell? Of the life and times of Wolfe Tone, Robert Emmet, Henry Grattan, or the occurrences of the eighteenth century? No—not even a single book in modern Irish dealing with the nation's history or its great people of any age.[32]

Obviously this lack was particularly frustrating for students in the league's own new history programs, as *An Claidheamh Soluis* acknowledged in March 1903: "Numerous candidates for the forthcoming Di-

---

30. *Trasna na Bóinne* (Across the Boyne) (Baile Átha Cliath: Sáirséal agus Dill, 1957), 141–42.

31. "Gleó na gCath," *ACS*, 23 January 1915.

32. "Trácht ar Bheatha Eoghain Uí Chomhraidh" (An essay on the life of Eugene O'Curry), *FL*, 5 August 1899. Pléimeann's source was Sara Atkinson's account of the scholar in her *Essays* (1896). "Is dona dealbh sinn, gan stair ár dtíre thíos againn le léigheadh i leabhraibh ion-láimhseálacha, go bhféadfaimís breith gan duadh ar chúntas ar gach nidh do bhain leis ár dtír is na haimsiribh d'imthigh tharainn. . . . Bhfuil aon leabhrán Gaedhilge againn ag tabhairt tráchta ar aimsiribh nó ar bheatha Dhomhnaill Uí Chonaill? ar aimsiribh nó ar bheatha Uolfe Tóne, Riobáird Emmet, Hannraí Grattan, nó ar imtheachtaibh na haoise a hocht déag? Ní'l, ná fiú aon leabhar amháin i nGaedhilg na haimsire seo ag trácht ar stair ár dtíre nó a mórdhaoine d'aon aois."

ploma Examinations have asked us to recommend History Text Books for the various courses. Unfortunately, no one has yet given us an Irish History written from the inside, and it is largely a question of choosing the least objectionable of a bad lot."[33] Most objectionable of the short-comings of this "bad lot" was their linguistic medium—English. For Gaelic intellectuals of the early Revival it was axiomatic that Irish should and ultimately would be the working language of any serious Irish historian. In the words of Father John O'Reilly,

> Ireland's history, literature, song, story, superstition, saga—all those outlets of the nation's mind which would give her true character to the world—all these are simply illegible without the Irish language. The best part of Ireland's history—the really Irish part—cannot be read at all without a knowledge of Gaelic. The right and genuine idea of Ireland—the true discernment of Irish affairs, of those lofty spirits who discuss them to our people abroad—can never be grasped through the medium of the English tongue.[34]

Moreover, English was not merely a passive barrier denying the historian access to "the right and genuine idea of Ireland"; rather its use actively distorted the researcher's perception of his subject, as the reviewer of Mícheál Breathnach's *Stair na hÉireann* (The history of Ireland) pointed out in 1910: "Writers in English can scarcely escape the spell of that language which compels them to write, to some extent, as foreigners." This critic then went on to warn that it was "safer to have our national history in Irish."[35] Specific examples of the dangers involved in writing national history in a foreign language had been spelled out by Seán Mac Giollarnáth the previous year: "The manner in which our history has been written is scarcely less tragic than the history itself. For centuries we have had no Irish historian. . . . Men who knew no Irish were unable to distinguish between our ancient history and literature, and they neglected or condemned both as fable. The early Christian period they smothered in miracles and magic, and the literature, commerce, and industry of the country they neglected altogether."[36] Conversely, for a Gaelic scholar there was believed to exist a

---

33. "Oideachas" (Education), *ACS*, 28 March 1903.
34. "The English Mind in Ireland," *FL*, 14 July 1900.
35. Review of *Stair na hÉireann*, part 2, by Mícheál Breathnach, *ACS*, 30 July 1910.
36. "The Teaching of History," editorial, *ACS*, 2 October 1909. See also the comments of "The O'Neill" in *The Leader*: "As regards these particular matters of Irish history and

natural, almost mystical, empathy amongst author, subject, medium, and audience. Thus in his preface to *Saothar Ár Sean i gCéin* (The work of our ancestors abroad), his study of early Christian Irish missionary activity, Seán Ua Ceallaigh ("Sgeilg") wrote: "No more suitable language has ever been created to bring the history of his ancestors and its meaning home to the mind of the young Irish person. History that is learned through Irish never loses its grip on the mind of an Irish person."[37]

With this high promise in mind, leaguers once again faced a clear and straightforward challenge. But this time the mechanism for its solution through the encouragement of Irish historical study and authorship lay ready to hand in the competitions of the local feiseanna and the annual national Oireachtas. The local festivals showed little imagination, in general simply organizing oral quiz contests in Irish history for young people[38] and running Irish essay contests, again frequently for young people, on historical topics of local interest. Thus the 1901 Leinster Feis solicited essays on Michael Dwyer;[39] the 1903 Muskerry Feis on the Whiteboys, "including a description of local episodes such as Cath Chéim an Fhiadh";[40] the 1903 Keating Feis in Clonmel on the Siege of Clonmel or the life of Father Sheehy;[41] the 1904 Sligo Feis on "the Book of Ballymote, the Book of Lecan, the Yellow Book of Lecan, the Carrowmore Cromlechs, the Druid's altar in the Calry Deerpark, the Sligo Abbey";[42] and the 1908 Castlebellingham Feis on Donnchadh Ua Cearbhaill, king of Airgíalla.[43]

---

literature, it is about time we treated of them in Irish. What between the Irish histories in English and the opinions in English of Matthew Arnold and Mr. Yeats, and so on about Irish literature, it is small wonder we've become mixed up and hazy in our ideas of both." ("Irish in Belfast," *The Leader*, 19 October 1907).

37. *Saothar Ár Sean i gCéin: Gearr Thuairisc ar Obair na Sean-Ghaedheal ar fuid na hEorpa* (The work of our ancestors abroad: A short account of the work of the medieval Irish throughout Europe) (Baile Átha Cliath: Cumann Bhuan-Choimeádta na Gaedhilge, 1904), 9. "Níor cumadh teanga eile riamh ní b'oireamhnaighe chum stair a shínsir agus a brigh do bhualadh isteach i n-intinn an Ghaedhil óig. An seanchus fhoghluimightear as an nGaedhilg, ní bhogann sé a ghreim de mheabhair an Ghaedhil go deo."

38. For an entirely random sample, see *ACS*, 14 February 1903 (Co. Mayo Feis); 28 March 1903 (Ballina, Co. Mayo); 25 April 1903 (Castlebellingham, Co. Louth); 6 June 1903 (Co. Wexford Feis); 22 April 1911 (Athlone, Co. Roscommon); 4 May 1912 (Dublin).

39. "List of Competitors in the Second Leinster Feis," *ACS*, 23 February 1901.

40. "Feis Mhúsgcaire agus Aonach Mhór Mhaghchromdha" (The Muskerry Feis and the Great Fair of Macroom), *ACS*, 6 June 1903.

41. "Feis an Chéitinnigh" (The Keating Feis), *ACS*, 4 July 1903.

42. "The Sligo Feis," *ACS*, 5 March 1904.

43. Séamus Ó Searcaigh, "Ó Chúige Uladh," *ACS*, 25 April 1908.

The organizers of the Oireachtas were more innovative and ambitious, regularly using the larger prizes and wider publicity available to them to channel Gaelic energies toward specific perceived needs.[44] Thus while the Oireachtas could sponsor the predictable essay contests—usually on an open topic like 1898's "Eachtra ó Stair na hÉireann" (an episode from Irish history)[45] or a subject of broad national significance like 1902's "Hugh O'Neill's Struggle against Elizabeth"[46]—it could also challenge competitors to produce a "Short History for Children" (1903),[47] or a "Civil and Social History of Ireland to the end of the 16th century" (1909).[48] In addition, the Oireachtas actively encouraged genuine creative work on Irish historical themes, sponsoring competitions for short historical fiction,[49] for a historical novel,[50] and for historical drama, for which it also provided the resources for full stage production.[51]

With all this activity astir, Peadar Mac Fhionnlaoich had in 1902 issued a direct challenge to his fellow Gaelic writers: "We have yet to reveal the history of Ireland."[52] As should be obvious from the foregoing, they rose to that challenge with focused energy, and by 1911 had generated a respectable body of historical essays in Irish as well as three useful history textbooks in the language: "Conán Maol's" *Éire:*

44. Some wanted the Oireachtas to be even more ambitious in this area. As early as 1898 Alice Milligan was urging the league to offer diplomas in "Gaelic Scholarship" through the Oireachtas. To be modeled on the Cambridge Higher Local Examinations, the proposed Oireachtas tests would cover, among other subjects, Irish literary history, "the social customs and government of Gaelic Ireland," "a knowledge of the territorial divisions and clans and Royal lines of ancient Ireland, and the history of all the most famous buildings," and "a period of history." Her suggestion was never acted on, although elements were incorporated into the curricula of the various Gaelic colleges, summer and other. See Alice L. Milligan, "Papers on the Organisation of the Gaelic Movement / No. 1.—A Suggestion for the Oireachtas," *FL*, 5 March 1898.

45. Donnchadh Ó Súilleabháin, *Scéal an Oireachtais*, 176.

46. "The Oireachtas, 1902 / List of Competitions," *ACS*, Duilleachán an Oireachtais, 21 September 1901. Even at this Oireachtas, however, essay topics of local interest were set for individual counties or specific regions. For example, the subject for Mayo writers was John McHale, while that for Leinster entrants was Lord Edward Fitzgerald. For a list of Oireachtas historical essay competitions and their winners, see Ó Súilleabháin, *Scéal an Oireachtais*, 176–77.

47. "The Oireachtas Committee," *ACS*, 17 October 1903.

48. "Oireachtas Literary Competitions," *ACS*, 19 June 1909.

49. See, for example, *Imtheachta an Oireachtais 1900*, 84; and Ó Súilleabháin, *Scéal an Oireachtais*, 173–74.

50. See Ó Súilleabháin, *Scéal an Oireachtais*, 173.

51. See Ó Súilleabháin, *Scéal an Oireachtais*, 182.

52. "An Litiordhacht Nua Gaedhilge" (The new literature in Irish), *ACS*, 11 October 1902. "Tá stair na hÉireann le nochtughadh againn fós."

Léigheachta ar Stair na hÉireann (Ireland: Lectures on the history of Ireland) (1907), a serious if uncritical treatment of national history through
the reign of Brian Bóroimhe; Eoghan Ó Neachtain's two-part *Stair-
Cheachta* (History lessons) (1905–7), an introduction for young readers;
and Mícheál Breathnach's three-part *Stair na hÉireann* (1909–11), a survey beginning with the arrival of the Celts and extending to the foundation of the Gaelic League.[53] When added to the growing corpus of
acceptably nationalist treatments of Irish history in English—the work
of Alice Stopford Green comes most immediately to mind[54]—these pioneering Gaelic efforts, however humble in retrospect, cleared the way
for creative explorations and interpretations of native history by Gaelic
writers and playwrights.

Two primary ambitions motivated the Gaelic author who turned to
historical themes. The first, noted above, was simply to correct the
distortions inflicted on the nation's history by the use of a foreign linguistic medium and its alien ethos. The second was to fill the enormous
gaps in Irish historiography left by writers ignorant of the national language of much of the nation's past and thus condemned to regard Irish
history "as starting with the Norman Invasion, bound up with the
varying fortunes of the Pale, and written of by none but Anglo-Irish
and Irish writers, whose point of view was always taken from the Bir-
mingham Tower."[55] In a 1904 *An Claidheamh Soluis* editorial, Pearse
addressed the problem from a more positive perspective, consciously
avoiding nativist exclusivism of the kind exemplified by the vague references to "race" into which Hyde, to Mac Néill's distress, often lapsed
"Gaelicism . . . is the traditional spirit of this land, the thing which
gives continuity to Irish history, the thing whose possession as something still vital and energetic makes the Ireland of to-day the same Ireland as the Ireland of history; the thing on whose loss would ensue the
death of Ireland."[56]

53. Mac Néill was among those who vetted historical works before their publication by
the league. See the mimeographed report of the Publications Committee ("Coisde na
Clobhann") for 20 April 1910 in the Fionán Mac Coluim Papers, National Library of
Ireland, MS. 24,405.

54. See, for example, the comments on her *The Making of Ireland and Its Undoing* by
"Brian" in "Books for Irish People to Read," *Guth na nGaedheal*, March 1910, 15.

55. "Dublin Notes," *ACS*, 2 February 1901.

56. "Ulster," editorial, *ACS*, 24 December 1904. Of course, given his own ethnic and
religious identity, Hyde could hardly be too insistent on this point, and Terence Brown
has rightly underscored his belief in "the powerful myth of Ireland's assimilative capaci-
ties." See Brown, *Ireland*, 44; and for a discussion of Hyde's use of racial terminology, D.
George Boyce, *Nationalism in Ireland*, 237–40. For a discussion of Mac Néill's rejection of
such language, see Hutchinson, *Dynamics*, 123–27. Joseph Lee has recently issued a caveat

In the minds of many Gaelic intellectuals an informed awareness of that vital and energetic Gaelicism was already in the process of being lost, even by patriotic Irish people with some grasp of isolated if worthy aspects of the nation's heritage. For example, in an 1899 essay entitled "The Pale and the Gael," D. P. Moran wrote: "We are proud of Grattan, Flood, Tone, Emmet and all the rest who dreamt and worked for an independent country, even though they had no conception of an Irish nation; but it is necessary that they be put in their place, and that place is not at the top as the only beacon lights to succeeding generations. The foundation of Ireland is the Gael, and the Gael must be the element that absorbs."[57] Writing sixteen years later, Seosamh Laoide ("Mac Tíre") seems to have felt that the intervening time had brought little improvement in authentic historical awareness for the mass of the Irish people: "Some of the Irish people are not unmindful of their heroes of past ages. We hear a lot about Emmet and Wolfe Tone, neither of whom, so far as is known, could speak a word of Irish or realised at all that the Irish language was a necessity to Irish Nationality. We do not hear so much about the older heroes who could speak Irish—if we except King Brian and two or three of the princely family of Tyrone we probably allow for all who are remembered to-day."[58]

Yet in their attempt to realize the second of these ambitions by reacquainting their compatriots with "the older heroes who could speak Irish," Gaelic writers often lost sight of the first by ignoring those significant periods of Irish history most prominent in the work of their

---

about reading into such appeals to race "the full range of subsequent sinister connotations." See Joseph J. Lee, *Ireland, 1912–1985: Politics and Society* (Cambridge: Cambridge University Press, 1989), 3.

57. In *The Philosophy of Irish Ireland* (Dublin: James Duffy, 1905), 36–37. This essay originally appeared in the *New Ireland Review* for July 1899. Once again it is important to note that, like Pearse, Moran, one of the most outspokenly Catholic Irish-Irelanders, here eschews references to "race" and is explicit in his belief that those of Protestant Anglo-Irish stock could be "absorbed" into a nation whose *cultural* identity was Gaelic. In *Nationalism in Ireland*, Boyce stresses the difficulty of this process of assimilation, writing: "The nationalist idea of the race, of the 'real nation' excluded all but the most enthusiastic and thick-skinned Irish Protestants" (387). But such de facto segregation was not necessarily intentional, and thus those guilty of it cannot with entire justice be called "exclusive nationalists" (251).

58. "A Monograph of a Scotch-Irish Hero," *ACS*, 29 May 1915. Laoide was here praising the book *Alasdair Mac Colla* by Eoin Mac Néill and Niall Mac Mhuireadhaigh, of which he himself was the editor. See also "Learning to Know Ourselves," editorial, *ACS*, 28 May 1910; and "E.," "The New Year and the Old Cause," *ACS*, 11 January 1913. "E." wrote: "The living heroes and the dead, what has been their aim? It is to make Ireland a Gaelic land, to give back to the Gael, whose claims to this country are not to be questioned, the language of his heart, the traditions of his past."

English-language counterparts. For instance, Dublin's long and eventful history—indeed the history of any important Irish town—is central in no Gaelic historical work with the exception of Tomás Ó Míodhcháin's slight and chronologically imprecise 1903 story "Taidhbhse an Phríosúin" (The ghost of the prison).[59] Furthermore, despite Donnchadh Pléimeann's counsel noted above, major figures like Sarsfield, Grattan, Tone and the United Irishmen, the Pikemen of Wexford, Emmet, O'Connell, Young Ireland, and the Fenian and Home Rule leaders are entirely absent from creative writing in Irish.[60] Indeed, whatever pride they might have taken in the pioneering accomplishments of Gaelic historians of Gaelic Ireland, even the most committed revivalists would have had to concede that for a satisfactorily inclusive picture of the Irish past, they would have to combine the historical perspectives available through both of the nation's languages.

As we turn to the creative works themselves, we may find it surprising that writers did not draw more inspiration from that most unimpeachably Gaelic period of Irish history before the arrival of the Normans, or even the Norse.[61] Ancient Ireland is, however, little more than a vague and rather exotic backdrop in Pearse's incomplete 1914 dual-language novel *An Choill / The Wood*, with its setting "a very long time ago, before the Gael in general received knowledge of the true illustrious God";[62] in a story like Mártan Ó Domhnaill's "Sgéal an Bhráthair nár Fhéad Focla Áirithe 'san Naomhadh Sailm ar Cheithre Fíchid do Thuigsint" (The story of a monk who could not understand certain

---

59. *ACS*, 23–30 May 1903.

60. Some of these figures did feature in nonfiction Gaelic works. For example, Máire Ní Chinnéide won a 1902 Oireachtas Prize with an essay on Lord Edward Fitzgerald (see Breathnach and Ní Mhurchú, *Beathaisnéis a Dó*, 80), and *UI* published a brief Gaelic biography of Emmet by "Giolla Bhríghde" in 1905, and biographies of Tone, Lord Edward, Thomas Russell, the Brothers Sheares, Henry Joy McCracken, and Oliver Bond, all by "Sean Duine Garsúin," in 1906. Indeed, there was even a 1911 Oireachtas Competition for an essay on Edmund Burke. See "The Literary Competitions," *ACS*, 12 August 1911. The winner was Séamus Mac Cormaic.

61. An tAthair Peadar did publish several rather extensive hagiographic essays on early Irish saints in the *Irish Rosary* from 1901 to 1905. See Shán Ó Cuív, "Materials for a Bibliography of the Very Reverend Peter Canon O'Leary, 1839–1920," supplement to *Celtica* 2, no. 2 (1954).

62. The only two installments of this work originally appeared in the *Irish Review* 4, nos. 41–42 (July–November 1914). The Irish text is available in *Na Scríbhinní Liteartha le Pádraig Mac Piarais*, ed. Ó Buachalla, 131–41; the English text in *The Literary Writings of Patrick Pearse: Writings in English*, ed. Ó Buachalla (Dublin: Mercier, 1979), 135–48. The story is set "tamall an-fhada ó shin, sula fuair Gaedhil i gcoitchinne eolas an fhír-Dhé fhorórdha."

words in the 89th psalm);[63] and in plays like the 1898 "Saint Patrick at Tara" scene translated by Pádraic Ó Beirne from Father O'Growney's *The Passing of Conall*, Hyde's 1902 *An Naomh ar Iarraidh* (The missing saint), Máire Ní Chinnéide's 1904 *Naomh Pádraig* (Saint Patrick),[64] Dinneen's 1909 *Comhairle Fithil* (The counsel of Fitheal),[65] Pearse's 1912 *An Rí* (*The King*), or Searloit Ní Dhúnlaing's 1915 *An Tobar Naomhtha* (The holy well).[66] Tadhg Ó Donnchadha was obviously more concerned with verisimilitude in his 1911 outdoor Oireachtas pageant *Feis na Teamhrach* (The festival of Tara).[67] Yet despite its dialogue, this production was in effect an extravagant visual re-creation of Ó Donnchadha's conception of the court of Cormac Mac Airt, and *Feis na Teamhrach* was thus a superficial if edificatory work, a talking tableau vivant rather than an authentic historical drama. Even thinner were two Gaelic "operas." Professor Paul McSwiney's *An Bárd 'gus an Fó* (The poet and the knight), subtitled "A Gaelic Idyll" and first performed at the Steinway Hall in New York as far back as 27 and 28 November 1884, was set at some unspecified time in the distant Gaelic past, "in the springtime of Life" (in Earrach a saoghail) [i.e., of the characters], and was a simple love story of a young Irish maiden and a soldier willing to fight "for the sacred rights of Erin" (chun saoirse 's ceirt na h-Éireann).[68] Tomás Ó Ceallaigh's 1909 *Eithne, nó Éan an Cheoil Bhinn* (Eithne, or The bird of the sweet music) was set "before the Foreigners came" (sul a dtáinig na Gaill), but is foggily allegoric and tells us nothing of the early history other than that Ireland was happier without foreign invaders.[69] The most original use of material from ancient Irish history was that in "Lucht Dlighe agus Géarchúise / Sgeul Aoir" (Lawyers and sharp people / A satirical story) by "Bhnsmmbhbhc" [*sic*], a brief tale set in

---

63. *Irish Rosary* 12, no. 5 (May 1908): 383–84.

64. I have not been able to locate a text of this play. It was produced twice by Dublin students in 1904, and is summarized in "A New Play," *ACS*, 17 December 1904; and in "I bhFochair na nGaedheal," *WF*, 12 December 1904.

65. *IG* 19, no. 2 (February 1909): 50–72; 19, no. 3 (March 1909): 109–23.

66. *An Tobar Naomhtha: Dráma Beag chun na Leanbh i gCóir Lae Fhéile Phádraig* (The holy well: A little play for the children for St. Patrick's Day) (Baile Átha Cliath: M. H. Mac Guill agus a Mhac, 1915). The action is set in the time of Patrick; the characters are "the pagan girls of Munster" (cailíní págánacha na Mumhan), all of whom are, needless to say, baptized by play's end.

67. *ACS*, 5–26 August 1911.

68. Professor Paul McSwiney, *An Bárd 'gus an Fó / A Gaelic Idyll*, in *An Gaodhal* 4, no. 2 (December 1884)–4, no. 4 (February 1885). Since the text is given in both Irish and English, I have used this English in the text. McSwiney seems to have composed the music as well.

69. (Dublin: M. H. Gill and Son, 1909).

Heaven and bringing together, among others, Saint Patrick, Fionn Mac Cumhaill, and Brian Bóroimhe.[70]

The reasons for this Gaelic failure to develop the imaginative potential of the early period are probably quite simple. They may, like their Anglo-Irish counterparts, have been blinded to the more prosaic history by the dazzling wealth of ancient literary tales to be adapted, modernized, or re-created, although their work in this area was similarly disappointing. Or, and this seems more probable, they may have been honestly intimidated by the complexities of that early history, complexities being confronted at just this time by their comrade Eoin Mac Néill in essays in English such as "Where Does Irish History Begin?" and others in Irish such as "Oghmoracht" (Ogham writing).[71] Furthermore, as William P. Ryan pointed out in his own series of popular essays on the *Lebor Gabála* scheme of early history,[72] a knowledge of modern spoken Irish would do little to unravel many of the philological, political, mythological, social, or legal dilemmas this new scholarly discipline would entail.[73] Gaelic writers in quest of historical raw material could

---

70. *An Lóchrann* 4, no. 4 (September–October 1911): 4.

71. "Where Does Irish History Begin?" appeared in the *New Ireland Review* 25 (March 1906): 1–18; "Oghmóracht" was serialized in *IG* from May 1908 to May 1909. For a full bibliography of his historical writings, see *The Scholar Revolutionary: Eoin Mac Néill, 1867–1945, and the Making of the New Ireland*, ed. F. X. Martin and F. J. Byrne (New York: Barnes and Noble, 1973), 344; and Byrne's essay in the volume, "Mac Néill the Historian" (17–36). In 1909 Mac Néill was appointed professor of early Irish history in the new National University.

72. This work, "Tús Staire na hÉireann: Sean-Sgéalta agus Sean-Déithe na nGaedheal" (The beginning of Irish history: The ancient stories and the ancient gods of the Irish) was serialized in *ACS* commencing on 24 October 1903.

73. See "The Background of Irish History," *ACS*, 14 March 1903. Ryan wrote: "Not only have we gone far towards spoiling the Irish historical perspective, but our general notion of antiquity in Ireland is either false or fantastic. Twice recently I noticed in very good Irish the hopelessly unhistorical assumption that the Gaels once dwelt in Egypt and that we, in fact, are descendants of the daughter of Pharaoh!" On the other hand, Ryan's own views on early Irish intellectual history could seem every bit as fantastic to some of his contemporaries. See, for example, his "An Múinteoir Taisdil, Bhergilius, agus an Sagairtín" (The traveling teacher, Virgil, and the little priest) and "Brugh na Bóinne agus an Domhan Thoir" (Newgrange and the Eastern world) in *ACS*, 2 November 1912; and 23 November 1912 respectively. Both pieces in revised form were incorporated into the novel *An Bhóinn agus an Bhóchna* (to be discussed in Chapter 7). Moreover, *ACS* felt compelled to append an editorial disclaimer to his 1912 essay "Spioradáltacht na Sean" (The spirituality of the ancients), writing, "Let it not be thought that *An Claidheamh* agrees with everything said in this essay." (Ná síltear go réidhteigheann *An Claidheamh* le gach a bhfuil ráidhte san aiste seo.) See Ryan, "Spioradáltacht," *ACS*, 14 December 1912. And the following month a reader wrote from New York City to call Ryan's work "rotten rubbish." See Henry Magee, letter, *ACS*, 25 January 1913. Ryan was defended by

certainly be forgiven if they failed to share Ryan's fascination with what was difficult in the study of Celtic Ireland: "The early legends, history, archaeology, and so on, have so many sides, and the material is so abundant, but unmeasured and unsifted, that the beginner is necessarily bewildered."[74] In fact, some credit is due them for not succumbing to any appreciable extent to the sort of ahistorical fantasizing that Ryan himself feared and that the scholar R. A. S. Macalister warned them against in a letter to *Fáinne an Lae* all the way from Palestine. Himself later the editor of *Lebor Gabála Éireann* (The book of invasions), a text that has been a fertile source of questionable theories for a millenium, Macalister was concerned about the ridicule that could be inspired by extravagant claims for the antiquity, reliability, and splendor of Irish historical records: "It is unnecessary to make such claims, for while science has rudely swept away many of the fancies of O'Flanagan, Vallancey, or even the much greater O'Curry, it has left enough to satisfy the patriotic feeling of any nation."[75]

Less explicable is the paucity of creative works on Brian Bóroimhe, particularly considering the respectable number of biographical pieces on him in Irish and the fact that Father John O'Carroll's "Amharca Cleasacha / Dramatic Scenes in Irish" set on the eve of Clontarf had appeared as early as the first number of *Irisleabhar na Gaedhilge* in November 1882.[76] While, as we will see below, O'Carroll does offer an interesting interpretation of Brian's character, his skits, with their long-winded set speeches in verse, were obviously intended not for production but rather for oratorical declamation, rather like Peadar Ua Laoghaire's later "Rosc Catha Bhriain i gCluain Tairbh" (Brian's battle

Mac Giollarnáth in an editorial response to Magee in this same issue, and defended himself in a letter published in *ACS* for 1 February 1913.

74. "London Notes," *ACS*, 24 January 1903. See also Ryan, "I mBaile 's i gCéin," *ACS*, 4 April 1903, where he wrote: "Irish history is something in regard to which most of us will believe anything except what is true; and while everything may go well and happily with the language movement, years may elapse before young Ireland as a whole has a proper conception of Irish history."

75. R. A. S. Macalister, "A Menace to the Irish Language / A Letter from Palestine," *FL*, 28 October 1899. Macalister explicitly identifies as the source of his concern some recent pieces that had appeared in *FL* itself, among them Dr. Shahan's "Let Us Save the Language." But Shahan had company. See Henebry, "Spread of Gaelic Study", *FL*, 21 April 1900; and Pádruig L. Uí Dhálaigh, "Fáilte an 'Chlaidimh Soluis' " (Welcome to *An Claidheamh Soluis*), *ACS*, 20 January 1900. The former essay was originally published in the *Boston Republic*; the latter is the text of a speech delivered in New York by Ó Dálaigh, who was an officer of the Boston Gaelic School.

76. *IG* 1, no. 1 (November 1882): 5–6; 1, no. 2 (December 1882): 33–38; 1, no. 3 (January 1883): 65–69; 1, no. 5 (March 1883): 151–62; 1, no. 8 (June 1883): 233–41.

cry at Clontarf), a favorite of competitors at early feiseanna.[77] O'Carroll's work, on the other hand, seems to have been forgotten soon after its publication. Even more obscure was the dramatic fragment "Dúnlaing Óg agus a Leannán Sidhe" (Young Dúnlaing and his otherworld lover"), collected in Kerry in 1898 and produced on a program with two of Pearse's plays at the Theatre of Ireland in Hardwicke Street in December 1915.[78]

Yet apart from O'Carroll's "scenes" and the 1916 *Oighreacht Bhriain* (Brian's legacy) by Sadhbh Trínnseach and Proinnsias Ua Súilleabháin, a copy of which I have been unable to locate,[79] the only creative treatment of Brian we have is Ua Laoghaire's extraordinary *Niamh* (1907), by far the most substantial (or at least longest) novel of the first decades of the Revival.[80] Perhaps the book's sheer bulk coupled with its author's formidable personality awed other Gaelic writers into creative silence on Brian. If so, more's the pity, for the book is radically flawed by, as Pearse pointed out, "the cardinal fault of being untrue—not merely to history . . . but to historical vraisemblance."[81] In addition to Ua

---

77. *FL*, 10 September 1898.

78. The piece, said to have been "enacted among the people up to sixty or seventy years ago," was merely a dialogue between the young warrior Dúnlaing and his otherworld lover the night before the battle of Clontarf. (Information from the program for the performance in the Pearse Museum at Sgoil Éanna, Rathfarnham.)

79. The work was advertised as "an historical semi-pageant play." It seems to have been produced twice, once by the students of Coláiste Eoghain Uí Chomhraidhe (Carrigaholt College), and once by Craobh na gCúig gCúigí in the Irish Theatre in Hardwicke Street. See "Gaelic Plays at the Irish Name [*sic*]," *ACS*, 9 December 1916. The Carrigaholt production may not have involved the final version of the play. In a report on the activities of Coláiste Eoghain Uí Chomhraidhe, it was described as "a 'pageant' on 'Mathghamhain, King of Thomond'" ("pageant" ar "Mathan, Rí Thuamhan"), directed by the author herself. See "In Iarthar Chláir / Coláiste Eoghain Uí Chomhraidhe" (In West Clare / Coláiste Eoghain Uí Chomhraidhe), *ACS*, 27 September 1916.

80. (Baile Átha Cliath: Muintir na Leabhar Gaedhilge, 1907).

81. "History and Romance," review of *Niamh*, *ACS*, 7 September 1907. On the other hand, Ua Laoghaire did have his champions. For example, Father O'Reilly wrote: "The personality of Brian, the character of Gormley, the court of Kincora, and the battle of Clontarf could hardly have fared better at the hands of Sir Walter Scott, given even that he knew Irish as well as Father Peter" (review of *Niamh*, *The Leader*, 31 August 1907). Tomás Ó Flanghaile agreed, lauding the book for, among other virtues, its educational value as history. See his review in *IG* 17, no. 10 (October 1907): 410–14. While waxing rhapsodic over the beauties of Ua Laoghaire's Irish—even suggesting the book would be reread to the point of memorization—Pádraig Mac Suibhne was skeptical about his reliability as a historian (Ó Chúige Mumhan," *ACS*, 7 September 1907):

> An tAthair Peadar and "Sgeilg" and "Conán Maol" have made a little god of Brian Bóroimhe. By no means do I agree that he was a person of the sort they conceive him to have been, and many agree with me. Who will put the other story before us?

Laoghaire's usual cantankerous editorializing on pet issues such as Irish importation of nasty English habits like the wearing of hats (55) or Irish tolerance for the duplicitous malice of English historians (84), the novel is rife with anachronisms and howling inaccuracies, most notably perhaps the introduction of a papal legate to tenth-century Ireland and the consistent interpretation of Brian's campaigns against the Norse and Norse-Irish, about whom Ua Laoghaire seems to have known virtually nothing, as a straightforward struggle between Irish Christianity and Scandinavian paganism (see, for example, 38–39). Significantly, when Ua Laoghaire thought of developing *Séadna* into a three-volume novel of ideas, one of which would bring the story to Tara at the time of Brian, he wrote to Mac Néill, then editor of *Irisleabhar na Gaedhilge*, where *Séadna* was being serialized: "It would be appropriate for me to acquire accurate knowledge of the affairs of that period. What do you think of my idea? Or if you find it a good idea which would serve the story, where could I get the knowledge I require?" Ua Laoghaire's lack of historical qualifications for this task no doubt weighed heavily in Mac Néill's decision not to publish the proposed sequels to *Séadna*, a decision that helped bring their friendship to a bitter conclusion.[82]

(Tá Dia beag déanta ag an Athair Peadar, agus ag "Sgeilg," agus ag "Conán Maol" de Bhrian Bóirimhe. Ní ghéillim i n-éan chor go raibh sé 'n-a dhuine de'n tsórt a cheapann siad-san agus tá mórán im' dhála. Cé chuirfidh an taobh eile de'n sgéal os ár gcomhair?)

82. Peadar Ua Laoghaire, letter to Eoin Mac Néill, 1 March 1897, quoted by Michael Tierney in *Eoin Mac Néill, Scholar and Man of Action, 1867–1945*, ed. F. X. Martin (Oxford: Clarendon, 1980), 37. For the rupture of their friendship, see Tierney, *Eoin Mac Néill*, 34–39; and Shán Ó Cuív, "Caradas nár Mhair: Peadar Ua Laoghaire agus Eoin Mac Néill" (A friendship that didn't last: Peadar Ua Laoghaire and Eoin Mac Néill), in *The Scholar Revolutionary*, ed. Martin and Byrne, 51–73, esp. 59–63. Ua Laoghaire was later to give all the credit for the publication of *Séadna* as a book to Norma Borthwick. See, for example, his letter to Tomás Ó Rathile of 19 December 1913 in the Ua Laoghaire Papers, National Library of Ireland, MS. G660. Even as fervent an admirer of An tAthair Peadar as Sister Mary Vincent ("Maol Muire") could dismiss *Niamh* as a serious historical novel:

But An tAthair Peadar was exceeding his abilities when he undertook the writing of a historical story. . . . He had virtually no knowledge of the history of that period. . . . There is nothing in the story that would suggest to someone that it dealt with the remote age of the Vikings.

(Ach bhí An tAthair Peadar ag dul thar a chómhacht nuair a thug sé fé sgéal startha do sgríobhadh. . . . Ní raibh aon eolas puinn ag an Athair Peadar ar stair na haoise sin. . . . Níl aon ní sa sgéal a chuirfeadh i n-iúl do dhuine gur bhain sé le haois imigéineamhail na Lochlannach.)

"Maol Muire," *An tAthair Peadar Ó Laoghaire agus a Shaothar*, 64–66. See also Muiris Ó Droighneáin, *Taighde i gComhair Stair Litridheachta na Nua-Ghaedhilge ó 1882 anuas* (Research toward a history of literature in Modern Irish from 1882 on) (Baile Átha Cliath: Oifig Díolta Foillseacháin Rialtais, 1936), 112–13.

To make things worse, there were ethical and ideological problems, as An tAthair Peadar, in common with all Gaelic writers who dealt with the period, had to face the distasteful fact that Brian was, after all, a usurper. Their solution never varied. The king was motivated not by personal or dynastic ambition, but by a vision, sadly premature, of Ireland as a unified and stable nation-state. For example, in his *Éire* "Conán Maol," having pronounced Brian worthy to stand "in comparison with the most important heroes in the history of the world" (i gcomórtas leis na fearaibh meanman is mó tábhacht i stair an domhain), weighed, then justified, his treatment of his predecessor Maelseachlhlainn: "It is said that it was not right to take the kingdom from Maelseachlainn, and that that deed set a bad precedent for other leaders after his death. There is probably a bit of truth in that, but I don't think that there was any other way, at that time, to make Ireland a strong kingdom."[83] Similarly, in his review of Seán Ua Ceallaigh's biography of Brian, Pearse noted that while Ua Ceallaigh omitted "the darker problems" of the king's career, he did not present "an undiscriminating panegyric," and that while he ignored the tragic result of Brian's failure, the weakening of Ireland that made possible a successful Norman invasion in the following century, he was right on target in his analysis of Brian's motives. According to Pearse, "this was no vulgar personal ambition. Brian doubtless saw that it was absolutely necessary that Ireland should be welded into a homogeneous political entity, and felt that he was the man to do it: seeing and feeling this, he was unscrupulous as to means."[84]

Only O'Carroll seemed willing to dwell on "the darker problems," depicting Brian at Clontarf as a man obsessed with doubt and guilt:

> Yet in this hour, of honour full and might,
> My heart can find no peace. One great dread fear
> Pursues me, that I did what was not just
> In raising up my power to this high state.
> Perhaps this strong right hand seems stained with guilt
> To the clear eyes of God, and therefore now,

83. "Conán Maol," *Éire: Léigheachta ar Stair na hÉireann* (Baile Átha Cliath: Clódhanna Teo., 1924), 115. "Deirtear nár chóir dó an ríoghacht do bhaint de Mhaelseachlainn, agus gur thug an bheart san droch-thaithighe do thaoiseachaibh eile i ndiaidh a bháis. Ní móide 'ná go bhfuil beagán de'n fhírinne sa mhéid sin, acht ní airighim go raibh aon chuma eile de réir na haimsire úd ar ríoghacht dhaingean do dhéanamh d'Éirinn."

84. "Brian Bóirmhe," review of *Brian Bóirmhe* by Seán Ua Ceallaigh, *ACS*, 9 March 1907. Darrell Figgis, who also admitted that Brian was "no rose-pink hero," likewise defended his aggressive nation-building. See "Brian Bóroimhe," *Guth na nGaedheal*, March 1914, 12–15.

Perhaps in very hour of victory,
His vengeance will descend upon my head.[85]

Moreover his Brian never explicitly claims a mission as nation-builder, instead wistfully maintaining that only duty keeps him on the throne and out of a monastery:

I must remain upon the trodden path,
I must here linger on among the things
That it were best for me to cast away . . .
Oh! blessed every prince of ancient Erin
To whom it was allowed to journey unto
The isle of Columbkille, to end his days.[86]

Nonetheless, even in O'Carroll's work Brian is presented as the sole force capable of unifying the Christian Irish against the pagan Norse, as his confessor (anamchara) Maolsuthain impresses on him:

Oh! King supreme and valiant, I have hope—
Hope deep and mighty—that a new age cometh,
Rich with true union, peace and amity,
Faith and devotion, charity and mercy;
When after this one war, the stranger foe
Shall feel for ever fear and awe of Erin;
And when in this fair land itself, its clans
Shall dwell in quiet on its plenteous soil,
And without strife or evil will, inhabit
This isle of saints, of sages, and of bards.[87]

85. O'Carroll, "Amharca Cleasacha," *IG* 1, no. 1 (November 1882): 6. All the translations here are those of O'Carroll himself. "Acht ins an uair so féin, lán cúmhachta, clú, / Ní bh-fuil síothcháin in mo chroidhe. Tá eagla orm, / An-mhó, uathbhásach, nach raibh ceart agam, / An méad a righneas air mo shon a dhéanadh. / B'fhéidir gur cionntach an lámh láidir so / I radharc Dé: 'gus air an adhbhar sin, / B'fhéidir go d-tuitfidh síos a dhíoghaltas / Go trom in uair na buaidhe air mo cheann."

86. O'Carroll, "Amharca Cleasacha," *IG* 1, no. 2 (December 1882): 35–36. "Caithfidh mé fanacht air an sean-chasán / Caithfidh mé fuireach fós ameasg na neitheadh / Dob' fheárr dham teilgean as mo chómhair go léir . . . / Och beannuighthe gach flaith na h-Éireann ársaidhe; / Aig a raibh cead dul go h-Í-Choluim-cille / Agus annsin fághail beatha a's fághail báis."

87. O'Carroll, "Amharca Cleasacha," *IG* 1, no. 2, 33. "A Áirdrigh Bhriain thréin, tá dóthchas orm, / Dóthchas an-mhór, go bh-fuil am nuadh le teacht, / Lán d'aondacht agus síothcháin, creideamh, cáirdeas, / Teas-charthannacht, fíor-chráibhtheacht, trócaire; / Go mbeidh air Ghallaibh 'n-déis an chatha-so / Eagla a's úmhlughadh romhainne go

Ua Laoghaire seems to have been untroubled by such scruples concerning the usurpation. Indeed, his startlingly democratic "Imperator Scotorum" is virtually compelled, by the Northerners themselves, to accept the High-Kingship, and only then with the acquiescence of Maelseachlainn: "High King, it is not fitting for me to do you any injustice. If it is the wish of the men of Ireland to give me this High Kingship, it is their right to give it to me. If it is their wish to keep it with you, it is their right to keep it with you."[88] Thereupon An tAthair Peadar metamorphosed might into right, presenting Maelseachlainn's "voluntary" submission to Brian's vision (and power) as confirmation of Irish political maturity and ethical superiority: "What would have been done over in England at any time in the past 800 years were it in England that that dispute occurred? What did Henry IV, the man who was called Bolingbroke, do when he took the kingdom of England from Richard II?"[89]

The following five centuries, centuries in which the language of the island was almost exclusively Irish, apparently failed to capture the Gaelic imagination. For the entire period—if we omit two short stories with generic medieval settings, the previously noted "Taidhbhse an Phríosúin" and what in effect is little more than a folktale, "Cuairt Currach na Slaodaighe" (The castle of Currach na Slaodaighe) (1903) by "Domhnall Balbh"—we seem to have only Micheál Mac Aodha's "Góimés" (Gomez), a story about the murder of a young Spaniard by the son of mayor Lynch of Galway, who eventually hanged the boy and gave a word to the English language,[90] Piaras Béaslaí's "Earc agus Áine," an essentially ahistorical love story that reads like a cross between *Romeo and Juliet* and the Deirdre tale,[91] and a single play, *Mac Cárthaigh Mór* by "Pádraig na Léime." A prizewinner staged at the 1908 Oireachtas, the play depicts, with due dramatic license, the heroic resistance of its eponymous protagonist against the advance into West Cork of the Normans under Meiler fitzHenry in the first decade of

---

bráth; / Agus go m-beidh Clanna Ghaedhil na h-Éireann / Go socaireach le chéile tríd an tír, / Le dóthain, gan aon troid nó tnúth ag aitreabh / Inse na naomh, na n-eolach a's na m-bárd."

88. Pp. 79–80. "A Áirdrigh, ní halaidh dhomh-sa aon éagcóir a dhéanamh ort. Má's toil le fearaibh Éireann an Árdrioghacht so thabhairt domsa isé a gceart í thabhairt dom. Má's é a dtoil í chimeád agatsa isé a gceart í chimeád agat."

89. P. 80. "Cad a dhéanfí thall i Sasana aon lá le hocht gcéad blian dá mba thall i Sasana a bheadh an t-imreas ar siúbhal? Cad a dhein an ceathramhadh Hamhraí, an fear ar a dtugtí Bolingbroke, nuair a bhain sé righeacht Shasana den tarna Risteárd?"

90. *WF*, 14 December 1907.

91. In *Earc agus Áine agus Scéalta Eile* (Earc and Áine and other stories) (Baile Átha Cliath: Oifig an tSoláthair, 1946), 7–46. The story was originally published in the *Freeman's Journal* in 1913.

the thirteenth century. The highlight of the production was no doubt an actual battle scene in which the foreigners were routed after a struggle conducted "closely, fiercely, dexterously for a while" (go tiugh fíochmhar aicillidhe ar feadh sgathaimh), leaving the triumphant Mac Cárthaigh and his Irish allies in command of the field.[92]

When Seosamh Laoide lamented in 1915 that "two or three of the princely families of Tyrone" were, with Brian Bóroimhe, the only Gaelic heroes known to modern Ireland, he was but acknowledging the obvious fact that his fellow Gaelic writers had devoted a disproportionate share of their scholarly and creative energy to the late sixteenth century. Yet this fascination with the period that saw the last stand of the native order was neither surprising nor fortuitous. For example, an anonymous contributor to *An Claidheamh Soluis* introduced his lengthy essay on Domhnall Ó Súilleabháin Bhéara with a direct reference to the unique significance of the age in which his subject struggled: "More than any other period through which our nation has passed, it is the sixteenth century I pronounce the most extraordinary."[93] Indeed, in a thoughtful and carefully reasoned 1903 essay one "Cú Cadhain" argued that the time of the Tyrone Wars was precisely the period most urgently in need of research and interpretation by Gaelic writers, even at the expense of essential work to establish the facts and publish the glories of early Irish history:

> The dominant note in the new Ireland is a note of strong recall. We have been turned in on ourselves and have recognised the necessity of taking up the historical thread where it has been broken. It is precisely the question as to where the thread has been broken and where weakened that should be engaging our most earnest attention at present. . . . I take it that the most convenient point for opening up the whole question would be the era of Elizabeth. The downfall of Kinsale was the last effort of an Irish National entity. If the reader opens his text-book of Irish History at that point he will find that the Gall takes up the

92. "Pádraig na Léime," *Mac Cárthaigh Mór: Dráma Éin-Ghníomha* (Mac Cárthaigh Mór: A one-act play) (Baile Átha Cliath: Connradh na Gaedhilge, 1908), 23–24. A photograph of the costumed cast of a Maynooth production of the play appeared in *Irisleabhar Mhuighe Nuadhad* (1914): 89.

93. Anonymous, "Gníomhartha Dhomhnaill Uí Shúilleabháin Bhéara: Aiste do Léigheadh os comhair Chumainn Ghaedhealaigh na hIolsgoile" (The deeds of Domhnall Ó Súilleabháin Bhéara: A paper read before the University Gaelic Society), *ACS*, 3 July 1909. "Thar gach ré dár ghabh an náisiún so thríd, do'n tseiseadh aois déag a mholaim-se barr éagcosamhlachta."

record there. As a result the period in which we are most interested as displaying the continuity of our native civilisation, and explaining even to the individual his connection with a past, is a tragic blank.

Having claimed that after Kinsale "the free clans of Ireland vanish from history like a stone dropped in a boghole" not to emerge until Catholic Emancipation in 1829, "Cú Cadhain" continued: "This is the big characteristic of those two hundred years of our national life—*the silence of the Gael*. Here is a question to which we must address ourselves, and I think there is no period which has such a human appeal for us all."[94]

Others seem to have agreed, as revivalists broke that silence on both the page and stage. The Desmond Wars of 1579–83 provided the background for what is generally considered the first Gaelic novel, Dinneen's *Cormac Ua Conaill* (1901), more a patriotic adventure story than a perceptive re-creation of the period and its tangled issues.[95] Munster's later involvement in the Tyrone Wars was the subject of Piaras Béaslaí's first play, *Coramac na Cuile* (produced at the Oireachtas in 1907; published in 1909), a drama that reinforced its inspirational patriotic theme through a romantic subplot in which the Gaelic firebrand Cormac Mac Cárthaigh wins the hand of the beauteous heroine Úna in defiance of two traiterous Anglicized enemies, her father, the Earl of Muskerry, and a rival suitor, "Donacha na Ngoul" (Donncha of the Foreigners), the son of the High Sheriff of Cork City and a bitter foe of Aodh Ó Néill, with whom Cormac is needless to say allied.[96]

Ó Néill and his fellow Ulsterman Aodh Ruadh Ó Domhnaill were, predictably and appropriately, the favorite protagonists of Gaelic historical writers, who invariably stressed their role as national leaders committed to the creation of a unified four-province state. Their status as heroes who transcended provincial rivalries is underscored by the fact that they fired the imagination not only of Ulstermen like Peadar Mac Fhionnlaoich and Éamonn Ó Néill,[97] but also that of Southerners like "Conán Maol," Seán Ua Ceallaigh, and even An tAthair Peadar. Con-

94. "Wanted—A History of Anglicisation," *ACS*, 16 May 1903.
95. (Baile Átha Cliath: Connradh na Gaedhilge, 1901).
96. (Dublin: James Duffy, 1909). The play was printed in the "simplified spelling" championed by several Munster writers of the period, of whom the most forceful and consistent was Shán Ó Cuív ("Seán Ó Caoimh" in the orthography he was attempting to replace).
97. See his essay "Eachtra Aodha Ruaidh: Mar Chaith Sé Nollaig a 1592 i gCaiseal Átha Cliath" (An adventure of Aodh Ruadh: How he spent Christmas 1592 in Dublin Castle), *WF*, 4 December 1915 (Christmas supplement).

nacht added its tribute when the Mayo-born Micheál Mhag Ruaidhrí dictated a lengthy and detailed biography of Aodh Ó Néill to William Shortall in 1903.[98]

Gaelic writers of fiction and nonfiction alike were in thorough agreement concerning the Ulstermen's personal and patriotic splendor—Pearse, for example, called Ó Néill "the most tremendous figure in our history" and a man who "had well-nigh been the most tremendous figure in the history of the world," and An tAthair Peadar wrote of Ó Néill and Ó Domhnaill that "it is not possible to find in the history of the world, except for the saints of the Church, two who were a greater credit to the country that gave them birth than those two."[99] Nevertheless, magnificent defeat rather than triumph dominated their work, producing a note of elegaic fatalism that Matthew Arnold would have no doubt found peculiarly Celtic and that at least one contemporary Celt, Liam Ua Domhnaill, found peculiarly annoying in Irish historical writing in both Irish and English:

> The fault that many people find with the history of Ireland is that the students who study it are always thinking about the work that was not done, with never a thought for the work to be done. In their opinion, there is too much "Minstrel Boy" and "Harp that Once" in it. Perhaps there is some truth to their view, for it is not through keening by the grave of Ireland that Ireland will be revived in the time to come.[100]

Most Gaelic writers on this period seem, however, to have preferred the graveside, with only "Conán Maol" in *Aodh Ó Néill* (1902) and Ua

98. Micheál Mhag Ruaidhrí ("Nochtadh na Fírinne"), *Beatha Aodha Uí Néill* (Baile Átha Cliath: Connradh na Gaedhilge, n.d.). The work won a prize at the 1903 Oireachtas. There were also some brief Irish passages in Tyrone-born Alice Milligan's *The Deliverance of Red Hugh: A Play in One Act and Two Scenes* (*WF*, 15 March 1902). The Irish was probably not written by Milligan herself.

99. See "Hugh O'Neill," review of *Beatha Aodha Uí Néill* by Micheál Mhag Ruaidhrí, *ACS*, 22 July 1905; and Ua Laoghaire, letter to Séamus Ó Dubhghaill, 25 November 1906, quoted by Ó Fiannachta in "Ag Cogarnaíl le Cara," *IMN* (1991): 119. "Measaim nach féidir a dh'fhághail i seanachus an domhain, lasmuich de naoimh na hEagailse, beirt is mó creideamhaint do'n tír a thug beatha dóibh ná an bheirt sin."

100. Liam Ua Domhnaill, "I mBaile Átha Cliath / Stair na hÉireann" (In Dublin / The history of Ireland), *ACS*, 25 April 1908. "Is é locht fhághann a lán daoine ar Stair na hÉireann go mbíonn na mic léighinn a dhéanas staidéar uirthi ag síor-smaoineamh ar an obair nár déanadh agus gan aon smaoineamh aca ar an obair a dhéanfar. Bíonn an iomarca 'Minstrel Boy' agus 'The Harp That Once' innti, dar leo. B'fhéidir go bhfuil roinnt de'n fhírinne aca; óir ní de dheasgaibh a bheith ag gol-chaoineadh le hais uaighe na hÉireann a déanfar Éire d'aithbheochain san aimsir atá le teacht."

Laoghaire in *An Bealach Buidhe* (*The Yellow Road*) (1906) focusing on moments of Gaelic success. Indeed, in her 1909 play *An Leoirghníomh* (The atonement), Searloit Ní Dhúnlaing even managed to turn the greatest of Irish victories, that at the Yellow Ford, into an occasion of inspirational mourning, as her protagonist Toirdhealbhach Ó Ruairc, who had once nearly betrayed the national cause, performs his fatal act of patriotic atonement on the battlefield and dies in the now forgiving arms of his fiancée Énid: "I have finished it, the work God obliged me to do as expiation for my evil deed. . . . The Foreigners are down, and Ireland is rising up. . . . Accept my blood and these pains that are rending me, and clean my lips from the shame that was burning them!"[101] Éamonn Ó Néill followed the story to its bitter end with the death of Ó Néill's son Aodh Óg in Roman exile in his 1901 one-acter *Na Díbeartaigh* (The exiles), also known as *Bás Aodha Óig Uí Néill* (The death of Aodh Óg Ó Néill). The play concludes on the dying man's despairing "O Ireland, Ireland . . ." (A Éire, Éire . . .)[102]

No single event or personality of the seventeenth century seems to have dominated the Gaelic imagination,[103] not even Eoghan Ruadh Ó Néill, although he was the protagonist of the episodic, pseudo-Shakespearean extravangaza *Eoghan Ruadh Ua Néill, nó Ar Son Tíre agus Creidimh* (Eoghan Ruadh Ua Néill, or For country and faith), a collaborative effort by two anonymous Maynooth students that ran for more than five hours on its initial production at the seminary in 1906.[104]

101. *An Leoirghníomh: Cluiche Trí Ghníomh* (The atonement: A play in three scenes), *ACS*, 21 August 1909. "Tá sé críochnuighthe agam, an obair do chuir Dia orm le déanamh mar shásamh im' dhroch-ghníomh. . . . Tá na Gaill ar lár agus tá Éire ag éirghe suas. . . . Glac mo chuid fola agus na pianta so atá dom' réabadh agus glan mo bheola ó'n náire a bhí á ndóghadh!"

102. *IG* 11, no. 129 (June 1901): 103–8. This must be the same play performed on 1 July 1903 at Mount Melleray under the title *Bas Aodha Óig Uí Néill* (The death of Aodh Óg Ó Néill). See "Gleó na gCath," *ACS*, 11 July 1903.

103. In April 1908 *ACS* welcomed the performance in Derry of a play commemorating the 300th anniversary of Cathaoir Ó Dochartaigh's abortive revolt. See "Cluiche Nua i nDoire" (A new play in Derry), *ACS*, 4 April 1908. While the *ACS* reference might imply that the work was in Irish, it is plain from the review in the *Derry Standard* that it was in English. See "Cahir O'Doherty at the Opera House," *Derry Standard*, 18 March 1908.

104. *Eoghan Ruadh Ua Néill, nó Ar Son Tíre agus Creidimh: Dráma Stardha ag Baint le Cogadh 1641, do Cumadh agus do Céad-Léirigheadh i gColáisde Phádraig i Maigh Nuadhad, Beirt Mhac-Léighinn d'Ullmhuigh agus do Chuir i n-Eagar do Chonnradh Chuilm Naomhtha* (Eoghan Ruadh Ua Néill, or For country and faith: A historical drama dealing with the 1641 war, composed and first produced at St. Patrick's College, Maynooth, two students prepared and edited it for the Columban League) (Baile Átha Cliath: M. H. Gill agus a Mhac, 1907). This play will also be discussed in Chapter 5.

Cromwell's siege and sack of Kilkenny is the subject of Breandán Ua Raghallaigh's bilingual "Sean-Sgeul ag Baint leis an Mainistir Dhuibh / A Tale of the Black Abbey," in which an old woman betrays the Dominicans in the town and as a result is cursed, so that "not a priest of her name was ever known from that day to this, so say the old people."[105] The Williamite Wars provided the background for Douglas Hyde's 1904 *Rígh Seumas* (King James), a thin farce in which the cowardly monarch escapes from Ireland hidden in a wine barrel;[106] for Micheál Mac Aodha's 1909 "Droichead Bhaile Átha Luain" (The bridge of Athlone), an edifying account of Irish heroism in defense of this bridge in 1691;[107] and for Pearse's incomplete play *Eoghan Gabha* (Eoghan the smith), of which we have only twenty-four handwritten pages constituting a complete first act and four pages of a second.[108] Neither Boyne nor Aughrim furnished the setting for Gaelic story or play. *Éamonn an Chnuic* (1909–10) by Micheál Ó Gríobhtha deals with the activities of the eponymous rapparee protagonist in Tipperary after the Irish surrender at Limerick.[109]

An interesting innovation in works dealing with this century was the introduction of Gaelic heroes whose triumphs were intellectual rather than martial. Thus in nonfiction we find a survey of "Sgríbhneoirí Staire Éireann san 17adh Aois" (Writers of Irish history in the seventeenth century) by Aonghus Mac Dóighrí,[110] and biographical accounts of Dubhaltach Mac Firbisigh by Eoghan Ó Neachtain in 1901[111] and of Geoffrey Keating by Risteárd Ó Foghludha in 1908.[112] In addition, Pea-

105. *Irish Rosary* 9, no. 4 (April 1905): 312–16. "Agus sé rud deir na sean-daoine ná facathas ó'n lá sain go dtí an lá indiu sagart dá sloinneadh." Ua Raghallaigh, who regularly published bilingual historical essays in the *Irish Rosary* at this time on topics ranging from the Célí Dé to the 1848 Rising, claimed to have written this story "just as it was told to myself."

106. (Dublin: M. H. Gill and Son, n.d.).

107. *ACS*, 16 January 1909.

108. See Porter, *P. H. Pearse*, 149, n. 6. I have not personally seen this MS., nor have I been able to track down the Hodges and Figgis catalogue in which it is described. It is not among the catalogues preserved in the National Library of Ireland.

109. *ACS*, 27 November 1909–25 June 1910.

110. *SF*, 23 May–4 July 1908.

111. *Dubhaltach Mac Firbisigh* (Baile Átha Cliath: Connradh na Gaedhilge, 1902).

112. Risteárd Ó Foghludha ("Fiachra Éilgeach"), *Saoghal-Ré Sheathrúin Céitinn: Sagart is Dochtúir san Diadhacht, Staruidhe, File, Ughdar, ⁊c. (The life of Geoffrey Keating: Priest and doctor of divinity, poet, author, etc.)* (Baile Átha Cliath: Muinntir an Ghoill, 1908). The essay originally appeared in *IG* in this same year. There was also a study of Keating's writings by Ernest Joynt ("An Buachaillín Buidhe") in 1903. See "Sgríbheanna Sheathrúin Chéitinn" (The writings of Geoffrey Keating), *Banba* 2, no. 3 (17 March 1903)–2, no. 7 (July 1903).

dar Mac Fhionnlaoich imaginatively re-created the arrival of the Franciscan historian Tadhg Ó Cléirigh at the castle of Feargal Ó Gadhra in Connacht in 1631. For his Ó Cléirigh the pen is indeed mightier than the sword, certainly than any English blade: "Let our descendants know the history of the country, and it is not credible that a people like us would yield to churls without faith, without refinement, without learning, without heart, without soul."[113] Tragically, the sword has its way in Piaras Béaslaí's first story in Irish, "Oidheadh Dhubhaltaigh" (The violent death of Dubhaltach), an account of the 1670 murder of Dubhaltach Mac Firbisigh by a drunken English soldier in County Sligo. The scholar is mourned by his student: "The paragon of learned men is dead. A foreign churl killed him, but his fame will be related when the lout of Luther's seed is in the chains of Hell."[114]

Not surprisingly, the majority of Gaelic historical fiction dealing with the eighteenth century focuses on the Rising of 1798. What is of interest, however, is that none of it is set where the Rising was planned—Belfast or Dublin—and little where it was most bloodily if briefly successful—Anglicized southern Leinster. Set in Wexford, "Sgéilín ar an Éirghe Amach i '98" (A little story about the Rising in '98) by "Art" deals with the killing of an innocent boy by the bayonets of soldiers searching for rebels hidden in a turf rick, and the subsequent death of the rebel leader in the last stand at Vinegar Hill.[115] In "Uaigh an Chroppí" (The croppy's grave) by "Cill Mhanntain," British troops in Wicklow torture and kill another young boy for refusing to betray Michael Dwyer.[116] But for most Gaelic writers, '98 was literally "Bliadhain na bhFranncach" (The Year of the French), and their stage the Irish-speaking West. The most substantial of these works are a novel by Seaghán Ua Ruaidhrí and plays by Mac Fhionnlaoich and Tomás Ó Ceallaigh. Ua Ruaidhrí's 1907 novel is actually titled *Bliadhain na bhFranncach*, but this title is somewhat misleading, as a good part of the

113. "An Bráthair Bocht," *ACS*, 3 April 1909. "Bíodh eolas staire na tíre ag ár sliocht agus ní inchreidte é go ngéillfeadh daoine mar sinne do bhodachaibh gan creideamh gan slacht gan múnadh gan croidhe gan anam."

114. In *Earc agus Áine agus Scéalta Eile*, 103. "Tá bile na n-ollamh ar lár. Daoi Gallda do leag é; ach beidh trácht ar a chlú agus an lópach de shíol Lútair i ngeimhleachaibh Ifrinn." Béaslaí said of the story: "I think that this is the first story I ever wrote in Irish. Perhaps I should call it a 'historical picture.' Dubhaltach Mac Firbisigh was killed exactly as is told in this story." (Measaim gurbh é an chéad sgéal Gaedhilge a sgríobhas riamh. Béidir gur chóra dhom 'peictiúir staireamhail' do ghairm de. Do marbhuigheadh Dubhaltach Mac Firbisigh díreach mar a innstear san sgéal so.) See "Réamh-Rádh" to *Earc agus Áine*, 3. The story originally appeared in the *Freeman's Journal* in 1913.

115. *UI*, 17 January 1903.

116. *Inis Fáil*, February 1908, 5–7; March 1908, 8–9.

narrative concerns a Mayoman's ultimately successful post-Rising quest for vengeance on a treacherous captain of the Yeomen. Ua Ruaidhrí does, however, attempt to elevate this personal revenge to the level of patriotic service, as when his protagonist on the eve of his departure from Ireland tells a comrade, "If we did not defeat the foreigners, it is neither your fault nor mine."[117] Nevertheless, as is frequently true of Gaelic historical fiction, the book is really just a simple adventure story set in the past. Mac Fhionnlaoich's 1903 *Tá na Francaighe ar an Muir* (The French are on the sea) is exceptional on several counts. It is set in Donegal; it celebrates Ulster Presbyterian loyalty to the ideals of the United Irish movement; and it ends on an optimistic note when two of the defeated Unitedmen return from exile to plan future resistance with a rebel who had stayed in Ireland.[118] Tomás Ó Ceallaigh's 1908 *An Fóghmhar* (The harvest) shows the strong influence of Yeats's *Cathleen Ni Houlihan*, which Ó Ceallaigh himself had translated into Irish in 1905. As in Yeats's play, a young man engaged to be married hears and follows the call of militant Ireland, although in Ó Ceallaigh's work the messenger is no allegoric crone, but rather a local United Irish activist. The play ends with the family's proud acceptance of their son's sacrifice: "Don't keen for a hero who died a glorious death as he did. That boy who died for Ireland will be sitting in a shining chair in God's Paradise tonight."[119] Cormac Ó hAirt, the hero of "Ní'l Aon Rud ann mar an Fhírinne" (There is nothing like the truth) (1904) by Seán P. Mac Éinrigh ("Tír Fhiachrach"), will spend his postrevolutionary life more humbly seated, for he survives Ballinamuck and escapes to America.[120] The two Mayo protagonists of "Sgéal Fíor ar Mhéirleachas Nochadh a hOcht" (A true story of villainy in '98), a historical folktale by Micheál Seodhach, likewise survive the Rising by duping Lord Cornwallis himself to pardon them although they have singlehandedly killed two local Orangemen and no fewer than sixteen British soldiers.[121] And finally, both the male and female protagonists of Pádraic Ó Conaire's play *An Droighneán Donn* are heroic veterans of the campaign

117. (Baile Átha Cliath: Connradh na Gaedhilge, 1907), 74. "Munar ghnoitheamar ar na Gaill, ní tusa ná mise is cionntach leis."

118. (Dublin: M. H. Gill and Son, n.d.). The play was published with an accompanying English translation.

119. (Baile Átha Cliath: M. H. Gill agus a Mhac, 1908), 38. "Ná caoin laoch a fuair bás glórmhar mar fuair seisean. An buachaill sin a fuair bás ar son na hÉireann is i gcathaoir lonnraigh i bhFlaitheas Dé bhéas sé i n-a shuidhe anocht."

120. *Inis Fáil*, August–September 1905.

121. *FL*, 11 February 1899. An English translation of the story was published in *UI*, 16 August 1902.

in Mayo, the woman having fought in men's clothing, although the play itself, set around 1801, is not really a historical work, dealing instead with the issue of the arranged marriage.[122]

Munster in the year of the Rising is the setting for several stories. Pádraig Stúndún's "Lasgadh an Athar Pheadair Uí Néill" (The flogging of Father Peadar Ó Néill) is an account of the brutal interrogation of a priest in Ballymacoda Co. Cork.[123] "Seaghán Ruadh an Ghaorthaidh" (Seaghán Ruadh of Gearagh), set around Macroom in 1798, relates the guerilla exploits of the eponymous hero against the Yeomen.[124] "Peadar Ua Siacháin" deals with a Cahirciveen man who saves a priest from searching soldiers in 1798 and later leads a revolt against the payment of tithes.[125] "An Spailpín Fánach" (The wandering spalpeen) is a tale of the activities of rapparees in and around Castleisland Co. Kerry. The author of this last story, "An Dairbhreach Dána," makes explicit from the outset his intention to vindicate the honor of his native province against the charge of cowardly inaction in '98: "The people of Munster are often criticized for holding back when there was need for fighting some hundred years ago or more. . . . If we go west from Leinster . . . we will find plenty of evidence that the ordinary people were not afraid of the Foreigners at any rate."[126] The story's protagonist, "Boc" Ó Gráda, ultimately commits suicide in London to escape the gallows for deeds committed in Ireland. A more glorious death on the field at Ballinahinch claims Conall Óg Ó Raghallaigh, the hero of Agnes O'Farrelly's 1905 Grádh agus Crádh (Love and torment), a story whose County Cavan setting is as close as Gaelic writers got to the Galltacht in their works on the '98. Again, despite its historical setting and exemplary theme, O'Farrelly's story is not a serious exploration of the Irish past, but rather a syrupy late Victorian tale of crossed love between Conall and the patriotic daughter of a cruel Anglicized landlord, just the sort of purple emotionalism that Father Henebry singled out for special

122. In Bairbre Rua agus Drámaí Eile, 28.

123. FL, 7 October 1899. The story is obviously based on fact, and Stúndún intended it to be read as history pure and simple. Father Ó Néill survived his ordeal and lived until 1835.

124. "Tadhg na Tuinne," "Seaghán Ruadh an Ghaorthaidh," UI, 16–23 April 1904. He is never taken, and dies peacefully in his bed.

125. "Fiadh," "Peadar Ua Siacháin," SF, 22 August 1908. This is an extraordinarily disjointed tale, dealing also with hedge schools, faction fighting, horse stealing, and the Otherworld!

126. ACS, 2–16 December 1905. "Is minic a cháintear muinntear Mumhan toisc leisce a bheith ortha nuair a bhí gábhadh le troid céad éigin bliadhan ó shoin is breise. . . . Má dhruidimíd ó Laighnibh siar . . . gheobhaimíd fiadnaise go leor nach amhlaidh a bhí eagla roimh na Gallaibh ar an sluagh, pé scéal é."

scorn in his discussion of O'Farrelly's work in a "Revival Irish" essay of January 1909: "Foreignism then in its most forbidding guise accosts us in the love themes of modern literature. We must shun it as the leprosy."[127]

Mention has already been made of stories dealing with the activities of the dispossessed rapparees of penal Ireland. The adventures of one such chivalrous Kerry outlaw, Risteárd de Barra, provided the action for "Conán Maol's" "Eachtra Risteáird" (The adventures of Richard) as early as 1898.[128] "Conán Maol" was also the author of the 1903 novella *Mac Fínghín Dubh,* which details the resistance of the Cork chieftain Ó Súilleabháin of Dóirín against the oppression of the Penal Laws, his self-exile to the Continent, and his despairing belief that he and his fellow aristocratic Wild Geese could better have served their country had they stayed and fought as did the peasant Whiteboys.[129] The sufferings of those who did stay were depicted by "Gruagach an Tobair" in "Dún-Mharbhughadh an tSagairt san Innis Faill" (The murder of the priest in Innis Faill). Set between Glengarriff and Kenmare in "17___," the story tells of a man who, denied the hand of a priest's sister in marriage, betrays the priest to the soldiers who kill him.[130] Qualms about what they could have done to stop such outrages afflict the valorous exiles of Tomás Ó hAodha's 1906 *Seabhac na Ceathramhan Caoile* (The hawk of Carrowkeel), a romantic and sentimental play set against the background of Irish heroism at Fontenoy, a battle the Wild Geese wish could have been fought on their native soil: "I would far prefer to break the power of the English at home—on the plains of Thomond, for example."[131] O hAodha fused Gaelic cultural and political nationalism in the person of his "Seabhac"; the young man not only fights England in the uniform of France, but is also the devoted son of the poet and scholar Mícheál Cuimín. What most impressed the play's Oireachtas audience, however, were the sound effects for the battle scene. Indeed, some were apparently so taken that they demanded an

127. *The Leader,* 9 January 1909. Henebry was writing specifically of the "love sentiment" in O'Farrelly's *An Cneamhaire* (1903).

128. In *An Buaiceas,* 52–75. The story was originally published in *IG* in 1898 and won an Oireachtas Prize for "sgéal eachtraidheachta" (an adventure story) that same year.

129. (Dublin: Irish Book, 1903).

130. *UI,* 14 May–16 July 1904.

131. *Seabhac na Ceathramhan Caoile: Dráma Cheithre Ghníomh* (The hawk of Carrowkeel: A four-act play) (Baile Átha Cliath: Connradh na Gaedhilge, 1906), 47. A picture of the costumed cast of the Maynooth production of this play appeared in *Irisleabhar Mhuighe Nuadhad* (1912): 51. "B'fhearr liom go mór cumhacht na Sasanach do bhriseadh ag baile—ar mhachairíbh Thuadh-Mhumhan, cuir i gcás."

immediate encore, and thus, in the words of William P. Ryan, "changed drama to comedy for the moment."[132]

It was a brief and entirely unpremeditated moment. The revivalists found little that was amusing in the nation's history. Moreover, in their works on the '98 they came face to face with the issue of full-blown physical-force republicanism, the dangers of exploring which would be intensified when they examined the more immediate past of the nineteenth century. A common response to this challenge was to evade it. For example, Father Dinneen presented the agony of the Famine in almost purely religious, or rather, sectarian, terms in his 1901 play *Creideamh agus Gorta* (Faith and famine). And while in his social history *Muinntear Chiarraidhe roimh an Droch-Shaoghal* (The people of Kerry before the Famine) (1905) he raged at the British government's callousness during the Famine,[133] the conclusion of his play, with its chorus of angels to bring the souls of starved Catholic children to their eternal reward, focused more on the spiritual compensations for earthly suffering than on the political and economic system that caused it.[134] "Creideamh agus Grádh" (Faith and love) a story written in 1903 by Tomás Ághas (Thomas Ashe), a republican who died in British custody of forced feeding in 1917, also opted for a religious and fatalistic reading of the Great Hunger. A relatively well-off Catholic farmer refuses to let Soupers use his barn and as a result, although sick with fever, is evicted to die on the road. His son must emigrate, and when he returns he finds his fiancée on her deathbed. His response is to become a Franciscan.[135] More aggressively sectarian is Tomás de Brett's Famine folktale "Leapthach" (1898), in which the widowed mother of a moronic son cold-bloodedly murders a Protestant minister to protect a crock of gold the boy has found.[136] Another folk-modeled tale, Seán Ó Muimhneacháin's

132. *The Pope's Green Island*, 300–301.

133. (Baile Átha Cliath: M. H. Gill agus a Mhac, 1905), 83.

134. *Creideamh agus Gorta: Traighidheacht Bhaineas le hAimsir an Droch-Shaoghail, 1847* (Faith and famine: A tragedy dealing with the time of the Famine, 1847) (Dublin: E. Ponsonby, 1901). In chapter 12 of *Muinntear Chiarraidhe*, also titled "Creideamh agus Gorta," Dinneen seems to see the Famine primarily as a test of Irish Catholic faith. Thus he blasts the "diabolic" (diabhlaidhe) work of the Soupers, claims that parents would rather have seen their children starve than turn Protestant, and offers a cautionary tale of a family that took both soup and children's clothing and then died before their intended reconciliation with the Church (86–87).

135. *An Lóchrann*, September 1918, 1–2. The story was submitted to *An Lóchrann* after Ashe's death by Micheál Ó Conchobhair, who also supplied the date of composition.

136. *FL*, 18 June 1898. When the investigating police later dig up a goat's skull from what they believe to be the minister's grave, the boy comments: "Oh! your minister was indeed a devil: look at the horns that have grown out of him since he was buried." (Och,

Procadóir na nDeachmhadh (The tithe collector) raises and then ducks the issues involved in the Tithe War. The peasants who find the collector's lost money feel no obligation to return it to him, but their keeping it is an utterly apolitical act, for they use their windfall purely for their own gain and then repay the man when they have made themselves rich.[137] More politically aware are the West Clare smugglers of Tomás Ó hAodha's serialized novel *Cuan an Óir* (The harbor of gold) (1913), whose creator provided them an explicitly political motive for their profitable activities: "A ship or two used to come in almost every single month, and they would not leave empty on their return. When John Bull made laws for his own benefit, and when the wool trade in Ireland was destroyed by the oppressive taxes imposed on the manufactures of the country, many a valuable cargo of Clare wool was sent abroad to spite honest John."[138]

Landlord tyranny and the specter of eviction are the subject of three important early Gaelic plays, Labhras Ua Tuathail's *Lá an Cíosa* (Rent day) (1903), Tomás Ó Ceallaigh's *Ar Thaoibh an Locha* (Beside the lake) (1908), and Hyde's *Maistín an Bhéarla* (The Bully of the English language) (1914). All three works dramatize the anguish of a farmer threat-

---

ba diabhal go cinnte do bhí in bhur ministeír: féach na h-adharca atá fásta as ó cuireadh é.) Incidentally, the fool later kills a Catholic priest, but that is done entirely by accident! Such often violent anti-Protestantism was, understandably if regrettably, common in the native folk tradition. One thinks, for example, of the tale in which the poet Aodhagán Ó Rathaille sees a minister's son hanging from a tree and exclaims: "Your fruit is good, tree, / May your fruit flourish on every branch, / Alas! that the trees of Ireland / are not full of your fruit every day." (Is maith do thoradh, a chrainn, / Rath do thoraidh air gach aon chraoibh, / Mo chreach! gan crainn Insi Fáil / Lán dod' thoradh gach aon lá.) See "Sean-Chuimhne Aodhagáin Uí Rathaille" (A Reminiscence of Aodhagán Ó Rathaille"), in *Dánta Aodhagáin Uí Rathaille / The Poems of Egan O'Rahilly*, ed. and trans. Patrick S. Dinneen (London: Irish Texts Society, 1900), 232–35.

137. (N.p.: n.p., 1907).

138. *ACS*, 13 September 1913. "Thagadh soitheach nó dhó isteach gach éin-mhí nach mór agus ní follamh a dh'imthighidís ag filleadh dhóibh. Nuair do dhein Seaghán Buidhe dlighthe ar mhaithe leis féin, agus nuair do scriosadh an cheárd olna i nÉirinn le truimeacht na cána do gearradh ar dhéantúsaibh na tíre, is mó last luachmhar d'olann Uí Bhriocáin do cuireadh anonn thar sáile le stainncín ar Sheaghán macánta."

They are not the only patriotic smugglers in Gaelic historical fiction. "Conán Maol's" *Mac Fínghín Dubh* also practices the trade, and the smugglers in Ua Ruaidhrí's *Bliadhain na bhFranncach*, while nervous about sheltering a rapparee, do so out of their hatred for foreign rule. On the other hand, although this rapparee himself takes pains to rob only the British and their allies, he nonetheless worries that his activity is morally degrading. See *Mac Fínghín Dubh*, 26; and *Bliadhain*, 45–62. In 1912 Seán Tóibín won a *WF* Oireachtas Prize for a love story involving what seem to be just plain smugglers until we learn at the end that some of the money they make is used to send a boy to Sgoil Éanna! See "Prize Gaelic Story," *WF*, 12 December 1913.

ened with the loss of his holding, and the first two resolve the crisis with a facile and unconvincing deus ex machina climax. In the former, the greedy landlord Manders seems to undergo an instantaneous conversion to human decency when his wife points out that he hasn't been a very nice person. At play's end, he sacks his unscrupulous agent and vows to do his utmost to keep his tenants safe, secure, and at home in Ireland by allowing them to buy out their holdings at bargain rates.[139] In Ó Ceallaigh's play, the threatened farmer is driven to the desperate decision to shoot his landlord, an act from which he is dissuaded by a neighbor who appeals to his pragmatic rather than moral sense, using arguments that could have been used against any form of physical resistance in nineteenth- and indeed early twentieth-century Ireland: "What good is the killing of a single villain? Villains will always be plentiful."[140] The play achieves a happy, but politically meaningless, ending when the farmer saves his daughter from the landlord's lecherous clutches by marrying her off to someone else, and then has his farm saved by the sudden arrival of a wealthy son from America. Given the increasing pressure on him from advanced nationalists, pressure that drove him to resignation as league president in 1915, Hyde's reading of nineteenth-century Irish history in *Maistín an Bhéarla* is understandable if equally unconvincing. In this play, the villain is the Anglicized Irish Anglicizer, the new national schoolmaster, while the potential savior of both peasantry and their language is the enlightened English landowner, here Lady Dromanore, whose "accidental" death is engineered by the master. For Hyde, at least in this play, the fault does not seem to be in the system itself but in those who adminster it abusively. Nevertheless, it should be noted that his is the only one of these three plays that ends tragically, with the noble heroine dead, the villain triumphant, and the worthy peasants in serious jeopardy.[141]

Father Dinneen's inability to resolve his own ambivalence about the

139. Labhras Ua Tuathail, *Lá an Chíosa*, *ACS*, 24 October–5 December 1903. Actually the play lacks a clear historical context and is included here because Pearse called it "a blending of the tragedy and comedy of the land war" on its performance at the 1903 Feis Chonnacht. See "Feis Chonnacht," *ACS*, 29 August 1903.

140. Tomás Ó Ceallaigh, *Ar Thaoibh an Locha*, in *An tAthair Tomás Ó Ceallaigh agus a Shaothar* (Father Tomás Ó Ceallaigh and his work), ed. An tAthair Tomás S. Ó Láimhín (Gaillimh: Complacht Foillsighe an Iarthair, Tóranta, 1943), 113. "Cé'n mhaith aon chladhaire amháin a mharbhadh? Beidh cladhairí go tiugh ann i gcomhnaidhe."

141. See Hyde, *Maistín an Bhéarla: Dráma Éin-Ghnímh* (Baile Átha Cliath: Oifig Díolta Foilseacháin Rialtais, 1934). The play was produced by the Gaelic acting company Na Cluicheoirí at the Abbey Theatre in February 1914. That Hyde was consciously challenging the growing physical-force movement within the league is evident from a favorable reference in the play to the nonviolent Daniel O'Connell (9).

morality of violence in face of oppression may explain why his un-published story "Cáit Ní Laoghaire—Scéal Bhaineas leis na Buachaillí Bána" (Cáit Ní Laoghaire—A story dealing with the Whiteboys) was never completed. A patriotic Whiteboy leader, having described the plunder of Ireland "by rabid wolves who have been crushing you and destroying you since you were born," seems to want to fire his troops to vengeance: "Don't give them respite or mercy, but relieve the dis-tress of your country without delay." But the narrative text states that he also explicitly tells them not to shed blood, and the story then breaks off.[142] Finished stories could be every bit as evasive, as is "Diarmaid Ó Ceallaigh" by "Pádraig na Léime," in which two land-grabbers end up dead, but with no blame attaching to anyone. The former owner of a farm accidentally shoots a man who took his farm as they wrestle over a gun. Years later, he faces the same man's son in a duel in Paris and is victorious—when his opponent dies of a heart attack! He is then able to return to Ireland and buy the now vacant ancestral land.[143]

More credible is the conscious and intentional agrarian violence in another of "Pádraig na Léime's" stories, "Is Mairg a Bhíonn Síos an Chéad Lá" (Woe to the one who is down on the first day); in Tomás Ó hAodha's "Brianach Mhóire"; in "Go hUair a Bháis" (To the hour of his death) by Pádraic Ó Conaire; and in "Dílseacht agus Tíorántacht" (Loyalty and tyranny) by Colm Ó Gaora ("An Gruagach Bán"). In the first, two men meet their deaths, one in Ireland and one in California, as the result of violence that has its roots in rack-renting, dishonest agency, and land grabbing.[144] In the second, a man whose mother dies on the street after eviction leads an ambush that wounds several police-men and soldiers—somehow killing none—and terrifies his landlord into stopping his tyrannous conduct.[145] In the third, a particularly loath-some Galway landlord ends his days "with a bullet shot through him"

142. Dinneen Papers, National Library of Ireland, MS. G827. The story is not dated. The leader refers to the plunder of Ireland "ag faolchonaibh nimhe atá do bhur mbru-ghadh agus do bhur mbascadh ó rugadh sibh," and exhorts his men: "Ná tugaidh spás ná trócaire acht reidhtighidh ceasna bhur dtíre gan moill." In "Peadar Ua Siacháin" by "Fiadh," the priest saved from soldiers urges his rescuer not to endanger his soul by pursuing and harming them. The local leader's plan is to capture them if necessary, though we are never told what he plans to do with them if he is successful. The dilemma never arises because the soldiers are sent off to suppress the Rising in Wexford. See "Pea-dar Ua Siacháin," SF, 22 August 1908.

143. WF, 11 March 1911. The story won a WF Oireachtas Prize in 1910.

144. "Pádraig na Léime" (Pádraig Ó Séaghdha, Cahirdaniel), "Is Mairg a Bhíonn Síos an Chéad Lá," WF, 12 March 1910. The story won a WF Oireachtas Prize in 1909.

145. Tomás Ó hAodha, "Brianach Mhóire," WF, 16 March 1912. The story won a WF Oireachtas Prize in 1911.

(agus piléar sgaoilte tríd).[146] In "Dílseacht agus Tíorántacht," set at some unspecified time during the reign of Victoria, "na Turais," Conamara Whiteboys, feel no compunction about running their homemade pikes through the bodies of constabulary and military. Less convincing than their violence is their success, as they rout a force of five hundred English soldiers. While Ó Gaora never links his formidable rural guerrillas with any specific organized resistance movement, he does take pains to emphasize that theirs is no local vendetta, however justified. In death they take their place in the national pantheon: "But there is one thing for which they will be distinguished forever, and that is that they died for their country and that they shed the last drop of their blood for Cathleen Ni Houlihan."[147] Violent confrontation is avoided in "An Piléir agus an Gabhar" (The peeler and the goat) by D. Ó Muimhneacháin, but the threat of it rings true even in this fundamentally comic tale. During the Land War, a cowardly RIC sergeant guarding the house of an evicted tenant knows he can expect no mercy if attacked by "Captain Moonlight" and his guerrilla band: "He knew full well that it is little heed that gentleman would pay to the "white flag" if it had to be raised. The Captain had no use for prisoners. . . . The Sergeant had no hope that the Captain, or the villains under him, would fight as they did in civilized nations."[148]

Common to virtually all Gaelic works about agrarian unrest is an unwillingness or perhaps even inability to confront the ideological implications of Irish economic distress. Consistently the problem is reduced to one of straightforward imperialism, political, economic, or cultural. Thus the actual system of landlordism, with its inherently inequable distribution of the means of earning a living, is never ques-

146. Pádraic Ó Conaire, "Go hUair a Bháis," *Guth na nGaedheal*, November 1904, 12–17.

147. *ACS*, 20 November 1909. "Acht aon rud amháin a mbeidh a shéala ortha go deo na ndeor, sé sin go bhfuair siad bás ar son a dtíre agus gur dhoirteadar an braon deireannach dá gcuid fola ar son Chaitlín ní hUallacháin." On the other hand, the sharp-eyed and unsentimental Pádraic Ó Conaire knew that such capacity for self-sacrifice was not universal among Irish countrymen. In his play *An Uadhacht*, the idealism of a now impoverished Land League organizer and his reliance on ethnic and class solidarity are dismissed as obtuse naiveté by his own brother. See Ó Conaire, *An Uadhacht*, in *Bairbre Rua agus Drámaí Eile*, 35.

148. *ACS*, 9 January 1909. "Do bhí a shár-fhios aige gur beag é toradh an duine uasail úd ar an 'mbrat bán' dá mbadh rud é gurbh' éigean é árdadh. Ní raibh aon ghnó de phríosúnaigh ag an gCaptaen. . . . Ní raibh puinn muinighine ag an Sárseant go ndéanfadh an Captaen, ná na bioránaigh a bhíodh fé, troid de réir mar dheinid ins na náisiúin síbhialta." Of course, Colm Ó Gaora was also quick to point out the sort of fate that awaited any of the "Moonlighters" should they be captured.

tioned, much less condemned, only the abuses of English or Anglicized landlords, and the ultimate solution of the economic crisis is seen as a virtually automatic and inevitable consequence of Gaelic reconquest of Ireland. The sole exception here is Séamus Ó Duirinne's 1905 Fenian play *Ar Son Baile agus Tíre* (For home and country), in which the rebel schoolmaster stresses the class basis of the national struggle: "We are watching them driving our neighbors out of their homes, throwing them out on the roads without shelter from the rain. Is this work the will of God? Patience is a good thing, and hasn't Father John often told us . . . not to spill a drop of blood, but look what we have as a result."[149]

Of course in dealing with the Fenian period the revivalists would, one would think, have had no place to hide from the dilemma of patriotic bloodshed. Nevertheless Tomás Ó hAodha at least somehow managed to sidestep such troubling issues implicit in his own choice of subject. In his 1903 novel *An Gioblachán* (The ragged man) he merely uses his protagonists's Fenian connections to lend politically correct excitement to a farfetched adventure yarn. "An Gioblachán" is an IRB organizer who has built up an arsenal in his elaborate cave hideout in West Clare. Ó hAodha devotes most of the story to a description of the cave's wonders, dismissing the Fenian defeat and the paralyzing divisions in the American Clan na Gael in a few pages. The only revolutionary act in the book, the Fenian's firing on his landlord, is negated when he learns with relieved conscience that the man had actually been killed by a lightening bolt that flashed simultaneously with his gunshot.[150]

Qualms of conscience also afflict the protagonist of "Aimsir na bhFígínídhe i nUíbh Ráthach" (The time of the Fenians in Iveragh) (1909), a "short novel" (úrscéal gairid) by "Pádraig na Léime." Cormac Ó Raghallaigh, the local Fenian leader, learns that one of his men is an informer but is dissuaded from killing him by the moral and religious pleas of his fiancée Nora. Although sorely tempted—the man's treachery has already caused the death of his brother Pádraig—Cormac spares him: "Thanks be to God that I am free from danger. If Pádraig is al-

149. *Ar Son Baile agus Tíre: Dráma Cheithre Ghníomha* (For home and country: A four-act play) (Baile Átha Cliath: Muintir Fhaellamhain, 1905), 2. "Támaoid ag féachaint orra ag ruagairt ár gcomharsain amach as a dtíghthibh, dá gcaitheamh amach ar na bóithribh gan clúdach ó'n bhfearthainn. Bé toil Dé an obair seo? Is maith an rud í an fhoighne agus nach minic a dubhairt An tAthair Seaghán linn . . . gan braon fola a dhortadh, acht féach cad tá dhá bhárr againn."

150. *An Gioblachán: Finnsgéal Nuadh-Dhéanta* (The ragged man: An original adventure story) (Baile Átha Cliath: Connradh na Gaedhilge, 1903), 80–82.

lowed to see me from the Home of the Bright Saints, he will be joyful tonight that my soul is free from mortal sin. . . . I will leave him to the judgment of the God of Glory, and may He forgive him all his evil deeds."[151] However ethically commendable, his act of mercy is tactically disastrous, for the man escapes and betrays the Fenians on the eve of the Rising. After the rout and the death of Cormac, another rebel is unwilling to wait on divine justice, himself strangling the informer in a fair fight. Betrayal and forgiveness are also at the heart of Micheál Ó Conchubhair's "An Dóibheart agus an Bharthanacht" (The evil deed and eternity), in which a group of American Fenians sheltering after the defeat praise their comrades and lament that "there wasn't a move we made that wasn't told to the English officials." Most of the men are former Union soldiers, but at least one is an ex-Confederate who informs on their leader. Years later, although fully aware of the man's treachery and having already saved his life on two separate occasions, this leader takes him in when he finds him homeless on the streets of San Francisco.[152] On the other hand, moral issues are avoided altogether in Domhnall Ó Súilliobháin's 1903 story "Bord an Fhín—Aimsir na bhFíníní" (Bord an Fhín—The time of the Fenians). Despite some impeccable nationalist rhetoric, Ó Súilliobháin drains all meaningful political content from his work by manipulating his ostensible plotline of British pursuit of a West Kerry Fenian leader into a virtual folktale savoring the farcical ineptitude of police and informers as their quarry escapes.[153] Even sillier was Muircheartach Ua Séaghdha's "An Seargeant agus an Gabhar, nó an tSlighe do Rug Cosa-Buidhe ar an bhFiannach" (The sergeant and the goat, or How "Yellow Legs" caught the Fenian), in which an RIC man is duped into shooting a mounted goat's head he thinks is the Fenian leader James Stephens.[154]

More forthright was the approach of Séamus Ó Duirinne, Patrick O'Shea ("Conán Maol"?), "Pádraig na Léime," and Patrick Pearse, all of whom embraced the Fenian cause without compromise or apology. In *Ar Son Baile agus Tíre*, Ó Duirinne's mouthpiece, the Fenian schoolmaster Uilliam Mac Craith, preaches class consciousness and republican separatism instead of random agrarian violence as the answer to the

151. *IG* 19, no. 3 (March 1909): 141. "Buidheachas le Dia go bhfuilim saor ó ghuais. Má tá sé ceadtha ag Pádraig mé fheiscint ó Áras na Naomh nGeal, beidh lúthgháir air anocht m'anam a bheith saor ón bpeacadh marbhthach. . . . Fágfad é fé bhreitheamhnas Dé na Glóire agus go maithfidh Sé a dhroichbhearta dhó."

152. *WF*, 11 March 1911. The story won a *WF* Oireachtas Prize in 1910. "Ní raibh cor d'ár chuireamar dínn nár innseadh d'oifigíbh Shasanna."

153. *IG* 13, no. 151 (April 1903): 262–67.

154. *WF*, 15 December 1900.

political, social, and economic oppression of rural Ireland (2–4). In addition, the play offers a rosy picture of clerical support for the cause when the local parish priest, despite his O'Connellite reservations about violence, blesses the men as they set out to fight: "I have often said that peace is best, but it is not possible to preserve it any longer. They want to sweep the Irish from the country, but I say that death is a hundred times better than for that disgrace to happen to us."[155] Significantly, to suppress the strains of "the Harp that Once," Ó Duirinne ended his play on the expectant eve of the Rising rather than on its bathetic aftermath.

"Pádraig na Léime," on the other hand, followed the Rising to its bitter and bloody end and beyond in "Aimsir na bhFígínídhe," as his rebels kill an informer and shoot down several pursuing RIC men as they make for a ship to take them into French exile. Although his story focuses largely on personal treachery and vengeance, it also features a debate between the martyred protagonist's cautious father and militant mother over the wisdom of armed resistance. Not surprisingly, she gets the best lines: "It is, at any rate, the glut of treacherous foreigners that has caused our plight, and it seems to me that one single hour of fighting on the battlefield would be better than a long, easy life under the hooves of the foreigners."[156] Furthermore, one of the rebels makes clear that while this battle has been lost, the war will go on: "The sword will be bared again some day for the freedom of this country" (186).[157] In Patrick O'Shea's "Fear na nGiobal" (The ragged man), the defeated Fenians fight their way out of Ireland into exile in Chicago, where they pledge that "we'll have our day over there" (beidh lá againn thall").[158] Fenians who didn't escape were the subject of an inspiring little tale of patriotic death in the "Ár dTeanga Féin" (Our own language) column of the United Irishman,[159] and of Micheál Ó Raghallaigh's 1903 "Micheál Mháirtín," the story of an old patriot who is overjoyed to learn of the revolt in 1867 and of his own son's involvement, but dies of a stroke

155. P. 20. "Is minic a dubhras gur b'í an tsíothcháin do b'fhearr, acht ní féidir í a choimeád níos sia. Teastuigheann uatha na hÉireannaigh do scuabadh as an dtír, acht deirim gur fearr an bás céad uair ná an tarcuisne sin do tharla dúinn."

156. IG 19, no. 4 (April 1909): 178. "Is iad iomairdí muirearach Shasana fé ndeara ár gcruadhchás, pé scéal é, agus b'fhearr aon-uair-a-chluig amháin, dar liom-sa, ag troid ar pháirc an bhuailte ná saoghal fada saoráideach fé chrúbaibh na nEachtranach."

157. "Nochtfar an claidheamh lá éigin arís ar son saoirse na tíre seo."

158. WF, 15 December 1900. The story won a WF Oireachtas Prize. This "Patrick O'Shea" is most likely "Conán Maol," as "Gruagach an Tobair" always used his pen name, and "Pádraig na Léime," who didn't acquire his pseudonym until 1907, identified himself before that time by indicating his home place of Cahirdaniel.

159. UI, 8 February 1902.

when he hears of their defeat and the boy's death. His last words are: "Twenty years from today Ireland will be free."[160]

The Irish text of *Owen*, Pearse's "little dramatic episode," no longer survives, but we do know that it was staged twice in the original in late 1913, and we have an obviously literal translation prepared by the author himself in 1915. Pearse set the play on 4 March 1867, the night before the Rising, and wrote of one of its productions: "At the St. Enda's performance we gave the play a western setting, the bigger boys wearing bawneens and the smaller boys the long frocks worn by children in the Connacht Gaedhealtacht."[161] The play offers a variant on Pearse's theme of messianic self-sacrifice, as his young hero dies holding off an RIC search party so that his Fenian schoolmaster can escape. However modest the work itself, in *Owen* themes developed by the revivalists in their writings on the Irish past are followed through to their logical conclusion, as history, on the eve of the Easter Rising, began to merge into prophecy.[162] Literally so, for on 11 March 1916, the *Weekly Freeman* began serialization of an Oireachtas Prize–winning story from the previous year. The story, Pádraig Ó Grádaigh's "Scéal Eachtra na Gé Fiadhaine" (The story of the adventure of "the Wild Goose"), deals with Volunteer drilling and gunrunning in the ship of the title. The third installment appeared on 22 April, two days before the Rising broke out; there seem to have been no more.[163]

160. *Banba* 2, no. 2 (1 February 1903): 129–31. "Dá fhichid bliadhain ó 'ndiu beidh Éire saor."

161. *Fianna*, n.s., no. 6 (December 1915): 16–17. It was, of course, one of Pearse's most cherished beliefs that Gaeltacht folk were instinctive republicans, a notion rejected out of hand by Father Francis Shaw in "The Canon of Irish History—A Challenge," *Studies* 61 (Summer 1972): 113–53.

162. Pearse's last work of fiction, the unfinished adventure story for boys *The Wandering Hawk*, published as a serial in *Fianna* from February 1915 to January 1916, also deals with the Fenian period. In *Fianna* each episode was said to have been originally written in Irish, but Séamas Ó Buachalla writes: "Pearse refers to it in his literary testament as having been written originally in English and not translated from the Irish as indicated in *Fianna*." See Ó Buachalla, "The Literary Works: A Bibliographic Guide," in *Literary Writings*, 10. The two most interesting aspects of this work are its depiction of a Catholic headmaster's support for the goals if not the methods of the Fenians and its forthright acceptance of violence. Describing his role as a schoolboy in a battle with a British gunboat, the narrator reports: "We blazed. I shot as cooly as if I had been firing at a row of Maggies at a fair. I saw men go down with as much satisfaction as I should have seen a Maggie topple. It was as interesting as, and not more exciting than, shooting Maggies. I felt a sort of artistic pleasure in doing my work well." See Pearse, *The Wandering Hawk*, in *Literary Writings*, ed. Ó Buachalla, 206, 232. Since the story breaks off incomplete, we do not know whether Pearse would here have faced the fact of Fenian defeat.

163. *WF*, 11 March–22 April 1916.

Before discussing those themes we should, however, examine the approach to historical scholarship prevalent among most of these early writers, for in no small degree the method was the message. The history of Gaelic Ireland was largely terra incognita at this time, and several Gaelic intellectuals were aware that its exploration would be a tricky and even perilous enterprise. The great pioneer in that venture was, of course, Eoin Mac Néill, of whom Francis John Byrne has written, "To Mac Néill belongs the credit of having dragged Celtic Ireland practically single-handed from the antiquarian mists into the light of history."[164] While none of his colleagues even began to approach Mac Néill's scholarly accomplishments, he was not alone in his efforts to dispel, or at least to urge others to dispel, those mists obscuring not only the Celtic past but also the history of the Gaelic nation right through the nineteenth century. For example in the introduction to his "Tús Staire na hÉireann" (The beginning of Irish history) William P. Ryan challenged contemporary Irish historians to begin the spadework for a broad social and cultural as well as political and military history of the country:

> There is a great task ahead of us before the history of Ireland will be entirely clear to us. The history of our country is extensive. . . . Therefore when we know about the kings and the heroes of the country, we don't know its history. We must also have knowledge of its ordinary life from age to age, knowledge of its laws, knowledge of its games and customs, knowledge of its music, knowledge of its poetry, knowledge of its schools, knowledge of everything connected with it.[165]

Liam Ua Domhnaill agreed, criticizing historians for their belief that "writers of history had only to raise the monuments of the past and to say a word or two about the people who lived in it. . . . They have too much childish talk about the kings, about their grandeur and about their glory, about the battles they won and the wealth they amassed, so that they forget altogether the people of the country and the condition

164. "Mac Néill the Historian," in *The Scholar Revolutionary*, 17.
165. *ACS*, 24 October, 1903. "Is mór an obair atá romhainn sul mar a bhéas stair na hÉireann ar fad soiléir dúinn. Is fíor-leathan an rud stair ár dtíre. . . . Dá bhrígh sin nuair atá eólus againn ar ríghthibh agus ar laochraibh na tíre níl a stair againn. Ní fuláir dúinn eólus ar a gnáth-shaoghal, ó aois go haois, eólus ar a dlíghthibh, eólus ar a cleasaibh agus a nósaibh, eólus ar a cuid ceóil, eólus ar a filidheacht, eólus ar a sgoileannaibh, eólus ar gach rud d'ár bhain léithi a bheith againn mar an gcéadna."

they were in."[166] Pádraig Ua Dálaigh was likewise fed up with the traditional approach to history, writing: "I, at any rate, would take more pleasure in learning how the people of the countryside amongst the mountains, plains, and glens of Ireland spent their lives, than how the great chieftains lived, fighting and wrangling and plundering each other and destroying their native land." Moreover, Ua Dálaigh saw such educational work as particularly appropriate for the novelist: "That's the sort of thing that would make for the kind of storytelling I have in mind, that is, the thing Scott did in Scotland and Liam Ó Coirealláin (or William Carleton) in Ireland."[167]

Reviewing an English-language history of County Mayo, Pádraic Ó Domhnalláin suggested some of the areas in need of further attention: "What about education? What about trade? What about the way the chieftains and princes lived? What about agriculture and what about fishing?"[168] His list was extended by "Cú Cadhain," who laid out a historiographical agenda comprehensive to the point of intimidation, arguing that the study of history

166. "I mBaile Átha Cliath," ACS, 11 April 1908. Ua Domhnaill criticized them for their belief "nach raibh le déanamh ag sgríbhneoiribh an tseanchais acht leacracha na seanaimsire do thógáil agus focal nó dhó a rádh i dtaobh na ndaoine do mhair innti. . . . Bíonn an iomad cainnte leanbaidhe aca fá na ríghthibh, fá n-a ngradam agus fá n-a mórdhacht, fá na cathannaibh do bhuaidheadar agus fá'n saidhbhreas do chnuasadar go dtí nach mbíonn aon chuimhneamh aca ar mhuinntir na tíre agus ar an mbail a bhí ortha."

Ua Domhnaill urged Irish historians to confront the political, social, and economic implications of the facts they unearthed:

When there is a mighty king full of worldly wealth and personal beauty, the people of the country are often under harsh oppression. Customarily wealth is amassed and castles built with the slavery and the destruction of the people.

(Nuair a bhíonn rí mór-chumhachtach ann agus é lán de mhaoin shaoghalta agus d'áilneacht pearsan, is minic a bhíonn muinntir na tíre fá dhaor-bhroid go cruaidh. De ghnáth cnuastar an saidhbhreas agus tógtar na caisleáin le sglábhaidheacht agus le sgrios na ndaoine.)

167. "Sgéaluidheacht" (Storytelling), editorial, ACS, 23 May 1914. "Agus ba thaithneamhaighe liomsa, ar aon chuma, eolas dfhagháil ar cionus do chaith muinntear na tuaithe a saoghail imeasg sléibhte is bánta is gleannta na hÉireann, ná ar cionus do chaith na taoisigh mhóra a saoghail ag troid, ag achrann is ag creachadh a chéile, agus ag milleadh a dtíre dhúthchais. . . . Sin é an rud do dhéanfadh an sórt Sgéaluidheachta atá agamsa i m'aigne .i. an rud do-rinne Scott i nAlbainn agus Liam Ó Coirealláin (nó William Carleton) i nÉirinn." Ua Dálaigh then went on to spell out the daunting qualifications such work would require, including historical knowledge and scholarly discrimination. In this regard it is worth noting that he was silent on the Gaelic historical fiction of his own time.

168. "Ó Chúige Chonnacht" (From the province of Connacht), ACS, 15 August 1908. "Céard fá'n oideachas? Céard fá'n tráchtáil? Céard fá'n gcaoi ar mhair na taoisigh agus na prionnsaí? Céard fá'n talmhuidheacht agus céard fá'n iasgaireacht?"

should satisfy us as to the nature of the institutions existing at any particular period . . . should introduce us to the active, formative portion of the community which supplied the fighting men and the governing element . . . should take cognizance of the dominant ideas of the time . . . should realise and reconstruct the past . . . going down as minutely into the details of everyday life as our authorities will allow.

"Cú Cadhain" also singled out what has become one of the principal themes of Irish cultural research in our own time, the uneasy balance between tradition and innovation throughout Irish history. Every institution was to be studied to discover "what strides it had made towards its maximum position at the time, or how far it had become a thing outworn and resisting assimilation."[169]

To be truthful, however, such intellectual adventurousness and sophistication were far from universal amongst Gaelic writers on historical topics, the majority of whom, it is safe to say, were avowed, closet, or instinctive Carlyleans in their hero-worship. While we occasionally get interesting bits of social history in the odd Gaelic essay like Dineen's *Leader* column on totemism,[170] Pearse's piece on early Irish "libraries,"[171] and Ó Foghludha's study of Keating; or more substantially in Dinneen's *Muinntear Chiarraidhe* and *An Saoghal i nEirinn* (Life in Ireland); Pádraic Ó Domhnalláin's "Conamara" (1914–15);[172] or the early chapters of Ua Laoghaire's *Mo Sgéal Féin*; more characteristic of Gaelic historical writing at this time is the recitation of litanies of the illustrious dead. Particularly in early exhortations to the study of the past, Irish history was conceived of as a straightforward series of heroic biographies. One such roll call, that of Donnchadh Pléimeann, has already been cited. Dinneen offered his own list for students in *Native History in*

169. "Wanted—A History of Anglicisation," *ACS*, 16 May 1903. To make such an analysis possible, Gaelic intellectuals welcomed the appearance of scholarly publications like *Archivum Hibernicum*. See Tadhg Ó Donnchadha's review of the first volume of this journal in "Leabhra" (Books), *ACS*, 22 February 1913.

170. "Geasa agus Toteime" (Taboos and totemism), *The Leader*, 9 July 1910.

171. "Leabharlanna sa tSean-Shaoghal" (Libraries in Antiquity), *An Leabharlann* 1, no. 2 (June 1905): 140–43. Pearse here showed a good familiarity with the annalistic sources of early Irish history, but could not resist the predictable invidious Eurocentric comparison: "When the English had no more literature or books than the black men of Africa have today, books and libraries were widespread in Ireland." (Nuair nach raibh de litridheacht ná de leabhraibh ag an Sasanach acht an oiread is tá ag fearaibh gorma na hAfraice indiu bhí leabhra agus leabharlanna go fairsing i nÉirinn.)

172. Ó Domhnalláin's "Conamara" ran in *ACS* from 19 December 1914 to 7 August 1915.

National Schools: "St. Patrick, St. Columbkille, Brian Boru, Henry the Second, Art Mac Murrogh, Earl of Desmond, Hugh O' Neill, Cromwell, Sarsfield, Swift, Grattan, O'Connell. On these dozen names, as pegs, the drapery of Irish History could be hung."[173] Indeed, for Dineen, without familiarity with "the deeds and character of the noblest and most heroic of her children," Irish history, "the knowledge of mother Erin," would be "as empty of meaning and absurd as the play of Hamlet robbed of the character of the prince of Denmark" (10). It would serve no purpose to list the minor personal variants of the litany or the scaled-down invocations of "the warriors and the heroes who always stood forth, who are standing forth today, and who will stand forth forever as a beacon, an example, and a cause for boasting for the family of the Gaels."[174] More to the point is that in practice this biographical fixation permeated Gaelic historical writing, including the two general texts published by the Gaelic League in the first decades of this century, Ó Neachtain's *Stair-Cheachta* and Breathnach's *Stair na hÉireann*. Even Mac Néill could momentarily succumb to the temptation: "Then, as a distinct chapter, the Norse inroads and settlements, with the story of Turgesius and Mael Sechnaill, and with the story of Gormlaith and Cormac and Niall Glundubh. After that the heroic career of Brian."[175]

As is evident from the prevalence of proper names in the titles of Gaelic historical works of nonfiction and fiction alike, for many revivalists the protagonist was the point. Their principal interest was in the

173. P. 19. To be fair, Dinneen also wrote: "Instead of taking names of historical characters the teacher might takes dates or events, and group the history round them, or both systems may be employed together" (20).

174. An tAthair Uáitéir Ó Conmhacáin, "Ár Náire nó Ár n-Onóir" (Our shame or our honor), *ACS*, 24 June 1899. Ó Conmhacáin praised "na gaisgidhigh agus an laochradh a sheas amach ariamh, atá i n-a seasamh amach andiu agus a sheasfas amach go bráth mar lóchrann agus mar shompla agus adhbhar gaisge ag Clann na n-Gaedheal."

175. Mac Néill, "The Teaching of History in Irish Schools," *ACS*, 28 October 1911, "Seanchaidhe na Samhna" supplement. Of course, nationalist historians writing in English were also fond 'of such roll calls of the illustrious departed, a practice parodied by Joyce in the Cyclops chapter of *Ulysses*, the chapter dominated by "The Citizen," a grotesque "patriot" and anti-Semite modeled in part on Michael Cusack, founder of the Gaelic Athletic Association and dedicated language revivalist. Joyce began his litany in orthodox fashion with "Cuchulin, Conn of hundred battles, Niall of nine hostages, Brian of Kincora, the Ardri Malachi, Art MacMurragh, Shane O'Neill. . . . Soggarth Eoghan O'Growney," but went on to include Irish figures like John L. Sullivan, "the Bold Soldier Boy," the Colleen Bawn, and the Lily of Killarney, as well as exotics like "the Mother of the Maccabees, the Last of the Mohicans, the Rose of Castille, the Man for Galway, The Man that Broke the Bank at Monte Carlo." See *Ulysses* (New York: Vintage, 1961), 296–97.

resurrection, or, in the case of story or play, the re-creation or invention of magnificent incarnations of the deathless if temporarily languishing spirit of Gaelicism. In this regard the near fabulous state of much Gaelic history was more enabling than embarrassing, freeing the writer from a slavish Anglo-Saxon attachment to mere fact. Reviewing Seán Ua Ceallaigh's *Beatha Bhreandáin* in 1915, one "P." acknowledged that "without doubt the truth is amplified a bit in our traditional history; there is too much heroism and magic in our traditional accounts of war, and perhaps miracles are referred to too often in the traditional stories dealing with piety and the Faith," but insisted that such an approach to history should be judged by indigenous criteria. He continued: "Let us stay with our own traditional history. Let us ignore foreignism. In God's name let us follow the path of the heroes."[176] Dinneen sounded a similarly ambivalent note more moderately: "The teaching of Native History, and of all history, it is scarcely necessary to say, should be scientific. It is truth that should be taught, not fable. That particular kind of fable known as legend has, however, its own place in historical teaching."[177] Even William P. Ryan could praise the "touch of romance" in another of Seán Ua Ceallaigh's histories, *Saothar Ár Sean i gCéin*, although he did insist that the imaginative factor be regulated: "He has

176. "Beatha Bhreandáin," *ACS*, 8 May 1915. "P." wrote that "gan amhras tá beagán i dteannta na fírinne i n-ár seanchus; baineann an iomad gaiscidh agus draoidheachta le seanchus cogaidh, agus b'fhéidir gur ro-mhinic a dheintear tagairt do mhíorbhailtibh 'san seanchus a chuireann síos ar dhiadhacht is ar an gcreideamh." Nonetheless, he concluded: "Claoidhimís le n-ár seanchus féin mar sin. Sgaoilimís thorainn an Ghalldacht. Leanaimís lorg na laochradh i n-ainm Dé."

In his review, Tadhg Ó Donnchadha put the emphasis on the book's historical value: "But the book's greatest and most important virtue is, it seems to me, the virtue of knowledge. It is brimming with knowledge about Brendan and about the Ireland of his time." (Acht isé an buadh is mó agus is tábhachtaighe ag an leabhar, dar liom, ná buadh an eoluis. Lomlán d'eolus ar Bhreandáin agus ar Éire lena linn, atá sé.) See "Cúrsaí an tSaoghail / Leabhar Nua," *ACS*, 13 March 1915.

177. *Native History*, 23. In "Breacadh Lae an Chreidimh ar Éirinn" (The dawn of the faith over Ireland), Dinneen suggested an interesting methodology for Irish social history:

I don't say that many of them can be found, but that the odd person can be found here and there—and they have been there in those [Irish-speaking] districts for ages—so that it would be possible to put together and reveal the traits of the ancient Gaels even if we had neither story nor poem from antiquity.

(Ní hé adeirim go bhfuighfidhe a lán aca acht go bhfuighidhe fo-dhuine annso is annsúd, agus go rabhadar le fagháil sna ceanntaraibh sin ós na ciantaibh, i dtreo gur bh'féidir tréithe na sean-Ghaedheal . . . do chur le chéile is d'fhoillsiughadh dá mba 'nar fhan scéal ná duain againn ón tseanaimsir.)
See "Breacadh Lae an Chreidimh ar Éirinn," *Guth na Bliadhna* 9, no. 4 (Autumn 1912): 493.

brought out the story element very happily, while conveying historic fact."[178]

Fidelity to historic fact doesn't seem to have troubled the usually scrupulous Pearse in his review of "Conán Maol's" *Éire* in 1907: "Personally we do not greatly care whether Clann Mhilidh came to Eire seventeen hundred years before Christ or four hundred years after; but it is to us and will be to others a real pleasure to get these vital pictures of *life* in olden Ireland, independently of any question as to the authenticity of names and dates."[179] Of course, the application of such casual academic criteria to early history conveniently opened the door for the admission of strictly literary characters to the Irish pantheon, on the grounds that, in the words of Peadar Mac Fhionnlaoich, "if Conchobar and Cú Chulainn and Fergus and Conall Cernach never lived, it is certain that the likes of them did."[180] Less explicable is Pearse's cavalier dismissal of almost any orthodox standards for historical credibility in his review of *Stair-Cheachta*, a work that was, after all, intended as a textbook for young readers: "He who would suppress a gracious legend on the mere ground that it is probably untrue is simply an iconoclast of the most objectionable description."[181] He needn't have worried. Iconoclasm was in chronically short supply in the early Revival, and legend graced the pages of much of the historical writing of the period.

Yet however broad the narrative license they allowed themselves, the revivalists worked within a strikingly narrow thematic range.[182] Of course, a rigorous and comprehensive theoretical study of the past was

178. U. Ó R., "A Chapter of Irish History," review of *Saothar Ár Sean i gCéin* by Seán Ua Ceallaigh, *ACS*, 10 June 1905.

179. "An Irish History of Ireland," review of *Éire* by "Conán Maol," *ACS*, 24 August 1907. To be fair, Pearse assumed that a more scholarly approach to history would evolve naturally in due course, writing in his review of Mhag Ruaidhrí's *Beatha Aodha Uí Néill*: "Philosophical history—the detailed analysis of character, the study of the causation of events, the probing to the heart of things—will come later on" (*ACS*, 22 July 1905).

180. *Conchubhar Mac Neasa: Stair-Sheanchas Curadh na Craobhruaidhe* (Baile Átha Cliath: Clódhanna, Teo., 1914), 77. "Munar mhair Conchubhar agus Cúchulainn agus Fearghus agus Conall Cearnach, is cinnte gur mhair a mac a samhla." Incidentally, Mac Fhionnlaoich's work, largely based on Keating, was in general accepted as history, although Seán Ó Ciarghusa ("Marbhán") introduced an ambiguous note of reservation in his review in *The Leader*: "In so far as it is history, it is the one book to read on its subject." See "Some Recent Irish Books," *The Leader*, 31 October 1914.

181. "An Irish History Primer," review of *Stair-Cheachta*, vol. 1, by Eoghan Ó Neachtain, *ACS*, 20 May 1905.

182. Needless to say, there were many parallels between the work of Gaelic historical writers and their nationalist counterparts in the English language. See, for example, Boyce's discussion of popular "Davisite" historians like A. M. Sullivan in *Nationalism*, 246–54.

never their main concern. In 1905 Pearse stated flatly "The Gaelic League is first, last, and always propagandist."[183] In this light, Irish history became a source to be mined for didactic and hortatory purposes, a task for which certain themes were peculiarly appropriate. The most obvious and fundamental was the essential and timeless nobility of the Gael, a nobility that, as An tAthair Peadar chided, had all too often been forgotten: "All of that shows that there was in Ireland long ago . . . a public nobility and a public submission to laws and to good, noble customs, the like of which it is not easy to see now in any race of people. These foreign scoundrels who now try to convince our people that there were nothing but savages in ancient Ireland, let them ponder that. And those of our own people who are all too willing to yield to the lies of those scoundrels, let them also ponder that."[184]

All revivalists would have agreed with Ua Laoghaire that Irish history, despite its pathos, provided an edifying chronicle of heroism and virtue and thus potent inspiration for a resurgent contemporary Gaelicism. Reviewing Dinneen's *Cormac Ua Conaill*, "F.P." wrote of the nation's past that "with all its sorrows and humiliations, it exhibits a more exalted type of human greatness and goodness than are to be found in the records of nations that have suffered less. . . . The Triumph of Mind and of Faith over bodily sufferings and death, is a higher sort of glory than the triumphs of armies on hard fought battle-fields."[185] For Pearse the task of the historian was to bring that glory home, a process that would, as he made clear in his review of the second volume of Ó Neachtain's *Stair-Cheachta*, of necessity have consequences: "A book of Irish history for the young folk of Ireland should be such a book as would set the heart aflame and kindle a desperate purpose in the brain."[186] And it was certainly Pearse who gave this tenet of the Revival creed its most memorable expression in a 1908 *An Claidheamh Soluis* editorial: "The old fairy tale is come true. Every night after the battle a veiled woman passes over the battlefield. She has a phial in one hand and a feather in the other. She dips the feather in the phial and touches

---

183. "The Old Year and the New," editorial, *ACS*, 30 December 1905.

184. *Niamh*, 84. "Taisbeánann an méid sin go léir go raibh i nÉirinn fadó . . . uaisleacht phoiblidhe, agus umhluigheacht phoiblidhe do dhlighthibh agus do nósaibh maithe uaisle, nach ró-fhuiriste a leithéid a dh'fheisgint anois i n-aon treabhchas daoine d'á bhfuil suas. Na ropairí Gallda so a mheasfadh a chur 'n-a luighe ar dhaoinibh anois ná raibh i n-Éirinn fadó ach daoine fiáine, deinidís machtnamh ar an méid sin. Agus an chuid d'ár ndaoine féin nár chuid ba lugha 'ná a fhonn ortha géilleadh d'éitheach na ropairí sin, deinidís machtnamh ar an méid sin." See also 130–31.

185. *The Leader*, 25 May 1901.

186. "Irish History for the Schools," review of *Stair-Cheachta*, vol. 2, by Eoghan Ó Neachtain, *ACS*, 29 June 1907. He felt Ó Neachtain's work required "just a little more vividness, just a little more rush and fervour in the narrative" to accomplish this purpose.

the brow of every dead man as she passes, and in the morning the host that was overthrown stands up again to arms. That woman, I think, must be Ireland. The feather must be the symbol of written history."[187]

Moreover, never, even in the darkest periods of Gaelic oppression, do such resurrected heroes betray either their national or ethical heritage. For instance, his British foes find incomprehensible the self-sacrifice of a patriotic rapparee in Ua Ruaidhrí's *Bliadhain na bhFranncach* (75) while in "Conán Maol's" "Eachtra Risteáird," the protagonist echoes John O'Leary's belief that "there are things that a man must not do to save a nation." Challenged by a fellow rebel to meet English repression with guerrilla ruthlessness, Risteárd de Barra declines: "God be with us. I would prefer to fight them in a manly and passionate manner than to throw them over a cliff in that way like wild animals."[188]

No such scruples trouble the enemy in the work of the revivalists. Foreigners, especially of course the English, were almost invariably depicted as base, cowardly, and treacherous. Thus in an essay urging Gaelic playwrights to make use of the abundant historical material available to them, "Pádraig na Léime" included among the themes they could not avoid confronting "the treachery of the foreigners" (feall na nEachtranach) and the "deviltry and cunning of the destroyers" (diabaluigheacht agus gliocas na scriosairidhe).[189] Indeed, a reading of the Irish history available in Irish at the time would seem to confirm the extraordinary 1917 editorial dictum of *An Claidheamh Soluis*: "An Irishman, however bad, is better than an Englishman (Gall), however good."[190]

187. "The Veiled Woman of the Battlefield," *ACS*, 3 March 1908.

188. "Conán Maol," "Eachtra Risteáird," in *An Buaiceas*, 61. "Ó Dia linn, dob' fhearr liom comhrac leo go fearamhail faobhrach 'ná iad do chaitheamh le faill mar sin ar nós beathadhach allta."

In Ó hAodha's *Cuan an Óir*, a Clare farmer tends a beacon fire all night to save the crew of a British revenue cutter that otherwise would have been wrecked as the result of a smugglers' trap. See *Cuan an Óir*, *ACS*, 13 September 1913. In like manner, the Fenian organizer of Pearse's English work *The Wandering Hawk*, having lured a British gunboat into running aground, arranges to have the crew rescued the next day. See Pearse, *The Wandering Hawk*, in *Literary Works*, ed. Ó Buachalla, 237–38. We should also, of course, recall here the forbearance shown a tyrannous landlord in *Ar Thaoibh an Locha* and the mercy accorded a known informer in "Aimsir na bhFígínídhe i nUíbh Ráthach."

189. "Pádraig na Léime," "Aiste / An Dráma i nÉirinn" (Essay / The drama in Ireland), *SF*, 13 November 1909.

190. "Cúrsaí an tSaoghail," *ACS*, 17 February 1917. "Is fearr Gaedheal dá dhonacht é, ná Gall dá fheabhas é." It should also be noted, however, that at least one Gaelic intellectual who urged the study of Irish history emphasized that such a study should not lead to xenophobia and chauvinism. In 1908 Liam Ua Domhnaill wrote ("I mBaile Átha Cliath," *ACS*, 25 April 1908):

It would be a good thing for Irishmen to understand their enemy, and it is possible to understand them without offering them a stupid and foolish contempt. . . . It is clear

The sole truly despicable character of undiluted Gaelic stock in a historical work of this period is the Munster king Conchubhar Ruadh Ó Donnchadha an Ghleanna, who betrays his loyal follower Earc by attempting to seduce Áine in Béaslaí's "Earc agus Áine." From such a perspective, even the unquestioned moral deficiency of a noted Gael could serve to highlight more profound virtues absent in his foreign foes and critics. Thus, having acknowledged the abduction of another man's wife by Seán an Díomais ("Shane the Proud") Ó Néill, "Conán Maol" commented: "He was nearly as bad as the English themselves in that way, except that *he* would admit his evil conduct, for he was no hypocrite, but a truthful man who would not conceal his fault."[191] There was little truth, much sin, and almost instinctive hypocrisy amongst the invaders who, unable to defeat the Irish fairly, "said to themselves that they would win by trickery and treachery what they had failed to win with the blade of a sword."[192] Confining ourselves solely to creative works, we find the loathesome Norseman Amhlaoibh in Ua Laoghaire's *Niamh*; a deformed Machiavellian Spaniard cribbed from Elizabethan convention in "Pádraig na Léime's" *Mac Cárthaigh Mór*; the treacherous Seagrave in "Conán Maol's" *Aodh Ó Néill*; the British authorities who kill their own puppet Earl of Muskerry in Béaslaí's *Coramac na Cuile*; the drunken soldier (piast de mheisceoir Ghallda) who kills the venerable Mac Firbisigh in the same author's "Oidheadh Dhubhaltaigh"; the bloodthirsty Yeomen, especially Bhaitéir Breac 'ac Bhaltair, in Ua Ruaidhrí's *Bliadhain na bhFranncach*; Dublin Castle's agents provocateurs in Ó hAodha's *An Gioblachán*. And the list goes on. Gaelic historians generally dismissed even allies from abroad as un-

---

that the reading of history benefits us in two ways: it strengthens national feeling and weakens provincialism and insularity. And look! We don't think that there are in Ireland today two other afflictions more widespread than lack of national feeling and provincialism.

(Badh mhaith an rud é d'Éireannachaibh a námhaid do thuigsin agus is féidir leo iad do thuigsin gan tarcuisne baoth amaideach do thabhairt dóibh. . . . Is léir go dtéidheann léigheamh na staire chun sochair dúinn ar dhá chuma: Neartuigheann sé an náisiúntacht agus laghduigheann sé an chúigeachas agus an oileánacht. Agus féach! Ní dóigh linn go bhfuil i nÉirinn indiu dhá ghalar eile níos fairsinge 'ná an mhínáisiúntacht agus an cúigeachas.);

191. *-Seaghán an Díomais: Blúirín as Stair na h-Éireann* (*Shane the Proud: A Fragment of Irish History*), (Dublin: Irish Book, 1901), 2. "Is suarach nach raibh sé chomh h-olc leis na Sasanaigh féin, acht amháin go n-admhóchadh seisean a dhroch-chleachtadh mar níor bha fímineach é, acht fear fírinneach ná ceilfeadh a chaim."

192. Micheál Ó Loingsigh, "Gáire an tSasanaigh" (The Englishman's laugh), *SF*, 1 May 1909. "Dubhradar leo féin go mbuaidhfidís le cleas is feallbheart an rud a theip ortha a ghabháil chuca le faobhar chlaidhimh."

reliable or worse, with the Spanish condemned for their obtuseness and timidity at Kinsale;[193] the French for their failure to assist Eoghan Ruadh Ó Néill[194] and for their lukewarm commitment at Aughrim[195] and in the Mayo of 1798;[196] and the Americans for their self-aggrandizing pettiness in the Fenian period.[197]

For Gaelic historical writers such political and military issues were, however, of secondary significance. Their primary concern was always with what D. P. Moran termed "the Battle of Two Civilizations."[198] Nor for most Gaels was there any confusion about the irreconcilable essence of those civilizations: language. What had sustained—indeed, preserved—the Irish as a distinct nationality through centuries of persecution was above all their devotion to their language, a point no serious student of Irish history could fail to grasp: "There is no doubt but that our language and our history are so closely interwoven that the two must be taken together to derive any fundamental benefit from them."[199] Generally, such devotion was given positive expression, as when Pearse praised the assimilative potential of the language and the "Gaelachas" it embodied as "the birthright of us all,"[200] or when Dinneen documented the realization of that potential in *Muinntear Chiarraidhe*: "Without a doubt people from England and from other places settled here and there throughout the county, but there are few of their descendants to be found today, and those who are left, what are they now but Gaels?"[201] Occasionally, however, revivalists have their characters prove their love of Irish through their contempt for English, as does "Diarmuid na Bolgaidhe" in "Conán Maol's" *Mac Fínghín Dubh*.[202]

193. Maíre Ní Shíthe, "Machtnamh ar Chath Chionn tSáile" (Thoughts on the battle of Kinsale), *ACS*, 20 November 1909.

194. *Eoghan Ruadh Ua Néill*, 10.

195. "Conán Maol," *Mac Fínghín Dubh*, 17. See also 20, 42, 46–47.

196. Ua Ruaidhrí, *Bliadhain na bhFranncach*, 20–21.

197. Ó hAodha, *An Gioblachán*, 106.

198. In *The Philosophy of Irish Ireland*, 94–114.

199. Éamonn Ó Donnchadha, "Ó Chúige Mumhan," *ACS*, 11 July 1908. "Níl aon amhras ná go bhfuil ár dteanga agus ár seanchas fighte chomh mór sain 'n-a chéile nach fuláir do'n dá thaobh gabháil le n-a chéile chum aon tairbhthe bhunadhasach a bhaint asta."

200. "Ulster," editorial, *ACS*, 24 December 1904.

201. P. 3. "Gan amhras do chuir daoine ó Shasana is ó áiteannaibh eile fútha annso is annsúd ar fuaid na conntae; acht ní mór dá sliocht le fagháil indiu, agus an méid atá ann díobh cad eile iad acht Gaedhil anois?"

202. P. 12. One is reminded here of Pearse's polemical praise of Jeremiah O'Donovan Rossa: "With Shane O'Neill he held it debasing to 'twist his mouth with English.' To him the Gael and the Gaelic ways were splendid and holy, worthy of all homage and all service: for the English he had a hatred that was tinctured with contempt. He looked

Similarly, in Hyde's *Rígh Seumas*, James II's ignorance of Irish and babbling in English are nearly as contemptible as his cowardice (24). Nowhere, however, is this negative note sounded more stridently than in accounts, like that in Mac Fhionnlaoich's *Eachtra Aodha Ruaidh Uí Dhómhnaill* (An exploit of Aodh Ruadh Ó Domhnaill), in which Aodh Ó Domhnaill orders his men to kill all captives ignorant of Irish.[203] Commenting on this action in his *Stair na hÉireann*, Mícheál Breathnach drew a linguistic rather than an ethical moral: "That is how a foreigner was recognized 300 years ago—hasn't there been a great change since!"[204] "P. Ó D." saw it as a change for the worse, apostrophizing Ó Domhnaill:

> And, Aodh Ruadh Ó Domhnaill, isn't it you who had the law and the good rule, that is, that the person who could not speak Irish was not Irish, but a foreigner. And everyone of their like that you ever met who didn't have Irish speech on his tongue, you hanged him on the spot. O my love, my heart's hero, you are the one who understood what the direct method is, and didn't you have the proper "Direct Method." And if you were alive today, wouldn't there be work for you?[205]

In the eyes of many, however, language had not been the sole spiritual sustenance of the Gael through the centuries of oppression. Despite the views of Protestants like Hyde, Ernest Joynt, "Conall Cearnach,"

---

upon them as an inferior race, morally and intellectually; he despised their civilisation; he mocked at their institutions and made them look ridiculous." See "O'Donovan Rossa—A Character Study," *Collected Works: Political Writings and Speeches*, 128.

203. (Baile Átha Cliath: M. H. Gill agus a Mhac, 1911), 7. This story won an Oireachtas Prize in 1898 and was first published in the *Weekly Freeman* as "Grádh Aodha Ruadh" (The love Of Aodh Ruadh) on 10 December of that year. In a report on a paper about Aodh Ruadh Ó Domhnaill read to the Central Branch in 1899, we find: "Special emphasis was laid on Ó Domhnaill's strenuous efforts on behalf of the national language, his hatred of the English extending not only to their invading arms and armies, but also their habits, thoughts, and speech." See "News of the Movement / Dublin (Central) Branch," *FL*, 30 December 1899.

204. Part 2, ed. Seosamh Laoide (Baile Átha Cliath: Connradh na Gaedhilge, 1910), 35. "Sin mar d'aithnighthí an Gall trí chéad bliadhain ó shoin—nach mór an t-athrughadh ó shoin!"

205. "Guth ar Sliabh" (A voice on a mountain), *ACS*, 28 November 1908. "Agus a Aoidh Uí Dhomhnaill nach agat do bhí an dlighe agus an riaghail mhaith .i. an té ná raibh Gaedhealg aige, nár Ghaedheal é acht Gall. Is gach éinne dá leithéidíbh dár casadh riamh ort is ná raibh friotal na Gaedhilge ar a dteangain aca níor dheinis leótha acht iad a chrocadh láithreach bonn. Ó mo ghraidhinn thú a laoich mo chroidhe is badh thú a thuig cad is modh direach ann agus nach agat do bhí an 'Modh Direach' ceart, agus dá mbeitheá i d'bheathaidh indiu nach agat do bheadh an obair?"

and Seosamh Laoide, or Catholics like Pearse, Ryan, and Mac Néill, Roman Catholicism seems only marginally less integral to genuine Irish nationality than is the language itself in these historical works.[206] Time and again the fight is one for the native land, culture, and faith. Thus Ua Laoghaire's Brian Bóroimhe is always presented as a champion of Christianity, and the author's anachronistic introduction of a papal legate underscores the fact that An tAthair Peadar had in mind no generic or pallidly ecumenical brand of Christianity, but rather full unity with and submission to the Holy See, as Brian makes clear in a toast welcoming the legate to Kincora: "He asked the company to drink to the health of the Pope. He praised the faith and he praised the Visible Head of the faith, and he promised, for himself and on behalf of all who were present of the nobles of the Gael, of the race of the Gael, that, with the help of God, the Gaelic race would be loyal to the faith as long as there would be a sun in the sky and people on earth."[207]

If anything, after the Reformation the distinction between Gael and Gall, Catholic and Protestant, was even starker than that between Christian and pagan. Dinneen's imprisoned Cormac Ua Conaill laments "the devastation of his tormented and tortured native land and the faith it had preserved without blemish despite its enemy."[208] The Aodh Ua Domhnaill of Ua Laoghaire's *An Bealach Buidhe* fires his troops with a simultaneous patriotic and pious fervor, and not necessarily in that order: "These foreigners are giving every kind of insult to the faith. If they are giving any insult worse than the others to the faith, it is the insult they give to the Virgin Mary. It is for the faith we are

206. Far more than the explicit sectarianism of many of the nativists discussed in Chapter 1, this almost instinctive equation of identity and creed supports the charge that the Revival, for all its noble claims of nonpolitical inclusiveness in a shared nationality, was de facto a Catholic movement, because, in the words of Moran, "the Irish nation is *de facto* a Catholic nation." See the discussion in Boyce, *Nationalism*, 242–43. The best defense can only be to acknowledge the accuracy of Moran's perception while pointing out that the league's official position was nonsectarian and that the sincerity of that position was accepted by more than a few Protestant nationalists. On the other hand, the argument that sectarian writers were speaking solely as individuals is undercut to a considerable extent by the fact that much of their work bears the league imprint.

207. Ua Laoghaire, *Niamh*, 47. "D'iar sé ar an gcuideachtain sláinte an Phápa dh'ól. Do mhol sé an Creideamh agus do mhol sé Ceann So-Fheicse an Chreidimh, agus do gheall sé, uaidh féin, agus thar cheann a raibh láithreach d'uaislibh Gaedheal, shíolrach Gaedheal, go mbeadh sliocht Gaedheal dílis do'n Chreideamh, le cúnamh Dé, an fhaid a bheadh grian ar spéir agus daoine ar talamh." Similar declarations of Irish devotion to the church can be found throughout the novel. See, for example, 8, 26, 32–33, 38, 61, 114, 178–80, 190–92, 214, 224–25, 252, 255, 274, 320–21, 327–28, 351, 355.

208. *Cormac Ua Conaill*, 13. Conall laments "dithe a dhúthchais chráidhte chéasda is an chreidimh do chongaibh sí gan teimheal gan spleádhachas dá námhaid."

fighting, for the faith and for Ireland."[209] As the title indicates, an identical fusion pervades the 1906 Maynooth play *Eoghan Ruadh Ua Néill, nó Ar Son Tíre agus Creidimh*, in which the protagonist rallies his forces on the eve of Benburb with a stirring sectarian appeal: "For your country and for your faith—for your wives and your children—for God and St. Patrick—drive your enemies over the sea! Be courageous and hopeful; be strong and bold; put your reliance in God and in the Blessed Virgin."[210]

Lay writers could be every bit as categorical on this point, as when Micheál Mhag Ruaidhrí consistently stresses the Catholicism of Aodh Ó Néill;[211] when "Conán Maol" has an old Gaelic chieftain wrap a rosary around his sword in *Mac Fínghín Dubh* (17); or when Agnes O'Farrelly describes the contempt felt by "the true Gaels" (na fíor-Ghaedhil) for those who betrayed "their people and their faith" (a muinntear agus a gcreideamh) and thus became "as English as the English themselves" (chomh Sacsanach leis na Sacsanachaibh féin).[212] Indeed, as has been noted, the only Gaelic historical writer who explicitly eschewed such sectarianism was the Ulsterman Peadar Mac Fhionnlaoich in his play *Tá na Francaighe ar an Muir* (see, for example, 13, 22).

Paradoxically, this virtual identification of faith and nationality violated a central tenet of the nationalist creed that had evolved from the revivalists' reading of Irish history. If the past had anything at all to teach the present it was the imperative necessity for Irish unity, and again and again the Gaelic historians isolated internal dissension as the radical tragedy of the national experience. Mícheál Breathnach offered the, literally, textbook statement of the theme in *Stair na hÉireann*: "As I have already said, and as I will say again, what always brought loss to the Irish was their lack of close union amongst themselves."[213] Less re-

---

209. (Baile Átha Cliath: Muintir na Leabhar Gaedhilge, 1906), 22. "Tá gach aon tsaghas easonóra ag na Gallaibh seo 'á thabhairt do'n Chreideamh. Má tá easonóir is measa 'ná chéile acu 'á thabhairt do'n Chreideamh is í an easonóir a thugaid siad do'n Mhaighdin Mhuire í. Ar son an Chreidimh iseadh atáimid-ne ag troid; ar son an Chreidimh agus ar son na hÉireann."

210. P. 97. "Ar son bhur tíre agus bhur gcreidimh—ar son bhur mban agus bhur gclainn—ar son Dé agus Naoimh Phádraig—ruagaidh bhur náimhde tar fairrge! Bídhidh misneamhail, dóchasach; bídhidh neartmhar, dána; cuiridh bhur muinighin i nDia agus 'sa' Mhaighdin bheannuighthe."

211. See, for example, *Beatha Aodha Uí Néill*, 13, 27, 83–84, 102–3.

212. O'Farrelly, *Grádh agus Crádh: Úirsgéilín* (Love and torment: A novella), (Baile Átha Cliath: Connradh na Gaedhilge, 1905), 5. O'Farrelly was, however, clear that such traitors were never very numerous (6).

213. Part 2, pp. 7–8. "Mar dubhairt mé cheana agus mar déarfas mé arís, 'sé rud a chaill do na Gaedhealaibh é i gcomhnuidhe gan an dlúth-mhuinnteardhas a bheith eatorra féin."

strained—indeed, near apocalyptic—was Pádraig Ua Dálaigh as he contemplated the catastrophe of Kinsale: "Woe to the territory and to the noble native land. Woe to the country and to the population in which kinfolk and brothers draw hand and sword against each other. Woe to the head and to the heart that counseled such fratricide. Woe to the brother who deserted his own people during the time of need and danger."[214]

Some Gaels saw such strife as the direct result of invasion and conquest, fantasizing for the earliest period of the nation's history a prelapsarian Pax Gadelica. Reviewing Arthur Ua Cléirigh's *The History of Ireland to the Coming of Henry II*, Pádraig Mac Suibhne could write: "Our great historical writers have always loved to work in the field of early Irish history, and no wonder. The early ages were our spacious times before sects and parties and cliques began their quarrels, obscuring from our vision the springs of action and the real life of the nation."[215] Significantly, however, the majority of Gaelic writers on history acknowledged that these centrifugal tendencies were entirely indigenous, predating any foreign interference in Irish affairs. For example, writing in *The Republic* in 1907, "Eoghan" admitted that: "We all know that it was disunity that put the Gaels under the feet of their enemies in every period. It saddens me to say that they were almost always fighting each other. Before the Vikings came into Ireland, the Gaels were at strife with each other day and night."[216] The "great important lesson" (ceacht mhór thábhachtach) Micheál Ó Luingsigh drew from the legendary sixth-century cursing and abandonment of Tara was that "it is our duty

---

214. "An Nodlaig i gCeann tSáile" (Christmas in Kinsale), *ACS*, 21 December 1901. "Is mairg don chríoch agus don chaomhdhuthaigh. Is mairg don tír agus don tuath ina bhfuil comhghaolta agus comhbhráithreacha ag tarraingt lámh agus lann i gcoinne a chéile. Is mairg don cheann agus don chroidhe a cheap agus a chomhairligh a leithéid de fhionghal. Is mairg don bhráthair a thréig a mhuintir féin le linn an ghábhaidh agus an bhaoghail." Ua Dálaigh was explicit concerning the contemporary relevance of this lament: "And are we free from these faults today? I fear that we are not, and if anyone is uncertain about that, he need only look around and notice what is happening in the country." (Agus an bhfuilmid saor ó na lochtaibh so indiu? Tá eagla orm nach bhfuilmid, agus má tá éigcinnteacht ar éinneach 'na thaoibh, ní gábhadh dó a dhéanamh acht breathnughadh thart timcheall agus imtheachta na tíre do thabhairt fá ndeara.)

215. *ACS*, 2 January 1909. See also "Ár dTeanga Féin / Seaghán Mac Aodhagáin Ó Cathasaigh" (Our own language / John Keegan Casey), *UI*, 26 April 1902.

216. "I n-Aontacht Tá Buaidh, i Scaipeadh Mío-Ádh" (In unity there is victory, in separation, misfortune), *The Republic* 1, no. 11 (21 February 1907): 7. The article concluded the following week. "Tá fhios againn uile gur ab í an easaontacht do chuir na Gaedhil fá chois a námhad ins gach uile aois. Is brónach liom a rádh go raibh siad ag troid le chéile i gcomhnaidhe nach mór. Sul a dtáinig na Lochlannaigh isteach i n-Éirinn, bhí na Gaedhil i n-achrann le chéile de ló agus d'oidhche."

to assist every man who is working for Ireland; that it is to our benefit to be loyal to each other; to be friendly and generous with each other; to have nothing to do with enmity or with spite."[217]

Only a few examples of this theme need be cited from the historical fiction and drama of the early Revival. In common with all Gaelic historical writers, Peadar Ua Laoghaire made his Brian Bóroimhe a self-consciously patriotic nation-builder committed to the permanent suppression of those petty personal, dynastic, and provincial rivalries that threatened Ireland with a full-scale Norse conquest: "Brian knew that there was danger and that the fact that it was so little understood made the danger greater. He also knew that there would be danger as long as the kings of Ireland were opposing each other, and fighting each other, and weakening each other as they were. Therefore, as soon as his power began to increase, he began bringing the other kings under his own control and compelling them to cooperate against the Scandinavians."[218] In "Pádraig na Léime's" *Mac Cárthaigh Mór*, Mac Cárthaigh and Ó hEidirsceoil unmask at the last moment a plot to set them against each other, and Mac Cárthaigh draws the orthodox moral: "It is together that we are strongest. As long as the Irish stand shoulder to shoulder there is no danger to us."[219] Dinneen's Cormac Ua Conaill realizes as a young man that the source of his nation's woes is the failure

217. "Tréigean na Teamhrach" (The desertion of Tara), *IG* 18, no. 11 (November 1908): 510. The lesson was "gurab é ár ndualgas cuidiughadh le gach fear atá ag oibriughadh ar son na Fódla; gurab é ár leas a bheith dílis dá chéile; a bheith cairdeamhail, carthannach le n-a chéile; gan bac ná baint a bheith againn le heasaontas ná le mioscais." The only work in which Irish disunity is a mere fact of narrative rather than thematic significance is Béaslaí's story "Earc agus Áine."

218. Ua Laoghaire, *Niamh*, 18. "Do thuig Brian go raibh an baoghal ann agus gur mhóide an baoghal a luígheadh a tuigeadh é. Thuig sé, leis, go mbéadh an baoghal ann an fhaid a bhéadh ríghthe Éirean ag gabháil i gcoinnibh a chéile, agus ag troid le n-a chéile, agus ag lagughadh a chéile mar a bhíodar. D'á bhrígh sin, chomh luath agus thusnuigh a chómhacht ar dhul i méid, do thusnuigh sé ar na ríghthibh eile do thabhairt fé n-a smacht féin, agus ar a chur feuchaint ortha oibriughadh a' lámhaibh a chéile i gcoinnibh na Lochlannach." See also 33–34, 53, 65–67, 77–84, 92–93, 98, 134, 138, 164, 187, 190, 196, 212–13, 232, 238. Irish civil strife after Brian's death at Clontarf obviously pained Ua Laoghaire. For instance, he writes of the coronation of Brian's son Donnchadh as High-King, but downplays the fact that his claim to the throne was widely rejected, and that he was in fact merely the king of Munster (352). Indeed, Ua Laoghaire seems to have wished to avoid the whole topic of post-Clontarf dissension: "This story is not, however, concerned with the Dál gCais nor with Mac Giolla Phádraig, but with Niamh, and with Caoilte, and with Conn." (Ní le Clainn Chais ná le Mac Giolla Phádraig a bhaineann an sgéal so, ámhthach, ach le Niamh, agus le Caoilte, agus le Conn") (342).

219. P. 23. "I dteannta a chéile is treise sinn. An fhaid is beidh Clanna Gaedheal guala ar ghualainn ní baoghal dúinn."

to achieve such fraternal solidarity, the fact that "the Irish chieftains hated each other more than they hated the English."[220]

When the united forces of the Gael do manage to direct their wrath against the common foe, they work wonders, as do, for example, Ua Laoghaire's Brian and his Ua Domhnaill, "Pádraig na Léime's" Mac Cárthaigh, "Conán Maol's" Aodh Ó Néill, and the Maynooth Aodh Ruadh Ua Néill. Yet it is precisely at such a moment of triumph, that of Ua Domhnaill in An tAthair Peadar's *An Bealach Buidhe*, that the radical fallacy in the Gaelic consensus concerning this theme is laid bare, as Aodh Ruadh, with naively ironic sectarianism, provides a simultaneous affirmation and subversion of what for revivalists was the core truth of Irish history: "If the Irish nobility were of one spirit and one mind against these foreigners, soon there would be little heard of foreigners in Ireland. With the will of the God of Glory and through the intercession of the Virgin Mary, may it not be long until we see the day that that is so!"[221]

Of course all Irish people, not just Gaelic activists, shared this obsession with the debilitating consequences of internal strife. After all, the period of our study experienced the Parnell bitterness, the split in the Irish Volunteers, and the Civil War. But Gaelic Leaguers had particularly urgent reasons to yearn for solidarity. In the first decade of this century the league was riven by acrimonious disputes, from debates about *cainnt na ndaoine* and "classical Irish" to bitter ad hominem arguments about the potential educational benefits for the language of the Irish Council Bill of 1907, the place of Irish in the school curriculum (the so-called fees question that came to a head in 1907–8 with the resignation of Dinneen and Ua Laoghaire from the league's Executive Committee), and the status of Irish in the new National University.[222]

220. *Cormac Ua Conaill*, 4. The problem is "gur fhuathadar na taoisigh Gaedhealacha a chéile níos mó ná d'fhuathadar na Sagsanaigh."
221. P. 32. "Dá mbeadh ríogra Éireann ar aon aigne agus ar aon íntinn i gcoinnibh na nGall so ba ró-ghearr go mbéadh beagán tuairisg ar Ghallaibh i n-Éirinn. Le toil Dé na Glóire agus tré impidhe na Maighdine Muire nára fada go bhfeicimíd an lá i n-a mbéidh san amhlaidh!"
222. For a discussion of all of these issues, see Ó Súilleabháin, *Cath na Gaeilge sa Chóras Oideachais*. For Pearse's role, see also Ó Súilleabháin, *An Piarsach agus Conradh na Gaeilge* (Pearse and the Gaelic League) (Baile Átha Cliath: Clódhanna, Teo., 1981), 102–15; and Ruth Dudley Edwards, *Patrick Pearse*, 69–89. For the other side, see Ó Conluain and Ó Céileachair, *An Duinníneach*, 176–200. In the circumstances, it is interesting to note that in 1906 Dinneen called "mutual forbearance" "the noblest fruit of self-sacrifice" in an appeal for Irish unity in *WF*. See "Self-Sacrificing Work for Ireland," *WF*, 22 September 1906. Of the relationship between Pearse and Brugha, the latter's biographer, Seán Ua Ceallaigh, wrote: "Indeed, I think that it must be said that he and Pearse were in agree-

As an undercurrent to these controversies ran the constant and prickly rivalry among supporters of the three major dialects of the language, all trying to establish their particular brand of Irish as the national standard.

Obviously these provincial linguistic rivalries frustrated more far-sighted revivalists for whom the language was potentially the most cohesive element in the nation. Just as disheartening was the fact that such jealousies could and did infect the study of the history that was projected as an almost equally inspirational force for unity. For instance, in the letter columns of *The Derry People* and of *An Claidheamh Soluis* in 1905, Ulster's Seaghán Mac a' Bháird, Munster's "Conán Maol," and assorted allies squared off over what the former saw as a disparagement of the north's role at Clontarf in the latter's *Éire*. Somewhat disingenuously Mac a' Bháird wrote: "Glorification of any province at the expense of the others is but a poor occupation for one calling himself an Irishman, and the sooner we learn to be Irish instead of provincial the better for our country."[223] Against this background and on the eve of the announcement of an extraordinary Ard-Fheis (General Meeting) to deal with the crisis precipitated by the actions of the "Wrecker Party" of Dinneen and Cathal Brugha, Pearse voiced the fears and affirmed the faith of the majority of his comrades in the spring of 1908: "There are those who fear that the fated moment which comes to most Irish movements has come to ours—the moment when each fighter, forgetting the presence of the common enemy, turns his sword against the breast of his brother, and the whole ends in a tumult of fratricidal strife. This fear we do not share. We have still an abiding faith in the sanity of Gaelic Leaguers."[224]

In the writing if not always in the making of history the revivalists were not without their share of both sanity and invention. Their creative works set in the Irish past contributed significantly to the liberation of the new Gaelic literature from a paralyzing reliance on contemporary rural subjects and themes, and established a tradition of historical fiction and drama that continues to the present. None of the historical works of our period are aesthetically successful, most are factually flawed and ideologically muddled, but all contributed to that

---

ment about nothing except the necessity of fighting for the freedom of Ireland when the time came." (Is dóigh liom go deimhin gur éigean a rádh ná raibh sé féin is an Piarsach ar aon intinn i dtaoibh éinnidhe acht amháin i dtaoibh riachtanas na troda ar son saoirse Éireann tráth tháinig an lá.) See Ua Ceallaigh ("Sceilg"), *Cathal Brugha* (Baile Átha Cliath: M. H. Mac an Ghoill agus a Mhac, 1942), 12.

223. *ACS*, 23 December 1905.

224. "The Crisis," editorial, *ACS*, 23 May 1908.

sense of a proud national identity that was perhaps the chief legacy of the "harmless cultural nationalists" of the early Gaelic League. Where we often see cardboard characters, implausible plots, and stilted dialogue, contemporary readers and audiences saw a half-forgotten, half-suppressed hidden Ireland restored to life, dignity, and relevance. It was in such works that Pearse, for example, first heard the Gaelic voices of "the dead generations" he summoned to his side in the Proclamation of Easter 1916.[225] Yet it is a much humbler document, the anonymous review of a 1907 performance of "Conán Maol's" *Aodh Ó Néill* in Cork City, that best captures the meaning of these historical works for their own time and place: "The Gael was filled with joy of heart, and the Foreigner and the Shoneen saw something that made them realize the sort of life there had been long ago and the sort of life the league intends to bring back again."[226]

225. One is reminded here of the conclusion of Tomás Ó Ceallaigh's *An Fóghmhar*, in which Séamus Ó Cuinn is confident that the men of '98 will be aided by "the people who preceded them . . . the heroes and the saints who are buried under these sods, and who are still, with the help of God, praying for Ireland and watching over their descendants" (na daoine chuaidh rómpa-san . . . na laochra agus na naoimh atá thíos fá iadhadh na bhfód ṣo, agus atá fós, le congnamh Dé, ag guidhe ar son na hÉireann agus ag faire ar a gclainn). See Ó Ceallaigh, *An Fóghmhar*, in *An tAthair Tomás Ó Ceallaigh*, ed. Ó Láimhín, 89.

226. "Cogarnach na gCraobh / I gCathair Chorcaighe" (The gossip of the Branches / In Cork City), *ACS*, 19 January 1907. "Bhí an Gaedheal líonta le áthas croidhe agus an Gall agus an Seoinín . . . do chonnaiceadar soin rud éigin do chuir i n-umhail dóibh cad é an saghas saoghail a bhí ann fadó agus cad é an saghas saoghail atá ceapaithe ag an gConradh do thabhairt thar n-ais arís."

4

"The Greatest of the Things Our Ancestors Did"

Modernizations and Adaptations of Early Irish Literature

In 1898 Robert Atkinson, Trinity College's professor of Sanskrit and comparative philology and Todd Professor of Celtic Languages at the Royal Irish Academy, outraged the Irish language movement with his disdainful dismissal of the entire corpus of early Irish literature in testimony before the Vice-Regal Commission on Intermediate Education: "I would say it would be difficult to find a book in ancient Irish in which there was not some passage so silly or so indecent as to give you a shock from which you would never recover during the rest of your life."[1] However Pecksniffian in retrospect, such a charge was delivered and taken in deadly earnest in late Victorian Dublin, and to have left it unchallenged would have seriously undermined the by then impressive

---

1. Quoted in "Trinity's Attack on the Irish Language," *ACS*, 24 January 1903. As the title indicates, Atkinson's criticism was directed at far more than just the ethical failings of medieval Irish literature.

growth of the language movement under the auspices of the Gaelic
League. Few familiar with the medieval sources would go so far as to
agree with Father Henebry that "Irish literature holds no indecent material. As the Irish people were and are pure, so is their literature pure in
its persistent spirit,"[2] and one need only imagine the probable reaction
of that scrupulously respectable cultural nationalist, Mrs. Kearney of
James Joyce's "A Mother," to appreciate why the league immediately
mobilized its forces to refute Atkinson[3] and in the process to do battle

2. "The Reverend Doctor Henebry on Trinity College," *ACS*, 10 June 1899. The
piece originally appeared in the United States in the *Saint Louis Star*. Henebry did acknowledge that the early tales, like the Bible, contain some "coarseness." See also "An
English Insitution in Ireland/Rev. Dr. Henebry on Trinity College," *FL*, 24 June 1899. In
the general critical vacuum concerning early Irish literature at this time, there was ample
scope for extravagant claims by both its admirers and foes. For example, Father Peter
Yorke, addressing the league's Central Branch in the Antient Concert Rooms in 1899,
proclaimed: "Outside the Sacrosanct literature there was none so unique, so beautiful, or
so instructive or full of human interest as the old Irish literature." See "Lecture by the
Rev. Peter C. Yorke, San Francisco," *ACS*, 16 September 1899. Disturbed by such hyperbole, the scholar Osborn Bergin lectured a University College, Dublin, audience in
1913: "I know that one or two modern writers have in the fervour of patriotic enthusiasm
declared that nowhere in the whole of Greek literature, not even in the Homeric poems, is
there anything so magnificent as the 'Táin bó Cúailgne.' I can only express my regret that
such absurd and extravagant claims should find either writers or readers." See "In the
Gaelic World," *WF*, 16 August 1913.
   3. See, for example, "Dr. Atkinson and Modern Gaelic," editorial, *FL*, 4 March 1899.
As this piece makes clear, Atkinson's English birth was a sore point. The Gaels also
mounted a sustained attack on Atkinson's qualifications as a scholar of Irish, their most
serious allegation being that he plagiarized the work of his assistant, John Fleming (Seán
Pléimeann). Thus, in 1907 "An Gae Bolga" wrote: "Many are of the opinion that some of
his best work was due to Flemming's [sic] assistance, and they point out the significant
fact that since Flemming's death Dr. Atkinson has published nothing." See "An Gae
Bolga," *A Talk about Irish Literature* (Dublin: M. H. Gill and Son, 1907), 2; and Richard
Henebry, "An English Institution in Ireland," *FL*, 24 June 1899. Peadar Ua Laoghaire
aggressively exposed Atkinson's deficiencies in modern Irish in "The Dismal Swamp"
(*FL*, 25 March, 22 April, 3 June 1899), and in 1900, the league reprinted this article along
with a February 1899 Ua Laoghaire letter to the *Freeman's Journal* on the subject in one of
its propaganda pamphlets, *The Irish Language and Irish Intermediate Education IX*. Ua
Laoghaire drew particular attention to Atkinson's difficulties with the copula, thus giving
rise to the memorable bit of doggerel, "Atkinson of T.C.D./Doesn't know the verb to
be." Nor were the language revivalists alone in their displeasure with the Trinity professor. Lady Gregory, for example, regretted the fact that "not only fellow-professors in
Trinity but undergraduates there have been influenced by his opinion, that Irish literature
is a thing to be despised." See "Notes" to *Gods and Fighting Men* (Toronto: Macmillan,
1976), 355–56. This book originally appeared in 1904.
   Time softened Gaelic resentment, however, and on his death Atkinson was paid a brief
but gracious tribute in *ACS* as a scholar who prepared facsimile editions of the *Book of
Leinster* (1880), the *Book of Ballymote* (1887), and the *Yellow Book of Lecan* (1896), and as

with the Anglophile establishment of the country's oldest university. Indeed, not only did the league summon its own most articulate advocates to address the commission—men like Mac Néill, Dinneen, and most important, Trinity alumnus Douglas Hyde, who later lampooned the faculty of his alma mater in his 1903 farce *Pleusgadh na Bulgóide, or The Bursting of the Bubble)*⁴—but it also solicited and published the testimony of the world's leading Celticists as to the linguistic, cultural, and aesthetic significance of early Irish literature.⁵

As was, however, to be true with frustrating frequency in days to come, forensic and moral victory in this controversy produced disappointingly mixed practical consequences. In this instance the commission's generally favorable recommendations concerning the place of the language in the curriculum were undercut by the government's appointment of the league's archfoe, Trinity provost John Pentland Mahaffey, to the Intermediate Education Board in 1901.⁶ Even more fun-

---

the editor of *The Passions and Homilies from the Leabhar Breac* (1887), Keating's *Trí Bior-Ghaoithe an Bháis* (1890), and the fifth and sixth volumes of the *Ancient Laws of Ireland* (1901), volume 6 being a glossary. Pearse wrote of Atkinson: "There's many a person who criticized the work of Atkinson who doesn't do his own work half as meticulously as Atkinson did his." (Is iomdha duine a cháineadh saothar Atcinson nach ndéanann a chuid oibre féin leath chomh beacht is a dhéanadh Atcinson a chuid oibresean.) See "Mion-Sgéala" (Brief notices), *ACS*, 18 January 1908. For a brief biography of Atkinson, see Breathnach and Ní Mhurchú, *Beathaisnéis a Dó*, 15–16.

4. Douglas Hyde, *Pleusgadh na Bulgóide; or the Bursting of the Bubble* (Baile Átha Cliath: Gill agus a Mhac, n.d.). The play, set in the Commom Room of "Coláiste na Bulgóide" (Bubble College) and featuring Mahaffy and Atkinson as main characters, was first performed at a Cumann na nGaedheal Samhain Festival on 2 November 1903. The published text came complete with notes to explain the jokes, including references to the writings of the Trinity dons. Atkinson and Mahaffy were also satirized in *The Conspirators: An Irish Tragedy in Five Acts* by "Shanganagh." The play commenced sporadic serialization in *UI* on 16 February 1901, with other installments on 22 March and 15 June. These are the only pieces I could find, and they do not complete the play. The work is said to have been written for the Irish Literary Theatre, but is not mentioned in Robert Hogan and James Kilroy's authoritative *The Irish Literary Theatre, 1899–1901*. In the play the Hyde character has speeches in Irish. "Shanganagh" also satirized Atkinson in two prose pieces, "Ár dTeanga Féin agus Ollamh Mac Aitcin" (Our own language and Professor Atkinson) and "The Voyage of Atcin, son of Chaos," supposedly from "Leabhar na hÉireannach Aonthuighthe" [sic]. Both pieces appeared in *UI*, the former on 29 November 1902, the latter on 20 December of the same year.

5. The testimony solicited by Hyde was published by *ACS* throughout 1900–1901. For a useful survey of the controversy, see Ó Súilleabháin, *Cath na Gaeilge sa Chóras Oideachais*. Hyde discusses his involvement in *Mise agus an Conradh*, 77–100. Dinneen's role is summarized in some detail in Ó Conluain and Ó Céileachair, *An Duinníneach*, 106–19.

6. Mahaffey had testified magisterially before the commission concerning the value of Irish literature although he knew absolutely nothing of the language. Several years later,

damentally, Gaelic intellectuals may have felt their euphoria over having faced down Queen Elizabeth's university tempered by their awareness that responsibility for promoting a more authentic and profound understanding of the early literature now rested squarely on their own shoulders.

This sense of obligation was not, of course, entirely new. Gaelic reviews of the various Anglo-Irish reworkings of the ancient tales often praised the good patriotic intentions and frequent artistic successes of writers like Yeats, Lady Gregory, and George Russell (AE), while consistently emphasizing that the true spirit of early Irish literature was inaccessible through the English language. Richard Henebry expressed this idea in categorical fashion in 1909: "In the *Táin Bó Cúailgne* it is different. To a person whose mind is charged with English it is strange, uncouth and foreign. To one reared Irish it is the same tune he has always heard; he knows it. But how define its tone, its atmosphere for the foreigners? It cannot be done, it is the other way, it differs in everything and entirely from the way of the strange people. Nor can it be translated."[7] Anglo-Irish writers might well achieve both aesthetic effect and critical acclaim with their versions of the early tales, but their works could never be more than literary halfway houses on the road to a re-Gaelicized Irish worldview. Even that most famous of all Anglo-Irish appropriations of the ancient epic material, Lady Gregory's *Cuchulain of Muirthemne*, was dismissed with polite condescension by William P. Ryan in his review for *The Leader*: "I believe that the work as a whole will do a temporary good, but we may trust that in ten or twenty years it will be regarded as entirely out of date, or as possessing a sort of historical interest as a specimen of the contrivances that served a purpose as Ireland returned from the desert."[8] The only fully legiti-

---

in 1914, he banned a meeting of Trinity's Gaelic Society when he learned it was to be addressed by "a man called Pearse." See Edwards, *Patrick Pearse*, 226–27.

7. "Revival Irish," *The Leader*, 16 January 1909. Peadar Ua Laoghaire had expressed virtually identical sentiments in a lecture nine years previously: "If I turn and read the same traditional matter in English all is changed. The reality is gone. . . . The words . . . are nothing but sound. . . . They have, of course, a certain meaning, but it is all the same to me whether they describe the traditions of Ireland or the traditions of China." See "The Irish Language," *FL*, 30 April 1898. More typical of the generally sympathetic Gaelic response to the efforts of Anglo-Irish writers in this area are the remarks of an anonymous critic in a review of A. H. Leahy's *Heroic Romances of Ireland*: "Leahy makes a useful attempt to bring the ancient romances alive in English, but they can only be properly understood in one language—Irish." (Tugann Mac Uí Laochaigh iarracht fhoghanta ar na sean-starthaibh a thabhairt amach san mBéarla, acht ní féidir iad a thuigsint i gceart i n-éin-teangain acht san nGaedhilg.) See *IG* 15, no. 3 (December 1905): 64.

8. "Kiltartan, Mr. Yeats, and Cúchulain," review of *Cuchulain of Muirthemne* by Lady

mate heirs of the creators of Cú Chulainn and Fionn Mac Cumhaill were to be those Irish writers who had remained true to the language of their heroes.

Those heirs had not, however, done much with that priceless patrimony. In the early years of the Revival a sore point for Gaelic intellectuals was the fact that Irish scholars had played and continued to play so secondary a role in the development of Celtic studies as an academic discipline. For example, in a 1900 *Fáinne an Lae* editorial note praising *Fled Bricrenn* (*Bricriu's Feast*), the most recent volume issued by the London-based Irish Texts Society, an organization whose work received uniformly favorable coverage in the Gaelic press, we read: "We wish we could claim the learned editor, Dr. Henderson, as an Irishman. Bookmaking, unless on horses, is an art not over well-known in Ireland, and it is well we should get an occasional lead."[9] Similarly, in a 1903 piece promoting the new School for Irish Learning, Tadhg Ó Donnchadha urged his fellow Gaels to seize this opportunity to atone for their past lack of scholarly initiative: "It were as well for us to pay attention to Old Irish and not to be leaving it to the Germans and other foreigners."[10] Apparently the Gaels welcomed this opportunity to acquire a firsthand knowledge of the traditions in which they took such pride: from its foundation as a six-week summer course in Old Irish taught by John Strachan,[11] the School for Irish Learning was followed

---

Gregory, *The Leader*, 5 July 1902. Lady Gregory herself may not have disagreed, in principle at least, writing in *Gods and Fighting Men* that as time passed people "will not be content with my redaction, but will go, first to the fuller versions of the best scholars, and then to the manuscripts themselves." See "Notes" to *Gods and Fighting Men*, 356.

9. "Notes," *FL*, 13 January 1900.

10. "An Scoil Shean-Ghaedhilge" (The school of Irish learning), *IG* 13, no. 155 (August 1903): 369. "Níor mhisde dhúinn aire a thabhairt do'n tSean-Ghaedhilge, agus gan bheith 'gá fágaint fé Ghearmánaigh is fé eachtrannaigh eile." See also "Gleó na gCath," *ACS*, 8 August 1903; and "Scoil na Sean-Ghaedhilge" (The school of Irish learning), *SF*, 16 July 1910. Due tribute was of course paid to a native scholar who undertook such work. See the editorial eulogy for Whitley Stokes in *ACS*, 24 April 1909; and "Fathach Neartmhar den tSeanaimsir" (A mighty giant of antiquity), Dinneen's obituary tribute to Standish Hayes O'Grady in *The Leader*, 30 October 1915.

11. See "A Summer School of Irish Studies," *ACS*, 27 June 1903; "Doctor Meyer's Project," *ACS*, 4 July 1903; and *Ériu* [the title of the school's journal], *SF*, 11 March 1911. From the outset, the Liverpool University professor Kuno Meyer was full of projects for himself and his Gaelic allies, calling in 1904 for "translation of the masterpieces of the older literature into modern Irish, editions of the literature buried in countless mss." See "A Plea for a Gaelic Academy," *ACS*, 31 December 1904. Pearse felt that the School of Irish Learning should undertake this task in its new journal *Ériu*: "One of the chief objects of this periodical will be the publication of collations and editions with translations into English (why not versions in Modern Irish?) of Ms. Materials bearing on Irish Litera-

with enthusiasm in the Gaelic and Irish-Ireland press and drew a significant percentage of its students from the language movement.[12] Indeed,
as early as 1904 Pearse could list among the triumphs of that movement
the fact that "young native scholars are commencing to delve into the
past of the language, and the dead bones of Old and Medieval Irish are
stirring again and donning flesh and graciousness."[13] Moreover, the
Gaelic League was soon to put such young scholars to work under its
own sponsorship, with Coláiste na Mumhan (The Munster College)
taking the lead in the summer of 1907 by offering courses in Old and
Middle Irish language and literature taught by Osborn Bergin.[14] By
1912 such courses seem to have become part of the core curriculum in
virtually every major Gaelic training college and summer school.[15]

Yet in an organization as populist and pragmatic as was the early
Gaelic League, the study of medieval Irish and its literature was soon
enlisted in the service of the modern language, although Pearse felt this
ambition would not be fully realizable while foreign scholars dominated
Celtic studies: "As long as our older literature continues to be edited by
foreign scholars it obviously will not have the instant awakening effect
it would have if done as part of a movement, by men of the movement.
We can only hope that we may soon see a race of Irish scholars spring-
ing up—who will retell our old tales in our own modern Irish speech."[16]
A similar suspicion of detached, or perhaps more accurately elitist,
scholarship is evident in a 1901 *An Claidheamh Soluis* review sar-

---

ture and History" ("The School of Irish Learning," *ACS*, 16 January 1904). A brief history of the school can be found in "The School of Irish Learning," *Scéala Scoil an Léinn
Cheiltigh/Newsletter of the School of Celtic Studies*, no. 3 (November 1989): 30–36.

12. See "Scoil na Sean-Ghaedhilge," *IG* 18, no. 8 (August 1908): 362–66.

13. "An Epoch of the Movement," review of *Foclóir Gaedhilge agus Béarla/An Irish-
English Dictionary* by Patrick S. Dinneen, *ACS*, 10 August 1904.

14. See "Coláiste na Mumhan," *ACS*, 20 April 1907. Bergin had been appointed to the
faculty of the School of Irish Learning the previous year.

15. See, for example, for Belfast, "Belfast Training College for Irish," *ACS*, 28 September 1907 (the teacher was Mrs. Arthur Hutton, who in 1907 translated the *Táin* into
English verse); for Clochaneely, Co. Donegal, Séamus Ó Searcaigh, "Árd-Sgoil Choluim
Cille" (The Colm Cille High School), *ACS*, 18 July 1908 (the teacher was Agnes O'Farrelly, and apparently the class was less than a rousing success; see *ACS*, 3 October 1908);
for Tourmakeady, Co. Mayo, "Old Irish in the Connacht College," *ACS*, 5 March 1910
(the teacher was Eoin Mac Néill); and for Carrigaholt, Co. Clare, "Colaísde Eoghain Uí
Chomhraidhe" (The Eugene O'Curry College), *ACS*, 6 July 1912 (the teacher was
Tomás Ua Nualláin). In 1915 the active and influential Dublin Craobh na gCúig gCúigí
initiated a class in Old Irish open to all leaguers as part of its regularly scheduled activities
for the year. The teacher was Máire Ní Bhroin. See "Craobh na gCúig gCúigi," *ACS*, 30
October 1915.

16. "Gleó na gCath," *ACS*, 8 August 1903.

castically dissenting from Thomas O'Neill Russell's praise of the work of the Royal Irish Academy in preserving Irish manuscripts: "The Irish manuscripts which the Academy has preserved, it has preserved with a vengeance. About the last thing in the world it would dream of doing is to destroy their value by causing them to be printed, for in that event people might actually read them!"[17] Unfortunately, putting the early literature before readers would involve difficulties more daunting than negotiating with unsympathetic librarians on Dawson Street.

Many tales and ballads about Fionn Mac Cumhaill did, of course, still survive in the Gaeltacht, and these were assiduously collected. As usual, the various feiseanna and the Oireachtas took the lead. For example, the 1902 Galway Feis, courtesy of Lady Gregory, offered prizes for "best collection in prose or verse of unpublished legends relating to the Fianna of Erin."[18] Fenian material also figured prominently in the annual generic folklore competitions of the Oireachtas, those along the lines of "a collection of previously unpublished folktales (or poems)." And in 1910 a more specific competition was sponsored for "previously un-published information about Diarmaid and Gráinne from the people of the Gaeltacht" (eolas ó mhuintir na Gaeltachta i dtaobh Dhiarmada agus Ghráinne nár foilsigheadh go fóill).[19] The fruits of such research ap-peared regularly in Gaelic journals from the pens of both established literary figures of the Revival like Peadar Mac Fhionnlaoich[20] and young writers just beginning to make themselves known, the most important of whom to first appear in this context was Séamus Ó Grianna, who published stories about both Cú Chulainn and Fionn.[21] Fenian tales

17. Review of *An Gaodhal* for September 1901, *ACS*, 10 December 1901. Arthur Griffith also blasted the RIA on its election of Atkinson as president in *UI*, 23 March 1901; and on 3 January 1903 called it "one of the most unprogressive and illiterate institu-tions in Ireland." Once again time healed some wounds, and a rather more favorable view of the RIA was offered by Tadhg Ó Donnchadha in "An tAcadamh" (The academy), editorial, *ACS*, 10 May 1914. Ó Donnchadha did, however, offer some rather prophetic criticism of the speed with which the academy was compiling and publishing its *Dictio-nary of the Irish Language*: "Indeed, if they continue in that way there is no one alive today who will see the end of the work." (An dagha, má leanaid siad ortha ar an gcuma soin níl éinne suas anois a chífidh deireadh an tsaothair.) The final fasciculus of the RIA *Dictionary* was published in 1976.

18. "Feis Chonnachta le Bheith i nGaillimh Lughnasa 20 agus 21, 1902/Syllabus" (The Connacht Feis to be held in Galway, 20 and 21 August 1902/Syllabus), *ACS*, 21 June 1902.

19. See Ó Súillebháin, *Scéal an Oireachtais*, 168–71; and Chapter 2.

20. See, for example, "Cú Uladh," "Thall 's i bhFus i dTír Chonaill," *ACS*, 26 April and 3 May 1902. Fenian lore was a regular feature in this series by Mac Fhionnlaoich.

21. See, for example, "Cúchulainn," in *Cú na gCleas agus Sgéalta Eile*, ed. Séamus Ó Searcaigh, 55–74; "Gaduigheacht Inis Dubháin" (The thievery of Inis Dubháin), *ACS*, 21

were also included in larger collections like the volumes of Oireachtas winners published by the league, and were issued in separate pamphlets like Seán Ó Cadhla's *Eachtra Fhinn Mhic Cumhaill le Seachrán na Sál gCam* (1906) or Tomás Mac Céidigh's *Céadtach Mac Fhinn as Éirinn* (Céadtach, the son of Fionn from Ireland) (1907).

Older Fenian material was in a language late enough to be accessible to those with a sound knowledge of modern Irish and thus could be and was edited by revivalists like Mac Néill, Pearse, Seán Ua Ceallaigh, and Pól Breathnach (Father Paul Walsh).[22] Some of this work, like "Filleadh na Féine (Filleadh Chaoilte Mhic Rónáin i n-Aimsir Phádraic)" (The return of the Fianna [The return of Caoilte Mac Rónáin in the time of Patrick]), "Fáistine Fhinn" (The prophecy of Fionn), "Mac Ghníomartha Fhinn" (The boyhood deeds of Fionn), or the account of the battle of Gowra (Cath Gabhra); modernizations of short excerpts from the medieval *Acallamh na Senórach* (The colloquy of the ancients),[23] or editions of ballads from Irish (and, as we will see in Chapter 6, from Scots Gaelic and Manx as well) appeared in *Irisleabhar na Gaedhilge*, *Irisleabhar Mhuighe Nuadhad*, *An Claidehamh Soluis*, and *An Sléibhteánach / The Mountaineer*.[24] Other offerings were considerably more sub-

---

December 1912; and "Oisín i nDiaidh na bhFiann" (Oisín after the Fianna), *ACS*, 17 October 1914. Folktales about Cú Chulainn like the one above are much rarer than those about Fionn, but see *Sgéal Chúchulainn ag Cuan Carn* (The story of Cú Chulainn at Cuan Carn), ed. Seosamh Laoide (Baile Átha Cliath: Connradh na Gaedhilge, 1906).

22. Breathnach was a versatile and meticulous scholar. In this particular context, see "Fianaighecht," his review of the state of Fenian scholarship, in *ACS*, 15 July 1911.

23. See "Filleadh na Féine (Filleadh Chaoilte Mhic Rónáin i n-Aimsir Phádraic: Sliocht as 'Agallamh na Senórach')," *ACS*, 22 December 1906; "Fáistine Fhinn," *ACS*, 3 August 1907; "Cinn Fhaoladh," "Mac Ghníomartha Fhinn," *SF*, 20 February 1909; and "Déise Mumhan" (The Decies of Munster), *An Sléibhteánach / The Mountaineer: Irisleabhar Choláiste Chnuic Mhellerí*, November 1912, 4–7. Three of these pieces were published without attribution. The first includes a modernization of the famous Ossianic poem on winter that begins "Scél lem dúib," a fact that might suggest Ó Donnchadha as the adapter. The work is not, however, mentioned in Diarmuid Ó hÉaluighthe's detailed bibliography for Ó Donnchadha. See "Clár Scríbhinní Thórna ó 1896 anuas go 1945" (A "Tórna" bibliography from 1896 to 1945), in *Féilscríbhinn Tórna* (A festschrift for "Tórna"), ed. Séamus Pender (Corcaigh: Cló Ollscoile Chorcaí, 1947), 225–58. The third was based on a less reliable text from the 1859 volume of the *Transactions of the Ossianic Society* even though Meyer had edited the tale in the first volume of *Ériu*. The fourth was based on the text in the *Transactions of the Ossianic Society* for 1854.

24. See, for example, "Fáisdine Fhinn" and "Ar Chruitire Fhinn Mhic Cumhaill" (Concerning the harper of Fionn Mac Cumhaill), *IG* 10, no. 112 (December 1898); "Bruigheann Ceise Corainn" and "Bruigheann Bheag na hAlmhaine," *Irisleabhar Mhuighe Nuadhad* (1907); and the poems edited with fairly extensive notes and commentary by "An Sgoláire Bocht" in his "Filidheacht" (Poetry) series in *ACS* in the winter and spring of 1911–12.

stantial. Mac Néill and Osborn Bergin published *Eachtra Lomnachtáin an tSléibhe Riffe* (The adventure of the naked one of Sliabh Riffe) in serial form in *Irisleabhar na Gaedhilge* in 1898–99 and as a book in 1901.[25] Mac Néill's still standard edition and translation of the first volume of *Duanaire Finn / The Poem Book of Finn* was issued by the Irish Texts Society in 1907.[26] Pearse edited three Fenian texts which will be discussed in more detail below. Ua Ceallaigh published a volume of Ossianic poems, *Leabhar na Laoitheadh* (The book of the lays) in 1912, a year after the first of two important collections of early modern Irish texts was produced by Maynooth's Cuallacht Chuilm Cille (Columban League), a scholarly student organization in which An tAthair Breathnach played a leading role. This volume, *Mil na mBeach* (The honey of the bees), an anthology that included several episodes from the Ulster Cycle as well as Fenian material, was followed in 1915 by *Gadaidhe Géar na Geamh-Oidhche* (The sharp thief of a winter's night), the most active contributor to which was Tomás Ó Gallchobhair.

Yet however impressive this work with the Fenian material, the fact nonetheless remained that with the exception of a few texts like the stories from Keating of the deaths of Cú Chulainn's son and of Medb published in *Éigse Suadh is Seanchaidh* (The learning of the sages and the storytellers) in 1909,[27] and more important, *Dearg-ruathar Chonaill Chernaig* (The red charge of Conall Cernach) and *Brisleach Mhór Mhaighe Muirtheimhne* (The great rout of Muirthemne Plain) edited by Seosamh Laoide from modern manuscripts,[28] the most distinctive treasures of the early literature, in particular the Ulster Cycle tales about Cú Chulainn, were locked away in a language unintelligible not only to the general reader, but to most informed students of Modern Irish as well. Thus for a knowledge of their own literary tradition, many fluent in the modern language were forced to consult the translations, especially those in English, accompanying editions prepared by their countryman

25. The work commenced serialization in *IG* 8, no. 94 (April 1898) and concluded in *IG* 9, no. 105 (March 1899). The book was published by the league.

26. The second volume of texts and the third volume containing the notes, glossary, indexes, etc. were edited by Gerard Murphy for the Irish Texts Society in 1933 and 1954 respectively.

27. See "Oidheadh Chonlaoich mic Con gCulainn" (The violent death of Conlaoch, son of Cú Chulainn) and "Fochain Bháis Mheidhbhe" (The cause of the death of Medb), in *Éigse Suadh is Seanchaidh: Sliocht do Shein-Leabhraibh an Chuid is Mó don Méid-se, idir Prós agus Filidheacht* (The learning of sages and storytellers: Excerpts from old books, both prose and poetry, for the most part) (Baile Átha Cliath: Muintir Ghoill [1909]). There were two versions of the former story, one from Keating.

28. The texts were published by the league in 1907 and 1915 respectively. Both deal with the death of Cú Chulainn.

Whitley Stokes or by foreigners like Meyer, Thurneysen, Windisch, de Jubainville, or Marstrander. Their abashment in so doing is evident in a 1900 letter from Muiris Ó Dubhdha to *An Claidheamh Soluis*: "We can't learn the ancient language of Ireland—we have enough work keeping the modern language alive. Therefore we can only read the ancient stories out of books in English. Isn't that a great shame?"[29]

Shameful or not, the inescapable fact remained that English was far less foreign to most readers of Modern Irish than was the language of much of the early literature. In such circumstances the appearance of scholarly editions with English translation and apparatus, and even more so of English-language "adaptations" of the early tales like those in Standish James O'Grady's *History of Ireland* (1878–80), Lady Gregory's *Cuchulain of Muirthemne* (1902), or A. H. Leahy's *Heroic Romances of Ireland* (1905–6) could legitimately be regarded as a threat to the Gaels' claim to a unique spiritual continuity with the Irish past. Indeed, in an editorial note in *An Claidheamh Soluis* in 1900 Mac Néill had expressed his reservations in dead earnest: "Reading translations exposes us to the danger of looking at things from the English standpoint; and it might be said that the better and more faithful a translation is the worse it is, for it will keep people from going to the original where alone the literature can be judged for what it is really worth."[30]

The Gaelic response to this threat was characteristically pragmatic. If the early literature could not be read as it stood, it would have to be modernized, in effect translated into the contemporary form of the language that was its only legitimate medium. As early as 1900 the Oireachtas, whose competitions were regularly used to encourage Gaelic writers to address specific perceived needs, offered a prize that

29. *ACS*, 23 June 1900. "Ní féidir linn sean-teanga na hÉireann d'fhoghluim—tá obair ár ndóithin againn agus an teanga nuadh-dhéanta do choimeád beo—mar gheall air sin ní féidir linn na sean-sgeulta do léigheadh acht as leabhraibh Beurla amháin. Nach mór an náire é sin?"

30. "Notes," *ACS*, 7 July 1900. Apparently, the league at one point planned to resolve this dilemma by enlisting Lady Gregory herself in their own literary modernization program. In October 1901, the Publication Committee, chaired by Hyde, announced "the forthcoming publication of a volume of tales from the Cú-chulainn Cycle, collected by Lady Gregory, and retold in easy, present-day Irish, by Dr. Hyde. The tales will be woven into a consecutive narrative, and will form an attractive and simple reading-book." See "Gaelic League/Publication Committee," *ACS*, 26 October 1901. This must be the same project referred to by Lady Gregory in her dedication of *Cuchulain*. It seems never to have materialized, for four years later Giollabhrighdhe Ó Catháin was exhorting his fellow Gaels: "The work Lady Gregory did in English should be being done in modern Irish as well by this time." (An obair do dhein an Bhaintighearna Gregorí i mBéarla, badh cheart í bheith dá dhéanamh san nua-Ghaedhilge leis, an taca so lá.) See Giollabhrighde Ó Catháin, letter, *IG* 14, no. 175 (April 1905): 776.

was to become a fixture in subsequent years for "the best modernised version of a tale or episode from Old or Middle Irish."[31] The prize drew an editorial welcome from *An Claidheamh Soluis*: "Valuable as our medieval literature is from many points of view, it is idle to deny that so long as it remains understandable only by those who have devoted years of study to it, it might as well, as far as the average speaker of Irish is concerned, be a foreign language. We must make the literature stored away in the Royal Irish Academy and in Trinity College available to the Aran Islander and to the Donegal Highlander."[32]

This view was unanimous among the Gaels; indeed, the necessity for modernizing the early tales was perhaps the literary policy on which nativists and progressives could most fully agree. The enthusiasm of the former should hardly be surprising. What is remarkable is the equally warm support for modernization as a fundamental element in the league's cultural program by the progressives who insisted that the new literature must confront the realities of twentieth-century European life. For example, discussing the problems involved in developing a Gaelic prose style both contemporary and true to its own traditions, William P. Ryan wrote: "The modernising (without changing the essential structure) and the publication of interesting older Irish will be one of the factors making for better things."[33] Eibhlín Nic Niocaill, a young woman whose enthusiasm for contemporary literature at times bordered on an iconoclasm that drew criticism from more conservative

---

31. "An t-Oireachtas, 1901/Further List of Competitions," *ACS*, 1 December 1900. Actually, the original competition was for "best modernisation of the text of an early Irish story of date previous to sixteenth century." The competition was never one of the more popular ones, and in 1906 Seaghán Mac Colgáin, having referred to it, asked, "Is the Oireachtas—the literary festival of the Gaelic League—doing anything directly to turn students towards the manuscripts which lie on shelves of the Royal Irish Academy, the Library of Trinity College, the Franciscan Library, and elsewhere?" See "Is the Progress of the Oireachtas Satisfactory?" *ACS*, 15 September 1906. In 1907 there was but one entry, and even that deemed unworthy of a prize, while in 1908 there were no submissions at all. The competition did, however, pick up somewhat in 1909. This sort of competition was obviously deemed too challenging for local feiseanna; only the 1904 Feis Bhaile Átha Cliath emulated the Oireachtas example, offering a prize for "best rendering in Modern Irish of any interesting extract not hitherto modernised from Old Irish or Middle Irish of a date prior to 1500 A.D." See the prospectus for the Feis, *ACS*, 19 December 1903.

32. "The Oireachtas," editorial, *ACS*, 9 March 1901. William Rooney was in entire agreement, calling modernization "after original work the most practical and the most necessary to be undertaken for the language." See "All Ireland," *UI*, 30 December 1899. This column was unsigned, but after Rooney's death Griffith acknowledged that it had been largely his work. See "All Ireland," *UI*, 18 May 1901.

33. "I mBaile 's i gCéin," *ACS*, 5 December 1903.

colleagues, went further, seeing modernization as an invaluable means of rooting a vibrant Gaelic future in a sound appreciation of a vibrant Gaelic past: "It is desirable that our older literature should be brought within the reach of all who have the future progress of our race at heart. This can best be done by means of modernised versions. . . . This, then, is one of the ways in which those who are willing to work for the future can prepare the way for the rise of the new literature."[34]

Mere enthusiasm, however universal, could not, of course, guarantee competence, much less success. As Muiris Ó Dubhdha wrote of modernization in his letter to An Claidheamh Soluis: "Perhaps that's an easy thing? Certainly! It's easy for the person who can do the trick."[35] Nor did the unanimity concerning the importance of the task extend to a consensus about how it should be accomplished, although all probably accepted the commonsense caveat of Tomás Ó Flannghaile: "The rendering of a piece from an ancient language into the modern living representative of the same tongue, no doubt, requires to be done with care and caution."[36]

Predictably the controversy centered around just what such care and caution were designed to protect and preserve from distortion the literal text or the ineffable and elusive spirit of the early tales.[37] The opposing viewpoints were delineated clearly in 1903 in the columns of An Claidheamh Soluis when Eleanor Hull and Peadar Mac Fhionnlaoich debated how best to give readers of the modern language a meaningful and valid understanding of the early literature. Hull stressed that a modernization should above all aim to capture "the heart and essence of

34. "Some Thoughts About the Future of Irish Literature," ACS, 12 June 1909. Her paper, originally delivered to a meeting of Cumann Náisiúnta na Mac Léigheann (Students' National Literary Society), apparently sparked a debate on the intriguing topic of "the value of a modernisation as opposed to a translation of our MSS." See "Cumann na Mac Léighinn," ACS, 12 June 1909. Several years later UCD students were still debating this topic following a lecture by Caitlín de Bhulbh on "Cad is Fiú an tSean-Ghaedhealg do Lucht Léighte agus Foghlumtha na Nua-Ghaedhilge?" (What is the value of Old Irish for readers and students of Modern Irish?) See "Cumann Gaedhealach na hIolscoile" (The University Gaelic Society), ACS, 15 February 1913.

35. ACS, 23 June 1900. "Is fuiriste an nídh sin, b'fhéidir? 'Seadh! Is fuiriste an nídh é leis an té is féidir leis an cleas do dhéanamh."

36. "The Youthful Exploits of Finn," in For The Tongue of the Gael: A Selection of Essays Literary and Historical, 2d ed. (Dublin: Sealy, Bryers, and Walker, 1907), 25.

37. This was, of course, the same dilemma that had faced the Anglo-Irish writers who had worked with this material since the early nineteenth century. See the discussion of their various responses, which were identical to those of their Gaelic counterparts, in Phillip L. Marcus, Yeats and the Beginnings of the Irish Renaissance (Ithaca: Cornell University Press, 1970), 223–40. I am indebted to Professor Marcus's extensive research for several of the references that follow.

the old romance," writing: "We greet any translation, any adaptation, however and wherever it comes. All are useful; and it may be that as yet, while the old literature is unfamiliar to most of us, some adaptation may be necessary to reconcile the mind to what is new to it, new because it is so old."[38]

Mac Fhionnlaoich's approach was more conservative: "In rendering old Irish into modern I conceive the best way to be to change as little as possible. . . . As to the style and form of the old romances, we may think that these could be improved upon, but our first business is to restore the original and make it common property before we proceed to "improve" it."[39] Mac Fhionnlaoich modified his views somewhat over the years. In a 1909 review of *Donnbó* by Henry Morris, he first spelled out what he meant by "restoring" an original: "We are indeed obliged to make some changes in the Old Irish so that it can be understood, for there are few people able to read Old Irish. The ancient words have to be removed and words common in the mouths of the people put in their place; a new twist has to be given to many of the words; and not infrequently an idiom that will be understood must be substituted for an idiom that would not be understood by Irish speakers of today." But then, having done so, he continued:

> Another thing, I am not saying that it is not possible to improve the stories themselves. We see from stories like *Bricriu's Feast* and *Congal Cláiringhneach* [both published by the Irish Texts Society] that the form of the ancient stories themselves, as they are found now, has been greatly corrupted from the form they had, in all probability, in their youth. I am not against all these changes when there is a reason for them; but that is not the same thing as writing them anew; and I would prefer to preserve and retain the form and style of the ancient stories except where there is a great need to make a change, and even then it should be made reluctantly and carefully, and with reverence as well.[40]

38. "'Style' in Old Irish Romance," *ACS*, 4 April 1903. Compare the approach of P. W. Joyce in his *Old Celtic Romances* (1879): "A translation may either follow the very words, or reproduce the life and spirit, of the original, but no translation can do both. If you render word for word, you lose the spirit; if you wish to give the spirit and the manner, you must depart from the exact words and frame your own phrases. I have chosen this latter course." See P. W. Joyce, Preface to *Old Celtic Romances* (London: David Nutt, 1894), vii.

39. Letter, *ACS*, 2 May 1903.

40. "Donnbó," review of *Donnbó agus Rígh-Sgéalta Eile* by "Fearghus Mac Róigh," *ACS*, 30 January 1909. Mac Fhionnlaoich began: "Tá sé d'fhiachaibh orainn go dearbhtha

The Oireachtas Committee responsible for judging entries in the modernization competition had from the outset favored a not entirely dissimilar position, although perhaps its vague invocation of "greater artistic success" would have been more acceptable to Hull than Mac Fhionnlaoich. The committee ruled: "Consistently with the preservation of the main outlines of the story, a certain re-handling of the theme will not be regarded as inadmissible, but competitors should note that any departure will only be considered as justified when a greater artistic success has thereby been achieved."[41] Oireachtas judges actually marked entrants down for unimaginative fidelity to the language of their originals, as we can read in an adjudicator's report on the 1901 competition: "The compositions . . . were all good, but they adhered too closely to the old texts, and hence were somewhat stiff."[42] These standards were maintained even in difficult circumstances. Thus in 1907 the sole entry in the competition was denied an award, in part because "some of the old language was left in the story" (do fágadh cuid de'n tsean-chainnt sa sgéal).[43] Gaelic literary critics in general agreed with this principle. For example, the adapter's retention of too many archaic words and phrases was the major and justified criticism directed at Thomas O'Neill Russell's *An Bóramha Laighean* (The Leinster tribute), a work that was never submitted to the Oireachtas.[44] On the other hand, adapters could go too far in the other direction, as is evident from the scathing dismissal of two of J. P. Craig's works in reviews in *Irisleabhar na Gaedhilge* and the *United Irishman*. The author of the former, probably Seosamh Laoide,

---

athrughadh éighinteach do chur ar an tsean-Ghaedhilg i modh 's gur féidir i thuigbheáil mar is beag duine a dtigh leis an tsean-Ghaedhilg do léigheadh. Caithfear na focla ársaidhe do sgriosadh amach agus focla atá coitchionn i mbéalaibh na ndaoine do chur in a n-ionad, caithfear casadh nuadh do chur ar mórán de na foclaibh agus ní annamh caithfear cor cainnte a thuigfear do chur i n-ionad cor cainnte nach dtuigfidhe ag Gaedhilgeoiríbh na haimsire seo." He continued: "Rud eile, chá deirim nárbh fhéidir feabhas do chur ar na sgéaltaibh iad féin. 'Tchímid ó sgéaltaibh mar 'Fleadh Bhricrinn' agus 'Congal Cláiringhneach' go bhfuil cruth na sean-sgéalta iad féin mar fághtar anois iad truaillighthe go mór ó'n chuma do bhí ortha, de réir cosamhalachta, i dtús a n-óige. Chan fhuil mé i n-aghaidh na hathruighthe seo go léir nuair bhíos fáth leo; ach ní hionann sa chás an méid seo uilig agus na sgéalta do sgríobhadh go húr-nuadh; agus b'fhearr liom féin cruth agus déanamh na sean-sgéal do choigilt agus do choimeád acht amháin nuair a bheadh gábhadh mór le hathrughadh do dhéanamh agus annsin féin é dhéanamh go mall agus go cúramach, agus go hurramach fosta."

41. "An t-Oireachtas, 1901 / Further List of Competitions," *ACS*, 15 September 1900.

42. See *Imtheachta an Oireachtais 1901*, 149.

43. See *ACS*, 17 August 1907, Duilleachán an Oireachtais.

44. See the unsigned review in *IG* 11, no. 126 (March 1901): 63–64. The work was, on the other hand, praised by an anonymous critic in *UI*. See "An Bhóramha Laighean," *UI*, 2 March 1901.

wrote: "This book is a *prácás* [potpourri] of provincialisms of the most pronounced type. . . . The same remarks apply to the author's other book *Clann Tuireann.*"[45]

Commenting on this controversy over how best to reacquaint contemporary Ireland with "the greatest of the things our ancestors did," William P. Ryan conceded: "The re-rendering will be no easy matter. To make it new, and comprehensible at Irish firesides or in Irish classes of our day, and at the same time to preserve its antique compass and epic flavour is a task that must try the most capable writer."[46] For better or worse at this very time the man whom many did consider the most capable, "the most original and most dramatic of modern Irish writers,"[47] was doing his utmost to bring to modern Irish readers *his* version of their lost literary heritage. The year 1900 saw the publication of Peadar Ua Laoghaire's *Bás Dhalláin* (The death of Dallán), a one-act play based on the opening section of *Tromdamh Guaire* and the first important Gaelic reworking of the ancient material if we leave aside the colorful but linguistically neutral tableaux vivants popular at league events from the turn of the century on.[48] Far more ambitious was Ua

45. See *IG* 12, no. 145 (October 1902): 159; and "A Student," "Dialect Irish," *UI*, 23 February 1901. Other critics were, however, less negative about Craig's approach. See the brief review of his *Clann Lir* in "Publications," *ACS*, 2 March 1901; and William P. Ryan's remarks on *Clann Tuireann* and *Clann Uisnigh* in "London Notes," *ACS*, 5 July 1902. Craig's work, which was not published under the auspices of the league, seems on the whole to have had little impact.

46. "I mBaile is i gCéin," *ACS*, 12 December 1903.

47. "Notes," *ACS*, 23 June 1900.

48. For an idea of what these tableaux looked like, see "The Feis Week in Belfast / Gaelic Festival and Tableaux," *FL*, 14 May 1898. Such tableaux retained their popularity at Gaelic festivals for years, and were a regular attraction in the annual Language Procession through Dublin. For the 1907 offerings, see "In and Around Baile Átha Cliath," *ACS*, 18 May 1907. The league also organized an occasional outdoor pageant drawing on ancient history and literature. For example, in July 1908, Craobh na gCúig gCúigí staged "a legendary pageant, entitled 'The Fate of the Children of Tuireann,' a synopsis of the story being read to the audience." See "Craobh na gCúig gCúigí," *ACS*, 11 July 1908. Pearse's three contributions to this genre will be discussed below. Irish-Irelanders also offered support to the occasional large-scale outdoor pageants staged in this period, particularly when the language was in some way involved. One such pageant was the Castleknock College production of *The Battle of Cnucha* in 1908, with its bardic recitation of the "Martial Ode of Cnucha" in Irish and an Irish "caoineadh" for "Coohal." See "Hibernicus," "The Castleknock Pageant," *The Leader*, 13 June 1908. Gaels must, however, have been disappointed by the most impressive of such efforts, that staged in 1910 by the Christian Brothers to celebrate their centenary in Cork. This pageant consisted of three "acts"—"Cúchulainn, the Boy Hero of the Gael," "The Story of Deirdre," and "Maeve the Warrior Queen"—performed by a cast of 500 boys and several horses. Each act was preceded by a spoken synopsis (in English) and accompanied by a

Laoghaire's adaptation of *Táin Bó Cúailnge* as a closet drama, which was serialized in the *Cork Weekly Examiner* in 1900–1901. An tAthair Peadar followed this work with a one-man publisher's list of modernizations: *Bricriu* (1901–4), *Eisirt* (1902–3) *Cath Chrionna* (The battle of Crionna) (1903), *An Craos-Deamhan* (The demon of gluttony) (1905), *Aodh Ruadh* (Red Hugh) (1905–8), *Ceallachán Caisil* (Ceallachán of Cashel) (1907), *Cath Ruis na Rí for Bóinn* (The battle of Rosnaree on the Boyne) (1907), *Lughaidh Mac Con* (1908), *Guaire* (1908–9), *An Cleasaidhe* (The trickster) (1909–10) and *Sliabh na mBan bhFionn* (Slievnamon) and *Cúán Fithise* (a proper name from the *Mionannála* [Minor annals] in *Silva Gadelica*) (1914). Ua Laoghaire often relied on English translations because of his lack of training in Middle Irish. He was always far more interested in providing colloquial and unadulterated "Irish" entertainment for native speakers than in meeting the scholarly criteria of academicians, a priority he made clear in a 1900 essay on a lecture by Kuno Meyer: "Is there any reason in the world why Irish Ireland should not swallow and assimilate Dr. Meyer, ancient MSS., philology, blackboard, chalk, and all? I see none, and I consider such a meal would be a very wholesome and a very invigorating one for Irish Ireland. Nothing could be more healthy than the contact of living Irish speakers and ancient Irish MSS."[49] Nor did he ever make any coherent or consistent effort to capture either the letter or the spirit of his originals.[50] Even so sympathetic a critic as Sister Mary Vincent could write of his efforts in this area: "It is best to read books like *Bricriu*, *Eisirt*, *An Cleasaidhe*, *An Craos-Deamhan*, etc., as original works without calling to mind the sources at all. They are best thought of in that way, for perhaps An tAthair Peadar's stories gain little when compared with the original tales."[51] Thus while his *Guaire* shows that he was capable of

---

"Bardic Choir" (singing, in English, songs like Moore's "Avenging and Bright"). For a detailed synopsis of this pageant, see R. J. Ray, "A Notable Pageant," *Journal of the Ivernian Society* 14, no. 13 (October–December 1911): 27–38. Significantly, this work does not seem to have drawn much comment in the Gaelic press with the exception of a report in *The Leader*. See, "Liam," "The Cork Pageant (With an 'Afterpiece')," *The Leader*, 16 September 1911.

49. Peter O'Leary, P.P., "Dr. Kuno Meyer's Lecture/Ourselves," *WF*, 6 June 1903.

50. For example, he could correspond at length in 1913 with the scholar Tomás Ó Rathaile (Thomas O'Rahilly) concerning his modernization *Sliabh na mBan bhFionn* without once asking him a question concerning the text, the whole correspondence being devoted to technical points of grammar and personal grievances against the league. His two letters to Ó Rathaile, one from 16 March and a much longer one from 19 December, along with the manuscript of *Sliabh na mBan bhFionn*, are in the Ua Laoghaire Papers, National Library of Ireland, MS. G660.

51. *An tAthair Peadar Ó Laoghaire agus a Shaothar*, 154. "Is fearr leabhair ar nós 'Bricriu,'

faithful modernization, he was also quick to alter or "emend" what he found unsatisfactory.

Ua Laoghaire was not, of course, alone in bowdlerizing his sources. Nor were his criteria for such editorial decisions all that different from those of Standish James O'Grady, who explained in his preface to *The History of Ireland* how he sorted the "essential" from that which was "wholly to be rejected:" "The nobler conception of any character is, of course, to be preferred to the ignoble."[52] Similarly, in his *Congal* (1872), Sir Samuel Ferguson suppressed what he called "inherent repugnancies too obstinate for reconcilement."[53] In her well-known dedication of *Cuchulain of Muirthemne* to "the people of Kiltartan," Lady Gregory informed them that "I left out a good deal I thought you would not care about for one reason or another."[54] To take just two examples, both of which as we will see involve changes identical to those made by Ua Laoghaire, her Maeve offers potential allies her "close friendship" in place of the "friendly thighs" of the original text, and is spared the humiliating and misogynistic menstrual weakness that afflicts the heroine in the tale's climactic battle.[55] On the other hand, Lady Gregory includes the scene in which "red-naked" women are sent to soothe the berserk frenzy of Cú Chulainn after his first martial exploit (33). Most Anglo-Irish adapters of this episode took one of three approaches. They omitted all reference to the nudity, as did Mrs. Hutton in her verse "translation" of the *Táin*. They added appropriate fig leaves, as did Standish James O'Grady, who has the women go to meet Cú Chulainn "in lowly wise, with exposed bosoms and hands crossed on their

---

'Eisirt,' 'An Cleasaidhe,' 'An Craos-Deamhan,' ⁊rl., do léigheamh gan chuimhneamh i n-aonchor ar na bun-sgéaltaibh, ach a cheapadh gur obair bunúsach iad, mar b'fhéidir nárbh fhearrde sgéalta an Athar Peadar a gcur i gcomparáid leis na leabhraibh bunaidh." Yet in 1907 Pádraig Mac Suibhne had recommended that readers make just such a comparative study of Ua Laoghaire's version of *Cath Ruis na Rí for Bóinn*, "to see his method and how he approaches the ancient tale" (féachaint cad é an nós oibre atá aige agus cionnus do ghabhann sé timcheall ar an sean-sgéal). See "Ó Chúige Mumhan," *ACS*, 2 November 1907. And in 1914, Tadhg Ó Donnchadha praised Ua Laoghaire's modernizations, writing "we find in them an account of the mind and spirit of the Gaels of antiquity" (geibhmíd ionntasan tuairisc ar mheoin agus ar aigne Gaedheal san tseanaimsir). See "Rudhraigheacht" (The Ulster Cycle), *ACS*, 10 October 1914.

52. *History of Ireland: The Heroic Period* (London: Sampson, Low, Searle, Marston and Rivington, 1878), xiii.

53. *Congal: A Poem in Four Books* (Dublin: Edward Ponsonby, 1872), vii.

54. "Dedication of the Irish Edition to the People of Kiltartan," in *Cuchulain of Muirthemne: The Story of the Men of the Red Branch of Ulster Arranged and Put into English by Lady Gregory with a Preface by W. B. Yeats* (Gerrards Cross: Colin Smythe, 1970), 5.

55. See *Cuchulain of Muirthemne*, 143, 204. I know of no adaptation from this period in either Irish or English that refers to Medb's menstruation.

breasts."[56] Or they obviated the problem through sheer verbosity, as did Aubrey De Vere in *The Foray of Queen Maeve* (1882)[57] or Standish Hayes O'Grady in "Cuchullin's Boy-Deeds" (1898). In the latter work, the women "reduce themselves critically to nature's garb, and without subterfuge of any kind troop out to meet him."[58]

As we will see, Gaelic critics and the adapters themselves could be equally presumptuous concerning the alteration of original texts. For example, in an *An Claidheamh Soluis* review of Standish James O' Grady's *In the Gates of the North*, "An Buailtean" praised the work precisely because of, rather than despite, the fact that "there is no pretension to exact scholarship, no wearisome following of the details of the story."[59] Furthermore, this attitude even extended to serious and sympathetic students of the early literature. Patrick Pearse, for example, believed that "the old world was in many ways less squeamish than the modern world, and, in so far as it was, the old world was undoubtedly a better and honester world,"[60] and argued that "the tales when presented to modern readers should not be shorn of their barbarism, or of their grotesqueness; and in fact that the barbaric and grotesque element belongs essentially to them."[61] Yet even he could inflict minor "refinements" on his edition of a Fenian tale like *Bruidhean Chaorthainn*, not to mention his later pageant *Macghníomhartha Chúchulainn.*[62]

"Minor" would not, however, be the appropriate description for An tAthair Peadar's "emendations." Indeed, he seems at times to have had a perverse psychic radar that homed in on precisely those texts with which he would have least sympathy. For example in *An Craos-Deamhan,* his version of *Aislinge Meic Con Glinne* (The vision of Mac Con-

---

56. *The Coming of Cuchulain* (London: Methuen, 1894), 159.

57. *The Foray of Queen Maeve and Other Legends of Ireland's Heroic Age* (London: Kegan Paul, Trench, 1882), 16.

58. "Cuchullin's Boy-Deeds," in *The Cúchullin Saga in Irish Literature: Being a Collection of Stories relating to the Hero Cúchullin, translated from the Irish by Various Scholars: Compiled and Edited with Introduction and Notes,* by Eleanor Hull (London: David Nutt, 1898), 153.

59. "The Hero of the Ford," review of *In the Gates of the North* by Standish O'Grady, *ACS,* 21 November 1908.

60. "In First Century Ireland," *ACS,* 4 January 1908.

61. "Gleó na gCath," *ACS,* 8 August 1903.

62. See *Bruidhean Chaorthainn: Sgéal Fiannaidheachta,* ed. Pearse (Baile Átha Cliath: Clódhanna Teoranta, 1912), 33. In the original Conán's buttocks are flayed as well. It is interesting to note that in a review of an edition of an Ulster version of this tale, Tomás Ua Concheanainn wrote: "There isn't an obscene word or phrase in it, and that is something that can't be said about other ancient stories." (Níl aon fhocal ná aon leagan cainnte gársamhail ann agus sin rud nach féidir a rádh i dtaoibh seansgéalta eile.) See Ua Concheanainn, "*Bruidheann Chaorthainn,*" review of *Bruidheann Chaorthainn* by "Feargus Mac Róigh," *ACS,* 28 October 1911.

glinne), he omitted the original's burlesque of the Crucifixion and entirely suppressed its zestful anticlericism, instead depicting the monks of Cork as a long-suffering and good-natured lot who teach Mac Conglinne an overdue and well-merited lesson. In fact, as Breandán Ó Buachalla has pointed out, he inverted the entire narrative perspective of the medieval tale: "In *Aisling Meic Conglinne* the author's sympathy is with Mac Conglinne, but in *An Craos-Deamhan*, his sympathy is with Mainchin [the abbot of Cork]."[63] In addition, Ua Laoghaire here as throughout his work freely inserted little lectures on pet issues, most notably a passage extolling native customs prior to the arrival of foreign contamination with the Normans,[64] and a brief temperance sermon: "The demon of drunkenness has now taken possession in many people . . . And far greater is the destruction and the ruin that he is doing than Cathal's Demon of Gluttony ever did" (120).[65] More drastic measures were required with the marvelously bawdy *Aided Fergusa Mic Léide* (The death of Fergus Mac Léide), parts of which were left discreetly untranslated by its editor Standish Hayes O'Grady and one of the tales Atkinson had in the forefront of his mind when he issued his famous denunciation of the moral temper of the early literature. An tAthair Peadar was, as usual, unfazed. He simply bowdlerized what he could, such as the passage in which the tiny people defecate in all the wells of Ulster,[66] and excised what he found utterly repugnant, such as the scene in which the massive Fergus jokes as he copulates with the pygmy queen.

Nor were his versions of two of the most significant Ulster Cycle tales free of what he no doubt saw as improvements. An tAthair Peadar wrote two plays based on the *Táin*. In *Méibh*, written for performance, he read the ancient tale as a temperance text, stressing that it was the arrogant drunkenness of the Connacht messengers that enraged the Ulsterman Dáire and caused him to refuse Medb the loan of his bull, thus

---

63. "An tAthair Peadar is Mac Conglinne" (An tAthair Peadar and Mac Conglinne), *Comhar* 29, no. 12 (December 1970): 8. "In *AMC* tá bá an údair le Mac Conglinne, ach in *ACD* is le Mainchín atá a bhá."

64. *An Craos-Deamhan* (Baile Átha Cliath: Brún agus Ó Nualláin, n.d.), 65–67. Having analyzed Ua Laoghaire's manipulation of *Aislinge Meic Conglinne* in some detail, Breandán Ó Buachalla concluded: "He made a Victorian moral fable out of a blasphemous Rabelaisian satire." (Dhein sé fabhailscéal morálta Victeoiriach de aoir raibiléiseach dhiamhaslach.) See "An tAthair Peadar is Mac Conglinne," 6–9.

65. "Tá seilbh anois ag craos-deamhan an mheisge istigh i n-a lán daoine. . . . Is mó go mór an milleadh agus an creachadh atá aige 'á dhéanamh 'ná mar a dhein Craos-Deamhan Chathail riamh."

66. *Eisirt* (Baile Átha Cliath: Muintir na Leabhar Gaedhilge, 1909), 68.

setting the war in motion.[67] In the earlier and far longer closet drama *Táin Bó Cúailnge*, he for the most part adhered to the dialogue of his *Book of Leinster* original, but radically reshaped the personality of Queen Meadhbh, allowing her to retain her Machiavellian forcefulness, but depriving her of her voracious sexuality. For example, the "friendly thighs" (cardes sliasta) offered to lure Dáire mac Fiachna (and others) in the ancient tale become a bland "special friendship" (caradas fé leith) in Ua Laoghaire's play,[68] and her thematically essential menstrual weakness during the final battle is reduced to a meaningless "some confusion" (measgán mearaidhe éigin) (246). Even more striking is his depiction of the redoubtable Connacht queen as a devoted mother to Fionnabhair, the daughter whom in the original she uses as a sexual bribe to dupe warriors into fighting Cú Chulainn: "You know well that there is nothing at all that I would not do to make you happy and to take and keep every source of trouble from you" (134–36).[69] Fionnabhair calls her "the best mother a child ever had" (an mháthair is fearr a bhí ag leanbh riamh) (136).

Fled Bricrend required less sanitization, but An tAthair Peadar did not relax his vigilance. Thus in his *Bricriu* the Ulster women somehow manage to keep their clothes in decorous order—well below the rumps to which they climb in the original!—during their mad dash for precedence,[70] and their warrior husbands swear unconvincingly "by this and that" (dar so agus súd) rather than invoking unacceptable tribal deities (66–67). Nonetheless, despite Ua Laoghaire's obvious shortcomings as an accurate modernizer—shortcomings sometimes noted and gently criticized in contemporary reviews[71]—his work was of considerable sig-

---

67. The play was produced at the 1903 Muskerry Feis. See "Múscraidheach," "Feis Mhúscraidhe" (The Muskerry Feis), *ACS*, 12 September 1903. It was not, however, published until 1910, when it was serialized in the *Irish Industrial Journal* from 7 May to 25 June.

68. *Táin Bó Cúailnge 'na Dhráma* (Baile Átha Cliath: Muintir na Leabhar Gaedhilge, 1915), 8–11.

69. "Tá a fhios agat go maith ná fuil ní ar bith ná déanfainn chun áthais a chur ort agus chun gach adhbhar buartha do thógáilt díot agus do choimeád uait." See also 34.

70. *Bricriu, nó "Is Fearr an t-Imreas 'ná an t-Uaigneas"* (Bricriu, or Strife is better than loneliness) (Baile Átha Cliath: Brún agus Ó Nualláin, n.d.), 20. Ua Laoghaire similarly manages to preserve the modesty of the itinerant Mac Conglinne by omitting reference to his habit of traveling about with his shirt hoisted over his buttocks.

71. See, for example, Pearse's comments in his review of *An Craos-Deamhan*: "We have here, in fact, the culmination of a fierce spirit of anti-clericalism or at any rate anti-monasticism, which several times emerges in Irish literature, and is not unknown in Irish folklore. . . . Needless to say, all this anti-clericalism is toned down in Father O'Leary's modern version to a good-humoured raillery which any 'monks of Cork' who happen to

nificance in giving Gaelic readers some sense of the extent, variety, and interest, if not the form or spirit, of the early literature.

Ua Laoghaire was not alone in his attempt to bring the old tales alive for a new audience. As early as 1891 Thomas D. Norris commenced serialization of "Extracts from Seanchus Mór [the most extensive early Irish law tract]" in *An Gaodhal*,[72] and Father O'Growney published modern Irish versions of two medieval *immram* (voyage) tales in *Irisleabhar na Gaedhilge*. In 1901 Thomas O'Neill Russell brought out his *Bóramha*, followed by his *Beatha Naoimh Brighde, or The Life of St. Brigit (from the Leabhar Breac)*,[73] works whose "modern" texts, in keeping with the author's championship of "classical" Irish, might strike some readers as only slightly less archaic than their exemplars! Also in 1901 Peadar Mac Fhionnlaoich put his principles into practice by submitting a modernization of *Fled Bricrend* to the Oireachtas, where it received a for him disappointing second prize, the winning entry being Tadhg Mac an Bháird's *Fleadh Dhúin na nGeadh; agus Mar Tugadh Cath Mhuighe Rátha* (The feast of Dún na nGeadh and how the battle of Magh Ráth was fought). Eight years later Mac Fhionnlaoich was still at work in this vein, publishing *Eachtra Néill Naoi nGiallaigh .i. Mar Tháinig Sé i Ríghe Éireann* (The adventure of Niall of the nine hostages, i.e., How he assumed the sovereignty of Ireland), *Easgáineadh na Teamhrach* (The cursing of Tara), and in predictably bowdlerized form, *Eisirt agus na Ríghthe* (Eisirt and the kings) from *Aided Fergusa Mic Léide*, of which he disingenuously wrote: "I have not altered the tale in any way, except to omit a few passages."[74]

Other important modernizations that will not be singled out for special comment are Tadhg Ó Donnchadha's "Ar Choisriceadh an Chéad Teampoill ar Talamh do Mhicheál Ard-Aingeal" (On the consecration

---

read the book will enjoy as hugely as the mere layman." See "An Irish Rabelais," *ACS*, 27 May 1905. Of the same work, Father Dinneen wrote: "His version is not a close modernisation of the old tale, departing as it does from it in many particulars; nevertheless it hangs together quite consistently, and is extremely readable." Incidentally, Dinneen incorporated his own quite lengthy temperance sermon in this piece (review of *An Craos-Deamhan, The Leader*, 6 May 1905). One "D.G." was also untroubled by the fact that Ua Laoghaire "does not slavishly follow the text of the Leabhar Breac," and claimed that his version can serve as "a specimen of the rich vein of humour possessed by our ancestors." See "Some New Books in Irish," *UI*, 27 May 1905.

72. "Extracts from Seanchus Mór (Ancient Brehon Laws)," *An Gaodhal*, February 1891–March 1893. Norris provided "Original as in Seanchus Mór," "Modern Form," and "English Translation," stating in the first installment that he was giving "Modern Irish as I understand it."

73. The work commenced serialization in *WF*, 31 May 1902.

74. "Eisirt agus na Ríghthe," *Irish Nation and Peasant*, 16 October 1909.

of the first church on Earth to the Archangel Michael), the winner of the first Oireachtas Prize for modernization;[75] *Leithsgéal Inghine Ghuilidhe* (The excuse of the daughter of Gulide) by "Ógánach";[76] three anonymous works, "Sgéala an Trír Chléireach Óg" (The Story of the three young clerics), "Aithbheóchan Bhreasail Mhic Dhiarmada" (The revival of Breasal Mac Diarmada), and *Breith Chúchulainn* (The birth of Cú Chulainn);[77] two versions of the medieval tale *Echtra Laegaire Meic Crimthainn* (The adventure of Laoghaire Mac Crimhthainn), one of them also providing the text in Esperanto;[78] Micheál Ó Dúnlainge's *Cath Mhaighe Mochruimhe* (The battle of Mag Mucrama);[79] *Bás Mheidhbhe* (The death of Medb) by "Éamonn";[80] *An Ceithearnach Caoilriabhaigh, Cath Fionntrágha* (The battle of Ventry), and *Eachtra Thaidhg Mhic Céin* (*The adventure of Tadhg Mac Céin*) by "An Seabhac";[81] Art Mag Uidhir's *Fraoich agus Fionnabhair* (Fraoich and Fionnabhair)[82] Éamonn Ua Néill's "Páis an Mhóir-sheisear do Chodail i nÉifis Caogadh ar Chéad Bliadhan Dóibh" (The suffering of the seven who slept

75. *Imtheachta an Oireachtais 1900*, 48–51. The text was from the *Leabhar Breac*.

76. *ACS*, 21 December 1901. His original was *Erchoitmed Ingine Gulide*.

77. *Sgéala an Trír Chléireach Óg*, IG 12, no. 142 (July 1902): 98–101; *Aithbheóchan Bhreasail Mhic Dhiarmada*, IG 12, no. 143 (August 1902): 113–14; *Breith Chúchulainn, Inis Fáil*, November 1906, 8–10. The originals were, respectively, *Sgéla an Trír Maccléireach* from *Leabhar Mhic Carrthaigh Riabhaigh, Aided Bresail Meic Diarmata*, and *Compert Con Culainn*.

78. Seán P. Mac Éinrigh, *Cúaird Laoghaire Mhic Chrimthainn go Maigh Meall* (The visit of Laoghaire Mac Crimthainn to the Plain of Delights), *Banba* 3, no. 1 (August 1904); and E. E. Fournier and R. B. White, *Eachtra Laoghaire Mhic Criomhthainn go Maigh Meall / The Visit of Leary, Son of Criffan, to the Plain of Delight* (Baile Átha Cliath: M. H. Gill and Son, 1907). The latter included the Esperanto version. The original was *Echtra Laegaire Maic Crimthainn*.

79. IG 17, no. 25 (September 1907)–18, no. 4 (April 1908). His main source was RIA 23.M.47. The original was *Cath Muige Mucrime*.

80. *An Connachtach*, December 1907. The original was *Aided Meidbe*.

81. *An Ceithearnach Caoilriabhaigh* commenced serialization in *An Lóchrann* in November 1908; and was published as a book by the league in 1910. *Cath Fionntrágha* and *Eachtra Thaidhg Mhic Céin* were also published by the league as books, the former in 1911, the latter in 1914. The originals were, respectively, *Echtra in Chethernaig Chaoilriabhaigh, Cath Finntrágha*, and *Echtra Thaidhg Meic Céin*. Incidentally, in 1910 Seán Mac Éinrigh complained to the league's Publications Committee that he also had been at work on a version of *Echtra in Cheithernaig*, and that publication of Ó Siochfhradha's modernization as a book would make his own redundant. See the mimeographed report of the committee's meeting for 20 April 1910 in the Fionán Mac Coluim Papers, National Library of Ireland, MS. 24,405. In 1912 the league did, however, publish another modernization of this very tale by Henry Morris as *Ceithearnach Uí Dhomhnaill, nó Eachtra an Cheithearnaigh Chaoil-Riabhaigh* (O'Donnell's kerne, or The adventure of the slender striped kerne).

82. IG 19, no. 4 (April 1909)–19, no. 5 (May 1909). The original was *Táin Bó Fraích*.

in Ephesus for 150 years);[83] Cormac Ó Cadhlaigh's *Eachtra Chondla Mic Chuinn Chéadchathaigh* (The adventure of Connla the son of Conn of the Hundred Battles);[84] and Eoghan Ó Neachtain's *Tochmarc Fhearbhlaidhe* (The wooing of Fearbhlaidh).[85] What made much of this work possible, of course, was the regular publication at this time of accessible scholarly editions, often with English translation, a fact underscored by the appearance in 1909 of a modernization of sections of *Imtheachta Aeniasa* (the Irish *Aeneid*) by "Donnchadh Bacach," two years after an edition and translation of the entire text was issued by the Irish Texts Society.[86]

In this same year of 1909 *An Claidheamh Soluis* commenced serialization of Mac Fhionnlaoich's retellings of Ulster Cycle tales, eventually published in book form in 1914 as *Conchobhar Mac Neasa: Stair-Sheanchas Curadh na Craobhruaidhe* (Conchobhar Mac Neasa: A historical account of the warriors of the Red Branch).[87] Based for the most part on the work of the seventeenth-century historian Geoffrey Keating rather than on the original texts, Mac Fhionnlaoich's work consistently bowdlerizes the tales, stripping them of disturbing elements of barbarism that would decrease their value as heroic exemplars for contemporary Anglicized Ireland. Furthermore, Mac Fhionnlaoich was uncertain, or perhaps more accurately unconcerned, as to whether these tales should be considered as reliable historical documents.[88] Thus while he often does include clearly fictional or mythological material such as Fergus's lopping off the tops of hills with his sword or the famous "pangs" of the Ulstermen, his work on the whole treats the early tales as history, an approach he defended rather petulantly at the conclusion of his book:

83. *An Lóchrann*, 3, no. 1 (December 1909): 3 and 7. The original was in the *Leabhar Breac* (Dublin: Royal Irish Academy, 1876), 189–90.

84. *An Lóchrann* 4, no. 1 (April 1911): 1. Ó Cadhlaigh also contributed "Ceisneamh Inghne Ghoil Átha Loigh" (The complaint of the daughter of Gol of Áth Loigh), a story in rather antiquated Irish about Feidhlimid mac Crimhthainn, in *An Lóchrann* 4, no. 12 (December 1912): 4–5.

85. (Baile Átha Cliath: Mac an Ghoill agus a Mhac, 1912).

86. "Cáirdeas Aonghusa agus Dídó" (The friendship of Aeneas and Dido"), *SF*, 27 March–17 April 1909.

87. Mac Fhionnlaoich had already published brief plot summaries of the "mythological" tales concerning the two battles of Moytura as "Prímh-Sgéalta na Sean-Ghaedheal" (The prime stories of the Ancient Gaels) in *ACS*, 11 and 25 April 1903. Other of "Sean-Sgéalta na nGaedheal" (The ancient stories of the Gaels) dealing with Irish pseudohistory were summarized anonymously in *Inis Fáil* from October to December 1904, and from September to December 1905.

88. It may be worth noting that an advertisement for the publisher, Clódhanna Teoranta, states that "the book is professedly the life story of the celebrated King of Ulster." See *ACS*, 19 June 1915. We should also recall that Mac Fhionnlaoich's ambivalence concerning the historical reliabilty of the early tales is, of course, present in Keating as well.

"We can't go back as far as them through writings or a definite attested account like the one we have for Brian Bóroimhe and the Battle of Clontarf, but if Conchobar and Cú Chulainn and Fergus and Conall Cernach did not live, we are certain that the like of them did. . . . Warrior Gaels like them lived at some time in some place, and it doesn't matter to us whether they lived in Emain Macha or not."[89]

His ambivalence on this point is entirely characteristic of his time and milieu, as is evident from even a glance at the treatment of the reign of Conchobar in Caitlín Nic Ghabhann's 1910 Oireachtas Prize-winning essay "Éire sa tSean-Aimsir" (Ireland in ancient times).[90] Many other Irish-Ireland literary figures, including Pearse, whose views will be discussed in more detail below, could be every bit as unclear, even cavalier, concerning the historicity of the early literature as was Standish James O'Grady. Thus Arthur Griffith wrote in 1910: "In our history—for Cuchullin is as historical a person as Napoleon—there is no figure which typifies the Gael as he does, and the nation should guard and treasure every memorial of him."[91] In their descriptions of two geographical locations that enshrined such memories, Ráth Cruachan, the home of the legendary Medb, and the Plain of Muirthemne, where much of the action of the *Táin* takes place, neither Tomás Ó hEidhin nor Peadar Ó Dubhdha questioned the factual accuracy of the early literature. Ó Dubhdha wrote: "The scene of the Táin is spread out before us. From the southwest came Medb in search of the bull. And from this fort below us Cú Chulainn went off in his chariot to meet his enemy and to slaughter and overthrow them."[92] Indeed, some felt that

89. *Conchubhar Mac Neasa: Stair-Sheanchas Curadh na Craobhruaidhe*, 77. "Ní féidir linn dul siar fhaid leo trí sgríbhinníbh nó cunntas cinnte dearbhtha amhail is tá againn ar Bhrian Bóirmhe is ar Chath Chluain Tairbh, ach murar mhair Conchubhar agus Cúchulainn is Feargus is Conall Cearnach, is cinnte linn gur mhair a mac a samhla. . . . Bhí a leithéid de laochraibh Gaedheal ann i n-am éigin i n-áit éigin agus is cuma dúinn ciaca mhair siad i nEamhain Macha nó nár mhair." Mac Fhionnlaoich clearly accepted the truth of O'Grady's dictum that "the legends . . . are the kind of history which a nation desires to possess." See *History of Ireland: The Bardic Period*, 22. And compare the view of AE: "What does it matter whether Cúchulain, Deirdre or Maeve ever lived or acted on earth, as legend relates of them? They are immortals and find bodies from generation to generation." See "The Antecedents of History," in *The Living Torch*, ed. Monk Gibbon (London: Macmillan, 1937), 134.

90. Nic Ghabhann's essay was serialized in *ACS* beginning on 25 September 1915, and again in "Pádraig Bán agus a Chairde" (Fair-haired Pádraig and his friends), a young readers' column, beginning on 11 March 1916.

91. "Cuchullin," *SF*, 9 April 1910. Griffith was praising the efforts of a group of people who had come together to buy Dún Dealgan, the legendary home of Cú Chulainn, for the Louth Archaeological Society, thereby preserving it from "vandals."

92. "An tOireachtas/Maigh Mhuirtheimne," *ACS*, 27 March 1915. "Tá láthair na Tána

the tales were reliable in quite specific detail, so that members of the Belfast Branch on a day's outing to the site of Emain Macha outside Armagh were told: "This hill was the site of Conor MacNessa's palace—the house of the Red Branch. On one side of it, beyond the fosse and the chariot-ridge, which are still to be seen, was the Druid's house in which Deirdre, the fateful child, was born. On the other side was the building where the sons of Usna were lodged after their return from Scotland under the guaranty of Fergus MacRoy."[93]

Fortunately, versions of central episodes of the *Táin* far more authentic than those offered by Mac Fhionnlaoich were made available when installments of John Strachan's invaluable Old Irish *Stories from the Táin* were accompanied by accurate modernizations in *Irisleabhar na Gaedhilge* in 1903–4.[94] Strachan's text was also the source for the faithful modernization *Giolla na Tána* (1912–13) by Tomás Ua Nualláin, who in the same year published an equally accurate *Comhrac Fir Diad* based on Ernst Windisch's edition of the *Book of Leinster Táin*.[95] Perhaps the most unexpected modernizer was Pádraic Ó Conaire, who wrote in "Sean-litridheacht na nGaedheal agus Nua-litridheacht na hEorpa" in 1908: "Don't bother with antiquarianism. Even though your fathers recounted excellent stories and composed beautiful and noble poetry, don't think that you will achieve the same results by having the same material to write about. The age of that ancient literature is long past."[96]

ós ár gcomhair leathta. Aniar-ndeas 'seadh mar tháinig Meadhbh ar lorg an tairbh. Agus as a' dún seo fúinn-ne 'seadh d'imthigh an Cú leis in a charbad i n-aircis a námhad a' cur áir agus cosgair ortha." See also Ó Dubhdha, "Dún Dealgan," *SF*, 29 October 1910. For Ó hEidhin, see "Ráth Cruachan," *ACS*, 28 November 1908. This essay had won a prize at the 1904 Oireachtas.

93. "Connradh na Gaedhilge / Belfast," *ACS*, 8 September 1900.

94. With the exception of two sections explicitly attributed to Eoghan Ó Neachtain (*IG* 14, no. 160, p. 161), these modernizations were published anonymously. William P. Ryan gives Tadhg Ó Donnchadha credit for the work in "I mBaile 's i gCéin," *ACS*, 12 December 1903; as does "Macha Maol," "An tIrisleabhar," *ACS*, 5 December 1903. The attribution certainly makes sense, although the work is not listed in the prose modernization subsection of Ó hÉaluighthe's bibliography. See "Clár Scríbhinní Thórna" in *Féil-scríbhinn Tórna*, 254.

95. Ua Nualláin also published the following modernizations: *Fath Catha Cnucha* (The cause of the battle of Cnucha) from the original *Fotha Catha Cnucha*, in *ACS*, 13 January 1912; "Ceann Cruaich" (a place-name) from Rawlinson B 502 in *ACS*, 27 January 1912; and "Caraidh na Fírinne" (The friend of the truth) from *Leabhar Breac*, in *ACS*, 17 February 1912 (pretty much a simple glossing of archaic words).

96. In *Aistí Uí Chonaire*, 51. "Ná bacaidh le sean-aimsireacht. Bíodh is gur ríomh bhur n-aithreacha sársgéalta, agus gur chumadar filidheacht aoibhinn uasal, ná ceapaidh go ndéanfaidh sibhse an obair chéadna ach an t-adhbhar céadna scríobhtha a bheith agaibh. Tá ré na seanlitridheachta úd thart le fada an lá."

Yet only two years previously his own versions of two of those "excellent stories" (sárscéalta), *Noínden Ulad* (The pangs of the Ulstermen) and *Serglige Con Culainn* (The wasting sickness of Cú Chulainn), appeared in the London Gaelic League journals *Guth na nGaedheal* and *Inis Fáil* respectively.[97] Perhaps the clearest indication of the degree to which this kind of work was perceived as central to the literary revival in the first decades of this century is the surprising involvement of a writer like Ó Conaire.

No such surprise attaches to the involvement, indeed immersion, of Ó Conaire's progressive comrade Pearse in the study and revival of the heroic literature, and Yeats's famous question from "The Statues" (1938) merely underscores the passion of Pearse's commitment:

> When Pearse summoned Cuchulain to his side,
> What stalked through the Post Office?

That commitment was lifelong; in addition to creating two pageants with Cú Chulainn as the central character, he referred regularly to the heroes of early Irish literature in his writings on all of the many topics that drew his attention as editor, educator, critic, and cultural and political activist.

Like others who learned their Irish from books in Dublin, Pearse's first direct encounter with the heroic literature was not through the linguistically challenging Ulster Cycle, but through the more popular and accessible tales of Fionn Mac Cumhaill available in modern manuscripts as well as in *Irisleabhar na Gaedhilge* and on the lips of native speakers. Thus in June 1900 he published the text of a lecture he had delivered at a league meeting on "An Fhiann agus an Fhiannaidheachd" (The Fenians and Fenian lore), a term-paper exercise largely concerned with the historicity of Fionn and his Fianna and bristling with refer-

---

97. "Lagar na nUltach" (The weakness of the Ulstermen), *Guth na nGaedheal* (March 1906); and "Seargadh Chúchulainn" (The withering sickness of Cú Chulainn), *Inis Fáil*, December 1906–February 1907. Ó Conaire was aware of his limitations as a scholar, writing of the linguistically difficult "Bríatharthecosc Con Culainn" (Cú Chulainn's instructions) interpolation in *Serglige*: "The language in it is extremely difficult and inscrutable, and therefore it will not be dealt with here." (Tá an chainnt atá ann rí-dheacair do–thuigsiona, agus mar sin de ní bacfar leis annseo.) Ó Conaire did, however, express interest in carrying on with this kind of work, noting of the subtale *Óenét Emire* (The only jealousy of Emer): "Perhaps we will have that story some other time." (B'fhéidir go mbeadh an sgéal úd againn uair eile.) See Ó Conaire, "Seargadh Chúchulainn," *Inis Fáil*, February 1907, 2.

ences to Continental Celticists and their theories.[98] And, as we have seen, within a few years he himself had sufficient mastery of the early modern Irish of the later Fenian tales to edit and publish three of them: *Bodach an Chóta Lachtna* (1903–4), *Tóraidheacht Fhiacail Ríogh Gréag* (with Eoghan Ó Neachtain in 1904), and *Bruidhean Chaorthainn* (1908).[99]

Even as he was establishing his scholarly credentials with this work on the Fenian material, he was beginning to immerse himself through translations in the Ulster Cycle. As early as his March 1897 lecture entitled "Gaelic Prose Literature" to the New Ireland Literary Society of which he was the seventeen-year-old president, he discussed "the knights of the Red Branch," quoted extensively from translations, and in words he could have used unchanged at the end of his life, affirmed his faith in the inspirational value of the early literature: "The self-same old epics . . . may still be inspiring and rejuvenating the heart of man, and lifting him to higher and nobler ideals."[100] In October of the same year he returned to this theme in "The Intellectual Future of the Gael," declaring:

> Fearghus, Conchubhar, Cúchulainn, Fionn, Oisín, Oscar—these were more to the Gael than mere names of great champions and warriors of a former time: they represented to him men who had gone before, who had fought the good fight. . . . And though well-nigh two thousand years have rolled away since those mighty heroes trod this land of ours, yet their spirit is not dead: it lives on in our irresistible, overmastering conviction that we, as a nation, are made for higher things.[101]

At the 22 February 1898 meeting of the New Ireland Literary Society, it was Patrick's brother—and in this case proxy—who delivered a

98. "An Fhiann agus an Fhiannaidheachd," *IG* 10, no. 117 (June 1900): 532–38. It is instructive to compare even this early essay with the less informed work on the subject by "Conán Maol" in "Fian Poetry," *Catholic Bulletin* 2, no. 7 (July 1912): 449–55.

99. In a note to his edition of *Bodach an Chóta Lachtna* in *ACS*, Pearse commented that the idea of publishing such material in *ACS* came to him in response to Father O'Reilly's "recent plea for the necessity of a close and sympathetic study of the existing examples of an Irish prose style, but more especially of the Ossianic romances." See "Bodach an Chóta Lachtna," *ACS*, 19 December 1903. Several months later, he commented that reader response to the edition "has convinced us that this is, on the whole, the class of matter which the Irish-reading public likes best" and announced that "tales from MS. sources—mainly unpublished ones—will be a leading feature of *An Claidheamh* during the coming year." See "Sinn Féin," *ACS*, 5 March 1904. Such material did indeed appear in *ACS*, but on an occasional, not regular, basis.

100. In *Three Lectures on Gaelic Topics*, 14, 31.

101. In *Three Lectures*, 55.

lecture entitled "Cúchulainn and the Red Branch Cycle" which, as Ruth Dudley Edwards has said, "shows all the signs of Patrick's fine Gaelic hand."[102] According to the report in *Fáinne an Lae*, Willie "sketched the origin of the Red Branch, and traced its influence on Irish history and literature. The feats of the Red Branch heroes . . . were vividly illustrated from numerous extracts from the 'Red Branch Epics.' . . . The commanding position occupied by Cúchulainn, to whom Mr. Pearse naturally devoted his chief attention, was placed in a clear, historic light." Not surprisingly, Patrick found the lecture an entirely edifying experience, and seconding the vote of thanks to the speaker "urged that the noble personality of Cúchulainn forms a true type of Gaelic nationality, full as it is of youthful life and vigour and hope."[103]

In his lecture "Irish Saga Literature" delivered to the Catholic Commercial Club on 5 January 1899, Pearse was a bit more explicit about the qualities he associated with this "true type of Gaelic nationality." *Fáinne an Lae* reported: "The last point to which he directed attention was the elevation of thought, the chivalrous love of what was great and noble; the purity and delicacy of conception that marked their whole Saga literature. Their heroes, while sometimes arrogant and willful, were invariably represented as men of noble impulse and elevated inspirations, incapable of mean actions, and, in short, what would now be called a 'thorough gentleman.'"[104] This bathetic picture of Cú Chulainn as a worthy candidate for admission to the Catholic Commercial Club is clearly a figment of the imagination of the occasionally priggish young Pearse who insisted on wearing morning clothes at formal functions of the league,[105] and whom Dinneen invariably called "P. Haitch Pearse" or "B.A.B.L.," a dig at the young man's fondness for citing his academic degrees.[106]

In the ensuing years of literary, political, and educational work, and especially with his founding of Sgoil Éanna in 1908, Pearse's faith in the

102. *Patrick Pearse*, 22.

103. "Gnótha na Gaedhilge" (Gaelic affairs), *FL*, 5 March 1898.

104. *FL*, 14 January 1899. Joseph Holloway was present and exasperated at this lecture, writing in his diary: "He was indiscriminately eulogistic to absurdity over his subject, and the adjectives he employed to describe the extracts which he read from the Sagas were beyond the bounds of reason when the stuff so praised became known to his listeners. . . . It is this absurd, unmeaning, almost fanatical praise that makes the few lovers of the Irish language left to us so unbearable and impractical to all broadminded people." See *Joseph Holloway's Abbey Theatre: A Selection from His Unpublished Journal "Impressions of a Dublin Playgoer,"* ed. Robert Hogan and Michael J. O'Neill (Carbondale: University of Southern Illinois Press, 1967), 4.

105. Edwards, *Patrick Pearse*, 89.

106. Ó Conluain and Ó Céileachair, *An Duinníneach*, 198.

pedagogical value of early Irish literature and his adoption of Cú Chulainn as an inspirational exemplar took on additional depth and significance. No longer was Ulster's champion merely a shadowy "true type of Gaelic nationality" or an absurdly anachronistic bourgeois Dubliner. Writing in *An Claidheamh Soluis* on 27 October 1906, at a time when his attention was almost entirely fixed on educational questions and he was evolving the theory and methods on which he would soon base his experiment at Sgoil Éanna, he exhorted his readers: "Our first counsel to Gaels is: let them have always before them a noble goal, an 'ideal' as the English speaker would say. Let us remember Cú Chulainn. Let his deeds and sayings or the deeds and sayings of some other hero like him be a guiding light shining gloriously in the sky before us."[107] When he opened Sgoil Éanna in September 1908, he put his convictions into very visible practice. As the new students arrived in the main hall at Cullenswood House, they faced a large mural of the boy Cú Chulainn taking arms, in accordance with their headmaster's belief that "it would be a noble thing to set somewhere where every boy that entered the school might see it a picture in which the boy Cúchulainn should be the central figure."[108] And lest the moral somehow be lost, he began telling his students the story of Cú Chulainn on their very first morning in their new school.[109] A young native speaker from Ros Muc, the future novelist Pádraic Óg Ó Conaire, claimed that the students were apt learners: "We weren't there long until we understood that it was Pearse's goal to make every student a 'Cú Chulainn,' for Cú Chulainn was his exemplar."[110]

In his history of Sgoil Éanna, *The Story of a Success*, Pearse said of the school: "I do not think that any religious community can ever have been knit together by a truer oneness of purpose or by a finer comradeship than ours."[111] This purpose was no less than "to recreate and per-

107. "Seanmóir" (Sermon), editorial, *ACS*, 27 October 1906. "Ár gcéad chomhairle do Ghaedhealaibh, bíodh cuspóir uasal, 'ideal' mar adéarfadh an Béarlóir, i gcomhnaidhe os a gcomhair amach aca. Cuimhnighmís ar Chúchulainn. Bíodh a ghníomhartha agus a ráidhte sin, nó gníomhartha agus ráidhte gaisgidhigh eile mar é, 'n-a réalt eolais ag lonnradh go glórmhar sa spéir os ár gcomhair."
108. "Our Heritage of Chivalry," editorial, *ACS*, 14 November 1908.
109. Desmond Ryan, *Remembering Sion*, 97.
110. "Cuimhní Scoil Éanna" (Memories of Sgoil Éanna) in *Cuimhní na bPiarsach* (Memories of the Pearses), cuid a 3 (part 3) (Baile Átha Cliath: Coiste Cuimhneacháin na bPiarsach, n.d.), 5. This booklet was issued for an annual Pearse memorial concert, and the letter from Senator Margaret Pearse at the beginning of the text is dated 11 January 1958. "Níorbh fhada ann dúinn gur thuigeamar gur chuspóir ag an bPiarsach 'Cúchulainn' a dhéanamh de gach mac léinn mar bhí Cúchulainn ina eisiompláir aige."
111. *Collected Works: The Story of a Success*, 1–2.

petuate in Éire the knightly tradition of the *macradh* [boy troop] of Emain Macha . . . the high tradition of Cúchulainn . . . the noble tradition of the Fianna . . . the Christlike tradition of Colm Cille" (7). For Pearse the headmaster, the educational system of early Ireland as he traced its outlines in the Ulster Cycle and saw it epitomized in its finest product, Cú Chulainn, offered a clear, detailed, concrete, and feasible inspiration for himself, his students, and all of Ireland: "Cú Chulainn himself may never have lived, and there may never have been a Boy-Corps at Eamhain; but the picture endures as the Gaels' idealisation of the kind of environment and the kind of fostering which go to the making of a perfect hero" (34).[112] And when he set forth the qualities of such a hero, he was a long way from the "thorough gentleman" of 1900: "The key note of the school life I desiderate is *effort* on the part of the child itself, struggle, self-sacrifice, self-discipline, for by these only does the soul rise to perfection" (37).

All was not, however, Spartan at Cullenswood House in 1908: the emphasis was on the young Cú Chulainn, a boy who practiced his virtues with exuberance, and not on the doomed warrior facing overwhelming odds. To celebrate the end of this first schoolyear, one of the happiest periods of his life, Pearse wrote and his students performed on the school grounds the first of his two Cú Chulainn pageants. He explained the motive and timing for the play in *An Macaomh*:

> It may be wondered why we have undertaken the comparatively ambitious project of a Cúchulainn Pageant so early in our career. The reason is that we were anxious to crown our first year's work with something worthy and symbolic; anxious to send our boys home with the knightly image of Cúchulainn in their hearts and his knightly words ringing in their ears. They will leave St. Enda's under the spell of the magic of their most beloved hero, the Macaomh who is, after all, the greatest figure in the epic of their country, indeed, as I think, the greatest in the epic of the world.[113]

112. Compare the views of Conn Ó Murchadha, "Ancient Irish and Greek Education," editorial, *ACS*, 10 April 1915; and those of Dinneen in "Breacadh Lae an Chreidimh ar Éirinn," *Guth na Bliadhna* 9, no. 4 (Autumn 1912): 483. Dinneen wrote: "We don't know, and we don't care, when Oisín lived, nor whether his like ever existed. . . . But whether Oisín existed or not, the ancient storyteller who conceived him did a fine job." (Ní fios dúinn, agus is cuma dhúinn, caithin do mhair Oisín, nó an raibh a leithéid riamh ann. . . . Acht cia aca bhí Oisín ann nó ná raibh, ba mhaith an mhaise ag an seanscéaluidhe do cheap é.)
113. *Story of a Success*, 26.

Pearse stressed his absolute fidelity to his original in writing this play, and thus it makes sense at this point to investigate the whole question of his sources for his ideas about Cú Chulainn and the Ulster Cycle in general. As in discussions of other aspects of Pearse's ideas and ideology, there is sharp disagreement concerning his firsthand knowledge of early Irish literature. Those under his personal spell were impressed by the breadth and depth of his scholarship. For example, his sister Mary Brigid Pearse recalled that "he had a fine collection of the old sagas; and he was a fluent translator at sight; it made no difference to him whether the stories were in Gaelic or English."[114] A former student, the historian Desmond Ryan, claimed: "His close study of Irish gave him that mastery over it which was later to make him one of the great Irish writers of to-day. He steeped his mind in the heroic literature of the Fionn and Cúchulainn cycles."[115] The classicist Stephen McKenna, who certainly understood the criteria of sound scholarship, thought that Pearse knew the native literature "as other men know their arithmetic,"[116] while more recently the Celticist David Greene has pronounced Pearse "deeply read in early Irish literature."[117] On the other hand, in his famous polemic essay on Pearse, Father Francis Shaw, also a scholar of early Irish literature, wrote: "To judge by his writings Pearse's knowledge of the Gaelic past of the country was slight rather than profound. Certainly his written work gives the impression that his acquaintance with Irish literature was not very wide. He falls back on lists of names and over and over again he uses the same quotations."[118]

While Shaw undoubtedly overstated his case here, it is impossible to ignore the fact that in his writings Pearse does refer to a very limited number of Ulster Cycle texts, and that in virtually every instance it is possible to identify the translation he used. This should, however, come as no surprise. Very few people in the early years of this century had any meaningful mastery of the Ulster Cycle tales, many of which were only then being competently edited. At worst, Pearse was an enthusiastic, knowledgable, and up-to-date amateur. For example, he

114. *The Home Life of Pádraig Pearse*, 84.
115. *The Man Called Pearse*, 30. See also Ó Searcaigh, *Pádraig Mac Piarais*, 38, 53. Ó Searcaigh was doubtless unconscious of the irony in his claim that in *Three Lectures on Gaelic Topics*, "he revealed thoughts the like of which had never before been heard in Ireland." (Nocht sé smaointe . . . nár cluineadh a leithéid roimhe sin i nÉirinn.)
116. "Martin Daly" [Stephen MacKenna], *Memories of the Dead* (Dublin: Powell, n.d.), 19.
117. *Writing in Irish To-day* (Dublin: Cultural Relations Committee of Ireland, 1972), 19.
118. "The Canon of Irish History: A Reappraisal," *Studies* 61, p. 130.

quotes several times from two of the translations in Eleanor Hull's 1898 *Cúchulainn Saga in Irish Literature—The Wooing of Emer (Tochmarc Emire)*[119] and *The Phantom Chariot of Cúchulainn (Siaburcharpat Con Culainn)*.[120] He also quotes from Father Edmund Hogan's 1892 translation *The Battle of Rosnaree (Cath Ruis na Rígh)*;[121] from Eugene O'Cúrry's 1859 translation of *The Sick-bed of Cúchulainn and the Only Jealousy of Eimer (Serglige Con Culainn ocus Óenét Emire)*;[122] from the translation of "The Fight of Ferdiad and Cúchulaind" from the *Táin* in O'Curry's *On the Manners and Customs of the Ancient Irish* (1873);[123] from the translation of the same section as "The Combat at the Ford" in A. H. Leahy's *Heroic Romances of Ireland* (1905);[124] and from Mrs. Arthur Hutton's verse translation of the *Book of Leinster Táin* (1907).[125] But more important, as will be discussed below, he owned and studied Ernst Windisch's 1905 edition of the *Book of Leinster Táin* with accompanying German translation.

Of course, in none of the writings to which Shaw makes reference, apart from those done while he was still a teenager just beginning to discover the Irish language and literary tradition, was Pearse dealing with the literature for its own sake.[126] He was not attempting detailed scholarly analyses of the tales, but rather using brief references or quo-

---

119. *Story of a Success*, 22, 34; and "Our Heritage of Chivalry," *ACS*, 14 November 1908. The translation of *The Wooing of Emer* found in Hull is that of Kuno Meyer originally published in the *Archaeological Review* in 1888.

120. *Story of a Success*, 35; and "Our Heritage of Chivalry." Hull used J. O'Beirne Crowe's translation of *The Phantom Chariot* that first appeared in the *Journal of the Royal Historical and Archaeological Association of Ireland* in 1871.

121. "Gaelic Prose Literature," in *Three Lectures*, 15.

122. "Some Aspects of Irish Literature," in *Collected Works: Songs of the Irish Rebels*, 134–35. In this same lecture Pearse refers to the tale of Cú Chulainn's death, and incorrectly identifies the woman to whom Emer sends Cú Chulainn for protection as Fann, not Niamh (135).

123. "Gaelic Prose Literature," in *Three Lectures*, 15–16.

124. "From a Hermitage," in *Collected Works: Political Writings and Speeches*, 158–59. Mary Colum recalled Pearse's frequently reading aloud from George Sigerson's translation of Cú Chulainn's lament for Fer Diad, "for he thought no poem represented such high chivalry. He would repeat it with intense emotion, his strange eyes aflame." See Mary Colum, *Life and the Dream* (Garden City, N.Y.: Doubleday, 1947), 164.

125. "Our Heritage of Chivalry," *ACS*, 14 November 1908. According to Séamas Ó Buachalla, this was the version of the epic most popular at Sgoil Éanna. See *The Letters of P. H. Pearse*, ed. Ó Buachalla, 440. It was reported in the midsummer 1909 issue of *An Macaomh* that "Mrs. Hutton would have been glad to know that we have on rolls a boy of 12 who has read through her 'Táin' twice, and is commencing it a third time" (87). Pearse reviewed her work favorably in *ACS* on 21 December 1907. By this time, however, he himself was working with the tale in the original.

126. The single exception is the 1913 lecture "Some Aspects of Irish Literature," in which he also confuses the names of characters, a sure sign of haste. See note 122 above.

tations to illustrate his ideas on a wide range of topics. Since many of these pieces were also written as reviews, editorials, or public lectures, and often no doubt prepared with a deadline bearing down—Pearse was a notorious procrastinator—he can hardly be blamed for not making translations of his own when adequate renderings of the brief passages he required lay ready to hand. Moreover, it should be noted that when he went to translations he looked for the best he could find. As early as 1900 in his lecture on Fionn he had shown a commendable knowledge of contemporary Celtic scholarship, and he always kept abreast of the field, as is obvious, for example, in his editorial obituary of Whitley Stokes in 1909.[127] Thus Father Shaw's statement that Pearse was largely reliant on "the infected source" of Standish James O'Grady for "many of his romantic notions about early Ireland"[128] is both disingenuous and misleading. Of course no one growing up with an interest in the Irish past in Pearse's time could have avoided the influence of O'Grady, and the young Pearse was undeniably captivated by the bombastic grandeur of O'Grady's imagination.[129] There can, for instance, be no doubt that Pearse's ideas about early Irish education were colored by O'Grady's depiction of the Ulster Boy Troop at school.[130] However unlike a writer like Yeats, Pearse was able, as a result of his serious study of Irish, to move well beyond the distortions of O'Grady. Denis Gwynn has recorded a conversation between Pearse and O'Grady in which Pearse corrected O'Grady's mispronunciation of Cú Chulainn's name as "Cutch-ulane." Gwynn writes: "O'Grady was overwhelmed by the discovery, and after a long pause informed Pearse that he would have written an entirely different book if he had known the correct sound of the name."[131] Pearse's own precise knowledge of that sound and much more enabled him to produce a different book of his own.

Of course, our clearest proof of the mature Pearse's ability to work with Ulster Cycle material is not reliant on anecdotal evidence, however amusing or suggestive: we have the text of his first Cú Chulainn

127. "Whitley Stokes," editorial, *ACS*, 24 April 1909.

128. "The Canon," *Studies* 61, p. 130.

129. AE, for example, wrote of "how deep was Pearse's love for the Cúchulainn whom O'Grady discovered or invented." See AE, "Standish O'Grady" in *The Living Torch*, 144. Other orthodox Gaels shared Pearse's respect for O'Grady. See "An Buailtean," "The Hero of the Ford," review of *In the Gates of the North* by O'Grady, *ACS*, 21 November 1908; and Seán Mac Giolla an Átha (i.e., Mac Giollarnáth), "The Return of the Fianna," a review of the production of O'Grady's *The Coming of Fionn* by the students of Sgoil Éanna, in *ACS*, 27 March 1909.

130. Compare O'Grady's account in *The Coming of Cuchulain*, 49–50; with Pearse's in *The Story of a Success*, 32–34.

131. *Edward Martyn and the Irish Revival* (London: Jonathan Cape, 1930), 245.

pageant, a play in three scenes presenting the boy's arrival at Emain, his acquistion of his heroic name, and his first taking of arms. The modern Irish of this pageant, *Macghníomhartha Chúchulainn* (The boyhood deeds of Cú Chulainn), follows with great fidelity the language of the *Book of Leinster* (henceforth referred to by its standard Irish abbreviation *LL*) *Táin*, a text Pearse owned in the German edition of Ernst Windisch. In *Remembering Sion*, Desmond Ryan refers to this book as "that much read edition of the *Cattle Spoil of Cúailnge*,"[132] and Pearse's personal copy does indeed survive in battered and incomplete condition at the Pearse Museum in the Sgoil Éanna building in Rathfarnham.[133] Introducing the published text of the play in *An Macaomh*, Pearse wrote: "I have extracted the story and a great part of the dialogue from the *Táin*, merely modernising (but altering as little as possible) the magnificent phrase of the original."[134] With regard to language, he is entirely correct; a close comparison of his pageant with the *LL* text shows that the only linguistic changes he made were those absolutely necessary to render the dialogue intelligible to an audience that knew modern Irish.[135] He is, however, somewhat less accurate when after listing a few trivial deviations from the original necessitated for the most part by production constraints, he claims that "for everything else I have authority."[136]

Before we investigate those changes, we should discuss his most important textual decision, his choice of the *LL Táin* over the version of the tale now called "Recension I" and contained in two manuscripts, *Lebor na hUidre* and the *Yellow Book of Lecan* (henceforth *LU* and *YBL*).[137] Too much should not be made of this preference, for writers adapting the *Táin* have almost without exception found the far more unified, consistent, and artistically crafted *LL* text a better source for their pur-

132. Pp. 159–60. Pearse could read German.

133. The first part of the book is lost, the text now beginning at 467. It is also worth noting that 622–23 in the Irish text are uncut, although these pages do not contain material used in the pageants.

134. Pearse, "By Way of Comment," *An Macaomh* 1, no. 1 (Midsummer 1909): 15.

135. For example, when Cathbad gives Sétanta his new name of Cú Chulainn, he says in *LL*: "Con cechlabat fir hÉrend ocus Alban inn n-ainm sin, ocus bat lána beóil fer hÉrend ocus Alban don anmuin sin" (Windisch's edition). Pearse renders this passage: "Cluinfidh fir Éireann agus Alban an t-ainm sin, agus beidh béil fear Éireann agus Alban lán den ainm sin." The meaning is identical: "The men of Ireland and Scotland will hear of that name, and the mouths of the men of Ireland and Scotland will be full of that name."

136. Pearse, "By Way of Comment," 15.

137. The motto under the Cú Chulainn mural at Cullenswood House was in the wording of the Recension I text.

poses.[138] Nevertheless, the sections of the *LU–YBL* version that Pearse required were readily available to him in the convenient form of Strachan's *Stories from the Táin*, the *Irisleabhar na Gaedhilge* series that had been issued as a booklet in 1908, and in English translation in Winifred Faraday's *The Cattle Raid of Cúalnge* (1904). However, even leaving aside more strictly aesthetic considerations, the *LU–YBL* recension was inappropriate for Pearse's didactic purpose. It contains two episodes hardly flattering to the youthful Cú Chulainn: his drubbing of fifty members of the Boy Troop and his subsequent hiding from their enraged parents under Conchobar's couch, and his slaying of a servant who dares to wake him too early in the morning. It also includes two entire episodes absent from *LL*: Cú Chulainn's retrieving the wounded Conchobar from a battlefield where he has to fight otherworld foes, and his defense of Ulster against twenty-seven invaders from "the Isles of Faiche." Thus, with his rejection of the *LU–YBL* redaction Pearse also rejected episodes that presented Cú Chulainn in a negative, in particular an excessively violent light, or that were marked by crude exaggeration or an unneccessary venture into the supernatural.

Having chosen *LL*, Pearse claimed that any departures from his original had "a sufficiently obvious purpose."[139] The most striking of these changes involve his omission of Cú Chulainn's fight with Culann's hound and of the single longest episode in the "Boyhood Deeds" section of the *Táin*, his expedition to the border, his combat with the sons of Nechtan Scéne, and his triumphal and terrible return to Emain where he is met and pacified by a troop of naked women, although the first two of these incidents are referred to in the choral songs that open the second and third scenes, and the third is presented in more modest form.[140] The "sufficiently obvious purpose" for these alterations is probably the simple inability of the Sgoil Éanna cast and crew to stage such spectacular scenes with the resources available to them. Staging problems may also have accounted in part for the omission of Cú Chulainn's bizarre physical appearance at the end of his adventure, although Pearse must have been relieved that he could thus avoid one of the elements of the Cú Chulainn story that most disturbed his fellow adapters like O'Grady and Lady Gregory.[141] And of course Pearse's reluctance to

138. Thomas Kinsella, who based his translation primarily on the Recension I text, discusses this issue in the introduction to his *The Táin* (London: Oxford University Press, 1969), x–xi.

139. "By Way of Comment," 15.

140. *Macghníomhartha Chúchulainn*, in *Na Scríbhinní Liteartha*, ed. Ó Buachalla, 146–47, 150.

141. Cú Chulainn's physical transformations, in particular the hideous *ríastrad*, shocked

send a bevy of naked women onto a suburban Dublin lawn before an audience of adolescent boys requires no further explanation.

There are, however, other deviations from the original for which the reasons are less "sufficiently obvious" and for which he had no authority but that of his own imagination. First of all, when Pearse's Cú Chulainn arrives at Emain, the boys ask him to take part in their game. In the LL Táin, he interferes in their hurling with no such invitation. Also, in the original tale the boys are clearly acting on the assumption that Cú Chulainn knows of and has chosen to disregard their geis (magical injunction) requiring that they put newcomers under their protection before accepting them as peers. When he later informs Conchobar that he had never heard of this geis, the arrogant Cú Chulainn of LL adds, "If I had known, I should have been on my guard against them."[142] Pearse's Cú Chulainn is far more self-effacing. Having claimed ignorance of the geis, he concedes, "If I had known I would have done it." (Dá mb'eol, dhéanfainn é.)[143] But then again he must be baffled by this whole business of geis since the boys themselves have already, through their almost spontaneous invitation to him, suspended the injunction.

An even more striking departure from the original occurs in the scene depicting Cú Chulainn's taking of arms. In the LL Táin as well as in all translations and adaptations of it with the important exception of O'Grady's, Cú Chulainn is said to have accidentally overheard the druid Cathbad's prophecy concerning the future fame of one who first took arms on that day. The boy then disingenuously tells Conchobar that he makes his request for arms at the instruction of Cathbad and thus gets his weapons through trickery. In Pearse's pageant, on the other hand, Cú Chulainn is explicitly identified as a member of Cathbad's class, the stage directions reading: "Cathbhadh comes on the green with Cú Chulainn and Follamhan and the other boys around him."[144] Furthermore, in Pearse's play it is Conchobar who comes to

---

the early adapters of the Ulster Cycle. O'Grady, for example, described the distorted Cú Chulainn thus: "His eyes blazed terribly in his head, and his face was fearful to look upon. Like a reed in a river so he quaked and trembled" (The Coming of Cuchulain, 155). For Aubrey De Vere, the ríastrad was "the rage from heaven" (The Foray of Queen Maeve, 22). Lady Gregory was even more discreet: "It was not his appearance he had on him, but the appearance of a god." See Cuchulain of Muirthemne, 169. Pearse himself called the ríastrad "a sort of Berserker rage" ("From a Hermitage," Collected Works: Political Writings, 158). For a sense of what the ríastrad involved in the original, see Kinsella, The Táin, 150–53.

142. Táin Bó Cúalnge from the Book of Leinster, ed. and trans. Cecile O'Rahilly (Dublin: Dublin Institute for Advanced Studies, 1967), 159–60.

143. Macghníomhartha Chúchulainn, in Na Scríbhinní Liteartha, 145.

144. Macghníomhartha Chúchulainn, in Na Scríbhinní Liteartha, 150–51. "Cathbhadh do theacht ar an bhfaithche agus Cúchulainn agus Follamhan agus an mhacradh ar cheana i

where Cú Chulainn stands off by himself after the class, whereas in *LL* the boy sets off purposefully to secure arms through verbal trickery as soon as he hears the prophecy.[145] Thus in Pearse's treatment Cú Chulainn has a right, indeed an obligation, to hear and act on Cathbad's teaching, and the druid's later anger at the use to which his instruction has been put is both unjust and unmotivated. Pearse also makes no mention in the text of Cú Chulainn's later wrangle with Conall Cernach at the border, where again using trickery he compels Conall to return to Emain and thus secures for himself the honorific duty of defending the frontier. We know that Pearse placed a very high premium on truthfulness, and was constantly urging his students to be worthy of the boast of the ancient Fianna of Fionn concerning "truth on our lips." Apparently when he found the Cú Chulainn of his sources trifling with the truth, he simply, silently, and perhaps even subconsciously, emended this flaw in his hero's ethical practice.

No text survives of Pearse's second Cú Chulainn pageant, *The Defence of the Ford* (1913), but we do have synopses of the action from the program for its performance in Croke Park, from a promotional announcement in *An Claidheamh Soluis*,[146] and, far more vividly, from an account too long to cite in full and too good to truncate in Sean O'Casey's autobiography and from a letter written by O'Casey to the *Irish Worker*. The letter reads: "Two hundred performers will take part in this pageant. Here will be shown the Boy Corps of Ulster hurling on the field. The news of Cúchulainn's wounding; the march of the boys to defend the frontiers till the Hero recovers; the scene of the men of Ireland around their Camp Fires; the attack by the Boy Corps of Ulster; and finally, in the last act, the 'Battle of the Ford' between the two Heroes, Cúchulainn and Feardiadh."[147] What O'Casey calls "acts" are called "parts" in *An Claidheamh Soluis*, and with such an enormous cast, including Pearse himself as a messenger, and such sweeping action—all of which was apparently played in just one hour[148]—it is plain that this was spectacle rather than drama and so may well have had no set text or

---

n-a thimcheall." O'Grady's revision is even more extreme, for his "Cathvah" directs his teaching specifically to Cú Chulainn, with whom he is alone at the time, and later goes himself to secure Conchobar's consent to arm the boy. See O'Grady, *History of Ireland: The Heroic Period*, 122–23.

145. *Macghníomhartha Chúchulainn*, in *Na Scríbhinní Liteartha*, 151.

146. "The Defence of the Ford," *ACS*, 31 May 1913.

147. "To *Irish Worker*," letter, 7 June 1913, *The Letters of Sean O'Casey*, ed. David Krause (New York: Macmillan, 1975), 78. See also O'Casey, *Drums under the Windows* (New York: Macmillan, 1960), 352–60.

148. See "Touching the St. Enda's Fete," *An Macaomh* 2, no. 2 (May 1913): 46.

dialogue, any more than did *The Fianna of Fionn* (1913), a piece that seems to have involved little more than Sgoil Éanna boys performing what Raymond Porter has called "a rhythmical march representing the activities of the ancient Fianna."[149] With *The Defence of the Ford*, Cú Chulainn ceased to play a prominent role in Pearse's writings, which were increasingly dominated by the more recent heroes of physical-force republicanism.

As a result of such shifts in emphasis, Pearse's intellectual development has too readily been seen as a progression through a series of discreet stages: cultural nationalism, political activism moving towards radical separatism, belief in messianic blood sacrifice; or, to embody that development in terms of successive role models: Cú Chulainn, Robert Emmet, Jesus Christ. Apparent confirmation of such a scheme can be found in Pearse's own words when he wrote after moving Sgoil Éanna from Cullenswood House to the Hermitage in Rathfarnham: "Whereas at Cullenswood House I spoke oftenest to our boys of Cú-chulainn and his compeers of the Gaelic prime, I have been speaking to them oftenest here of Robert Emmet and the heroes of the last stand. Cúchulainn was our greatest inspiration at Cullenswood; Robert Emmet has been our greatest inspiration here."[150] Yet Desmond Ryan, who knew him intimately, has warned against such a simplistically linear view of Pearse's thought: "Development may be traced in his writings, but no essential change."[151] Ryan, a graduate of Sgoil Éanna, felt that "Cú Chulainn moved with Sgoil Éanna to the Hermitage, but settled down and became an invisible member of the school staff."[152] In addition, if Cú Chulainn moved with the school to Rathfarnham, Emmet and other heroes of the more recent nationalist pantheon had likewise been present in Cullenswood House. In an account of a visit to the Cullenswood Sgoil Éanna, Liam Ua Domhnaill mentions Emmet's as among the names inscribed on the wall of the main classroom,[153] and the names of other members of this hall of fame are provided by Desmond Ryan in a recollection of his own time at the school. Ryan here

149. See "The Defence of the Ford," *ACS*, 31 May 1913; and Porter, *P. H. Pearse*, 96. In the spring of 1909, the Sgoil Éanna boys produced Standish O'Grady's *The Coming of Fionn* at the school, a production of which Seán Mac Giollarnáth wrote: "The boys played as if they were perfectly at home in the ways of the Fianna, as if captured by the spirit of the ancient heroes." See "The Return of the Fianna," *ACS*, 27 March 1909.

150. *Story of a Success*, 53–54.

151. *The Man Called Pearse*, 10. Eavan Boland has written of Pearse: "He was an extremely consistent man; his ideas underwent a process of accretion rather than of change." See "Aspects of Pearse," *Dublin Magazine* 5, no. 1 (Spring 1966): 49.

152. *The Man Called Pearse*, 83.

153. "I mBaile Átha Cliath," *ACS*, 12 September 1908.

describes his first day at Cullenswood House where, after passing the
Cú Chulainn mural, he entered this classroom "where in Gaelic letter-
ing names of heroes, saints, and sages circle the wainscotting: Brian of
the Tributes, Owen Roe, Sarsfield, Tone, Colmcille, Patrick, Keating,
John Mac Hale, Thomas Davis. Over the mantlepiece hangs a picture
of the Christ child."[154]

This reference to the Christ child brings us to Pearse's most daring,
indeed to some a blasphemous, identification, that of Cú Chulainn with
Christ and ultimately of himself with both. Pearse was not, however,
the first to suggest this parallel. As John V. Kelleher has made clear, the
medieval Christian redactors of the Ulster Cycle consistently attempted
to associate its principal hero with Christ.[155] Nor were later writers reluctant to see affinities. Thus the account of Cú Chulainn's death in
Standish James O'Grady's *History* is rich in echoes of the events of
Good Friday: "Thereat the sun darkened, and the earth trembled, and a
wail of agony from immortal mouths shrilled across the land, and a
pale panic smote the vast host of Meave when, with a crash, fell that
pillar of heroism, and that flame of the warlike valour of Erin was
extinguished."[156] But Pearse had the conviction and nerve to make the
identification full and explicit, as he did in the 1913 lecture "Some Aspects of Irish Literature:"

> The story of Cúchulainn symbolizes the redemption of man by a
> sinless God. The curse of primal sin lies upon a people; new and
> personal sin brings doom to their doors; they are powerless to
> save themselves; a youth free from the curse, akin with them
> through his mother but through his father divine, redeems them
> by his valour; and his own death comes from it. I do not mean
> that the *Táin* is a conscious allegory: but there is the story in its
> essence, and it is like a retelling (or is it a foretelling?) of the
> story of Calvary.[157]

This idea was by no means a new one for Pearse in 1913; in the same

154. *Remembering Sion*, 95.
155. "The *Táin* and the Annals," *Ériu* 22 (1971): 121–
156. *History of Ireland: Cuculain and His Contemporaries*
Marston, and Rivington, 1880), 342.
157. "Some Aspects of Irish Literature," in *Collected V*
Séamus Ó Grianna was particularly taken by this idea,
Cú Chulainn." (An dóigh ar thuig sé Cúchulainn.) S⟨
Fáil (Men of Ireland) (Dún Dealgan: Cló-Lucht "an Scr
congruity of Pearse's view with the original mediev
material, see Kelleher, "*Táin*," *Ériu* 22, pp. 121–22.

1909 issue of *An Macaomh* in which he published *Macghníomhartha Chúchulainn* he wrote that all Irish boys should follow the example of Cú Chulainn, "for that youth lost his life before he would lose his honor," and compared this heroic sacrifice to that of another boy who, "although he himself was guiltless" (gidh go raibh sé féin neamh-chionntach), gave his life "for the sins of his people" (ar son cionnta a chinidh).[158] Indeed, as early as 1905 Pearse presented Christ as a Jewish patriot: "Christ, our Exemplar, wept over Jerusalem, the fallen capital of his nation."[159] And in 1906, he urged the readers of *An Claidheamh Soluis* to "follow in the wake of the Heroes," for in this command lay "the very *summa* of natural and Christian ethics."[160] The boys entering the main lobby of Cullenswood House may have been most impressed by the Cú Chulainn mural, but they would also have seen in the same hall Beatrice Elvery's painting of Christ as a boy, naked to the waist and with arms outstretched in the cruciform position,[161] and soon thereafter must have realized that the time set aside by Pearse for the recitation of stories about Cú Chulainn was invariably right after that devoted to religious instruction.[162]

While Pearse's "thorough gentleman" of 1900 and his later Gaelic messiah bear little resemblance to each other, both were rooted in their creator's lifelong quest for worthy ideals, a search we have already seen leading him in his fiction to a Gaeltacht almost entirely the product of

158. "Réamhsgéal" (Preface), 5–6. "Óir do chaill an macaomh sin a bheatha sul dá gcaillfeadh sé a eineach."

159. "A Christmas Sermon," editorial, *ACS*, 23 December 1905. Again, this idea was not unique to Pearse. In 1901 Father Patrick Kavanagh delivered a lecture to Maud Gonne's Inghinidhe na hÉireann on "Patriotism: True and False" which a *UI* correspondent characterized as "of a semi-religious character" ("Limerick Notes," *UI*, 23 March 1901). And after the Rising, An Bráthair Benedict drew the sharpest possible parallel between the suffering of Christ and that of Ireland and her patriots in "Éire—Náisiún Céasta" (Ireland—A tormented nation). See *An Síoladóir* 1, no. 3 (December 1920): 93–105.

160. "'Seoda na Sean' [The treasures of the ancients] and Some Reflections," editorial, *ACS*, 12 May 1906.

161. Pádhraic Óg Ó Conaire, "Cuimhní Scoil Éanna," in *Cuimhní na bPiarsach*, 6. A reproduction of this painting along with several photographs of Sgoil Éanna, including some from the pageants, can be seen in Séamas Ó Buachalla's *Pádraig Mac Piarais agus Éire lena Linn* (Patrick Pearse and the Ireland of his time) (Baile Átha Cliath: Cló Mercier, 1979), 39–64. When the school moved to the Hermitage, Elvery's picture was hung near ortrait of Wolfe Tone. See "Sgoil Éanna," *ACS*, 23 August 1913.

Desmond Ryan, *Story of a Success*, 90. *The Story of a Success* was edited by Ryan rse's execution. The first four chapters are slightly revised versions of Pearse's Comment" essays in *An Macaomh*; the final chapter is by Ryan.

his own imagination. Joseph J. Lee has written of him that "the extent to which Pearse thought tactically tends to be overlooked in the fascination with the more exotic aspects of his character."[163] In 1900 he needed some noble Gaelic model to assert in the face of the Anglicized tawdriness he saw all around him; too immature, however, to transcend his own stolidly bourgeois Victorian upbringing, he was unable to conceive of that model except in terms derived from the value system of the very milieu he wished to indict. With growing intellectual self-confidence, his idealism ceased to be a mere reaction to what he experienced as the soullessness of contemporary society, and his image of Cú Chulainn became increasingly antithetical and challenging to the smug West Britonism of repectable Dublin. The hero became a symbol of "the starkness of the antique world" (*Story of a Success*, 63), and was held up to the boys at Sgoil Éanna as an exemplar of "struggle, self-sacrifice, self-discipline" (36), whom they were to emulate by being "brave and unselfish, truthful and pure" (7). And his own Cú Chulainn of the *Macghníomhartha* would be endowed with precisely those virtues, even at the expense of strict fidelity to the original text.

As his despair over Ireland's political and, more important, her spiritual servility deepened, his conception of Cú Chulainn underwent a further transformation. The individualistic, character-building self-sacrifice of the first pageant became the messianic offering of self for one's people of *The Defence of the Ford*, and the implicit parallels between Cú Chulainn and Christ noted in earlier writings came to be asserted as a virtual convergence. In the five years before his execution, Pearse explored this theme of messianic blood sacrifice in four plays in addition to *The Defence of the Ford*: *An Pháis*, an Irish Passion Play staged at the Abbey Theatre in Holy Week of 1911; the one-act "morality" (fáithchluiche) *An Rí* (The king), first produced by the students of Sgoil Éanna on the school's grounds in June 1912; *The Master*, performed at the Hardwicke Street Irish Theatre in May 1915; and *The Singer*, written in 1915, but not produced until after his death. While it is impossible to read anything Pearse wrote about the events and symbols of Easter without thinking of his own subsequent role in the Rising, it would be inappropriate, unjust, and flat-out wrong to reduce his Passion Play to personal or political allegory. While no text survives, we do have synopses as well as a few glowing reviews that make it clear that his primary motive in writing the play was religious and that he succeeded in creating a theatrical experience as dignified as it was genuinely mov-

---

163. *Ireland, 1912–1985*, 26. Lee does continue: "Nevertheless his intense nature did rebel against exclusively tactical argument."

ing.[164] In *An Rí*, on the other hand, it seems entirely justified to hear the voice of Pearse in the words of his innocent boy hero going out to die in successful defense of his people after the failure of their sinful and world-weary king: "I will do a king's duty. . . . I welcome death if that is what is ordained for me."[165] In *The Master*, on the other hand, redemption is achieved through a courageous young boy's act of faith, not his teacher's apparent sacrifice of fame and power or willingness to surrender his own life, an offer his royal foe dismisses with near contempt: "What will that prove? Men die for false things, for ridiculous things, for evil things. What vile cause has not its heroes? Though you were to die here with joy and laughter you would not prove your cause a true one."[166] There was, however, nothing vile, false, or ridiculous about the cause championed by MacDara in *The Singer*, the work in which Pearse explicitly merged the orthodox notion of spiritual salvation through the sacrifice of Christ with his personal vision of national redemption through the willed death of the patriotic martyr. In lines that are undoubtedly the best-known from any of Pearse's creative work, MacDara sets off to face the foreigners, crying out: "One man can free a people as one Man redeemed the world. I will take no pike, I will go into the battle with bare hands. I will stand up before the Gall as Christ hung naked before men on the tree."[167]

Yet as early as 1910 Pearse was already beginning to read his first Cú Chulainn pageant in this light. Recalling his pride in his students after they had concluded the 1909–10 schoolyear with a performance of the pageant at the Castlebellingham Feis in County Louth, "Cúchulainn's country" as he called it, he wondered "whether, if ever I need them for

164. In what Séamas Ó Buachalla calls his "literary testament," Pearse described the manuscript of *An Pháis* as being "in a fragmentary state and not finished for publication." See Ó Buachalla, "The Literary Works: A Bibliographical Guide," in *Literary Works*, ed. Ó Buachalla, 17. A detailed synopsis is available in the program for the Abbey performances. For anecdotal and critical information about the play, see *The Story of a Success*, 101–8; Mary Bulfin, "Pádraig Pearse among His Pupils," in *The Home Life of Pádraig Pearse*, ed. Mary Brigid Pearse, 122–23; Mary Colum, *Life and the Dream*, 157 (Colum took the part of Mary Magdalene); Máire Nic Shiubhlaigh, *The Splendid Years: Recollections of Máire Nic Shiubhlaigh as told to Edward Kenny* (Dublin: James Duffy, 1955), 145–46; "The Passion Play," *ACS*, 8 April 1911; R. O D., "Dráma na Páise" (The Passion Play), *An t-Éireannach*, no. 11 (May 1911): 2; and Padraic Colum, review of Pearse's Passion Play, *Irish Review* 1, no. 3 (May 1911): 107–8.

165. In *Collected Works: Scríbhinní [Writings]*, 18. "Déanfad dualgas Ríogh. . . . Mo chion an bás, má's é orduighthear dhom."

166. In *Collected Works: Plays, Stories, Poems*, 98. While the boy is undaunted in the face of death, it is important to note that it is the king's will, not his own desire for martyrdom, that has put him in danger.

167. In *Collected Works: Plays, Stories, Poems*, 44.

any great service, they will rally, as many of them have promised to do
. . . holding faith to the inspiration and tradition I have tried to give
them."[168] In a 1908 *An Claidheamh Soluis* editorial he had spelled out
what form such youthful service might take, writing of a Sgoil Éanna
outing to Sliabh Rua:

> There are heights to be held in Ireland to–day against the En-
> glish. Are they all manned? Are the defenders at their posts? Are
> their weapons primed? Are their teeth set for resistance? How
> long will they hold out? Then another thought came: could we
> but garrison our hills with these boys and other boys such as
> these, what need to fear? And why not so garrison them? Why
> not set every Irish child a sentinel on a height, to watch and
> ward it, and hold it even to the death, because it is a part of
> Ireland? Our hills and fords and our frontiers want such young
> defenders. *It is for us and for our fellow-teachers to train the young
> hands and fire the young hearts.* We shall find apt pupils.[169]

But were such pupils found at Sgoil Éanna, and were they so trained
and fired? Here the question of Pearse's proselytism, even manipulation, of his students becomes unavoidable. Denis Gwynn, perhaps the
most academically gifted graduate of the school, stated of Pearse after
1914: "Even before I had left the school myself, three years earlier, he
had already begun more or less consciously, and with the conviction
that he was performing a sacred duty, to educate his boys in the idea
that they must look forward to one day taking part in a war of Irish
independence. The idea had grown logically enough out of the interesting program with which he had begun."[170] Yet Desmond Ryan, another
of Sgoil Éanna's prize pupils, has explicity refuted Gwynn's charge:

> But even here in the Hermitage there was no undue political
> propaganda except where Irish history retold is itself a very
> powerful visualisation of the great men and the great glories and
> great mistakes of the past and a very powerful incentive to youth
> to seek future national movements free from time-weary blun-

168. *Story of a Success*, 69–70.
169. "On Sliabh Ruadh," editorial, *ACS*, 31 October 1908. Emphasis in original.
Compare the views of "An Buailtean" with regard to the heroic literature: "No sane mind
can regret that the best of those tales should be universally known in the Ireland of
today, when we want young men of honour and strength and tenacity to hold the fords,
and the gaps of danger throughout the land." See "An Buailtean," "The Hero of the
Ford," review of *In the Gates of the North* by S. J. O'Grady, *ACS*, 21 November 1908.
170. "Patrick Pearse," *Dublin Review*, 172, no. 344 (January–March 1923): 95–96.

ders. Those of his pupils who eventually took part in the 1916 Insurrection might well have done so had they never met Pearse, for great as Pearse was as a kindler to action he cannot be held responsible for the home associations and the national movements which had already moulded the characters and outlook of the odd twenty or so senior and ex-students of his who joined him. Probably the associations of the Hermitage swayed Pearse more than Pearse swayed the majority of his pupils.[171]

And of course Pearse himself denied that he ever tried to indoctrinate his students, writing, "I do not mean that we have ever carried on anything like a political or revolutionary propaganda among the boys," but then going on to add that "we have allowed them to feel that no one can finely live who hoards up life too jealously; that one must be generous in service, and withal joyous, accounting even supreme sacrifices slight."[172]

At all events, on 28 November 1910, Pearse organized a troop of Na Fianna Éireann at Sgoil Éanna, among whose officers was John Dowling, the brother of the boy who played Cú Chulainn in *Macghníomhartha Chúchulainn*.[173] A Fianna drill was on the program of the school fete at which *The Defence of the Ford* was performed, and in fact such exercises seem to have composed the "plot" of *The Fianna of Fionn*. Among the cast of the former pageant was "a whole army . . . of heroes" brought along by "the bold Colbert," a Fianna leader who was later to share Pearse's fate in 1916.[174] Pearse may well have never actively pressured, much less recruited, his students in the cause of physical-force republicanism, but could he have been unaware of the influence on them of his own passionate creed and forceful personality? That he understood such influence could be all but irresistible is evident from his description of the effect of the Fenian Owen Kilgallon on his students in *The Wandering Hawk*:

---

171. *Remembering Sion*, 118. Ryan says of Gwynn: "Denis Gwynn's total lack of humour, political prepossessions and post-war disillusion colour his otherwise living portrait of Pearse, whom he regarded more truly when he was in actual touch with Pearse in Cullenswood House" (161). It may also be worth noting that Gwynn played Conchubhar in *Macghníomhartha Chúchulainn*. (Ryan was a humble "watcher!") See the program for the performance of 22 June 1909 in the National Library of Ireland. At any rate, the above discussion should make clear that the dismissal of Pearse's disclaimer as "merely a semantic quibble" by Cairns and Richards is as unjust as it is uninformed. See Cairns and Richards, *Writing Ireland*, 110.

172. *Story of a Success*, 78.

173. See *An Macaomh*, 2, no. 3 [sic] (Christmas 1910): 79.

174. Ryan, *Remembering Sion*, 167.

The man was gaining a strange ascendancy over us. He had said or done nothing extraordinary; he had on the whole been silent and reserved; to the Fenian conversation, a conversation which had turned all our minds into new paths, paths which seemed wonderful and adventurous and perilous, he had contributed only a sentence or two; and yet from that time on he dominated us. I do not think he aimed at exercising more than the ordinary ascendancy of a teacher; certainly he put forward no special effort, made use of no particular arts. In thinking of him now, after I have known three generations of men, it seems clear to me that the quality in virtue of which he ruled us, as I believe he would have ruled any others he might have come in contact with, was just an elemental simplicity and truth.[175]

Perhaps the most suggestive answer to this whole question is provided by his famous dream about "a pupil of mine, one of our boys at St. Enda's, standing alone upon a platform above a mighty sea of people; and I understood that he was about to die there for some august cause, Ireland's or another." Pearse shared the dream with his students and recorded their reaction: "But what recurs to me now is that when I said that I could not wish for any of them a happier destiny than to die thus in the defence of some true thing, they did not seem in any way surprised, for it fitted in with all we had been teaching them at St. Enda's."[176] Immediately following this passage is the explicit denial of indoctrination cited above. And whether or not the daytime Pearse could consciously face the question of his role in their choice, he was deeply proud of those Sgoil Éanna students and graduates who elected to march with him into rebellion in 1916.[177]

Whatever Pearse may have expected to stalk through the GPO in Easter Week, that expectation was based on a long evolutionary process of thought. Throughout his life he remained constant in his attempt to revive the ethos of heroic Ireland in the service of national resurgence. If his concept of that ethos and his image of its greatest champion changed with time and was always significantly different from that of the original tales, neither development nor discrepancy was the result of conscious manipulation on his part. He was too serious and honest not to subordinate superficial consistency to his own steadily deepening un-

175. In *Literary Writings*, ed. Ó Buachalla, 170–71.

176. *Story of a Success*, 76–77.

177. A list of Sgoil Éanna boys who served in the Rising can be found in Louis Le Roux's *Patrick H. Pearse*, 372.

derstanding of what he saw as the real meaning of the early literature and the true needs of the contemporary nation.[178]

Pearse was, as we have seen, unique only in the fervor of his commitment to making the heroic literature and its values vital forces in modern Irish life. Unfortunately, as we have also seen, this unanimous Gaelic agreement concerning the significance and relevance of the work did not extend to even a rough consensus about critical methodology or translational fidelity. Thus, while scholars like Tadhg Ó Donnchadha or Tomás Ua Nualláin dedicated themselves to providing meticulously accurate modernizations, other writers, most notably Ua Laoghaire, never hesitated to alter texts as they saw fit. Such deviations from the original were not, however, by any means haphazard or purely idiosyncratic, nor were they always the result of an Irish Victorian squeamishness. There were three widely accepted rationales for modernization. The first was grounded in an awareness, shared by native and foreign scholars unaffiliated with the language movement as well as by Gaelic Leaguers, of the linguistic, historical, and cultural significance of the early literature. The other two were, however, more intimately bound up with the immediate practical and ideological concerns of the Revival and its literary adherents.

Most literary Gaels saw the ancient tales rather simplistically as models of pure native prose unsullied by foreign influences. The young Pearse developed this idea in some detail in the Royal University magazine St. Stephen's in 1901: "The ancient literature we had long ago grew from ourselves. . . . Unless this new literature being established grows from ourselves, we will be none the better for it. It won't be Irish literature at all, but a half-Irish, half-English mishmash . . . thus if we want to establish a truly Irish modern literature, we must, first of all, have an exact knowledge of the beautiful and noble ancient literature we already have."[179] It is in precisely such terms that Eoin Mac Néill

178. Joseph Lee has written of Pearse: "He was an honest thinker, and his non-sequitors spring from logical confusion, not from ideological expediency." See *The Modernisation of Irish Society, 1848–1918*, The Gill History of Ireland 10 (Dublin: Gill and Macmillan, 1973), 148.

179. "Litridheacht Nua-Dhéanta," *St. Stephen's: A Record of University Life* 1, no. 1 (June 1901): 10. "An tsean-litridheacht do bhí againn i n-allód, uainn féin d-fhás sí. . . . Muna bhfásfaidh an nua-litridheacht so atá dhá cur ar bun uainn féin, ní féirrde sinn í. Ní litridheacht Ghaedhilge bhéas innti ar chor ar bith, ach praiseach leath-Ghaedhilge leath-Bhéarla. . . . Má's mian linn, mar sin, nua-litridheacht fhíor-Ghaedhilge 'chur ar bun, caithfimíd sa gcéadchás de, eolas cruinn a bheith againn ar an sean-litridheacht uasail aoibhinn atá againn cheana." Among the reasons Pearse offered for publishing tales like *Bodach an Chóta Lachtna* in *ACS* was that he would be thereby "placing before them models of form and style from the vast treasure-house of Early Modern Irish Literature"

welcomed the Oireachtas Prize for modernization in an editorial in *An Claidheamh Soluis* the same year, stating that by putting the ancient tales into modern Irish, "we shall be laying securely the foundations of a modern literature, and shall, moreover, be placing purely native models before the builders of that literature."[180] An anonymous contributor to *Sinn Féin* (perhaps Tadhg Ó Donnchadha) was insistent on this point in a series of essays on the School for Irish Learning that appeared in 1910 and 1911. Focussing throughout on the question "Where is the standard?" (Cá bhfuil an caighdeán?),[181] he wrote: "For the writers who are to come, it is Old and Middle Irish that will provide the model. In accordance with it they will compose and give shape to their thoughts. Without it, we are certain that their work will not be a native growth of the language and that there will be in it the influence of some other literature that the particular author knows well."[182] While Ó Donnchadha himself was elsewhere more open to the possibility of foreign influence, stating that the more languages an aspiring Gaelic writer knew the better, he was adamant that such influence could be no more than secondary: "And the writer must come to know what is ancient. . . . The literature of his own country in antiquity, that is the '*sine qua non.*'"[183] And of course it is hardly surprising to find Father Richard Henebry championing his own uncompromising variant of this fundamentally nativist position: "Old Irish must become the study of our boys in school just as Latin and Greek. . . . And after a knowledge of spoken Irish the classical literature, whether good Modern, Middle, or Old Irish, must be the source from which we draw material for our Irish writings. And it must be the exclusive source."[184] As we have al-

---

and so rendering "an important service to writers and would-be writers of Irish." See "Bodach an Chóta Lachtna," *ACS*, 19 December 1903.

180. "The Oireachtas," editorial, *ACS*, 9 March 1901.

181. "Scoil na Sean-Ghaedhilge," *SF*, 21 January 1911.

182. "Éiriu," *SF*, 11 March 1911. "Dos na scríobhnóiridhibh atá le teacht is í an tSean agus an Mheadhon-Ghaedhilg an múnla. Dá réir cumfaid agus cuirfid cruth ar a smaointibh. Gan í tuigtear dúinn nach féidir leis an saothar teacht ó dhuthchas na teangan agus go mbeadh rian leitridheachta éigin eile uirthi ar n-a mbeadh dlúitheolas ag an scríobhnóir." See also "Scoil na Sean-Ghaedhilge," *SF*, 16 July 1910. While not listed in the Ó hÉaluighthe bibliography of his writings, in theme and style these pieces seem to me to be the work of Ó Donnchadha.

183. Ó Donnchadha, "Deascán Díoghluma / An Seanléigheann" (Miscellany / The old learning), *ACS*, 5 September 1914. "Agus ní fuláir don scríbhneoir eólus a chur ar an sean. . . . Litridheacht a theangan féin i n-allód, siné an 'sine qua non.'"

184. Letter, *ACS*, 28 February 1903. See also Henebry, "Best Method of Learning Irish," *ACS*, 5 July 1902; and Peadar Mac Fhionnlaoich, letter, *IG* 14, no. 174 (March 1905): 753. Agreement on this point was not quite unanimous. Louis H. Victory, who

ready discussed, for Henebry "good" literature in Modern Irish pretty much ended with Keating.

The third rationale for the Gaels' commitment to resurrecting the heroes of the ancient literature was clearly ideological. Writing in 1902 in *Éire go Bragh*, the journal of the Newry Branch of the league, one "Bodhbh Dearg" made explicit the inspirational potential of the early tales for contemporary Ireland: "It is a commonplace that a study of our pre-historic legends would go far to infuse into our composition a much needed element, to wit, a reasoned racial pride, fructifying into a desire to emulate amid the changed conditions of to-day the heroic deeds of the men of old."[185] Pearse was by no means alone in his apotheosis of Cú Chulainn or in his belief that "the story of those Fianna of Fionn should be part of the daily thought of every Irish boy."[186] Nor was such ethical guidance to be limited to the young. Writing in May 1909, Charlotte Deasy offered the ancient heroes as relatively self-evident models of right conduct for their twentieth-century descendants: "The ideals of the Gael are as high and as fine as those of any country, and in no way do they deserve to be cast aside. We have but to read what was written of our ancient heroes to know the standard demanded of Irishmen in those days. Allowing for the difference of times, allowing for a certain high-flown language, there remains much in these descriptions to serve as an example in the present."[187] Even the occasionally sardonic and iconoclastic William P. Ryan, having underscored the perhaps obvious point that "there are few Irishmen as fine or as steadfast as Cú Chulainn," could write: "We can't make true literature from corrupt and contemptible things, even if they are up-to-date, but we can make true literature from things that happened before St. Pat-

---

identified himself as an "Irish-Irelander," wrote in *The Leader* that if too much emphasis was placed on the early tales as literary models, "we are likely to be deluged, not with modern literary masterpieces, either Irish or Anglo-Irish, but we shall have instead a crude, semi-barbaric, and formless conglomeration of works which will in no sense bear the impress of literature, but which will bear the indelible imprint of their incoherent and unliterary originals." See "The Irish Scorn of English Literature," *The Leader*, 7 October 1905.

185. "A King's Treasure: About the Cúchullin Saga," *Éire go Bragh: A Monthly Bi-lingual Magazine for the Preservation and Promotion of the Language, Industries, Music, Art, and Literature of Ireland*, February 1902, 4.

186. "The Fianna of Fionn," *Fianna Handbook* (Dublin: Central Council of Na Fianna Éireann, n.d.), 151. Indeed, the views of the hardheaded Arthur Griffith differ not at all from those of Pearse: "There is none of the Greek heroes to compare in simple manhood with Cuchullin. He said and did nothing mean. He shines the sun of the noble band who formed the first order of chivalry the world remembers—the Red Branch." See "Cuchullin," *SF*, 9 April 1910.

187. S. Ni Dh. [Charlotte Deasy], "Nobless Oblige," *ACS*, 8 May 1909.

rick came to Ireland, if they be noble and fitting. Great deeds! Great thoughts! They don't become outdated. They are always contemporary. They live forever."[188] Thus conscious of a virtual duty to offer the high heroism of the early native literature as an antidote to "the cheap smartness, the glare, the coarse materialism and sensuality of the modern world," Gaelic modernizers and adapters would have felt little compunction about what they saw as the minor and justified smoothing out of a few unrepresentative ethical rough spots in their sources.[189]

Reviewing the work of the Irish Texts Society in 1902, William P. Ryan wrote that "scholarship even at the best is obviously not so important as good creative work, yet scholarship very often tends to save the creative artist toil and trouble. The Texts Society is furnishing rich material on the whole, and other men and minds can turn it to their own purposes in intellectual Ireland."[190] Considering the liberties taken by the adapters—"men and minds" with some claim to Gaelic scholarship—with what were supposedly translations of established texts, it would hardly have been surprising had they enthusiastically availed themselves of the greater freedom allowed by the opportunity to "turn this rich material to their own purposes" in creative reworkings of the ancient tales or in entirely original works based on characters and motifs from the early literature. Pearse for one felt that the early literature could offer its own precedents for such evolution, even experimentation, calling the story of Diarmaid and Gráinne (*Tóruigheacht Dhiarmada agus Ghráinne*) "neither more nor less than a novel . . . one of the greatest and one of the most interesting historical novels ever written,"[191] and

188. "Cainnt agus Litridheacht" (Talk and literature), *ACS*, 22 November 1902. "Is beag Éireannach atá chomh breagh, chomh seasmhach le Cú Chulainn. . . . Ní féidir linn fíor-litridheacht do dhéanamh as rudaibh truaillighthe tarcuisneacha, giodh go bhfuilid i ngluaiseacht na haimsire, acht is féidir linn fíor-litridheacht do cheapadh as rudaibh a thuit amach sul ar tháinig Naomh Pádraig go hÉirinn, má's rud é go rabhdar uasal oireamhnach. Mór-ghníomha! Mór-smaointe!—ní éirigheann siad-san 'seanda.' Tá siad-san 'chómhaimseardha' i gcomhnuidhe. Maireann siad go síorraidhe."

189. That such ideas were very much a part of the cultural climate of the time is evident from Yeats's comments in his preface to Lady Gregory's *Cuchulain*:

If we will tell these stories to our children the Land will begin again to be a Holy Land, as it was before men began to give their hearts to Greece and Rome and Judea. When I was a child I had only to climb the hill behind the house to see long, blue, ragged hills flowing along the southern horizon. What beauty was lost to me, what depth of emotion is still perhaps lacking in me, because nobody told me, not even the merchant captains who knew everything, that Cruachan of the Enchantments lay behind those long, blue, ragged hills!

See Yeats, Preface to *Cuchulain of Muirthemne* by Lady Gregory, 16–17.

190. "London Notes," *ACS*, 22 February 1902.

191. "Gaelic Prose Literature," in *Three Lectures on Gaelic Topics*, 14.

its heroine "the Hedda Gabler of Irish literature."[192] Precedent or no, such experimentation was, however, virtually nonexistent in the early years of this century, and modernizations far outnumber original works throughout our period, a fact that baffled the anonymous reviewer of An tAthair Peadar's *An Cleasaidhe* in 1914: "What prevents a person from setting Fionn and Oisín and Oscar, or Conchobar and Fergus and Cú Chulainn to doing once again deeds in which Irish speakers would take interest? What prevents him from reviving them for us, from praising their old talents, and bestowing on them new and modern talents?" This critic also had some intriguing suggestions about the directions such creative license might follow: "Let's take for example the thumb of Fionn Mac Cumhaill. There is now a great demand for those things called detective stories in English. Wouldn't it be possible to create fine stories of that sort based on the virtue that was in Fionn's thumb? They would beat Sherlock Holmes hands down on his best day."[193]

Unfortunately, Gaelic writers entirely ignored this marvelous suggestion, and we have no *At Swim-Two-Birds* or *King Goshawk and the Birds* in Irish.[194] Instead, the handful of original material drawing on heroic characters or motifs consists of innocuous parodies like Tadhg Mac Suibhne's "Radharc ar an nGadaidhe Dubh" (A look at the Black Thief), an account of a day's outing by London Gaelic Leaguers;[195] humorous movement allegories like Seán P. Mac Éinrigh's "An Sean-Rí / Sgéal

192. "Aspects of Irish Literature," in *Complete Works: Songs of the Irish Rebels*, 142.

193. "Leabhra/*An Cleasaidhe*" (Books/*An Cleasaidhe*), *ACS*, 17 January 1913. "Cadé an bac a bheadh ar dhuine Fionn agus Oisín agus Oscar, nó neachtracha Conchubhar agus Fearghus agus Cúchulainn a chur arís ag déanamh gníomhartha go gcuirfeadh muinntir na Gaedhilge suim ionnta? Cadé an bac air iad d'aithbheódhchaint dúinn agus a seancháilidheachta a mholadh, agus cáilidheachta nua an lae indiu do bhronnadh ortha? . . . Cuirimís i gcás órdóg Fhinn Mhic Cumhaill. Tá an-éileamh anois ar na hearraí seo go dtugtar detective stories ortha sa Bhéarla. Nár bhreágh na scéalta dhen tsórd soin do bhféidir a cheapadh ar an mbuaidh sin a bhí i nórdóig Fhinn? Do bhuaidhfidís caoch ar Sherlock Holmes an lá do bhfhearr a bhí sé."

194. More understandable in light of technical and financial restraints, Gaelic artists did not explore the cinematic possibilities suggested by "Seán Óg" Ó Caomhánaigh in 1913: "Where is my Cú Chulainn and my Emer? my Fionn Mac Cumhaill and my white-toothed Diarmuid Ó Duibhne and his Gráinne, my Oisín, oh yes, my Oisín and my Patrick? . . . Think of the *Táin Bó Cúailnge* on the screen!" (Cá bhfuil mo Chúchulainn agus m'Emher? mo Fhionn Mac Cumhaill agus mo Dhiarmuid déidgheal Ó Duibhne agus a Ghráinne, mo Oisín, ó, seadh, mo Oisín agus mo Phádraig? . . . Cuimhnigh ar an 'Táin Bó Cúalainge' bheith ar an scáine!" See "An Scáine agus an Ghaedhilg," *ACS*, 8 February 1913.

195. *ACS*, 19 August 1899.

Úr-Nuadh Déanta ar Nós Sean-Sgéil" (The old king / A contemporary story modeled on an ancient story), with its royal figure "Gaedheal" and its protagonist Dubhghlas (Douglas) of Connacht;[196] brief propaganda pieces like "Oisín ag Teagasc Gaedhilge i mBéal Feirste" (Oisín teaching Irish in Belfast);[197] or more ambitiously, the sui generis "Eachtra Chonáin Uí Cheallaigh" (The adventure of Conán Ó Ceallaigh) and "Eachtra Déidheanach na bhFiann" (The last adventure of the Fianna), two exercises in sterile narrative and linguistic antiquarianism by Father Henebry.[198] The cleverest of the lot came from San Francisco, California, where "Mac Mic Mhairéid Ní Thaidhg" borrowed freely from tales of Fionn's Fianna in his humorous story of Father Peter Yorke's epic battles with the Know-Nothing American Protective Association and with *seoinín* Irish-American politicians.[199]

The reason for the general lack of artistic initiative may, of course, be all too simple. Truly creative work demands greater literary sophistication and command than does the modernization of a set text. Nonetheless, at this time of abundant enthusiasm, when good patriotic intentions were often sufficient compensation for undistinguished aesthetic achievement, mere lack of talent is not an adequate explanation for the limited number of original Gaelic works or reworkings inspired by the early literature. The real challenge of such work may have been both more profound and more intractable. Many Gaels seem to have honestly questioned the very possibility of re-creating the ancient world in any coherent or meaningful sense, and, chastened by what they saw as the undeniable Anglo-Irish failure in this regard, were wary of the pitfalls into which their often less scrupulous literary brethren had recklessly tumbled: "Where information and knowledge failed them they resorted to imaginings or conjectures, and hence we have had too much that is fantastic. We have had a little of Cúchulainn and a great deal of modern fancy and phantasms."[200] And apparently for once some Gaels felt that this Anglo-Irish failure was not purely or even primarily linguistic, and that their own fidelity to the language of their heroes was

196. *ACS*, 27 December 1902–31 January 1903.

197. *ACS*, 26 December 1908. Pearse's English-language Fenian sketch, "The Second Return of Oisín," was precisely this sort of piece, conscripting an ancient hero into the service of the Revival. See *ACS*, 12 August 1905, Duilleachán an Oireachtais; 26 August 1905, Duilleachán an Oireachtais.

198. In *Scríbhne Risteird de Hindeberg*, 157–64; 165–86.

199. "Oscar na Féinne 'ghá Chur i gCompráid leis an Athair Ó Floinn; nó Oscar na Ficheadh Sinnsire" (Oscar of the Fianna compared to Father O'Flynn [i.e., Yorke]; or Oscar of the twentieth century"), *ACS*, 12 July–9 August 1902.

200. William P. Ryan, "Kiltartan, Mr. Yeats, and Cúchulain," *The Leader*, 5 July 1902.

no guarantee of artistic empathy, much less success.[201] Even writers committed to such work seem to have shared this pessimism. Thus in 1902 Mac Fhionnlaoich, having pronounced ancient Irish literature "as polished and as well-crafted as any literature in Europe," wrote: "It's no use for us to speak of Cú Chulainn or of Fionn Mac Cumhaill or of Deirdre or of Gráinne. They had their day, and we cannot resurrect them."[202] Reviewing Tomás Ó Ceallaigh's play *Deirdre* on its production at the 1909 Oireachtas, Pearse theorized in similar vein on why he found the work ultimately disappointing: "Perhaps it is a vain thing for moderns to essay the old theme. As we move farther away from the gods we lose more and more of the divine creative breath which of old breathed life into clay, making it godlike."[203] Paradoxically, Pearse's own *Macghníomhartha Chúchulainn*, prompted almost identical reservations from Thomas MacDonagh, a man whose heroic death in 1916 was to make him, with Pearse, one of Cú Chulainn's heirs in a new national orthodoxy. Writing in *An Macaomh*, MacDonagh concluded: "Some in our day or after may make a great new literature in the tradition of this old world of Early Irish Literature. But I rather expect that the literature of tomorrow will be in terms of the life of tomorrow, and that the old world is too different, too far apart, too wronged now. . . . We cannot pray to the old gods. . . . History is between us and our heroes."[204]

Yet if the stern heroic ethos of *Táin Bó Cúailnge* was suspected of being ultimately inaccessible to the modern mind, there was one ancient tale whose appeal seemed genuinely universal. The Deirdre story captivated the Gaels as thoroughly as it did their Anglo-Irish counterparts,

---

201. Paradoxically, the failure of Gaelic writers to challenge Anglo-Irish re-creations of the heroic literature with original work of their own ceded, at least in part, to those writing in English the opportunity to fulfill what John Hutchinson sees as one of the principal roles of the artist in movements of cultural nationalism, to "create out of the collective experience of the people, preserved in historical legends, and dramatize their lessons for the present." See Hutchinson, *Dynamics*, 15. As we have seen in the Chapter 3, Gaelic writers were more successful with history, however legendary, than they were with legends, however historical.

202. "An Litiordhacht Nua Gaedhilge," *ACS*, 11 and 18 October 1902. Mac Fhionnlaoich said the literature was "chomh snasta is chomh slachtmhar le litiordhacht ar bith 'san Eoroip," but went on: "Níl gar dúinn trácht ar Choin Chulainn nó ar Fhionn Mac Cumhaill, nó ar Dheirdre nó ar Ghráinne. Bhí a lá féin aca siúd, agus ní féidir iad d'aithbheodhadh." Compare the views of Mícheál Breathnach in "Lean Lorg na Laochra" (Follow the path of the heroes), in *Sgríbhinní Mhíchíl Bhreathnaigh*, 44.

203. "The Plays," *ACS*, 14 August 1909.

204. "Notes for a Lecture on Ancient Irish Literature," *An Macaomh* 2, no. 2 (May 1913): 13. This essay was reprinted in *Literature in Ireland* (1916).

and it is thus remarkable that Tomás Ó Ceallaigh's drama *Deirdre* is the only published creative refashioning of this tale in Irish from the early years of the Revival.[205] Like Yeats, Synge, AE, and later James Stephens, Ó Ceallaigh was principally fascinated by the tale's depiction of tragic fated love—although as befits a priest his passion is a bit more pallid—and only secondarily with his own interpretive notions of other themes in the work. Nonetheless, while he offers a generally straightforward dramatization of a more genteel late version of the tale—a version that has Deirdre die romantically of grief at, not in, Naisi's grave—he does make significant changes in the motivation of Conchobar, changes with a clear ideological intention rooted in the philosophy of the Revival.

In 1894 Eoin Mac Néill insisted that early Irish literature, regardless of its province of origin, was distinguished by a profound awareness of Ireland as a self-consciously distinctive cultural and national unit: "One of the clearest marks of ancient Irish literature is the mark or note of nationality . . . a positive conscious nationality, which consists in a constant recognition of the unity and community of the Gaelic race, and in the recognition of Ireland as its chief home and ancient patrimony, and as one of the dearest objects of its affections."[206] Fifteen years later, Riobárd Ua Fhloinn [Robert Lynd] gave Mac Néill's doctrine a contemporary relevance as he praised what he called the nation's "imagination-builders," its writers in English and, more important, in Irish, who were offering their fellow citizens

> the idea and the vision of the oneness of Ireland—the spiritual unity that, however dimly felt, binds the Orange ship-builder of Belfast to the sickled peasant of Connacht and the cattle-driver of Tipperary, that binds Professor Mahaffy and Cardinal Logue and Lord Ashtown in the one bundle of national life. I say that no man can realise this unity to the full and remain exactly the same in his political ideals as he was before, and I say that no man—no Irishman, at any rate, except the merest grammarian—

205. Seosamh Ó Néill won the 190? ireachtas Prize for a short play with a work of which the adjudicators reported: "This is the old story of Deirdre told well in dramatic form. The language of the competitor is not nearly so good as that of many of the others, but as a drama it deserves the prize." The play seems never to have been published, perhaps because of its linguistic shortcomings. See "Some Extracts from the Adjudicators' Reports," *ACS*, 23 May 1903, Duilleachán an Oireachtais.

206. "Characteristics of Irish Literature," *IG* 5, no. 5 (August 1894): 75. This piece originally appeared in *New Ireland Review* for May 1894.

can study the Irish language and read the old literature of the Irish people without realising that unity with a new clearness.[207]

The ancient literature could, then, like the nation's history, be a vital force that not only bound present to past, but also linked all Ireland in a shared and magnificent heritage.

This nationalist ideology—an ideology that as we saw in Chapter 3 seemed all too often threatened by the myriad provincial and even parochial squabbles in the movement[208]—is at the heart of Ó Ceallaigh's play. His exiles express a longing for Ireland itself, not just for their home province of Ulster: "I would rather be wretched and poor in Ireland than exiled from her for life, even if I were king of all Scotland."[209] But most significant is the playwright's transformation of Conchobar into a failed prophet of the European nation-state. While Ó Ceallaigh's king retains his exemplar's deceitful thirst for vengeance, his explicit motivation is not so much personal vindication as a desire to assert the legitimate authority of a centralized state as a step toward the political unification of Ireland under a single monarchy: "My desire was that the Red Branch would hold sway over all so that this island of the Gaels would be under the authority of one king—so that a kingdom and a succession would be established the like of which had never yet been seen in the world" (27).[210] Viewed in this light, the killing of Naisi and his brothers is not exclusively an act of jealous rage, but rather to some extent an execution carried out "as punishment for breaking my law" (i ndíol mo reacht do bhriseadh).[211] That no contemporary critic

207. "Literature and Politics," SF, 27 February 1909.
208. Some of the principal divisive issues troubling the league have been discussed in Chapter 3. Pearse for one lamented the bitterly personal tone that often suffused these debates, and in 1906 invoked shared heroes in an attempt to bring leaguers together again. Looking back on the simpler early days of the movement, he wrote: "There was about the League of those days some of the gallant *insouciance* of youth: we were like so many young Cúchulainns setting out on the journey to Eamhain Macha, and taking bat and ball to 'shorten the way.' Yet for all our youthful 'irresponsibility'—the word was often flung at us—there was in our hearts, as there was in that of Cúchulainn, the sternness of a great purpose." See "A Plea for Brotherhood," editorial, ACS, 28 July 1906.
209. *Deirdre* (Baile Átha Cliath: Connradh na Gaedhilge, 1909), 18. "Do b'annsa liom bheith dealbh bocht i nÉirinn 'ná bheith ar dhíbirt uaithi le mo bheo, siúd is go mbéinn im' rígh ar Albain uile." Of course, such sentiments were also in line with the league's vigorous propaganda campaign against emigration.
210. "Do b'é mo mhian go rachadh an Craobh-Ruadh i réim thar réim go mbéadh an t-oileán so na nGaedheal fá smacht aon ríogh amháin—go ndéanfaidhe ríoghacht is réim do chur ar bun nach bhfacthas fós a leithéid ar an domhan."
211. P. 33. As was discussed in Chapter 3, Brian Bóroimhe was similarly perceived as a pioneer nation-builder, a view that enabled Gaelic writers of history and historical fiction to condone his otherwise troubling usurpation of the "High-Kingship."

noted such a fundamental, ideologically motivated revision of the original tale is our most powerful confirmation of how closely Ó Ceallaigh
was in tune with prevailing Gaelic orthodoxy.[212]

The only other major Gaelic creative work inspired by the early literature was Seán Ua Ceallaigh's 1912 Oireachtas play *Cú Chulainn is Cú
Roí* (published as *Cú Roí*). Ua Ceallaigh showed some nerve here, for
he was dealing with sensitive material. In the original *Aided Con Roí*
(The death of Cú Roí), the paradigmatic Irish hero Cú Chulainn is
bested and humiliated by the awesome Kerry warrior Cú Roí, whom
he later attacks and kills in his sleep with the assistance of Cú Roí's wife
Bláthnaid. Unlike Séamus Ó Dubhghaill and "An Dairbhreach Dána"
(Ua Ceallaigh himself), both of whom wrote stories based on folk versions of this tale,[213] Ua Ceallaigh confronted Cú Chulainn's treachery
head-on, having the murder committed right onstage. Nevertheless,
despite his own Kerry chauvinism, Ua Ceallaigh's depiction of the national hero's perfidy does mitigate the savagery of the original in three
significant instances. First of all, his Cú Chulainn actually awakens his
sleeping foe, even if only to immediately dispatch him.[214] Second and
more important, Ua Ceallaigh provides the Ulster warrior with a more
ethically legitimate motive for vengeance than does the medieval redac-

212. It is worth noting that the only contemporary critic who commented on the
prominence accorded Conchobhar in the play entirely misunderstood Ó Ceallaigh's intention, writing:

> Father O'Kelly in his play has made a good deal of the character of Conchubhar,
> High King of Uladh, and it is easy to understand what an appeal this character, this
> king who was prepared to do treacherous things to regain possession of Deirdre,
> made to the dramatist. In the first act I thought Father O'Kelly scored distinctly in
> handling this character. . . . In the last act, however, I thought the dramatist gave too
> much reign to Conchubhar, and that Deirdre and her lover were sacrificed to him.

See B., "Deirdre," review of the 1909 Oireachtas production of Ó Ceallaigh's *Deirdre*,
SF, 11 August 1909.

213. See "An Dairbhreach Dána," "Aideadh Chonroí" (The violent death of Cú Roí),
ACS, 20 and 27 January 1906; and Séamus Ó Dubhghaill, "Cathair Conroí" (Cú Roí's
Fort), in *Cathair Conroí agus Sgéalta Eile* (Cú Roí's fort and other stories) (Baile Átha
Cliath: Connradh na Gaedhilge, 1907). The story was originally written for the 1902
Oireachtas. Perhaps predictably, Ua Ceallaigh and Ó Dubhghaill were both Kerrymen.
As "An Dairbhreach Dána" Ua Ceallaigh was aware that his presentation of Cú Chulainn
in an unfavorable light could cause resentment, particularly among Ulstermen: "It's not
likely that all Ulstermen will agree with my version, but what harm if we do have a little
controversy about the episode." (Ní móide go n-aontóchaidh Ultaigh uile lem' innsint-se,
acht cad é an díoghbháil má bhíonn conspóid bheag féin againn i dtaoibh an eachtra.) See
ACS, 20 January 1906.

214. *Cú Roí* (Baile Átha Cliath: Muinntear Ghuill, n.d.), 31. "An Dairbhreach Dána"
has the awakened Cú Roí provided with weapons, although he is still overwhelmed by
superior numbers. In Ó Dubhghaill's story there is no reference to the killing; Cú Roí is
simply, and with no explanation, found dead.

tor. Whereas in the original tale Bláthnaid is presented primarily as a prize of war to be contested by Cú Roí and Cú Chulainn and only secondarily as a woman in whom Cú Chulainn is interested, in Ua Ceallaigh's play their romantic relationship is emphasized from the hero's opening speech (1–2).[215] And third, in the play she explicitly appeals to Cú Chulainn to rescue her from Cú Roí (15–17). On the whole, however, with the possible minor exception of the story "Béal Cú agus Conall Cearnach" by Henry Morris, Ua Ceallaigh's play is the modern Irish work that most faithfully re-creates its original even in its disturbingly unedifying aspects.[216] This fidelity may account for its apparent lack of success among the Gaels.[217]

The Gaelic attempt to reincarnate the epic heroes must, unfortunately, be judged a failure. A major factor here was that the league and its writers indirectly allowed one of their most articulate foes to set their agenda. Prior to Atkinson's 1898 diatribe, modernization was an insignificant element in the Gaelic literary program, with even O'Growney's 1891 efforts mostly forgotten.[218] The Trinity scholar's well-publicized taunts in effect drove many Gaelic writers to accept a challenge for which they were both ill-prepared and ill-suited. Even more important, it seems in retrospect that the task they set themselves was in the final analysis impossible, for they were attempting to achieve simultaneously two irreconcilable goals. On the one hand, they felt an obligation to preserve the tales accurately, to avoid, indeed to redress, what they saw as the Anglo-Irish writers' unscrupulous manipulation and distortion of their sources.[219] On the other hand, they adhered, of-

215. See also 13 for a sentimental love scene between the hero and Bláthnaid.

216. In Morris's story, based not on the Middle Irish original, *Aided Cheit Maic Mágach* (The death of Cet Mac Mágach), but on Samuel Ferguson's poem "The Healing of Conall Carnach," the Connachtman Béal Cú plots with his sons to murder the Ulterman Conall through treachery. Conall outwits them, duping the sons into killing their own father. See "Béal Cú agus Conall Cearnach," in *Donnbó agus Rígh-Sgéalta Eile* (Derry: Messrs. O'Breslin, 1909), 31–46.

217. See, for example, the review by "Caor," "The Oireachtas Plays," *ACS*, 20 July 1912. Unfairly, though conveniently for ideological reasons, "Caor" places the blame for Cú Chulainn's treachery on Bláthnaid, "the evil genius of two heroes of Irish history . . . a woman of passion and of great parts, one who possessed little conscience and who had a power over men." On the other hand, *Cú Roí* was given a very favorable review by "Eibhle" in the Kerry-based *An Lóchrann*. See "Eibhle," "Cú Roí," *An Lóchrann* 4, no. 11 (August–September 1912).

218. See, for example, Mac Néill's comments in June 1900: "Father O'Growney was, we believe, the first who saw the need of building up the literature of modern Irish on the foundations of the past. His work has been little heard of" ("Notes," *ACS*, 23 June 1900.)

219. As we have seen, however, the Gaels could distort their sources in much the same way and for precisely the same reasons as some of those they criticized. Standish James

ten it seems unconsciously, to an ideology that insisted on taking the early tales as explicit, noble, and anachronistically ethical and patriotic models for an emerging de-Anglicized Ireland. Either way the Gaels were handling holy writ, and it is hardly surprising that most of them were sufficiently intimidated to forego a genuine personal exegesis. Thus, despite the early enthusiasms of writers like Ua Laoghaire and Mac Fhionnlaoich, and the contributions of scholars like Tadhg Ó Donnchadha and Tomás Ua Nualláin—or in our own time of Proinsias Mac Cana and Tomás Ó Floinn—if the ancient tales have entered the home of the Aran Islander or Donegal Highlander, they have not done so in their native language. While over the past ninety years native scholars, many of them alumni/alumnae of the Gaelic League, have prepared meticulous editions of early texts with accurate translations and critical apparatus in English, we still await the fulfillment of "Bodhbh Dearg's" confident prediction that "we shall soon have in our hands the greatest of Irish romances, the *Táin Bó Cúailnge*, done into modern Irish."[220]

O'Grady was, for example, regarded as "at one and the same time one of our most pleasing of National writers, and one of the most unscrupulous manipulators of historical facts" ("Tír-Chonaill Notes," *ACS*, 8 September 1900). Yet in many ways the pleasure he provided Gaels with his glowing depictions of the Irish heroic past was a function of just this "unscrupulous" manipulation of his originals, a manipulation rooted in what Phillip Marcus has dubbed the "good story" approach to ancient source material. Explaining his objections to AE's dramatization of the Deirdre tale in 1902 from an ideological perspective identical to that of Ua Laoghaire, O'Grady wrote: "If we lose Concobhar [*sic*] we lose the Red Branch, for we cannot continue to believe in those who were the knights and followers of such a captain as the scoundrel of the 'Deirdre' story. So, we lose the heroic period altogether, unless we can remake it, building it up anew out of the centres of honour, faithfulness, courage, and affection which we know are in the literature." See "Open Letter to AE," *All Ireland Review* 3, no. 7 (19 April 1902): 100.

220. "A King's Treasure," *Éire go Bragh*, February 1902, 4. This prophecy may at long last be fulfilled, for Niall Ó Dónaill is currently at work on a modern Irish version of the *Táin*. See "Agallamh na Míosa: Liam Ó Muirthile ag Cainnt leis an Dochtúir Niall Ó Dónaill" (The interview of the month: Liam Ó Muirthile speaking with Doctor Niall Ó Dónaill), *Comhar* 48, no. 4 (April 1989): 8.

5

Uneasy Alliance

The Gaelic Revival and the "Irish" Renaissance

In May 1899 a self-righteous nineteen year old Patrick Pearse declared war on the Irish Literary Theatre and its attempt to create a new national literature for Ireland in the English language. Writing to the editor of *An Claidheamh Soluis*, Pearse proclaimed: "If we once admit the Irish literature in English idea, then the language movement is a mistake. Mr. Yeats' precious 'Irish' Literary Theatre may, if it develops, give the Gaelic League more trouble than the Atkinson–Mahaffy combination. Let us strangle it at its birth."[1] Despite the youthful hyperbole, Pearse's major premise here was by no means idiosyncratic in Gaelic circles. The same idea had already been advanced by writers more influential than the then obscure Pearse in forums more impressive than the correspondence column. In an editorial in the 22 January 1898 *Fáinne an Lae* we find an attack on "the great host of people in Ireland for the past hundred years or so who believe it is possible to

1. Letter, *ACS*, 20 May 1899.

create a national literature for this country in a foreign language."[2]
Again, on 23 April 1898, *Fáinne an Lae* referred to "that strange sect
who maintain that Irish may be written in English, and who, while
ignorant of any 'Celtic' language, write and talk much of a 'Celtic'
movement."[3] In an editorial note in *An Claidheamh Soluis* the month
immediately prior to Pearse's letter, Eoin Mac Néill had remarked with
mock incredulity: "But there are to be found people who try to per-
suade themselves that Irish literature may mean literature in the English
language. This heresy has done more to provincialise Ireland than has
the Act of Union."[4] In fact on 6 May 1899, Pearse's attack on Yeats and
his colleagues had actually been anticipated on the editorial page of *An
Claidheamh Soluis*: "Such 'Irish' dramatists are far more the servants of
English Imperialism than is their counterpart of the Munster Fusiliers,
the Connacht Rangers or the Enniskillings."[5] Even the dying Father
Eugene O'Growney felt strongly enough on this point to write from
Arizona to the New York *Irish World* in January 1899 that "you may
say that we could have a literature which while in the English language,
would be truly Irish in sentiment and thought. This looks well in theory, but in practice it fails to work out."[6]

Not only did this idea take form early in the history of the Revival
and its press, it also persisted throughout the first two decades of this
century as both the Gaelic and the Anglo-Irish movements gained
strength and influence. Particularly virulent were the attacks of D. P.
Moran in *The Leader*. Moran, who memorably christened AE "the
Hairy Fairy," who called Synge's *Riders to the Sea* "the corpse curtain
raiser,"[7] and who frequently referred to Yeats as "Pensioner Yeats" after
the poet accepted a Civil List grant in 1910, made his views clear in the
inaugural issue of his journal:

2. "Litridheacht Náisiúnta" (National literature), editorial, *FL*, 22 January 1898. The
attack was on "sluagh mór daoine i nÉirinn, le céad bliadhan nó mar sin, dhá cheapadh
gur féidir litridheacht náisiúnta do chruthughadh do'n tír seo as teangaidh Ghallda."

3. "Notes," *FL*, 23 April 1898.

4. "Debasing Literature: Its Antidote," editorial, *ACS*, 29 April 1899.

5. "Notes," *ACS*, 6 May 1899.

6. "*The Irish World* Language Fund," in *Leabhar an Athar Eoghan*, ed. O'Farrelly, 257.
Alan Titley has written that the founding of the Gaelic League was itself an attempt "to
refute the opinion that the country's literature could be based on the unique English
spoken in Ireland" ("séanadh a thabhairt don tuairim go bhféadfaí litríocht na tíre a
thógáil ar Bhéarla faoi leith na hÉireann"). See Titley, "Litríocht na Gaeilge, Litríocht an
Bhéarla, agus Irish Literature" (Literature in Irish, literature in English, and Irish literature) *Scríobh*, 5 (1981): 127.

7. "'The Eloquent Mr. Dempsey' at the Abbey Theatre," *The Leader*, 27 January
1906.

We deny the possible existence of such a thing as Irish literature in the English language, but literature concerning Ireland written in English—and which we will always refer to as Anglo-Irish Literature—we recognise as something which will probably always remain with us. We will deal with that with discrimination, but with a due sense of the dignity of Ireland and the respect due her, even when people purport to disclose her thought through the medium of a foreign language.[8]

Father Patrick Dinneen, who, as we have seen, could be quite open and eclectic in his tastes, was on this point even less restrained than his close friend Moran, telling a league audience: "With a foreign language come foreign modes of thought, foreign ideals in art and literature, foreign customs, foreign manners, the spread of all that is debasing in foreign literature. . . . No genuine native school of literature, or of art, can ever be created from foreign or Anglo-Irish models.[9]

While often lacking the rhetorical flamboyance of Moran or Dinneen, Gaelic League spokespersons closed ideological ranks on this point. For example, in January 1900 Peadar Mac Fhionnlaoich urged leaguers who attended lectures on Irish literature that only dealt with Anglo-Irish writing to politely but firmly recite their creed "that it is not right to call writings or literature of that kind Irish, for they are English writings or literature." Mac Fhionnlaoich assured them they would meet with little cogent opposition, for "there is no answer at all to be given to this."[10] In addition, An Claidheamh Soluis regularly articulated this position under several editorial regimes, most notably in two extended debates on the "Irishness" of Anglo-Irish literature, the first with T. C.

---

8. Editorial, *The Leader*, 1 September 1900. Among the virtues for which *ACS* congratulated its new "ally" *The Leader* was its willingness to confront "the heresy of Irish literature in English." See "Review," *ACS*, 8 September 1900. Actually, Moran's tone was a bit more conciliatory in the second issue of his journal: "Of course we grant—our experience tells us—that the distinctly Irish genius can now and again strike a distinct note in the English language. But it is of rare occurrence." See "The 'Leader' and Some Representative Men," *The Leader*, 8 September 1900. Moran's own 1905 novel *Tom O'Kelly* was, of course, in English, although "Imaal" did entitle his review of the work in *The Leader* (23 December 1905) "A New Sort of Anglo-Irish Novel."

9. "The Irish Language Revival Movement," in *Lectures on the Irish Language Movement*, 42–43.

10. "Tuairisg ó'n Tuaisceart" (Report from the North), *ACS*, 27 January 1900. He believed "nár chóir an ainm Éireannach do thabhairt ar sgríbhinnibh nó ar litirdheacht de'n tsamhail úd nó gur sgríbhinní nó litirdheacht gaill-bhéarla iad. . . . Níl freagra ar bith le tabhairt ar so."

Murray in 1899, the second with Seamas MacManus in 1903.[11] In his editorial response to MacManus's contention that Anglo-Irish writing was a valid component of Irish national literature, Eoghan Ó Neachtain flatly rejected the very term "Anglo-Irish:"

> It has really been invented as a sort of half-way house, in which certain English writers may rest, flattering themselves with the thought that what they write is not English literature, and yet not Irish literature, to be sure; but something with the virtues of both—"Anglo-Irish" literature. "Irish or Anglo-Irish?" Neither:—"English."[12]

Four years later, with the *Playboy of the Western World* row still fresh in mind, Pearse, now editor of *An Claidheamh Soluis*, defended himself against Éamonn Ceannt's charge that he was soft on Anglo-Irish literature with a ringing restatement of league policy: "Literature which is in Irish is Irish literature; literature which is not in Irish is not Irish literature."[13] And Eoin Mac Néill, despite his cordial personal relations with leading Anglo-Irish writers, similarly denied them a primary role in the building of a distinctively Irish identity, writing in a 1909 pamphlet: "In Ireland there is no possible foundation for a national culture except the national language. It can easily be shown that an attempt to base Irish

11. Murray's debate with Mac Néill, which also involved Moran and C. J. Murphy, ran in *ACS* from 24 June to 16 September 1899. For the MacManus controversy, see *ACS*, 3–24 January 1903. Moran's critical assault on the Brooke–Rolleston *A Treasury of Irish Poetry* sparked the third sustained debate on this question in the Gaelic or Irish-Ireland press in 1900–1901. See *The Leader*, 1 December 1900–9 February 1901.

12. "Irish or Anglo-Irish," editorial, *ACS*, 10 January 1903. Moran dissented on this point, defending the use of the term "Anglo-Irish," "for it, or some equivalent, is the only proper phrase, as far as we can see, to meet the case." See "Current Affairs," *The Leader*, 17 January 1903.

13. Editorial response to a letter from Éamonn Ceannt, *ACS*, 13 April 1907. That Pearse never fully resolved his ambivalences about Irish writing in English is evident from the reflections of his friend and former student Desmond Ryan (*The Man Called Pearse*, 19–20):

> Rightly or wrongly . . . Pearse's whole mental attitude was antagonistic to Anglo-Irish literature. The very words Anglo-Irish he detested and denied their validity, although, unlike certain perfervid propagandists, his knowledge of the work of Irish men and women was as appreciative and exact as his knowledge of English literature itself. . . . But speaking generally, Pearse practiced bilingualism to the detriment of the English language in Ireland, working and striving for the final battle between the two languages. . . . Your Anglo-Irish writers, he contended, brought only fame to English literature and could never be true representatives of Irish literature. A special niche might be set apart for them in English literature, it is true, but at the best they only retarded the rise of a literature in Irish.

culture on the English language can only result in provincialising Irish life."[14]

While Gaelic aggressiveness abated as relationships between the language and Anglo-Irish movements warmed somewhat after the death of Synge, there was never compromise on this central article of the Gaelic literary faith. For example, in April 1911 Seán Ó Cuill wrote in *Sinn Féin*:

> I hold that the adding of another book to the Nation's Library is a work that a patriot may feel proud of. But an Irish patriot cannot share that pride, no matter how well he may write of his Fatherland or his Mother tongue, if he writes in English. Because no work in English, no matter how good—no nor in German, nor Italian, nor French, nor Spanish—can be admitted (except in the department for foreign masterpieces) into Éire's Library. *That Library Must be Irish.* (emphasis in original)[15]

Writing in the same journal, Seán Ó Caomhánaigh agreed in March of the following year: "It was always my opinion that work in English, however good, is of little benefit to Ireland, and that opinion has still not wavered. My opinion was that it had not been and could not be anything but an addition to English literature: many share that same opinion with me.[16] As the official organ of the movement, *An Claidheamh Soluis* felt obliged to affirm this fact periodically, as it did in a September 1912 editorial entitled "Irish Literature": "To sustain our

14. Quoted by Daniel Corkery in *What's This About the Gaelic League?* (Dublin: Gaelic League, 1942), 25. Mac Néill's position here was not a new one. As early as 1897 he had editorialized in *Irisleabhar na Gaedhilge*: "The Anglo-Irish or Hiberno-English idea of a National Irish literature is daily becoming a more evident delusion. That literature itself has failed to obtain any hold whatsoever on the Irish mind." See "Past, Present and Future," *IG* 8, no. 85 (May 1897): 3. Donal McCartney argues that it was in deference to the wishes of Hyde that Mac Néill refrained from even stronger criticisms of the Anglo-Irish movement. See "Mac Néill and Irish Ireland," in *The Scholar Revolutionary*, 93. The distinction between the views of Hyde on this point and those of Mac Néill is also stressed by Michael Tierney in his biography of the latter: "The rejection of the literary revival by Mac Néill and those who thought like him was absolute. They were prepared to admire its products as they admired Shakespeare, but further than this they would not go." See Tierney, *Eoin MacNéill*, 67.

15. "Why Not Write Something in Irish?" *SF*, 1 April 1911.

16. "Trí Chlódhanna" (Three publications), *SF*, 23 March 1912. "Dob é mo bharamhail féin riamh gur beag an mhaith d'Éirinn saothar dá fheabhas i mBeurla, agus ní dheaghaidh aon lagughadh ar an mbaramhail san agam fós. B'í mo thuairim ná raibh agus ná feudfadh a bheith ann ach breis ar an litridheacht Bheurla: tá mórán ar an dtuairim gceudna san liom."

own claim to it we have of set purpose chosen the title adopted for this article. Though the term is still applied to Irishmen's efforts in the English language such an employment thereof remains just as false as when it first obtained currency. In other words, there can be no Irish literature except the Irish language be its medium.[17] Three years later, Tadhg Ó Donnchadha turned to that medium to make the same point, answering his gloating question "Where are the 'Celtic Noters' or the 'Irish Ibsens' today?" with the assertion that their apparent disappearance was a sign "that there will never be a drama or a literature in Ireland until it is written in Irish. There will be no true Culture in this country if it is not a Gaelic Culture."[18]

As is clear from both the melodramatic threats of the young Pearse's letter and the more considered judgments of an older Pearse and other Gaels, there were those in the language movement who saw Anglo-Irish literature as not merely irrelevant to the definition of a distinct modern Irish culture, but as hostile to it. For these writers, Anglo-Irish literature was, in the words of D. P. Moran, "one of the most glaring frauds that the credulous Irish people ever swallowed."[19] Ernest Blythe remembered this as a fairly widespread view among Gaels in the early years of this century: "I thought, as did many young leaguers at that time, that an English language writer couldn't but be an enemy of Ireland."[20] Naturally this attitude found expression in the Gaelic press.

---

17. *ACS*, 14 September 1912. Lest this view seem entirely the product of wishful thinking, it should be remembered that it was shared at various points in their careers by some of the most prominent Anglo-Irish literary figures. Yeats himself, speaking in New York in 1904, recalled: "When this great movement [the Gaelic League] appeared in Ireland, it looked for a time as if there was nothing for men like myself to do." See William Butler Yeats, *Uncollected Prose*, ed. John P. Frayne and Colton Johnson (London: Macmillan, 1975), 2:323. See also Yeats's "The Literary Movement in Ireland," in *Ideals in Ireland* (London: Unicorn, 1901), 90; and his comments on the future of Gaelic literature as reported in *ACS*, 5 March 1904. Even Sean O'Casey could write as late as 1913: "We are out to overthrow England's language, her political government of our country, good and bad; her degrading social system." See "'Euchan' and Ireland, a Challenge to Verbal Combat," in *Feathers from the Green Crow: Sean O'Casey, 1905–1925*, ed. Robert Hogan (London: Macmillan, 1963), 93.

18. "Cultúr" (Culture), *ACS*, 13 February 1915. "Cá bhfuil na 'Celtic Noters' nó na 'Irish Ibsens' indiu?" Their disappearance was a sign "ná beidh aon dráma ná litridheacht i nÉirinn go deo nó go mbeidh siad i nGaedhilg. Ní bheidh aon Chultúr ceart san tir seo muna Cultúr Gaedhealach é."

19. "The Future of the Irish Nation," in *The Philosophy of Irish Ireland*, 22.

20. Earnán de Blaghd (Ernest Blythe), *Slán le hUltaibh* (Farewell to Ulster) (Baile Átha Cliath: Sáirséal agus Dill, 1971), 46. "Cheapas, mar a cheap a lán Conrathóirí óga an t-am úd, nach bhféadfadh scríbhneoir Béarla gan a bheith ina namhaid d'Éirinn."

Thus in June 1899 *An Claidheamh Soluis* stated flatly: "The so-called Irish Literary movement is a hindrance and not a help to a genuine revival."[21] A fortnight later another editorial developed this idea:

> Any movement whose end is the creation of works in English is in its essence English. With such a movement we have no quarrel till it call itself Irish and national, thereby setting up a wrong ideal, and confusing and obscuring the minds of the people with regard to what constitutes nationality and a national literature. The leaders in such a movement, whether they be New Irelanders or Irish Literary Movement men, are some of the most seductive, and therefore most dangerous emissaries of Anglicisation.[22]

What is most interesting and significant here is the suggestion that Anglo-Irish literature was most dangerous in its appeal, that is in its aesthetic success and beauty. This idea is found as early as 1897 in Mac Néill's favorable review of George Sigerson's *Bards of the Gael and Gall* in *Irisleabhar na Gaedhilge*: "Indeed, to those ignorant of Irish literature I should hesitate to recommend the reading of Doctor Sigerson's translations, lest they should say, 'This is good enough for us. It cannot have been better in the Irish.'"[23] It was also Mac Néill who made explicit the Gaels' fear of the alluring power of Anglo-Irish literature in an *An Claidheamh Soluis* editorial on "The Irish Literary Movement": "Its effect upon the great mass of the people, however, will be to make them forget that it is only the second-best thing; the more excellent it is the more will they be inclined to give it an exaggerated value and to rest content with a maimed and defective product to the great detriment of the fairer, perfect and ideal embodiment of the national spirit—that in the national tongue."[24] He made the same point in his congratulatory letter to Lady Gregory on publication of *Cuchulain of Muirthemne*, a letter whose jocular tone cannot totally mask a serious and widely shared concern: "A few more books like it, and the Gaelic League will want to suppress you on a double indictment, to wit, depriving the Irish language of her sole right to express the innermost Irish mind, and

21. "Notes," *ACS*, 10 June 1899.
22. "Notes," *ACS*, 24 June 1899.
23. Eoin Mac Néill ("Mac Léighinn"), "A Vindication of Ancient Irish Culture," review of *Bards of the Gael and Gall* by George Sigerson, *IG* 8, no. 89 (September 1897): 81.
24. *ACS*, 26 September 1899.

secondly, investing the Anglo-Irish language with a literary dignity it
has never hitherto possessed."[25]

We are a long way from bog-trotting philistinism here. If anything,
many Gaels had an acute sense of the beauty of Anglo-Irish literature
and were more likely to be dazzled by the achievements of their contemporaries than blind to their artistic triumphs. Indeed, in 1908 Pearse
could go so far as to say: "We are loathe to say it, but it is the plain
truth, and it is no help to hide the truth. Most of the beautiful, profound thoughts being expressed amongst the Irish today are being expressed in English."[26] As we will see, Yeats and other Anglo-Irish
writers—with the glaring exception of Synge—usually received fair
play or better from the Gaels as artists, if not as fully and authentically
Irish artists.[27]

25. Letter, quoted by Lady Gregory in *Seventy Years: Being an Autobiography of Lady
Gregory*, ed. Colin Smythe (Gerrards Cross: Colin Smythe, 1974), 402.

26. "Sgríbhneoirí" (Writers), *ACS*, 1 February 1908. "Is beag linn é rádh, ach 'sí an
fhírinne lom í agus ní cabhair an fhírinne a cheilt, gurab i mBéarla nochtuightear bunáite
dá bhfuil dá nochtughadh de smaointibh áilne doimhne i measg Gaedheal indiu." Two
years previously, Mícheál Ó Brasaire had written in *IG*: "We often speak of the intellectual vigor found throughout Ireland today. But take my word for it that it is the intellect
of the Anglo-Irish, and that the intellect of the true Gaels is as yet a dull and lifeless
thing." (Is minic sinn ag trácht ar bhrigh intlidheachta an lae indiu ar fuaid na hÉireann;
acht tuigidh uaim-se gur intlidheacht na nGall-Gaedheal í, agus go bhfuil an intlidheacht
sin na bhfíor-Ghaedheal 'n-a spreas gan borradh gan bíodhgadh fós.) See "Éirghidh, a
Ghiollaí Leisceamhla!" (Wake up, lazy lads!), *IG* 16, no. 10 (June 1906): 146.

27. See Pearse's comments in "About Literature," *ACS*, 29 April 1905, where he
wrote: "That Mr. Russell and his confreres ought to cease writing poetry because they do
not know Irish we have, of course, never suggested. As literature we rate their work
high. We regret that it has not been done in Irish, that it might be altogether ours. But we
prefer that it should be done in English than that it should remain undone." While Douglas Hyde lived up to William P. Ryan's characterization of him as "tolerance personified"
by never actively entering this debate, in his preface to his early collection of poems *Úbhla
de'n Chraoibh* (Apples from the branch), he quietly took a stand much like that of Pearse
above:

> I would prefer to produce one sweet stanza in the language I am now writing than to
> compose a full book of verse in English. For if there were any value in my English
> verse, the profit of it would not go to my mother, Ireland, but to my stepmother,
> England.

(B'fhearr liom aon rann binn amháin do thabhairt uaim ann san teangaidh atá mé d'á
sgríobh anois, ná lán leabhair de bhéarsuigheacht do chumadh ann san mBéarla. Óir
dá mbeidheadh aon mhaith ann mo bhéarsuigheacht Béarla, ní do mo mháthair Éire
do rachadh sé i dtairbhe, ach do mo leas-mháthair Sacsana.)
See "Roimhrádh" (Preface) to *Úbhla de'n Chraoibh* (Dublin: M. H. Gill and Son, 1900), v.
Typical of Hyde's diplomatic approach to the public discussion of Anglo-Irish literature
are his comments in the course of a speech on intermediate education: "Anglo-Irish literature, which would at least have the merit of interesting our people in themselves is ig-

Such warm openness toward Irish writers of English was even more evident amongst articulate and influential members of the London Gaelic League than it was among their counterparts in Dublin.[28] The positive response of people like William P. Ryan, P. S. Ua hÉigeartaigh (P. S. O'Hegarty), and Robert Lynd no doubt had its origins in many factors besides cultivated personal taste, chief amongst them direct involvement in the polyglot literary scene of the imperial capital, the exile's sharpened appreciation of the distinctively Irish quality of much Irish writing whatever its linguistic medium, and a simple national pride in the recognition accorded their countrymen by the English literary establishment.

The critical independence of the Londoners was most notably apparent, as we will see below, in their friendly interest in George Bernard Shaw, in their consistent support for the Abbey Theatre, whose company was received with informed enthusiasm on its regular visits to England, and most strikingly in their fair and generous response to the work of Synge, including *The Playboy of the Western World*. At times this independence led at least Lynd and Ua hÉigeartaigh perilously close to heresy in their deviation from accepted Gaelic opinion. For example, in a review of new verse collections by Padraic Colum and Joseph Campbell in the London League's official organ *Inis Fáil* in 1908, Lynd asserted: "The fact that they are written in English ought not to chill the enthusiasm of the welcome we on our part give them. They are Irish of the Irish in their music and in their moods. They are essentially the result of the awakening of the Irish national spirit just as are the stories of Pádraic Ó Conaire or the historical studies of Conán Maol."[29] Three years later, having conceded that Ireland could never produce "a great national literature" in English, Lynd claimed of Colum and Yeats: "They write about Ireland and for Ireland, and the fact that they write in English does not make their work unnational any more than a Gaelic League propagandist speech in English is unnational. . . . We must have literature, whether we speak Irish or not."[30]

---

nored." See "The Intermediate System / The Mansion House Meeting / Speech of Dr. Douglas Hyde," *ACS*, 4 February 1911.

28. London leaguers did, however, applaud Father Michael Moloney for a lengthy address in which, among many other things, he said: "Anglo-Irish literature is, at best, but a province of English. . . . Anglo-Irish literature is a narrow region of stunted productions; the wild Celtic genius does not take kindly to that soil." See "The London Gaelic League / Fine Address by Father Moloney," *ACS*, 13 October 1900.

29. R. Ua F., "Two Poets," review of *Wild Earth* by Padraic Colum and *The Gilly of Christ* by Seosamh Mac Cathmhaoil, *Inis Fáil*, January 1908, 6–7.

30. "Muskerryism / A Note on National Criticism," *An t-Éireannach*, September 1910, 4. Lynd was, however, more orthodox in his insistence that that literature be "national"

In both London and Dublin, the appreciation of the aesthetic excellences of Anglo-Irish writing often led to a willingness to see its creators as allies, rather than foes, in the struggle to forge a new national identity in literature. Such was certainly the view of Douglas Hyde, who of course came forward as one of the original "guarantors" of the Irish Literary Theatre and remained a lifelong friend of Yeats and Lady Gregory. It was, however, an older and wiser Pearse who gave clearest expression to this more open attitude in a personal letter to Lady Gregory: "I have been trying in *An Claidheamh Soluis* to promote a closer comradeship between the Gaelic League and the Irish National Theatre and Anglo-Irish writers generally. After all we are all allies."[31] More important, he was to express this same idea in print, writing in April 1905: "We recognise in the Irish National Theatre, so long as it is true to its best instincts, not a danger to, but an ally of, the language movement."[32] But again, this idea was not a new one. In January 1899 William Rooney, a popular and zealous nationalist and student of the language, urged members of Dublin's Celtic Literary Society, of which he was president, to offer Anglo-Irish writers a role in the Revival: "It is a narrow view, considering the circumstances, to say that all effort must be concentrated in purely Gaelic channels. It means that men who otherwise might do good, men with sympathies wholly Irish, are to be shut off from all participation in the uprise of the nation because fortune did not favour them with a Gaelic mother, and consequently they cannot reach above mediocrity in the language of their own land."[33] He

---

in spirit if not in language: "It is more important just now that we should encourage middling literature in a really Irish vein than that we should praise better technical work conceived in an English or an Anglo-Irish spirit. Not that we love literature less, but that we love nationality more, believing, moreover, that a healthy nationality is the only possible basis of any widespread and permanent literary or artistic movement." See "A Plea for Extremists," *Uladh: A Literary and Critical Magazine* 1, no. 4 (September 1905): 16.

31. "To Lady Gregory," 29 April 1905, *The Letters of P. H. Pearse*, ed. Ó Buachalla, 94. That Pearse was not merely flattering the influential Lady Gregory is shown in a letter to Séamus Ó Dubhghaill written when he was canvasing support for his candidacy for the editorship of *ACS*. Pearse included among his detailed suggestions for editorial changes: "Each issue would contain at least one literary article in English, dealing with some phase of Irish Ireland. These should be written by the best English writers at the disposal of the League. Such names as Lady Gregory, Stephen Gwynn, W.P. Ryan, Edward Martyn, W.B. Yeats, F.A. Fahy, Miss Hull and hosts of others occur to me." See "To J.J. Doyle," 27 February 1903, *Letters*, 71–72.

32. "About Literature," *ACS*, 22 April 1905. In light of subsequent controversies, his reservation may sound ominous; it need not have done so at the time it was published.

33. "A Recent Irish Literature," in *The Prose Writings of William Rooney* (Dublin: M. H. Gill and Son, 1909), 68.

again espoused this view in December of the same year in the *United Irishman*, a paper whose editorial position was always favorable to what Griffith called "Irish-Beurla" literature.[34] Writing as "Shel Martin," Rooney posed the question "Is There an Anglo-Irish Literature?" and answered in the affirmative, although he did add that "the truest and best Irish literature must seek expression in the Irish language."[35]

Six months later, one Anglo-Irish writer, the future Abbey playwright Thomas C. Murray, suggested in general terms what that role might be: "To my mind, at least, the literary renaissance is a tributary, not a negative current to the broad stream of the Gaelic revival. . . . The fact is, there is a great dividing gulf between Anglicisation pure and simple and the propaganda of the Gaelic League. The natural bridge between them is the literary movement."[36] An tAthair Peadar felt that one nineteenth-century Anglo-Irish writer, Thomas Davis, had attempted just such a mediation: "He understood that it was best to make use of English until Irish could be employed, to make a sort of bridge out of English so that one could go over to Irish."[37] Ua Laoghaire was not, however, impressed with the use subsequent Anglo-Irish poets had made of Davis's bridge: "They stayed standing on the bridge. They were neither here nor there. They made songs. They weren't English songs and they weren't Irish songs. They were no use at all."[38] In fact, Ua Laoghaire came to believe that the changed circumstances created

34. For example, *UI* agreed with Murray and MacManus in their respective debates with *ACS*, with Griffith in 1903 calling the view that Irish national literature must be in Irish "this erratic view," and declaring the term "Anglo-Irish" "offensive as well as erroneous." He preferred "Irish-Beurla literature." See "All Ireland," *UI*, 1 July 1899; and "All Ireland," *UI*, 17 January 1903. Rooney was probably the author of the former piece; Griffith doubtless of the latter. In 1901 the regular *UI* contributor "Cuguan" wrote: "To understand Irish is very good—to understand that you are an Irishman is better." See "Irish Books," *UI*, 20 July 1901.

35. *UI*, 26 August 1899.

36. Letter, *ACS*, 15 July 1899.

37. "An Drochad" (The bridge), in *Sgothbhualadh*, 146. "Thuig sé gur bh'fhearr úsáid a dhéanamh de'n Bhéarla go dtí go bhféadfaí an Ghaeluinn do shaothrú; sórd drochaid a dhéanamh de'n Bhéarla i dtreó go bhféadfaí dul anonn mar a raibh an Ghaeluinn." Rooney was in agreement with An tAthair Peadar on this point, although he obviously foresaw the voyage as a longer one than did Ua Laoghaire: "I do not seek to claim as an end an Anglo-Irish literature. I only point it out as one of the roads, and the surest road, that can be travelled by those long dissociated from Gaelic thought and treasure." See "A Recent Irish Literature," in *Prose Writings*, 70.

38. "Cé Atá Ciontach?" (Who is responsible?) in *Sgothbhualadh*, 148. "D'fhanadar 'n-a seasamh ar an ndrochad. Ní rabhadar thall ná abhus. Dheineadar abhráin. Níorbh' abhráin Bhéarla iad agus níorbh' abhráin Ghaedhealacha iad. Ní raibh aon mhaith thall ná abhus ionta."

by the Gaelic Revival had rendered the bridge itself obsolete: "It is a
foolish thing for people to be imagining in their minds that people can
have *Irish* literature and that literature *in English*. . . . I will tell you
what happens to a thing which people imagine to be English and Irish
at the same time. It turns out in the end to be neither English nor Irish.[39]
    The London Gaels were generally more optimistic. For example,
William P. Ryan, then London correspondent for *An Claidheamh Soluis*,
wrote with a slight shift of metaphor in February 1903: "Some Gaelic
Leaguers hurry a little haughtily past half-way houses, and shake their
heads over those who bide therein. We, on the other hand, believe that
Gaelic Leaguers ought to concern themselves in one way or another
with nearly everything that happens in all the Irelands or half-Irelands.[40]
Nine years later, Robert Lynd drew on similar voyage imagery to make
the same point even more forcefully: "Mr. Yeats and Synge and AE
and the others who have given us literature in English, represent a
movement towards the old high road of national tradition and advance,
as well as our writers in Irish like Padraic O Conaire and Canon
O'Leary."[41]
    Yet if most Gaels were more inclined to see the Anglo-Irish writers
as friends rather than foes in the campaign against Anglicization, there
was never any question that the alliance was one of equals. In December 1899 *Fáinne an Lae* clearly defined the place of Yeats and company
in the battle line: "We must regard our Anglo-Irish writers as skirmishers, as foreign agents, as sappers and miners, but not as our main
force."[42] Six months later, the paper returned to this idea in a comment
on the work of "Fiona Macleod": "The English writings of three or
four neo-Celts do not make up a Celtic movement such as is stirring
the Celtic nations to their very depths. They may be forerunners,
scouts, or what you like. In future ages they may be looked upon as
apostles of the Transition."[43] In fact a contributor to *Fáinne an Lae* had

39. "Tadhg agus Donnchadha," *ACS*, 15 July 1899. An tAthair Peadar provided his
own English translation for this dialogue: "Is amadánta an obair do dhaoínibh bheith 'ghá
cheapadh 'na n-aigne go bhféadfadh daoíne litireacht Ghaodhalach do bheith acu agus an
litireacht san i mBéarla. . . . 'Neósfadsa dhuit cad imthigheann ar an rud a meastar bheith
Gallda agus Gaodhalach i n-aonfheacht, ní bhíonn sé Gallda 'ná Gaodhalach ar ball."
    40. "London Notes," *ACS*, 21 February 1903.
    41. "Literature in Ireland," *An t-Éireannach*, January 1912, 12.
    42. "Notes," *FL*, 30 December 1899.
    43. "Notes," *FL*, 16 June 1900. Compare the views of "Angus Óg": "It should be the
care of those entrusted with the work of rebuilding the national mind of Ireland that
while the work of reviving Gaelic is proceeding, the mind of Anglo-Ireland is fed on
healthy Anglo-Irish literature." Since "Angus Óg" also believed that "a nation's intellectual appetite must be satisfied, and Gaelic literature is not yet equal to the task," he

pondered just the sort of work these scouts and skirmishers could be up and doing. Having reported on a Yeats speech in Gort in which the poet had apologized for his inability to use Irish in his own work, the correspondent outlined how such a well-intentioned master of English could serve the cause: "Why wouldn't he prepare material for translation into Irish? . . . There's nothing in the world that Irish needs more than good material for translation. . . . If our English speakers and our Irish-speakers cooperated, we could establish a fine literature."[44] The project never materialized. Another intriguing proposal never implemented was advanced in *The Leader* by W. T Stead ("Chanel") to insure that foot soldiers for the Revival showed proper initiative and loyalty to the cause they were being allowed to serve: "I suggest that future Anglo-Irish poets should be compelled to append to each lyric, as a guarantee of good faith, a certificate stating what part of O'Growney they have arrived at, e.g., "A Sonnet to Leonora" (guttural aspiration). 'The Rejected Lover's Complaint' (eclipsis). We would thus be enabled to gauge accurately the fervour of the lyrist's enthusiasm for the Gaelic language."[45]

In effect, the Gaels expected Anglo-Irish writers to hasten the extinction of their own literary species, an outcome that was at any rate seen as inevitable in the cultural evolution of the nation. For most Gaelic intellectuals, however broad-minded, the Anglo-Irish "renaissance" was, in Pearse's phrase, "a movement of defeat"[46] that would wither to irrelevance with the coming "de-Anglicisation" of Ireland. In June 1900, *Fáinne an Lae* prophesied: "Anglo-Irish literature must and will

---

obviously doubted the imminence of the "Transition." See "Angus Óg," "An Anglo-Irish Library," *SF*, 30 December 1911.

One Anglo-Irish writer who was quick to accept this subordinate role was Edward Martyn, who wrote to *ACS* in July 1900: "For what is the modern Irish literary movement in the English language but a preparation for the grand movement in the Irish language that is to follow. We, the forerunners, have the spirit and sentiment, but as yet not the language of the Celt. . . . We are determined to pursue our course, thus paving the way for the great genius of the future, who, if we are faithful, will surely come, like a Goethe, to shed world-wide glory on our rescued Irish speech." See letter, *ACS*, 14 July 1900. At this same time Martyn also produced a propaganda pamphlet for the league entitled *Ireland's Battle for Her Language*.

44. "Dubhghlas de híde san Iarthar" (Douglas Hyde in the West), *FL*, 5 August 1899. "Ca chuige ná déanfadh sé ádhbhar aistí i gcomhair a n-aistrighthe go Gaedhilg d'ullamhughadh. . . . Ní'l rud ar domhan is mó theastuigheas ó'n nGaedhilg ná ádhbhar maith chum aistrighthe. . . . Dá gcuirfeadh ár mBéarlóirí Éireannacha agus ár nGaedhilgeoirí le chéile, is breágh an litridheacht do chuirfidís ar bun."

45. "Gaelicophile Poetry and Two New Poets," review of *Through the Ivory Gate* by Thomas MacDonagh and *Lays of the Moy* by Gerald Griffin, *The Leader*, 31 January 1903.

46. "A Movement of Defeat," *ACS*, 6 February 1904.

suffer in this time of transition. Our poets and prose writers feel that they are something which is only half the real thing. They stand aside and await the coming of the Gaelic school."[47] As we saw in Chapter 4, William P. Ryan in 1902 identified Lady Gregory as one sincere and patriotic Anglo-Irish writer who would soon have to make this sacrifice, when her *Cuchulain of Muirthemne* became no more than "a specimen of the contrivances that served a useful purpose as Ireland returned from the desert."[48]

Irish-Ireland has, of course, stayed in the desert a bit longer than the ten or twenty years Ryan forecast, but a 1914 *An Claidheamh Soluis* editorial makes clear that more than a decade after his prophecy Gaels continued to share his belief that history was with them: "The 'Imperial' literature produced in Ireland is already in decay. Pegeen Mike, no less than Mickey Free, is already a withered wretch, but Deirdre, Sétanta, Gráinne, Brighdín Bhéasach, Sighle Ní Ghadhra, they are for ever."[49] Nor could cultural orthodoxy and nationalist fervor win redemptive exemption; even the most committed and politically correct writing in English was ultimately doomed to irrelevance, as one "Mac an Chuill" acknowledged in *The Leader*: "Anglo-Irish plays, Anglo-Irish literature, an Anglo-Irish review like the *Leader*, are but transitory things doing their little work of the day, and will be lost and forgotten when Ireland realises herself and ceases to be West British."[50] Fortunately, however, *Fáinne an Lae* had an assignment to keep these redundant literati gainfully occupied in the future: "When our Gaelic literature has reached maturity . . . the question of a new Anglo-Irish school of writers may well come up for discussion. But its task will not be then to create an 'Irish' literature in English, with a 'Gaelic flavour,' but to interpret the new thoughts and conceptions evolved from the heart of the Gaelic race to an outside world through the medium of a *lingua franca* inferior in power and subtlety, but more widely disseminated."[51]

It was, of course, the assertion by Yeats and his colleagues, through

47. "Notes," *FL*, 23 June 1900.
48. "Kiltartan, Mr. Yeats and Cúchulain," review of *Cuchulain of Muirthemne* by Lady Gregory, *The Leader*, 5 July 1902.
49. "Ancestor Worship," editorial, *ACS*, 18 April 1914.
50. "An Irish Play and an English Afterpiece," *The Leader*, 2 November 1901. For more of the same, see Séamas Ó Conghaile, "Nationality in Drama," *SF*, 23 January 1909; and "Ros Fáilghe," "Anglo-Ireland," *SF*, 19 October 1912. "Ros Fáilghe" was gracious in anticipated victory: "Not without poignant regret does one admit the utter impossibility of Anglo-Ireland continuing to exist."
51. "Notes," *FL*, 23 June 1900.

the foundation of the Irish Literary Theatre and later the Abbey, that that lingua franca was a valid medium for the creation of a self-consciously Irish literature that first focused the hostile attention of revivalists on contemporary Anglo-Irish writers. Yet, paradoxically, all of the leading figures in the Anglo-Irish dramatic movement that culminated in the Abbey claimed a commitment to the creation of a modern drama in Irish, and several of them, most notably Lady Gregory, Edward Martyn, and the Brothers Fay, backed up that claim with concrete contributions, both financial and artistic.[52] In his early days as a drama critic for the United Irishman, Frank Fay's pronouncements would have satisfied the most ideologically rigorous Gaelic partisan. For example, in May 1901 he proclaimed: "An Irish Theatre must, of course, express itself solely in the Irish language; otherwise it would have no raison d'etre."[53] His brother Willie acted to make such a theater possible, by directing, despite his own lack of proficiency in Irish, Mac Fhionnlaoich's Eilís agus an Bhean Déirce for Maud Gonne's Inghinidhe na hÉireann in August 1901; Casadh an tSúgáin for the Literary Theatre in October of that year; and Dinneen's An Tobar Draoidheachta for the league's Keating Branch in November 1902.[54] Moreover, Willie played a leading role, as did George Moore, in organizing the league's first traveling company to take Gaelic theater to the provinces, staging Dinneen's play in Killarney and Tralee before its opening in the capital. In later years Synge and Martyn both argued persuasively for the formation of such itinerant Gaelic companies, a project that remained for years a frustratingly unfulfilled dream.[55]

52. Yeats also took an early interest in the possibilities of Gaelic drama. For example, in a speech to the Árd-Chraobh of the league he advised Gaelic playwrights to keep their plays short and simple and to focus on "the treasures of the Irish language." See "Central Branch Sgóruidheacht / Address by Mr. W. B. Yeats," ACS, 27 October 1900. Ten years later the poet addressed the Árd-Chraobh on "The Theatre and Ireland." See "A Lecture by Mr. Yeats," ACS, 5 March 1910.

53. "Mr. Yeats and the Stage," in Towards a National Theatre: The Dramatic Criticism of Frank J. Fay, ed. Robert Hogan (Dublin: Dolmen, 1970), 50.

54. Fay discusses these activities in W. G. Fay and Catherine Carswell, The Fays of the Abbey Theatre: An Autobiographical Record (New York: Harcourt, Brace, 1935), 113–15. Robert Hogan and James Kilroy discuss the roles of Moore and Fay in the production in The Irish Literary Theatre, 1899–1901, vol. 1 of The Modern Irish Drama: A Documentary History) (Dublin: Dolmen, 1975), 92–95. One of the actors, under the pen name "Duine Acu" (One of them), has left an amusing account of the rehearsals under both Fay and Moore in "Casadh an tSúgáin," Banba 1, no. 1 (December 1901): 7–8.

55. Martyn's ideas, outlined in a letter to the editor of the Freeman's Journal published on 26 April 1907 provoked considerable discussion, almost all of it in favor of the scheme. See, for example, "I bhFochair na nGaedheal," WF, 4 May 1907; and P., "An tArdán Maol" (The bare stage), UI, 28 December 1907. Martyn did actually sponsor a brief

Such generous openness was, moreoever, reciprocated from the Gaelic side. Drama was not an indigenous Gaelic genre, although several intriguing fragments survive from the nineteenth century. One of these, "Dúnlaing Óg agus a Leannán Sidhe," a dialogue set on the eve of the Battle of Clontarf and said to have been "enacted among the people up to sixty or seventy years ago" was staged in 1915;[56] three others were collected from the oral narration of Tadhg Ó Conchubhair of Lispole, Co. Kerry by Fionán Mac Coluim ("Finghín na Leamhna") and published in An Lóchrann. Of the three—"Caismirt na gCearc" (The battle of the hens),[57] "An Dá Dhrúncaer" (The two drunkards),[58] and "Bruighean an Bhacaigh le Cáit" (The quarrel of the beggar with Cáit)[59]—the first two are attributed to Muiris Ó Gríbhghín, "who lived in Gleann na Mínáirde over eighty years ago" (do mhair i nGleann na Mínáirde os cionn cheithre fichid bliain ó shoin). All three of these little skits involve multiple characters and actual simple stage directions.

However suggestive, these fragments did not, however, constitute anything even remotely resembling a theatrical tradition, and so the creation of an Irish-language theater would demand flexibility in the search for models. Predictably revivalists conducted a vigorous debate over just what those models should be. For the nativists, the truest and safest exemplars were implicit in the Gaelic tradition, in the inherently dramatic quality of the Ossianic dialogues between St. Patrick and Oisín whose most important compilation is the twelfth-century Acallamh na Senórach (Colloquy of the ancients), and in the histrionic recitational style of the seanchaí, whose repertoire was, moreover, certain to include modern versions of the Ossianic material. But others, including some nativists, felt that models of considerably greater aesthetic sophis-

---

theatrical tour of the Connacht Gaeltacht in the summer of 1912. See "Cluada Cheabhsa," "Sgéal ón Iarthar" (News from the West), ACS, 27 July 1912.

56. This information is from the program for the performance at the Hardwicke Street Irish Theatre in May 1915 in the collection of the Pearse Museum at Sgoil Éanna, Rathfarnham. Tadhg Ó Donnchadha claimed that the fragment was believed to be "at least 300 years old" (trí chéad bliadhain d'aois ar a laighead), and ACS proclaimed that its existence "disproved . . . the accepted statement that native Irish literature had never evolved a drama." See Ó Donnchadha, "Sean-Dráma Gaedhilge" (An old Gaelic drama), ACS, 22 May 1915; "The St. Enda's Plays," ACS, 22 May 1915; and Hogan, Burnham, and Poteet, The Rise of the Realists, 397.

57. An Lóchrann 3, no. 1 (December 1909)–3, no. 2 (January 1910).

58. An Lóchrann, April–August 1918.

59. An Lóchrann, November–December 1918. The composer of this piece is not named, but the informant, Tadhg Ó Conchubhair, told Mac Coluim that he once knew much more of it (a lán eile dhe), but that he had forgotten it, having first learned it more than sixty years before (An Lóchrann, December 1918, 7).

tication and cultural relevance lay to hand in the work of their country-men who wrote in English. Their conviction seems to have been borne out by the fact that the first three Gaelic plays—as distinct from tab-leaux vivants or scenes like O'Carroll's Brian Bóroimhe material writ-ten purely as literary exercises—were translations of Anglo-Irish works: [60] Eoghan Ó Neachtain's unperformed version of Dion Boucicault's *The Colleen Bawn* in 1895;[61] Pádraic Ó Beirne's "Saint Patrick at Tara" scene from O'Growney's *The Passing of Conall* in 1898;[62] and Micheál Mhag Ruaidhrí's rendering of John Cannon's farcical sketch *The Dentist* in the same year.

Gaelic interest in and support for the new Anglo-Irish drama move-ment also found expression in the generally positive coverage of its growth in the Gaelic press. Thus in January 1900 *Fáinne an Lae* wel-comed the upcoming productions of the Irish Literary Theatre—all in English—and warmly embraced the group as an ally in the Irish-Ireland cause: "We heartily wish success to the Society, not so much for what they have done, or even for what they are now doing, but for the manifest intention they have to struggle against being foreigners in their own country."[63] Of course, revivalists felt the finest proof of this noble intention would be the production of a play in Irish, but an awareness of the difficulty involved caused them to approach even this cherished ambition with a rather startling diffidence. For example, after the furor over *The Countess Cathleen* had subsided, *Fáinne an Lae* editorialized: "But now that there is a lull in the storm I may be permitted to regret that this attempt to create a new theatre was not assisted by some little

60. In his brief introduction to the first of Fr. O'Carroll's "Amharca Cleasacha / Dramatic Scenes," David Comyn tantalizingly stated: "Its true beginnings have already been made by some good translations of portions of English drama." See *IG* 1, no. 1 (November 1882): 18. None of these seem, however, to have survived.

61. In his reliable *Taighde i gComhair Stair Litridheachta*, Ó Droighneáin calls Ó Neach-tain's work "the first translation of a play into Irish" (an chéad aistriú go Gaedhilg ar dhráma) (93). Unfortunately I have been unable to find a copy of this edition of the *Pilot* in either Dublin or Galway.

62. There has been some confusion about both the author and translator of this work. The scene was published in *WF* on 10 December 1898, with the translator given as Patrick O'Byrne and the following note: "The drama has been written by a celebrated student of Irish history, and a prominent member of the Gaelic League, who desires to have his identity concealed." Alice Milligan, who was chiefly responsible for the performance of the scene in Belfast and Derry following its initial production at Aonach Thír-Chonaill, identified O'Growney as the author of the play and Ó Beirne as the translator of the scene in a letter to *ACS* published on 30 August 1913. See also her 21 January 1899 letter to the *Daily Express*, quoted by Hogan and Kilroy, *The Irish Literary Theatre*, 52–54.

63. "Notes," *FL*, 27 January 1900.

essay in Gaelic. Not a long play, of course, but some little thing—a
sketch, say, just to see how people would take the novelty."[64] All was,
however, changed utterly by the stirringly successful production of *Casadh an tSúgáin*, a triumph that led to a greater, indeed excessive, confidence on the part of some enthusiasts, among them the critic for *An
Claidheamh Soluis*. Having commented favorably on the Yeats–Moore
collaboration *Diarmuid and Grania*, he lavished praise on Hyde's play,
concluding with the assertion that Gaelic drama was now the wave of
the future, and "the Gaelic drama will drive the English drama out of
the country, and the Irish-speakers will control the Irish stage. We
think English will be driven from the stage entirely within a few more
years."[65]

Whatever can be said for the loyalty of a person willing to jettison his
erstwhile allies with such unseemly haste, he was no prophet. In fact,
instead of driving Anglo-Irish plays from the public stage, the Gaelic
drama was itself soon to be exiled to the Rotunda, the Antient Concert
Rooms, and, even more frequently, to obscure parish halls in both
Dublin and the provinces. As the Anglo-Irish playwrights, directors,
and actors perfected their art with growing sophistication, the gap between them and their Gaelic counterparts yawned ever wider. The reasons were not far to seek, nor were they unknown to even the most
ardent theatrical revivalist. Quite simply, there were no Gaelic plays,
no Gaelic actors, and no Gaelic audiences. Even Bernard Doyle, the
publisher of *Fáinne an Lae*, could but ruefully agree with George
Moore's assessment that while a Gaelic play was an absolute cultural
imperative, few in any theater would actually be able to understand
one. Having noted the keen interest his dog took in human conversation, Doyle continued: "Most of us at the Gaelic play will be in the
position of the retriever. We will be dying to understand what is going
forward, and will be most anxious to impress our neighbors with the
intelligent interest we are taking in the performance. Yet we will be
able to do no more than listen for some familiar word so that we may
be able to wag our tails with effusion." Doyle suggested that he and his
fellow retrievers be provided with a translation to take with them so
that they might "wag their heads, as well as their tails, wisely, if not
intelligently."[66]

---

64. "Notes," *FL*, 20 May 1899.
65. "*Casadh an tSúgáin*," *ACS*, 26 October 1901. "Buailfidh an dráma Gaedhealach an
ceann Sasanach amach as an tír, agus beidh stáitse na hÉireann ag na Gaedhilgeoiribh.
Díbreofar is dóigh liom an Béarla de'n stáitse go léir i gceann beagán bliadhanta eile."
66. "Notes," *FL*, 17 March 1900. Not all revivalists were so pessimistic. *ACS* com-

While Doyle's own ignorance of the language undoubtedly caused him to overstate his case, comments on the linguistic competence of the audience were a regular feature of Gaelic drama criticism in the first decade of this century. When the "Saint Patrick at Tara" scene was performed in Derry in April 1899, readers of *Fáinne an Lae* were informed that "the audience thoroughly enjoyed the piece, though it was presented in a vernacular foreign to probably most of them."[67] The situation was not necessarily better in the south. When Dinneen's *An Tobar Draoidheachta* was staged in Dunmanway, Co. Cork, in May 1902, a local critic for *An Muimhneach Óg* pronounced the acting "first-class" and asserted that the play was "generally enjoyed even by people who did not understand a word of Irish."[68] Peadar Mac Fhionnlaoich, a Belfast production of whose *Eilís agus an Bhean Déirce* was apparently a success, although "the audience, as a whole, could not follow the work,"[69] was aware of the problem, and his sensitivity to the limitations of Gaelic playgoers was praised by one critic, who wrote of his 1902 *Miondrámanna* (Little plays): "The plots are, of course, quite simple, so that the pieces may be easily staged, and in fact easily followed by an audience which consists mainly of learners."[70] When an audience consisted of something other than learners, the fact merited comment. *An Claidheamh Soluis* reported of a production of *Casadh an tSúgáin* in Ballaghadereen, Co. Roscommon, that "the best thing is that many who were present understood Irish."[71] This problem was to persist, and while the nucleus of a Gaelic audience was slowly coalescing in the first fifteen years of this century, few revivalists would have faulted Padraic Colum's sympathetic assessment of the situation in 1910: "For a long time there will be, in the general audience for Irish plays, many who do not know the language, or know it imperfectly, many who, in Mark Twain's phrase, "average it up." A play depending on subtility of char-

---

mented that Moore "evidently spoke in complete ignorance of the extent to which the Irish language movement has taken hold in the city of Dublin, and in the suburbs." See "Glimmerings of the Dawn," editorial, *ACS*, 3 March 1900.

67. "Gaelic Dramatic Performance in Derry," *FL*, 15 April 1899.

68. "Thall is i bhFus," *An Muimhneach Óg: Irisleabhar Míosamhail chun Cabrughadh leis an Dream atá d'Iaraidh Éire Dhéanamh Gaedhealach* (The young Munsterman: A monthly journal to aid those who are trying to Gaelicize Ireland) 1, no. 2 (June 1903): 5.

69. "Ulster Notes," *ACS*, 10 November 1900.

70. "Leabhra Nua" (New books), *ACS*, 7 February 1903.

71. "Gaedhilgeoir," " 'Casadh an tSúgáin' agus Cuirm Cheoil Ghaedhealach i mBealach-a'-Doirín" ("Casadh an tSúgáin" and a Gaelic concert in Ballaghaderreen), *ACS*, 22 February 1902. "An chuid is fearr de bhí tuigsint ar Ghaedhilg ag a lán d'á raibh i láthair."

acterisation and refinement of nature could not be a success with such an audience."[72]

Linguistic competence was, of course, even more essential on the other side of the footlights. Again, the Gaels were painfully aware of the challenge confronting them here. Welcoming the news that the directors of the Literary Theatre planned to produce a play in Irish, *Fáinne an Lae* urged them not to lose heart in face of the obstacles, particularly the major one: "Where will they find enough Irish speakers who know how to act and who can spend time together practicing their acting and rehearsing?"[73] This question was to be posed with distressing frequency in the early years of the Gaelic dramatic movement, and the answer was to remain maddeningly elusive. In 1904 one "Ardánach" reminded those interested in staging a play in Irish that it was absolutely essential that the director know the language well, but then continued stoically: "It does great damage to the Gaelic drama to put people on stage who don't have an idea in the world what the words they say mean. It's difficult to find suitable people everywhere, and it's likely that we will have to put up with what we now have until we get something better."[74] A similar resignation is evident in the February 1903 *An Claidheamh Soluis* review of the league's most ambitious theatrical undertaking to that date, the production of four original plays at the Rotunda. The critic judged the evening a success, but acknowledged that "of course there were slips here and there, both in the acting and in the pronunciation of Irish."[75] When the actors were fluent in the language, as in the Ballaghadereen production of *Casadh an tSúgáin*, the achievement was noted with pride: "They had Irish as fluent and natural as if they had been speaking it from the cradle."[76] With this background in mind, the Oireachtas Committee was by no means belaboring the obvious when it insisted in 1907 that "it is a *sine qua non* that the principal parts in any

72. "Some Notes on Dramatic Method," *ACS*, 27 August 1910.

73. "An Theatre Éireannach" (The Irish theatre), *FL*, 3 March 1900. "Cá bhfuighid siad Gaedhilgeoirí a ndóthain a bheas eolgach ar ghníomhthóireacht agus a fhéadfas a n-aimsir do chaitheamh i dteannta a chéile ag déanamh taithighe agus roimh-aithris ar a ngníomhthóireacht?"

74. "Árdánach," "Árdán na Gaedhilge" (The Irish language stage), *IG* 13, no. 151 (April 1903): 272. "Is mór an díoghbháil i n-aghaidh dráma na Gaedhilge, daoine do chur ar an árdán agus ná feadair siad ó thalamh an domhain cad é an bhrigh atá leis an méid cainte adeirid. Is deacair daoine oireamhnacha d'fhaghái l ins gach aon áit, agus is dócha go gcaithfimíd cur suas leis an earra atá againn go dtí go bhfuighmíd ceann níos fearr."

75. "Notes," *ACS*, 21 February 1903.

76. "Gaedhilgeoir," "Casadh an tSúgáin," *ACS*, 22 February 1902. "Bhí an Ghaedhilg chomh blasta agus chomh nádúrtha aca agus dá mbeidís d'á labhairt ó bhíodar 'sa chliabhán."

play adopted shall be filled by competent Irish speakers."[77] Seven years later, Tadhg Ó Donnchadha suggested even stricter standards, since "the best play that could be written would be destroyed unless those staging it were native Irish speakers." Ó Donnchadha's patience seems to have been wearing thin: "If one goes to hear a drama there [in Dublin], half of what is said cannot be heard or understood. There are traces of English on the speech . . . so that any Irish-speaker who goes there is disgusted."[78]

The ability to pronounce the language in which a play is written is obviously a minimal qualification for an actor. To make things worse, in the case of Irish those best situated to acquire a mastery of the language were precisely those worst situated to see, much less learn, the art of the stage. Thus it is hardly surprising that early critics of Gaelic performances focused almost exclusively on the good intentions of those involved, as did John Boland in his review of a Kerry production of Dinneen's *Creideamh agus Gorta*:

> To the performance as a whole the highest praise can be given. The actors were practically word-perfect, and the services of the prompter were but little required. Defects due to inexperience of stage management were evident, such as the tendency to over-hurried delivery, with the consequent loss of accentuation; whilst a natural feeling of shyness caused the impersonators of the female characters to deliver their lines more to the back of the stage than to the audience. But these are obvious defects which a little experience will easily remedy.[79]

Boland was, perhaps, a bit too optimistic, nor were the "obvious defects" limited to the hinterlands. In a July 1906 *An Claidheamh Soluis* editorial, Pearse confessed: "Bluntly, we have hitherto got very little acting in Irish that has risen above the painfully mediocre. . . . Two things are wrong. The first thing is that most of those who have essayed the actor's art in Irish do not know how to speak. They can only

77. "The Oireachtas Committee," *ACS*, 5 January 1907.
78. "Dráma na Gaedhilge" (Irish language drama), *ACS*, 6 June 1914. "An cluiche is fearr do bfhéidir a scríobhadh do loitfidhe é mura mbeadh an Ghaedhilg ó dhúthchas ag lucht a léirighthe. . . . Má théightear ag éisteacht le dráma ann [i mBaile Átha Cliath], ní féidir a leath dá n-abarthar a chloisint ná a thuigsint. Bíonn blas an Bhéarla ar an gcainnt . . . i dtreo go mbíonn déistean ar aon Ghaedhilgeoir a théigheann ann."
79. John P. Boland, M.P., " 'Creideamh agus Gorta' at Glenbeigh," *ACS*, 8 February 1902.

talk. The second is that they . . . or perhaps those responsible for their training are enslaved by English conventions and mannerisms."[80]

In a series of reviews and leaders throughout 1906 and 1907, Pearse commented at some length on Gaelic stagecraft, praising what excellences he found and suggesting practical steps to improve the more numerous shortcomings. That he understood the magnitude of the challenge is apparent despite the diplomatic tone of his comments welcoming the publication of Tomás Ó Ceallaigh's *An Fóghmhar* in April 1908: "It has dramatic motive and coherency. It has statement, crisis, and catastrophe. It is entirely actable. To do it full justice, indeed, it would require acting of a high order, and we doubt if any body of Irish players we have seen would be altogether equal to it."[81] Piaras Béaslaí also began his long career in Gaelic theater at this time, winning a 1907 *Irisleabhar na Gaedhilge* contest, and in the process inspiring a lively debate, with an essay on "Aistigheacht" (Acting).[82] Perhaps the most striking indication of the magnitude of the problem facing the Gaelic director and actor is the fact that Béaslaí, for all his sound advice, could not save his own first play, *Coramac na Cuile*, from the sins of its time and milieu: "The staging and the acting do not call for much com-

---

80. "Irish Acting," editorial, *ACS*, 7 July 1906. For example, "Duine Aca" says of the rehearsals for *Casadh an tSúgáin*:

> None of us had ever been an actor on a stage before that. And along with that there wasn't a person there that wouldn't have some other business to keep him from the rehearsal for a night or two during the week. We would be missing one person tonight and someone else tomorrow night. . . . But there was no cure for that, since every one of us had his own business to take care of, and acting was not our livelihood.

> (Ní raibh éinne againn 'n-a aisteoir ar ardán riamh roimhe sin. . . . N-a theannta soin, ní raibh duine ann, ná beadh gnó éigint eile gá choimeád ó'n gceacht meabhruighthe, oidhche nó dhó i rith na seachtmhaine. Bheadh duine i n-éagmuis orainn anocht, agus duine eile ist oidhche i mbárach. . . . Ní raibh éin-leigheas air seo, mar bhí a ghnó féin le déanamh ag gach éinne againn, agus níor bh'aisteóracht ba slighe mhaireamhna dhúinne.)

See "Duine Acu," "Casadh an tSúgáin," *Banba* 1, no. 1 (December 1901): 7. On the other hand, Pearse was aware of the potential for a powerful naive authenticity in the acting of such players, writing of the forthcoming visit of the Tawin group from the Galway Gaeltacht: "In kind, the Tawin actors are comparable to no modern actors of which we can think, unless it be the great peasant-actors of Ober Ammergau." See "Gleó na gCath," *ACS*, 14 November 1903.

81. "A 'Claidheamh' Play," review of *An Fóghmhar* by An tAthair Tomás Ó Ceallaigh, *ACS*, 25 April 1908.

82. "Liúdaidhe Óg" [Piaras Béaslaí], "Aistigheacht," *IG* 17, no. 19 (March 1907): 289–92.

ment. Both are bound to be, at present, amateurish in Irish plays."[83]

Gaelic awareness of this inescapable amateurism must have been made particularly galling by contrast. While the Anglo-Irish movement was building a company of superbly gifted professionals to produce a growing repertoire of fine and varied plays in a permanent, subsidized theater under the management of a genius, the Gaels were rehearsing their crude one-acters after work, when and where they could, in preparation for what was usually a one-shot performance in a rented or donated hall. Given these daunting conditions it is understandable that no true Gaelic dramatic companies were organized until 1912. The need was, however, felt from quite early on. In December 1903, *Banba* called for the foundation of a centralized "Gaelic Institute," since "under the existing order of things, no real development of the Irish drama is possible."[84] The following month, one "Diarmuid" urged "the establishment of a society or department or committee under the direct auspices of the Gaelic League for the presentation or performance of plays in Irish," on the grounds that "dramatic talent is a very rare commodity, and it would be quite accidental, therefore, if any one branch contained players sufficient in quantity AND quality to perform a play satisfactorily."[85] Several such temporary or ad hoc groups did arise in individual branches. For example, the league's Munster-dominated Keating Branch, which had provided most of the actors for the Literary Theatre's *Casadh an tSúgáin*, continued to play a leading role in keeping the language on the Dublin stage, even taking the boards at the Abbey with Dinneen's *Creideamh agus Gorta* in October 1905.[86] Five years later, the Abbey hosted another league branch with theatrical ambitions when Craobh Mhic Éil staged William P. Ryan's *An tOide as Tír na nÓg* (The teacher from the Land of the Young) for a "big audience."[87] Also committed to the development of Gaelic drama in the capital was Craobh na gCúig gCúigí, whose years of hard work were apparently paying dividends by 1912: "The players of Craobh na gCúig gCúigí . . . especially the women players, have set themselves the task of learning the art of presenting plays, and they are meeting with considerable success."[88] More in line with the plan advanced by "Diarmuid," the Central

83. "Seán," "Cormac na Coille," *ACS*, 18 May 1907.

84. Untitled notes, *Banba* 2, no. 9 (December 1903): 293. Seán Ua Ceallaigh was editor of *Banba*.

85. "Diarmuid," "Irish Drama," *ACS*, 30 January 1904.

86. See "Cuirm Cheoil na Samhna" (The Samhain concert), *ACS*, 4 November 1905.

87. "An tOide as Tír na nÓg," *ACS*, 19 November 1910.

88. "Irish Players," *ACS*, 11 May 1912.

Branch (Árd-Chraobh) of the league took advantage of its position not only to coordinate theatrical activities in Dublin on a citywide basis, but also, from 1907 on, to form its own company from the various Dublin branches to stage plays at the Oireachtas.[89]

Outside of the league, the most active Gaelic players were the students of Sgoil Éanna, several of whose productions we have already discussed. They not only performed works by Pearse and others at the school, but also at the Hardwicke Street Irish Theatre, and, in 1910, 1911, and 1913, at the Abbey. Their 1911 Abbey performance of Pearse's *An Pháis* was a notable triumph, in the words of Máire Nic Shiubhlaigh "probably the most outstanding Gaelic production seen in Dublin before 1916."[90] Padraic Colum was even more impressed, calling it "in a sense . . . the first serious theatre piece in Irish," and predicting "if its production ever be made an annual event it might create a tradition of acting and dramatic writing in Irish."[91]

Meanwhile, in the eagerness to establish such a tradition efforts were being duplicated and precious talent spread thin, a distressing situation that prompted recurrent calls for the formation of a central, stable troupe that would perform Gaelic plays in Dublin throughout the year, unlike groups such as Cumann na nAisteoirí Náisiúnta (National players society), for whom plays in Irish were undertaken as an occasional patriotic duty, or the short-lived Na Saoirseantóirí, who came together only in the weeks immediately prior to the Oireachtas.[92] Thus

---

89. Pearse found their 1907 debut "amateurish," but added: "The Árd-Chraobh players are steadily improving, and their *blas* [accent] leaves nothing to be desired." See "The Oireachtas / The Story of the Week," *ACS*, 17 August 1907.

90. *The Splendid Years*, 145–46.

91. Editorial, *Irish Review* 1, no. 3 (May 1911): 107–8.

92. Na Saoirseantóirí produced Tomás Ó hAodha's full-length historical drama *Seabhac na Ceathramhan Caoile* at the 1906 Oireachtas. Despite the involvement of actors who were members of the league, the National Players Society was in effect an Anglo-Irish company associated with Maud Gonne's Inghinidhe na hÉireann. It did, however, produce the occasional Gaelic play like Hyde's bilingual farce *Pleusgadh na Bulgóide* in 1903 or *Liúdaidhe Óg na Leargadh Móire* (Seamus MacManus's *The Lad from Largymore*) in 1906 and at the 1907 Oireachtas. Moreover, this was apparently the company Martyn had in mind for his proposed tour of the Gaeltachtaí. See Robert Hogan and James Kilroy, *The Abbey Theatre: The Years of Synge, 1905–1909*, vol. 3 of *A Documentary History of the Modern Irish Drama* (Dublin: Dolmen, 1978), 189–90. Hogan and Kilroy do, however, exaggerate the league's (as opposed to individual leaguers') role in the society, no doubt largely due to a confusion between Cumann na nGaedheal, the political organization that on occasion sponsored the society's plays, and Conradh na Gaedhilge (the Gaelic League). Thus the 1905 Samhain Festival of Cumann na nGaedheal is mistakenly identified as a Gaelic League event in *The Years of Synge* (46). Note how Pearse differentiates the various groups in "Cluicheoireacht Ghaedhealach," *ACS*, 2 March 1907. See note 93. See also

in March 1907, with the *Playboy* row only a month in the past, Pearse praised the technical proficiency of the Abbey company and lamented: "Isn't it a great pity we don't have a troupe of Irish speakers with the opportunity to practice acting from week to week as do the English speakers of the Abbey Theatre? Perhaps if the Theatre of Ireland and the 'National Players' and the people from the Árd-Chraobh and the Keating Branch put their heads together on this question some profit would come of it."[93] The difficulties and frustrations of trying to stage plays with amateur actors working together for only a few weeks were spelled out in 1909 by Séamus Ó Conghaile, whose solution was for the league to form "a Stock Company of Gaelic players" drawn from graduates of the dramatic classes held by various Dublin branches.[94] Nothing came of his scheme, but his call for some coordinated approach to the problem was repeated in an *An Claidheamh Soluis* editorial the following year: "Stage talent is rare, and it is only by uniting all our forces that we can hope to make any progress toward a truly Irish theatre. For this reason we hope that all our Gaelic League dramatic companies in the city will unite immediately after the Oireachtas to form a permanent society of Gaelic actors."[95]

Apparently Seán Ó Caomhánaigh saw little sign of progress in this direction over the years; commenting on the 1912 Oireachtas plays, he wrote: "Until a truly Gaelic theatre is established where we will have plays month after month, little benefit will come from sporadic efforts like these. It is not possible to do justice to a play without trained actors, and it is foolish to expect that from anyone who is not always working with plays. Acting is an art in itself and a difficult one, and it is not in one play or two that it can be learned."[96] Unknown to Ó

"Coming Events," *ACS*, 28 October 1905 for an announcement touting the upcoming dramatic endeavors of Cumann na nGaedheal.

93. "Cluicheoireacht Ghaedhealach" (Irish acting), editorial, *ACS*, 2 March 1907. "Nach mór an truagh é gan buidhean Ghaedhilgeoirí againn agus caoi aca ar chleachtadh a dhéanamh ar an gcluicheoireacht ó sheachtmhain go seachtmhain, mar tá ag Béarlóiribh Amharclainne na Mainistreach? B'fhéidir, dá gcuirfeadh Cluicheoirí na hÉireann, na 'Cluicheoirí Náisiúnta,' agus muinntir na hÁrd-Chraoibhe agus Chraoibh an Chéitinnigh a gcomhairle i gceann a chéile ar an gceist seo, go dtiocfadh tairbhe as."

94. "A School of Irish Acting," *ACS*, 31 July 1909, Uimhir an Oireachtais 1909 (Oireachtas 1909 number).

95. "An tOireachtas," *ACS*, 16 July 1910. See also "A Company of Gaelic Actors," *ACS*, 6 August 1910.

96. "Críochnugh an Oireachtais" (The end of the Oireachtas), *SF*, 13 July 1912. "Go dtí go gcuirtear amharclann fíor-Ghaedhealach ar bun mara mbeidh cluichidhe ó mhí go mí againn is beag toradh a thiocfas de iarrachtaibh taodhmanacha mar seo. Ní féidir a cheart féin a thabhairt do chluiche gan aisteóiridhe oilte, agus is aimideach a shúil sin le

Caomhánaigh, things were, however, happening and happening quickly. Only three months after his complaint Gaels were informed: "A small group of Gaels in the city is about to establish an acting society and they want to get help from members of all branches. What they want is help and advice from people who have acting ability in order to form and to maintain and to strengthen one solid, permanent society for Gaelic acting."[97] This group, Na hAisteoirí, was led by Béaslaí, whose translation of a French play formed part of the inaugural program at league headquarters in Parnell Square in April 1913. Only days after this announcement, Na Cluicheoirí, another serious Gaelic company that had been organized earlier in the year, brought a full evening of drama to the Abbey itself. Largely composed of members of the Árd-Chraobh, Na Cluicheoirí were to have a spectacular year in 1913, with an excursion to Spiddal in the Conamara Gaeltacht in August, and an ambitious return to the Abbey with a full program of Abbey plays in Irish translation.[98] It was, however, Béaslaí's Na hAisteoirí who were to have the greatest inspirational and practical impact on Gaelic drama in both Dublin and the provinces.[99] Indeed, the success of their 1914 production of Béaslaí's *Cluiche Cártaidhe* (A game of cards) in the capital— a production like several by Na Cluicheoirí not bound up with the Oireachtas schedule—actually gave "Pádraig na Léime" the confidence to pay a backhanded tribute to the Abbey, writing: "However excellent

h-aoin'ne ná bíonn i gcómhnaidhe ag gabháil de chluichidhibh. Ealadha innte féin agus ealadha achrannach 'seadh aisteóireacht agus ní i gcluiche ná i dhá gcluiche is féidir í d'fhoghluim."

97. "Beirt Bhan," "Cumann Cluicheoireachta" (An acting society), *ACS*, 12 October 1912. "Tá dream beag Gaedheal sa gCathair ar tí cumann cluichtheoireachta do chur ar bun agus b'áil leo congnamh d'fhagháil ó dhaltaibh na gcraobh uile. Is é rud atá uatha cabhair agus comhairle ó dhaoinibh a bhfuil féith na haisteoireachta ionnta agus aon chumann seasamhach láidir do thabhairt le chéile agus do chothughadh agus do neartughadh le haghaidh aisteoireachta Gaedhilge."

98. "Na Cluicheoirí fá'n dTuaith" (Na Cluicheoirí in the country), *ACS*, 23 August 1913. For a balanced view of the technical and linguistic competence of Na Cluicheoirí, see "Irish Plays at the Abbey," *SF*, 28 February 1914.

99. Relations between the two companies seem to have been strained at best, as Crawford Neil made clear in *Sinn Féin* in November 1913: "Na Cluicheoirí are the living voices of that Gaelic revelation. There is a very strong body of players, Na hAisteoirí, which might well have kept Samhain festival with our friends on Monday night last at the Abbey; but since they consider the existence of Na Cluicheoirí an insult to their well-known competence, their sincere rivalry will be very welcome, not in newspaper comments, but upon the stage." See Neil, "Féile na Samhain [*sic*]," *SF*, 29 November 1913. See also "Crooked Shaun," "Plays in Gaelic," *SF*, 26 April 1913; and the letters from Micheál Ó Foghludha and Béaslaí quoted in "Irish in the Theatre," *SF*, 3 May 1913.

the English-language actors of the Abbey Theatre, it is not likely that they have boasting rights over Na hAisteoirí now."[100]

According to a report on Na hAisteoirí reprinted in *An Claidheamh Soluis* in this same year, "their greatest successes have been in the comparatively unspoiled country places."[101] This opinion seems to be confirmed by the account of their summer tour of Cork and Kerry written by one of the actors themselves. In terms and tone that re-create the atmosphere of the earliest Gaelic productions in rural Irish-speaking communities, "Aisteoir" recalled a performance in Inchigeela in West Cork: "The hall was full, the people crowding each other, the Irish speakers coming in search of entertainment and fun and delight, and they got entertainment and fun and delight. The delight that was in their hearts was to be heard in their laughter. Weren't they pleased with Na hAisteoirí!"[102] Of course the most lasting contribution of Na hAisteoirí was that the group provided the nucleus from which Gearóid Ó Lochlainn formed his An Comhar Drámuidheachta, the company that brought serious Gaelic drama into the Abbey on a regular basis in the early years of the Free State.[103]

One of the major factors contributing to the success of Na hAisteoirí was Béaslaí's talent for creating clever and technically proficient plays. The shortage of stageable vehicles had bedeviled Gaelic producers and actors from the birth of their dramatic movement. Of course there had, quite simply, been no acting scripts in Irish before 1898, and thus a Gaelic repertoire had to be built from nothing. The major impetus for this work came again from local feiseanna and particularly from the Oireachtas. As early as May 1900, the Macroom Feis produced An tAt-

100. "Cluiche Cártaidhe," *ACS*, 4 April 1914. "Dá fheabhas iad Aisteoiridhe an Bhéarla i nAmharclainn na Mainistreach, ní móide go mbeadh a lán le maoidheamh aca ar na hAisteoiribh fé láthair."

101. "Impressions of the Oireachtas / Bards and Dramatists," *ACS*, 22 August 1914. The report originally appeared in the *Daily Herald*.

102. "Turas na nAisteoirí" (The tour of Na hAisteoirí), *ACS*, 5 September 1914. Other installments of this account ran in *ACS* on 12, 19, and 26 September. "Bhí an halla lán, na daoine ag brughadh ar a chéile, na Gaedhilgeoirí ag teacht ar lorg suilt a's grinn a's aoibhnis agus is aca a bhí an sult a's an greann a's an t-aoibhneas. Bhí an t-aoibhneas a bhí istigh 'na gcroidhthibh le h-aireachtaint 'na ngáire. Munab iad a bhí sásta le na hAisteoiribh!" Na hAisteoirí organized this tour to coincide with their performance at that year's Oireachtas in Killarney. Unfortunately such large-scale undertakings proved beyond the resources of Na hAisteoirí, although the unrest in the country after 1916, unrest in which Béaslaí as a Volunteer officer was to be deeply involved, may have rendered such projects moot.

103. See Gearóid Ó Lochlainn, *Ealaín na hAmharclainne* (The art of the theater) (Baile Átha Cliath: Clódhanna Teoranta, 1966), 31–33.

hair Peadar's *Tadhg Saor*,[104] and the following March the Leinster Feis offered a prize for "the best acting of a short Irish dramatic sketch, tragedy or comedy."[105] Many other regional gatherings would follow this lead. Of more significance, from its inception the national Oireachtas pledged itself to the fostering of "dramatic sketches in Irish,"[106] and first included drama among its competitions in 1901. Subsequently, the festival used its awards not only to encourage the writing of Gaelic plays, but also to channel that writing toward what were defined as key theatrical needs.[107] Among Oireachtas Prize categories over the years were: "a short play for children" (1906); "a three-act historical play" (1907); "a one-act bilingual play involving propaganda for Irish" (1910); and "a translation of a play from another language into Irish" (1912 and thereafter).[108] In addition, the Oireachtas was, after 1903, by far the single most important showcase for Gaelic theater, and it placed an increasing emphasis on the stageworthiness of award-winning plays, ultimately deciding in 1909 that the first prize for drama would not be awarded until the various contenders had actually been produced at the festival.[109]

On a more theoretical level, the Oireachtas sponsored competitions for essays on the theater in 1907, 1909, and 1911, the 1911 prize being shared by two practicing playwrights, Tomás Ó hAodha and Pádraic Ó Conaire.[110] Nor were such essays mere academic or linguistic exercises. While the Oireachtas and the feiseanna were presiding at the creation of a native drama, some nativists (and others) were worried about the principles that would govern its growth, and warned that this long-standing literary vacuum should not be filled with mere imitations of foreign models, however aesthetically impressive. Even Pearse, in his first year as editor of *An Claidheamh Soluis*, could express reservations

---

104. "A Big Day in Macroom," *FL*, 26 May 1900.

105. "The Leinster Feis," *ACS*, 30 March 1901.

106. The pledge was made on 25 August 1896 in a resolution at a meeting called to discuss plans for the first Oireachtas. See Preface to *Imtheachta an Oireachtais, 1897*, 7.

107. The role of the Oireachtas in the development of Gaelic drama is discussed by Donncha Ó Súilleabháin in *Scéal an Oireachtais*, 68–83. Among the judges in the drama competitions over the years were some of the leading figures in Gaelic theater and literature in general, among them Hyde, Mac Fhionnlaoich, "Conán Maol," Tomás Ó hAodha, and Thomas MacDonagh. See the various minutes of Coiste an Oireachtais (the Oireachtas Committee) in the Fionán Mac Coluim Papers, National Library of Ireland, MS. 24,403.

108. See Ó Súilleabháin, *Scéal an Oireachtais*, 181–84.

109. "Oireachtas Competitions," *ACS*, 27 March 1909.

110. Ó Conaire's essay was serialized in *ACS* beginning on 19 August 1911, and has been reprinted in *Aistí Phádraic Uí Chonaire*, 59–75.

about the potential influence of English plays, many of which were brought to Ireland by British companies touring the "provinces": "Everyone knows that the world of the Irish and the world of the English are not alike, and that it is therefore necessary for the dramas of the two countries to have no similarity at all to each other."[111] An unapologetically aggressive statement of the nativist case was made by one "An Rábaire" in 1906:

> The fact remains that Irish drama, if it develops at all, will grow in its own way, naturally, out of humble beginnings. It will not be generated in the incubators of artificial *sgoláirí* [scholars] in Dublin, nor in the hothouse of editorial leading articles. It must be popular if it is to do anything at all. It must appeal to the taste of the ordinary Irish-speaking Gael. . . . Any more ambitious efforts that have been made are only calculated to inspire regret.[112]

The following year, "Goll Mac Móirne," reacting to Edward Martyn's call for the formation of an itinerant dramatic company to tour the Gaeltachtaí, questioned whether Gaelic drama and acting should not be allowed to evolve from native roots in their own time rather than through the forced grafting of standards proper to the Anglicized capital: "If we want to develop Gaelic acting—in the old style as you might say—I think that it is best to give free rein to the gestures and skills native to Irish speakers, rather than impose on them 'the people from Dublin' or from anywhere else to show them how to act, with those outsiders perhaps imitating in many points the acting of foreigners."[113]

111. "Dráma na nGaedheal," editorial, *ACS*, 14 November 1903. "Tá a fhios ag an saoghal nach mar a chéile saoghal na nÉireannach agus saoghal na Sasanach, agus, dá bhrígh sin, gur éigean do dhrámanna an dá thír bheith gan cosamhlacht ar bith aca le chéile." The occasion of this editorial was the visit to Dublin of the Tawin players; see note 80. One may compare here the views of Tadhg Ó Donnchadha more than a decade later: "The speech and the gestures of the English speaker are not like the speech and the carriage of the Irish speaker, and the sooner Irish-language actors understand that the better." (Ní mar a chéile cainnt ná goití an Bhéarlóra agus cainnt is iomchur an Ghaedhilgeora: agus níl dá luaithe dá dtuigfidh aisteoirí na Gaedhilge soin nach amhlaidh is fearr.) Ó Donnchadha's category of "English speakers" doubtless included those born and raised in Ireland. See "Dráma na Gaedhilge," *ACS*, 6 June 1914.

112. "Irish Plays and Critics," *IG* 16, no. 10 (June 1906): 145. "An Rábaire" was jabbing at Pearse in this piece. Pearse responded in "Mion-Sgéala," *ACS*, 20 October 1906.

113. "Baramhail an Mhairtínigh" (Mr. Martyn's opinion), *ACS*, 1 June 1907. "Má's rud é gur maith linn gníomhaidheacht Ghaedhealach—ar an sean-nós mar adéarfá—a oileamhaint sa tír, sílim féin gur fearr dúinn cead a gcos a thabhairt do na goitíbh agus do na healadhnaibh atá ins na Gaedhilgeoiríbh ó nádúir, thar a bheith ag tarraingt isteach

Despite their paranoia about the shadowy power of Dublin's handful
of Gaelic literati, proponents of this brand of theatrical protectionism
had a point. "Humble" and "popular" little comedies designed to amuse
"the ordinary Irish-speaking Gael" were undoubtedly the most successful productions on the Gaelic stage in the first decade of this century.
Plays like Ua Laoghaire's *Tadhg Saor*, "Domhnall na Gréine's" *Lá na
nAmadán*, or Ó hAodha's *Seaghán na Sguab* may have been short on
catharsis, but they were full of idiomatic Irish, good-natured humor,
and, as we have seen in Chapter 2, an edifying view of the wit and
wisdom of the Irish-speaking peasantry. And that peasantry seems to
have responded with authentic delight when they saw such plays, often
starring their friends, in the local parish hall. For example, at a performance of Ua Laoghaire's *An Sprid* in Rossmore, Co. Cork, "the people
were just about dying with the laughter, and they were almost crawling
on top of each other at the back of the hall trying to get a better look at
everything."[114] It would be hard to imagine any of these plays being
seriously revived anywhere today, but before we dismiss the lot, we
should remember that as cosmopolitan a critic as William P. Ryan
could find such sketches a source of "general and unaffected delight,"[115]
and that both Yeats and Synge were genuinely amused and moved by
the most famous representative of the genre, Hyde's *Casadh an tSúgáin*.

It was not, however, plays like these, several of them the work of
their own number, that concerned some nativists. Rather, they worried
about the direction a more self-consciously artistic Gaelic theater might

---

'muinntir Bhl'á Cliath' nó 'Bhl'á' ar bith eile orthu le tasbáint dóibh an chaoi le gníomh-
haidheacht a dhéanamh agus iad-san b'fhéidir ag aithris in go leor pointí ar
ghníomhaidheacht na nGall." Such views were not necessarily the result of provincial
ignorance. In November 1913, Éamonn Ua Tuathail, after a brief survey of contemporary European theater, urged Na hAisteoirí and Na Cluicheoirí, whose work he appreciated, to study the language and style of the *seanchaí*, for "the Gaeltacht is where Irish
language drama will succeed and contribute most." (Is í an Ghaedhealtacht an áit is mó a
mbeidh rath agus tairbhe ar dhrámuigheacht Ghaedhilge.) See "Drámanna Dúinn Féin,"
editorial, *ACS*, 29 November 1913. See also the views of Tadhg Ó Donnchadha, who
stressed that Gaelic drama would have to grow "naturally from the customs and the
language of the Irish" (go nádúrtha as nósaibh agus as teangain na nGaedheal), avoiding in
particular "the influence of the English language" (anáil an Bhéarla). But he also believed
that after this natural evolution had occurred, "there will be no harm in letting in foreign
material" (ní miste an t-iasacht a sgaoileadh chuige). See "Dráma na Gaedhilge," *ACS*, 6
June 1914.

114. "Dul Amudha," "'An Sprid' i Rosmhóir" (*An Sprid* in Rossmore), *ACS*, 3 January 1903. "Bhí . . . na daoine go léir i riochtaibh a n-anam do chailleamhaint a' gáirí agus
iad anuas ar a chéile nach mór sa cheann thíos do'n halla a d'iarraidh radharc níos fearr
d'fhagháil ar gach nidh."

115. "London Notes," *ACS*, 20 December 1902.

take, especially when it left the *poitín* and potatoes behind and aspired to tragedy or the interpretation of Irish history and legend. From the nativist perspective, such elevated subjects and themes could only be safely developed in a theater rooted in indigenous models. For example, *Fáinne an Lae*, having identified the medieval Ossianic tales as "the nearest thing to stage dialogues which we possess," less convincingly argued that they should therefore be taken as "the starting point" for a "truly Irish National theatre."[116] The other major potential native source for dramatic inspiration was the narrative style of the traditional *seanchaí*, which Seán Mac Giollarnáth regarded as the fertile "soil" from which Gaelic acting would have to grow and in which could be rooted lessons learned farther afield.[117] Tomás Ó Máille developed this idea in 1917 in "Taidhbhearc Ghaedhealach" (Gaelic theater), as he wrote of listening to traditional storytellers:

116. "Notes," *FL*, 23 September 1899. *FL* was here echoing Alice Milligan, who, in her *Daily Express* letter mentioned above, called the Ossianic dialogues "the nearest approach to drama in an ancient native literature." See Hogan and Kilroy, *The Irish Literary Theatre*, 53. In 1913, in the lecture deprecating the extravagant claims made for early Irish literature by some Gaels, Osborn Bergin said that "it was greatly to be regretted that medieval Ireland never produced a drama, for in our romantic and semi-historical tales there was admirable dramatic stuff, and the storytellers are at their very best in rapid, pointed and natural dialogue." The example he offered was from the Ulster Cycle tale *Scéla Mucce Meic Dathó* (The story of Mac Dathó's pig). See "In the Gaelic World," *WF*, 16 August 1913.

117. "The Stage," editorial, *ACS*, 15 January 1910. Mac Giollarnáth may also be the author of the unsigned 1917 "Cúrsaí an tSaoghail" column in *ACS* in which the stage work of native speakers from Ring, Co. Waterford, was clearly being offered as a model of sorts. Beginning with the admission that "Gaelic drama henceforth has not been an entirely natural growth (ní fás nádúrtha ar fad a bhí san drámaidheacht Ghaedhilge go dtí seo), he said of the Ring troupe:

> The long recitation the Ring players performed was not a drama, at least learned people would not call an effort of that sort a drama, but the conversation in it was simple, and the speech rhythms were natural and followed the usage of the people, and the speech was said in a natural manner without timidity or shyness, and the performance drew a big laugh from the audience.

> (An píosa fada cainte a léirigh cluicheoirí na Rinne níor dhráma é, nó ní thiubharfadh lucht léighinn dráma ar aiste dá shórt, ach bhí an comhrádh go simplidhe ann, agus dul na cainte de réir meoin agus nós cainte na ndaoine, agus dubhradh an chaint go nádúrtha gan sgáth ná cúthaileacht, agus bhain an léiriú gáire mór as an lucht éisteachta.)

See "Cúrsaí an tSaoghail," *ACS*, 18 August 1917. See also Pearse's suggestion to Na Cluicheoirí that they travel to the Gaeltacht to learn from native speakers and storytellers. Pearse offered his advice from the stage of the Abbey on an evening when Na Cluicheoirí were performing at the theater. See "Beirt," "Ag Dul ar Aghaidh" (Making progress), *ACS*, 29 November 1913.

You would think you were listening to the people speaking to each other and that you were watching them as he described them. You would think that you could see the clothes and the gear they had on. You would think you could see the expression they would have when they spoke to one another, whether it were friendly or hostile. . . . That is the way we did it in Ireland. In other countries they had another way. The story would first be composed, but instead of telling it all by mouth, every action in it would be presented or shown in front of the people who were present.[118]

Yet although the Ossianic dialogues did indeed provide the framework for what is usually called the first "play" in Irish, the "Saint Patrick at Tara" scene—the honor more properly belongs to Paul McSwiney's *An Bárd 'gus an Fó*—and although the *seanchaí* could offer a wealth of native lore and a fine-tuned mastery of incident and dialogue expressed in elegant, subtle, and precise Irish, neither of these sources had ever generated anything like a complete play, a fact lamented by "Pádraig na Léime" in 1909: "It is a great source of regret for us that we lack native writing for the stage as a model for our task now."[119]

Father Dinneen, himself one of the first to attempt the genre in Irish, moved beyond regret to confront the problem with forthright honesty in a 1906 reply to a critic who had objected to his use of the loanword *dráma*: "Now I think that one who knows only Irish cannot have an adequate idea of what the term drama implies."[120] Some of the initial efforts in Gaelic stagecraft suggest that their authors shared the ignorance of Dinneen's monoglot. Repeatedly, reviews of early performances and dramatic publications question whether these works should

118. Editorial, *An Stoc* 1, no. 3 (February–March 1918): 4. "Shílfeá go mbeitheá ag éisteacht leis na daoine ag caint le chéile agus go mbeitheá ag breathnú orthu do réir mar bheadh seisean ag cur síos orthu. Shílfeá go bhfeicfeá an aghaidh a bhéarfaidís ar a chéile nuair bheidís ag caint, dhá mbu aghaidh carad í nó aghaidh námhad. . . . Sin é an reacht a bhíodh ar bun i n-Éirinn. I dtíortha eile bhíodh bealach eile acu. Ghnítí an sgéal a cheapadh i dtosach ach i n-áit a innsean ar fad i gcaint bhéil déanfaidhe gach gníomh dhá mbeadh ann a fhoilsiú nó a thaidhbhsiú os comhair na ndaoine a bheadh sa láthair." Ó Máille did acknowledge that "there was nothing of that sort here in Ireland until it came in with the foreign culture" (ní raibh aon cheo den tsórt sin ar bun i n-Éirinn go dtáinig sé isteach leis an nGalldacht), but said that it was essential to develop theatrical art even if it was a foreign importation.

119. "Aiste: An Dráma i nÉirinn," *SF*, 23 October 1909. "Is mór an t-adhbhar áithbhéile dhúinne gan scríobhnóireacht dhúthchais i gcómhair an árdáin a bheith mar shompladh fé n-ár gcúram anois."

120. "Iasacht Focal san nGaedhilg," *IG* 16, no. 7 (March 1906): 97.

have been written as plays at all. For example, in 1904 one "E." affirmed that "our Irish drama is moving along right lines," but continued: "Some of the drama we have got so far, however, would form
better subject matter for stories. Many of our dramatists do not seem to
realize what drama actually is; and they frequently rush off and cast into
dramatic form every plot that suggests itself to them."[121] Three years
later, Pearse returned to this problem, classifying the majority of Gaelic
plays as "mere narratives, long or short, divided into so many 'Acts'
and 'Scenes' instead of chapters, and on the strength of this posing as
'drama.'"[122] And, according to Seán Ó Caomhánaigh, things weren't
much better in 1913: "We have no suitable, stageable plays, and the
plays we do have lack polish and theatrical expertise because our playwrights do not have a precise knowledge of stagecraft, something very
important for the writing of plays. That is why most of our 'plays' are
stories and not plays."[123]

An tAthair Peadar and other nativist pioneers of the Gaelic stage may
well have felt a self-righteous scorn for imported dramatic theories and
practices, and may have believed that their own efforts were as
throughly Irish as their language, but even a superficial glance at the
recurring faults of their most ambitious plays reveals that they were
enthralled by the work of the playwrights most of them knew best or
admired most, the nineteenth-century melodramatists and, more important, the Elizabethans. Few serious Gaelic dramatists heeded the
1904 warning of "Connla Caol:" "Some of our Irish writers in drama
have wasted effort in trying to breathe new life into the Elizabethan
conventions, which are as dead to-day as their founders."[124] Again and
again, critics urged playwrights to reduce the number of scene divisions, set changes, subplots, and characters, and to avoid long-winded
bouts of purple rhetoric. For example, in a July 1903 review of Mac
Fhionnlaoich's *Tá na Francaigh ar an Muir*, "E." pointed out that the
author had fallen into "the mistake so common in nearly all recently
written plays in Irish," and continued "it is scarcely right to have five

121. "Recent Plays," *ACS*, 1 October 1904.
122. "Plays and Players," editorial, *ACS*, 30 March 1907. See also his comments on Ua
Laoghaire's shortcomings as a playwright in "A New Aodh Ruadh Play," review of *An
Bealach Buidhe* by An tAthair Peadar Ua Laoghaire, *ACS*, 5 January 1907.
123. "Gluaiseacht na Cluichidheachta" (The Dramatic Movement), *SF*, 19 April 1913.
"Níl aon cluichidhe oireamhnach inléirighthe againn; na cluichidhe atá againn, tá ceal
deismireachta agus cleasaidheachta an árdáin ortha, de dheascaibh ná fuil eólas cruinn ag
ár scríobhnóiridhibh cluiche ar chéird an árdáin, nidh antábhachta do scríobh chluiche. Sin
é an fáth gur sceul an chuid is mó dár gcluichidhibh agus nách cluiche."
124. "Árdán na Gaedhilge" (The Irish language stage), *Inis Fáil*, December 1904, 6.

acts, entailing numerous changes of scene in a play which can be read in a quarter of an hour."[125] Indeed, the Oireachtas Committee was repeatedly compelled to set out in detail just what it considered a stageable work, as in its regulations governing the competition for three-act plays: "No act should contain more than one scene. Competitors are requested to bear in mind that the number of speaking parts should be limited, as far as is consistent with the treatment of the subject. Simplicity of scenery and dress are also recommended."[126]

The playwrights, however, chafed under such restrictions. "E." may have acknowledged that "perhaps we are still at the *Ralph Royster Doyster* or the *Gammer Gurton's Needle* stage,"[127] but the dramatists often wanted all the color and scope of Shakespeare or even Boucicault in a one-act skit. The editorial staff at *Banba* were, for example, stupefied by the special effects involved in Séamus Ó Dubhghaill's one-acter *Muinntear Chillmhuire nó Bó i bPoll* (The people of Cill Mhuire, or A cow in a hole) which they published in 1903:

> We will present the first volume of *Banba* to anyone who will tell us how a wave can be set in motion on the stage, how seven men can gather around a bog-hole there and pull a cow out of it with ropes and sacks, how the cow can be kept on the stage with water and mud flowing from her sides, how she can be driven from there to the byre, how,—how,—how will the *drama* be put on the stage, that is what we want to know. It's not easy to do, but it must be possible. Let everyone have his answer to us by the first of June.[128]

If anything, bigger ambitions created bigger problems. Ua Laoghaire's one-act Aodh Ó Néill play *An Bealach Buidhe* has eight scenes, all with different settings, and nine speaking parts, plus extras; while "Conán Maol's" play about the same hero has seven scenes with six sets, and

125. "A New Play," *ACS*, 4 July 1903.

126. "The Oireachtas Committee / Literary Competitions for 1910," *ACS*, 2 October 1909.

127. "Recent Plays," *ACS*, 1 October 1904.

128. *Banba* 2, no. 6 (June 1903): 210–14. The editorial note cited is on 214. "Tabhairfimíd an chéad leabhar de *Bhanba* arís do'n té 'neosfaidh dúinn cionnus a chuirfidhe tonn ar bogadh ar an árdán, cionnus a chruinneochadh móir-sheisear fear timcheall puill phludaigh ann, agus bó do tharrac amach as le téadaibh agus le málaibh, cionnus fhéadfaidhe an bhó do choimeád 'na leidhpín ar an árdán agus uisce is pluda ag scéitheadh ó na slineánaibh, cionnus thiomáinfidhe as san go dtí an cró í, cionnus, —cionnus, —cionnus a chuirfear an *dráma* ar an árdán, sin é tá uainn. Ní fuiriste é dhéanamh, acht ní fuláir ná gur féidir é. Bíodh freagra gach duine againn fé'n chéad lá de'n Mheitheamh."

more than twenty characters. The specter of Shakespeare was most banefully obvious in what is still the most extravagant play ever staged in the Irish language, the Maynooth *Eoghan Ruadh Ua Néill*, first performed at the seminary in December 1906. This five-act play with a cast of twenty plus ran more than five hours and caused even the in-house reviewer of *Irisleabhar Mhuighe Nuadhad* to temper his otherwise glowing report with the admission that "the influence of that supreme foreign author" (rian an phríomh-ughdair ghallda soin) is everywhere apparent, and "that the author of this play is no Shakespeare yet" (ná fuil ughdar an dráma so 'n-a Shacspeare fós).[129] When the play was staged in Cork, one "Lee" was considerably less impressed, charging that the author had allowed "his mind [to] swing wild on the Shakespearean tradition," and, more damningly, that the resultant play was Irish in language alone.[130] His comments stirred a predictable controversy, and he did little to assuage any wounded feelings when he pronounced Padraic Colum's Anglo-Irish play *The Land* a more genuinely Irish creation than was *Eoghan Ruadh*: "'The Land' could not have been writen by anyone but an Irishman . . . and 'Eoghan Ruadh' could."[131]

Such views may have been heresy for some revivalists, but others had already acknowledged the national significance of the Anglo-Irish theater movement. They were, for example, impressed by the Theatre of Ireland, which split from the Abbey in 1906 and whose promise to include Gaelic plays in its repertoire was fulfilled with its productions of Tadhg Ó Donnchadha's translation of *The Land* at the 1906 Oireachtas, its collaboration with the players of the Árd-Chraobh in staging Tomás Ó Ceallaigh's *Deirdre* at the 1909 Oireachtas, and its production of Tomás Mac Domhnaill's *Áine agus Caoimhghín* at the 1910 festival.[132] Many Gaels also welcomed the successor of the Theatre of Ireland, the Hardwicke Street Irish Theatre, which also pledged itself to put the Irish language on the stage and which did produce several Gaelic plays in the years after its founding in 1914.[133] Especially notable for the revivalists was the program presented in May 1915, when the Irish The-

129. "Sinne agus Ar Sean-Cháirde" (Ourselves and our old friends), *Irisleabhar Mhuighe Nuadhad* (1906–7): 51.

130. "Peculiar Propagandism," *The Leader*, 16 November 1907.

131. "Irish Drama," *The Leader*, 7 December 1907.

132. See *ACS*, 14 August 1909; 13 August 1910. The group did not appear at the 1911 Oireachtas, a fact that prompted a warning from *ACS* that their preoccupation with drama in English would lead to "early death and the sacrifice of lasting fame." See "Plays," *ACS*, 4 March 1911.

133. For a full account of the activities of this company, including their Gaelic productions, see William J. Feeney, *Drama in Hardwicke Street: A History of the Irish Theatre Company* (Rutherford, N.J.: Fairleigh Dickinson University Press, 1984).

atre hosted the Sgoil Éanna players for an evening of two of Pearse's plays, *Íosagán* and *The Master*, as well as a lecture by Pearse entitled "The Irish Style of Dramatic Speaking," illustrated by what was called "the performance of the only surviving fragment of an Irish drama prior to the language revival, 'Dúnlaing Óg and his Leannán Sidhe.'"[134]

However appreciative the interest of revivalists in these groups, they never forgot that the real center of the Anglo-Irish dramatic world remained on Abbey Street. Such acknowledgment of the Theatre's significance did not, however, extend to unaninimity concerning the way it exerted its cultural and linguistic influence on the nation. The vociferous involvement of some revivalists, notable among them Piaras Béaslaí,[135] in the disturbances surrounding *The Playboy of the Western World* in 1907 has blinded most scholars of Anglo-Irish literature to the diversity and seriousness of Gaelic reservations concerning the Abbey. For example, the disappointment that is a frequent note in Gaelic commentary on the Theatre only serves to underscore the high ambitions many in the Revival had for it. Thus, in a controversy to be revived on Broadway in 1990, Yeats was lambasted in the columns of *An Claidheamh Soluis* when he brought the English Mrs. Patrick Campbell to Dublin to play the Irish heroine Deirdre: "It is to be feared that the Irish Literary Theatre is becoming more Anglicised. Their Anglo-Irish actors are not sufficiently English now. They have to bring real English people over from London."[136] For Tadhg Ó Donnchadha, such casting decisions were only a logical consequence of the Theatre's radical failure. Commenting on the Scottish theater scene in 1914, Ó Donnchadha quoted Ruaraidh Erskine with approval: "He says that Yeats and Lady Gregory failed to establish a national drama because they neglected the national language. . . . Ruaidhrí is right there, at any rate. It is good news for them in Scotland that they don't have an 'Abbey Theatre or a "school" of red-herring Anglo-Scottish dramatists, to do battle with or seek to circumvent.'"[137]

134. This information is again from the program in the Pearse Museum at Sgoil Éanna.
135. See James Kilroy, *The Playboy Riots* (Dublin: Dolmen, 1971), 49–51, 85, 89.
136. "I mBaile Átha Cliath," *ACS*, 23 November 1907. "Ag dul i nGalltacht atá an Irish Literary Theatre, is baoghlach. Níl cluicheoirí Gall-Ghaedhealach sáthach Gallda aca anois. Caithfidh siad fíor-Ghaill a thabhairt anall as Lonndain."
137. "Ceilteachas / 'An Mhainistir'" (Celtic affairs / "The Abbey"), *ACS*, 27 June 1914. "Deir sé gur theip ar Yeats agus an Bhaintighearna Gréagóir dráma náisiúnta a chur ar bun toisc go ndearnadar faillighe san teangain dúthchais. . . . Tá an ceart ag Ruaidhrí san méid sin, acht go háirithe. Is maith an scéala dóibh i nAlbain ná fuil aca 'Abbey Theatre or "school" of red-herring Anglo-Scottish dramatists, to do battle with or seek to circumvent.'" Erskine's essay "Gaelic Drama" was serialized in the summer and autumn

At the more strident end of the critical spectrum, we find "Pádraig na Léime," who, in an outraged review of the 1912 Abbey production of Lennox Robinson's *Patriots*, added premeditated treachery if not downright treason to the Theatre's catalogue of sins. Yet even here it is important to note the sense of a betrayed common cause underlying his diatribe: "I had faith in these people when they went to work at first. It wasn't long before they betrayed us. . . . The directors of this work were involved with the traitors who have been detroying us for years and years. They think they still have us down, but they're wrong."[138]

Significantly, "Pádraig's" intemperance as well as the strictly ideological nature of his attack were immediately challenged by one "Fear na Feirste," who insisted on judging the Theatre's work on its artistic merits. Having admitted that he enjoyed some of the Abbey's productions while "others disgust me" (cuireann cuid eile díobh déistean orm), he continued: "I don't wish to say anything about how Pádraig na Léime slanders the Theatre itself. I would say this much: I think it's right to have confidence in the people who created and who staged a drama as true—although it was a bitter truth—as 'Patriots' at this time of abasement."[139] Three years later, one "Feargus" echoed this sane and sensible open-mindedness when he took *An Claidheamh Soluis* to task for its low-key but sustained editorial and publicity bias in favor of Edward Martyn's Hardwicke Street Company at the expense of the Abbey. Expressing his impatience with Gaelic sniping at and snubbing of the Abbey in light of its real contributions over more than a decade, "Feargus" wrote:

> Querelous references to the Abbey Theatre will only prove repellent or wearisome. Many of us happen to have seen a number of Abbey plays, and to have read others, and we know what

1913 and spring 1914 issues of his journal *Guth na Bliadhna*; the quotes used by Ó Donnchadha are from the spring 1914 issue, in which he called Synge and Lady Gregory "'situation' hunting eavesdroppers." For Ó Donnchadha's immediate response to Synge's *Playboy*, see "'Art' ar Iarraidh" ("Art" wanting), *ACS*, 9 February 1907.

138. "Ó'n Deisceart" (From the South), *ACS*, 27 July 1912. "Bhí ionntaoibh agam as an ndream seo an uair chuireadar chun na hoibre 'san chéad eascadh. Níor bh'fada gur fhealladar orainn. . . . Bhí baint ag lucht stiúirighthe na hoibre seo leis na fealltóiribh atá dhár milleadh le faid de bhliadhantaibh. Measaid go bhfuil cos ar bolg aca orainn fós de dheallramh, acht tá dearmhad ortha."

139. "Searbhas na Fírinne" (The bitterness of the truth), *ACS*, 10 August 1912. "Ní mian liom aon rud a rádh fá dtaobh de'n mhaslughadh a ghníos Pádraig na Léime ar an Amharclann féin. Adéarfainn an méid seo: is dóigh liom gur chóir ionntaoibh a bheith againn as an dream do cheap agus do léirigh dráma chomh fíor—gidh gur searbhas na fírinne atá ann—le 'Patriots' i n-aimsir seo na n-inísliughadh."

they are, and what they are not. The Abbey has given us a share
of work that is poetical and beautiful, a good deal that is sincere
and expressive, and not a little that is entertaining. For some of
the offerings I do not care, but I can still believe in the honesty
of the writers. The latter-day development of petulance in regard
to the Abbey is an unhealthy sign: it says little for the Gaels
(more or less) concerned.[140]

More important, even in the heat of the *Playboy* debate, Pearse took
no satisfaction in what seemed to him at the time the definitive schism
between the two national literary movements. Thus while in his famous editorial on "The Passing of Anglo-Irish Drama," he pronounced
Synge's play "indefensible" and Yeats's behavior "lamentable," he also
dismissed the antics of the rioters as "puerile" and "inept." For him
there were no winners in this fiasco: "On both sides there have been
mock-heroics and hysterics; on both a shameful lack of tolerance and
broadmindedness; on both an even more painful want of that saving
sense of humour which in his most tense and electric moments never
deserts the genuine Gael." Real sadness rather than any sense of vindication, much less gloating triumphalism, colored his concluding prophecy that "as for Anglo-Irish drama—it is the beginning of the end."[141]
    Yet within a month of this editorial he himself was already contribut-
ing, albeit with marked reservations, to the reestablishment of the generally cordial relations that had prevailed between the two literary
movements since the days of the Irish Literary Theatre, writing that
"even the Abbey, be it good or evil, is at any rate an emanation from
the soil of Ireland."[142] And by the following year, much, if not all, was

140. "The Abbey Theatre and the Gael," letter, *ACS*, 16 January 1915. In 1911 a similar defense of the Theatre had been provided by Tadhg Ó Donnchadha's sister Cáit: "And
although it's not possible to agree with much that is presented by them, that does not
mean that we do not have a duty to go to their aid." (Agus cé nach féidir a bheith ar aon
intinn le n-a lán a foillsightear aca, ní fhágann san gan é bheith de dhualgas orainn dul n-a
gcabhair.) See "Amharclann na Mainistreach" (The Abbey Theatre), *ACS*, 11 February
1911.
    141. "The Passing of Anglo-Irish Drama," editorial, *ACS*, 9 February 1907.
    142. "A Note on Acting," *ACS*, 6 April 1907. Pearse was here echoing comments he
himself had made the previous year: "It appears that the fame of the dramatists and actors
of the Abbey is spreading. If so, we don't mind. Although their product doesn't always
have the proper flavor, it is the product of this country." (Samhluigheann sé go bhfuil cáil
drámadóirí agus cluithcheoirí na Mainistreach ag leathadh. Ní miste linn, má tá. Cé nach
mbíonn an blas ceart ar a ndéantús i gcomhnaidhe, is é déantús na tíre seo é.) See "Mion-
Sgéala," *ACS*, 17 November 1906. Even in the midst of the *Playboy* controversy, Pearse
never lost sight of the aesthetic significance of the Abbey's accomplishment. Thus in

forgiven, and Pearse could conclude a brief report on a lecture by Lady Gregory to the league's Árd-Chraobh with a tribute to her theater: "Some writers and players of the Abbey may have sinned against our dearest sentiments, but the good they have done outweighs all their shortcomings, and while we deprecate indiscreet praise we must in justice admit that those who have succeeded in founding a home-made theatre, and who successfully run it independently of the worst influences of the modern decadent English stage deserve well of their nation."[143] And he was willing to preach this lesson to the young, as he did when he chaired a debate on "Is the work of the Abbey Theatre good or bad?" (An maith nó olc í obair Amharclainn na Mainistreach?) at University College, Dublin, in March 1911. The report of the debate in the *National Student* records that many cogent opinions were expressed, with most speaking in favor of the Theatre. Pearse summarized the debate and then "the chairman gave his own opinion on the Abbey Theatre. It is a theatre, he thought, that will leave its mark on the history of Ireland. That the Abbey Theatre had been founded was a good thing done."[144] But perhaps Pádraic Ó Conaire's retrospective view from 1918 most accurately sums up the mature Gaelic attitude to, even pride in, Yeats's Abbey: "We didn't even have that many Anglo-Irish plays when the Abbey Theatre was founded, but Yeats and his companions were not long at work before they had provided a good crop of plays. And the new Anglo-Irish plays surpassed the plays being

---

March 1907, his reference to "the fizzling out" of the Abbey is immediately qualified by the phrase "at least as a National force." See "Plays and Players," *ACS*, 30 March 1907.

143. "Drama," *ACS*, 21 November 1908. He also claimed to prefer the work of the Ulster Literary Theatre to the Abbey, writing ("Mion-Sgéala," *ACS*, 2 May 1908):

> There is more humanity and more Gaelicism in their plays than there is in the majority of the plays that are seen in the Abbey Theatre. The Belfast writers understand the life of the average Ulsterman better than the Dublin writers understand the life of the average Connachtman or Munsterman.

(Is mó de'n daonnacht agus de'n Ghaedhealtacht atá ag baint le n-a gcuid cluichí 'ná mar atá le furmhór na gcluichí dá bhfeictear i nAmharclainn na Mainistreach. Is fearr a thuigeas sgríbhneoirí Bhéal Feirste gnáth-shaoghal an Ultaigh 'ná mar thuigeas sgríbhneoirí Bhaile Átha Cliath gnáth-shaoghal an Chonnachtaigh nó an Mhuimhnigh.)

144. T. Ó M., "Cumann Gaedhealach Choláiste na hIolscoile" (The Gaelic Society of the University College), *National Student* 1, no. 4 (April 1911): 116. "Dorigne an cathairleóir . . . a thuairm féin do thabhairt ar Amharclann na Mainistreach. Amharclann iseadh é, dar leis, fhágfas a rian ar stair na h-Éireann. Amharclann na Mainistreach bheith curtha ar bun, sin rud maith deunta."

produced in England."[145] At any rate, it is of utmost importance to re-member that while the *Playboy* episode was both bitter and divisive, the wounds did heal with surprising speed, and to view opinions expressed in the flush of controversy as paradigmatic of Gaelic response to the Anglo-Irish movement is to indulge in caricature.

London Gaels, for whom the visits of the Abbey company generated considerable cultural and social excitement, were always less equivocal in their support of the Theatre's work, even at its most controversial in the work of Synge. For example, in 1908 P. S. Ua hÉigeartaigh wrote:

> Criticism of the Abbey on the ground that it is not national seems to me to be absurd. The best Irish one-act play yet writ-ten, "Riders to the Sea," is an Abbey play, and, of the others, "Kathleen Ni Houlihan," "The Rising of the Moon," and "The Gaol Gate" are undeniably national: while the remainder are na-tional in the broad sense.[146]

Writing in *Irish Freedom* four years later, Ua hÉigeartaigh challenged Gaels to examine their own consciences before attacking the Abbey for its failure to produce plays in Irish: "Has anybody ever submitted a play in Irish to them? Has the Gaelic League ever asked them to do a play in Irish, or helped them to organise an Irish side to their company? And above all, what encouragement have they had in their uphill upbuilding of drama in Ireland from the Gaelic League, and what support from Gaelic Leaguers?"[147] The Londoners certainly felt that that support had been earned, as is evident from the tribute offered in 1910 by an anony-mous contributor to *An t-Éireannach* who claimed to speak for the entire Gaelic community in exile: "We can all be proud of the astonishing ability of the writers and players associated with the Abbey Theatre."[148] The following year Ua hÉigeartaigh succinctly expressed what the Ab-bey and its London productions meant to himself and his Gaelic com-rades: "The annual visit of the Abbey Theatre Company is one of the

145. "Drámannaí," in *Aistí Uí Chonaire*, 129. The essay was originally published in *The Irishman*, 28 September 1918. "Is beag dráma Gall-Ghaedhealach féin a bhí againn nuair cuireadh Amharclann na Mainistreach ar bun, acht ní raibh an obair i bhfad ar siubhal ag an Yéatsach agus ag a chomhluadar go raibh barr maith drámannaí soláthruighthe aca. Agus sháruigh na drámannaí nuadh Gall-Ghaedhealacha na drámannaí bhí ghá léiriughadh i Sasana."

146. "Dramatic Criticism and Sanity," *Inis Fáil*, January 1908, 10–11.

147. "Art and the Nation," *Irish Freedom*, May 1912, 2.

148. "The Irish National Theatre," *An t-Éireannach*, July 1910, 1.

annuals which, with the Aonach and the Festival, make life in London less unbearable for Irish-Irelanders."[149]

Dubliners, for whom the Abbey lacked the magic of novelty, were more skeptical. In particular, many Gaels found the Abbey, however sincere and occasionally successful in its battle against vulgar Anglicization, as "oppressively slow" in its march "Irish-wards" as its predecessor, the Irish Literary Theatre. Their impatience was voiced by *An Claidheamh Soluis* in an editorial entitled "The Stage": "We have not classed the 'Abbey' with the other houses, because Mr. Yeats deserves well of Ireland for many reasons. . . . but he is making no attempt at the Gaelicising of the Irish stage, or at the creation of a purely Irish drama. . . . The production of plays in English is not to be condemned, but it is questionable if a Theatre from which plays in Irish are excluded, can be called Irish."[150] It was, however, "E. Ó N." who in a review of the work of Na hAisteoirí most memorably captured the Gaels' simultaneous fascination with and suspicion of the work of the Abbey: "We all may enjoy the Abbey Theatre and admire it, but unknown to us Gaelic Leaguers it is tyrannising over us, and silently trampling on our hopes of an Irish dramatic movement. Everything is so perfect in the Abbey that the Gaelic League feels ashamed of its occasional little dramatic attempts. Beautifully staged and performed plays in English are a danger to our hopes for self-expression in Irish—our language."[151]

Yet if Gaelic drama was ever to cease embarrassing even its partisans, it was going to have to be staged adequately if not beautifully, and performed competently if not splendidly. Unlike "E. Ó N.," many involved with Gaelic theater felt that these were precisely the areas in which the Anglo-Irish movement, particularly the Abbey, could most inspire and instruct its literary poor relation. As early as 1904, "Connla Caol" had urged those developing an Irish-language theater to turn for models to their more established and sophisticated counterparts in Dublin: "A little talent is a dangerous thing, and I do not see how a close study of stage literature, especially modern stage literature, can be dispensed with. . . . The plays produced by the Irish National Theatre Company may be studied to advantage, especially for the harmony in setting and the artistic restraint in acting."[152] Pearse developed this idea

149. "The Abbey Players' Visit," *An t-Éireannach*, August 1911, 11.

150. *ACS*, 15 January 1910.

151. "Na hAisteoirí," *ACS*, 19 April 1913. For a more optimistic view of the influence the Abbey's excellence could have on Gaelic theatre, see Cáit Ní Dhonnchadha, "Amharclann na Mainistreach," *ACS*, 11 February 1911.

152. "Árdán na Gaedhilge," *Inis Fáil*, December 1904, 6.

in much greater detail in "A Note on Acting" in April 1907, specifically
listing some of the practical lessons Gaelic actors and directors could
learn from a visit to the Theatre of Ireland or the Abbey.[153] In 1911, one
"Ú.," having suggested an obvious solution to the central problem of
the Gaelic theatrical movement—that the Abbey actors learn the language and take the lead in the production of plays in Irish—went on to
offer a more realistic alternative: "No thoughtful person would say that
the Abbey is a Gaelic theater, but even so, it is possible to learn a great
deal there. Irish speakers concerned with the production of Gaelic plays
could do nothing more profitable than to go watch the acting there
now and again."[154]

If Gaelic actors were, however, to miraculously master their craft as
fully as had the Fays, Sara Allgood, or Máire Nic Shiubhlaigh, where
would they find the plays to showcase their skills? As has been noted,
there were only a handful of Gaelic plays at this time, and the vast
majority of those were either brief knockabout farces, woodenly
orthodox propaganda pieces, or unwieldy, pseudo-Shakespearean
melodramas. There was also, however, a precedent for the translation
of Anglo–Irish plays into Irish, a precedent several influential revivalists
saw offering the best immediate source of relatively sophisticated plays
to challenge and thereby develop the technical and aesthetic talents of
crew and cast while simultaneously providing long-suffering Dublin
audiences with a much-needed new perspective on, if not escape from,
the cabin kitchen or castle hall. Furthermore, not only would such plays
be Irish in subject, setting, and theme; they would also be familiar in
their English incarnation to an audience with a shaky command of
Irish. The logic of this approach was spelled out in *Sinn Féin* in 1913:
"The production of popular plays in the dress in which they should
originally have have been and are at last, properly clothed [i.e., the Irish
language] is a wise proceeding: for those who know the plays in English can have proof that, first, Gaelic plays are worth doing, second,
that these mere translations, by their familiarity and competent work-

---

153. *ACS*, 6 April 1907. The previous year he had urged revivalists "to pay an occasional visit to the Abbey Theatre," where they would be put "in touch with the best
contemporary ideals." See "Irish Acting," editorial, *ACS*, 7 July 1906. His 1907 editorial
drew a strong letter of protest from Éamonn Ceannt, who wrote that "the *Claidheamh* is
no place for booming the literary efforts of English-speaking people born in Ireland"
(*ACS*, 13 April 1907).
154. "Cluichtheoireacht" (Acting), *ACS*, 14 January 1911. "Ní abróchadh duine tuig-
sionach ar bith gur amharclann Ghaedhealach an 'Mhainistir,' acht munab eadh féin is
féidir mórán a fhoghluim innte. Ní fhéadfadh Gaedhilgeoirí a bhíos baint aca le léiriughadh drámanna Gaedhilge rud níos tairbhighe do dhéanamh ná dul ag féachaint ar na
cluichtheoiríbh ansin anois agus arís."

manship, will do more to educate public taste for the Gaelic drama than
original work would."[155] As early as April 1899, with no original Gaelic
drama yet in sight, *Fáinne an Lae* had suggested that league branches use
translations to put Irish on the stage,[156] and the following year the paper
gave considerable publicity to George Moore's advice to would-be Gaelic dramatists: "Translate an Irish play into Irish—I mean a play like
Mr. Yeats' 'Land of Heart's Desire,' which only requires translation
into Irish to make it thoroughly and entirely Irish."[157] At this very time,
one Anglo-Irish writer, Alice Milligan, was willing to offer her work as
trial material for Moore's scheme, sending her *The Last Feast of the
Fianna* to Douglas Hyde for translation into Irish. Hyde's letter thanking her for the book makes plain, however, that he did not share
Moore's confidence about the inherent ease of this translation process:
"I don't think your artist who will turn into good idiomatic and above
all intelligent Irish all you have written, lives. Anyhow I should not like
to undertake it!"[158]

Pragmatism was a keynote of the early Revival, and translation was
viewed here as the quickest solution to immediate needs. As is obvious
from the wistful note so common in Gaelic reviews of Abbey productions—"a pity we don't have plays like this in Irish" (truagh gan
cluithchíbh mar so againn i nGaedhilg)[159]—the revivalists wanted origi-

155. "Plays in Gaelic," *SF*, 22 November 1913. The translations referred to here were
those staged by Na Cluicheoirí at the Abbey in November 1913. They will be discussed
below. Compare the views of Crawford Neil on the same plays: "It was wise to choose
three translations for production, though it appeared to be questionable; good for the
player and listener; for the first, because he could walk an old road with a new gait,
learning his steps by familiar ways, and the latter could see how much finer the new gait
was even on the old road." See Neil, "Féile na Samhain [*sic*]," *SF*, 29 November 1913.
Thomas MacDonagh also recommended the translation of Anglo-Irish classics to provide
a repertoire for his proposed touring company for the Gaeltacht. See "For Plays in Irish:
A Suggestion," *An Macaomh* 2, no. 1 (Christmas 1910): 40–42.

156. "A Gaelic Theatre," *FL*, 4 February 1899.

157. "An Irish Play / Interview with Mr. George Moore," *FL*, 3 March 1900. Among
Moore's schemes was his well-known plan that he would write a play in French that Lady
Gregory would put into English for Tadhg Ó Donnchadha to translate into Irish! See
Moore, *Hail and Farewell!* (New York: Appleton, 1925), 1:309.

158. Letter to Alice Milligan, no date, but obviously 1900. Carl Racine of Boston
College found this letter bound in the front of an autographed copy of *The Last Feast of
the Fianna* in Harvard's Widener Library. Milligan later stated that "my Ossianic trilogy
was written with a view to translation into Irish, and has never been translated." See Alice
Milligan, "Historical Drama," *SF*, 26 June 1909. *Last Feast* was staged outdoors in Donnybrook by Craobh na gCúig gCúigí in 1906. See "Cogarnach na gCraobh," *ACS*, 9
June 1906. The play was finally translated into Irish by Risteárd Ó Foghludha and published in his *Naoi nGearra Chluichí* (Nine short plays) in 1930.

159. "The Mineral Workers," *ACS*, 3 November 1906.

nal plays of all kinds. Most were also realists, however; aware that such plays could only come after a period of apprenticeship and that meanwhile actors were in search of scripts and audiences in search of entertainment, they looked to the rich resources of their English-speaking compatriots. Nor did they delay once they had accepted the logic of this course. As has been noted, the first three Gaelic plays were translated from Anglo-Irish originals, and in 1901 the first play to win an Oireachtas prize was *Suipéar Dhiarmada Mac Pháidín*, not a translation, but rather an adaptation by Máire Ní Shíthe of MacManus's story "Jerry MacFadyeen's Supper."[160] MacManus was at this time an enthusiastic and highly respected member of the league whose literary activities were closely monitored in the Gaelic press. Therefore it is hardly surprising that, with his full blessing, three of his plays eventually appeared in Irish: *An Fear Cruadh-Chroidheach* (*The Hard-Hearted Man*), translated by Tomás Ua Concheanainn in 1905[161]; *Liúdaidhe Óg na Leargadh Móire* (*The Lad from Largymore*), translated by Seán Ua Ceallaigh in 1906; and *Eiséirghe Dhonncha* (*The Resurrection of Dinny O'Dowd*), translated by "An Seabhac" in 1913. Given the current critical consensus on MacManus, it should be stressed that the Gaels were not blind to his literary shortcomings, which were given a definitive summation by Louis J. Walsh in what was on the whole a favorable review of *An Fear Cruadh-Chroidheach* in *The Leader*: "At his worst, in his strained attempts at wit, his ill-conceived plots and feeble denouements, his bathos, buffoonery, and mean 'stage Irishmanism,' it were hard to find him a fitting compeer."[162] Indeed, the general Gaelic attitude to his work in both the original and in Irish provides a clear indication of just

160. *Imtheachta an Oireachtais, 1901*, 127. The story was published in *WF*, 13 January 1900. In addition, the libretto of Butler's opera *Muirgheis* was originally written for translation into Irish, a project that seems to have fallen through due to a dearth of singers competent in the language. See Pearse's comments in "Gleó na gCath," *ACS*, 5 December 1903; and Edward Martyn's review of the first performance in *ACS*, 19 December 1903. Pearse wrote: "On the whole we think it better that the opera should be produced in English than that it should be produced in parrot Irish."

161. Writing to *UI* in 1905, MacManus said of his collaboration with Ua Concheanainn: "Thomas O'Concannon is responsible for more than the mere translation of the play. He it was who not only directed my attention to the theme, but laid down the lines on which it should run. The bones of the play, I would say, are O'Concannon's." He concluded by calling Ua Concheanainn "joint author with me." See "All Ireland," *UI*, 12 August 1905.

162. "An Irish-Ireland Play," *The Leader*, 26 August 1905. His review provoked a debate in which MacManus himself participated. Pearse took a kinder view of MacManus's shortcomings in his review of *Liúdaidhe Óg na Leargadh Móire* on its publication, stating that he was "never a philosopher, but only a genial and kindly observer." See "A Playlet," *ACS*, 17 February 1906.

what they hoped to gain from such ventures in dramatic translation. Tomás Ó Ceallaigh pronounced *An Fear Cruadh-Chroidheach* "a distinct advantage over anything we have had so far,"[163] while Robert Lynd saw *Liúdaidhe Óg na Leargadh Móire* as "almost an ideal play to produce at the present stage in our language and dramatic revival."[164] Reviews of the published texts and performances of these translations leave no doubt about what the Gaels saw as their function "at the present stage:" they were workable and well-built plays worth going to see in which the language would be stretched comfortably and adapted to deal with fresh subject matter and, perhaps, more sophisticated themes and more developed characterizations. They were, in effect, to be a preparation not a proxy for original drama in Irish. And at the time, the wisdom of this policy seemed confirmed by the popularity of *Liúdaidhe Óg na Leargadh Móire* with actors and audiences at league entertainments up and down the country.

Plays like those of MacManus could not, of course, satisfy those who wanted a more profound dramatic portrayal of Irish life in the Irish language. George Moore had suggested that one of Yeats's plays be put into Irish, and his advice was eventually acted on in 1904, when Tomás Ó Ceallaigh took first prize at the annual Comóradh na Samhna festival of Cumann na nGaedheal with his *Caitlín Ní Uallacháin* (*Cathleen Ni Houlihan*). The work was welcomed with rapture by Pearse in *An Claidheamh Soluis*: "It is a beautiful rerendering of the most beautiful play that has been written in Ireland in our time."[165] Nor was his enthusiasm in any way diminished when he saw the play on stage at the 1905 Oireachtas: "Fr. O'Kelly has performed a feat which we had scarcely imagined possible. He has produced an Irish version which does not suffer considerably by comparison with Mr. Yeats' beautiful original."[166] Significantly, and predictably, Ó Ceallaigh's own concern was not limited to the aesthetic impact of his work on its audience; as he wrote in the preface to the play on its publication in 1905: "I have appended a glossary in preference to an ordered vocabulary as being more helpful

163. "A Propagandist Play," *ACS*, 14 October 1905. Ó Ceallaigh also said of the work that it "may well be taken to mark the beginning of serious Irish Drama," but the bulk of his review makes plain that his emphasis was on beginnings rather than on seriousness. *UI* had high praise for the play in both the original and translation, drawing particular attention to its value as antiemigration propaganda. See "All Ireland," *UI*, 5 August 1905.

164. "An Irish Theatre in London," *Inis Fáil*, February 1907, 8.

165. "New Plays," *ACS*, 12 August 1905.

166. "The Plays," *ACS*, 19 August 1905. *UI* pronounced Ó Ceallaigh's version superior to its original, though tribute was paid Yeats as well since "the idiom of the play, as well as the spirit, is peculiarly Irish, and the Irish language is its natural, although not its original, attire." See "All Ireland," *UI*, 19 August 1905.

to students who may have an opportunity of seeing a performance of the play with this booklet in their hands."[167] While never as popular as *Liúdaidhe Óg na Leargadh Móire*, Ó Ceallaigh's translation did bring Yeats to the Gaeltacht and remained a fixture in the Gaelic repertoire for years to come.

In 1906, literary Gaels looked forward with some eagerness to an Oireachtas production of the Gaelic version of a play by the author whom Pearse had called "the most considerable among the little band of Anglo-Irish dramatists . . . the most powerful and original mind in the present-day literary movement."[168] Tadhg Ó Donnchadha's translation of Padraic Colum's *The Land* was, however, somewhat of a disappointment onstage, and the play does not seem to have been revived in our period.[169] Another of Colum's plays, the one-act *The Miracle of the Corn*, was twice translated into Irish, by Tomás Ó Ceallaigh as *Arbhar Dé* (God's corn) in 1908, and by Eoghan Ó Súilleabháin as *Míorbhúil an Arbhair* (The miracle of the corn) in 1911. Neither version seems to have ever been produced. Other major translations were Máire Ní Shíthe's *Cití* (Mary Butler's *Kitty*) in 1902; Pádraic Ó Máille's *An Roilleán Draoidheachta* (John Hamilton's *The Magic Sieve*) in 1908; "An Seabhac's" *Dubhairt Sé Dabhairt Sé* (Lady Gregory's *Spreading the News*) and Liam Ua Domhnaill's *Fé Bhrigh na Mionn* (Rutherford Mayne's *The Troth*) in 1911;[170] the Micheál Mhag Ruaidhrí–Seán Mac Giollarnáth col-

167. An tAthair Tomás Ó Ceallaigh, "Réamh-Fhocal" (Foreword) to *Caitlín Ní Uallacháin: Dráma Náisiúnta* (Dublin: M. H. Gill and Son, 1905), 3.

168. "Plays and Players," editorial, *ACS*, 30 March 1907.

169. Pearse discussed "the comparative failure of 'The Land' to 'go' in Irish" in "The Plays," *ACS*, 18 August 1906. Actually, he had anticipated some problems with this translation, "because we are not convinced that there exists between the minds of Tadhg Ó Donnchadha and Padraic Colum that secret and indefinable sympathy which would enable the one to give a perfect and satisfying translation of the other." See "Irish Acting," *ACS*, 7 July 1906. One "Gaillimh" seems to have agreed, suggesting in 1905 that Tomás Ó Ceallaigh do the translation. See "Gaillimh," "Stray Impressions at the Oireachtas," *UI*, 2 September 1905. The cantankerous "An Rábaire" didn't think much of the original play, but did praise Ó Donnchadha for managing to put "a garment that smells of Irish on thoughts that would never occur to a country Gael from one end of the year to the next" (culaith ar a bhfuil balath Gaedhealach do smaointe ná ritheadh le Gaedheal na tuaithe ó cheann ceann na bliadhna). See "Clódhanna Nua," *IG* 16, no. 14 (October 1906): 224. Apparently the production was somewaht jinxed right from the rehearsal stage. See Hogan and Kilroy, *The Years of Synge*, 104–5. The play was revived by An Comhar Drámuidheachta in the Abbey in October 1928. See Donncha Ó Súilleabháin, "Tús agus Fás na Drámaíochta i nGaeilge (III)" (The beginning and growth of drama in Irish), *Ardán* (Summer 1972): 3.

170. A report in *ACS* in December 1913 stated that Na Cluicheoirí were rehearsing *An Liúdramán*, a translation by Eoghan Ó Neachtain of Mayne's *The Drone*. Ó Neachtain's

laboration *Mac na Mná Déirce* (Seamus O'Kelly's *The Shuiler's Child*) in 1913;[171] and, the following year, Piaras Béaslaí's *Cluiche Cártaidhe* (A game of cards), an adaptation of *Three Weeks after a Marriage* by the eighteenth-century Irish playwright Arthur Murphy.[172] Na Cluicheoirí's successful productions of the Gregory and O'Kelly plays both in Dublin and in the Gaeltacht inspired a call from "B.M." for more such efforts: "Translations of such Anglo-Irish plays as 'Birthright,' 'The Building Fund,' 'The Mineral Workers,' and 'The Country Dressmaker' will help us to finer and subtler drama."[173] The omission of Synge here was probably no oversight; as we will see, many revivalists never forgave him for the *Playboy*. Nonetheless, we do have intriguing references to a translation of *Riders to the Sea* by Tomás Mac Domhnaill, who taught at Sgoil Éanna. The play was tentatively scheduled for production by the Theatre of Ireland at the 1910 Oireachtas, but, according to *An Claidheamh Soluis*, was canceled due to "some difficulty . . . as to the acting rights."[174] More details were provided by Mac Domhnaill himself in his preface to another of his plays, *Áine agus Cao-*

---

version was published in 1932, but I can find no record of its publication or performance in the period under discussion in this study. See "Drámaí" (Plays), *ACS*, 20 December 1913.

171. After seeing the production of this play by Na Cluicheoirí with Máire Nic Shiubhlaigh in the title role, Arthur Griffith pronounced it "drama, real drama, great drama, of our own," and went on to proclaim that 1913 would be remembered as the year that saw "the birth of a great Irish drama—speaking to the world in the tongue of Ireland." See Griffith, "Great Drama in the Irish Language," *SF*, 12 July 1913. This piece was originally published in the *Southern Cross* in Buenos Aires in June of the same year. See also "Irish Plays on the Public Stage," *SF*, 10 May 1913.

172. There was some controversy over whether this play should be considered an actual translation. Béaslaí himself denied that it was, writing of his source: "It set me thinking and I composed a play as a result. It is for all practical purposes a new play." (Chuir sé ag machtnamh mé agus cheapas dráma dá bharr. Is cuma nó dráma nodh é.) Commenting on this assertion, *ACS* nonetheless pronounced the play a translation. See "Dráma Nua nó Aistriú?" (A new play or a translation?), *ACS*, 11 April 1914.

173. "A Note on Gaelic Plays," *ACS*, 17 May 1913. Oddly, "B.M." was suspicious of the Abbey itself: "It would be well for Na Cluicheoirí not to consciously model itself on the Abbey Theatre; for the Abbey to-day is not in a healthy or progressive condition. The springs of its first inspiration have dried up. The enthusiasm of the Gael for the language ought to keep alive a similar Gaelic movement and lead it to something larger than the Abbey could ever have hoped to be, since its life was restricted by an alien language." Incidentally, *An Oighreacht*, a translation of T. C. Murray's *Birthright*, was staged by the Irish Theatre Company in 1916. See Feeney, *Drama in Hardwicke Street*, 128. The translator was Máire Ní Shíothcháin.

174. "Drama Competitions," *ACS*, 4 June 1910. The play was certainly scheduled for performance as late as May 1910 according to the minutes of the Oireachtas Committee for 7 May 1910 in the Fionán Mac Coluim Papers, National Library of Ireland, MS. 24,403.

imhghín: "When I sought permission from the publishers, it seemed that it would take me God knows how long to get all of the rights involved with it."[175] Whatever the problem, the Gaels thereby lost their chance to experience in Irish what all too many of them regarded as Synge's only acceptable play.

In a pessimistic survey of "The Stage" in January 1910, Seán Mac Giollarnáth exempted the Abbey from his general condemnation, while nonetheless accusing it of having failed to provide leadership in the development of a genuinely national drama, that is, one in Irish. Yet by 1913, despite the difficulties its own resident company continued to have in learning the language, the Theatre's management was by no means excluding Irish from its stage. For example, on St. Patrick's Day of that year, with the Number One company on tour in America, the Abbey's School of Acting successfully produced Hyde's *An Tincéir agus an tSidheog* (The tinker and the fairy) at the Theatre.[176] In addition, several of the works performed on the Abbey stage by the visiting Gaelic companies were themselves translated Abbey plays, a development that culminated—although those involved were mercifully unaware that this was the high point of their achievement—on the evening of 24 November 1913, when Na Cluicheoirí brought Irish versions of Yeats, Gregory, and Mayne to the Abbey.[177] Revivalists would obviously have preferred to see the regular production of sophisticated original drama in Irish by the permanent professional company of the "National Theatre," but they were clear-sighted enough to be proud of what they had

175. "Réamhrádh" (Preface) to *Áine agus Caoimhghín: Dráma Éin-Ghníomha* (Áine and Caoimhghín: A one-act play) (Baile Átha Cliath: Connradh na Gaedhilge, 1910), v. "Nuair d'iarras cead ar na foillsightheoiríbh facthas dom go dtóigfeadh sé orm—ag Dia tá 'fhios cé 'fhaid—gach ceart dá raibh ag baint dhó d'fhagháil." According to Mac Domhnaill, Pearse had expressed interest in publishing the translation in *ACS* though he never did so. See Declan Kiberd, *Synge and the Irish Language* (London: Macmillan, 1979), 244–45. Writing in the school magazine, another Sgoil Éanna faculty member, Thomas MacDonagh, had suggested the translation of this play in 1910. See "For Plays in Irish: A Suggestion," *An Macaomh* 2, no. 1, 42.

176. See Hogan, Burnham, and Poteet, *The Abbey Theatre: The Rise of the Realists*, 176–78; and M., "Fuireann Cluicheoirí na Mainistreach" (The Abbey acting company), *ACS*, 24 February 1912. E. R. Dix had pointed out to Gaels that a large attendance was essential if they wanted the Abbey to know there was a demand for such plays, and warned, "If such does not take place it is almost certain that no other effort of the kind will be made." See E. R. Dix, letter, *ACS*, 17 February 1912. Seán Ó Caomhánaigh attended the play with "Fada Fánach" but while he was impressed with the turnout, his companion was angry that important members of the movement were not present and that the Gaelic text of the program was full of spelling errors. See Ó Caomhánaigh, "Catharach Nuadh," *SF*, 24 February 1912.

177. "The Stage," editorial, *ACS*, 15 January 1910.

achieved. And with Yeats and Lady Gregory on the boards of the Abbey in Irish, the high optimism of Robert Lynd may well have seemed prophetic: "We may look at the triumph of the Gall-Gael in the field of dramatic literature as a mere hint and omen of what the Gael and the Gall-Gael combined will one day be able to accomplish in the sphere of a truly national drama."[178]

Of course, as we have seen, unquestioned Gaelic orthodoxy would not allow any such combination to be one of equals, and even for the most broad-minded Gaelic progressives any Anglo-Irish movement could achieve its only real validity as a lesser, if temporarily broader and more imposing, tributary of the Gaelic Revival. The universality of this assumption of necessity colored the Gaelic response to all Irish writers in English, from the most naive generator of nationalistic rhymes for the provincial press to the winner of the 1923 Nobel Prize in literature. What, however, could be done with those Anglo-Irish writers who had lacked a contemporary Gaelic movement to which they could subordinate themselves? The answer was simple: they were written off. Thus in his favorable review of Mícheál Breathnach's translation of Charles Kickham's *Knockagow*, Pearse could admit that it had never occurred to him to read Kickham, and could ask: "How comes it that we who have heard persistently the call of Gaelic Ireland, of Puritan England, of enthusiastic France, of metaphysical Germany, have never even for a moment heard the call of Anglo-Ireland?" While he went on to qualify this statement a bit, his dismissal of the corpus of nineteenth-century Irish writing in English is unmistakable: "Wolfe Tone's *Autobiography*, Mitchell's *Jail Journal* and certain noble ballads of the Young Irelanders and others, —these alone of all that Ireland has thought and written in English have ever appealed to us. We can feel a kinship on the one hand with An tAthair Peadar Ua Laoghaire and on the other with, say, William Makepeace Thackeray: we can feel none with Lever, Lover, or even with Carleton and Griffin."[179]

Most of his fellow revivalists would have agreed; we hear virtually nothing about any nineteenth-century Anglo-Irish writers with the exception of the poet-patriot Thomas Davis, for whom there was universal affection and whose high-minded nationalism was given enhanced significance in Gaelic eyes by his championing of the national language

178. "An Irish Theatre in London," *Inis Fáil*, February 1907, 8. This piece must have been written just prior to the production of *The Playboy of the Western World* in Dublin.

179. "Literature, Translations, and 'Cnoc na nGabha,'" *ACS*, 27 October 1906. The dismissal of Carleton by Pearse and other Gaelic intellectuals is in retrospect striking. Carleton (Liam Ó Coirealláin) does receive a passing word of praise as a historical novelist from Pádraig Ua Dálaigh in "Sgéaluidheacht," editorial, *ACS*, 23 May 1914.

(a point underscored by both Ua Laoghaire and Dinneen in their essays on the poet).[180] Yet never did appreciation of the national service performed by Davis and the other Young Irelanders cloud the central issue. In the words of Robert Lynd, the work of Davis and his comrades "was in its aim the literature of an Irish nation, but in its expression it was still the literature of something like an English colony."[181] The other major Anglo-Irish poet of the nineteenth century, Thomas Moore, most interested revivalists as the occasion for discussions about translation inspired by Archbishop MacHale's 1842 Irish versions of his *Melodies* and the subsequent efforts of other translators around the turn of the century.[182] However Thomas O'Neill Russell, Seán Ó Caomhánaigh, Dinneen, Hyde, and the anonymous author of the *Weekly Freeman's* "I bhFochair na nGaedheal" column could all defend Moore's literary reputation, the first limiting his approbation to the poet's work in the preservation of Gaelic melodies, the second offering generous praise, the third wondering whether his dismissal by English critics was the result of anti-Irish or anti-Catholic prejudice, the fourth noting his seminal role in inspiring Ascendancy interest in Irish culture in the nineteenth century, and the fifth calling him "the superb Irish poet who is lying in a foreign grave" (an sár-fhile Gaedhealach atá 'na luighe i n-uaigh iasachta).[183] Concerning other Anglo-Irish writers there was virtual silence.

The situation is entirely different with regard to Yeats's Anglo-Irish movement, the leader of which was of enormous interest to the Gaels. All of Yeats's pronouncements and activities were scrupulously monitored and evaluated in the Gaelic and Irish-Ireland press. The stormy relation between Yeats and Arthur Griffith, in whose the *United Irish-*

---

180. For Ua Laoghaire, see "Fiuchadh Fola" (Boiling blood) and "An Drochad" (The bridge) in *Sgothbhualadh*, 143–46 (both essays originally appeared in *The Leader* in August 1904); for Dinneen, see "Níor Bhain le Ní nár Shlachtuigh" (He graced all he touched), *The Leader*, 12 December 1914. For Davis's own views on the Irish language, see "Our National Language," in *Prose Writings of Thomas Davis. Edited with an Introduction, by T. W. Rolleston* (London: Walter Scott, n.d.), 158–65.

181. "Literature and Politics," *SF*, 27 February 1909.

182. The popularity of Moore as a source for translation into Irish will be considered in the next chapter.

183. See Thomas O'Neill Russell, "Thomas Moore," *UI*, 30 March 1901 (originally a St. Patrick's Day lecture to the National Literary Society); Seán Ó Caomhánaigh, "Catharach Nuadh," *SF*, 27 May 1911; Patrick Dinneen, "Lucht Measta na Litridheachta / Tomás Ua Mórdha File" (Literary critics / Thomas Moore, poet), *The Leader*, 1 January 1916; Hyde, *Mise agus an Connradh*, 14; and "I bhFochair na nGaedheal," *WF*, 19 April 1904 (the use of the adjective "Gaedhealach," meaning both "Irish" and "Gaelic," is interesting).

man the poet once published on a regular basis, has been chronicled in detail more than once, and hence need only be summarized here. In an unsigned 1900 piece entitled "The Literary Movement in Ireland," the author, probably Griffith himself, says: "Mr. Yeats hopes much for Ireland from the new writers. If they were all as good Irish Nationalists as Mr. Yeats himself, we should hope too."[184] The following year, one of the paper's regular literary critics, "Cuguan," pronounced Yeats "the greatest of living poets and the greatest of Irish poets" since "he has interpreted the Celt to the world and to the Celt himself, and the Celt is exceeding fortunate in having a great artist for his interpreter."[185] But Yeats's support in *Samhain* of Synge's *In the Shadow of the Glen*, a play Griffith called "Mr. Synge's adaptation of the old Greek libel on womanhood," both angered and baffled Griffith, as is evident from his comments in January 1905: "Because we appraise at their full value the services Mr. Yeats has rendered and can render Ireland, we have reference to his articles in *Samhain* with a frankness he will not misunderstand . . . we trust he will come to agree with us that only by turning their backs on London can Irish men of letters serve as reasonably, Ireland and their own souls."[186] Whatever the two men agreed about, it was not Synge, and the discussion became more heated and even abusive in the months and years that followed,[187] so that by 1906 there was an unpleasant snideness in Griffith's comment on a letter from a disgruntled member of the National Theatre Society: "The letter reveals the very regrettable condition of affairs which could not have arisen if Mr. Yeats had followed the advice we gave a few years ago in these columns. Everybody will be sorry for the conversion of our best lyric poet into a limited liability company."[188] Needless to say, the *Playboy* controversy further embittered the relationship. Writing on "The Freedom of the Theatre" on 9 February 1907, Griffith was dismissive: "As to his country, Mr. Yeats claimed on Monday night that he had served it, and the claim is just. He served it unselfishly in the past. He has ceased to serve it now—to our regret."[189] If after this break Griffith was usually fair-

---

184. "The Literary Movement in Ireland," *UI*, 6 January 1900.

185. "Mr. Yeats's Poems," review of *Poems* by Yeats, *UI*, 27 April 1901.

186. Untitled notes, *UI*, 7 January 1905.

187. See, for example, the letter from Yeats and the response from Griffith in *UI*, 17 October 1903, the same issue in which the playlet *In a Real Wicklow Glen* by "Conn" (Griffith?) appeared; and the letters from Yeats and responses from Griffith concerning *The Well of the Saints*, in *UI*, 28 January, 4 and 11 February 1905. Nevertheless, it should also be noted that *UI* serialized Ó Ceallaigh's translation of *Cathleen Ni Houlihan* beginning on 11 February 1905.

188. "All Ireland," *UI*, 10 March 1906.

189. "The Freedom of the Theatre," *UI*, 9 February 1907.

minded enough to publish both his opponent's own combative letters
and favorable comments on his literary work,[190] he nonetheless never
relented in his criticism of what he saw as Yeats's apostasy. For example, he berated him for his neglect of the Irish language at the Abbey,[191]
and asserted that the young man who "wrote so fiercely in our columns
against those Irish who paid 'ignoble loyalty' to Queen Victoria" bore
the same relation to "the Mr. Yeats who has secured a weekly pension
from the Strangers" that "a wild dog has to a Duchess's pug."[192]

Moran's snide dislike of the poet he once dubbed "our Irish Bun-
thorne,"[193] has already been noted. For the most part he shared with
Griffith a primary belief that Yeats had deserted the national cause, that
his work was characterized by an irrelevant and exclusive aestheticism,
an epicene mysticism parading itself as Celtic spirituality:

> We have nothing to say against symbolism—provided we un-
> derstand it. Our "Celtic" symbolists appear to us to have coined
> their own symbols independently, so that before you could un-
> derstand one of their poems you should go through a course of
> lectures in the particular technique of their symbolism. . . . Even
> Mr. Yeats does not understand us, and he has yet to write even
> one line that will strike a chord of the Irish heart. He dreams
> dreams. They may be very beautiful and "Celtic," but they are
> not ours.[194]

190. See, for example, W. E. Fay, "The Catechist," *UI*, 29 June 1907; the letter from
P. S. Ua hÉigeartaigh quoted in "Irish Ireland," *UI*, 26 September 1908; and Michael
Orkney, "William Butler Yeats / A Character Sketch," *SF*, 6 November 1909. Griffith
probably took more pleasure in negative assessments like those of "S." in "Mr. Yeats and
the British Association," *UI*, 19 September 1908; or of Arald de Blácam in "A Poet in
Error," *SF*, 6 July 1912.

191. See "Ireland and the Theatre," *SF*, 12 March 1910. He was here attacking Yeats
for his address to a meeting of the league's Central Branch where the poet had been
praised by both Hyde and Pearse.

192. "Mistaken Identity," *SF*, 25 January 1913.

193. "Current Affairs," *The Leader*, 16 September 1911.

194. "More Muddle," review of *A Treasury of Irish Poetry*, ed. Stopford Brooke and
T. W. Rolleston, *The Leader*, 22 December 1900. In an editorial reply to a letter praising
Yeats (9 February 1901), Moran wrote: "We only quarrel with the poet of a coterie when
he is regarded as the poet of a nation." Suspicion of Yeats and his colleagues on class
grounds, a persistent undercurrent in Gaelic criticism at the time, was given its most
explicit expression by Bernard Reid in 1914. Speaking of the arts in general, he wrote:
"As happened, in a manner, in the later Anglo–Irish literary movement, they have become attached to a class, the toy of an aristocratic ascendancy, at worst voicing only its
prejudices, at best satisfying only its sentiments; but never thus can they be the authentic

A similar concern was linked with criticism of the poet on more ortho-dox linguistic grounds by Mary Butler in a 1908 review of *Samhain* in the feminist journal *Bean na hÉireann*: "Mr. Yeats writes of all writers of the period that preceded the present literary revival as if they were mere West Britons. Does he think that a tinge of mysticism, an occasional use of Irish idiom, an acquaintance with Irish mythology, makes verse written in English anything other than English verse?"[195]

On the whole, however, positive judgments of the poet far outweigh the negative, and the youthful Pearse's contemptuous dismissal of him as "a mere English poet of the third or fourth rank"[196] is utterly unrepre-sentative. For example, in *Fáinne an Lae*, we read: "But no one will deny that Mr. Yeats strives most earnestly to follow the lead of the old Gaelic writers; whether he succeeds in giving expression to the true Gaelic spirit is a point to be decided by an admiring public."[197] In 1904, An tAthair Tomás Ó Ceallaigh, who translated *Cathleen Ni Houlihan* into Irish the following year, seems to have allowed his admiration of Yeats to carry him perilously close to heresy in his personal decision on this point: "It seems not unnatural to expect that the peculiar qualities of the Celtic nature should shine through the work of an Irishman, even when he writes in English, giving a lustre which is recognisably Irish."[198] Avoiding comment on this "Celtic note" controversy, Pearse in Octo-ber 1905 simply proclaimed *Cathleen Ni Houlihan* "the most beautiful piece of prose that has been produced by an Irishman in our day,"[199] while three years later he wrote of the poet: "We may not all agree with his theories on art and literature, but we cannot forget that he has spent his life in an endeavour to free our ideas from the trammels of foreign thought, or that it was through his writings that many of us made our first acquaintance with our early traditions and literature. He has never ceased to work for Ireland."[200] With the *Playboy* bitterness fresh in

utterance of a nation, or be possessed of vitality or a national style." See "The New Dispensation," *ACS*, 18 July 1914.

195. Review of *Samhain* (1908), *Bean na hÉireann* 1, no. 3 (January 1909): 3.

196. Letter, *ACS*, 20 May 1899.

197. "A Gaelic Theatre," *FL*, 4 February 1899.

198. "The Future of Literature in Ireland," in *An tAthair Tomás Ó Ceallaigh agus a Shaothar*, 283.

199. Review of *Caitlín Ní Uallacháin*, translation of Yeats's *Cathleen Ni Houlihan* by Tomás Ó Ceallaigh, *ACS*, 10 July 1905.

200. "The Gael in Trinity," *ACS*, 28 November 1908. Yeats's artistic integrity and willingness to resist baneful foreign cultural influences were foremost in Pearse's mind when he praised the poet for defying Dublin Castle to stage Shaw's *The Shewing-Up of Blanco Posnet* in 1909: "When Yeats isn't going against public opinion he's going 'against

mind, it was precisely Yeats's service to the national cause that one "Brian Donn" invoked in *Inis Fáil* in 1907: "It is given to few men to do so much fine work for Ireland as he has done. It will be little short of a tragedy if the breach between him and Irish Nationalism, instead of being healed, grows still wider."[201] Pádraig Ua hÉigeartaigh was disgusted by what was going on at home, writing to Griffith's *United Irishman* to defend "the greatest living Irish poet" and "the only National Theatre there is in Ireland": "The cold shoulder which has for some years past been given in Nationalist circles in Dublin to the National Theatre Society, and the constant depreciation of Mr. Yeats, have been not a little puzzling to those who live outside Dublin. . . . They [attacks on Yeats] commenced with the outcry against 'In the Shadow of the Glen,' an outcry ridiculous in the extreme, and ever since they have gone on increasing in virulence and in personality."[202] Writing elsewhere Ua hÉigeartaigh made clear that for him Yeats was far more than an ally in the revivalist cause: "If I were to have to choose between Shakespeare and Yeats now, I don't know which one I should choose, but at any rate I read Yeats many times more often."[203] Less effusive, but no less laudatory, was Seán Mac Giollarnáth, writing in calmer times in *An Claidheamh Soluis* three years later: "When Mr. Yeats speaks on the conditions under which literature is created, on the attitude that encourages its growth, he has the wisdom of a sage, and Ireland owes him much for the example he has set in his devotion to literary ideals, even when she cannot agree with the ideals which Mr. Yeats sometimes holds before her."[204]

---

the Government.' He's a fighter. God preserve him, for we keenly need his like in Ireland." (Nuair nach mbíonn an Yéatsach ag dul i n-aghaidh baramhla an phobail bíonn sé ag dul 'i n-aghaidh an Riaghaltais.' Fear troda is eadh é. Nár lagaidh Dia é, mar tá a leithéid ag teastáil go géar uainn i nÉirinn.) See "Sgéala ar an nGaoith" (Stories on the wind), *ACS*, 4 September 1909.

201. "The Dublin Actors in London," *Inis Fáil*, July 1907, 9. This tribute was particularly noteworthy, for "Brian Donn" was the London Gael most skeptical of the claims of the Anglo-Irish movement. For example, in this very essay he wrote that Yeats's theater could only "pretend" to be an Irish national theater, and the previous year he had called the "National Theatre Company" "a very arrogant title" for the Abbey players. See "Is Dublin a Dead City?" *Inis Fáil*, January 1906, 9.

202. Pádraig Ua hÉigeartaigh, letter, quoted in "Irish Ireland/Mr. Yeats and the British Association," *UI*, 26 September 1908. Griffith flatly rejected Ua hÉigeartaigh's interpretation.

203. "W. B. Yeats, Dramatist," *Inis Fáil*, March 1907, 4.

204. "Ireland and the Theatre," *ACS*, 19 March 1910. Mac Giollarnáth was here commenting on a lecture Yeats delivered to the league's Central Branch in Dublin, with Hyde in the chair and Pearse offering the motion to thank the lecturer. Hyde opened the proceedings by reminding the audience that "Mr. W. B. Yeats had given them in Ireland a

Nevertheless, despite such tributes, the fact remains that Yeats's stature in Gaelic eyes was in general proportionate to his espousal of Gaelic ideals. Once again, the Anglo-Irish writer, however gifted and feted, was to be a self-sacrificing foot soldier in the advance of the Revival. In August 1898 *Fáinne an Lae* celebrated Yeats's enlistment in the cause: "Mr. Yeats, who might do for us what Kollar, with his patriotic poems full of sorrow and passion and hope, did for the Czech movement . . . has taken up Irish as a serious study and has already, we are informed, made considerable progress therein. . . . We look forward confidently to original work in his own language from Mr. Yeats."[205] In March 1904, Pearse commented editorially on a Yeats speech in the United States in which the poet praised the Gaelic League and stressed the central role of the language in the creation of a new Irish literature:

> It is a matter of congratulations that Mr. Yeats has come to see the inadequacy of the literary movement with which he has been mainly associated to touch the heart of Ireland or to utter Ireland's soul. He is now precisely at the same point as the Gaelic League, which holds that literary work in English, however largely it may draw its inspiration from Ireland, is at best only propagandist. We confess that we regard such an admission from Mr. Yeats as valuable, for it represents a conclusion arrived at by a long process of thought. In a sense, too, it is a courageous admission, for by a kind of self-denying ordinance, it shuts out Mr. Yeats's own work from the Valhalla of Irish literature.[206]

Two years later, Pearse granted Yeats a more actively creative role in the Revival while still barring his work from the Gaelic Valhalla: "As for writers in English, they interest us only when they directly or indirectly help on our work, as, we think, Mr. Yeats himself has done in 'Cathleen Ni Houlihan,' in 'On the King's Threshold' and 'On Baile's Strand.'"[207] Nor was there ever much question in Pearse's mind about the ultimate significance of even a Yeats: "When all is said and done, a Roibeárd Weldon making homely rhymes by the fireside in the Déise is nearer the heart of Ireland, is accomplishing a nobler work for Ireland,

---

theatre of their own, for which they had sincerely to thank him." See "The Theatre and Ireland / Lecture by Mr. W. B. Yeats," *SF*, 12 March 1910. Yeats's opinions on the Irish theatre, and in particular the place of the Irish language in its future, were also praised by Pádraic Ó Domhnalláin after he heard the poet deliver a lecture on the subject in Galway. See "Ó Chúige Chonnacht," *ACS*, 3 October 1908.

205. "Notes," *FL*, 27 August 1898.
206. "Mr. Yeats on His Failure," *ACS*, 5 March 1904.
207. "Mr. Yeats on the Drama," *ACS*, 28 January 1905.

is from every point of view of greater moment to Ireland, than a W. B.
Yeats trying over elaborate cadences to the accompaniment of a zither
in a Dublin drawingroom."[208]

In effect, despite his growing appreciation of Yeats's genius, Pearse
continued to see the Yeatsian "renaissance" as "a movement of defeat":

> Unlike most Gaelic Leaguers, we have a sincere admiration for
> much of the work of Mr. Yeats, Mr. Russell, and the other po-
> ets and dramatists of what, without irreverence, we may call the
> Celtic Twilight School. We believe that their work is the finest
> that is being done in our time in English. But do Mr. Yeats and
> his fellows hold a place in the intellectual present of Ireland com-
> parable to that held, say, by An tAthair Peadar or Conán Maol?
> Mr. Yeats with a possible audience of four million is much less
> of a force in Ireland than An tAthair Peadar or Conán Maol with
> a possible audience of half a million. . . . The future is with the
> Gael.[209]

If for Yeats most Gaels had a healthy respect even in disagreement,
for Synge many felt bitter hostility throughout his lifetime. There is no
need to rehash in detail here Declan Kiberd's account of Synge's stormy
relationship with the Irish-Ireland movement.[210] Griffith was especially
and consistently savage, returning again and again to his central objec-
tion to the playwright's work: "His peasants are not Irish, and the language they speak is pure Whitechapel."[211] Griffith was at one with the
Dublin Gaels here, and a few quotes from the movement's press should
serve to illustrate the nature and extent of the revivalists' enmity. Even
in his generous letter to Lady Gregory previously cited, Pearse could

208. "A Word to Our Readers," *ACS*, 21 December 1907. Compare Griffith's far more
extreme view that "we must proclaim that the edifice of English education and English
literature we have built up in this country is not worth a Gaelic verse on the lips of a
Connemara peasant or a Blasket Islander." See "The Native Speaker," editorial, *SF*, 28
January 1911.

209. "Some Thoughts," *ACS*, 10 February 1906. Five years later, one "D.C." [Daniel
Corkery?] underscored what was at stake if such optimism was misplaced: "When we let
go of our own language we laid the seeds of our mental destruction. . . . It is true that, in
spite of the loss of our own tongue, a distinctive character has often marked Irish writings, so that an Anglo-Irish literature has sprung up. This bears a certain relation to the
past. But as time goes on and as we get mentally further from that past, this character will
die out, and for all intents and purposes there will be but one common literature in these
countries." See "Wanted—A National Literature," *The Leader*, 6 April 1912.

210. See *Synge and the Irish Language*, and "John Millington Synge agus Athbheochan na
Gaeilge," (Synge and the Irish language revival), *Scríobh* 4 (1979): 221–33.

211. "All Ireland," *UI*, 11 February 1905.

write: "Plays like Mr. Synge's, however, discourage me."[212] In a brief review of *The Well of the Saints* in 1905 he made plain the reasons for this discouragement: "Some impurity of mind adheres to everything that comes from the hand of this author. He has another failing as well, and it's no small failing. He doesn't understand the mind of the Gael, and we fear he never will."[213] That same year he pondered Yeats's "strange infatuation which makes him see a great dramatist in Mr. Synge,"[214] and offered the Abbey some unsolicited advice in a favorable notice of Lady Gregory's *Kincora*: "Let them stay clear of rubbish like 'The Well of the Saints' and 'In the Shadow of the Glen.'"[215] Pearse was here fully representative of mainstream Gaelic opinion at the time. During his life all of Synge's work, with the exception of *Riders to the Sea*, was condemned in the Dublin Gaelic press, and even that play was ridiculed in the *Leader* and in *An Claidheamh Soluis* in February 1906: "Except for the pampooties, the people who were on the stage had no more connection with the people of Inis Mean than they did with the people of Hong Kong."[216] *Playboy* was seen as only a more extreme expression of this central failing, as is clear from Micheál Mhag Ruaidhrí's letter to the *United Irishman* after seeing the play: "He began writing a drama to put the manners, modesty, and meekness of the women of Mayo in foreign words and to show their deeds as they spoke those words on the un-national stage of the Abbey Theatre in the City of the Pale."[217]

---

212. 29 April 1905, *Letters*, 94.

213. "Mion-Sgéala," *ACS*, 11 February 1905. "Leanann neamh ghlaine éigin intinne do gach aon rud thigeas ó láimh an ughdair seo. Easbaidh eile atá air, agus ní beag an easbaidh í, ní thuigeann sé aigneadh an Ghaedhil, agus is baoghalach linn nach dtuigfidh go deo."

214. "About Literature," *ACS*, 22 April 1905.

215. "Mion-Sgéala," *ACS*, 15 April 1905. "Seachnaidís drabhfhuigheall de shaghas 'The Well of the Saints' agus 'In the Shadow of the Glen.'"

216. "Ráflaí" (Rumors), *ACS*, 2 March 1906. "Taobh amuigh de na brógaibh úr-leathair, ní raibh gaol ná cosmhalacht ag na daoinibh do bhí ar an árdán le muintir Inis Meadhon thar mar bhí acu le muintir Hong-Cong." Synge's perceived exoticism was also attacked by a critic in *Irisleabhar na Gaedhilge*, who wrote of one of the Aran articles that appeared in *An Gaodhal*: "Mr. J. M. Synge, whoever he be, appears to be inclined to look down at the natives of Arann from a very high eminence indeed. He discourses of them in a quasi-learned style, as if they were some tribe of central Africa, instead of Irish islanders of simple and unaffected manners." See "Clódhanna Nua" (New publications), *IG* 11, no. 128 (May 1901): 95. As we have seen, however, *Riders to the Sea* was translated into Irish by Tomás Mac Domhnaill.

217. Micheál Mhag Ruaidhrí, letter, quoted in "Irish Ireland," *UI*, 16 February 1907. "Thoisigh sé ag sgríobhadh dráma le modhamhalacht, macántacht, agus mánlacht ban Conntae Mhuigheo a chur i mbriathraibh Gallcanta agus a ngníomhartha a theasbáint i

As has been noted, London Gaels differed sharply and consistently from their Dublin counterparts in their reception of Synge. For example, commenting in February 1907 on Synge's essay "The Vagrants of Wicklow," an anonymous reviewer in *Inis Fáil* wrote with unintentionally ironic understatement that the piece "reminds us, that, on the whole, Gaelic Leaguers have not appreciated Synge at anything like his real value."[218] Responding to events in Dublin, where a *Leader* columnist had written that should the Abbey continue to produce work like the *Playboy* "criticism must eventually take the form of a cabbage,"[219] London Gaels offered a welcome sense of proportion. Thus, having noted "the attempted muzzling" of J. M. Synge, *Inis Fáil* editorialized:

> The play is about as unreal a thing as ever was written about Ireland. It is as unreal as a fairy-tale. It is a kind of fairy-tale, indeed, in which the characters are all bad. It is the least important piece of work that Mr. Synge has yet done, being for the most part a mere condensation of all the eccentric and grotesque things he ever heard or imagined. There is imagination in it, however, and so it can be read with interest—sometimes, with artistic delight. Still, looked at as a whole, it is mediocre. It did not deserve to be hissed to death.[220]

Similar insistence on judging the play by aesthetic rather than political or moral criteria is evident in Ua hÉigeartaigh's comments in June 1907. Emphasizing that the play was flawed by "over-expression" that

---

gceann na briathra ar áilléar neamh-náisiúnta i n-Amharclainn na Mainistreach i gCathair na nGall-Teorann." Mhag Ruaidhrí also attacked the play in "Dhá Chéad Bliadhain Deireannach, a Ghrádh, Nach Fada an Suan É?" (The last two hundred years, love, isn't that a long sleep?), *ACS*, 9 February 1907. At least Mhag Ruaidhrí had seen the play. Tomás Breach attacked it in *An Lóchrann* contingent on whether "the accounts we have seen of it are true." See "The Stage Irishman and Anti-Irish or Music Hall Songs," *An Lóchrann* 1, no. 1 (March 1907): 6.

218. Review of *The Shanachie*, *Inis Fáil*, February 1907, 5.

219. "Avis," "The Playboys in the Abbey," *The Leader*, 2 February 1907.

220. "Notes of the Month," *Inis Fáil*, April 1907, 3. "Brian Donn" agreed. Calling *Playboy* "tedious," he wrote: "We do not imagine that 'The Playboy' will be heard of very much in the future." The notion that Synge's imagination gravitated to the bizarre and unwholesome was a recurrent one in Gaelic criticism on both sides of the Irish Sea. For example, an *Inis Fáil* reviewer commented on one of his West Kerry sketches: "One feels, however, that his interest in them is primarily an interest in the abnormal and unusual and that normal happenings make no impression on him." See review of *The Shanachie*, *Inis Fáil*, October 1907, 5–6. Similarly, years later Lynd wrote: "But in the wildly overelaborated tale of 'The Playboy' we see a man of limited vitality straining after monstrous effects which could only be achieved by a Rabelais." See "Literature in Ireland," *An t-Éireannach*, January 1912, 12.

is "deliberate," Ua hÉigeartaigh called *Playboy* "Mr. Synge's worst play from the literary point of view," adding: "The play is not a libel; it is only a bad play." Significantly, what made this failure most disappointing for Ua hÉigeartaigh was his belief that Synge and Padraic Colum were "the two writers who 'get' our peasantry best . . . giving us plays utterly devoid of that colourless simplicity which tradition, literary tradition that is, ascribes to them."[221] Such an opinion, expressed in certain circles in Dublin at the time, might well have merited its author his very own critical cabbage.

The passage of time, and especially the playwright's premature death in March 1909, sharpened Ua hÉigeartaigh's appreciation of Synge's unique vision and artistic integrity. For example, after seeing an Abbey production of *The Well of the Saints* in Sloane Square in the summer of 1909, he lamented:

> "The Well of the Saints" was finely played, with just the right amount of reserve in the acting, and it, and parts of "The Playboy" made me feel what Ireland lost in Mr. Synge's wild imaginative power. That wild imagination which flashed into a wild exaggeration in some parts of "The Playboy" would assuredly have quieted down again to harden him into the greatest of our dramatists. . . . The play was both attacked and defended on wrong grounds. The things for which it was attacked are mere excrescences on it, which obscure the central idea, but do not detract from its worth. A calmer generation will see this more clearly.[222]

Such calmer clarity found expression in Robert Lynd's insightful obituary of Synge in *Inis Fáil* the month after the playwright's death. Although he still saw *Playboy* as "only a caricature of Synge's really good work," he pronounced *Riders to the Sea* "immortal," a work "even an Irish-speaking Ireland will have to translate and make its own," and concluded: "Synge, like Mr. Yeats, has helped to bring to birth in Ireland an ideal of literary form that is likely to outlast the use of the English language as a literary medium among us. . . . Heap up their faults as you will, you must admit that few men have served Ireland

221. ("Sarsfield"), "Holding the Mirror," *Inis Fáil*, June 1907, 8. In 1912, Lynd was to call *Playboy* "a sort of literary forgery on Irish life, just as Macpherson's 'Ossian' was a forgery on Gaelic literature. . . . I use the word 'forgery,' of course, not in the sense that Synge aimed at anything dishonest, but that he accomplished something untrue." See "Literature in Ireland," *An t-Éireannach*, January 1912, 12.

222. "Ireland in Sloane Square," *Inis Fáil*, July 1909, 4.

better in their generation according to the light given to them. They have helped to give Ireland a new dignity among the nations."[223]

Even in Dublin time and reflection made it possible for a few Gaels to accept and even treasure Synge. A year after the playwright's death Art Mag Uidhir wrote in *An Claidheamh Soluis*: "Synge was a Gael among men. He was far more Gaelic than Eoghan Ruadh Ó Súilleabháin. . . . Colum Cille and Synge were of the same blood."[224] Of course, the most dramatic change of mind and heart about Synge was that of Pearse, who wrote in "From a Hermitage" in June 1913: "When a man like Synge, a man in whose sad heart there glowed a true love of Ireland, one of the two or three men who have in our time made Ireland considerable in the eyes of the world, uses strange symbols which we do not understand, we cry out that he has blasphemed and we proceed to crucify him."[225]

Nevertheless, for most Gaels, Synge remained the "Evil Spirit"[226] of the Anglo-Irish movement, and they would have agreed with Cáit Ní Dhonnchadha, who in 1911 wrote that she still found much of his work alien and distasteful: "It is said that he had a beautiful dramatic talent, but whatever misfortune afflicted him, he never really succeeded in feeling affection for the people of his own country. It is difficult to speak with patience or with the respect due the dead if one is to properly discuss some of his work."[227]

---

223. "J. M. Synge," *Inis Fáil*, April 1909, 4. See also the perceptive appreciation by Patrick Hogan, who praised Synge not only for *Riders*, but also for his understanding of the Irish peasant evident in *In the Shadow of the Glen*. Of *Playboy* Hogan wrote: "It is a piece of genuine art, but it should never have been presented as a picture of Irish life, and so far as we have read the play and its criticisms it was never judged aright." See "Synge and His Writings," *An t-Éireannach*, September 1912, 7–8.

224. "John M. Synge," *ACS*, 30 April 1910. The author was identified as Art Mag Uidhir when the piece was reprinted in the *National Student* 4, no.1 (November 1913): 20. Mag Uidhir pronounced *The Well of the Saints*, along with the *Táin* and the poem "Slán le Pádraig Sáirséil," "the three masterworks of the Gael" (trí bhárr na nGaedheal). "Gaedheal ar fearaibh iseadh Synge. Is Gaedhealaighe go mór é ná Eoghan Ruadh Ó Súilleabháin. . . . Aon-fhuil do Cholum Cille agus do Synge." Indeed, in 1912 the Widow Quin of *Playboy* was quoted as an authority on the "parching peelers, and the juries fill their stomachs selling judgments of the English law." See "English Law and the Irish Language," *ACS*, 8 February 1912. Even Griffith's *Sinn Féin* moderated its stance toward the late playwright. See, for example, William Bulfin, "Synge as Playwright / A Criticism by 'Che Buono,'" *SF*, 2 April 1910; and A. de Blácam, "Synge," *SF*, 5 October 1912.

225. In *Collected Works: Political Writings and Speeches*, 145.

226. "The Passing of Anglo-Irish Drama," *ACS*, 9 February 1907.

227. "Amharclann na Mainistreach," *ACS*, 11 February 1911. "Tá sé amuigh air go raibh féith áluinn cluichtheachta ann, acht pé donas a bhí ag gabháil dó is beag má éirigh

If the London Gaels had better things to say about Synge than did their comrades in Dublin, they had much more to say about Shaw. Although in 1901 Griffith could include him with Russell and Moore as one of "the three Georges" in his response to a letter asking about "the greatest Irish literary men of the present day,"[228] on the whole G.B.S. seems to have inspired little interest in his native city, and that little negative, particularly when he made light of the cause: "Mr. Shaw made himself ridiculous when a couple of weeks ago he betrayed an unusual prejudice, for one claiming to be Irish, against the national language of this country. . . . What is really wrong with Mr. Shaw is that he has been a West Briton quite unknown to himself. He discovered the fact a fortnight ago and is very angry ever since."[229] Indeed, when Shaw's work did make news in Gaelic circles, after the Abbey defied Dublin Castle and staged *The Shewing-Up of Blanco Posnet* in 1909, the playwright himself was mentioned almost as an afterthought, the focus being on Irish theatrical independence and the heroes Yeats and Lady Gregory. Pearse wrote:

> We take no more interest in the literary fate of Mr. George Bernard Shaw than an orthodox Hebrew of the House of Judah may be imagined to have taken in the fate of an erring member of one of the mislaid Tribes. So far as the Gael is concerned, Mr. George Bernard Shaw belongs "to the legion of the lost ones, to the cohort of the damned." . . . Yet we are interested in the situation which the putting on of Mr. Shaw's play by the Directors of the Abbey Theatre has precipitated. The action of the directors may have been wise or foolish, but the fact remains that they are now making a fight for Irish freedom from an English censorship. Mr. Shaw and "Blanco Posnet" have no more to do with the case than the flowers that bloom in the spring.[230]

But not even Yeats's apparent defiance of the Castle could impress Moran, who blasted the poet for embroiling the Abbey in a purely English squabble that could lead to the introduction of British censor-

---

riamh leis taithneamh a thabhairt do phobal a thíre féin. Ba dheacair labhairt le foidhne nó leis an urraim is dúil do'n mharbh ag cur síos le hoireamhaint ar chuid dá cheapadóireacht."

228. "Answers to Correspondents," *UI*, 7 September 1901.

229. "Mr. Shaw Angry," *ACS*, 22 October 1910. Griffith's is certainly the attitude toward Shaw that Sean O'Casey remembered as typical of Irish Irelanders. See *Drums under the Windows*, 253.

230. "An English Censorship in Ireland," *ACS*, 28 August 1909.

ship to Ireland.[231] Griffith, for whom Shaw was "England's chartered jester" and "the cleverest flatterer England has hired,"[232] shared this view, writing in *Sinn Féin*: "Bernard Shaw is a very brilliant Irishman who gave up his country to capture the British public. Now that he and the British public have quarrelled, there is no reason why we should take part in the squabble."[233] And in Dublin, Shaw seems at times to have been considered the most irrelevantly Anglo of all contemporary Anglo-Irish writers, so that while Peadar Mac Fhionnlaoich could acknowledge that the plays of Sheridan, Goldsmith, and Shaw were "of the highest quality," he could then go on to ask, "What appeal have they to an Irishman more than Shakespeare's or J.M. Barrie's?"[234] In like manner, William P. Ryan, reviewing MacDonagh's *Literature in Ireland*, stated: "There are many writers who were born in Ireland—from Goldsmith and Sheridan to George Bernard Shaw—and it would be futile for us to seek this Irish Mode in their writings."[235]

On the other hand, in London, where the playwright was approaching the prolific height of his powers and popularity, G.B.S was harder to ignore, although some Gaels there felt he deserved such treatment: "He has just sufficient Irish nature to feel out of his element, but he has not enough to enable him to interpret Irish ideas or Irish character. . . . Not wholly through his own fault he is lost to his own race, and, through that fact, is virtually lost to humanity—it is highly improbable that he can make any permanent contribution to literature."[236] William P. Ryan, at the time resident in London, was even sharper in his condemnation of Shavian irreverence for Gaelic League ideals, which he apparently felt the playwright, perhaps subconsciously, shared: "He has got now into the habit of jesting about his deepest convictions. It serves with the Anglican, but the Gael regards it with impatience, mingled with some wholesale contempt."[237] For most of the Londoners, however, there seems to have been some amused affection for G.B.S., an affection that comes through in the little 1905 skit "Two Dramatists— A Tragic Moment on a Mountain" from *Guth na nGaedheal*. Set on "a mountainside along which mystic shadows are flitting," the playlet

231. See "Current Affairs," *The Leader*, 4 September 1909.
232. "The New Stage Irishman," *SF*, 19 March 1910.
233. "The Castle and the Theatre," editorial, *SF*, 21 August 1909.
234. "Feis Bhéilfeirste," *ACS*, 2 May 1914.
235. "Tomás Mac Donnchadha," *ACS*, 2 September 1916. "Tá iomadh sgríbhneoir a rugadh i nÉirinn—ó Goldsmith agus Sheridan go dtí George Bernard Shaw—agus do bheadh sé fánach againn bheith ar lorg an Mhodha Éireannaigh seo i n-a sgríbhinní."
236. "The Sad State of G.B.S.," *Inis Fáil*, December 1904, 4.
237. "London Notes," *ACS*, 23 March 1901.

spoofs both Shaw and Yeats with witty good humor. Frustrated that the Yeats figure is not shocked by his iconoclasm, the Shaw figure pledges that "this day must I eat a steak, make a commonplace remark, and die," and then exits "tearing his latest hundred-page preface."[238] Also, the suspicion that Shaw's deepest convictions might just be evolving in the right direction meant that he was not beyond redemption. Thus in 1907 Ua hÉigeartaigh wrote: "Many will resent my saying that his genius is essentially Irish, but at any rate it isn't English."[239] In fact the playwright's nationality was primary in Ua hÉigeartaigh's praise of the Abbey for staging *Blanco Posnet*: "The Abbey Company has been criticised a good deal for accepting the play and criticised most unjustly. As the work of an Irishman, offered to them, they are quite right to take it and play it, and the event has justified them, as in the case of the 'Playboy.' "[240]

Some London Gaels, themselves exiles to whom the Revival had brought both purpose and zest, also seem to have believed that G.B.S. could share their commitment, turning his prodigious energy into native channels. Praising the preface to *John Bull's Other Island* in *Inis Fáil* in 1907, "Brian Donn" fantasized: "He does not yet understand the point of view of the Gaelic League, but he has only to continue for another five years along his present line of thinking in order to become a faithful student of O'Growney and a regular contributor to—perhaps ultimately even editor of—*Inis Fáil*."[241]

Of other Anglo-Irish writers, Lady Gregory, who always maintained close personal relations with the league and its leaders and who occasionally contributed to *An Claidheamh Soluis*, was almost invariably treated with respect and affection, even by Moran.[242] Typical is Pearse's

238. "Iniscreabhain," "Two Dramatists—A Tragic Moment on a Mountain," *Guth na nGaedheal*, March 1905, 23–24.

239. "Holding the Mirror," *Inis Fáil*, June 1907, 9.

240. "The Oireachtas Dramas—and Others," *Inis Fáil*, September 1909, 5.

241. "George Bernard Shaw and Ireland," *Inis Fáil*, August 1907, 9. See also "George Bernard Shaw and Gaelic" (*Inis Fáil*, February 1906, 6): "On whatever pretext he joins us, however, he is sure to be a sufficiently popular figure in our classes for beginners."

242. For example, Moran called her *Devorgilla* "the best play we have yet seen at the Abbey" ("Current Affairs," *The Leader*, 9 November 1907). See also the highly positive review of her *Seven Short Plays* by Seán Ó Ciarghusa ("Marbhán") in *The Leader*, 18 September 1909. Of course, when she and Yeats took *Playboy* to the United States in 1911, Moran was willing to excommunicate her not only from the movement, but from the race: "Probably Pensioner Yeats and Lady Gregory have not a drop of Irish blood in their veins, but finding the mere Irish in a weak state after the Penal Laws and the persecutions, they would attempt to enforce their wills on the nation." See "Current Affairs," *The Leader*, 16 December 1911.

brief review of *The Jackdaw* in March 1907: "Lady Gregory is an extraordinary woman. Here's another play she has composed, and it is
funnier than anything that has come from her pen yet."[243] Two years
later, in a review of her *Seven Short Plays*, Pearse pronounced her work
fit for production even by Gaelic League branches at official league
functions: "Lady Gregory's plays are not in any sense propagandist, but
are simple pictures of Irish life, tragic and humorous. As plays they
have met with great popularity, and may safely be recommended to
Gaelic League Companies who still find it necessary to stage English
plays."[244]

Another major and highly visible Anglo-Irish figure was less fortunate. AE (George Russell) received considerably less notice in the Gaelic
press, although Pearse, despite reservations about his aestheticism, did
call him "a true artist, thinking conscientiously, and giving of the best
that is in him";[245] Pearse even admitted that he preferred Russell's play
Deirdre to that of Yeats.[246] Usually, however, *An Claidheamh Soluis*
seems to have been more interested in Russell in his role as traveling
agent for the Irish Agricultural Organisation Society and editor of its
organ the *Irish Homestead*, chiding him for his linguistic inadequacy for
these posts, but on the whole impressed by his commitment and competence: "Mr. Russell writes in English and he does not wholly understand the Irish-speaking people of places like Connemara, in whose
lives he finds 'not a redeeming feature,' but his gospel of local patriotism is so sound and convincing that we have to regard him as one of

243. "Cluicheoireacht Ghaedhealach," *ACS*, 2 March 1907. "Is éachtach an bhean í
Baintighearna Gréagóir. Seo cluiche eile curtha i ndiaidh a chéile aici, agus í níos sult-
mhaire 'ná aon nidh dá dtáinig ó n-a láimh fós." See also his comments on *Kincora*
("Mion-Sgéala," *ACS*, 15 April 1905); and on *The Gaol Gate* ("Mion-Sgéala," *ACS*, 3
November 1906). The Londoners also enjoyed Lady Gregory's work, at least most of the
time. For example, reviewing *The Bogie Men* and *Coats* in 1912, Ua hÉigeartaigh wrote:
"Lady Gregory has established a record in writing the two worst plays of this generation,
as well as two or three of the best." See "The Abbey Players / More Reflections," *An
t-Éireannach*, August 1912, 8.

244. Review of *Seven Short Plays* by Lady Gregory, *ACS*, 31 July 1909, Duilleachán an
Oireachtais. One Gaelic intellectual who would have dissented was Tadhg Ó Donnchadha, who wrote of *The Kiltartan Wonder Book*: "Don't books in broken English go a
long ways from home—in the name of Ireland! Thus are many people outside of Ireland—and some inside Ireland as well—deceived concerning the native characteristics of
Ireland." (Nach fada ó bhaile a théigheann leabhair Bhéarla bhriste—i n-ainm na hÉireann! Mar sin a curtar púicín ar a lán daoine leathsmuigh d'Éirinn—agus roinnt daoine
leathstigh d'Éirinn leis—i dtaobh fiornós dúthchais na hÉireann.) See "Ceilteachas,"
ACS, 18 January 1913.

245. "About Literature," *ACS*, 29 April 1905.

246. "Mion-Sgéala," *ACS*, 21 December 1907.

the most valuable forces in the Ireland that is in the making."[247] The many facets of AE's creativity were brought most sharply into a Gaelic focus by William P. Ryan in his serialized 1915–16 novel *An Bhóinn agus an Bhóchna*, where Russell, under the name Feargus Ó Ruanaidhe, is presented as a polymath *bodhisattva* from a Celtic Golden Age: "Fergus is a marvelous man. He takes as much interest in potatoes as in mysticism, in sowing as in the Cosmos, in bees as in Brahma. When I listen to him I feel that the human race is noble and that Ireland is a noble, bountiful, spiritual land. I feel that I am near Tír na nÓg."[248]

Edward Martyn, whose significant contributions to the league were financial as well as propagandist, was accorded near deference by the Revival press, with even Pádraic Ó Conaire offering his quite literal blessing (beannacht) on his soul in 1927.[249] Gaelic inflation of Martyn's contribution to the cultural revival culminated in a 1915 *An Claidheamh Soluis* editorial by Crawford Neil in which Martyn was proclaimed "the strongest mind of the earliest Irish Literary Theatre," and a man who

247. "A Book for Nation Builders," review of *Co-operation and Nationality* by AE, *ACS*, 23 March 1912. *ACS* was, of course, aware of Russell's varied cultural contributions. For example, his paintings on exhibit at the Oireachtas of 1911 were singled out for special praise. See "The Arts Exhibition," *ACS*, 5 August 1911.

248. *An Bhóinn agus an Bhóchna*, *ACS*, 30 October 1915. "Is iongantach an duine é Feargus; cuireann sé an oiread suime i bprátaí agus i bhfisidheacht, i gcuraidheacht agus sa gcosmos, i mbeacha agus i mBrahma. Airighim agus mé ag cloisint dó gurab uasal an cine daonna agus gur fial fairsing spriodálta an tír í Éire. Airighim go mbím i n-aice le Tír na nÓg." Actually, an almost identical assessment of Russell had been offered readers of *ACS* three years previous by one "Clóca" (Ryan again?):

> There isn't anyone who knows George Russell (AE) who doesn't know that he is a multifaceted man. Poet, artist, painter, playwright, newspaper editor, a fine debater about literature, art, the life of rural people, etc. He is no more happy speaking about pictures, poetry or the like in literary company than speaking amongst farmers about good fertilizer, the best way to make butter or to set hens laying.

> (Níl aonne a bhfuil aithne aige ar Sheoirse Ruiséal (A.E.) ná gur b'eol dó gur il-thréitheach an duine é sin. File, gaisteoir, peictiúrí, scríobhnóir cluiche, eagarthóir páipéir, aighneastóir breagh ar litridheacht, ealadhain, tuath-shaoghal na ndaoine, ⁊c. Ní sonaidighe leis labhairt ar pheictiúiríbh, fhilidheacht agus a lithéid ameasc cuideachtan liteardha ná ameasc na bhfeirmeoirí ar leasughadh maith, an tslighe is fearr chun ime do dhéanamh, nó cearca do chur ar breith.)

See "Fada Fánach" (Wandering afar), *ACS*, 23 November 1912. See also Aonghus Ó Duibhne, "The New Druids at Home: An Evening with Thinkers and Workers in New Ireland," *Saothar na h-Éireann*, November 1913, 28–31 ("Gerald Newman" is the AE figure here).

249. Pádraic Ó Conaire, "Obair Shamhraidh: Feiseanna agus Eile" (Summer work: Feiseanna and other things), in *Iriseoireacht Uí Chonaire*, 183. Martyn died in 1924; this piece originally appeared in the *Connacht Sentinel* on 12 July 1927. Ó Conaire was praising Martyn specifically for his work with Irish music.

"remained dominantly Gaelic and sensible" while "his friends Yeats and Moore pursued fantasy to the ends of the earth."[250] Interestingly, a London Gaelic critic, removed from the proximate influence of the Martyn paunch and purse, could view his work with a more jaundiced eye: "Mr. Edward Martyn is still intellectually where Europe was some fifteen or twenty years ago, that is to say he is still trying to 'do' Ibsen. I am afraid it will not do. . . . Mr. Martyn has read his Ibsen not wisely but too well."[251]

A healthy, and well-merited, skepticism was the dominant Dublin response to George Moore from the time of his 1901 return to his native land to save the Irish language. For example, in September of that year Moran wrote: "We have often speculated as to how long Mr. George Moore will stay in this country, and we have often thought about two years will give him enough of it, and that then we may expect him to go away and tell us fairly what he thinks of this green immortal nation."[252] Of course, in keeping with the prevailing Gaelic attitude toward Anglo-Irish writers, Moore was warmly welcomed when he expressed a willingness to serve in the ranks of the Revival by championing Gaelic drama or providing original short stories expressly for translation into Irish. Nevertheless, even at his most flamboyantly committed, the Gaels seemed unable to take him entirely in earnest: "Suddenly we hear the sweet strains of a fairy *tiompán*, and the curtain flies up to discover Mr. Moore pushing aside the mummers (as is his wont) with one hand, while with the other he presents us with the acting copy of a play in Gaelic."[253] Predictably, when Moore lost inter-

250. "An Irish Theatre," *ACS*, 9 January 1915. Reid's editorial and the regular laudatory references to Martyn's Hardwicke Street Irish Theatre in *ACS* in 1914–15 seem to have been intended at least in part to annoy what Reid called "the Abbey Press Bureau," where "unpleasant little peasant atrocities . . . are manufactured *ad nauseam*." See also "The Irish Theatre," *ACS*, 24 April 1915.

251. A. de Blácain [sic], "Some Recent Books," review of, inter alia, *Grangecolman* by Edward Martyn, *An t-Éireannach*, June 1912, 11.

252. "The Irritation of Mr. George Moore," *The Leader*, 28 September 1901. *UI*, which in general treated Moore fairly, could share this skepticism. See "All Ireland," 10 February 1900. Commenting on Moore's conversion to Protestantism two years later, Moran claimed, with justice in this instance, to speak for the movement: "Irish-Ireland, somehow, never took much notice of the 'convert.' It regarded him with a large amount of suspicion when it interested itself at all in the now 'saved' gentleman." See "Current Affairs," *The Leader*, 3 October 1903.

253. "Notes," *FL*, 3 March 1900. This bemusement was apparently shared by the actors whom Moore directed in Hyde's *Casadh an tSúgáin*, a play whose language was unknown to him. See "Duine Acu," "*Casadh an tSúgáin*," *Banba* 1, no. 1 (December 1901): 7–8. Griffith, on the other hand, wondered about the political implications motivating Moore's commitment to Gaelic drama. See untitled notes, *UI*, 6 July 1901.

est in the Revival, the Gaels as quickly lost interest in him: "Mr. George Moore, too, has now gone back to his old love, and he is now trying to hold up Gaelic League leaders for the laughter of London drawingrooms in an English review."[254] Thereafter he became for many "the very notorious George Moore . . . an evil genius,"[255] "the godless hedonist" who "has pinned [sic] a false notion of his friend [Martyn in *Hail and Farewell*] for English boors to see."[256]

Whatever the sentiments about English boors, English-based Gaels found Moore, back in England from 1911 on, more important and amusing than did their fellows across the Irish Sea. For example, an editorial note in *An t-Éireannach* for March 1910 forthrightly acknowledged "the loss to Irish literature of a genius like Mr. Moore's," and went on to ponder the corresponding loss for the author himself: "And we are not sure that Mr. Moore would not have found an intimate knowledge of traditional Ireland something more than compensation for the chocolates and the civilisation of Paris where he wore the 'blonde beard à la capoule.'"[257] Ua hÉigeartaigh, whose willingness to espouse the heterodox we have already encountered, would actually suggest in a thoughtful 1912 review of *Hail and Farewell!* that the basic responsibility for this mutual loss lie with the Gaels: "One has only to read this book, the candid and sincere account of the contact of a man of genius of Irish blood and birth, and French intellect, with the Gaelic League to see that it failed to hold him because of something lacking in it which cannot be more clearly defined than by a certain lack of courageous vitality."[258]

The revivalists' regular equation of Anglo-Irish willingness to serve the cause with literary promise or accomplishment is apparent from even a glance at a short list of the writers most consistently and/or highly praised in the Gaelic press. While always denying that the English language could adequately or authentically express the Irish soul,

254. "The Abbey Theatre and 'The Playboy,'" *ACS*, 6 January 1912.

255. "The 'Donnybrook Fair' Irishman," *ACS*, 14 November 1914. Moore is here also said to have "deserted us to play the stage Irishman in London."

256. Reid, "An Irish Theatre," *ACS*, 9 January 1915.

257. "Notes of the Month / George Moore and Ireland / How Mr. Moore Nearly Saved Irish," *Inis Fáil*, March 1910, 2–3.

258. "Non-Moral Moore," review of *Hail and Farewell!* by George Moore, *An t-Éireannach*, December 1912, 3. The following month Sarah MacDermott dissented from Ua hÉigeartaigh's praise, writing that "Moore is only of the 'artistic temperament' and not an artist." See "Superficial Moore / An Appreciation and a Difference," *An t-Éireannach*, January 1913, 5–6. Surprisingly, Moore's *Hail and Farewell!* was greeted with some enthusiasm in *SF* in reviews by Griffith and Arald de Blácam. See "George Moore—His Book," *SF*, 30 December 1911; and "Bozzy Moore," *SF*, 19 October 1912.

many revivalists nonethless claimed to find an ineffable Gaelic aura in
the work of such authors as "Eithne Carbery," Brian O'Higgins ("Brian
na Banban"), Mary Butler,[259] the Reverend P. A. Doyle,[260] and Carbery's husband Seamus MacManus. Gaelic enthusiasm for MacManus,
whose critical stock is appropriately at an all-time and perhaps permanent low, is both striking and, at least on the surface, troubling, a reaction that, as we have seen in the discussion of his plays, was shared by
some at the time. In June 1902, the Glasgow Branch of the league actually named itself the Seamus MacManus Branch, an honor accorded
only one other Anglo-Irish writer, Thomas Davis. Gaelic affection for
MacManus even survived what *An Claidheamh Soluis* called his "unrepentant" defense of Anglo-Irish literature in January 1903: "I consider
that you can have an Irish literature as easily as you can have an Irish
linen or Irish soap, irrespective of the language ingredient; and if you
stamp, and advertise, and tell about your Irish linen and your Irish soap
in English, or in Choctaw, they are still Irish linen and Irish soap—not
Anglo-Irish or Choctaw-Irish because of that ingredient."[261] Of course,
MacManus always remained a loyal supporter of the league, touting it
in America, where he spent more and more of his time, contributing
essays (in English) to *An Claidheamh Soluis*, allowing translation of his
plays and of a book of stories,[262] and funding Oireachtas prizes. In return for all these services the league and its official organ reported his
activities at home and abroad, and, more important, treated his literary
work with invariable seriousness and respect.[263] For example, when

259. See, for example, "A Soul and the Movement," Pearse's review of her *The Ring of
Day*, *ACS*, 29 September 1906. In 1902 the league published translations by Tomás Ua
Concheanainn of three of her stories under the title *Blátha Bealtaine* (The flowers of May).
    260. In October 1915, *ACS* called his *The Hook in the Harvest*, then on stage at Dublin's
Father Mathew Hall, "one of the most faithful representations of Irish life ever put on the
stage." See "'The Hook in the Harvest,' and Dublin Theatres," *ACS*, 30 October 1915.
    261. Seamus MacManus, letter, *ACS*, 3 January 1903. It was with such views in mind
that *Banba* dissented when MacManus was appointed to the league's Executive Committee (Coiste Gnótha), calling him "a man of doubtful orthodoxy." See untitled notes,
Banba 2, no. 2 (1 February 1903): 137.
    262. The book of stories was *An Pleidhseam: Trí Sgéalta Draoidheachta ó Thírchonaill*
(The foolishness: Three otherworld stories from Donegal), translated by Peadar Mac
Fhionnlaoich (Dublin: An Cló-Chumann, 1903). The title page indicates that MacManus
originally collected these stories in Irish, for Mac Fhionnlaoich is said to have put them
"back into Irish" (ar ais go Gaedhilg).
    263. See, for example, Pearse's previously cited reviews of three of his plays in *ACS*, 7
October 1905, 14 October 1905, and 17 February 1906, and the following, all favorable,
reviews in *UI* or *SF*: 5 January 1910 (*Donegal Fairy Tales*), 11 April 1903 (*A Lad of the
O'Friels*), and 9 June 1906 (*A Lad of the O'Friels*). In 1900, *UI* (probably Rooney) wrote
that "we know of very few Irish writers whose works might be recommended as more
healthy and more native than his." See "All Ireland," *UI*, 3 March 1900.

MacManus was appointed to an academic post at Notre Dame University in 1908, Pearse wrote: "There are few people in whom one finds the storyteller's genius one finds in Seamus MacManus, and we often say to ourselves that it is a great pity that we have no one at all able to compose stories in Irish as he is able to do in English."[264] While it should be emphasized that there is absolutely no reason to doubt the integrity or sincerity of either party to this informal arrangement, it is also worth noting that the London Gaels seem to have paid little heed to either MacManus or his work.[265]

In his review of a posthumous collection of verse by Carbery, "Conán Maol" provided an exaggerated and florid statement of the principal Gaelic criterion for accepting the validity, albeit partial, of some Anglo-Irish writing: "It is a great pity that 'The Four Winds of Eirinn' is written in English. It is, however, only an English crust, for its whole substance is Gaelic. The mind and heart of the most Gaelic woman of my time is everywhere in the sixty-eight poems in the book."[266] The work of Brian O'Higgins met both this criterion and that of service to the movement, as is evident from Mary Butler's review of his The Voice of Banba in 1907: "The spirit of Brian's work is frankly and vehemently of Irish-Ireland, and for the cause of the Conradh he works indefatigably in Eoghan Ó Gramhna's country."[267] Séamus Ó Searcaigh had similar praise for his story collection Glimpses of Glen-na-Mona: "You can't read it without noticing that it was a Gael who understands his people and his ancestors who wrote the stories in it."[268] Yet despite his impeccable national credentials, the fact that his work was in English could still draw a mild rebuke from Pearse in 1908:

264. "Séamus Mac Maghnuis," ACS, 1 August 1908. "Is beag duine atá le fagháil a bhfuil féith an sgéalaidhe ann mar tá sé i Séamus Mac Maghnuis, agus is minic a dubhairt muid linn féin go mba mhór an truagh nach bhfuil duine ar bith againn atá i n-ann sgéalta a chumadh dúinn sa Ghaedhilg mar atá seisean i n-ann a dhéanta sa mBéarla."

265. One may, however, wonder if MacManus was in William P. Ryan's mind when he expressed his disgust with "a strange and distressing conglomeration which passes for 'Irish dialect' . . . simply broken English, of course, with an occasional Irish word wrongly spelled." See "London Notes," ACS, 2 November 1901.

266. Review of The Four Winds of Eirinn by Eithne Carbery, ACS, 21 June 1902. "Is mór an truagh gur i Sagsbhéarla atá 'The Four Winds of Eirinn' sgríobhtha. Ní fhuil act sgreamh Sagsbhéarla air ar a shon sain, mar is Gaedhealach é a chabhail agus a chorp. Tá intinn is croidhe na mná ba Ghaedhealaighe lem' linn ó bhun bárr ins na hocht dánta is trí fichid atá 'san leabhar."

267. "A Bilingual Poet," review of The Voice of Banba by "Brian na Banban," ACS, 20 April 1907. See also the comments of "An Leipreachán" in "Cois Leasa na nGaedheal" (By the fort of the Gaels), WF, 20 May 1905.

268. "Ó Chúige Uladh," ACS, 8 February 1908. "Ní thig leat a léigheadh gan tabhairt fá dear gur Gaedheal a thuigeas a mhuinntir féin agus a shinnsear a sgríobh na sgéalta atá ann."

"Our only regret about Brian's books is that they are not in Irish. Why does he not turn to Irish authorship as a number of our young writers have already successfully done?"[269] In 1912, he did, publishing *Síol na Saoirse* (The seed of freedom), a work that was predictably welcomed in two reviews, one in Irish and one in English, in the same issue of *An Claidheamh Soluis*, "Manannán" writing: "But yesterday, Irish life and thought seemed dead in Leinster. To-day the mind of a countryman of Ó Neachtain, O'Carolan, and O'Growney gives birth to a book in direct descent from the singers of the olden time."[270] However, although O'Higgins was to have a lengthy and prolific career as poet, publisher of the nationalist *Wolfe Tone Annual*, and designer of Irish greeting cards among other things, most of his literary output was to be in English, with his very next publication, *Signal Fires* (1912), already reverting to bilingualism.[271]

Perhaps most gratifying of all for the Gaels, these earnest minor writers knew their place, as Mary Butler acknowledged with quintessentially proper self-effacement in the preface to her story collection *A Bunch of Rushes*: "My only regret, and it is a poignant one, is that I cannot, at present at any rate, submit to my country people a work written in their own language and my own."[272] Yet here again we must avoid the simplistic conclusion that the league issued its imprimatur solely to boost the reputations of safely second-rate camp followers from the Anglo-Irish side. Padraic Colum and James Stephens, two other writers in English believed to have captured to a striking degree the elusive Gaelic spirit, were by no means either safe or second-rate. In a glowing review of Colum's *The Land* in *An Claidheamh Soluis*, Seosamh Ó Néill wrote: "It is a great pity that this book was written in English, for it has nothing to do with English or the Galltacht; it is

269. "A New Book by Brian na Banban," review of *By a Hearth in Eirinn* by "Brian na Banban," *ACS*, 12 December 1908.

270. "File Gaedhealach" (A Gaelic poet), review of *Síol na Saoirse* by Brian Ó hUigín, *ACS*, 30 July 1910, Uimhir an Oireachtais. See also "File Gaedhealach," *ACS*, 30 July 1910; and "Síol na Saoirse," *SF*, 9 July 1910.

271. For a summary of O'Higgins's career, see the various articles in the special issue of *Feasta* dedicated to him in July 1982.

272. Quoted in "Anglo-Irish Literature," review of *A Bundle of Rushes* by Mary Butler, *ACS*, 5 January 1901. Her self-effacement was applauded by this *ACS* critic: "There is Anglo-Irish literature, and Anglo-Irish literature. There are some who write such literature, and think it can express all Ireland well enough, and that there is no need to revive Irish to really express the Irish mind. On the other hand, there are writers who well know the limitations of such literature, and fully recognise that while it has undoubted value, yet it cannot claim to express Ireland in the fullest sense. Of the latter class is Miss Butler."

Gaelic from start to finish. . . . Gaelic from the bone to the marrow."[273] We have already noted Pearse's glowing opinion of Colum as "the writer who in intellectual stature, as in breadth and depth of vision, must henceforth be acknowledged the most considerable among the little band of Anglo-Irish dramatists." Even Moran was favorably impressed, applying what for many revivalists were the most rigorous critical criteria in his review of the Theatre of Ireland's 1907 production of *The Fiddler's House*: "We thoroughly enjoyed Mr. Colum's latest piece. We enjoyed it as we would enjoy sitting down and listening for an hour or so in the corner of a farmer's house when the people might be discussing their various interests."[274]

Colum was also one Anglo-Irish author on whose virtues Dublin and London could agree. We have already noted Ua hÉigeartaigh's judgment that with Synge Colum was one of "our" two writers "who 'get' our peasantry best," and Lynd's praise of Colum and Campbell as "Irish of the Irish," and one who, like Yeats, wrote "about Ireland and for Ireland." "Brian Donn" went a step farther, putting Colum a notch above his Anglo-Irish contemporaries: "Mr. Yeats expresses beautifully the soul of Mr. Yeats, Mr. Synge expresses in a curious and fascinating way the soul of Mr. Synge, but Mr. Colum comes near expressing the soul of modern Ireland."[275] Predictably, of course, as Colum continued to write exclusively in English and drifted from active involvement in the Gaelic movement, reservations arose and criticism sharpened: "Write in English and you immediately qualify as an intellectual tin god, you are hailed as an Irish Ibsen by the 'Art for Art's sake' votaries, your plays are hailed all over Anglo-Saxondom, from Canada to New Zealand, you may even get a Civil List Pension, you may, in short, become a Bernard Shaw, a W. B. Yeats, or a Padraic Colum."[276]

Like Colum, Stephens was admired by the Gaels both for his creative work, particularly *The Crock of Gold*, and for his serious interest in the language: "Stephens is an Irishman (Éireannach) and a Gael (Gaedheal)

---

273. Review of *The Land* by Padraic Colum, *ACS*, 7 January 1905. "Is mór cás an leabhar so ar na scríobhadh i mBéarla, óir baint ná páirt ní'l aige le Béarla nó le Galldacht; Gaodhalach 'seadh é ó thús go deire. . . . Gaodhalach ó'n gcnámh go dtí an smúsach."
274. "Current Afairs," *The Leader*, 30 March 1907.
275. "Is Dublin a Dead City?" *Inis Fáil*, January 1906, 9. See also the two glowing reviews of *The Land* in *UI*, the first by Maurice Joy on 24 June 1905, the second by Delia O'Dwyer on 16 December 1905.
276. "A Word of Encouragement," *ACS*, 29 April 1911. His *Thomas Muskerry* certainly stirred up considerable controversy in the pages of *SF* concerning his place in the national movement, a controversy in which Colum gave as good as he got. See, for example, X., "Muskerryism," *SF*, 16 July 1910; and Colum, "Muskerryism—A Reply to 'X.,'" *SF*, 23 July 1910.

to the marrow. Although he is only beginning to learn Irish, he has a superb knowledge of the way our old storytellers told stories."[277] In a brief note on Stephens's winning the Polignac Prize for *The Crock of Gold*, Eoin Ó Searcaigh emphasized the novel's Gaelic spirit while at the same time pointing out what he saw as the healthy influence of An tAthair Peadar on its author: "'The Crock of Gold' is a very Gaelic book. There is a big piece from 'Eisirt' woven into it."[278] Even more extravagant in his praise of and claims for this novel's Gaelicism was Arald de Blácam: "I have just come back to London from Tír na nÓg. In other words, I have just finished my second reading of James Stephens' new book 'The Crock of Gold.' . . . The style of writing—the artful play on Gaelic idiom—the thrilling allusions wrapt in the names of Angus Óg and the man Mac Cul, these indeed shew that we are recovering our heritage, that we are learning the magic that is in the Gaelic tongue, and the poetry that is in myths and legends."[279] The reviewer for *Sinn Féin*, a paper to which Stephens himself contributed on a regular basis, was in full agreement, although many revivalists must have questioned his use of O'Grady as a standard by which to judge mastery of Gaelic mythology: "Since Mr. O'Grady descended into that hades of half-forgotten heroes and made them live and move again for us, I know of no writer save James Stephens who walks amongst the gods and heroes with so assured a step."[280] Such enthusiasm extended to Stephens's work without such obvious Gaelic influences, as is evident in the lengthy *An Claidheamh Soluis* review of *The Insurrection in Dublin* (1916): "The opinions of Stephens himself are interesting and courageous, for they are the opinions of a perceptive, truthful man. Stephens is a person without timidity or fear. He feels in his heart and he under-

---

277. "Buailtean," "An Sgéalaidhe Gaedhealach" (The Gaelic storyteller), *ACS*, 26 October 1912. "Éireannach 'seadh Mac Stiopháin agus Gaedheal go smior é. Cé nach bhfuil sé acht ag tosnughadh ar an nGaedhilg d'fhoghluim tá sár-eolas aige ar an nós sgéalaidheacht a bhí ag ár sean-sgéalaidhe." Leaguers like "Buailtean" must also have been impressed when Stephens was able to take a part in a Gaelic play, *An Croiteachán* (The hunchback), Éamonn Ó Néill's translation of Coppée's *Le Luthier de Crémone*, at the 1911 Oireachtas. See "The Plays," *ACS*, 29 July 1911. For a detailed discussion of Stephens's interest in and work with the Irish language, see Joyce Flynn, "The Route to the *Táin*: James Stephens' Preparation for His Unfinished Epic," *Proceedings of the Harvard Celtic Colloquium* 1 (1981): 125–44.

278. "Craobh na nUghdar" (The Authors' Branch), *ACS*, 6 December 1913. "Leabhar an-Ghaedhealach is eadh 'an Corcán Óir.' Tá slíocht mór 'd'Eisirt' sníomtha isteach ann."

279. "Out of the Crock," review of *The Crock of Gold* by James Stephens, *An t-Éireannach*, May 1913, 2.

280. "S. O'S.," "The Crock of Gold," *SF*, 9 November 1912.

stands in his head that 'the knee is nearer than the ankle.' He is a Gael and he is on the side of the Gaels."[281]

Unfortunately, in the years following independence a writer like Colum or Stephens might conceivably be accepted as "Éireannach," but would rarely be honored as "Gaedheal." Declan Kiberd has lamented "the self-imposed quarantine,"[282] in which Gaelic writers confined themselves after the founding of Saorstát Éireann, and of "the false border between the two literatures" (an teorainn bhréige idir an dá litríocht)[283] that intellectually partitions the country to this day. As we have seen, the roots of this stultifying rigidity go well back into the early days of the language revival. Yet contemporaneous with Gaelic hostility toward and rejection of Anglo-Irish literature was a sincere and sensitive appreciation of the accomplishments of Irish writers of English. While most Gaels may not have been willing to accept their Anglo-Irish counterparts as full partners in the war against Anglicization, they often welcomed, even invited, their support and praised their contributions. Tragically, this liberating vision of an authentically bilingual Irish literary culture was fractured in the political and ideological upheavals of the independence struggle. The adolescent Pearse's strident 1899 letter is not infrequently quoted as representative of pigheaded Gaelic hostility to the Anglo-Irish "renaissance." Too little is heard of the more thoughtful and no less representative views of a *Fáinne an Lae*

---

281. "Cúrsaí an tSaoghail" (Current affairs), *ACS*, 28 October 1916. "Tá baramhla Mhic Stiopháin féin spéiseamhail agus misneamhail mar gur baramhla fir thuigsionaigh fhírinnigh iad. Duine gan sgáth ná faithchíos 'seadh Séamus Mac Stiopháin. Mothuigheann sé ina chroidhe, agus tuigeann sé ina cheann gur goire an glún ná an rúitín. Gaedheal is ea é agus tá sé ar thaobh na nGaedheal." Piaras Béaslaí also expressed admiration for "the vigorous Dublin English" of *The Charwoman's Daughter* in one of his essays on the challenge of writing Gaelic fiction about English-speaking Ireland. See Béaslaí, "Language and Literature," *SF*, 30 March 1912. There were, of course, some reservations. Stephens's *Insurrections* received a chilly welcome in *ACS* in May 1909: "A new book was published in Dublin the other day. There isn't a word of Irish in it, but here's a sample of the English—'Old Snarly Gob.'" (Cuireadh amach leabhar dánta i mBaile Átha Cliath an lá cheana. Ní raibh focal Gaedhilge ann, acht, ag seo sampla de'n Bhéarla—"Old Snarly Gob.") See "Sgéala ar an nGaoith," *ACS*, 22 May 1909. In an *ACS* review of the *Irish Review* in 1911, we read: "The poets of 'The Irish Review' are not new. They are Padraic Colum, James Stephens, and Thomas MacDonagh. They have nothing to sing of, and consequently they fail to raise any worthy note." See "*The Irish Review*," *ACS*, 11 March 1911.

282. *Synge and the Irish Language*, 6.

283. "Seán Ó Ríordáin: File Angla-Éireannach" (Seán Ó Ríordáin: An Anglo-Irish poet), in *An Duine is Dual: Aistí ar Sheán Ó Ríordáin* (The natural person: Essays on Seán Ó Ríordáin), ed. Eoghan Ó hAnluain (Baile Átha Cliath: An Clóchomhar, 1980), 93.

contributor less than a year later: "It is not right for us to forget that English is here and that it will, it seems, be used by the Irish as long as it is used by the English themselves. . . . In the best sense we will have two languages from now on, and it is worthwhile to cultivate both of them to the best of our ability."[284]

284. "Nuaidheacht" (News), *FL*, 24 February 1900. "Ní ceart dúinn a dhearmad go bhfuil an Béarla ann, agus go mbeidh sé i núsáid ag Gaedhealaibh de réir deallraimh an fhaid agus beidh sé i n-úsáid ag na Sasanachaibh féin. . . . 'San toisg is fearr, beidh dá theanga againn feasta, agus is fiú an bheirt acu do shaothrú go dícheallach."

6

Unwise and Unlovable?

The Question of Translation

In the years following the creation by the Irish Free State of the publishing agency An Gúm, translations into Irish came in a flood as Gaelic writers seized the chance to make a pound for every thousand words put into the language. Yet many of the finest writers found this work futile and even embittering. It is said that Seosamh Mac Grianna would tie his leg to his writing table to keep him at work,[1] and his brother Séamus Ó Grianna felt that his own involvement in the translation scheme was well-nigh sinful![2] Máirtín Ó Cadhain, who also did work for An Gúm, dismissed the agency's translation efforts in a few weary sentences: "Most of the work done by An Gúm . . . was translation, preponderantly from English. Many have commented on the futility of it. Most of the translations were of third or fourth rate books, or of mere trashy books."[3] But perhaps the last word should be left

1. See Máirtín Ó Cadhain, *Páipéir Bhána agus Páipéir Bhreaca* (Blank pages and written pages) (Baile Átha Cliath: An Clóchomhar, 1969), 35.
2. See Séamus Ó Grianna, *Saoghal Corrach* (An uneasy life) (Corcaigh: Cló Mercier, 1981). This work was originally published in 1945.
3. "Irish Prose in the Twentieth Century," in *Literature in Celtic Countries* (Cardiff: University of Wales Press, 1971), 150.

with a sympathetic scholarly outsider, Fred Norris Robinson, a member of the Society for the Preservation of the Irish Language, the founder of Harvard's Department of Celtic Languages, and the collector who put together the nucleus of Widener Library's holdings in modern Irish literature, including translations: "Though a Gaelic speaker might well find it convenient to read Lucian or Cervantes in Irish, it is hard to believe he would prefer a Gaelic version to the original of *Treasure Island* or *Three Men in a Boat.*"[4]

Whatever or whoever else can be blamed for An Gúm's translation policy, there had been no lack of debate about the role and significance of translation in the half-century prior to its implementation. As early as 1877 the Society for the Preservation of the Irish Language listed among its goals: "To encourage the production of a Modern Irish Literature—original or translated."[5] A start had already been made in this direction with the publication of Tomás Ó Fiannachtaigh's translation of Maria Edgeworth's "Forgive and Forget" and "Rosanna" in 1833,[6] and especially with the appearance of the first edition of Archbishop MacHale's translations from Moore's *Melodies* in 1842. This work was reprinted many times in the nineteenth century despite a growing awareness of its linguistic and literary deficiencies.[7] MacHale's example was followed by a host of Gaels in the early years of the Revival, and translations of all kinds of poems—with Moore again a particular favorite—appeared in the Gaelic press in the 1880s and 1890s. Among well-known poems put into Irish were Callanan's "Gougane-Barra" in 1883,[8] Mahoney's "The Bells of Shandon" in 1886,[9] Davis's "The Men

---

4. Quoted by Máirtín Ó Cadhain, "Conradh na Gaeilge agus an Litríocht," in *The Gaelic League Idea*, ed. Ó Tuama, 61. On the other hand, Professor Proinsias Mac Cana of the Dublin Institute for Advanced Studies has told me of how useful he found such translations when he himself was first studying Irish. It may also be noted that the Gaelic *Three Men in a Boat* (*Triúr Fear i mBád*), translated by León Ó Broin in 1932, is a good read.

5. See Máirín Ní Mhuiríosa, *Réamhchonraitheoirí*, 6.

6. See Breandán Ó Buachalla, *I mBéal Feirste Cois Cuain* (In Belfast by the bay) (Baile Átha Cliath: An Clóchomhar, 1968), 85–86. This is probably the translation of "Rosanna" read by M. J. Mulrenin at a Gaelic League meeting in the summer of 1898. See "Gnótha na Gaedhilge" (Gaelic affairs), *FL*, 2 July 1898.

7. See, for example, the review of T. O'Neill Russell's edition of MacHale's translations in *IG* 10, no. 110 (October 1899): 31–32.

8. "Gúgán Barra," trans. Domhnall Ua Loingsigh, *IG* 1, no. 7 (May 1883): 219–20.

9. "Cloga Sheandúin," trans. Rev. Mr. O'Malley, *IG* 2, no. 23 (1886): 344. This translation originally appeared in the *Tuam News*.

from Tipperary" in 1892,[10] "The Star-Spangled Banner" in 1898,[11] and T. P. Sullivan's "God Save Ireland" in 1899.[12]

While the majority of these translators seemed to see this work as an amusing word game and were unsystematically translating whatever caught their fancy, others were pondering the role translation could or should play in the revival of the language as a literary medium. Disagreements were sharp, and some of the most thoughtful revivalists cautioned against what they saw as the danger to the language of a sudden influx of foreign, particularly English, models. For example, in 1901 Peadar Ua Laoghaire, who later translated a great deal of material (though none of it English), provided an unadulterated nativist perspective on the question:

> Are there not in the past history and traditions of our own race boundless fields teeming with food for thought? They are fields which have never been trodden by the feet of the foreigner. Equipped with our own Irish Language exactly as we find it, still full of life and vigour in the mouths of our native Irish speakers, we have it in our power to draw out of those native fields an abundance of literary wealth which will be a far wholesomer possession both for ourselves and for our readers than any imported materials.[13]

From the other end of the ideological spectrum, William P. Ryan wrote the following year: "Let us first 'possess' Ireland, socially and spiritually, and then we can naturally assimilate other cultures. . . . Once things essentially Irish have become real and vital good translations, to healthy minds, can be a source of stimulation."[14] Another writer framed the issue in more practical terms in a review of a volume of translated

10. "Tiobraid Árann," trans. Pádruig Ó Laoghaire, *IG* 4, no. 42 (December 1892): 174–75.

11. "An Bhratach Gheal-Réaltach," trans. Eugene O'Growney, *An Gaodhal* 13, no. 1 (July 1898): 5.

12. "A Dhia Saor Éire," trans. Domhnall Ó Loingsigh, *FL*, 2 January 1899.

13. "Irish Prose Composition," *The Leader*, 13 July 1901.

14. "Irish and Translation," *UI*, 22 March 1902. Writing from London several months later, Ryan developed this idea at greater length: "Some people have highly optimistic views as to what wholesale translations into Irish might achieve just now. Most of them, good in themselves, would probably fall quite 'flat' for the present. Native study must first strengthen and steady the native mind, and native creations carry it artistically onward. Then, by all means, let us have foreign masterpieces in good Irish." See "London Notes," *ACS*, 1 November 1902.

Anglo-Irish stories: "As translation is not in itself a necessity, it seems a pity that any good, original writers should be tied down to it."[15]

A more extreme version of this concern was voiced by the anonymous reviewer of Pádraig Ó Súilleabháin's translation of stories from George Moore's *The Untilled Field*: "There is so much difference between the Gaelic and the English way of telling a story that it would be best to leave the literature of each language in the language in which it was composed. Let the foreigners compose their own literature . . . but let the Gaels compose in Irish, and don't tamper with the very nature of Irish or a mess will be made of both languages."[16] This was to remain an issue that blurred the usual ideological allegiances, and so we find the Oxford-educated progressive Giollabhrighde Ó Catháin revealing a good deal of this same fear of translation in his contribution to the debate fought out on the issue in the pages of *Irisleabhar na Gaedhilge* in 1904 and 1905: "If we start translating a large number of foreign books into Irish, the result will be that we will lose the natural beauty of the language and distort its form. We have a special heritage: let us go our own way; let us keep and preserve it and the world will be grateful to us in the end."[17]

Even Father Richard Henebry and Pearse could find common ground in their suspicion of translation. As early as 1892, with MacHale's translation of Moore in mind, Henebry was warning: "But there must be no foreign admixture. English idioms, mannerisms, style, system of thought must be rigidly eschewed."[18] In 1905 his opinions were unchanged: "In the matter of books and writings we must eschew all material written by people who did not know the language well, as well as all translations from the English. Especially translations from English

---

15. "Book Notices," *Irish Rosary* 6, no. 6 (June 1902): 490.

16. "Notes," *ACS*, 14 June 1902. " Tá an oiread do dhifrigheacht idir an bealach Gaedhealach agus an bealach Gallda ar sgéal d'innsint agus go mb'fhearr, ar a laghad, litridheacht gach éan teangaidh d'fhágáil insa' teangaidh inar cumadh í. Cumadh na Gaill a litridheacht féin . . . ach cumadh na Gaedhil i nGaedhilg, agus ná sgartar an nádúr Gaedhealach ó'n nGaedhilg, nó déanfar praiseach do'n dá theangaidh." Oddly enough, the anonymous book reviewer for the *Irish Rosary*, in all probability the same person cited immediately above, commented favorably on this translation the very next month, although he did have reservations about the subject matter of one of the stories, "An Deoraidhe" (The exile). See "Book Notices," *Irish Rosary* 6, no. 7 (July 1902).

17. Letter, *IG* 14, no. 175 (April 1905): 776. "Dá gcromfamaois ar Ghaedhilg do chur ar a lán leabhar iasachta, sé bheadh dá bharr againn ná an áilneacht ba dhual di riamh do chailleamhaint agus atharrughadh crotha do chur uirthi. Tá oighreacht fé leith againn féin: leanamaois dár slighe féin, coinghibhmís agus coimeádaimís í agus beidh an saoghal mór buidheach go deo dhínn i ndeireadh na dála."

18. "A Plea for Prose," *IG* 4, no. 41 (June 1892): 143.

poetry; we must shut our eyes and stop our ears against that, it is not to be classed, it is a nameless terror."[19] Pearse, while never quite so flamboyant, used his influence as editor of *An Claidheamh Soluis* to de-emphasize the role of translation in the development of a new literature. Reviewing Tadhg Ó Donnchadha's version of Padraic Colum's *The Land* in 1906, Pearse wrote: "The comparative failure of 'The Land' to 'go' in Irish warns us once again that, except under the happiest combination of circumstances, translations are invariably unwise."[20]

Pearse was, however, willing to admit that such happy concatenations could occur and that there was, therefore, a place for translation in the Revival, as is clear from his highly favorable review of Mícheál Breathnach's version of Charles Kickham's *Knocknagow* in 1906,[21] and from his comments on the same work as "a noble piece of literature" in his lengthy editorial obituary for Breathnach in 1908.[22] Moreover, in his comments on Edward Martyn's call for translation in 1907, he could both downplay the potential contribution of such work, writing that "the need of a great translation is apt to be over-rated," and concede that "a distinguished translation of a world-classic would unquestionably benefit the literary movement in Irish."[23] In fact Pearse had already taken this more moderate position two years earlier, in a 1905 review of two translations, Donnchadh Pléimeann's *Eachtra na nArgonátach* (The adventure of the Argonauts) and Tadhg Ó Murchadha's *Toradh na Gaedhilge ar Aitheasc agus ar Ghréithribh na nGaedheal* (The effect of the Irish language on the speech and on the talents of the Irish): "Irish writers have hitherto been chary of translation, and wisely so; but we must not carry our chariness too far. Provided always that the translator be a master of both languages, provided further that he have a sound critical instinct, provided finally and chiefly that he be a really creative writer

19. "Best Method of Learning Irish," *ACS*, 5 July 1902. Henebry did, however, feel that the Irish language in the hands of one who had mastered it had all the resources necessary for translation from any language. See his "Do Theagosc Gach Foghlama as Gaedhilg," in *Scríbhne Risteird de Hindeberg*, 72.

20. "The Oireachtas," *ACS*, 18 August 1906. If only to justify my chapter title, I should also quote Mac Néill's 1901 editorial response to a letter in *ACS*: "As regards translations we are not in love with them, though at times they are not without their uses." See *ACS*, 5 October 1901.

21. "Literature, Translations, and 'Cnoc na nGabha,'" *ACS*, 27 October 1906.

22. "Mícheál Breathnach," *ACS*, 7 November 1908. His comments on the book in this piece are, however, almost entirely focused on its linguistic value as "the vastest storehouse of untarnished Irish idiom that has been gathered together in our time." Thus he felt publication of *Cnoc na nGabha* "did Irish literature a mighty service" and, more important, that it "did the living Irish of Connacht an incalculable service."

23. "Wanted—A Translation," *ACS*, 4 May 1907.

not a mere copyist, nothing but good ought to result from the rendition into Irish of the masterpieces of the world's literature." However, when he applied these rigorous standards he judged successful only Ua Laoghaire's modernizations of early Irish tales, which he called, accurately, "not so much translations as retellings."[24]

Actually, there is evidence that Ua Laoghaire himself shared this more balanced view that the danger lay not in translation itself, but rather in bad translation. In two articles in *Fáinne an Lae* in 1899, he offered "Some Hints as to How English Literary Matter Should Be Translated into Irish," concluding his series of practical suggestions with a warning to those unable to follow them: "If you are unable to do it yet, aim at it and you very soon will. But do not TORTURE US WITH YOUR TRANSLATIONS. THEY ARE BY FAR THE MOST DEADLY ELEMENT IN THE DISEASE WHICH IS KILLING OUR LANGUAGE. They effectively disgust and repel the most courageous of native Irish speakers."[25]

While Ua Laoghaire's lifelong concern was for such native speakers, many of the literary revivalists, including Pearse, were more interested in the new audience seeking more sophisticated material in Irish. Here translation was seen by some as a ready and healthy remedy for the paucity of worthwhile reading available in the language. Thus in March 1899, *Fáinne an Lae* pleaded: "Would it not be possible for a combination of our writers to turn out at least a couple of volumes of new work in prose and verse? They might very well include translations, which in the hands of many of our writers, would be practically original works."[26] Donnchadh Pléimeann was especially forceful in his rejection of the most common arguments advanced against translation:

> In the time of our ancestors, they did not object to the translation into Irish of the most famous stories of other European

24. "Irish Prose," *ACS*, 21 October 1905. One might well wonder how he could reconcile his fondness for An tAthair Peadar's modernizations with the stricter standards for translation he laid down in his review of *Cnoc na nGabha* in 1906: "Someone has preached the heresy that a translation ought to read as if it were an original creation. . . . We protest. The ideal translation would make on the reader the same impression as the original in the original language. The ideal is obviously impossible of attainment. Yet it should be striven towards." See "Literature, Translations, and 'Cnoc na nGabha,'" *ACS*, 27 October 1906. The image of An tAthair Peadar as a heretic unbenownst to himself is an intriguing one.

25. "Some Hints as to How English Literary Matter Should Be Translated into Irish," *FL*, 21 January 1899. The capitalization is Ua Laoghaire's. See also his "Seachain Beus Iasachta" (Avoid foreign usage), *FL*, 30 April 1898.

26. "Notes," *FL*, 25 March 1899.

countries, though they themselves had a very powerful and vivid literature at the time. And why should we have doubts about it now, when everybody says we have nothing interesting to read? Is it that it is thought that our Irish minds would be corrupted by reading in Irish what we read constantly in English? Or is it that the beauty of the language would become tarnished by use and by absorbing the rich thought of the best known foreign authors? But I do not believe that at all. If a number of celebrated books were translated into Irish, it would gladden our students and place good examples before our speakers of Irish.[27]

Maud Joynt argued that translation had been instrumental in the literary development of English, Italian, and German, and concluded: "The one thing which . . . is wanted above all others at the present moment, is a number of good translations into Gaelic. . . . Why should we not prepare the way for the coming poet of the Gaelic race, by providing him with books worth reading in his native tongue? We need not be afraid of impairing his originality or his racial and political instincts by so doing."[28] C. S. Boswell, a contributor to the *Irisleabhar na Gaedhilge* debate on translation, echoed Joynt's ideas about the seminal role of translation in the early development of a language as a literary medium, and argued: "The number of writers capable, at any given time, of producing original works of sterling value must needs be small; but there will be many more who have sufficient knowledge of Irish to make a readable translation from a standard foreign writer, ancient or modern." Boswell felt that in this way writers could supply "an imperative necessity if Irish is to be widely read," that being "a copious supply of matter interesting to read . . . of matter worth reading."[29]

In 1907 Edward Martyn breathed new life into the controversy in a letter to the *Freeman's Journal* published under the title "Suggestions to the Gaelic League." Arguing that with the language in decline it was essential to "find out what have been the most potent means used in the

27. Quoted by Pádraig Mac Suibhne in "Donnchadh Pléimeann: His Thoughts and His Works," *ACS*, 10 September 1904.

28. "The Future of the Irish Language," *FL*, 23 June 1900. This article originally appeared in the *New Ireland Review*.

29. Letter, *IG* 14, no. 173 (February 1905): 736. Tomás Ó Flannghaile shared these high hopes for translation into Irish. See his essay "Archbishop MacHale," in *For the Tongue of the Gael*, 271–72. Ó Flannghaile's own translations are collected in Donnchadh Ó Liatháin's *Tomás Ó Flannghaile: Scoláire agus File* (Tomás Ó Flannghaile: Scholar and poet) (Baile Átha Cliath: Oifig an tSoláthair, n.d.), 79–93.

successful language revivals on the Continent, and to carefully apply
the same so that they may have an equal effect in Ireland," Martyn
urged "that there should be made without delay, a really fine translation
of some master work of the world's literature." Anticipating the usual
objections, he continued: "If we had some such work in Irish, it would
be a model and inspiration to future authors. Of course, some will say
that we have many original writers now in Irish. We have, no doubt;
but the people with interesting ideas do not know Irish at all or well
enough, and those who know Irish do not appear to have very much to
say."[30]

The predicted, but not always predictable, some did indeed object.
For example, P. S. Ua hÉigeartaigh wrote from London: "Translations
will come naturally enough when there is a natural intellectual demand
for them; if they are forced on us deliberately before we are ready for
them they will fail of their effect."[31] On the other hand, the author of
the regular Gaelic column in the *Freeman's Journal* was impatient with
such reservations, writing vigorously in support of Martyn: "I have had
to tolerate senseless speech from people who don't understand. One
hears talk about 'our own thoughts' and 'our own talent.' The nonsense
is already being bandied about again. We are told 'to stand on our own
feet' and so on. Fine easy talk, but words won't feed the friars. And no
more so will nonsense nourish readers of Irish."[32] Pondering the problem of the "book famine in country places," the *Sinn Féin* contributor
John Brennan agreed, although his choice of suitable authors for translation may have raised some orthodox eyebrows; along with Tone,
Davis, and Mitchell, he included Balzac, Hugo, Poe, and Thoreau, concluding with the question: "What hard-worked Gael would not feel joy
on coming in at night to find a Gaelic edition of H.G. Wells ready for

30. *Freeman's Journal*, 26 April 1907.
31. "An Original Literature in Modern Irish," *Inis Fáil*, July 1907, 11. Among the
works suggested by Martyn for translation was the *Arabian Nights*. When Irish versions of
some of these tales appeared in 1908 in the Irish of "Fergus Finnbhéil," the controversy
was renewed, with Ua hÉigeartaigh (as "Sarsfield") again expressing serious concerns.
See Ua hÉigeartaigh, "The Revival of Irish Literature," *Inis Fáil*, October 1908, 9–10.
32. "I bhFochair na nGaedheal" (Amongst the Gaels), *Freeman's Journal*, 27 April 1907.
"B'éigean dom foighneamh le cainnt gan chiall ó lucht na mí-thuigse. D'airigheadh
ráiméis i dtaobh 'ár smaointe féin' agus 'ár ngustail féin.' Tá an ráiméis dhá spiúnadh arís
cheana féin. Deirtear dúinn 'seasamh ar a mbonnaibh féin' agus mar sin de. Cainnt
bhreagh bhog, acht ní bheathóchadh na briathra na bráithre. Ní mó ná soin a
bheathóchaidh ráiméis lucht léighte na Gaedhilge." This columnist dismissed fears like
those of Ua hÉigeartaigh because he believed that "we now have writers who could truly
Gaelicize any book to which they directed their efforts." (Tá scríbhneoirí againn anois a
chuirfeadh cruth fíor-Ghaedhealach ar aon leabhar acht cur chuige.)

his amusement; who would not delight in Samuel Butler's works translated into Gaelic?"[33] Not all proponents of translation were so sophisticated or discriminating; some called for, and indeed produced, renderings into Irish of almost anything to put into the hands of newly created readers. But most agreed with Boswell and Brennan that the real need was for translations that these readers would find intellectually and imaginatively satisfying. For such revivalists, the real importance of translation was as a catalyst to the shaping of Irish as a twentieth-century literary language. Thus in a 1900 *Fáinne an Lae* editorial we read: "Let us look around now. There is a supply of delightful food that will nourish Irish to be found without trouble in the literatures of the countries around us, and after our sick language tastes that healthy new food, a desire for new things will come back to it, and Gaels aren't Gaels unless they provide something new to satisfy that desire."[34] Liam Ua Domhnaill saw translation as a direct challenge to Gaelic writers to confront the twentieth century: "It is being said that a very famous book is going to be translated into Irish. That is a good thing. Perhaps 'Gaelic writers will abandon their deep sleep.' Perhaps they will wake up and see that it is now 1908. Perhaps they will realize that a great change has come over the world in the past 300 years."[35] Stephen MacKenna agreed, emphasizing that if writers did not come to terms with that fact the language itself was in peril. His suggestion was that native speakers and learners familiar with European literature should pool their resources through collaborative efforts:

33. "Influences in Ireland II/Book Famine in Country Places," *SF*, 21 August 1909.
34. "Sgéalta Nua" (New stories), *FL*, 24 February 1900. "Féachaimís tímcheall i n-am, tá lón de bhiadh áluinn a bheathóchas an Ghaedhilg le fáil gan duadh i litridheachtaibh na dtíortha n-ár gcomh-fhogus, agus tar éis blaiseadh de'n bhiadh nua folláin sin dár dteanga bhreoite, tiocfaidh fonn na nuaidheachta uirthi arís, agus ní Gaedhil na Gaedhil muna ndéanfaid soláthar nua a shásóchas an fonn sain." It is interesting to note that John Brennan used more bizarre gastronomic imagery to make the same point in his 1909 *SF* piece cited above, note 33: "Since the Gaelic League published our ancient literature we are becoming literary cannibals; we have devoured our ancestors with ferocious appetite. . . . Let us devour the offspring of other races, and see how our literature will thrive on the fare."
35. "Aistriughadh" (Translation), *ACS*, 8 February 1908. "Táthar dhá rádh go bhfuiltear chun leabhar mór-chlúmhail d'aistriughadh gus an nGaedhilg. Is maith an sgéal é. B'fhéidir 'go dtréigfeadh sgríbhneoirí na Gaedhilge a dtrom-shuan.' B'fhéidir go ndúiseochaidís agus go bhfeicfidís gurab í bliadhain míle, naoi gcéad agus a hocht atá ann fá láthair. B'fhéidir go bhfeicfidhe dóibh go dtáinig athrughadh mór ar an saoghal le trí céad bliadhain." The book was Tadhg Ó Murchadha's translation of *Robinson Crusoe*, published the following year. The phrase Ua Domhnaill puts in quotation marks is from Mac Néill's famous essay "Tréigidh Bhur dTrom-Shuan" (Abandon your deep sleep).

We must have in Irish just such matter, the contemporary expression of personal thought, as we read or hear or utter in any
other language. If this cannot be, Irish dies inevitably. . . . As
the matter stands, the one hope seems, to myself at least, to lie in
a constant collaboration—and, I venture to say, collaboration
mainly on translation. French, Italian, English, Spanish, German, Latin, and Greek, these literatures contain immense masses
of matter quite suitable for translation for the satisfaction of all
the varied minds that now take pleasure in Irish.[36]

A similar if less ominous exhortation was the dominant note in a 12
February 1916 An Claideahmh Soluis editorial: "Translation will benefit
the Irish language if it is done well, and the foreign product will teach
the writer's craft to Gaelic authors. Gaelic writers are not backwards,
but not many of them can be compared with contemporary foreign
authors. There is no lack of material for the writers themselves, nor a
lack of Irish, but neither the material itself nor the excellence of the Irish
makes for a finished story or play unless the composition is good."[37]
    One work that Ua Domhnaill saw as offering precisely such an inspi-
rational challenge was Eoghan Ó Neachtain's translation of John Mitchell's Jail Journal, "the best and most important book that has been published in a long while."[38] The book's educational potential was certainly
foremost in the minds of both Sinn Féin reviewers of the work, Peadar
Ó Maicín writing, with an eye to Father O'Reilly's dismissal of the
literary potential of cainnt na ndaoine: "Eoghan Ó Neachtain's translation
of the 'Jail Journal' is a striking example of how the most abstruse terms
and involved figures of speech may be rendered into easy and readable
Irish provided the writer be competent to undertake the task."[39]
"G. Ó C." went beyond the work's merely linguistic excellence in a
long review of the second installment of the translation three years

    36. Stephen MacKenna (Stiofán Mac Énna), "The Conscript of 1813: A Correction and
a Suggestion," SF, 7 February 1914. MacKenna himself participated in such a collaboration with Seán Ó Caomhánaigh. See note 66.
    37. "Na Sgríbhneoirí agus an tOireachtas" (The writers and the Oireachtas). "Rachaidh
an t-aistriú i dtairbhe do'n Ghaedhilg má déantar go maith é agus múinfidh an déantús
iasachta ceárd an sgríbhneóra d'ughdaraibh na Gaedhilge. Níl sgríbhneoirí na Gaedhilge ar
deireadh, ach ní féidir mórán aca a chur suas is anuas le ughdaraibh iasachta an lae indiu.
Níl easpaidh adhbhar ar ár sgríbhneoiríbh féin, ná easpaidh Gaedhilge ach ní chuireann an
t-adhbhar féin nó feabhas Gaedhilge, slacht ar sgéal nó dráma muna mbíonn an cheapadóireacht go maith."
    38. "Leabhair Nua" (New books), ACS, 27 August 1910. "Isé an leabhar is fearr agus is
tábhachtaighe de na leabharaibh Gaedhilge é do foillsigheadh le fada d'aimsir."
    39. "Books in Irish," SF, 11 February 1911.

later. Having pronounced Breathnach's *Cnoc na Gabha* and Ó Neach-tain's *Irisleabhar Phríosúin Sheagháin Mhistéil*, both translations of Anglo-Irish classics, the most intellectually satisfying books in modern Irish, this critic stressed the crucial importance of such works for the revival of Irish as a literary language: "This world is a world of struggle. No language and no people will live if they don't adapt to the concerns and the advance of the world. . . . In this book you will see Irish going out in a lively way into the world God created, instead of staying in its narrow enclosure and in the four walls of its prison, thinking about itself."[40]

While some nativists were provincial enough to feel both snug and smug in the four walls of a narrowly defined Gaelic tradition, prog-ressives were scornful of such false security, and many saw translation as opening an obvious escape route from such claustrophobic cultural isolation. Thus, as noted in Chapter 5, the plays of some Anglo-Irish contemporaries were read and Gaelicized with enthusiasm, an enthusi-asm that to a lesser extent carried over into other areas. For example, entering into the debate about translation of English classics inspired by Ó Murchadha's *Robinson Crúsó*, "Glenomera" was skeptical of the value of such work, but unequivocal in his support of bringing into Irish "such really Irish authors as Griffin, Edgeworth, Banim, Justin McCar-thy, Kickham, Burke, and a host of others," stating that "when Gaelic literature has been enriched by the translation of the great Irish writers of English, it will then be time enough for translators to turn their attention to the works of purely English authors."[41] As we saw in the previous chapter, not all Gaels had such eclectic tastes in Anglo-Irish writing, so in a review Ó Neachtain's rendering of Mitchell, an anony-mous *Sinn Féin* reviewer spelled out the broad criteria for determining which Anglo-Irish texts merited such linguistic elevation: "It is a much debated question as to how far translations from foreign languages are serviceable to the upbuilding of a modern Irish literature. The con-sensus of opinion would seem to indicate that modern Irish literature ought to include translations of the best works of those Anglo-Irish writers whose sympathies were national, and who had anything in them of what is called the Gaelic spirit."

40. "*Irisleabhar* an Mhistéalaigh" (Mitchell's *Journal*), *ACS*, 25 March 1911. "Saoghal troda is eadh an saoghal so. . . . Ní mhairfidh teanga nó muinntir muna gcuirfear i n-oireamhaint iad do ghnóthaibh agus do dhul-ar-aghaidh an tsaoghail. . . . Chífeá ans an leabhar so an Ghaedhilg ag dul amach go haerach fá'n saoghal a chruthaigh Dia . . . i n-áit fanamhaint i n-a cuibhreann chumhang agus i n-a ceithre ballaibh de charcair ag smuaineadh fúithí féin."
41. "Glenomera," letter, *WF*, 10 June 1905.

This critic went on claim that in addition to "some of the best-known Irish National songs . . . many prose pieces have been successfully turned into Irish."[42] "Many," however, seems a relative term here; apart from the dramas, there really wasn't all that much: three stories ("An Déirc" / "Alms-giving," "An Gúna-Phósta / "The Wedding Gown," and "Tóir Mhic Uí Dhíomasuigh" / "The Clerk's Quest") from George Moore's *The Untilled Field* that appeared in the *New Ireland Review* in 1902 in the Irish of Tadhg Ó Donnchadha, as well as a volume of stories from the same collection translated by Pádraig Ó Súilleabháin as *An tÚr-Ghort* and published that same year; the collection of Donegal tales by MacManus translated by Mac Fhionnlaoich as *An Pleidhseam* in 1903; the Mitchell and Kickham[43] books already noted; and an eclectic miscellany of works characterized more by nationality and "Gaelic spirit" than by literary excellence. Despite the Kickham and Moore titles above, Anglo-Irish fiction was poorly represented. Indeed, it might be more accurate to say it was misrepresented, for what we find is often as second-rate as it is sparse: a collection of Mary Butler's stories translated by Tomás Ua Concheanainn as *Blátha Bealtaine*,[44] a dire, self-righteous antiemigration tale, *Seosamh Ó Callanáin (Joe Callinan)* by N. F. Degidon,[45] "Ar Thóir Gháirdín Phárrthais" ("In Quest of Paradise") by Lily MacManus,[46] stories by Attie O'Brien[47] and John Sherlock,[48] and an anonymous story of the Cork peasantry.[49] There were as

42. "New Irish Books," *SF*, 10 June 1911. The author made plain the nature of the contribution such prose translations could make to the Revival: "Where the translation has been well done no more suitable reading practice can be put in the hands of the student who is acquainted with the original."

43. In March 1917 an unnamed reader wrote to inform *ACS* that he had already translated half of Kickham's *Sally Kavanagh* into Irish, and wanted to know whether anyone else was at work on the same book before he completed the project. See "Sally Kavanagh," *ACS*, 3 March 1917. This translation seems never to have been published. A translation of the novel by Máirtín Ó Cadhain was published by An Gúm in 1932 and has recently been reissued in the standard orthography.

44. (Baile Átha Cliath: Connradh na Gaedhilge, 1902).

45. Trans. "D. Ó C." (Baile Átha Cliath: Oifig "An Teachtaire Éireannaigh," 1908).

46. Lily MacManus (Lil Nic Mhághnuis), "Ar Thóir Gháirdín Phárrthais," trans. "Uachtar Ard," *ACS*, 21 and 28 July 1906.

47. Attie O'Brien, "Tobar na h-Inighine Cúl-Buidhe" (The well of the yellow-haired maiden), *An Gaodhal* 7, no. 1 (December 1888)-7, no. 4 (July 1889). No translator's name is given. The work originally appeared in the *Irish Catholic*. The English title given here is a translation of the Irish as I have not been able to locate O'Brien's story.

48. John Sherlock (Síorlaoich), "An Chloch" (The stone), *National Student* 6, no. 1 (December 1915): 10–12. No translator's name is given.

49. "Peig—Sgéal Daoine Tuaithe i gConndae Corcaighe, Éire" (Peg—A story of coun-

well, of course, translations of a fair number of usually patriotic poems like those of Davis, Rooney's "The Men of the West," or Ingram's "The Memory of the Dead."[50] No doubt patriotism also inspired the two Irish versions of Emmet's Speech from the Dock as "Domairm Báis Riobairt Emet" and "Óráid Emmet roimh a Dhaoradh"[51] and of an 1892 address on the language by the parliamentarian William O'Brien.[52] More surprising is the translation of AE's open letter to the "Master of Dublin" during the 1913 Lockout as "Stad ag Lucht Oibre agus Bataí dá gClaoidheadh" ("A Strike by the Workers and Clubs Beating Them").[53]

Those of progressive outlook on this question did not, however, restrict their efforts to their own country. In fact, the anonymous author of the "Cois Leasa na nGaedheal" column in the *Weekly Freeman*, while acknowledging that Anglo-Irish literature "formed the foundation of all my own voluntary reading," argued that literature could look after itself, and that Gaelic writers had a more pressing agenda: "Bearing in mind that we have to teach the language to the whole nation, I should therefore say, from my own experience, let our people read in the original the works of our really Irish writers of English, and let the men who still possess pure idiomatic Gaelic and are able to use it, give us in that tongue the works which the people of all Europe have thought it

---

try people in County Cork, Ireland), *WF*, 16 March 1901. Neither author nor translator is identified, although the story did win a *WF* Oireachtas Prize.

50. This song was translated at least three times in our period, by Hyde, by An tAthair Uáitéir Ó Conmhacáin, and by Tadhg Ó Donnchadha. The young Pearse got himself into trouble for criticizing the Hyde translation as "not Irish." See "Notes," *FL*, 22 July 1899.

51. "Domairm Báis Riobairt Emet," trans. Michael Logan, *An Gaodhal* 1, no. 7 (April 1882)—1, no. 12 (September 1882); and "Óráid Emmet roimh a Dhaoradh," trans. Tadhg Ó Murchadha, *FL*, 17 June 1899, special Duilleachán section.

52. William O'Brien, *Toradh na Gaedhilge ar Aitheasc agus ar Ghréithribh na nGaedheal*, trans. Tadhg Ó Murchadha (Baile Átha Cliath: Connradh na Gaedhilge, 1905). In 1898, there was an Oireachtas Prize offered for the translation of this 1892 speech, but it was not awarded. Éamonn Ó Donnchadha saw, inexplicably, Ó Murchadha's translation as a genuine milestone: "This translation is well-nigh the first attempt ever made by our Gaelic writers to take hold of their own language for the purpose of communicating to us the events and characteristics of the modern world." (Is beag ná gurab é an t-athar-rughadh so an chéad iarracht riamh a deineadh ag ár sgríbhneoiríbh Gaedhilge chun a dteanga féin do ghabháil chucha d'fhonn imtheachta agus éirimí an nua-shaoghail do chur i n-umhail dúinn.") See Ó Donnchadha, "Ó Chúige Mumhan," *ACS*, 7 December 1907.

53. George Russell, "Stad ag Lucht Oibre agus Bataí dá gClaoidheadh," *ACS*, 13 September 1913. The piece was most likely translated by William P. Ryan, whose own essay in support of the strikers, "Cúis na bhFear Oibre" (The workers' cause), precedes it.

worth their while to borrow into their own." His goal was thus "to get as many as possible of the world's classics turned into Irish, precedence, for obvious reasons, to be given to work in languages other than English."[54] Many agreed, seeing translation as the primary practical means available to them for the implementation of their program to reestablish the literary contacts that Gaelic Ireland had historically maintained with the rest of Europe and thereby to challenge and in the long run supplant the English language's monopoly in Irish intellectual life. The scorn of writers like Pearse and Ó Conaire for the linguistic solipsism of their Anglicized contemporaries and their corresponding enthusiasm about literary developments on the Continent have of course already been discussed. In 1920 Ó Conaire stressed the need for more translation precisely because it could do so much to give Gaels a share in the excitement of these developments. In a piece addressed to his fellow authors, Ó Conaire wrote: "If a good portion of the most important books in European literature could be put into Irish, it would be a great thing for the writer reliant on Irish and English, and for the reader as well. It would let them both know that there is a mind other than the British mind and that there is a world other than the world they already know."[55] But two full decades earlier a *Fáinne an Lae* correspondent was already drawing attention to a translation prize at the Dungarvan Feis and urging writers to set to work on what he clearly saw as a very long-term project:

> If we are to have a Gaelic literature—that is to say, if the Gaelic language is to live—it must live during the coming century largely by translation. . . . At present we are dependent altogether upon what the English write, or what they choose to translate for us. Given a new literature in Gaelic and a new race of scholars we should have the pick of the thoughts of the world. . . . It is a far cry, to be sure, from the Dungarvan Feis to

54. "Cois Leasa na nGaedheal," *WF*, 17 June 1905. This author did, however, say that he would prefer a translation of *Robinson Crusoe* to anything by any of the Anglo-Irish authors mentioned by "Glenomera."

55. "Clódhanna / Brostaighidh, a Lucht na bPeann!" in *Iriseoireacht Uí Chonaire*, 93. This piece originally appeared in the *Shamrock and Irish Emerald* for 20 November 1920. "Dá bhféadfaí mór-chuid de na leabhra is mó le rádh i litríocht na hEorpa chur i nGaedhilge, ba mhór an rud é do'n sgríobhnóir atá taobh le Gaedhilge agus Béarla, agus do'n léightheoir freisin. Chuirfeadh sé i gcéill dóibh beirt go bhfuil aigne nach Briotánach ann agus go bhfuil saoghal ann seachas an saoghal atá ar aithne aca cheana." Ó Conaire was also enthusiastic about the original translation policy of An Gúm. See "Ar Aghaidh Libh, a Sgríobhnóirí!" (Forward, writers!), in *Iriseoireacht*, 118. This piece originally appeared in the *Connacht Sentinel* for 1 November 1927.

the literature of Europe, but Dungarvan shows us how we may start upon the journey.[56]

Typically, the Oireachtas was to take up this project on a more ambitious scale, offering its first prize for translation as early as 1898.[57] However, probably due to the recurring controversy about the value of such work, regular competitions specifically devoted to translation were not announced until 1912, at which time annual prizes began to be offered for the translation of plays into Irish.[58] And it wasn't until 1916 that a prize was offered "to the person who will best put into Irish or who will rewrite in Irish a foreign story of not more than 10,000 words" (don té is fearr a chuirfidh i nGaedhilg nó a aithscríobhas i nGaedhilg scéal iasachta ná beidh thar 10,000 focal ann).[59] These flexible criteria may well account for the immediate success of the competition, An Claidheamh Soluis reporting that "the literary entry has been very fair, the translation of a foreign story being the most popular."[60] The winner of this first competition was Tomás Ó hEidhne for his version of Hawthorne's "The Great Stone Face" as "An tEudan Mór Cloch."[61]

Yet despite the popularity of this particular competition, few Gaelic writers committed themselves to such work on a sustained basis, and the tiny number of translations into Irish had little impact on the new literature in the early years of the Revival. I have already discussed in Chapter 1 the ideological reasons that caused most Gaels to avoid English literature, although it should also be noted that the author of the "Cois Leasa na nGaedheal" column, despite his opposition to wide-scale translation from English, felt the league should pay Tadhg Ó Murchadha a salary "which would enable him to devote all his time to the translation of classics of English literature for them."[62] That it was real-

56. "Notes," FL, 16 December 1899.

57. This was the unawarded prize for the translation of O'Brien's oration noted above. See the list of Oireachtas competitions in FL, 28 May 1898.

58. See Ó Súilleabháin, Scéal an Oireachtais, 183–84.

59. "Clár an Oireachtais, 1916/An Roinn Liteardha" (The program of the Oireachtas, 1916/The literary division), ACS, 20 November 1915. In the unsettled circumstances after 1916, the competition did not become an annual event until 1920.

60. "Oireachtas Notes," ACS, 15 July 1916. A serious attempt was made to maintain standards, all competitors being required to submit the text of their original. Nevertheless, ACS felt that it might be better, certainly easier for the judges, if further restrictions were imposed: "In future it would be well to specify certain works." See "Toradh an Oireachtais" (The results of the Oireachtas), ACS, 12 August 1916. This suggestion was not implemented.

61. The story began serialization in ACS on 18 November 1916.

62. "Cois Leasa na nGaedheal," WF, 3 June 1905. According to this author, Osborn Bergin also felt Ó Murchadha should focus on translating English classics.

ized such work would involve both considerable time and effort is apparent from the comments of the two Gaels who undertook the biggest projects in this area, Ó Murchadha and Dinneen. Prefacing his *Eachtra Robinson Crúsó*, Ó Murchadha discussed the difficulty of finding Irish equivalents for various technical terms, and then went on to broaden the scope of his complaint: "The thoughts and ideas in 'Robinson Crusoe' are altogether foreign to the thoughts and ideas of the tales I heard told in my youth, a fact which in itself made this translation all the more difficult."[63] Dinneen agreed, stating in his preface to *Duan na Nodlag* that he had stayed "as close to the original as the difference of idiom of the two languages permitted," but that "it need scarcely be said that several passages of the *Carol* present considerable difficulty to the translator, as many terms are used for which there are no very obvious Irish equivalents, and as, moreover, Dickens's style and language in his descriptive and rhetorical passages are extremely un-Irish."[64]

No ideological ambiguities clouded the task of translation from other languages, but again the output was somewhat disappointing, with a handful of writers producing a disproportionate share of the work. Thus from the French there came, along with several stories,[65] Seán Ó Caomhánaigh's translation of Ercmann-Chartrian's *L'Histoire d'un conscript de 1813* as "Togthán a 1813"[66] and Tadhg Ó Donnchadha's *Mór-Timcheall an Domhain Uile i 80 Lá* and *Tartur ó Thrascoin*, serialized versions of Verne's *Le Tour du monde en 80 jours* and Daudet's *Aventures*

---

63. "Roimhrádh" to *Eachtra Robinson Crúsó: Cuid I* (The adventure of Robinson Crusoe: Part I) (Baile Átha Cliath: Clódhanna, Teo., 1909), n.p.

64. Preface to *Duan na Nodlag*, 3–4.

65. See, for example, "Búm-Búm," a translation by Seaghán P. Mac Éinrigh of a story by Jules Clarédie, *ACS*, 1 April 1902; Donnchadh Ó Laoghaire's versions of two stories by Archbishop Fénelon as "Eachtra an Rígh Alfaroute agus Claraphile" (The Adventure of King Alfaroute and Claraphile) and "Eachtra na Sean-Bhainrighne agus an Chailín ó'n dTuath" (The adventure of the old queen and the girl from the country), in *An Lóchrann*, May and June 1909 respectively. Tadhg Ó Donnchadha's translation of Madame Présensée's children's story "Seulette," *SF*, 15 May–10 July 1909; Tomás Mac Domhnaill's "Elicsir an Athar Góisir" from Daudet's "L'Élixir du Révérend Père Gaucher," *ACS*, 14 December 1912; and Art Mag Uidhir's "Cathamh Aimsire" (Divertissement) from Pascal's *Penseés*, *National Student* 4, no. 5 (April 1914): 118.

66. Ó Caomhánaigh's work commenced serialization in *SF* on 31 January 1914. Stephen MacKenna was listed as co-translator, but in the following week's *SF*, MacKenna downplayed his role in the project, claiming he had done "little more than break the French into something like manageable Gaelic form" and to have kept "the final result simple against the tendency of the tutor [Ó Caomhánaigh] to be too lofty and luscious and obscure." See MacKenna, "The Conscript of 1813: A Correction and a Suggestion," *SF*, 7 February 1914. MacKenna's name was removed beginning with the fourth installment (21 February 1914).

prodigieuses de Tartarin de Tarascon respectively.[67] In addition there were translations of the following plays: Dufresny's *L'Esprit de contradiction*,[68] Molière's *Le Bourgeois gentilhomme* and *Le Médecin malgré lui*,[69] Coppée's *Le Luthier de Crémone* (twice),[70] Labiche's *La Fille bien gardée*,[71] and Moinaux's *Les Deux sourds*.[72] From the German came a handful of stories like the folktales "An t-Iasgaire agus a Bhain-Chéile" (The fisherman and his wife)[73] translated by "M. Ua C." and Máire Ní Eadhra's version of "An Lispín Draoidheachta" (The magic frog);[74] or Máire Ní Shíthe's "Bean Léigheannta nó Deagh-Chócaire; nó Togha agus Rogha agus Togha Eile" (A learned woman or a good cook, or The best choice and another choice).[75] More extensive were Pléimeann's *Eachtra na nArgonátach*, a translation of one of the stories in Niebuhr's *Griechische Heroen-Geschichte*;[76] a collection of tales from the Brothers

67. *Mór-thimpeall an Domhan* was serialized in the *Irish Weekly Independent* from 30 November 1912 to 1 November 1913. *Tartur* commenced serialization in *ACS* on 6 November 1915. Suggesting that Ó Donnchadha's work be released in book form, one *ACS* correspondent stressed the liberating potential of solid translations of modern work in words that echo those of Stephen MacKenna quoted above: "The Tórna-Verne story took us round the world in Irish: 'twas the greatest relief from the cow at the well and the fairy in the fort, and it gave us models for nearly all that is said and done in the modern world of trains, and shops, and ships, and social small talk." See K. M'S., "Tórna's Translation of 'Round the World,'" letter, *ACS*, 25 September 1915.

68. The play was translated by Liam Ua Domhnaill as *An Bhean Mhí-Chomhairleach* (The woman who couldn't be counseled) and staged at the 1907 Oireachtas.

69. See "The Publication Committee," *ACS*, 4 May 1907, where the committee announced: "Financial concerns forced cancellation of the publication of Máire Nic Shíthigh's translation" of *Le Bourgeois gentilhomme*. I have found no further reference to the work. *Le Médecin malgré lui* was translated by Fionán Ó Loingsigh and won an Oireachtas Prize in 1914.

70. The former was translated by Éamonn Ó Néill as *An Croiteachán* (The hunchback) and staged at the 1911 Oireachtas; the latter as *An Bheidhlín* by Eoghan Ó Máille and serialized in *ACS*, 28 November 1914 to 2 January 1915.

71. The play was translated by Máire Ní Chonaill as *An Cailín a Shiubhladh 'na Codladh* (The girl who walked in her sleep) and serialized in *ACS* beginning in December 1912. This was also one of seven entrants in the Oireachtas Competition for translated plays in 1912. See "Sgéala an Oireachtais," *ACS*, 22 June 1912.

72. The play was translated by Piaras Béaslaí and staged by Na hAisteoirí in 1913.

73. M. Ua C., "An t-Iasgaire agus a Bhain-Chéile: Sgeul-Síghe Gearmánach [A German fairy tale]," *An Gaodhal* 10, no.1 (July 1893)—10, no. 2 (August 1893).

74. *ACS*, 2 January 1909.

75. *ACS*, 27 April 1907. The author of the original is given as "Síle Beuren Hahn." Ní Shíthe also translated "Eachtra an Bhosga" (The adventure of the box) from the German of an unidentified author in *ACS*, 11 May 1907.

76. *Eachtra na nArgonátach*, trans. Donnchadh Pléimeann (Baile Átha Cliath: Connradh na Gaedhilge, 1904). *ACS* reported on the death of Pléimeann that "just before his death he was projecting a series of translations from Niebuhr's 'Grieschische Heroen-Ge-

Grimm translated by J. P. Craig as *Sgéalta Sgiúrtha* (Lively stories);[77]
Piaras Béaslaí's *Eachtra Pheadair Schlemiel* from Adelbert Von Cha-
misso's novel *Peter Schlemihls wundersame Geschichte*;[78] and the Reverend
T. Jones's bilingual Irish and English version of Father Hans Jacob's
"Aus dem Leben eines Unglücklicher."[79] Following the precedent of
MacHale's translation of the fifth through eighth books of the *Iliad* and
John O'Donovan's translation of a speech by Achilles in book 1 of the
same poem,[80] several authors turned to Classical literature for source
material. Among these works were An tAthair Peadar's translations of
the Aesop stories as *Aesop a Tháinig go hÉirinn* (The Aesop who came to
Ireland),[81] of Sallust's *Catilinae Coniuratio* (1913), and of Lucian's "Dialogue of the Gods" (1924); Liam Ó Rinn's translation of Plato's *Apology*;[82] and Tomás Ua Nualláin's version of the first eleven books of
Aristotle's *Nicomachean Ethics*.[83] Among miscellaneous translations were

---

schichte,' entitled the 'Exploits of Hercules,' for the Irish Department of the 'Independent.'" See "Notes," *ACS*, 25 August 1900.

77. See "New Books," *ACS*, 21 January 1911. Seosamh Ó Cléirigh made other European fairy tales available to young readers of Irish through his retellings in *Sáimhín Sógh*
(A merry mood) (Baile Átha Cliath: Clódhanna Teo., 1915).

78. Piaras Béaslaí, *Eachtra Pheadair Schlemihl* (Baile Átha Cliath: Muintir na Leabhar
Gaedhilge, 1909).

79. Rev. T. Jones, "An Scuab de na-a bhfuil caithte dhe shaoghal aindeiseóra / The
Birch, from the Life of an Unlucky One," *Catholic Bulletin*, February–December 1914.

80. MacHale published books 5 and 6 in 1860, 7 and 8 in 1869. O'Donovan's translation was published in *IG* 2, no. 21 (1885): 287–88. An Irish version of Virgil's *Bucolics*
was published in the *Tuam News* in the late nineteenth century. See Ó Maolmhuaidh,
Athair na hAthbheochana, 105.

81. Five booklets of this material with accompanying English translation were published between September 1900 and September 1902. The five parts were edited into a
single volume (without translation) by Norma Borthwick in 1903, with a second edition
in 1904 and an English translation the same year. A version in the "simplified spelling,"
edited by Bergin, appeared in 1911. Borthwick published another collection of Ua
Laoghaire's Aesop material in 1910, with a second edition in 1916. Ua Laoghaire was in
all probability working from English versions of these tales. See "Maol Muire," *An tAthair Peadar Ó Laoghaire*, 121–23.

82. This translation, "Socrates á Chosaint Féin" (Socrates defending himself), appeared
in *Irish Freedom* from October 1913 to March 1914.

83. This translation from "Leabhar Aristodeil ar a nGlaetar *Béasgna Nichómach*" (The
book by Aristotle called *Nicomachean Ethics*) was serialized in *ACS* from January to May
1912. There was also a lengthy prose retelling of *The Iliad* by Mícheál Ó Cuileanáin in *An
Lóchrann* from June 1908 to February 1910. In the minutes of the league's Publications
Committee (Coisde na gClobhann) for 20 April 1910, there is note that the committee
had received from Tomás Ua Nualláin the manuscript of a work he had translated from
Latin to Irish but that the committee had felt that book would be more appropriate for the
Irish Texts Society. It was never published by the ITS either. Information from the
Fionán Mac Coluim Papers, National Library of Ireland, MS. 24,405.

"Tír-Ghrádh de réir San Tomáis d'Acuin" (Patriotism according to Saint Thomas Aquinas), a rendering of a few paragraphs from *Secundus Secundae* by "Maolmhuire";[84] "Eachtra agus Imtheachta an Chaiptín Cuellar" ("Captain Cuellar's Narrative of His Adventures in Ireland");[85] "Feargus Finnbhéil's" *Finnsgéalta na hAraibe*;[86] "An t-Asal Malluighthe" (The cursed ass), a story translated from an English version of an Arabic tale;[87] Máire Ní Eadhra's "Sinbeád Máirnéalach" (Sinbad the sailor);[88] Gearóid Ó Lochlainn's "Dhá Sgéilín ó Theanga na hAraibe" (Two little stories from the Arabic);[89] Liam Ó Rinn's versions of Kropotkin's *Fields, Factories, and Workshops*[90] and of three stories by Tolstoy;[91] a Chekhov story by Colm Ó Lochlann and Froinsias Ó Conghaile;[92] Ua Laoghaire's *Don Cíochóté*, a loose retelling based on Jarvis's English translation of the first part of Cervantes's novel;[93] Gearóid Ó Loch-

84. "Maolmhuire," "Tír-Ghrádh de réir San Tomáis d'Acuin," *ACS*, 31 August 1907.

85. There were three translations of Cuellar's Spanish narrative into English between 1893 and 1897, one by Joseph P. O'Reilly, one by Robert Crawford and one by Henry Dwight Sedgwick. Cuellar was a survivor of the Spanish Armada.

86. This book, subtitled "Cuid I" (Part I), was published in 1908. It was based on either Scots Gaelic or English versions of eight of the stories. In a review in *The Leader*, Seán Ó Ciarghusa described the author's approach as retaining the framework of his originals while retelling them "in his own way in Irish." See "Two New Books," *The Leader*, 29 August 1908. A Scots Gaelic version of some of these stories, "translated from the English expurgated edition," was published as *Sgeulachdan Arabianacha* (Arabian stories) in 1898. See "Our Celtic Bookshelf," *FL*, 28 January 1899.

87. "An t-Asal Malluighthe," *IG* 8, no. 92 (December 1897): 131–3. The English version by "Zara" was entitled "The Enchanted Ass."

88. This story commenced a lengthy and sporadic serialization in *ACS* on 6 July 1907. Ní Eadhra's source was "an sgéal i nGaedhilg na hAlban" (the story in Scots Gaelic).

89. *ACS*, 14 September 1912. Ó Lochlainn did not know Arabic.

90. Under the title *Saothar Fear nDomhan* (The work of the men of the world) this translation from the English commenced serialization in *Irish Freedom* in December 1912 and, with a few exceptions, ran monthly until November 1914. See also "Fear na Feirsde," "Sgéala na Feirsde" (Belfast news), *ACS*, 14 December 1912. It was then reprinted in *ACS* beginning on 24 March 1917. The work was received with enthusiasm by "Béarlóir." See "Aistriughchán go Gaedhilg" (Translation to Irish), *An t-Éireannach*, January 1913, 2.

91. Micheál Mhag Ruaidhrí, "An Maistín agus an Geampa Aráin" (The mastiff and the lump of bread), *ACS* Uimhir an Oireachtais, 31 July 1909 (from an English version of the story); Liam Ó Rinn, "Chíonn Dia an Fhírinne, acht Feitheann" (God sees the truth but waits"), *SF*, 11 July–1 August 1914; and "Ina Phrisúnach ar Shliabh Caucais" (A Prisoner on Mount Caucus), *SF*, 8–22 August 1914. (This story breaks off incomplete at this point.)

92. Colm Ó Lochlainn and Froinsias Ó Conghaile, "Gorta" (Famine), *National Student* 4, no. 6 (June 1914): 144–46.

93. This translation was serialized in *Glór na Ly* in 1913, and in *SF*, again in the "simplified spelling," throughout 1913–14, and was published in book form in 1922. For

lainn's versions of three Norwegian folktales from Asbjörnsen and Moe's *Norske Folkeeventyr*;[94] a volume of stories by Hans Christian Andersen translated by Norma Borthwick as *Leabhairín na Leanbh* (The children's little book),[95] as well as the odd story from Andersen put into Irish by "Ros Fáilghe";[96] and, startlingly, "Arigata no Kichibei," a piece of transliterated Japanese with Irish translation that appeared in *An t-Eorópach* in 1899.[97] In addition, 1908 saw the appearance of three translations of Fitzgerald's *Rubaiyat*, one by Tadhg Ó Donnchadha,[98] and two by Gaels resident in America.[99]

If the number of translations from Continental languages was disappointing, the failure to bring the literature of fellow Celts into Irish is on the surface even more striking, particularly in light of the enthusiastic Gaelic support for revival movements in the other Celtic realms and

---

comments on Ua Laoghaire's cavalier approach to his original, see "Maol Muire," *An tAthair Peadar Ó Laoghaire*, 123–26. "Conall Cearnach" (Feardorcha Ó Conaill), who edited the text for its publication as a book, makes the startling claim that Ua Laoghaire's version provides "the Quintessence of Quixote" and is "in some respects . . . superior to the original." See his preface to *Don Cíochóté*, trans. Peadar Ua Laoghaire (Baile Átha Cliath: Brún agus Ó Nóláin, 1922), iv. In 1911 *ACS* announced that the Irish Texts Society was planning to issue a collection of Spanish stories by Juan Pérez de Montalbán in Irish translation by Tomás Ó Raghallaigh. The book never appeared. See "The Irish Texts Society," *ACS*, 13 May 1911.

94. Gearóid Ó Lochlainn, "Seanscéalta Lochlannach" (Norse folktales), *SF*, 30 July–1 October 1910. Ó Lochlainn may well have been translating from the original Norwegian (*Landsmál*).

95. *Leabhairín na Leanbh: Roinnt Sgéilíní a Tógadh a' Sgéaltaibh H. C. Andersen. Norma Bhortuic do Chuir Gaidhilg ortha* (Baile Átha Cliath: Muintir na Leabhar Gaedhilge, 1913). A version of this same book, edited by Osborn Bergin, had appeared the previous year in the "simplified spelling" as *Leouirín na Leanav*. Borthwick was most likely working with English versions of the stories.

96. See "Holgar Dánach," *ACS*, 19 October 1912; "An Bosga Teineadh" ("Fyrtojet"), *ACS*, 9 September 1916; and "An Sgáthdhuine" ("Skyggen"), *ACS*, 16 November 1916. Without knowing the identity of "Ros Fáilghe" it is not possible to say whether (s)he knew Danish; the fact that (s)he provides the Danish titles of the stories does, however, suggest (s)he did.

97. "Arigata no Kichibei," *An t-Eorópach* 1, no. 2 (October 1899): 14. In its brief six-issue life this bravely cosmopolitan Trinity College publication printed several interesting translations, among them one of Antony's funeral oration from *Julius Caesar* (vol. 1, no. 1, June 1899, 2–3); and one of Bret Harte's "Plain Language from Truthful James" (vol. 1, no. 5, May 1900, 40).

98. "Rubáiyát Omar Khayyám," *SF*, 26 December 1908.

99. One of these was sent to *ACS* by one Seán Ó Siúrtáin, "a good Gael who had never seen Ireland" (deagh-Ghaedheal nach bhfaca tír na hÉireann riamh). See "Mion-Sgéala," *ACS*, 25 January 1908. The other, by Eoin Ua Cearbhiúil, was published in America as *Rubaiiat Ro Chan Omar Caiiam* (Chicago: J. J. Collins' Sons, n.d.). The translator himself dates his work 2 September 1908.

the awareness that their triumphs and failures had special relevance for the Irish situation. Thus in the first sentence of his prize-winning 1899 Oireachtas essay on "An Múnadh Bheireann Breatain, .i. Muintear Bhreathanach, d'Éireannachaibh i dTaobh le a dTeangaidh Dhúthchais do Choimeád Beó / What Wales Can Teach Ireland as to the Preservation of Celtic Speech," Peadar Mac Fhionnlaoich confessed: "There is nothing related to keeping a language alive that the Welsh can't teach the Irish, for they have kept their language alive, and we have well nigh lost ours."[100] While not all Gaels were quite so impressed by their P-Celtic cousins, Mac Fhionnlaoich did accurately reflect not only a widespread belief in the importance of other movements for "the preservation of Celtic speech," but also an equally widespread acceptance of the fact that for the time being at least the Irish would be the pupils and not the teachers in any Celtic renaissance.

Such ideas were by no means new. As early as 1863, Canon Ulick Bourke had in the preface to the first edition of his *Easy Lessons or Self-Instruction in Irish* urged the Irish to emulate the Welsh, and he returned to this theme in the first number of his short-lived periodical *The Keltic Journal and Educator* in January 1869.[101] In the 1880s *Irisleabhar na Gaedhilge* was monitoring developments in Wales and Scotland, and then and thereafter the "Notes" and "News of the Movement" columns in the journal frequently commented on important events in these two countries. For example, in December 1892 readers were told of the foundation of the Scottish Mòd,[102] while in July 1897 it was reported that "for the first time a Welsh play was presented to a London audience. . . . The play is an adaptation of the well-known Welsh novel 'Rhys Lewis,' and was performed by a company of amateurs from Bale."[103]

In addition, reviews of Scottish Gaelic, though not of Welsh, publications were a regular feature of *Irisleabhar na Gaedhilge* from the 1880s on. Typically short and superficial, these reviews were symptomatic of the Irish movement's attitude to its Celtic counterparts at this time; they were obviously intended to draw attention to work worthy of emulation rather than to offer any meaningful intellectual or literary criticism. Characteristic is the following passage from an article on the 1897 Mòd that included comments on three new books in Scots Gaelic:

100. *Imtheachta an Oireachtais, 1899*, 43. "Ní'l aon nidh bhaineas le teangaidh do choimeád beó nach dtigh le Breathnachaibh 'mhúnadh d'Éireannachaibh, óir chongbhaigheadar siad-san a dteanga beó agus ní mór ná go bhfuil ar dteanga-ne caillte againn."

101. See Ó Maolmhuaidh, *Athair na hAthbheochana*, 69, 96.

102. "Notes," *IG* 4, no. 43 (December 1892): 167.

103. "News of the Movement," *IG* 8, no. 87 (July 1897): 37.

We don't want to set up a rivalry between Tadhg and Domhnall, but we cannot let this matter pass without mentioning one way in which the people over there surpass us, i.e., they publish more literature of the kind that is suitable for the average person. We have received three Gaelic books that have just been published in Scotland, and we couldn't help but say to ourselves that it is a great shame and pity for us that we don't have the like in Ireland.[104]

The same note was sounded more pithily in 1894 by the reviewer of the second volume of Cameron's *Reliquae Celticae*: "This is one of those numerous Gaelic publications which do honour to Scotland and put Ireland to shame."[105]

If the appearance of a handful of grammars and readers could touch off such feelings of inadequacy, we can well imagine how revivalists felt when they read of the Welsh Eisteddfod or even of its humbler Scottish counterpart, the Mòd, both of which festivals were covered regularly by *Irisleabhar na Gaedhilge*. In 1894 the *Irisleabhar* correspondent was so carried away by the Eisteddfod ceremonies that he allowed an inexcusable touch of monarchism into his report: "The Welsh National Eisteddfod has been celebrated with more than ordinary brilliancy this year. . . . The Prince and Princess of Wales, and the Princesses Victoria and Maud, and a number of the aristocracy underwent the curious ceremony of initiation."[106] Most Gaels were less bedazzled, but their usual reaction to these assemblies remained envy coupled with a desire to see something similar or even grander in their own land. For example, in an essay submitted to a contest sponsored by the Royal Irish Academy in 1874, Canon Bourke recommended the establishment of "Eisteddfod Gaelach."[107] But there was still no such institution on the horizon in 1890 when Father Eugene O'Growney extolled the Eistedd-

---

104. "An Mòd Gaedhealach," *IG* 8, no. 90 (August 1897): 98. "Níor mhaith linn comórtas do thógáil idir Thadhg agus Domhnall, acht ní fheudfamaoid an sgeul do sgaoileadh tharainn gan tráchd ar bhuaidh amháin atá ag an mbuidhin thall orainn féin, .i. tuilleadh litridheachd bheith fá chló aca de'n chineál is oireamhnaighe mar adhbhar léighte do'n choitcheanntachd. Fuaramar trí leabhair Ghaedhilge atá tar éis a gclóbhuailte i nAlbain, agus níor fheudamar gan a rádh linn féin gur mór a náire agus a thruaighe dhúinn gan a samhail do bheith againn i nÉirinn."

105. Review of *Reliquae Celticae*, vol. 2, by Alexander Cameron, *IG* 5, no. 9 (December 1894): 143.

106. Untitled notes, *IG* 5, no. 5 (August 1894): 65.

107. See Ó Maolmhuaidh, *Athair na hAthbheochana*, 192. For the competition itself, one for essays on the state of the language and its written and oral literature in each of the provinces, see Ó Maolmhuaidh, 106.

fod as a potent symbol of Welsh vitality for which Irish had no counter-part.[108]

While few of his colleagues could have missed O'Growney's obvious corollary, at the time of his essay they had no organization even re-motely capable of managing such an enterprise. But with the birth of the Gaelic League in 1893 and its extraordinary subsequent growth, ho-rizons could be and were expanded; in 1896 a meeting of representatives from league branches voted to hold the first Oireachtas the following May. Editorializing on the upcoming festival in January 1897, *Iris-leabhar na Gaedhilge* paid tribute to the Welsh inspiration of the Oireachtas: "We hope to see the Oireachtas, in course of time, do for Irish what the Eisteddfod has done for Welsh."[109] At the opening cere-mony on 17 May J. J. O'Meara was effusive in his appreciation of Welsh goodwill: "In Wales they hold a similar gathering periodically, and it is encouraging to members of the Gaelic League that they have had the sympathy of those who have been foremost in the work in Wales."[110] Several of those very leaders from Wales were present that day as official representatives of the Eisteddfod, and their attendance established the precedent for exchanges of delegates between the Oireachtas and the Eisteddfod and later between the Oireachtas and the Mòd. In fact, as time went on Welsh and Scottish participation was less passive, and singers from both countries were received with enthusiasm at subsequent Oireachtas concerts.[111]

This low-key, pragmatic sense of shared obstacles and objectives, a kind of lower-case pan-celticism, was soon to be threatened by the bat-tle within the Gaelic movement over Pan-Celticism in very large capital letters. A full discussion of this controversy falls outside the scope of this study; I and others have discussed its political and bureaucratic as-pects elsewhere.[112] Here it is sufficient to say that Pan-Celticism was merely one battlefield in the larger, longer, and even more confusing ideological and literary war within Gaelic circles that is the subject of this study. Nonetheless, while some aspects of the Pan-Celtic squabble

---

108. "The National Language," in *Leabhar an Athar Eoghan*, 231–37. This essay originally appeared in the *Irish Ecclesiastical Review* in November 1890.

109. "An tOireachtas," *IG* 7, no. 9 (January 1897): 130.

110. *Imtheachta an Oireachtais, 1897*, 15.

111. See, for example, *Imtheachta an Oireachtais, 1899*, where we are told that Miss Bronwen Jones's rendition of four Welsh songs "evoked loud applause," and that Miss Emily MacDonald performed two Scots Gaelic songs "in her best style" (21).

112. See Edwards, *Patrick Pearse*, 31–36; and Philip O'Leary, "'Children of the Same Mother': Gaelic Relations with the Other Celtic Revival Movements, 1882–1916," *Proceedings of the Harvard Celtic Colloquium* 6 (1986): 101–30.

can be dismissed as pretexts for fighting out other, often unrelated, issues, and while much of its very real virulence must unfortunately be attributed to personal animosity, we cannot overlook that amid the political maneuvering, name-calling, and recriminations, important cultural and literary concerns were being addressed and debated.

The chief voice of the institutional Irish Pan-Celts who eventually brought the Pan-Celtic Congress to Dublin in August 1901 was *Fáinne an Lae*, which from its inception under the management of Bernard Doyle had been an enthusiastic and on the whole informative chronicler of Celtic affairs, and whose coverage extended to Brittany, the Isle of Man, and Cornwall as well as to Wales and Scotland. For example, *Fáinne an Lae* greeted the Manx Language Society on its foundation in 1899: "Let us welcome the Manx nation into our Celtic brotherhood. It is small, but it is sturdy and vigorous. Ellan Vannin [the Isle of Man] is not *only* a pleasure ground for Lancashire trippers. There is a Celtic fire still burning among the embers."[113] As time passed and as opposition to organized Pan-Celticism was mobilized, *Fáinne an Lae* preached its gospel with an increasingly florid partisanship, culminating in a pledge of allegiance to "Celtia," a map of which was published in the edition of 6 January 1899 along with the following explanation:

> "Celtia" or "Keltia" is the name adopted at Cardiff last year for the aggregate territory of the Five Celtic Nations, i.e., those nationalities whose surviving, or rather reviving, national language belongs to the Celtic family of Indo-European languages. That definition leaves the questions of blood-relationship, of historical connection, of racial purity, and of political status altogether on one side. "Celtia" has an actual existence in the hearts of those who speak and love their Celtic language, and are in sympathy with the parallel efforts of their kinsfolk across the sea. . . . The five nations are linked together, however far apart may lie their political or religious tendencies.[114]

Whether this inchoate optimism was motivated by genuine naivete or tactical disingenuousness, it failed either to convince or inspire the

---

113. "The Manx Gaelic Movement," *FL*, 1 April 1899. Developments on Man attracted a disproportionate amount of ink in *FL*, perhaps on the basis that "the Isle of Man is the point of extreme danger. If Manx can be saved, Gaelic and Welsh are safe beyond further doubt" ("Notes," *FL*, 11 March 1899).

114. "Celtia," *FL*, 6 January 1900. The ubiquitous use of kinship terminology by the Pan-Celts sheds an odd light on their explicit bracketing of "questions" of blood relationship or racial kinship.

opponents of institutional Pan-Celticism, who found their forum in March 1899, when the league's Executive Committee, fed up with Doyle's *Fáinne an Lae* for a variety of reasons, inaugurated *An Claidheamh Soluis* as the league's official organ.[115] Initially and for months thereafter, the debate over Pan-Celticism was conducted with depressing personal nastiness in the now rival journals. Still, on 27 May 1899, *An Claidheamh Soluis* took a step back and laid out the intellectual and ideological case against official Irish affiliation with the Pan-Celtic movement. First of all, the aims of the Pan-Celts, "in so far as they can be ascertained," were pronounced "impracticable." *An Claidheamh Soluis* pointed out that, with the exception of Scots Gaelic, with whose language movement cordial relations had always been maintained apart from any institutional structure, the other Celtic languages were foreign and unintelligible to Irish speakers. Consequently, the "innate racial sympathy," that mystical bond that united "Celtia," was a chimera. Second, *An Claidheamh Soluis* stressed that for the Irish the real issue was the survival of their own language and that the struggle to save it would absorb all their energies. The third and fourth objections can be summed up as the repudiation of "a reversion to the old bad tradition of seeking foreign aid instead of relying on our own good selves."[116]

Both Ruth Dudley Edwards in her biography of Pearse and Hutchinson in *The Dynamics of Cultural Nationalism* supplement the list of reservations in *An Claidheamh Soluis* with two less enlightened motives rooted in ethnic and sectarian exclusivism. Emphasizing that the Irish Pan-Celts had ties with the gentry and with Dublin Castle and that they were disproportionately Protestant, and noting what she calls "their more cosmopolitan attitudes," Edwards resurrects the old dichotomy

115. According to Hyde, the last straw was Doyle's sponsorship of a fund-raising drive to finance an Irish-English dictionary at precisely the same time the league's Executive Committee was preparing the annual Language Fund appeal. See *Mise agus an Conradh*, 71. The diplomatic Hyde avoided taking a public stand on the Pan-Celtic issue, although he was apparently sympathetic to the movement. See Tierney, *Eoin Mac Néill*, 31.

116. "The Gaelic League and the Pan-Celtic Movement," editorial, *ACS*, 2 September 1899. This editorial was presumably by Mac Néill. The dismissal of any sort of mystical "racialism" is certainly in keeping with his resolute opposition to any such definitions of Irish identity. See the perceptive discussion of Mac Néill's philosophy of nationality in Hutchinson, *Dynamics*, 120–27. This official position with regard to the other Celtic movements did not vary throughout our period. In a January 1917 *ACS* editorial, we read: "We may best assist each other by doing, each body of us, our utmost in our own countries. . . . *Is mairg an té nach dtugann aire dá ghnó féin.* [Woe to the person who doesn't pay attention to his own business.] The more we concern ourselves with purely Irish affairs the more we shall be able to contribute to the common fund of Celtic endeavour." See "How to Help the Celt," editorial, *ACS*, 13 January 1917. This editorial was written in response to a piece in Erskine's *The Scottish Review*.

that condemns Gaelic revivalists in general as cultural jingoists blocking the constructive activities of their Anglo-Irish betters.[117] Focusing his attention on Mac Néill and more convincingly on Moran, Hutchinson reduces opposition to the institutional Pan-Celtic movement to unvarnished sectarianism.[118] The evidence does not, however, support such simplistic readings. Personal attacks on the Pan-Celts there were, and some of them, especially those on E. E. Fournier, reveal an ugly, ignorant, and even inappropriate xenophobia.[119] Nevertheless, with the exception of An tAthair Peadar, Moran, and to a lesser extent Dinneen, those here identified as thinkers with nativist tendencies, seem to have taken little ideological interest in the Pan-Celtic question. And even if one accepts the entirely plausible possibility that class or more likely religious sensibilities played a key role in the opposition to Pan-Celticism of some Catholics or that some Protestants like T. W. Rolleston found the league's ambiance Catholic sectarian, the fact is that after personal passions cooled, the League's official position was generous and moderate, simply stating that "the objectives comprised under the title of Pan-Celticism extend beyond the scope of the Gaelic League," but that "individual members of the Gaelic League are absolutely free in their personal capacity to take any course they please with regard to Pan-Celticism." This statement from September 1899 concluded with a return to the de facto league position before the controversy flared up: "We desire to maintain the fullest and most cordial friendship between the language movements in Ireland and in the other countries that have retained their Celtic speech."[120] Indeed, the crucial *An Claidheamh Soluis*

117. *Patrick Pearse*, 31–32.
118. *Dynamics*, 124, 180.
119. Fournier, a Breton by birth, was abused savagely and unjustly throughout this controversy, the most frequent gibe being directed at his non-Irish background. Thus on 12 August 1899 *ACS* inaccurately labeled him "an Englishman of Hugenot extraction now resident in County Dublin," while even five years later, in a report on the 1904 Pan-Celtic Congress, Moran could still comment sarcastically that there was "nothing very Irish about that name" ("Current Affairs," *The Leader*, 10 September 1904). In fact, Fournier was as deeply committed to the Irish language movement as he was to Pan-Celticism, and, at the very time he was being ridiculed as a foreigner, he won an 1899 Oireachtas Prize for a compilation of technical terms in Irish (see *Imtheachta an Oireachtais, 1899*, 165–66) and organized a successful *feis* on Tory Island off the Donegal coast (see *FL*, 16 September 1899). In addition to modern Irish he knew Scots Gaelic, Welsh, Breton, and Manx, and could work with texts in earlier forms of the language, as is evident from his modernization, *Eachtra Laoghaire Mhic Criomthainn go Maigh Meall*, noted in Chapter 4. On his marriage in 1906 Pearse called him "one who has given as unselfish and brilliant service to the Irish language movement as anyone we know" (see *ACS*, 31 March 1906).
120. "The Gaelic League and the Pan-Celtic Movement," editorial, *ACS*, 2 September 1899.

editorial of 27 May 1899 could hardly be more forthright in its rejection of narrow nativism and espousal of the progressive cosmopolitanism Edwards seems to see as a hallmark of the institutional Pan-Celts: "Of course there is sympathy because of their language question with both Wales and Brittany—so there is with the Provençals, the Flemings, the Finns, the Poles, and the Czechs."[121] And in comments inspired by a later Pan-Celtic Congress, an anonymous London Gaelic Leaguer exposed the fallacious roots of institutional Pan-Celticism, while bringing his own inclusive, no-nonsense broad-mindedness quite literally home:

> We are not Pan-Celts ourselves—and for this reason. We are working for the building up of the Irish nation—a nation which will be an Irish Ireland rather than a Celtic Ireland—a nation in which the Irish-born Celt and Saxon, the Irish-born Dane and the Irish-born Norman, shall live together as brothers. The Irishman of Saxon or Norman or Danish blood is of vastly more importance to the Gaelic League than the man of Celtic origin who belongs to any other nation. Our objects are national, not (in the narrow sense of the word) racial.[122]

For some, however, the prospect of such contemporary diversity did awaken a longing for a simpler time. Thus, in his essay "Celtic Ideals and Modern Ideas" in *Sinn Féin* in 1911, Thomas Kelly wrote: "As a check to the spread of many 'modern' ideas there can hardly be a stronger barrier than the bulwark of Celtic Idealism. . . . In the spirit of Celtic idealism we have an antidote to present-day commercialism."[123] But no Gaelic thinker of any real influence could countenance the luxury of living in or attempting to re-create such an irrelevant dreamworld, and it is, therefore, rather remarkable that what now appears to be the league's most compelling motive for distancing itself from Pan-Celticism was not even mentioned in the well-reasoned formal list of objections in the May 1899 editorial. Instead, it was voiced in a conten-

---

121. "The Pan-Celtic Congress." *FL* had explicitly charged opponents of Pan-Celticism with "parochialism:" "The parochialism that would confine our efforts within the confines of Ireland, and even within the limits of one organization in Ireland, is one of the many evidences of that slavishness that foully born in the ruins of Limerick, has marked us more deeply than the sun has burnt the America negro" ("Notes," *FL*, 6 May 1899).

122. "Notes of the Month / The Pan-Celts," *Inis Fáil*, October 1907, 4. The writer does add on a conciliatory note: "We are Pan-Celts in one sense of the word, however. We wish to see successful language revivals such as our own among all the Celtic peoples, and believe that the world would be immensely richer, for instance, by the uprising of a thoroughly Welsh Wales or a Scotch Scotland."

123. *SF*, 15 July 1911. On the same page of this issue of *SF* there appeared a piece on "Celtic Alliance" by "Éireannach."

tious and controversial *An Claidheamh Soluis* editorial in August of that year. One of the items on the agenda of the Irish Pan-Celts was the creation of an Irish Bardic Assembly modelled on the Welsh Gorsedd; to help set up this organization, the Gorsedd itself was invited to perform its rituals in Dublin during the Pan-Celtic Congress.[124] Invoking impeccably progressive criteria, the August *An Claidheamh Soluis* editorial not only condemned this specific invitation, but also questioned the rationale underlying the pomp of any such assembly: "The force of the Irish movement comes from the people's seeing in it a national and economic weapon. Once let the movement get a vague, a fantastic, or an antiquarian character and the edge is taken off our sword. . . . The rank and file up and down the country would lose faith in a 'golden age' and 'tenth-century Irish' movement."[125]

After the Executive Committee's policy statement the following month, *An Claidheamh Soluis* in effect withdrew from the fray, leaving this significant point unexplored. It was, however, taken up in July 1901 by An tAthair Peadar in *The Leader*,[126] and more fully and savagely the following month by the editor of that journal, D. P. Moran, in his report on the Pan-Celtic Congress. Recalling the visit of the Gorsedd to Dublin, Moran was dismissive: "It was a miniature Eisteddfod while it lasted, and an object lesson to us, the moral of which I take to be 'Do ye *not* likewise.' Can a nation be saved by jack-acting—I can't call it play-acting? What is the meaning of all this Bard and Druid business?. . . . Is there any *real* historical foundation for the thing, and if so, how much?" Claiming that the Irish had "quite enough sunbursting and make-believe already," Moran warned against "this trick of celebrating the absolutely dead and forgotten" as "a thing which can only draw down ridicule on any movement intended to be serious."[127]

He had a point. *Fáinne an Lae* at times showed an unhealthy fascination with the antiquarian trappings of the Gorsedd, as in its florid account of the ceremony at which the Irish Pan-Celt Lord Castletown was proclaimed "Arweinydd y Celtiaid" (The Leader of the Celts), and at which the Bretons and Welsh joined two halves of a broken sword

---

124. See "The Pan-Celtic Congress / Meeting of the General Committee," *FL*, 27 May 1899.

125. "Irish Hospitality," *ACS*, 12 August 1899.

126. Letter, *The Leader*, 31 August 1901.

127. "Some Pan-Celtic Comicalities," *The Leader*, 31 August 1901. A similarly sardonic view of the proceedings was taken by "M.L.R." in "At the Pan-Celtic Congress," *UI*, 31 August 1901. On the whole, *UI* distanced itself somewhat from league policy on this issue, even calling the May 1899 *ACS* editorial "utterly uncalled for." See "All Ireland," *UI*, 10 June 1899.

"as a symbol of the re-union of the sundered races."[128] Nor could progressives, already striving to dissipate the Anglo-Irish Celtic Twilight,
have been reassured when *Fáinne an Lae* called forth aid from the mists
of a Tennysonian past in the person of King Arthur: "He will come
again, and it may be that our own Fionn Mac Cumhal will wake from
his slumbers and conclude with Arthur that 'alliance' with the thought
of which Keating buried the thought of feuds between brothers, the
children of the same mother."[129] Possibly to put Fionn at his ease should
he decide to return for the 1899 Eisteddfod, the Irish Pan-Celts presented their invitation to the Gorsedd "in old Irish of the early tenth
century."[130]

Without a doubt the most striking example of the effect such heady
medievalism could have on a susceptible mind is provided by a series of
essays that appeared in *Fáinne an Lae* during late 1899 and early 1900
from the pen of "An Sgoláire Bocht." Impressed by the willingness of
the Gorsedd bards to undertake the task of constructing the stone circle
essential to their rituals in a Dublin field,[131] "An Sgoláire Bocht" urged
Gaels to emulate their dedication to the past by holding their own "traditional" *Aonach* (Fair) in a proper *caiseal* (stone fort). In proposing several sites for the *Aonach*—a spot between Christchurch and St Patrick's
Cathedrals, Stephen's Green, or the Phoenix Park—he pointed out that
"nothing would be necessary but the erection of the circular wall of dry
stone or of earth faced with sods," the gate of which was to open south
and be wide enough "for the passage of at least three horses harnessed
abreast."[132] With the logistic problems of the *Aonach* solved to his satisfaction, he could turn to weightier concerns of spiritual protocol, discussing the *geasa* (taboos or injunctions) that would have to be observed
by the modern-day counterparts of the King of Leinster and the King of
Ireland. After a complicated exploration of the geography of Dublin, he

128. "The Welsh Eisteddfod," *FL*, 22 July 1899. See also "The Bardic Gorsedd," *FL*, 7
January 1899. The latter piece defended the authenticity of the ceremony "which has been
handed down historically from the twelfth century, and traditionally through the last
2,000 years." For a discussion of the history of many of these Welsh rituals, see Emyr
Humphreys, *The Taliesin Tradition: A Quest for Welsh Identity* (London: Black Raven,
1983); and Prys Morgan, "From a Death to a View: The Hunt for the Welsh Past in the
Romantic Period," in *The Invention of Tradition*, ed. Eric Hobsbawm and Terence Ranger
(Cambridge: Cambridge University Press, 1984), 43–100.
129. "The Coming Eisteddfod," *FL*, 8 July 1899.
130. "The Coming Eisteddfod," *FL*, 8 July 1899. The invitation was prepared by the
Celticist Heinrich Zimmer ("Notes," *FL*, 5 August 1899), and read by Osborn Bergin
("Notes," *FL*, 22 July 1899).
131. "Notes," *FL*, 5 August 1899.
132. "An Sgoláire Bocht," "Gaelic Costume," *FL*, 17 February 1900.

had the answer: "Taking the two Geasa together, the Aonach should not meet at the north side on Wednesday under any circumstances, nor at either side on Monday if the programme require that the river should be crossed."[133] The extraordinary project of "An Sgoláire Bocht" offers a colorful and entirely sui generis confirmation of the progressive view that, however impressive and meaningful their traditional ceremonies were for the Welsh, any attempt to transplant this sort of creative anachronism to Ireland would be disastrous. If not a "burlesquing" of "the sacred relics of antiquity," to use Ua Laoghaire's phrase,[134] the institutional Pan-Celts' obsession with pompous rituals of dubious authenticity was at best a distracting irrelevance and at worst a real threat to the Revival's claim on the attention and loyalty of twentieth-century Ireland.

On the other hand, the efforts of fellow Celts to confront head-on the challenges of the new century were supported by virtually all revivalists. Even during the most virulent phase of the Pan-Celtic debate, both *Fáinne an Lae* and *An Claidheamh Soluis*, as well as *Irisleabhar na Gaedhilge*, continued to discuss and draw lessons from experiments and accomplishments throughout the Celtic world. Predictably, much of this concern focused on practical matters, such as education, but literary concerns were not entirely ignored, as is evident from the many reviews of new Celtic publications that appeared in all three journals throughout this period, although these reviews still tended to be brief notices drawing the attention of Gaels to models worthy of emulation rather than true critical evaluations.[135] *Fáinne an Lae* took the lead here, introducing on 28 January 1899 "Our Celtic Bookshelf," a weekly column providing concise reports on "the more important recent additions to Celtic literature."[136] *Fáinne an Lae* also published more substantial essays on cultural developments in Brittany and Cornwall by the Breton poet François Jaffrennou,[137] and in several perceptive and informative articles introduced Gaels to the Breton drama revival.[138] In addi-

---

133. "An Sgoláire Bocht," "Gaelic Costume," *FL*, 3 March 1900.

134. Peadar Ua Laoghaire, letter, *The Leader*, 27 July 1901.

135. Typical is the tone of a brief reference to a booklet of saints' lives in Breton: "This brought home forcibly to our mind how very backward we are in this respect ourselves. An immense amount of good could be done if similar booklets were published in Irish." See "Notes," *ACS*, 18 August 1900.

136. *FL*, 28 January 1899.

137. See "Our Breton Brethren / Interesting Letter," *FL*, 9 April 1898; "The Breton Theatre," *FL*, 16 July 1898; and "The Cornish Language," *FL*, 24 June 1899.

138. See E. E. Fournier's review of the mystery play *Sant Gwennole*, *FL*, 3 September 1898; "A New Breton Play," *FL*, 15 July 1899; or "The Breton Festival at Vannes," *FL*, 30 September 1899. In addition, *FL* serialized Heinrich Zimmer's "The Celtic Movement in Brittany" from 24 March to 26 May 1900.

tion, *Fáinne an Lae* actually published work in Scots Gaelic and Manx.[139]

With the passions of controversy in the past, *An Claidheamh Soluis* significantly expanded its coverage of Celtic affairs under the editorship of Pearse and that of his successor Seán Mac Giollarnáth. Himself a former member of the Irish committee of the Pan-Celtic Congress as well as the league's official representative to the 1899 Eisteddfod and Mòd, Pearse now eschewed explicit Pan-Celticism in favor of a more objective approach to what could be learned from fellow Celts. He also fostered a growing conviction that the Irish need no longer be merely the students of the Celtic world. With their confidence deepening as their movement gained strength and influence and as the first important works in their new literature began to appear, the Irish were now ready to teach and occasionally even chastise as well as learn from their Celtic counterparts. They were especially eager to share the lessons of their success with their fellow Gaels in Scotland, whom they encouraged to Gaelicize the Mòd,[140] to establish a periodical press,[141] and to expand and popularize the activities of An Cumann Gaidhleach along the lines of the Gaelic League.[142] Motivated by this same spirit, William P. Ryan was even more daring, suggesting to the Welsh ways to improve the Eisteddfod: "That the Eisteddfod has been as thoroughly national or as vigorously literary as it might have been is more than doubtful; as in Welsh life generally the musical, or perhaps we ought to say the singing, side has been developed at the expense of others."[143]

With this renewed pragmatism and their heightened awareness of their own achievements, the Gaels now preferred to look toward those Celtic realms where things were actually happening, focusing on Wales, Scotland, and to a considerably lesser extent, Brittany,[144] while on the whole ignoring the somewhat haphazard linguistic developments on

139. See, for example, "Sgéal ó Alban" (A story from Scotland), *FL*, 30 April 1898; and E. E. Fournier, "A Manx Ossianic Song/'Fionn as Oisín,'" *FL*, 16 December 1899.

140. Contrast Séamus Ó Dubhghaill's account of the 1902 Mòd (*ACS*, 4 October 1902) with his report on the 1906 gathering (*ACS*, 13 October 1906).

141. See, for example, "A Highland Appreciation," *ACS*, 28 October 1905; and "Alba," *ACS*, 25 May 1907.

142. See, for example, "In the Highlands," *ACS*, 20 May 1905; and "Éire and Alba," *ACS*, 2 March 1907.

143. *Lessons from Modern Language Movements*, 31. See also "Wanted—A Welsh Eisteddfod," editorial, *ACS*, 5 November 1904.

144. See, for example, "Fleid," "Amharclann sa Bhreatain" (A theater in Brittany), *ACS*, 15 August 1914. Actually *FL* had covered Breton developments far better than *ACS* was able to do until Tadhg Ó Donnchadha turned his attention to Brittany in 1912–13.

Man[145] and in Cornwall.[146] In particular, the unique claims of the Scottish Gaels continued to be recognized, as they had been since the 1880s,[147] and there were regular and lengthy reports on the Mòd and generally favorable reviews of a wide range of Scottish publications. Under the editorship of Tadhg Ó Donnchadha from 1902 to 1909, such reviews of Scots Gaelic works in *Irisleabhar na Gaedhilge* finally began to move beyond mere publicity notices to something approaching genuine criticism. Moreover, while the emphasis tended to remain on what the Irish could learn from the Scots, the lessons were becoming more sophisticated. For example, the anonymous reviewer (probably Ó Donnchadha himself) of *Oiteagan o'n Iar* (Breezes from the West) by Iain Mac Cormaig, felt the book offered "a lesson to be learned by every writer we have over here" (ceacht le foghluim ag an uile scríbhneoir dá bhfuil againn abhus) and explained that "Iain is chiefly concerned with the ordinary life of the present day . . . and we in Ireland should not forget that when we set out to write original fiction."[148]

Furthermore, under Pearse and then Mac Giollarnáth, *An Claidheamh*

145. The very first number of *ACS* greeted the new "Manx Association for the Revival of the Manx Language" on 18 March 1899. When nine months later the president of this group apparently opposed as impractical any attempt to revive Manx as a spoken language, *ACS* dismissed the organization out of hand: "The Manx Language Society can hardly expect to be taken seriously henceforward on this side of the water." See "Notes," *ACS*, 2 December 1899. *ACS* did, however, report favorably on the translation of terms like "root beer" and "chip potato" in the Manx-language version of a 1907 law regulating shops on the island. See "The Capabilities of Manx," *ACS*, 28 December 1907. In addition, *ACS* published Laoide's edition of "'Tóiteán Tighe Fhinn' [The burning of Fionn's house']/The Manx Version of It" with interlinear Irish translation in the issue for 6 August 1910.

146. Apart from the somewhat startled editorial welcome to "The Celtic Cornish Society" ("We had been under the impression that the Cornish Language was dead.") in *ACS*, 19 April 1902; and the report that Cornwall had achieved "admission . . . to the rank of a Celtic nation" at the 1904 Pan-Celtic Congress (*ACS*, 10 September 1904), the Cornish movement was almost entirely ignored by the Gaelic press. For example, *ACS* flatly rejected Robert Walling's assertion that the Cornish would always remain Celts despite the loss of their language. See "The Resurrection of Cornwall," *ACS*, 31 August 1912.

147. Indeed, in March 1894 *IG* had simply incorporated its "Scottish Gaelic" or "Scottish Gaelic Notes" column into "Gaelic Notes," its survey of Irish language news. While *UI* could see the sense of holding the institutional Pan-Celts at arm's length in 1899, it also felt that there was "no reason why the approaching Oireachtas should not be availed of for a possible conference of the Gaelic elements of that federation." See "All Ireland," *UI*, 22 April 1899.

148. "Clódhanna Nua" (New publications), *IG* 18, no. 5 (May 1908): 235. "Isé gnáth-shaoghal an lae indiu is mó atá ag déanamh buartha do Iain . . . agus níor mhiste dhúinn-ne i nÉirinn gan an méid sin a leigean ar dí-chuimhneamh nuair a chuirimíd chum sgéalta nuadhéanta a cheapadh."

Soluis established a close relationship with the Scots Gaelic Catholic monthly *Guth na Bliadhna*, and when in 1905 its editor Ruaraidh Erskine made a plea for "reciprocity," "the restoration of that correspondence which used to exist between Éire and Alba,"[149] Pearse "heartily endorsed" the sentiment: "The dwellers on the two sides of Sruth na Maoile have in many things common traditions, and to a large extent common problems. Why not then . . . an *entente cordial* between the Gael of Scotia Major and the Gael of Scotia Minor?"[150] In fact, Dinneen had already explored this shared heritage in an essay in *Guth na Bliadhna* in the summer of 1905:

> There is no great difference between the Gaelic of Ireland and the Gaelic of Scotland. The Gaelic of Ireland is read and understood in Scotland; the Gaelic of Scotland is read and understood in Ireland. There is respect for the musicians and singers of Ireland in Scotland, and respect for the musicians and singers of Scotland in Ireland. Their language is the same; their tunes are the same; their music is the same; their ancestry is the same—much of it at any rate—and it is proper that their heart and spirit be the same. May God never allow enmity to come between them.[151]

149. "Malairteachd" (Reciprocity), *ACS*, 25 November 1905. See also his editorial "Gaelic Confederation," *Guth na Bliadhna* 3, no. 1 (Winter 1906): 11–25. He developed the political implications of this initiative in "Éirinn is Albainn" (Ireland and Scotland), *Guth na Bliadhna* 8, no. 1 (Winter 1911): 1–12.

150. "Reciprocity," editorial, *ACS*, 25 November 1905. See also Giollabhrighde Ó Catháin, "Malairteachd," *ACS*, 30 December 1905. Ó Catháin went beyond Irish-Scottish "reciprocity" to full-blown vintage Pan-Celticism: "Finally, we are Celts; which means that we have a lion's share to perform in the establishing and vivifying that Nova Celtia which the seers of these days foresee will bring a new element, a new current to the thought and the life of the world in the future."

His views sparked no condemnation; the acrimony of at least one intramural Gaelic row had been neutralized. On the other hand, the resultant "reciprocity" itself seems to have been so unobtrusive that Peadar Mac Fhionnlaoich could feel the need to call for some sort of "Scottish alliance" in a 1911 letter to *Sinn Féin*: "Without any formal alliance it will be all to the good that we should know fully what is being done to hold on to the Gaelic on each side of the strait." See Mac Fhionnlaoich, letter, *SF*, 15 July 1911.

151. "Éire agus Alba" (Ireland and Scotland), *Guth na Bliadhna* 2, no. 3 (Summer 1905): 235–36. "Níl aon deifridheacht mhór idir Ghaedhilg na hÉireann is Ghaedhilg na hAlban. Léightear is tuigtear Gaedhealg na hÉireann i nAlbain; léightear is tuigtear Gaedhealg na hAlban i nÉirinn. Bíonn meas ar cheoltóiridhibh is ar amhránuidhthibh Éireann i nAlbain agus meas ar cheoltóiridhibh is amhránuidhthibh Alban i nÉirinn. Is ionann a dteanga; is ionann a gcuid fonn; is ionann a gceol; is ionann a sinsear—nó a lán de—agus budh chóir gur bh'ionann an croidhe bheadh aca is gur bh'ionann a spioraid. Nár leigidh Dia go dtiocfadh eascairdeas eatortha go deo." Other prominent revivalists who espoused similar views in *Guth na Bliadhna* were "Conán Maol" and Peadar Mac Fhionnlaoich. See "Conán

In literary terms, this "reciprocity" was expressed not only through reviews,[152] but also through scholarly linguistic discussions of Scots Gaelic like the one that dominated the "Ceist agus Freagra" (Question and answer) column of *An Claidheamh Soluis* in the first half of 1904,[153] and through the many annotated editions of Scots Gaelic poetry and prose published in the paper between 1910 and 1912,[154] the two most extensive being "Oidheadh Fraoich Mhic Fhiodhaigh" (The violent death of Fraoch Mac Fhiodaigh) and "Cos Chéin Mhic Mhaoilmhuaidh" (The leg of Cian Mac Maoilmhuaidh), both edited by Seosamh Laoide in 1912.[155]

Gaelic interest in the Welsh movement continued to center as it had always done on education and public life, the widespread practical recognition of Welsh in the nation's schools and the commitment of Welsh officials to use and lobby for the language. Unlike Welsh teachers and politicians, Welsh creative writers were virtually ignored in the Gaelic press, no doubt for the same simple reason as always: few involved in the Gaelic literary movement could read them. Thus, apart from the work of Tadhg Ó Donnchahda to be disussed below, the only translation we have from Welsh in this period is "Hata Sheáin Mhic Eoin," Caitlín de Bhulbh's version of Daniel Owen's "Het Jac Jones" (Jack Jones's hat).[156] Significantly, even Pearse's references to Welsh literature in *An Claidheamh Soluis* were limited to such occasions as his conventional editorial obituary for the "arch-druid" of the Welsh Gorsedd,

---

Maol," "Focailín" (A little word), *Guth na Bliadhna* 2, no. 4 (Autumn 1905): 308–10; and Mac Fhionnlaoich, "An t-Albanach in Éirinn" (The Scot in Ireland), *Guth na Bliadhna* 9, no. 3 (Summer 1912): 379–86. An tAthair Peadar's views were essentially identical with those of Dinneen on this point. See his letter to Séamus Ó Dubhghaill of 7 May 1906 quoted by Ó Fiannachta in "Ag Cogarnaíl le Cara," *IMN* (1991): 118.

152. The publication of such reviews continued throughout our period. See, for example, Lloyd's reviews of *Eachdraidhean-Beatha nan Albannach Iomraiteach Ud: Uilleam Uallas, Iain Knox, agus Rob Ruadh* (The life exploits of those famous Scotsmen: William Wallace, John Knox, and Rob Roy) and *Gille a' Bhuidseir, The Wizard's Gillie and Other Tales, Ancient Legends of the Scottish Gael* in *ACS*, 11 July 1914 and 16 October 1915 respectively; and the anonymous review of the magazine *Guth na Bliadhna* in *ACS*, 19 August 1916.

153. The leading participants in this debate about the degree to which Scots Gaelic had been "corrupted" since its divergence from Irish were the Scot Colum Mac Phartholain and the Irishman Seaghán S. Mac a' Bháird.

154. See, for example, the poems of Màiri Nic Leoid edited by Art Mag Uidhir, *ACS*, 5 February 1905 and 29 January 1910; or the series of Scots Gaelic songs published in the "Guth na mBárd" (The voice of the poets) column of *ACS* throughout the latter half of 1911.

155. Both appeared in *ACS*, the former on 13 July 1912; the latter from 7 September to 19 October of the same year.

156. Caitlín de Bhulbh, "Hata Sheáin Mhic Eoin," *ACS*, 24 October 1914.

Hwfa Môn,[157] or his passing remarks on John Morris Jones's Welsh translation of the *Rubaiyat*.[158]

This ignorance of creative developments in Wales, the Celtic country which, after all, had by far the most extensive corpus of contemporary literature, was at last, though single-handedly, enlightened by Tadhg Ó Donnchadha, a former Pan-Celt who not only never lost his initial enthusiasm for the cause, but also actually learned other Celtic languages. In addition, he seems to have been able to envision creative ways to adapt useful elements from the other Celtic languages and literatures to Irish conditions. Nor was he timid in his adaptations. For example, in 1903 he was one of the founders of Árd-Chúirt na hÉigse (originally Árd-Chúirt Shocaide na Suadh), a Munster-based group of poets and scholars including Dinneen, Béaslaí, and Risteárd Ó Foghludha ("Fiachra Éilgeach"), dedicted to preserving the integrity of the Irish poetic tradition, in particular the intricate patterns of sound, metre, and rhyme. In a 1912 review Ó Donnchadha stressed the Celtic roots of this kind of poetic assembly and explicitly identified it as a (lower-case) *gorsedd*.[159] More dramatically, at their 1914 meeting, the Ard-Chúirt voted "to take immediate steps to organize Cumann na hÉigse on the lines of the Welsh Gorsedd," a decision reported without comment by *An Claidheamh Soluis*.[160] Yet despite the conservatism of its members with regard to native versecraft, Árd-Chúirt na hÉigse was on the whole a corrective and constructive force on the literary scene and never went in for the artificial antiquarianism that had so legitimately alarmed many Gaels when the (upper-case) Gorsedd visited Dublin in 1901.[161]

With his sound knowledge of both Welsh and Breton, Ó Donnchadha was able to turn the "Ceilteachas" (Celtic affairs) column he began in *An Claidheamh Soluis* in November 1912 into something radically different from the previous Celtic literary columns, "Our Celtic Bookshelf" in *Fáinne an Lae* and "From the Celtic Press" in *An Claidheamh Soluis*.[162] As has been noted, these earlier features rarely went much beyond a few informational sentences announcing the ap-

157. "Hwfa Môn," editorial, *ACS*, 25 November 1905.
158. "Mion-Sgéala," *ACS*, 18 January 1908.
159. "An Bhriotáin agus a Teanga," *ACS*, 12 October 1912.
160. "Na Báird" (The bards), *ACS*, 8 August 1914. According to the *Weekly Freeman* column "In the Gaelic World," the project had also been discussed in 1911 but nothing had come of it. See "In the Gaelic World," *WF*, 13 January 1912.
161. Its members did share the well-nigh universal Gaelic use of picturesque pseudonyms and often added a curious symbol after these pseudonyms when they appeared in print.
162. The "Clódhanna Nua" column of *IG* also regularly noted the publication of books in Scots Gaelic or Welsh.

pearance of a new work, almost invariably one in Irish or Scots Gaelic. "Ceilteachas," on the other hand, even when commenting on several journals in a single review essay, seldom failed to provide a critical summary of their contents. Furthermore, Ó Donnchadha regularly used the column to introduce his Revival colleagues to broad developments in Celtic literature as well as to the work of individual Celtic authors.[163] For example, in October 1912 his review of the Pan-Celt Jaffrennou's *La Genèse d'un mouvement* turned into a lengthy essay entitled "An Bhriotáin agus a Teanga" (Brittany and her language),[164] and two months later he returned to the work of Jaffrennou ("Taldir") with a long review of the second volume of *Les Poèmes de Taldir / Barzaz Taldir*.[165] This essay included a biographical account of the poet, a sympathetic discussion of his work for Pan-Celticism, and, most significant, translations of several of his poems into Irish. Ó Donnchadha used this same approach in an even more extensive review of *Gwaith Barddonol Cybi* (The poetic work of "Cybi" [Robert Evans]);[166] in his four-part survey of "Filidheacht sa Bhreatnais" (Poetry in Welsh);[167] in his six-part review of Ifor Williams's edition of *Cywyddau Dafydd ap Gwilym a'i Gyfoeswyr* (The Cywydd poems of Dafydd ap Gwilym and his contemporaries);[168] and in his four-part review of *Gwaith Siôn Cent* (The work of Siôn Cent).[169]

Yet while Ó Donnchadha's review essays were a new departure in making possible a broader and deeper Irish understanding of Celtic literatures, in one important way he deviated little from the old utilitarian approach to developments in the other Celtic revival movements, repeatedly emphasizing the pedagogic value of the simpler texts he re-

163. His first such venture into Celtic studies was "Filidheacht na Breathnaise" (Welsh poetry) in the Oireachtas supplement of *ACS*, 31 July 1909. This piece included an Irish translation of a poem by Huw Morus (1622–1709). Ó Donnchadha did not limit himself to literary issues. For example, he discussed Welsh painting in two *ACS* columns in 1914. See "Láimhealadhna sa Bhreatain" (Art in Wales), review of *Celf yng Nghymru* (Art in Wales) by T. Matthews, *ACS*, 7 and 14 March 1914; and "Deascán Díoghluma / Ealadhna sa Bhreatain" (Miscellany / Art in Wales), *ACS*, 26 September 1914.

164. *ACS*, 5 and 12 October 1912.

165. "Taldir," *ACS*, 14 and 28 December 1912.

166. "Gwaith Barddonol Cybi," *ACS*, 3–24 May 1913.

167. "Filidheacht sa Bhreatnais," *ACS*, 30 May–20 June 1914.

168. "Dafydd ap Gwilym," *ACS*, 17 April–22 May 1915.

169. "Siôn Cent," *ACS*, 5–26 June 1915. See also his four-part review of Thomas Gwynn Jones's study *Emrys ap Iwan: Dysgawdr, LLenor, Cenedlgarwr* (Emrys ap Iwan: Teacher, man of letters, patriot), *ACS*, 28 June–26 July 1913. There were no translations in this essay.

viewed,[170] and rarely losing an opportunity to lecture Gaelic literatteurs about what they could learn from their linguistic cousins:

> The reason I write so much about developments involving the native language in Wales is that we have much to learn from the people of that country—with regard to loyalty to the native language and the tireless accompanying desire to set that language firmly on its feet. Those are traits well worth praising in them; and it would be a fine day for Ireland and for the Irish language if the Irish would imitate their brothers on the other side of the Irish Sea and keep the soul of this country uncorrupted by the alien as they do.[171]

Despite the apparent unadulterated nativism of this passage, Ó Donnchadha was, as we have seen, a polyglot European and an active translator from several languages. In his study of the other Celtic literatures, especially that of Wales, he seems at this time to have found a possible resolution of this ambivalence. The work of fellow Celts offered inspiration simultaneously foreign and familiar and so could serve as a source from which the new Gaelic literature could draw with a significantly reduced danger of "alien" corruption. From this perspective there is no contradiction whatsoever between the lines quoted above and his (almost) unreserved acceptance of "foreign" influences in the final installment of "Dafydd ap Gwilym:"

> It is a good thing, however, to look around us now and again, and to learn about the work being done in other languages. If we want Irish to flourish again, we must nourish it in the meantime

170. For example, he wrote of the Welsh monthly *Cymru* (*Wales*), with specific reference to the short stories of Thomas Gwynn Jones: "Indeed, I don't think it would be possible to find a better aid for learning Welsh than this paper." (Go deimhin, ní dóigh liom gur bhféidir áis eile do bfhearr d'fhagháil chum na Breatnaise d'fhoghluim 'ná an páipéar so.) See "Ceilteachas," *ACS*, 1 March 1913. He also urged Gaelic writers to follow the lead of their Welsh counterparts in producing literature for children. See "Deascán Díoghluma / Oideachas agus Náisiúntacht" (Miscellany / Education and nationality), *ACS*, 17 October 1914.

171. "Sión Cent—I," *ACS*, 5 June 1915. "Isé fáth go scríobhaimse an oiread san ar chúrsaí na teangan dúthchais sa Bhreatain ná a lán a bheith le foghluim againne ó mhuinntir na tíre sin—chomh fada agus a théigheann dílseacht don teangain dúthchais, agus an dúil dochlaoidhte a thagann dá dhruim chun na teangan do chur go daingean ar a bonnaibh. Is mór is ionmholta na tréithe sin ionnta súd; agus ba rómhaith an lá d'Éirinn agus don Ghaedhilg é dá ndéanfaidís Gaedhil aithris ar a mbráithribh gaoil ar an dtaobh thall de Mhuir Mheann, agus anam na tíre seo a choimeád gan truailliú ón iasacht mar a dhéinid siadsan é."

with a dash of the foreign. New thoughts and new arts and new literary devices, those are what we need. It is things of that sort from foreign languages that will excite our own writers to emulate them. And if the foreign is a good thing, it is essential to be careful about it and to filter it clean before it is used.[172]

At any rate, whatever the ideological or even psychological source of his fascination with other Celtic literatures, the lessons he derived from them and set for his colleagues could be both sophisticated and challenging. For instance, he urged Gaelic poets (and by implication prose writers) to follow the example of "Cybi" by widening the scope of their work to include political and social themes of contemporary relevance;[173] he discussed the initiative and ingenuity of Welsh publishers;[174] he contrasted the willingness of Welsh academics to make use of the language in all aspects of their work with the Irish practice of preparing scholarly commentaries and apparatus in English;[175] he praised Jaffrennou's approach to technical terminology, a blend of borrowings from the French and coinings from native roots, in his *Giriadur Gallek ha Brezonek / Dictionnaire Français-Breton*;[176] and he told those interested in Gaelic theater of Breton successes in staging native drama in the provinces.[177]

Unfortunately, as we have seen, few of Ó Donnchadha's colleagues had the ability to read the poems of "Cybi" or the plays of Jaffrennou in the original, and therefore his greatest contribution to Irish understand-

---

172. "Dafydd ap Gwilym—VI," *ACS*, 22 May 1915. "Is maith an rud, amh, féachaint timcheall orainn anois agus arís, agus eólus d'fhagháil ar an saothrú atá dhá dhéanamh i dteangthaibh eile. Má's mian linn athfhás do theacht ar an nGaedhilg ní mór dúinn í bheathú idir dhá linn ar steall den iasacht. Smaointe nua, agus ealadhna nua, agus 'giúirléidí' nua litridheachta, is iad atá i n-easnamh orainn. Solaoidí dá sórd a teangthaibh iasachta iseadh a ghríosóidh ár scríbhneóirí féin chun aithris ortha. Acht má's maith é an t-iasacht, ní mór beith cúramach n-a thaobh agus é scagadh glan sara mbaintear feidhm as."

173. "Gwaith Barddonol Cybi—III," *ACS*, 24 May 1913. See also his review of Thomas Gwynn Jones's travel book *Y Môr Canoldir a'r Aifft* (The Mediterranean Sea and Egypt), *ACS*, 1 February 1913. In this review Ó Donnchadha asked: "When will one of our writers be able to pay a visit to some foreign country and write a worthwhile, enjoyable book for us on his return home?" (Cathain a bheidh ar a chumas ag duine dár scríbhneóiríbhne cuaird a thabhairt i dtír éigin iasachta, agus leabhar fóghanta taithneamhach a scríobhadh dúinn d'éis casadh a-bhaile dhó?)

174. "Siôn Cent—I," *ACS*, 5 June 1915.

175. "Dafydd ap Gwilym—I," *ACS*, 17 April 1915.

176. "Ceilteachas / Foclóir Briotáinise" (Celtic affairs / A Breton dictionary), *ACS*, 2 May 1914.

177. "An Bhriotáin agus a Teanga—II," *ACS*, 12 October 1912.

ing of writing in the Celtic languages, even on the most rudimenatary, literal level, was his work in translation. His first such effort, a version from the Welsh he titled "An Gadhar 'na Shean-Aois" (The dog in his old age) appeared in *Celtia* as early as April 1901, and, as has been noted, he included translations from both Welsh and Breton in review essays for his "Ceilteachas" column.[178] He did not, however, limit himself to the occasional translation to illustrate a review. In 1912 appeared *Guth ón mBreatain .i. Llais o Gymru* (A voice from Wales), a collection of forty-one poems translated from the Welsh and ranging from the work of the fourteenth-century master Dafydd ap Gwilym to that of nineteenth-century bards. Characteristically, even in this, his most ambitious and impressive contribution to genuine pan-Celtic understanding, Ó Donnchadha was explicit that his motivation was in good part didactic, pointing out in his bilingual Irish-Welsh preface that Welsh literature was well ahead of Irish in its ability to deal with the modern world, and asserting: "I think it [Welsh] can best help us to understand how our own language must be guided along that difficult and rough passage until a safe harbor is reached, that is, until Irish is able to meet the demands of a language of learning and culture."[179]

With *Guth ón mBreatain* Ó Donnchadha pioneered an initiative in the Gaels' attempt to come to terms with their Celtic heritage. Speaking as an unrepentant Pan-Celt, he urged them to follow his lead: "If the efforts in this book serve to make Gaels aware of the ways of thought of their Celtic kinfolk, the path will be cleared for acquaintance and friendship. It is in the interest of both to bind themselves in an alliance of friendship, for the same power is the enemy of both, and it is an enemy without pity."[180] His rallying cry went unheeded, and despite all the expressions of interest and goodwill, the Celtic literatures either in the original or in translation were to have no significant influence whatsoever on Irish writing during the Revival, or, for that matter, afterward. And the reason is depressingly obvious. Gaelic interest in the

---

178. For a list of his translations from the Celtic languages, see Ó hÉaluighthe's "Clár Sgríbhinní Thórna," in *Féilscríbhinn Tórna*, 239–44.

179. "Réamhrádh" (Preface) to *Guth ón mBreatain/Llais o Gymru* (Baile Átha Cliath: M. H. Gill agus a Mhac, 1912), 4. "Is í, dar liomsa, is fearr do chuirfidh i dtuigsint dúinn an chuma nach fuláir ár dteanga féin do stiúradh an ród achrannach cnapánach soin, go dtí go sroisfear cuan na sábhála, .i. go mbeidh ar chumas na Gaedhilge freagairt do riachtnaisíbh teangan léighinn is ealadhan."

180. "Réamhrádh" to *Guth*, 5. "Má fóghnaid na hiarrachtaí sa leabhar so chun eólus a thabhairt do Ghaedhealaibh ar oibriughadh aigne a gcombráthar Ceiltigh, réidhfear an bóthar chun aitheantais is chun caradais. Níor mhiste dhóibh araon connradh caradais do cheangal le chéile, de bhrígh gurab é an chomhacht chéadna is namhaid dóibh, agus gur namhaid gan trócaire é."

literatures of other Celtic cultures foundered on the simple inability or
unwillingness of revivalists, many of them of course recent students of
Irish, to learn either Welsh, Breton, or indeed Scots Gaelic, a language
many of them seem to have felt absolved from studying because it was
consistently classified as a mere dialect of Irish.[181] The almost apologetic
opening sentence of Máirtín Ó Cadhain's preface to *Bás nó Beatha?*
(Death or life?), his translation of Saunders Lewis's *Tynged yr Iaith* (The
fate of the language), a work published fifty years after *Guth ón mBreatain*, underscores the failure of Ó Donnchadha's vision of a vibrant
Celtic cultural alliance nourished by translation: "I thought that it
would be worthwhile to translate this essay, *Tynged yr Iaith*. It has a
direct relevance for Irish as well even if that is not immediately clear."[182]

   To balance this lengthy tale of high hopes come to naught, we may
turn to areas in which the call for translation was answered promptly
and with some adequacy. One such venture was the provision of religious literature in Irish. Here there was, of course, a significant tradition of translation in the nineteenth century and before. Indeed, there
were three modern Gaelic versions of *Imitatio Christi*, two from the
eighteenth century and one from the nineteenth. Of the older texts, one
remained in manuscript throughout our period, while the other, by an
anonymous Ulster priest, was edited and published in 1915 by An tAthair Domhnall Ó Tuathail.[183] The nineteenth-century translation by An
tAthair Domhnall Ó Súilliobháin, had, on the other hand, appeared as
Searcleanamhaint Chríost (The loving following of Christ) as early as
1822 (with new editions in 1886 and 1908).[184] In addition, Archbishop

181. Translations from Scots Gaelic and Manx were, for example, specifically excluded
from the translation competition of the 1902 Feis Laighean agus Midhe. See "Feis
Laighean agus Midhe" (The Leinster and Meath Feis), *ACS*, 18 January 1902.

182. "Réamhrá" to *Bás nó Beatha?* (Death or life?), a translation of Saunders Lewis's
Tynged yr Iaith (The destiny of the language) (Baile Átha Cliath: Sáirséal agus Dill, 1963),
7. "Cheap mé gurbh fhiú Gaeilge a chur ar an léacht so, *Tynged yr Iaith*. Tá dlúthbhaint
aige leis an nGaeilge freisin cé nach léar sin ar an gcéad iarra."

183. *Tóraidheacht na bhFíreun ar Lorg Chríosda. Sagart Éigin i n-aice le Dúnphádraig a
d'Aistrigh 1762. Domhnall Ó Tuathail, Sagart, a Chuir i n-Eagar* (The search of the just for
Christ. Translated by a priest from near Downpatrick in 1762. Edited by Father Domhnall Ó Tuathail) (Baile Átha Cliath: M. H. Gill agus a Mhac, 1915). It is worth noting
that the *ACS* reviewer emphasized the potential linguistic as well as spiritual benefits of
the book: "It represents a piece of real literature in the old language, untouched by English influences either in style, idiom, or vocabulary. We believe it will become dear to
many, both for its language and its theme." See "Air Lorg Chríosda," *ACS*, 13 February
1915. For a brief discussion of these three translations of the *Imitatio*, see T. F. O'Rahilly,
letter, *SF*, 10 December 1910.

184. See "Searc-Leanamhaint Chríost," *ACS*, 5 November 1910; and "Searc-Leanamhaint Chríost," *SF*, 26 November 1910.

MacHale published a catechism, a prayerbook, a Stations of the Cross, and a translation of the *Pentateuch*.[185] His protégé, Canon Ulick Bourke, was almost as productive in this area, producing over the years translations of selections from the work of Saint Alphonsus Liguori, of the papal bull *Ineffabilis* (concerning the Immaculate Conception of the Blessed Virgin), and of the "Magnificat."[186] In 1813 the poet Seaghán Ó Conaill published *Eagna Fhírinneach; nó Smaointighthe do gach lá do'n tSeachdmhuin*, (*True Wisdom, or Considerations for every day of the Week*), a translation of the English version of a work on Catholic doctrine originally in Italian.[187] Challenor's *Think Well On't: or, Reflections on the Great Truths of the Christian Religion* was translated by Eoghan Ua Caomhánaigh and published in 1820.[188] Reverend Bernard Callan produced an Irish prayerbook, including some translated hymns, under the English title *The Spiritual Rose* in 1825, and Reverend Jonathan Furlong brought out another prayerbook, *Compánach an Chríostaigh* (The Christian's companion), and its abridged version *Carad an Chríostaigh* (The Christian's Friend) in 1842.[189]

Considering the number of Irish-speaking Catholics and the fact that priests, who often had a sound knowledge of Latin, played a leading role in the Revival, a continued productive interest in the translation of religious literature is hardly surprising. Much of this translated material was merely functional: sermons in *An Gaodhall* in 1887 and 1889;[190] bilingual and Gaelic catechisms, the latter by An tAthair Peadar,[191] a col-

185. For MacHale's translations of religious works, see Nollaig Ó Muraíle, "Staid na Gaeilge i gConnachta in Aimsir Sheáin Mhic Héil" (The status of Irish in Connacht in the time of John MacHale), in *Leon an Iarthair*, ed. Ní Cheannain, 57–58, 65–66.

186. Ó Maolmhuaidh, *Athair na hAthbheochana*, 33, 78–81, 170–71. Ó Maolmhuaidh gives excerpts from his translation of *Ineffabilis* and the text of his "Magnificat."

187. See Mac Uí Loingsigh, "Seaghán Ó Conaill," *ACS*, 29 April 1905. The author of the Italian original was Paolo Segneri; the English translation used by Ó Conaill had been published in Cork in 1795.

188. This book, which included the English and Irish text, was published in Dublin by John Coyne.

189. See the review of *An Casán go Flaitheamhnas* (The path to Paradise) by Rev. J. E. Nolan, O.D.C., *IG* 1, no. 10 (August 1883): 319.

190. "Neamh" (Heaven) ran in *An Gaodhal* from November 1887 to June 1888; "Seanmóir ar Lá an Bhreitheamhnais" (A sermon on the Day of Judgment) commenced a lengthy serialization in January 1889.

191. *An Teagasg Críostaighe Gearr* (The short catechism) (Baile Átha Cliath: M. H. Gill agus a Mhac, 1899). Ua Laoghaire's translation of *The Little Catechism of the Rosary* was serialized in the *Irish Rosary* from October to December 1900. Father Dinneen also worked on a translation of a catechism. There is an incomplete and undated version among his papers, with pages cut from an unidentified catechism in English facing his handwritten Irish rendering (National Library of Ireland, MS. G825).

lection of hymns,[192] a Litany of the Blessed Virgin,[193] and a booklet of sickbed prayers[194] in 1899; an Irish version of the bishops' Synodal Pastoral,[195] and a manual on receiving Extreme Unction,[196] in 1901; translations of liturgical readings,[197] the Rosary,[198] and the Stations of the Cross in 1902;[199] a prayerbook[200] and more liturgical readings[201] in 1904; the "Magnificat" in 1905;[202] the *De Profundis* in 1906;[203] and a life of St. Brigid in 1909.[204] More substantial were John Fleming's 1882–83 "Comhráidhte Deighbheusacha / Moral Discourses" from the English of Father Patrick O'Keefe;[205] Ó Donnchadha's 1902 *Duanaire Phádraig* (St. Patrick's poem book), a collection of religious verse translated from the English;[206] and Father Dinneen's 1906 *Faoistin Naomh-Phádraig* (St. Patrick's confession), a volume that included the Latin original of the *Con-*

---

192. The book, titled *Dánta Diadha Coitcheanna* (Common hymns), was translated by An tAthair Micheál Mac Eochagáin, C.SS.R. It was published in Belfast. See the brief notice in *ACS*, 13 May 1899.

193. "The Litany of the Blessed Virgin in Irish," *Irish Rosary* 3, no. 11 (November 1899): 600. The translator is not identified.

194. "A Method of Meditating on the Mysteries for the Use of the Sick / An Paidrín le hAghaidh Othar / Cionnus is in-déanta machtnamh ar rúndiamhraibh na Coróineach Mhuire," *Irish Rosary* 3, no. 12 (December 1899): 650–1. The translator is not identified.

195. This translation by Father Michael O'Hickey was pronounced the Gaelic publishing event of the year by *ACS* on 13 April 1901.

196. See the notice in *ACS*, 10 May 1901.

197. An tAthair Clement Ó Lughnaidh, *Na hEpistile agus na Soisgéula do réir na n-Domhnach agus na Saoire tríd an mBliadhain secundum Missále Romanum* (The Epistles and Gospels for the Sundays and feast days of the year according to the Roman missal) (Áth Cliath: Sealy, Bryers agus Walcer, 1902).

198. The translator was a Father Ua Nualláin.

199. The translator was Seaghán Mac a' Bháird.

200. *Leabhar Urnaighthe* (A book of prayers) (Baile Átha Cliath: Comhlucht na Fírinne Catoilice, 1904). The translator, identified as "Sagart Riaghalta" (A regular priest), was An tAthair Maurus Ó Faoláin. See Breathnach and Ní Mhurchú, *Beathaisnéis a hAon*, 70.

201. *Na h-Epistlí agus na Soisgéil do na Domhnaighibh agus Laethibh Saoire ar na d-Tarraingt go Gaedhilc (agus an Sacs-Bheurla ós a coinne) le Seaghán S. Mac A' Bháird / The Epistles and Gospels for the Sundays and the Holidays Translated into Irish (with the English opposite) by John C. Ward* (Baile Átha Cliath: Brún agus Ó Nualláin, 1904).

202. An tAthair Uáitéir Ó Conmhacáin, "An t-Árdmholadh," *Irish Rosary* 9, no. 12 (December 1905): 984.

203. Brother D. B. Magh Craith, O.P., "De Profundis," *Irish Rosary* 10, no. 11 (November 1906): 872.

204. The author was "a Redemptorist Father;" the translator Micheál Ó Floinn. See "An Seabhac," "Cainnt na nDaoine," review of *Beatha Bhrighde* (The life of Brigid), *ACS*, 28 August 1909.

205. John Fleming, "Comhráidhte Deighbheusacha / Moral Discourses," *IG* 1, no. 2 (December 1882)–1, no. 9 (July 1883).

206. See the favorable review in *ACS*, 7 June 1902.

fessio along with versions in both Irish and English.[207] In addition to the 1886 and 1908 editions of Ó Súilliobháin's *Searcleanamhaint Chríost* noted above, two other major translations of religious material from the past appeared in new editions: Séamus Ó Murchadha's 1910 revised version of Bishop O'Donnell's New Testament Gospels;[208] and Seán Ó Caomhánaigh's 1912 *Sailm Dháibhidh Bheidel*, the Psalms in the seventeenth-century translation of Archbishop Bedell.[209] The indefatigable Peadar Ua Laoghaire was characteristically ambitious and prolific, publishing a book of liturgical readings in 1902[210] and his own version of the *Imitatio* in 1914,[211] and producing a translation of the entire Bible between 1911 and 1916, although only the Gospels and the Acts of the Apostles have ever been published, the former in 1915, the latter in 1922.[212]

In a more worldly sphere, translation was, as we have seen in the previous chapter, advanced as a logical means to midwife, nourish, and sustain a Gaelic theater starved for both stageworthy plays and competent players. Predictably, Gaelic translators of a theatrical bent focused

207. Patrick Dinneen, *Faoistin Naomh-Phádraig i Laidin, i nGaedhilg, agus i mBéarla* (St. Patrick's "Confessio" in Latin, in Irish, and in English) (Baile Átha Cliath: M. H. Gill agus a Mhac, 1906).

208. *Tiomna Nuadh Ár dTighearna agus Ár Slánaightheóra Íosa Críost ar n-a Tarraing go Fírinneach as Gréigis go Gaoidheilg le h-Uilliam Ó Domhnaill ar n-a glanadh as ar n-a leasughadh go nuadh le Séamas É. Ó Murchadha* (The New Testament of Our Lord and Savior Jesus Christ translated faithfully from Greek to Irish, newly corrected and emended by Séamas É. Ó Murchadha) (Baile Átha Cliath: Hodges, Figgis agus a gCuideachta 1910). See the review in "Clódhanna Nuadh," *SF*, 11 February 1911. It is also interesting to note that in 1909 Liam Ua Domhnaill welcomed the publication by the Catholic Truth Society of Scotland of Father Mac Eachainn's Scots Gaelic translation *An Cath Spriodail* (The spiritual battle), pointing out that it could be of use to Irish readers as well. See "Review / *An Cath Spriodail*," *ACS*, 17 April 1909.

209. *Sailm Dháibhidh Bheidel dréir Láimhscíbhinne Bunaidhe Liam Bheidil, Easbog* (Bedell's Psalms of David according to the original manuscript of Bishop William Bedell), ed. Seán Mac Murchadha Caomhánach (Dublin: Hanna and Neale, 1912). Ó Caomhánaigh published this work under a grand form of his name he favored at the time. *SF* drew attention to the great linguistic value of the book: "For in this work we have the Irish language, not as it was written by the learned of the seventeenth century, but as it was spoken by the people." See "Sailm Dháibhidh," *SF*, 6 July 1912.

210. *An Sóisgéal as Leabhar an Aifrinn* (The Gospel from the missal (Dublin: Irish Book, 1902).

211. He found Ó Súilliobháin's translation an exercise in the dreaded "Gaedhluinn Uasal." See "Gaedhluinn 'Uasal,'" *An Crann*, no. 4 (The feast day of St. Adhamhnán, 1917), 4.

212. See "Maol Muire," *An tAthair Peadar Ó Laoghaire*, 126–33. For a full list of An tAthair Peadar's religious translations, see Shán Ó Cuív, "Materials for a Bibliography of the Very Reverend Peter Canon O'Leary, 1839–1920," supplement to *Celtica* 2, no. 2 (1954).

on the plays they knew best in the "foreign" language with which they were most comfortable, the Anglo–Irish dramas of their contemporaries, a body of work that, in George Moore's phrase, "only requires translation into Irish to make it thoroughly and entirely Irish." They did not, however, limit themselves exclusively to drama in the English language, and the several previously noted French plays brought into Irish, all of which were, incidentally, transposed to an Irish setting, must also have provided welcome relief from the rustic misadventures of much original Gaelic drama. Such was certainly the case with Liam Ua Domhnaill's *An Bhean Mhí-Chomhairleach*, of whose successful production at the 1907 Oireachtas Pearse remarked that "it strikes a higher artistic note than either of the other Oireachtas plays of this year."[213] As with the translations of Anglo–Irish plays, these works were seen as primarily important for the help they could offer in the development of a more technically and aesthetically mature Gaelic theater.[214] Thus in 1910 Padraic Colum urged Gaels to turn to Molière to learn "the art, or rather the artifice, of the theatre," and pointed out that translations of such works would be especially appealing to "the general audience for Irish plays," many of whom "do not know the language or know it imperfectly."[215] Of course the clearest indication of the value of a judicious use of translations was the success of Na hAisteoirí and, to a lesser extent, of Na Cluicheoirí, both of which amateur groups performed Gaelic versions of Anglo–Irish and French dramas as well as increasingly sophisticated original plays in the second decade of this century.

The early years of the Revival were a time of vitality, openness, and often exuberantly creative responses to the challenge of building a new literature from the ground up. Faced with this daunting task, the more daring revivalists were willing to look for help wherever it could be found, and translation was too obvious an aid to ignore. While literary Gaels may not really have needed Tadhg Ó Murchadha's *Robinson Crúsó* or Dinneen's *Christmas Carol*, it is nonetheless certain that they gained an inspirational sense of their own glorious past through the modernizations of earlier tales and poems discussed in Chapter 4, as well as a growing confidence in the present and for the future through

---

213. "The Oireachtas," editorial, *ACS*, 17 August 1907.

214. See, for example, the lengthy comments of "Ú." in "Cluichtheoireacht" (Acting), *ACS*, 14 January 1911. After urging the production of translations, he wrote: "The production would help to teach them the art of the stage. Until we have good actors, our writers won't make any progress." (Chuideochadh an léiriughadh go mór le ealadhain an árdáin do mhúnadh dóibh. Go dtí go mbéidh cluichtheoirí go maith againn ní bhéidh dul ar aghaidh ins na sgríbhneoiríbh.)

215. "Some Notes on Dramatic Method," *ACS*, 27 August 1910.

their ability to convey satisfactorily in Irish a wide range of modern literary subjects and themes, even in genres, like drama, previously undeveloped in the language. If a later generation did little but fill shelves with translations of English titles most Gaels preferred to read in the original if at all, the blame cannot with justice be placed on the zestful innovators who created the Gaelic Revival.

7

Displaced Persons

Urban Life in the New Prose
to the Founding of the Free State

"I myself think a meal of potatoes once a day or a couple of
lumps with my dinner a fine thing. But I must be hard to satisfy because I don't want potatoes three times a day whether they be the potatoes of Micheál Thaidhg or the potatoes of Tomás Mhuiris."[1] Thus
one "Tomás na dTuras" lamented the monotonous literary diet served
up to readers of Irish in the early years of this century. However valuable from a linguistic or pedagogic point of view and however commendable as pioneering efforts in the creation of a modern Gaelic prose,
booklets like Séamus Ó Dubhghaill's *Prátaí Mhichíl Thaidhg* (The potatoes of Micheál Thaidhg) must at times have sorely tested the good
intentions of many sophisticated urban language revivalists. Indeed one

---

1. Letter, *IG* 14, no. 175 (April 1905): 777. "Is dóigh liom féin gur maith an rud béile
de phrátaidhibh 'sa ló nó cúpla cnap i gcomhair mo dhinnéir. Acht is dócha gur deacair
mé shásamh ós rud é ná réidhtigheann prátaidhe liom trí huaire san ló is cuma cia 'ca
Prátaidhe Mhichíl Thaidhg iad nó prátaidhe Thomáis Mhuiris."

Dublin Gael complained tongue-in-cheek that through his reading he had acquired a truly impressive and entirely useless familiarity with the practices and accoutrements of farm life: "I have no land, ploughed or fallow, except for the amount in which a few shoots grow in the window, not to mention grain or grass, livestock, horses, or beehives. And it's not only that I don't have them, but it's very rarely I even see them, except for the horses I see going through the town in which I live."[2]

While most urban revivalists no doubt shared this frustration, not all of them saw the problem as a source of humor. As early as 1898 one "Fear na Cathrach" (The city man) had jolted readers of *Fáinne an Lae* with a stark pronouncement that called into question the central tenet of Gaelic League ideology, the indissoluble link between the language and the historic Irish nation: "If Irish is only suited for the country, it's not a national language at all, but only a poor dialect that's not worth discussion or debate. It will be dead before the question is settled."[3] The main concern of "Fear na Cathrach" was with the creation of a contemporary literature in Irish, and he saw no hope of such a literature emerging from the various exercises in "cainnt na ndaoine," which then formed the bulk of the corpus of modern Gaelic prose. Declaring that a new literature would require a fresh force and vigor, he argued, "This new spirit will not come from the country. It is not the people who have no connection with the great movements of the world who will give it to us. Generally they wait for direction from the towns. . . . The flood-tide of city life is swifter and stronger than the slow, almost stagnant stream of country life."[4]

Others agreed with his sense of urgency. Reviewing the bilingual propaganda play *Obair!* in 1909, "S.D." (perhaps Charlotte Deasy) wrote of the rural preoccupations of Gaelic drama: "If there are no people in Ireland worthy of stage treatment except policemen, widows, and corrupt magistrates, it is about time we gave up the ideal of a national

2. "Tíoghbhasach," "Gaeth ag Fear Luinge gan Lón" (A wind for a boatman without provisions), *ACS*, 13 April 1901. "Níl talamh agam, ithir ná bán, acht an méid bhfásann cúpla fiúisí ann sa bhfuinneoig, gan trácht ar arbhar ná féar, ar eallach, ar chaiplibh, ná ar bheachlann. Ní hé amháin nach bhfuil agam, ach is fíor-annamh do gheibhim amharc orra, muna mbeith na caiple do chím ag dul thríd an mbaile mór so i bhfuil mo chomhnaidhe."
3. "Gaedhilg na Cathrach" (City Irish), *FL*, 20 August 1898. "Má's do'n tuaith amháin oireas an Ghaedhilg, ní teanga náisiúin í ar aon chor, acht canamhaint bhocht nach fiú aighneas ná díospóireacht 'n-a taoibh. Beidh sí marbh sul a mbeidh an cheist réidthighte."
4. "Gaedhilg na Cathrach," *FL*, 16 July 1898. "Ní as an dtuaith a thiocfas an spiorad nua seo. Ní hiad na daoine atá gan aon bhaint le mór-ghluaiseachtaibh an domhain a bhéarfas dúinn é. Is amhlaidh is gnáthach leo súd bheith ag feitheamh le teagasg na mbailtí mór. . . . Is mire agus is boirbe go mór tonn-tuile beathadh na cathrach 'ná sruthán mall meirbhshiubhlach na beathadh tuatha."

drama."⁵ Art Mag Uidhir had seen the stakes even higher the previous year, arguing that unless the Irish language was grafted to urban life without delay, the Revival itself was doomed to ultimate irrelevance: "Usually the people of keenest intellect and greatest education live in the towns. It is from the towns that the literature and the newspapers and the books that are read throughout the countryside come. If the towns are foreign, the majority of the literature that comes from them cannot but be foreign. . . . When the country people see these things, who will tell me that their respect for the Irish language will be increased?"⁶

While few Gaels presented their views as cogently or categorically as "Fear na Cathrach" or Mag Uidhir, their challenge to Gaelic writers to turn their backs on sterile ruralism and to take on the complexities of contemporary urban life was to be sounded repeatedly in the decades to follow. For example, in February 1902 one "Seang Siúir" rather diffidently took issue with a lecture by Dinneen in which the speaker seemed to deny the cities any constructive role in the revival: "But what about the cities? Can't they be Gaelic? It's not only in the provinces that a national language is 'at home.' We must also remember the towns, for they are a true part of the nation as well."⁷ Two years later Micheál Ó Máille laid much of the blame for the continuing perception of Irish as a moribund rustic language on the timidity of Gaelic writers: "They have Irish in which to write nonsense, but they don't have the courage to settle a difficult question or even to say anything about it in Irish. . . . Anything the old folks haven't talked about they won't talk about. . . . But we know this much: they are keeping Irish on the mountains and on the bogs, and leaving the fertile, profitable land to the foreign crowd."⁸

---

5. "Book Reviews," *Irish Rosary* 13, no. 7 (July 1909): 558.

6. "An Tarna Teanga" (The second language), *ACS*, 2 May 1908. Mag Uidhir's essay was serialized in three parts, the others appearing in *ACS* on 25 April and 9 May 1908. "Is gnáthach gur ar na bailtibh móra chomhnnuigheann na daoine is géire inntleacht agus is mó sgolaidheacht. Is ós na bailtibh móra thagann an litridheacht, na páipéirí nuadhachta, agus na leabhartha, a léightear ar fuaid na tuaithe. Má bhíonn na bailte móra Gallda, ní féidir gan furmhór na litridheachta a thagann asta bheith Gallda. . . . Nuair a chífidh muinntir na tuaithe na neithe sin, cia dhéarfaidh liom go méadófar a meas ar an nGaedhilg?"

7. "Canamhain agus Teanga" (Dialect and language), *ACS*, 22 February 1902. "Acht cad atá ar na cathrachaibh? Nach féidir leo-san a bheith Gaedhealach? Ní hé amháin 'sna paróistidhibh go bhfuil aon teanga náisiúnta 'sa bhaile'. Caithfimid cuimhniughadh ar na bailtibh freisin; óir is fíor-roinn de'n náisiún iad-san mar an gcéadna."

8. "An Talamh Spíonta" (The exhausted land), *ACS*, 1 October 1904. "Tá an Ghaedhilg aca le seafóid a sgríobhadh innti, acht níl sé de mhisneach aca ceist dheacair a réidhteach i nGaedhilg ná smid a rádh fúithi. . . . Rud ar bith nár thrácht na sean-daoine

Seán Ó Caomhánaigh saw little improvement by 1911: "What in the world is wrong with our writers that they don't give over the road, the field, the ass, the glen, the hill, and so many other things that have glazed my eyes and deafened my ears, and face the city, the interesting places in it, the crowd that ceaselessly travels its streets, the fine buildings, the curious things, and the thousands of occurrences that happen constantly in it?"[9] Ironically, in his own controversial novel *Fánaí* Ó Caomhánaigh failed to heed this advice, although to be fair he did break with tradition in his setting: his horses, hills, and glens are in North Dakota. Of course, the most influential voice calling for a truly modern Gaelic literature was that of Patrick Pearse, who proclaimed in 1906: "This is the twentieth century; and no literature can take root in the twentieth century which is not of the twentieth century. We want no Gothic revival."[10]

Unfortunately, neither good intentions nor artistic courage would be sufficient to root the language in the rather exotic soil of twentieth-century urban life. Most Gaels, including "Fear na Cathrach" and Pearse, would probably have accepted Father O'Reilly's assertion that "modern life has not spoken Irish. There is no such thing as a native speaker of modern life in Irish. There is no such thing as a native speaker of the thoughts of any present-day educated man. There is no such thing as a native speaker who can speak Irish away on any subject you like to draw down to him up-to-date."[11] Father Patrick Dineen was more hopeful; in his address "The Irish Language the National Language of Ireland," he acknowledged that Irish was "some sixty or seventy years behindhand as a cultured speech," but then went on set a challenge: "It will obviously take a long time and much hard work to repair the ravages that long neglect and positive ill-treatment have made upon it."[12]

---

air níl siad-san ag dul ag trácht air. . . . Acht tá a fhios againn an méid seo: go bhfuil siad ag coinneál na Gaedhilge istigh ar na sléibhtibh agus ar na portachaibh, agus ag fágáil na bpáirceanna maith mín tairbheach ag an dream Gallda."

9. "Catharach Nua," *SF*, 29 April 1911. "Cad tá ar ár scríobhnóiridhibh in ao' chor ná leigid díobh an bothán, an gort, an t-asal, an gleann, an cnoc, agus a liach rud eile go bhfuil scáird curtha im shúilibh aca agus allaoir ar mo chluasaibh agus aghaidh a thabhairt ar an gcathair, ar na h-áiteannaibh inspéisighthe atá innte, ar an sluagh a thaisdealas a sráideannaibh gan sos, ar na fóirgneamhaibh bhreághtha, ar na rudaidhibh aite, agus ar na mílte teagmhas a thárluigheas go mion minic innte."

10. "About Literature," *ACS*, 26 May 1906.

11. O'Reilly, *Native Speaker*, 27. O'Reilly was obviously grinding his usual "Classical Irish" axe here.

12. In *Lectures on the Irish Language Movement*, 29. See also the assessment in the 1908 annual report of the Kinsale Coiste Ceanntair of the Gaelic League: "At present the Irish

Such hard work would have to be directed at two fundamental obstacles, one obvious and practical, one elusively ideological. First of all, as the Dublin Gael mentioned above humorously lamented, Irish was rich in the vocabulary of rural life but almost devoid of words for urban inventions and developments. It was, in the words of Eibhlín Nic Niocaill "an imperfect instrument . . . in the fact that it has yet to be adapted to modern ideas."[13] With the sound pragmatism so characteristic of the early Revival, the Gaels attacked the problem from several angles, and one of the movement's earliest and most telling public triumphs involved the refutation of this charge that modern spoken Irish was incapable of conveying the complexities of late nineteenth-century life. In 1896, T. W. Rolleston proposed an experiment to test the thesis. He would choose two representative prose pieces in English for Hyde to translate into Irish. Hyde's versions would then be given to Mac Néill for translation back into English, and the entire exercise published in the *Daily Independent*. Hyde's success was so pronounced that Rolleston himself joined the league and was eventually to testify in its behalf before the Intermediate Education Commission.[14] Such exercises were no mere public relations stunts, as Eoin Mac Néill made clear in a 1903 review of E. E. Fournier's *English-Irish Dictionary*. After expressing reservations about some of Fournier's neologisms, Mac Néill continued:

> But let us hope that the writers of Irish who are doing so little to conquer modern life for the language will refrain from stoning Mr. Fournier. Beyond doubt, the absence of technical terms for things of modern development is the constant cause of a like vacuity in the courage-containing region of the average Irish-speaker's brain, and a fairly just cause too. Why should not an

language is 300 years behind the times. It may be suitable enough for agricultural business and the somewhat primitive conditions of rural life in Ireland. But it is altogether unfit to meet the requirements and complexities of modern life." (*ACS*, 8 February 1908). This issue continued to trouble Dinneen, who wrote in the Scottish journal *Guth na Bliadhna* in 1911: "It's no good producing books that only suit a world that is gone. . . . If we want to preserve Irish we must cultivate it so that it will be suitable for the affairs of the present day." (Ní haon mhaitheas bheith ag soláthar leabhar ná hoireann acht do'n saoghal atá caithte. . . . Má's maith linn an Ghaedhealg do bhuanughadh caithfeam í shaothrughadh i dtreo go mbeidh sí oireamhnach do chúrsaidhe an lae inniu.") See Dinneen, "Saothrughadh na Teangan," *Guth na Bliadhna* 8, no. 4 (Autumn 1911): 382.

13. "Some Thoughts about the Future of Irish Literature," *ACS*, 12 June 1909.

14. See Hyde, *Mise agus an Conradh*, 62. The pieces Rolleston selected were from George Henry Lewes's *Life of Goethe* and Karl Pearson's *Grammar of Science*. See Tierney, *Eoin Mac Néill*, 31.

Irish-speaker be able to talk about "galvanised corrugated iron" without falling back on English?[15]

To make such conversations more likely, in 1902 the Oireachtas offered a prize for the best list of Irish words dealing with banking, accounting, and insurance, and in the following year a prize for medical terms. Similar prizes were offered for different subject areas in subsequent years.[16] On a more systematic basis, in 1903 Seaghán Ua Cearbhaill proposed the creation of an "Irish Academy" to meet weekly in Dublin to debate and eventually to determine a standardized Irish vocabulary for new and technical subjects,[17] and in 1905 interested Gaels did come together in Dublin to discuss the whole question of new terminology. Pearse welcomed the formation of this ad hoc group with a statement of the task facing them: "We have been at work now for more than twelve years, writing nothing but 'cainnt na daoine.' We have great respect for 'cainnt na ndaoine,' but there are many things about which the 'people' speak nothing, good, bad, or indifferent."[18] Apparently this committee stirred some interest: throughout 1906 An Claidheamh Soluis frequently published articles discussing terminology as well as lists of suggested new terms for such areas as philosophy and politics, and in 1907 the league officially appointed "Coiste na dTéarmaí" to research, draw up, and propose new words.[19] Pronouncing the Irish "a race of philologists by temperament," Diarmuid Trínseach welcomed the committee and underscored the importance and urgency of its work given the contemporary state of Irish: "Limited by such restrictions a language cannot long survive in the Europe of the twentieth century. Either we must provide a Gaelic word to cover the whole field of modern ideas, or the movement must fall to the ground and Gaelic be convicted of irremediable poverty."[20]

15. "An English Irish Dictionary," ACS, 4 July 1903.
16. For a list of the competitions and winners, see Ó Súilleabháin, Scéal an Oireachtais, 138–39. There were also competitions for technical terms in 1899, 1900, and 1901, but these competitions involved more traditional areas like agriculture and fishing.
17. "Wanted—An Irish Academy," letter, ACS, 28 November 1903. Ua Cearbhaill suggested as Irish names for this academy "Coisde Breitheamhnais na hÉireann" (The judgment committee of Ireland) or "Coisde na bhFocal" (The words committee).
18. "Cúirt na Pléidhe" (The court of discussion), ACS, 16 December 1905. "Tá muid ag soláthar anois le breis agus dhá bhliadhain déag, agus gan dá sgríobhadh againn acht 'cainnt na ndaoine.' Is mór é ár meas ar chainnt na ndaoine, acht is iomdha rud nach gcainntigheann na daoine orra olc, maith, ná cuibheasach."
19. Séamus Ó Muirgheasa, "Coiste na dTéarmaí" (The terminology committee), ACS, 12 January 1907.
20. "Coisde na dTéarmaí," UI, 12 October 1907. Not everyone was convinced of the

Other Gaels put their own theories into practice. In 1909 Tomás P. Ua Nualláin published *Sanas Gramadaigh: An English-Irish Vocabulary*, a collection of some nine hundred technical terms gleaned largely from native manuscripts and matched with approximate English equivalents.[21] Over the years several other writers produced occasional essays on specific topics in which they earnestly created or cultivated a new technical lexicon. Among such efforts were "Cad Is 'Darwinism' Ann?" (What is "Darwinism"?) by "Tighearnach," with a glossary explaining terms like "bithrothlas" (organic evolution) and "substaint cheomhar" (nebulous matter),[22] and the lengthy "An Gaedhael 'n-a Fheallsamhain" (The Gael as philosopher) by Giollabhrighde Ó Catháin, in which the reader of *An Claidheamh Soluis* was provided with an expression for the "continuity and discreteness of space" (sírleanamhaint agus biothroinnteacht an achair) among other things.[23] On a more popular level, in November 1910 *An Claidheamh Soluis* commenced serialization of Séamus Ó Dubhghaill's "Cainnt na Cathrach / City Chats," an Oireachtas Prize–winning series of conversational sketches dealing with city life: "The phrase-book will help speakers of Irish to converse freely on city affairs, and will obviate the difficulty of creating terms in Irish for things not commonly known to Irish speakers of the Gaeltacht, and for which Irish names have not been generally known."[24] Just how well Irish could express "things not commonly known to Irish speakers of the

value of such a committee. Writing in 1911, Peadar Ó Maicín stressed the need for the language to grow and expand in a more natural and empirical fashion: "And if Irish is ever going to have its vocabulary enriched and extended it is by means of newspapers it will be brought about, not by such institutions as Coisde na dTéarmaí, not by piling up dictionaries full of words that will never be used." See Ó Maicín, "Glór na Ly" (the name of a Munster weekly newspaper), *SF*, 24 June 1911.

21. See also the review of Ua Nualláin's work by "S," *ACS*, 26 June 1909. Surprisingly, in his review of a Breton-French dictionary, Tadhg Ó Donnchadha indicated that he would be less rigorous in his insistence on native sources for new coinings, writing: "There are few terms from the wide world of the sciences that one will not find in it. And I notice that he is not reluctant about drawing in loanwords from French. . . . But there are a large number of words composed from Celtic roots." (Is beag téarma i ndomhan bhfairsing na gceard ná faghfar ann. Agus tugaim fé ndeara ná bíonn scornn air i dtaobh focail a tharraing ar iasacht ón bhFraingcis. . . . Acht tá anachuid focal arna gceapadh a préamhchaibh ceilteacha.) See "Ceilteachas," *ACS*, 2 May 1914.

22. "Cad Is 'Darwinism' Ann?," *ACS*, 12 September 1908. Following his glossary, the author added a note: "I am not too satisfied with some of the terms above; perhaps some of the readers of *An Claidheamh* would try to improve them." (Nílim ró-shásta le cuid de na téarmaibh so thuas; b'fhéidir go dtuibhrfadh [sic] cuid de léightheóiríbh 'An Chlaidhimh' fá leas a chur orra.)

23. Ó Catháin's essay commenced serialization in *ACS*, 3 October 1908.

24. "The Oireachtas and the Ard-Fheis," editorial, *ACS*, 13 August 1910.

Gaeltacht" was demonstrated by the native speaker Tomás Ua Concheanainn, who in 1911 published a series of essays dealing with current and often controversial affairs, acccompanying each piece with a frequently quite extensive and even intimidating glossary. For example, his "An Telefón / Ag Comhrádh idir Eabhrac Nua agus Sicágó" (The telephone / Conversing between New York and Chicago") involved no fewer than forty-seven notes glossing neologisms.[25] As we will shortly see, this question of terminology also troubled those pioneering Gaelic creative writers who dealt with urban life, some of whom nevertheless faced the challenge with a certain self-conscious bravado.[26]

However daunting was the task of forging a vocabulary for new and often exotic concepts, it was precisely the sort of job the early Gaelic League relished, one best attacked through committees, propaganda, and plain hard work. The other obstacle facing those attempting to write of contemporary urban life in Irish was far more formidable, for it touched on the deep-seated and often unconscious preconceptions and prejudices of many revivalists, not all of them provincial nativists. In the very same issue of Fáinne an Lae in which "Fear na Cathrach" concluded his eloquent call for Irish speakers to reclaim the cities and thus establish the language on a truly national basis, the paper's editor wrote, in a different context: "Dublin is the great English language city and an enemy of Irish. . . . And it is the place from which the countryside has most been Anglicized."[27] Much has been written of the romantic roots of the various nineteenth-century European nationalisms and their exaltation of the indigenous, racially and culturally pure peasantry of any particular countryside over the jaded and compromised cosmopolitans of supranational urban society. Ireland was no exception, wit-

25. Tomás Ua Concheanainn, "An Telefón / Ag Comhrádh idir Eabhrac Nua agus Sicágó," ACS, 25 November 1911.

26. The debate about new and technical terminology simmered throughout our period. See, for example, the 1918 call from "Giolla" for a Gaelic Academy in "Acadamh Gaedhilge" (FL, 10 August 1918), a piece that caused Piaras Béaslaí to comment in an editorial of the same title the following month (14 September) that "there is little that is new in this world. It's nothing new for people to be singing that tune at any rate." (Is beag rud nua ar an saoghal so. Ní haon rud nua an port son ar siubhal age daoinibh, ach go háirithe.) And in 1921 T. R. O'Rahilly's "On Borrowed Words in Irish / The Purist Nuisance" (Misneach, 30 April) sparked a heated debate involving, among others, Peadar Mac Fhionnlaoich. See his "Focla Iasachta" (Foreign words), Misneach, 2 July 1921.

27. "Is Iomdha Tigh i mBaile Átha Cliath; Is Iomdha Sliabh ar Bheagán Bó; Is Iomdha Fear Dubh ag Éirghe Liath; Is Iomdha Croidhe Fial ar Bheagán Stóir" (There's many a house in Dublin; There's many a mountain with few cows; There's many a black-haired man turning grey; There's many a generous heart with little wealth), editorial, FL, 20 August 1898. "Cathair mhór an Bhéarla agus namha do'n Ghaedhilg Baile Átha Cliath. . . . Agus 'sí an áit is mó as ar béarluigheadh riamh an tuaith."

nessing, in the words of William Irwin Thompson, a concerted effort by Gaelic nationalists "to present against the fragmented collective of Ireland's vestigial feudalism and primitive capitalism, an image of the beautiful community of moor and glen."[28]

The rather abstract dichotomy outlined by Thompson found more vivid expression in the writings of many revivalists:

> Behind me I was leaving anglicisation with all its hideousness and soulless materialism, its big smoking chimnies and prison-like factories (called commercial property) where thousands of Irishmen and Irishwomen in their struggle for a sordid existence forget they have a soul. Before me lay the Gaedhealtacht where the spiritual passionate Gael with his simple beautiful customs, speaking his own language and singing his own sweet songs, lived as God intended that he should.[29]

Séamus Ó Dubhghaill, author of "Cainnt na Cathrach / City Chats," was even more lurid in his picture of the dangers of urban corruption:

> Some day England's power will be broken. Where there is growth there will be decline and there will be withering and there will be decay. This sickness has already come over England, where the cities seem to show an advanced decay and a withered state. They are much like cancers on a person's body or worms in a sheep's groin. The poison of the cities will spew out into the country. Some of it has already spewed out. If we want to protect ourselves from the poison, our only protective shields are the grace of God and the Irish language.[30]

This link between God, Gaelic, and country life was, of course, a central article of the nativist creed. Thus in a 1909 dialogue, one "An Brat Do-Fheicse" argued that urban Gaels should abandon Dublin to set up

---

28. *The Imagination of an Insurrection, Dublin, Easter 1916: A Study of an Ideological Movement* (New York: Harper and Row, 1972), 41–42.

29. "Fear an Oileáin," "In the Gaedhealtacht," *ACS*, 15 June 1907.

30. Letter, *ACS*, 24 May 1913. "Brisfear ar neart Sasana lá éigin. 'San áit n-a bhfuil fás beidh meathadh, agus beidh seothadh agus beidh lobhadh. Tá an galar so tagaithe cheana féin ar Shasana, mar a bheadh treas lobhadh nó dóigh-chríonn ins na cathrachaibh. Níl ionnta so acht mar a bheadh othraistí ar chorp an duine, nó mar a bheadh cnuimhe i mbléin chaerach. Sceithfidh nimh na gcathrach amach fé'n dtuaith. Tá cuid de sceithte cheana. Má is maith linn-ne sinn féin a chosaint ar an nimh seo níl de sciath cosanta againn acht grásda Dé agus an Ghaedhilg." See also Ó Dubhghaill's "An Chathair 's an Tuath / The City v. the Country," *ACS*, 1 and 8 July 1911.

an Irish-speaking suburb in the nearby countryside. The author had no doubt that the enterprise would find divine favor; as one of the characters in the skit proclaims:

> A wise sage once said "God created the country and people created the towns." God, praise be ever His, did create the country. The prophet said: "God created the peoples of the world for a healthy life and there is no mortal poison in his laws." Those laws weren't enough for the people. They built cities in which there was mortal poison and that poison has been killing them with every passing day.[31]

One revivalist was even more specific about the nature of the poison whose antidote was clean country living. Speaking of the urban workers, he wrote: "They love their wives and families, and they take pleasure in the clean little house and the garden for the children. The bright sun and the happiness of the country agree with them. If they cleared out of the city, there would be an end to drunkenness and ill-health."[32]

Nor were such ideas limited to provincials or homesick urban exiles. In a paradox common throughout nineteenth-century nationalist movements, the apotheosis of rural life was often most forcefully expressed in the work of sophisticated and genuinely cosmopolitan urban thinkers. Thus even Pádraic Ó Conaire could extol farming as "the most ancient and noble craft practiced by the human race" (an cheird is ársa agus is uaisle dá gcleachtuigheann an cineadh daonna),[33] while Pearse could state that "for the writing of imaginative literature residence in the country has the great advantage of leaving the author free from the stress and worry of city life. . . . The artificiality of the town

---

31. "An Baile Gaedhealach" (The Gaelic town), *ACS*, 1 May 1909. "Adubhairt saoi tuigseanach, tráth: 'Is é Dia do rinne an tuath agus is iad na daoine do rinne na bailtí móra.' Do cheap Dia, moladh go deo leis, an tuath. Adeir an fáigh: 'Do cheap Dia cineacha an domhain chum sláinte is níl aon nimh mharbhthach i n-a dhlighthibh.' Níor leor do na cineachaibh na dlighthe. Do thógadar cathracha i n-a raibh an nimh marbhthach is bíonn an nimh sin ghá marbhughadh ó lá go céile."

32. "Cathair Nua" (A new city), *ACS*, 4 April 1914. "Grádhuigheann siad a gcuid ban is a gclann, agus taithuigheann leo féin an teach beag glan agus an garrdha le haghaidh na bpáistí. Reídhtigheann an ghrian gheal leo agus aoibhneas na tuaithe. Dá mbeidís glanta as an gcathair bheadh deire leis an meisge agus leis an drochshláinte."

33. "Talmhaidheacht" (Farming), *Guth na Gaedheal* (March 1909): 4. See also Ní Chionnaith, "An Rómánsachas i Scríbhneoireacht Uí Chonaire," *An tUltach* 68, no. 4 (April 1991): 33.

is the bane of all true art."[34] In an editorial diatribe against "debasing" literature from England, Dubliner Bernard Doyle traced the source of that literature's moral fetor to its urban milieu: "Of the quality of much of this literature there can hardly be two opinions—it is produced in corrupt and overcivilised cities, and faithfully reflects their tone. When not frankly pagan or immoral ("realistic" is the modern shibboleth), it is vapid and inane."[35]

One of the starkest condemnations of the suffocating and corrupting effect of such "overcivilised" urban life was delivered by Eoin Mac Néill, who, having rhapsodized over the beauties of the countryside, contrasted the sturdily independent farmer with the harassed city dweller: "He is not like the city man with four walls around him, south, north, east, and west. . . . If he [the city man] sees the sun in the morning he won't see it again till day's end. The cool breeze he would let into his house wouldn't carry the fragrance of sea, wood, or turf, but the foul smell of thousands of chimnies." Mac Néill's lesson, delivered entirely in capital letters, was: "There is no independent man on earth except for the man who has enough land for himself rent-free."[36]

Such vehemence is, of course, the mark of the propagandist, and propaganda was, as we have seen, one of the most important and successful activities of the early Gaelic League. In their paradoxical glorification of a life they must have known full well they could not share, Mac Néill and other urban Gaels were offering a weighted answer to one of the most pressing questions facing the Revival. Lacking the educated nationalists' awareness of their priceless heritage and their own

34. "An t-Oireachtas," *ACS*, 20 February 1909. To be fair, Pearse was writing here to encourage young rural writers to enter the Oireachtas competitions.

35. "The Remedy against Debasing Literature," editorial, *FL*, 12 March 1898.

36. "Saoghal na Tuaithe" (Country life), *ACS*, 22 January 1910. "Ní hionann é agus fear na cathrach, ceithre bhalla ina thimcheall theas thuaidh thoir is thiar. . . . Má fheiceann sé an ghrian ar maidin nach bhfeicfidh sé arís go dubh í. An ghaoth fhionnfhuar do leigfadh sé isteach ina árus, ní hé boladh cumhra na farraige, na coilleadh, is na móna bheadh uirthi acht boladh bréan na mílte simléar." Mac Néill's lesson was: "NÍL ÉINFHEAR NEAMHSPLEADHACH AR AN DOMHAN ACHT FEAR A BHFUIL A DHÍOL FÉIN DE THALAMH GAN CHÍOS AIGE." It is striking how closely the urban progressive Mac Néill's picture of the city parallels that of the rural nativist Peadar Ua Laoghaire, who wrote of American cities that their residents suffered "without getting the fill of their lungs or the fill of their mouths of healthy wind by night or day, but rather the foul, unhealthy wind of the city, a wind that had gathered to itself every kind of foul smell from every corner of the city" (gan lán cléibh 'ná lán béil de ghaoith fholáin fhághail do ló ná d'oídhche, ach droch ghaoith mhí-fholáin na catharach, gaoth a bhí tar éis an uile shaghas droch bhaluith a bhailiú' chúichi ó gach droch chúinne de'n chathair). See Ua Laoghaire, "Neamhchoitchianta" ("Distinguished"), in *Sgothbhualadh*, 110. This essay was originally published in *The Leader* on 9 April 1904.

responsibility for its preservation, native speakers were deserting the Gaeltacht for the perceived economic and social opportunities of the cities. The challenge for the revivalists was, bluntly, how to keep them down on the farm. One response to that challenge was a flood of anti-emigration propaganda zeroing in on the hellish foreign cities that enticed the unsuspecting rural exile. As we have seen in Chapter 2, Gaelic creative writers and dramatists took up this theme with enthusiasm, one of the more popular Gaelic plays of the time being Lorcán Ua Tuathail's 1906 *An Deoraidhe*, subtitled "A Play against Emigration," in which a woman returns from America exhausted and dying to warn the young people of her townland of the poverty that awaits them in exile. On a more pedestrian level, the Gaelic press frequently reported on the economic miseries of both workers and the unemployed in American cities, pointing out that if native-born Americans were struggling to survive, there was little hope for immigrants.[37] Nor were the dangers facing Irish rural people in the United States merely physical or financial. Propagandists emphasized the religious and moral apathy of Americans and presented frightening tales and even statistics of the Irish deserting the faith in the baneful atmosphere of the urban slum.[38]

Of course England was in many ways even more dangerous than America. It was closer, its class divisions more profound, and its moral climate particularly noxious. Thus in 1906 "An Rúnaire Beag" presented a dire portrait of Christmas Eve in Manchester: "Eleven o'clock, and out from every drinking hall poured a stream of human misery; again are the young in the majority, and the future wives and mothers of England roll in the gutters." Not surprisingly a ruckus breaks out, and as the drunken brawlers are led away by the police, the author hears one woman cursing with "the blas of Munster": "And I know that if only she had stayed home she would now be on her way to Midnight Mass."[39] As we will see in our discussion of the urban fiction of Pádraic Ó Conaire, London was even more intimidating, not least, paradoxically, for the ethnic diversity to which the Irish themselves contributed:

37. See, for example, "An Imirce" (Emigration), editorial, *ACS*, 18 January 1913.
38. See the discussion in Chapter 2, as well as Seán S. Ó Gormáin, J.C.D., "An Imirce agus an Míchreideamh" (Emigration and loss of faith), *ACS*, 11 March 1911; and O' Farrelly, *The Reign of Humbug*, 11.
39. "An Rúnaire Beag," "The Other Side," *ACS*, 5 May 1906. See also the virtually identical picture in "Sgéala ó na Chúig Cúigí / Imirce na nGaedheal as Éirinn" (News from the four provinces / The emigration of the Gaels from Ireland"), *ACS*, 5 September 1903.

For a long time the rabble of the world has found refuge in London, people who could not make a living in their own countries and those who intend to overthrow the crowned heads. . . . The number of foreigners has increased from day to day so that today they have a corner of London to themselves. "When a goat enters church, it doesn't stop until it goes on the altar." That's the way it was with the foreigners in London. They made it their own.[40]

With direct experience of all these problems, the London Branch of the league in 1904 urged "all who have influence at home to warn intending emigrants against taking their chances in London," a city already filled with Irish people, "young and old, some of them quite destitute, and in any case pathetically unfitted for London circumstances."[41] The English capital was condemned by, of all people, an English lord in the 1911 short story "Gach Duine agus a Cheobhrán Féin air" ("Everyone has his own blind spot") by "Liam." The man falls in love with a young Irish country woman who has survived all of her mother's attempts to give her fashionable urban pseudosophistication. The couple live briefly and unhappily in London before returning to the Irish countryside because, in the words of the story's Lord Colchester: "I don't like London. It is nothing but a graveyard. The bad air and the bad life of the city kill everyone who goes into it. The second generation barely survives and there is no third generation. If it were not for the cursed fascination that country people have for London, London would be depopulated within a hundred years."[42]

The heroine of this story finds Dublin little better: "The young girl hated the city; the day they would spend on Grafton Street would seem

40. "Mearaidhthe i Lúndain" (Madmen in London), *SF*, 15 January 1911. "Lé fada tá dídean lé faghail ag díoscar an domhain i Lúndain, ag daoinibh ná faigheadh maireachtaint in a dtír féin, agus aca so atá ar tí na gceann Corónach do bhaint dá dtreóir. . . . Mheudaigh líon na n-eachtaranach ó lá go lá sa tslighe go bhfuil cúil de Lúndain aca chúcha féin indiubh. 'Nuair théigheann an gabhar in teampall ní stadann sé go dtéigheann sé ar an altóir.' Sin mar bhí ag sna h-eachtaranachaibh i Lúndain. Dheineadar a gcuid féin de."

41. "Cogarnach na gCraobh / Sasana," *ACS*, 9 January 1904.

42. *ACS*, 28 October 1911, "Seanchaidhe na Samhna" supplement. "Ní mian liom Lonndain. Níl inti acht roilig. Marbhuigheann droch-aer agus droch-shaoghal na cathrach an uile dhuine a théas inti. Is ar éigean a mhaireann an dara sliocht agus ní bhíonn an tríomhadh sliocht ann. Muna mbeadh an dúil mhalluighthe atá ag muintir na tuaithe i Lonndain bheadh Lonndain gan daoine i gceann céad bliadhan."

longer to her than a week at the foot of Sliabh Ruadh."[43] And most revivalists would have agreed that their own capital was in no way a satisfactory home for rural people, especially native speakers.[44] Indeed, for many Gaels Dublin was the most insidious of all cities, both for its alluring proximity and for its plausible but fraudulent claim to be Irish.[45] In an essay that prompted considerable debate in 1913, "Conán Maol," urging the league to move its headquarters out of Dublin, argued: "The Gaels are heading into a wild and profound wilderness and they will be swallowed up. If you do not believe that, you are deaf or blind. Neither Dublin nor anything connected with Dublin will save the Gaels from the abyss."[46] Less apocalyptic was Séamus Ó Dubhghaill in "An Chathair 's an Tuath," one of his "City Chats" which he himself appropriately rendered "The City v. the Country." Two suburbanites, distressed by the effect of Dublin's smog on their view, ponder why anyone would choose to live there. They decide the answer is "the big pay" (an pagh mór) and the bright lights, which entice rural youth "as the light of the candle lures the moth in the night-time so that it is singed, and that's how it is with many who come into the city. There are many

43. "Liam," "Gach Duine," ACS, 28 October 1911, "Seanchaidhe na Samhna" supplement. "B'fhuath leis an gcailín óg an chathair; agus an lá chaithfidís i Sráid Gh_____ b'fhuide léi é ná seachtmhain fé bhun an tSléibhhe Ruaidh."

44. For a survey of the depiction of Dublin in Irish language literature from the time of the Revival, see Eoghan Ó hAnluain, "Baile Átha Cliath i Nua-Litríocht na Gaeilge" (Dublin in modern Gaelic literature), Scríobh 4 (1979): 25–46. Ó hAnluain himself makes no claim to be comprehensive, calling his essay "a quite impressionistic compilation or gathering of the most obvious references to Dublin in that literature" (díolaimiú nó tiomsú atá impriseanaíoch go maith ar na tagartí is follasaí do Bhaile Átha Cliath ar fud na litríochta sin) (25).

45. One can only imagine what they thought of Belfast, since the only time it features in Gaelic literature at this time it is merely a train stop for two Dublin nationalists on their way to crash and confront a meeting of Ulster Orangemen in Proinnsias Áirmeas's comic story "Teacht agus Imtheacht an Ghiolla Dheacair Óig" (The coming and going of the young Difficult Lad), ACS, 28 December 1912. The title of the story is a play on the title of a Fenian tale.

46. "Fáith an Sgeil" (The meaning of the story), ACS, 10 May 1913. "Tá na Gaedhil ag déanamh ar fhásach fhiadhain dhuibheagánach agus báithfear iad. Muna gcreidir an méid sin taoi bodhar nó dall. Ní choisgfidh Bleácliath 'ná éin nidh a bhaineann le Bleácliath an Gaedheal ó'n duibheagán." The idea was not a new one, Diarmaid Ua Cruadhlaoich and "Pádraig na Léime" having championed it on more than one occasion in SF and ACS respectively the previous year. See, for example, Ua Cruadhlaoich, "The Gaedhealtacht," SF, 27 January 1912; and "Pádraig na Léime," "Sgéala na Seachtmhaine / Ó'n Deisceart" (The news of the week / From the south), ACS, 20 July 1912. For this particular controversy, see also letters from "Conán Maol" and others in the May 1913 issues of ACS.

people who come into cities and there are many who are singed and burned in them."[47]

Of course, the city's unforgivably dreadful slums provided Gaelic propagandists with abundant, verifiable, and effective images with which to affright country folk thinking of moving to the capital: "It would be difficult to describe those narrow, dark lanes of Dublin. A person would have to live in them to see how dirty, how smoky, how lonely, how hungry, how unnatural they are. Walk through one of them and your journey will affect you for a month."[48] Again, the moral climate was even more desperate: "A while ago we saw six score children in a single lane. They were out on the dirty paving-stones. They had nothing to see above them but a little bright line of sky and nothing to hear but the great howl of the city. There were drunkards swaying past, cursing. And the young were learning and drinking in every evil habit there was to be seen just as they had drunk in their mothers' milk."[49] And in the absence of a concerned and supportive community, such urban poverty was infinitely more painful and degrading than the rural variety: "If a traveler approaches a house in the city, he is met with inhospitality on the threshold. If he stands in a sheltered corner to let the stormy weather pass him by, a policeman rousts him out. The hardship doesn't allow him to be quiet and at rest, and the law and the

47. Séamus Ó Dubhghaill, "An Chathair agus an Tuath / The City v. the Country," *ACS*, 8 July 1911. Country people are enticed by the city "mar a mheallann solus na coinnle an feidhleachán istoidhche chun go loisctear é; agus sin é mar a bhíonn an scéal agá lán a thagann isteach 'sa chathair. Is iomdha duine a thagann isteach ionnta 's is iomdha duine a loisctear is a dóightear ionnta."

48. Liam Ua Domhnaill, "Ar Chuairt sa Ghaedhealtacht" (On a visit in the Gaeltacht), *ACS*, 8 December 1906. "Ba dheacair cur síos ar na sráidínibh caola dorcha soin Bhaile Átha Cliath. Níor mhór do dhuine comhnaidhe ionnta chun go bhfeicfeadh sé chomh salach, chomh deatamhail, chomh huaigneach, chomh hocrach, chomh mí-nádúrtha, is atáid. Siubhal trí sráidín aca is goillfidh do thuras ort go ceann míosa." See also "Fearghus Finnbhéil" (Diarmuid Ó Foghludha), "Cúrsaidhe an tSaoghail," *ACS*, 17 June 1899; "Ú.," "De na Bochtaibh" (Concerning the poor), *ACS*, 10 December 1910; William P. Ryan, "Cúis na bhFear Oibre," *ACS*, 13 September 1913; and anonymous, "Treabh gan Talamh gan Tíoghbhas" (A class without land, without housing), *ACS*, 27 September 1913.

49. "Cathair Nua," *ACS*, 4 April 1914. "Chonnaiceamar tamall ó shoin sé sgór páistí i n-aon tsráidín amháin. Amuich ar na leacracha salacha bhíodar. Ní raibh le feiceál aca os a gcionn ach líne beag geal de'n spéir agus ní raibh le clos aca ach uaill mhór na cathrach. Bhí lucht meisge ag lúbadh thart agus ag asgáinigh agus gach droch-bhéas dá raibh le feiceál dá fhoghluim agus dá dhiúl ag an aos óg mar do dhiúladar bainne a máthar." This piece was illustrated with six photographs of slum neighborhoods.

inhospitality of the rich people don't allow him to be at rest or content."[50]

Yet whatever their insensitivity to the poor, wealthy and socially successful people were viewed as potentially valuable converts to the cause, and not just for their money. Late Victorian Dublin had an acutely tuned sense of respectability, and people like Pearse, who invariably wore formal dress to the Oireachtas, believed that it was important for Gaels to show themselves every bit as polished as their Anglophile counterparts.[51] Mary Butler for one stressed that only the cultivation of the most punctilious social etiquette would enable the movement "to make converts of the shopper in Grafton Street, the flâneur in Stephen's Green."[52] And Oxford-educated Giollabhrighde Ó Catháin asked his fellow revivalists to imagine the effect on such modish shoppers and idlers "when another Gael and yourself in the highest of collars, impeccable ties, and patent-leather boots, talk Irish for an hour in a crowded railway carriage."[53] Such conversations, albeit imaginary, are the material of Séamus Ó Dubhghaill's series of "City Chats." His urban Gaels are prosperous middle-class people who live in comfortably furnished homes, employ domestic help, and worry about current events, debating, for example, the need for protectionist trade legislation.[54]

One must, however, wonder how many such conversations actually took place on Grafton Street or in Merrion Square. And if they didn't, how could Gaelic writers deal creatively with the lives of the people who lived and worked there? The answer of the vast majority of those writers seems to have been that they couldn't. The only Gaelic works of the early Revival that deal explicitly and exclusively with the life of urban middle-class characters other than language activists are *Beart Nótaí* (A bundle of [bank-] notes), a 1902 play by Máire Ní Shíthe and Eilís Ní Mhurchadha; Máire Ní Chinnéide's 1907 story "An Mótor"; Ní Chinnéide's 1908 one-act temperance melodrama *An Dúthchas* (Heri-

50. "Ú.," "De na Bochtaibh," *ACS*, 10 December 1910. "Má bhuaileann aistreánach isteach chuig teach sa gcathair bíonn an doicheall ar tháirsigh an dorais roimhe. Má sheasann sé i gcúinne fasgamhail leis an síon do leigint thart cuireann síothmhaor an ruaig air. Ní leigeann an t-anró do bheith ciúin socair, agus ní leigeann dlighe agus doicheall na daoine saidhbhir do bheith socair ná sásta."

51. See Edwards, *Patrick Pearse*, 46–48; and Ó Súilleabháin, *An Piarsach agus Conradh na Gaeilge*, 65.

52. Mary Butler (Máire de Buitléir Bean Thomáis Uí Nualláin), "Proper Pride," editorial, *ACS*, 22 January 1916. See also "Rúnaidhe an Chúigir," "The 'Cooking' of Dublin, Five O'Clock Teas, and Other Matters. According to the Mind of 'An Cúigear,' " editorial, *ACS*, 11 December 1915.

53. "Branches—Hustle!" *ACS*, 31 July 1909.

54. See, for example, Séamus Ó Dubhghaill, "Cainnt na Cathrach / City Chats," *ACS*, 21 January and 18 March 1911.

tage); and Mrs. McDonough Mahoney's 1909 story "An Cara Feall-
tach" (The treacherous friend). The first, set in "the garden of a suburban house" (gáirdín tighe in gar do'n chathair), deals with the theft and
recovery of a sizable sum of money from middle-class people wealthy
enough to invest in American railways.[55] The second is a cautionary tale
of automotive safety.[56] The third has a cast of "ladies and gentlemen"
(mná uaisle agus daoine uaisle) living in "some city in Ireland" (cathair
éigin i n-Éirinn), employing servants, receiving telegrams, hosting dinner parties, and drinking "Chateau Lafitte."[57] And the fourth is a love
story whose protagonist is a well-off Dublin barrister important
enough to be sent to Boston and New York for a year on banking
business.[58] Of course, even more alien to the language than such well-
off folk were the poor of O'Casey's Dublin, for whom the Irish lan-

55. Máire Ní Shíthe and Eilís Ní Mhurchadha, *Beart Nótaí: Dráma Dhá Ghníomh, Dráma
Suilt* (A comedy in two acts) (Baile Átha Cliath: Cuideachta Bhanba, 1904). The play was
first produced in Belfast in October 1902. The thief is at first assumed to have gone to
America, "for that is where every good-for-nothing and every cowardly rogue flees"
(mar is ann a theitheann gach beag-mhaith agus gach cladhaire rógaire) (29).
    56. Máire Ní Chinnéide, "An Mótor: Sgéal," *Irish Rosary* 9, no. 5 (May 1907): 382–87.
    57. Máire Ní Chinnéide, *An Dúthchas: Dráma Éin-Ghníomha* (Baile Átha Cliath: Con-
nradh na Gaedhilge, 1908). It is worth noting that Ó Lochlainn's An Comhar Drámuidheachta chose *An Dúthchas* for their first production at the Abbey on 12 November
1923. See Breathnach and Ní Mhurchú, *Beathaisnéis a Dó*, 80. The failure of Gaelic playwrights in particular to turn to the rich material of urban life for plays with which to
appeal to urban audiences must have both surprised and frustrated "Pádraig na Léime,"
who in his 1909 essay on drama wrote:
    It is clear to anyone that it is in places where every kind of person is gathered to-
    gether—the thief and the honest person, and the bad and the good—that it is there
    one sees many things that would provide good material for a play. Life is usually
    dour and quiet in the country, and the routine is the same from one end of the year
    to the next.

    (Is léir d'éinne gur i n-áiteannaibh mar a mbíonn gach saghas duine bailighthe i
    dteannta chéile—an cladhaire agus an duine macánta, agus an t-olc agus an mhaith go
    bhfeictear nidhthe líonmhara annsúd a dhéanfadh bun maith dráma. Bíonn saoghal
    dúr ciúin fé an dtuaith de ghnáth agus is é an réim chéadna ann ó cheann ceann na
    bliadhna.)
See "Pádraig na Léime," "Aiste / An Dráma i nÉirinn," *SF*, 13 November 1909. There
were Oireachtas competitions for essays on drama in both 1907 and 1909. This essay must
have been written for one of the two.
    58. Mrs. McDonough Mahoney, "An Cara Fealltach," *WF*, 11 December 1909. The
story won a *WF* Oireachtas Prize that year. For the sake of completeness we may also
note the bilingual story "Mothalainín agus a Chuideachta / Fuzzy and His Comrades," a
children's story of the adventures of a country kitten taken in by a well-off middle-class
family. See "Mothalainín agus a Chuideachta," *Catholic Bulletin*, May 1912–December
1913. The story was apparently originally written in English and then translated into Irish
by Seán Ua Ceallaigh ("Mogh Ruith"). The author of the English text is not identified.

guage must have seemed an exotic irrelevance. With these specific challenges no doubt in mind, Eibhlín Nic Niocaill went to the heart of the
problem in her perceptive and still provocative address to Cumann Náisiúnta na Mac Léighinn:

> Hardly less openly avowed than the principle that we ought to
> support Irish manufacture, is the prejudice that compels him
> who writes in Irish to deal with Irish subjects and personages.
> This is no slight limitation; for it confines the author, in so far as
> he deals with modern life in story or drama, to one class of the
> people of this country. . . . The result is that peasant life forms
> the whole theme of modern Irish fiction and drama. We are too
> conscious still with regard to the Irish language to be able to
> accept the fact that people who would not be speaking it in real
> life, are doing so in a story or on the stage; our train of thought
> would be continually interrupted by the improbability of the
> thing.[59]

The role of the urban writer, particularly one for whom Irish was an
acquired language, was debated at length in the pages of *Sinn Féin* in
the first months of 1912. The Liverpool-born Dubliner Piaras Béaslaí,
whose own pioneering efforts in several fields we have already encountered, provided a blunt and selfless summary of the central issue: "The
writer of Irish literature should be able to draw on the life around him
for his material. To put it as simply as possible: —Literature should
grow out of life. *An Irish literature must grow out of an Irish-speaking life.*
It cannot grow out of the English-speaking, English-thinking life of
Dublin."[60]
One "Sruhire" was quick to take issue with Béaslaí's dictum, writing:
"I think that view is utterly false. I think literature is not a thing of
growing but of making, and I take it that literature in any language can
be made out of anything. . . . Given the sensitive soul, the artist zest,
the full mastery of a language, we may get any literature anywhere—
French literature in Connemara or in Iveragh, Gaelic literature in Blá'
Cliath or on King Haakon's Plateau." Indeed, "Sruhire" was willing to
go much farther, throwing down a gauntlet to all the rural nativists
whose champion in this particular debate was Diarmaid Ua Cruadhlaoich, who had actually begun the controversy by quoting a conversation with Béaslaí and by praising the folk-oriented material in *An*

59. "Some Thoughts," *ACS*, 12 June 1909.
60. "Literature and the Gaedhealdacht," letter, *SF*, 16 March 1912. Emphasis in the
original.

Lóchrann at the expense of the work published in *An Claidheamh Soluis*, whose writers and readers alike he characterized as "'scholars' in the Galltacht" who liked "Englishy Irish" and had "an English outlook on life."[61] No doubt to the amazement and disgust of people like Ua Cruadhlaoich, "Sruhire" argued: "I think that by the side of the kind of reading—true literature it may well be—that the Gaoltacht is likely to give us, we may very well have, indeed must have, a literature that the Gaoltacht would reject utterly, whether with disgust and fierce denial or with simple noncomprehension—a non-understanding that might be due sometimes to strangeness of subject and idea, sometimes to strangeness of cadence and construction and even of words."[62]

In his first contribution to the debate, his clarification of what he had said in the conversation quoted by Ua Cruadhlaoich, Béaslaí was emphatic on a fundamental point with direct personal application, stating:

> I do not want to stop people from writing Irish just because they live in Dublin. I certainly do not intend to stop writing myself. But I do want our school of Gaelic League writers in Dublin to get out of their heads the idea that Irish literature depends on us. The most we can hope to do is to produce a "faked" artificial product, —an exotic plant reared in glasshouses, not a healthy natural growth from the sod. No doubt it is necessary to produce these hothouse plants for some time to come, until the sod is ready. We do it for patriotic and propagandist reasons, not for literary reasons.[63]

Béaslaí repeated this extraordinary assessment of the motivation and literary worth of what was, after all, a significant percentage of Revival literature in his second contribution to the debate. Stressing the fact that "there is no lack of intensely interesting life in Ireland full of drama and poetry; no lack of passion and intellectual stir; all of which would provide the material of a fine literature," he went on to acknowledge that

61. Diarmaid Ua Cruadhlaoich, "The Gaedhealtacht," *SF*, 27 January 1912. At least one contributor to *An Lóchrann* agreed. See the attack on the learned Irish of urban Leaguers by "Caol Cruga Mac Criomhthain," in "Gaedhilge Bhaile Átha Cliath" (Dublin Irish), *An Lóchrann* 2, no. 3 (November 1908): 2.

62. "Language and Literature," *SF*, 23 March 1912. See also the views of Peadar Ó Maicín, who in a piece predating the controversy involving Béaslaí, wrote of Gaelic authors that "they may make the Gap of Dunloe or Bride Street the scene of their novels, and yet have no fear but that the result will be Irish literature if they themselves really know the language." See Ó Maicín, "The Simplified Spelling and Other Matters," *SF*, 27 May 1911.

63. "Literature and the Gaedhealdacht," *SF*, 16 March 1912.

"the overwhelming preponderance of that life is of the Galltacht." Consequently, "it will be necessary to deal with the English-speaking life of Ireland in Irish. It is, indeed, 'not a counsel of ease.' In fact, it is a devilish hard job—and it involves a great loss of literary value. But writers will be found to make that sacrifice for the sake of Ireland."[64]

Of course, the more modest the literary effort, the less intimidated writers might be by the difficulty of their task. And some of the early Gaelic forays into the city were modest indeed, as was the literary value available for patriotic sacrifice. Influenced by the success of instructional dialogues like Ó Dubhghaill's "Beirt Fhear ó'n dTuaith" (Two men from the country), a few writers produced little conversational sketches with city settings. Ó Dubhghaill himself brought his Aodh and Diarmaid to the Oireachtas in Dublin, where they ruminated comically on big-city wonders like the tram.[65] The earliest such city dialogues seem to have been a pair titled "Beirt Bhuachaillí ón gCathair" by one "Seaghán." Both of these little skits center on feeble bilingual puns.[66] In 1910 An Claidheamh Soluis published "Domhnach na Gaedhilge / Turas ó Bhéalfeirste go hÁth Cliath" by Piaras Béaslaí ("Pilib a' Chleite"), the only point of which seems to have been the introduction of railroad terminology.[67] The most famous representative of this subgenre was Ó Dubhghaill's "Cainnt na Cathrach," which commenced its lengthy serialization on 26 November 1910, having won an Oireachtas Prize that year in recognition of its "practical usefulness" in "helping intelligent townspeople to talk freely in idiomatic Irish upon their customary concerns and pleasures."[68] The second prizewinner in this competition, Domhnall Ó Murchadha's Beirt Ghaedhilgeoirí 'na gComhnaidhe 'sa Chathair, was published as a book in 1915. Among the more interesting "customary concerns and pleasures" discussed therein are the killing of a horse by a downed wire, the suffragist movement, and a particularly scandalous local divorce trial.[69]

64. "Language and Literature," letter, SF, 30 March 1912.

65. "Beirt Fhear ó'n dTuaith" (Two men from the country), ACS, 14 June 1902.

66. "Seaghán," "Beirt Bhuachaillí ón gCathair" (Two boys from the city), ACS, 31 August and 5 October 1901.

67. (Irish language Sunday / A trip from Belfast to Dublin) ACS, 22 October and 26 November 1910.

68. "The Oireachtas Committee / Literary Competitions for 1910," ACS, 2 October 1909.

69. (Two Irish speakers living in the city), ed. Seosamh Laoide (Baile Átha Cliath: Clódhanna Teoranta, 1915). Ó Dubhghaill's nerve in making his Irish speakers true city folk probably earned him his first-place finish over Ó Murchadha, whose characters were, in the words of Laoide, "two or more native speakers of Irish fresh from the country, and just settled down in the city, hence as yet truly native and unspoiled by the overwhelming

Other writers were, at first glance, more ambitious, writing little stories, or perhaps more properly anecdotes, with urban settings. As early as St. Patrick's Day 1899 *Fáinne an Lae* published two such tales, one anonymous[70] and one by Stefán Seoigheach, a Conamara man living in Boston.[71] However, while the former is set in London and the latter in Cork, in neither is the urban background of any relevance. Three months later *Fáinne an Lae* published a more original story set in Paris. Once again, however, the setting is altogether arbitrary, and the story has nothing to do with Paris, or any other city for that matter.[72] In the following year *Fáinne an Lae* published three more such stories, one set in Waterford,[73] one in "a town" (baile mór),[74] and one involving a visit to Dublin.[75] All three are once again folktales in which the ostensibly urban setting plays no role. Slightly more sophisticated is the 1905 "Micheál na mBréag" (Michael of the lies) by "R. O'F.," a rural story dealing with the misadventures of the protagonist, some occurring in London, a setting of which we get no real sense at all.[76]

With this background in mind, Pádraic Ó Conaire's achievement in the mature and artistic treatment of urban themes in Irish is even more remarkable; indeed, to some his initiative was premature if not downright subversive. Thus looking back on *Deoraidheacht* in 1922, "Conall Cearnach" wrote: "Pádraic Ó Conaire did a bold thing writing about London in Conamara Irish. There is only one thing wrong with this— it's not natural. Writing in Irish about certain matters in life is like writing about them in Latin."[77] But for the new generation of Irish readers rising up with the Revival, his urban fiction could be a genuine

---

Anglicisation which is the ruling principle in all Irish cities." See Laoide, "The Gaedhilgeoir in the City," review of *Beirt Ghaedhilgeoirí 'na gComhnaidhe 'sa Chathair, ACS*, 1 August 1915. Ó Murchadha himself was from Valentia Island, and made unapologetic use of his native dialect in the book.

70. Anonymous, "Molann an Déirc Sí an Cheird is Fearr Í" (Praise charity, It's the best craft), *FL*, Duilleachán do'n Fhéile Pádruig (St. Patrick's Day supplement), 1899.

71. Steafán Seoigheach, "Séamus Ó Murchadha," *FL*, Duilleachán do'n Fhéile Pádruig, 1899.

72. Anonymous, "An tAmadán" (The fool), *FL*, 17 June 1899.

73. Anonymous, "Madradh an Dlíghtheora" (The lawyer's dog), *FL*, 3 February 1900.

74. "Sliabh Díle," "Boladh na Feola agus Torann an Airgid" (The smell of meat and the sound of money), *FL*, 3 February 1900.

75. Anonymous, "An Chaoi do Fuair Muintir na Ceapacha a gCuid Beurla" (How the people of Ceapach got their English), *FL*, 26 May 1900.

76. *UI*, 23–30 December 1905.

77. Quoted by Muiris Ó Droighneáin in *Taighde*, 148. "Ba dhána an rud do rinne Pádraic Ó Conaire agus sgríobhadh ar Londain as Gaedhilg Chonamara. Níl de locht air, acht ná fuil sé nádúrtha. . . . Ionann sgríobhadh i nGaedhilg ar chúrsaí áirithe an tsaoghail agus sgríobhadh sa Laidin."

revelation. For example, writing of *Seacht mBuaidh an Éirghe-Amach*, León Ó Broin recalled: "The book was a revelation to me and a source of great inspiration. Before it arrived on the market, I had begun to believe that contemporary Irish literature, by some peculiar twist of fate, was destined to concern itself with the banalities of agricultural life and as I was a city youth myself, the unhappy feeling which that belief engendered was a thing I had to do battle with or alternatively to surrender my growing interest in the national language."[78] An tAthair Cathaoir Ó Braonáin's judgment on the same collection was succinctly definitive: "Pádraic Ó Conaire has killed Cock Robin, and we who see him die must be grateful for the arrow."[79]

Yet although he did, as we know from the accounts left by his friends, immerse himself in both the sordid and sophisticated sides of life in London, alternately carousing with the outcasts on the Embankment and debating the latest literary news from Europe with other Irish intellectual émigrés, Ó Conaire never became a city man. His principal focus was always on the impact of the city on those coming from a rural, particularly Gaeltacht, background. Rarely was that impact salutary. His cities, and to some extent even his towns, are hostile places, in William P. Ryan's phrase "an unloving and unlovely environment,"[80] at times not that far removed from the stereotyped centers of sin warned against by antiemigration propagandists: "It's many a wonder I saw during that time. Big strong men who had no chance to get work begging for charity at the side of the street. . . . Women being tormented; children being beaten. And the Man with the Hooves sitting on high mocking them all."[81]

Frequently Ó Conaire presents the city, especially London, as actively hostile rather than merely indifferent: "In other towns, when a person is in trouble, when he is ashamed and downcast and humbled, it

---

78. "Pádraic Ó Conaire," *Capuchin Annual* (1934): 254.

79. Review of *Seacht mBuaidh an Éirghe-Amach*, *Studies* 7 (1918): 520. Ó Conaire fully understood the significance of what he was doing. In a 1928 essay urging the immediate Gaelicization of Galway City, he wrote: "Death is in store for any language that is not spoken widely and generally in some town or city." (An bás atá i ndán d'aon teangain nach labhartar go fóirleathan agus go coitchiannta i mbaile mór nó i gcathair éigin.) See Ó Conaire, "Ar Triail. Machtnamh Chinn Bliana" (On trial. A year's-end reflection), in *Iriseoireacht Uí Chonaire*, 206. This essay originally appeared in the *Connacht Sentinel* for 3 January 1928.

80. *The Pope's Green Island*, 287.

81. Pádraic Ó Conaire, "Fan go Fóill" ("Wait a while"), in *Nora Mharcuis Bhig*, 33. "Is iomdha iongantas a chonacas i rith na haimsire sin. Fir mhóra thréana nach raibh aon ghoir aca obair 'fhágháil ag éileamh déirce leathtaobh sráide. . . . Mná dhá gcéasadh. Páisdí dhá gcríonadh. Agus fear na gcrúb 'n-a shuidhe i n-áirde ag magadh fúthu uile."

doesn't seem to him that the things around him—the houses, the walls, the street itself—are trying to do anything to him, but in London a person like that thinks that the big gloomy houses would knock him down, would fall on him to crush him into the ground—if they thought it worth their while to make the effort for something so contemptible."[82] In such an environment people not only lose their dignity, but also their humanity, as in this description of elderly poor people picking through hotel trash bins: "When some of them came on a piece of bread or meat, you'd see them seizing it with their fingers and cleaning the filth from the grimy food with their fingernails. As they bent over those tin containers in the half light of the morning with the big hotels looking down on them derisively, they were like a flock of terrible, hungry, huge birds picking a person's bones with their large bony claws in a desert."[83] Such bestial imagery is pervasive in *Deoraidheacht*. At one point the protagonist Micheál Ó Maoláin sees the homeless in a city park as "jellyfish left on the beach after the tide" (smugairlí rón a d'fhágfaí ar an tráigh i ndiaidh taoille) (126). Loungers around a publichouse door are compared to "the horseflies that suck the blood of horses and cows" (na creabhair a bhíos ag súghadh fola na gcapall agus na mbó) (73). The windows of surrounding buildings seem to Ó Maoláin "like the eyes of an evil animal displeased with the human race" (geall le súilibh ainmhidhe uilc nár thaitnigh an cineadh daonna leis) (124), while the Thames becomes "a hideous monster" (ollphiast fhuathmhar) and London itself "that monster with thousands of lights, thousands of eyes, thousands of precious stones flashing in its skin" (an ollphiast úd a bhfuil na mílte míle solus, na mílte míle súil, na mílte míle cloch luachmhar ag deallramh 'n-a chraiceann) (74). Nor is such imagery limited to the nightmarish world of *Deoraidheacht*. Half-asleep on her way to Dublin, Nóra Mharcuis Bhig imagines the train to be "some wild animal . . . a fiery dragon taking her to some horrible wasteland" (ainmhidhe éigin allta . . . dragún tine . . . ghá tabhairt go

82. Pádriac Ó Conaire, *Deoraidheacht* (Baile Átha Cliath: Cló Talbot, 1973), 75. "I mbailtibh móra eile, nuair atá duine i gcruadh-chás, nuair atá náire agus ceannfaoi agus umhlaidheacht air, feictear dhó nach bhfuil na rudaí atá 'n-a thimcheall—na tighthe, na ballaí, an tsráid féin—ag iarraidh aon cheó a dhéanamh air, ach i Lonndain ceapann duine de'n tsaghas sin go gcuirfeadh na tighthe móra gruamdha dhá chois é—go dtuitfeadh siad air lena bhrúghadh síos 'san talamh—dá mb'fhiú leó an trioblóid sin a chur orra féin i ngeall ar shuarachán mar é."

83. *Deoraidheacht*, 75. "Nuair a thiocfadh cuid aca ar ruainne aráin nó feóla d'fheicfeá iad ag breith air le n-a méaraibh caola tanaidhe, agus ag glanadh an tsalachair de'n bhiadh bhrocach sin le n-a gcuid iongan. . . . Ag cromadh os cionn na soitheach stáin úd dóibh, i mbreac-sholas na maidne, agus na tighthe móra aoidheachta ag féachaint anuas orra go sgigeamhail, ba gheall le sgata éan mór uathbhásach ocrasach allta iad a bheadh ag piocadh cnámha duine le n-a mór-chrobhaibh garbh-chnámhach' i bhfásach."

fásach éigin uathbhásach).[84] Similarly, in "An Ceol agus an Cuimhne" (Music and memory), the storm outside a London boardinghouse is compared to "thousands of mad wild animals trying to get a hold of you" (mílte beithidheach allta buile . . . ag iarraidh greim fhágháil ort).[85]

Compounding the sense of ubiquitous threat, Ó Conaire's densely populated desert lacks reassuring landmarks; while he depicts his cityscapes with vividly concrete imagery, he offers few precise geographical references. "Conall Cearnach" could write that he found it hard to identify the city of Deoraidheacht with the London he himself knew, and Tomás Ó Broin has noted "a vague, unworldly atmosphere" (atmaisféar neamhshaolta éiginnte) that characterizes Ó Conaire's depiction of both London and his native Galway. Ó Broin writes of Deoraidheacht: "We don't encounter any of the usual names known throughout the world, Hyde Park, Marble Arch, Piccadilly. It is no exaggeration to say that Ó Conaire is trying to make the city unrecognizable."[86] Naturally this vagueness contributes to his characters' uneasiness and alienation, their awareness of being out of touch with their immediate surroundings, and it is this sense of being lost in a faceless crowd that most torments his urban protagonists.[87] Even the antinational detective of "Bé an tSiopa Seandachta" (The woman of the antique shop), a man for whom the anonymity of Dublin has been a protection throughout his career, falls victim to this dehumanizing isolation when, guilt-stricken, he suffers a breakdown after the Rising he has helped to betray. Walking the streets of the city, he seeks in vain for a cure he knows would be surer than drugs, "a little word of praise, a little word that would put vigor and life in him again" (focal beag molta, focal beag a chuirfeadh brígh agus borradh ann arís).[88] Unable to find such consolation, even from his fellow detectives, he is driven to suicide.

84. Ó Conaire, "Nóra Mharcuis Bhig," 7.

85. Ó Conaire, "An Ceol agus an Cuimhne," in Síol Éabha, no pagination.

86. "Deoraíocht: Réamhchainteanna agus Iarbhreitheanna" (Deoraíocht: Preliminary remarks and reflective judgments), Feasta 29, no. 5 (May 1976): 7. "Ní chastar linn aon chuid de na gnáthainmneacha atá ar eolas ar fud an domhain, Hyde Park, Marble Arch, Piccadilly. Ní áibhéile é a rá go bhfuil Ó Conaire ag iarraidh an chathair a dhéanamh do-aitheanta."

87. Compare the picture drawn by "An Dairbhreach Dána" in "Amudha i mBabilean" (Astray in Babylon), ACS, 22 June 1901. For a critical discussion of such alienation in Ó Conaire's fiction, see Bernard Ó Maoldomhnaigh, "Anam ar Strae: Staidéar ar Deoraíocht" (A soul astray: A study of Deoraíocht), IMN (1971): 97–107; Pádraig Ó Croiligh, "Go nGoilleann an Bhróg: Samhlaíocht Phádraig Uí Chonaire" (Until the shoe pinches: The imagination of Pádraic Ó Conaire), IMN (1968): 59–70; and Tomás Ó Broin, Saoirse Anama Uí Chonaire (Ó Conaire's freedom of soul) (Gaillimh: Officina Typographica, 1984), 3–4.

88. Ó Conaire, "Bé an tSiopa Seandachta," in Seacht mBuaidh an Éirghe-Amach, 141. It is

Such urban alienation is even more devastating for Ó Conaire's Gaeltacht exiles who, often driven to the city to escape the penury and con-
striction of rural life, find themselves trapped anew in the specious freedom of urban indifference, a point the author underscores by either
leaving his city characters nameless or by identifying them mostly or
solely by descriptive epithets like "The Big Man" (An Fear Mór), "The
Red-haired Woman" (An Bhean Ruadh), "The Fat Woman" (An Bhean
Ramhar), or "The Sallow Little Man" (An Fear Beag Buidhe). By contrast, the names of his rural people, names like Nóra Mharcuis Bhig or
Páidín Mháire, identify not only the characters as individuals, but also
their roots and place in a wider community. No such community is
possible for his city people, who are painfully unable to establish any
real communication or intimacy with the masses that surround them.
Thus in *Deoraidheacht* Ó Maoláin is initially amazed and ultimately outraged when Londoners pay no attention to him as he learns to walk
again after having been mutilated in a traffic accident: "Everyone had
his own story and I had my own great sad story. I began thinking. I
had to get through the rest of my life in this wretched condition. I
began to resent these people who were going by me actively and
quickly, able to use their legs. I thought they should at least look at me.
A person who was learning to walk again. A person who had been at
death's door and escaped."[89] Such indifference degenerates into true malevolence in "Fan go Fóill" ("Hold on there"), when the commotion
surrounding the death of an Irish exile occasions only abuse and complaints about being disturbed from fellow occupants of a London flop-
house: "The people who had been around us shortly before were falling
asleep again. Some of them were grumbling that they had been awakened. Others were ridiculing the Scotsman because he had gone for the
priest."[90]

Ó Conaire's chief device for conveying the sense of isolation in the
midst of company is what Pádraig Ó Croiligh has labeled "the major

worth noting that Eoghan Ó hAnluain has called this story "the closest thing we have in
Irish to the standard Joycean description in *Dubliners*" (an rud is gaire . . . don
ghnáthchursíos ag Joyce in *Dubliners* atá againn sa Ghaeilge). See Ó hAnluain, "Baile Átha
Cliath," *Scríobh* 4, p. 29.

89. *Deoraidheacht*, 2. "A sgéal féin ag gach éinne agus mo sgéal mór brónach agam féin.
Thosuigheas ag machtnamh. Bhí orm mo shaoghal a chur dhíom ar an an-chaoi seo.
Tháinic olc orm do na daoinibh seo a bhí ag dul tharm go beó tapaidh agus lúth na ngéag
aca. Cheapas go ba chóir dóibh féachaint orm ar a laighead. Duine a bhí ag foghluim
coisidheachta an ath-uair! Duine a bhí i mbéal an bháis agus a tháinic as."

90. "Fan go Fóill," in *Nóra Mharcuis Bhig*, 36. "Na daoine a bhí timcheall orainn ar ball
beag, bhíodar ag tuitim 'n-a gcodladh ath-uair. Cuid aca ag clamhsán gur dúisigheadh
iad. Cuid eile ag magadh faoi'n Albanach go ndeacha sé i gcoinne an tsagairt."

symbol of the window" (mór-íomhá na fuinneoige), stressing that windows make possible a superficial contact between people while obstructing true communication.[91] In story after story Ó Conaire's characters, boxed up in tiny, shabby, cell-like rooms, stare from windows at a world from which they are cut off yet in which they long to share. Thus Nóra Mharcuis Bhig, desperately homesick and eager for human warmth after her arrival in London, learns that her communion with the passersby is no more meaningful when she goes among them than it was when she merely watched from her window: "But the same thoughts were pressing in on her outside on the street amongst the people as had been inside."[92] In Deoraidheacht paranoia compounds the loneliness of Ó Maoláin: "When I sat at the window looking out at the street and at the people going by, the loneliness and the homesickness would be so great that I would have to go out amongst people. But I would be so gloomy and sorrowful that I would think they were all mocking me, that they loathed me, that they hated me."[93] The extent of his enforced isolation is brought brutally home to him one night when he learns that the neighbor he has watched kissing his wife and concerning whose family life he has embroidered a sentimental fantasy has beaten the woman to death in a drunken rage (103, 124).

Ó Conaire's most developed use of window symbolism occurs in "Neill." In this story a Galway woman spends nineteen years looking out her window into the window of the woman who stole away her fiancé and whose humiliation is the object of her life. Virtually all of Neill's contact with the world is through her window, and thus she has lost her sense of reality as well as all possibility of genuine communication, much less human sympathy. Even when she at one point wishes to reach out to the woman whose life she has finally destroyed, she is powerless to leave her window: "She saw Brighid Ní Ruadháin in the room going back and forth, back and forth, ceaselessly. She saw her white, tormented face; but when the other woman saw her, she would leave the window. And when Neill saw her going away, she felt a strong urge to go to her and to seek forgiveness. But she did not go."[94]

<hr>

91. "Ní Cúng le Duine an Saol: Sracfhéachaint ar 'Neill' Uí Chonaire" (A person doesn't find life confining: A glance at Ó Conaire's 'Neill' "), IMN (1970): 85, 91.

92. "Nóra Mharcuis Bhig," 9. "Acht bhíodh na smaointe céadna ag brúghadh isteach uirthi amuigh ar an tsráid i measg na ndaoine díreach mar bhí istigh."

93. P. 9. "Nuair a shuidhinn ag fuinneóig ag dearcadh amach ar an tsráid, agus ar na daoinibh bhí ag gabháil thart . . . bhíodh an t-uaigneas agus an cumha chomh mór sin ar mo chroidhe is go mbíodh orm éirighe agus a dhul i láthair na cuideachtan. Ach le chomh duairc dolásach is bhínn, cheapainn go mbídís uile go léir ag magadh fúm; go raibh olc aca dhom; go raibh gráin aca orm."

94. In Síol Éabha, no pagination. "Chonnaic sí Brighid Ní Ruadháin san tseomra agus í

Yet even when Ó Conaire's urban characters do leave their windows and make contact with other people, that contact remains superficial, for they have little to offer and no courage to offer it. In "An tSoch-raoid cois Tuinne" (The funeral by the sea), Ó Conaire explicitly con-trasts this modern shallowness with the primitive passion and sincerity of the Gaeltacht as given voice in the keen: "Some of us in this new age think it shameful to look too deeply into the heart of a person who is emotionally moved, for we think that it is not permissable for a person to probe some of the mysterious secrets of this life or to reveal the mysterious secrets in our own hearts to friend or to enemy. These peo-ple didn't think that way."[95]

Indeed it could be said of many of his urban characters that they have neither true friends nor real enemies. Even when a marriage sours, as happens in "M'Fhile Caol Dubh" (My dark slender poet), deep emo-tions are not necessarily stirred, and the wife can summarize the situa-tion without rancor: "My husband—what can I say but that the pair of us were tired of each other? Tired of each other —yes, that's the most suitable word . . . lack of interest and emotional weariness were de-stroying life for the two of us."[96] Her existence, sufficient in material comforts, is spiritually barren: "There are hundreds and hundreds of us rich women living pleasant, insignificant lives—shopping in the after-noon, tea, with backbiting of neighbors and friends afterwards, the train home, the man of the house snoring over the newspaper."[97]

Obviously, such a routine destroys even the possibility of meaningful thought or accomplishment, and in "Ná Leig Sinn i gCathughadh" (Lead us not into temptation), Ó Conaire's parable of the corruption and prostitution of an artist, the sculptor's only hope for personal and

---

ag imtheacht anonn 's anall, anonn 's anall, gan faoiseamh. Chonnaic sí . . . a haghaidh bán cráidhte; acht nuair d'fheiceadh an bhean thall í d'imtheochadh sí ó'n bhfuinneoig. Agus nuair d'fheiceadh an bhean i bhfus ag imtheacht í, bhíodh fonn mór uirthi a dhul chuici . . . agus maitheamhnas a iarraidh uirthi. Acht ní dheachaidh."

95. In *Cubhar na dTonn*, 6. "Is náireach le cuid againn ar an saoghal nuadh seo féachaint ródhoimhin i gcroidhe duine agus é corruighthe, mar is dóigh linn nach ceadmhach do dhuine sgrúdú dhéanamh ar chuid de rúnaibh diamhaire an tsaoghail seo, nó na rúnta diamhaire 'n-ár gcroidhe féin a nochtadh do charaid ná do namhaid. Níor mar sin do'n phobul seo."

96. In *Seacht mBuaidh*, 168. "Bhí m'fhear—céard is féidir liom a rádh acht go raibh an bheirt againn sáthach tuirseach dá chéile? Tuirseach dá chéile—seadh, sin é an focal is feileamhnaighe. . . . An neamhshuim agus an tuirse chroidhe bhí ag milleadh an tsaoghail orainn beirt." Yet ironically it is her unassuming husband, not her romantic lover, who performs the genuine and fatal act of heroism for love of her.

97. P. 168. "Tá na céadta agus na céadta againn de mhnáibh saidhbhre agus saoghal suairc suarach ghá chaitheamh aca—ag siopadóireacht sa tráthnóna, tae agus cáineadh na gcomharsan agus na gcarad n-a dhiaidh, an traen abhaile, fear an tighe ag srannadh ós cionn an pháipéir nuaidheachta."

creative integrity is to abandon the city: "The life he had spent, towns, amusement, the company of beautiful women—they were all nothing compared to the work he had to do."[98] Lured back by the woman he loves, he is enmeshed again in "the world's enchantments" (geasa an tsaoghail), and his vision irredeemably perverted: "And he understood precisely how the nobility had ebbed from him and how the baseness had grown; he understood how his work had been changed as his own mind and heart and soul had been changed."[99]

In *An Chéad Chloch* (The first stone), the 1914 collection that includes "Ná Leig Sinn i gCathughadh," Ó Conaire shifted his urban focus from Galway, London, and Dublin to Athens, Jerusalem, and imaginary cities of the Far East, and in the process redefined the horizons of modern Gaelic fiction.[100] Of his first reading of *An Chéad Chloch*, the future novelist Seosamh Mac Grianna, who until then was attempting to write in English, recalled: "When I read this book I stopped putting English words to the music of my spirit. I believed that it was possible to write a noble, poetic literature in Irish. That book tasted to me like wine would taste to a person who had never known there was anything in the world but water."[101] It would be hard to imagine places much farther from Micheál Thaidhg's potato patch or Pearse's dunghill than biblical Palestine or the exotic lands inhabited by "na hAibitínigh" under their king Alum-ba or "na Pártigh" under the mighty Cann-Aman. Of the eight stories in the collection, the first four—"An Chéad Chloch," "An Coimhthigheach a Raibh Aghaidh an Bháis air" (The stranger with the face of death), "Teatrarc na Gaililí" (The Tetrarch of Galilee), and "Baintreabhach an Fhíona agus a Mac" (The wine widow and her

98. In *An Chéad Chloch*, ed. Pádraigín Riggs (Corcaigh: Cló Mercier, 1978), 99. "An saoghal a bhí caithte aige, bailte móra, caitheamh aimsire, comhluadar ban áluinn—ní raibh ionnta uile acht neamhní i gcomórtas leis an obair a bhí le déanamh aige."

99. P. 105. "Agus do thuig sé go beacht cé mar thráigh an uaisleacht uaidh agus cé mar thuill an ísleacht; do thuig sé cé mar hathruigheadh a shaothar de réir mar hathruigheadh a mheón agus a chroidhe agus a anam féin."

100. All the stories in the collection were originally published in *ACS* between 1909 and 1912. His were not, of course, the *only* stories with exotic settings in the early Revival. For example, in 1905 Maolmhuire Mac Mághnusa set his "Ciriolca an Chalaidh" (Ciriolca of the harbor) by the Volga with a main character named Isaiah Macineocof. Despite these curiosities there is no indication that the story is a translation. See "Ciriolca an Chalaidh," *UI*, 4 November–2 December 1905.

101. "Pádraic Ó Conaire," in *Pádraic Ó Conaire agus Aistí Eile* (Pádraic Ó Conaire and other essays) (Baile Átha Cliath: Oifig an tSoláthair, 1969), 5. The book was originally published in 1936. "Nuair a léigh mé an leabhar seo stad mé a chur focal Béarla le ceól m'aignidh. Chreid mé go mb'fhéidir litridheacht uasal fhileamhanta a sgríobhadh i nGaedhilge. Bhí blas ar an leabhar agam mar bhéadh blas ar fhíon ag an té nach rabh a fhios aige go dtí sin go rabh ar an tsaoghal ach uisge."

son)—deal with material from the Bible, as Ó Conaire re-creates the pre-Gospel life of the woman taken in adultery, and the post-Gospel lives of Lazarus, the Tetrarch of Galilee who ordered the beheading of John the Baptist, and the men who gave the crucified Christ vinegar to drink and pierced his side. The other stories—"Aba-Cána-Lú," "Cleamhnas san Oirthear" (Matchmaking in the Orient), "Díoghaltas na mBan" (Women's revenge), and "Ná Leig Sinn i gCathughadh"— deal in quasi-allegorical fashion with, respectively, racial and cultural genocide, state regulation of private behavior, the battle between the sexes, and, of course, the personal integrity of the artist.

While Ó Conaire's treatment of women is for a modern reader the most interesting and controversial aspect of the book, the author's contemporaries were doubtless as or even more intrigued by its settings, including its cities.[102] Often these are little more than exotic backdrops: Athens the place where the lover of the adultress studies philosophy, Damascus the city that intrigues the world-weary Saul of Tarsus, Rome the distant imperial capital. But there are recognizable elements of the Ó Conaire city here as well. Variety and license, for example, characterize the Jerusalem of "Teatrarc na Gaililí" and "Baintreach an Fhíona." For the noble Roman Caius, this translates into little more than sexual opportunity, as he fantasizes about "the women of Jerusalem . . . their skin is soft and fragrant, smooth and sleek . . . their shoulders are firm and strong and well-shaped; their breasts round and white, splendid and milky—delightful for the son, be he young or be he old."[103] It should come as no surprise that An tAthair Peadar included An Chéad Chloch among the books he wanted removed from the university curriculum![104] For other characters in these stories, the extraordinary ethnic diversity of Ó Conaire's Jerusalem makes possible the practice of their own het-

102. See, for example, the review by "Cú Laighean" in ACS, 12 September 1914. "Cú Laighean" wrote: "It is a great thing for the Irish language that material for fiction is being sought outside of Ireland itself. That will benefit the language and its literature." (Is mór an nídh don Ghaedhilg go bhfuiltear ag cuardach leathsmuigh d'Éirinn féin ag lorg adhbhar scéalaidheachta. Raghaidh soin i dtairbhthe don teangain, agus dá litridheacht.)

103. "Baintreabhach an Fhíona agus a Mac," in An Chéad Chloch, 55. "Mná Iarúsalem . . . bíonn a gcneas go bog cumhartha agus go sleamhain slíochta . . . bíonn a nguailne go cruaidh láidir deágh-chumtha; a gcíocha go cruinn bán agus go lonrach bleachtmhar, — aoibhinn don mhac, bíodh sé óg nó bíodh sé críonna."

104. In his letter complaining of Ó Conaire's work, Ua Laoghaire specifically commented on the morality of the title story of this collection and on the depiction of Salome's dance in "Teatrarc na Gaililí." Curiously, while the other books Ua Laoghaire condemned were removed from the curriculum, An Chéad Chloch seems to have been left in place. See "An tAthair Peadar agus An Craoibhín: Conspóid faoi Phádraic Ó Conaire," in Pádraic Ó Conaire: Clocha ar a Charn, ed. de Bhaldraithe, 101–6.

erodox faith, Christianity.[105] What Ó Conaire's cities offer is, however, not tolerance, but indifference, and so when passions are aroused, there are no human ties to moderate them. Thus while his country folk and villagers, Palestinians or Galwegians, indulge in nasty spite and backbiting, their hatred is personal and has some limits. In his cities, on the other hand, such animosities can and do erupt into actual persecution and violence, like the mockery with which Lazarus is assailed in Jerusalem, or the stonings threatened in "An Chéad Chloch" and carried out in "Baintreabhach an Fhíona."[106]

Ó Conaire was a true pioneer in his willingness to deal seriously with authentic urban themes in Irish. Furthermore, although he did not usually confront head-on the central challenge of putting Irish into the mouths of people who in actuality would not have known the language—he sidestepped the issue through the geographically and temporally remote settings of the stories in *An Chéad Chloch*, and virtually all of his modern urban characters are native speakers in exile—he did show that the language possessed the flexibility to treat entirely new things and thoughts in a natural and artistic manner. Nonetheless, however firm his commitment to bringing Irish into the twentieth century, and however great his own debt to the intellectual freedom and ferment of urban life, he invariably saw the city through the eyes of an outsider, remaining in many ways as suspicious as any Gaeltacht nativist of "the false civilization of the age" (sibhéaltacht bréige na haoise).[107]

Despite his pride in his own Corca Dhuibhne Gaeltacht background, Seán Ó Caomhánaigh could be as daring as Ó Conaire in his willingness to confront urban life in Irish. We have already noted his April 1911 indictment of fellow Gaelic authors for their timid obsession with

105. See, for example, Ó Conaire, "Baintreabhach an Fhíona," in *An Chéad Chloch*, 46–47.

106. For Lazarus, see Ó Conaire, "An Coimhthigheach," 27; for the stonings, "An Chéad Chloch," 17–18; "Baintreabhach an Fhíona," 60–61 (all in *An Chéad Chloch*).

107. "Amuigh faoi'n bhFásach" (Out in the wilderness), in *Béal an Uaignis*, 20. Alan Titley comments on one aspect of this civilization that Ó Conaire found particularly distressing, advanced industrial capitalism, and offers suggestions for a Marxist reading of *Deoraidheacht*. Yet, having done so he then concludes: "As well as being a superb novel, *Deoraíocht* is a very fine example of a book that grew out of the living dialectic involving the life of the author, the historical circumstances from which he emerged, and the literary forms available to him in his time. It would be presumptuous for anyone to favor any one of these factors over the others." (I leataobh ó bheith ina úrscéal den scoth, is sampla an-bhreá é *Deoraíocht* de leabhar a d'fhás as an dialactaic bheo idir saol an údair, na cúinsí staire ar de é agus na foirmeacha liteartha a raibh fáil aige orthu lena linn. Ba dhána an mhaise do dhuine ar bith a thabharfadh a cheart seachas a chéile d'aon cheann ar bith díobh sin.) See Titley, *An tÚrscéal*, 207; 219–25.

rural subject matter, an indictment voiced in the first installment of "Catharach Nuadh" (A new urbanite), his regular *Sinn Féin* column on an Irish speaker's life in Dublin. Also, like Ó Conaire, he had little of Béaslaí's caution and reserve, a fact made clear in his ambitious opening apologia: "I will go to see every marvel in this marvelous city, I will visit every place worth seeing, I will go to the theaters, I will go to see beautiful pictures, I will make visits if I am invited. And I will hold fast to the language, even if I have to do some damage. It must speak in the future. Farewell to the countryside now; henceforth I am a city man."[108] The extent of his success can be gauged by a glance at some of the subjects to which he devoted subsequent columns: predictable Gaelic League activities like an outing at Sgoil Éanna (17 June 1911), or the Jones Road festival of Irish sports and music (8 July 1911); political demonstrations like that held on Beresford Place for Irish independence (1 July 1911), the annual march to Wolfe Tone's grave at Bodenstown (15 July 1911), and even a Unionist meeting (13 May 1911); evenings at the theater (24 June 1912), including the Abbey (24 February 1912); a visit to the movies (9 March 1912); and run-ins with the Dublin Metropolitan Police (20 May 1911).

Most striking about Ó Caomhánaigh is his real fascination with the variety and complexity of life in the city. There would be no ruralist propaganda in his essays: "When I set out to write of the city, I decided to pay attention to and to examine both sides of life here, and I have been doing that without prejudice. I think that it is proper for a writer to be as truthful to life as the historian is to the subject of his treatise."[109] Needless to say, there is plenty of urban awfulness in his columns, with a particular and accurate emphasis on the poverty of so many Dubliners. Thus in a scene reminiscent of *Deoraidheacht*, he could juxtapose virtual starvation with fashionable luxury: "They were all going the same direction in one great long row, every kind of person, from the

108. Seán Ó Caomhánaigh, "Catharach Nua," *SF*, 29 April 1911. "Raighead ag feuchaint ar gach iongtas san gcathair iongtaigh seo, beurfad cuaird ar gach aon áit is fiú d'fheiscint, raighead go dtís na h-amharclannaibh, raighead ag feuchaint ar pheictiúiridhibh áilne, deunfad cuairdeanna má fhaighim an cuireadh. Agus claoidfhead an teanga dá mbeadh orm díobháil do dheunamh. Caithfidh sí labhairt feasda. Slán beó leis an dtuaith anois; is cathrach feasda mé." The comment of the *SF* Gaelic editor is worth noting: "This person wants to do something extraordinary." (Tá fonn air seo . . . rud euchtach do dhéanamh.)

109. "Catharach Nuadh," *SF*, 19 August 1911. "Nuair chuireas romham tagairt ar an gcathair chinneas ar dhá thaobh na beatha annso do thabhairt fé ndeara agus do scrúdughadh, agus tá san dhá dheunamh agam gan chlaon. Dar liom gur ceart don scríobhnóir bheith chomh fírinneach don mbeatha agus bhíonn an staraidhe do stáid a thráchtais."

ugly old woman who was searching in the refuse bins on the sidewalk
in front of some big, arrogant house to the dandy with his tall hat, his
walking stick, his gloves, and his cigar."[110] Or again, he could ponder
what the night meant to his fellow citizens of different classes: "O
night! Sometimes you soothe a person's mind, and sometimes you torment it. Aren't you lovely to the person who can lay his head on a
featherbed? Aren't you lonely to the person whose bed is made for him
on the hard step of a doorway?"[111]

What is more interesting, however, about Ó Caomhánaigh is his
willingness to go beyond this familiar dichotomy, to anticipate Liam Ó
Rinn in his authentic delight for his adopted city:

> I reached Stephen's Green. The place was like a great black spot.
> You would hear the occasional cry of a duck—that was all. I
> continued to the top of Grafton Street. It was almost deserted,
> and you would hardly believe your eyes that it was the same
> street you had seen previously at four o'clock in the afternoon. I
> like it at a time like that and I said to myself: "I now have almost
> to myself this street that everyone longs to be on on a fine after-
> noon."[112]

In a piece in November 1911, he discussed his fascination with a hidden
Dublin, areas and aspects of the city ignored by even its natives.[113] Undoubtedly his most striking discovery was the single family urban
"Gaeltacht" he came on in O'Casey's North City slums: "Here in the
midst of filth and poverty, living in a single room, with but little

110. "Catharach Nuadh," SF, 6 May 1911. "Bhíodar go léir ag gabháil an bealach
ceudna in aon tsraith mhóir fhada amháin, gach saghas duine ón sean-mnaoi ghránda a
bhí ag cuardach go cíocrach na n-árus smúite ar an bpáille os chómhair tighe móir cean-
nárdaigh éigin go dtín staigín go n-a bhairéad árd, a mhaide láimhe, a láimhne, agus a
thúdóg." See also "Catharach Nuadh," SF, 10 June 1911.
111. "Catharach Nuadh," SF, 20 May 1911. "Á! a oidhche, uaireannta maoluigheann tú
meín an duine, uaireannta chiapann tú í. Nach aoibhinn tú don té gur féidir leis a cheann
do leigeant ar leabaidh chlúimh? Nach diamhair tú don té go gcóirighir a leabaidh dó ar
an gcéim chruaidh i mbéal dorais?"
112. "Catharach Nuadh," SF, 20 May 1911. "Shroiceas Faithche Stiofáin. Bhí an áit
mar ball mór dubh. Chloisfeá foth-scread lachan—sin a raibh. Chuireas díom go bárr
Sráide Ghraiftean. Bhí sí tréigthe beagnach agus ní mór go gcreidfeá do shúile gur b'í an
tsráid cheudna í a connac ar a ceathair a chlog um thráthnóna roimhe sin. Taithnigheann
sí liom ar a lithéid d'uain agus dubhairt liom féin: 'An tsráid seo go mbíonn tnúth gach
n-aon léithe um thráthnóna breágh tá sí nach mór fúm féin anois.'" See also his detailed
description of O'Connell Street on an ordinary day in "Catharach Nuadh," SF, 2 December 1911.
113. "Catharach Nuadh," SF, 18 November 1911.

knowledge of the country, having seen the smooth and the rough, having tasted the sweet and the bitter, separated altogether from Gaelic Ireland, there was a couple to be found with Ireland in their hearts."[114]

From 25 November 1911 to 3 February 1912, Ó Caomhánaigh used his column for what looks like an inchoate serialized short story about a friend of his who, thwarted in love, falls into poverty and despair. Predictably, the horrors of urban degradation are given prominence in the tale: "In my walks I have seen and noticed things that would make your hair stand up on your head and would make you vomit with their obscenity; I have heard savage words that would make you wish you didn't have ears to hear them."[115] But once again the city's greatest terror is the profound loneliness that can be experienced there: "When I went out, there would not be mountains, fields, sea, or islands, or 'God be with you,' but alien miseries, bare houses, crowds that did not know me. Wasn't it odious to think of them? What misfortune imposed on me the fate to be in this condition? But wait—weren't the throngs on every side of me in the same condition?"[116] Yet even though this young man at one point considers suicide,[117] he manages to pull himself together, in effect thinking and willing his way to a personal stoicism, a philosophy he acknowledges he could only have developed in the intellectual ferment of the city.[118] The tale concludes with a story within a story in which a young man from the country now resident in Dublin performs an act of heroism in a fire on Dame Street and thus wins the hand of his beloved.[119]

At the end of the following year and into 1914 Ó Caomhánaigh serialized another story of urban life in Sinn Féin. "An Truaghán Truaig" (The pitiful wretch) is an Ó Conairesque tale of the seamy underside of

---

114. "Catharach Nuadh," SF, 19 August 1911. "Annsúd i lár salachair agus dealbhais, in a gcómhnaidhe in aon tseomra amháin, gan aca ach beagán eolais ar an dtír, mín agus garbh feicthe aca, milis agus searbh blaiste aca, deighilte ar fad ó Éirinn Gaedhealach, bhí le fághail beirt go raibh Éire in a gcroidhe."

115. "Catharach Nuadh," SF, 6 January 1912. "Ar mo shiubhaltaibh tá nidhthe feicthe agus tugtha fé ndeara agam a chuirfeadh an ghruaig n-a seasamh ar do cheann le draostachta agus a chuirfeadh ag úirleacan tú, tá bréithre borba cloiste agam go mb'fheárr leat ná beadh cluasa ort le n-a gclos."

116. "Catharach Nuadh," SF, 30 December 1911. "Ar ghabháil amach ní bheadh sléibhte, guirt, farraige, ná oileáin, ná 'Dia dhuit,' ach cráidheanna cóimhtheacha, lomthighthe, sluaighthe nár bh'eól dóibh mé. Nár ghráineamhail a machtnamh? Cad é an crann a chaith an Chinneamhaint orm go mbein ar an aiste? Ach fan, ná raibh an toisc cheudna ag an ndrong a bhí ar gach taobh chomh maith?"

117. "Catharach Nuadh," SF, 6 January 1912.

118. "Catharach Nuadh," SF, 13 January 1912.

119. "Catharach Nuadh," SF, 27 January and 3 February 1912.

Dublin life (saoghal íochtarach na cathrach).[120] While the narrator, himself a poor and sometimes even homeless man from the country, is at first bewitched by the city and hopes he will one day be able to experience all its wonders, he quickly realizes that there is an entirely different Dublin about which the comfortable middle class knows nothing.[121] He then goes on to tell of his sporadic meetings and growing fascination with the story's title character, a crippled newspaper vendor, beggar, and free-lance fence who ends his days in the city morgue, killed when hit by a car. And if the manner of his demise is reminiscent of Micheál Ó Maoláin's disabling accident in *Deoraidheacht*, other incidents also reveal the influence of Ó Conaire's novel. On more than one occasion, the beggar is depicted as a beast: "The penny fell into the mud and he thrust himself after it like a hungry dog after a bone."[122] Ó Caomhánaigh also shared Ó Conaire's willingness to introduce the language into shockingly new settings, like the morgue or a brothel that, despite the author's discretion, must have scandalized some readers, particularly since, in anticipation of both Joyce and O' Casey, he introduced religious and patriotic icons into this sordid milieu: "On the walls, a few pictures, one of them above the door of Robert Emmet in the dock delivering his oration, another one above the mantle by the lamp, a holy picture. When I saw these in such a place, I shook my head and sighed."[123]

The next major Gaelic attempt to write of city life, the 1911 novel *Eoghan Paor* by "Conán Maol," is a decidedly peculiar production, "a frankly sensational novel" in the words of one contemporary critic.[124] It deals with the schemes of Eoghan Paor, alias Parheim, a Kerry exile who has become the world's richest man, to free his native land by buying, populating, and fortifying all the hills in Ireland. This kind of light escapist fiction with a contemporary setting was certainly a new

120. "An Truaghán Truaig," *SF*, 3 January 1914. The story commenced serialization on 13 December 1913 and ran to 17 January 1914, where it broke off and does not seem to have been resumed.

121. "An Truaghán," *SF*, 13 December 1913.

122. "An Truaghán," *SF*, 20 December 1913. "Thuit an phingin sa laithig agus raid sé é féin 'n-a diaidh mar gadhar ocrach i ndiaidh cnáimh feóla."

123. "An Truaghán," *SF*, 3 January 1914. "Ar na fallaidhibh beagán peictiúirí, ceann aca os cionn dorais Riobárd Eimit san ndug ag deunamh a óráide, an ceann eile os cionn an chlabhair le h-ais an lampa peictiúir beannuighthe. Ar a bhfeicsint seo dhom in a lithéid d'áit chroitheas mo cheann agus baineadh osna ionam." In a touch that also foreshadowed O'Casey, he introduced a young woman dying of consumption into this raucous setting.

124. "In the Gaelic World," *WF*, 10 February 1912. While conceding that " 'Conán Maol' has certainly gotten away from the beaten track of storytelling in Irish," this critic felt that "the picture is too highly coloured altogether."

development in Irish, and "Conán" seems to have relished his role as trailblazer.[125] A critic once remarked that the future of Irish could be regarded as secure when Seosamh Mac Grianna provided an Irish term for fish and chips. If this be a valid criterion, the date of the language's salvation must be brought forward three decades, for two of the main characters of Ó Séaghdha's novel run a chipper in London.[126] Nor did "Conán" limit himself to small business— stockbroking, medicine, and plush restaurants also figure prominently and on the whole successfully, if self-consciously, in the novel. Yet despite this success and despite his own personal familiarity with urban life in Cardiff, Belfast, and London, "Conán" saw the city through suspicious eyes. Like Ó Conaire he frequently emphasizes urban poverty, most notably in a scene in which a group of desperate men pressing forward in search of work as dockers inadvertently shove several of their number off a pier.[127] He also makes clear that many of London's poor are Irish country people who regret their mistake in coming and would go home if they could.[128] Even more to the point, as in Ó Conaire's city stories the bleakest aspect of urban life is not its physical poverty but its cold spiritual barrenness and apathy. Thus when the heroine, Gobnait, attempts to make a living as a street musician she is startled and hurt by the indifference of the passersby: "The crowds of people went past her, but each of them had his own business and had no interest in her. If it so happened that she fell over on the street a crowd of them would gather around her as was their custom. Some of them would be stretching their necks over the shoulders of the rest to get a look at her, but no sooner would a constable come towards them than they would scatter, each of them to his own affairs, and they would think of her no more."[129] No doubt speaking for the author, one Irish sailor long based

125. See the lengthy editorial review welcoming the novel in ACS, 16 December 1911.
126. See Ó hAnluain, "Baile Átha Cliath," Scríobh 4, p. 36. A fish-and-chip shop ("tigh an éisc agus na slisínidhe") also appeared in Ó Caomhánaigh's "Catharach Nuadh," SF, 10 June 1911. That such developments were taken seriously by language revivalists is evident from the delight with which ACS commented on the new terminology for "ice cream," "chip potato," and "herb beer" used in the Manx version of laws enacted on the Isle of Man in 1907. See "The Capabilities of Manx," ACS, 28 December 1907.
127. "Conán Maol," Eoghan Paor (Baile Átha Cliath: M. H. Gill agus a Mhac, 1911), 22. He was, of course, speaking from experience here. See his grim 1902 description of the underside of London life in "An Síc Córa" (The moment of justice), Banba 1, no. 3 (May 1902): 65–67.
128. "Conán Maol," Eoghan Paor, 89.
129. "Conán Maol," Eoghan Paor, 42. "Ghabh na sluaighte daoine tháirse, ach bhí a ghnó féin ag gach duine aca, agus níor chuireadar suim innte-se. Da dtárlóchadh go dtuitfeadh sí i gceann a cos ar an tsráid bhaileóchadh sgata aca 'na timcheall mar is gnáthach

in London tries to open the eyes of a newly arrived exile blinded by the sheer size and excitement of the city: "I prefer villages where the people are nice and comfortable and gentle with each other to a lonely city like London where you wouldn't see your next door neighbor from one end of the year to the next."[130]

While "Conán" was even more daring than Ó Conaire in his willingness to put Irish into the mouths of highly unlikely people like London financiers, the majority of his characters were, not surprisingly, native speakers. However, unlike Ó Conaire, he provided these homesick and disoriented Gaels with at least a temporary haven in which to seek refuge. William P. Ryan once described the London Gaelic League as "a city apart" (cathair fá leith) in which there was "light and joy . . . 'l'idéalisme' and 'le romanticisme'" (solus agus sógh . . . "l'idéalisme" agus "le romanticisme"),[131] and as "a sort of intellectual and spiritual Garden City."[132] The existence of the London League with its neighborly activities makes life in the metropolis bearable for Gobnait, and thereby leaves Ó Séaghdha's London a less irredeemably bleak place than is Ó Conaire's.[133] Of course even the London League is seen as a purely temporary expedient; the real home of the exiles will in future be on the fortified, free, and Gaelic hillsides of their native land.[134]

In his own short novel *Caoimhghín Ó Cearnaigh* (1913), Ryan gave creative expression to his notion that Gaelic "cities apart" could some-

---

leo. Bheadh cuid aca ag síneadh a muineáil thar guailnibh na coda eile i gcomhair radhairc d'fhághail uirthe, acht ní túisge bhuailfeadh consábla 'na treó 'ná go sgaipfeadh na daoine sin, gach ceann aca chum a ghnótha féin, agus ní chuimhneóchaidís uirthe níos mó."

130. "Conán Maol," *Eoghan Paor*, 6. "B'fhearr liom bailtí beaga go mbeadh na daoine go deas compórdach, ceannsa le chéile ionnta 'ná cathair uaigneach mar Lunduin ná feicfeá an fear a bheadh 'n-a chómhnuidhe i mbéal do dhoruis ó cheann ceann de'n bhliadhain."

131. "Sgríbhinní Mhíchíl Bhreathnaigh" (The writings of Mícheál Breathnach), *ACS*, 2 August 1913.

132. "I mBaile 's i gCéin," *ACS*, 17 October 1903. See also Pádraic Ó Domhnalláin's picture of the London League in "Gaedhil i gCéin" (Gaels abroad), *ACS*, 30 October 1909.

133. See, for example, "Conán Maol," *Eoghan Paor*, 54–55, 88.

134. London Gaelic Leaguers were given a more urgent reason to leave the city in "Spéar-Ruathar i Lúndan" (An air-raid in London) by "É Féin," in which a league meeting is disrupted during World War I by a German bombing raid. The piece includes a vivid description of Londoners sleeping in a tube station at the foot of an escalator (staidhre a bhí ag síor-ghluaiseacht), "a phrase Irish-speakers of the true Gaeltacht will not understand" (ní thuigfidh Gaedhilgeoirí na fíor-Ghaedhealtachta an abairt sin). See "É Féin," "Spéar-Ruathar i Lúndan," *ACS*, 20 October 1917. The airplane figures more benignly in Peadar Ó Dubhdha's *Ar Lorg an tSeanchaidhe* (On the trail of the storyteller), an adventure tale for young people in which the protagonists whiz around Ireland by air. See *Ar Lorg an tSeanchaidhe* (Dundalk: Dundalgan, 1915).

how exist within otherwise unsympathetic urban boundaries.[135] Once again the protagonist is an outsider, a native speaker drawn to the city, Dublin in this instance, by the prospect of a challenging environment for his intellectual talents: "He thought that Dublin was as wonderful as Tara in the time of Cormac Mac Airt or Emain Macha when the young Cú Chulainn set out for it."[136] Not surprisingly, disillusionment sets in, accompanied by the usual sense of loneliness and alienation: "But now and again sadness and a terrible loneliness would come over him without his knowing why. . . . He thought at those times that both himself and the human race were exiles—banished on account of some dreadful crime from the birthright of their souls and ignorant of the road that would bring them home."[137] His judgment on the city at this point echoes that of Ó Conaire: "Dublin is a wasteland" (Fásach is eadh Baile Átha Cliath) (8).

Fortunately for him, at this moment of near despair Caoimhghín discovers an oasis in the Gaelic League. Ryan was only following precedent when, like "Conán Maol" and others, he drew on the varied educational, political, and especially social activities of the League to provide the language a credible halfway house if not a veritable shelter on its literary arrival in the unsympathetic linguistic and cultural atmosphere of the capital. For example, in D. Ó Riain's "Cáit Ní Dhuibhir," a pair of young Gaeltacht lovers seem to make their sole contact with

135. Ó Caomhánaigh gave the novel a lukewarm review in SF, enjoying Ryan's re-creation of the Dublin League, but finding the book's love plot "insipid and un-Gaelic" (leamh neamh-Ghaedhealach). See "Dhá Leabhar Nuadha: Léirmheas" (Two new books: A review), SF, 25 October 1913. Aisling Ní Dhonnchadha has recently discussed this novel with a focus on issues for the most part different from those explored here in "'Caoimhín Ó Cearnaigh': Úrscéal de Chuid na hAthbheochana" (Caoimhghín Ó Cearnaigh: A novel of the revival), in An tÚrscéal sa Ghaeilge (The novel in Irish), Léachtaí Cholm Cille 21 (1991): 154–74.

136. Caoimhghín Ó Cearnaigh: Sgéal Úrnua (Caoimhghín Ó Cearnaigh: A novel) (Baile Átha Cliath: Clódhanna Teoranta, 1913), 2. The novel was originally published as a serial in Ryan's paper, the Irish Nation and Peasant in 1910. "Cheap sé go raibh Baile Átha Cliath chomh hiongantach agus do bhí Teamhair i n-aimsir Chormaic Mhic Airt, nó Eamhain Mhacha ar dul do Chúchulainn Óg ar a triall." Caoimhghín's was an enthusiasm that Ryan himself shared, for a while at least, a fact that no doubt inspired him to create in this novel what Eoghan Ó hAnluain has called "the first modern creative work that tried to show the contemporary life of the city through the eyes of an Irish speaker" (an chéad saothar cruthaitheach nua-aoiseach a d'fhéach le saol comhaimseartha na cathrach a thaispeáint trí shúil Gaeilgeora). See Ó hAnluain, "Baile Átha Cliath," Scríobh 4, 32.

137. P. 8. "Acht anois agus arís tháinig dólás agus uaigneas uathbhásach air gan fios cé'n fáth. . . . Shaoil sé annsin go raibh seisean, agus an cineadh daonna, 'na ndeoraidhthe—díbeartha mar gheall ar choir mhilltigh éigin, ó dhúthchas a n-anamann, agus gan eolas aca ar bhealach a bhfillte."

Dublin through the insulating medium of the league, and are thereby
impressed "that the city people had far more interest in Irish than did
the people who were living in the very heart of the Gaeltacht."[138] Despite their essentially urban occupations, all of Ryan's characters are
likewise committed language revivalists. Nor did Ryan see any contradiction in coupling movement activism with his own pet philosophical
and spiritual concerns. In a 1903 review of Ó Dubhghaill's *Cathair Conroí agus Sgéalta Eile*, he had written:

> The battle for Irish will not be won till we are able to habitually
> and naturally discuss in Irish every interest of our lives and
> thoughts. . . . Had we books on those interests in natural and
> thoughtful Irish, progress would be easier for the plain reason
> that we would have food for thought and material for speech;
> the elementary fact that speaking pre-supposes something to
> speak about, and the more thought and point there are in it, the
> better is the speech likely to be, is often forgotten. To a student
> who desires to discuss science, philosophy, and so on in Irish it
> is a poor consolation to be put off with something about the
> weather or his ancestors.[139]

Ryan does not deny his own characters such intellectual sustenance, but
he also manages to make the philosophic conversations that lie at the
thematic center of the book—and that may well have struck some
readers at the time as exotic if not downright "un-Gaelic"— seem natural enough at informal sessions in An Stad, a shop on North Frederick
Street frequented by Irish speakers, or among friends during Oireachtas
week.[140] Gaelic Dublin, Ryan's city within a city, thus offers the best of

138. *ACS*, 17 April 1909. They are impressed "go raibh i bhfad níos mo suime ag
muinntir na cathrach sa nGaedhilg ná mar a bhí ag na daoinibh bhí 'n-a gcomhnuidhe i
gceartlár na Gaedhealtachta." In Peadar Mac Fhionnlaoich's "An Gath Gréine" (The ray of
sunshine), three earnest but less than fluent Dublin Gaelic Leaguers vie for the hand of a
beautiful native speaker, who finally agrees to marry the man with the best Irish! See Mac
Fhionnlaoich, "An Gath Gréine," *ACS*, 5 June 1909. See also the much less self-conscious
treatment of middle-class urban affairs in Liam Ua Domhnaill's "Inntleacht Bhan"
(Women's ingenuity), an amusing little love story involving two Gaelic Leaguers on the
Dublin-Waterford train (*ACS*, 24 December 1909).

139. "Review / Mr. Doyle's Stories for Children," *ACS*, 18 July 1903.

140. See, for example, Ryan, *Caoimhghín Ó Cearnaigh*, 7, 28–31. "An Seabhac" wrote
that "although it is, as it were, in the exact center of Dublin shoneenism, it is unlikely that
there is a more Gaelic spot in all of Ireland today." (Cé go bhfuil sé i gceart-lár Sheó-
iníneachta Átha Cliath, mar atá, ní móide go bhfuil ball eile níos Gaedhealaighe i nÉirinn
uile indiu.) See "Stad na nGaedhilgeoirí," *Banba* 1, no. 3 (May 1902): 89–92. See also the

both worlds, the intellectual freedom of the capital and the warmly supportive communal spirit of the countryside.[141] Caoimhghín himself at one point expresses what is in effect the stereotypical dichotomy between rural and urban life, except in this instance he is discussing two distinctive life-styles, both of which could be practiced within the city itself: "When I am at a céilí or visiting by the fireside or in any Irish-language group, I think that Christ is with us. When I am in the towns during the day, that doesn't seem to be so" (26).[142] During Oireachtas week the two cities seem briefly coterminous as hundreds of Gaels turn Dublin into a big Irish-speaking village, and the conclusion of the festival leaves Caoimhghín frustrated by the gap between the Dublin that Oireachtas week proves could be and the mundane, Anglicized city it actually is: "They thought it a pity that the Oireachtas couldn't always be there as the city of Tara with all its joy was there from the beginning of the year to its end in the time long past. Wouldn't it be delightful for modern Gaels to be able to come from the countryside as often as they wished and find the Oireachtas in its full glory waiting for them in Dublin!"[143]

While Ryan's Ó Cearnaigh is as much an exile in the city as are any of Ó Conaire's or "Conán's" characters, he differs from them in accepting the city as his home and committing himself to reshaping it according to his vision of what the capital of a Gaelic nation should be. In

---

entry on Cathal Mac Garbhaigh, the owner of An Stad, in Breathnach and Ní Mhurchú, *Beathaisnéis a Dó*, 56–58.

141. There were conflicting views on the extent and vitality of the Dublin Gaelic community. Thus in a 1914 *ACS* editorial by "Caor," we read: "A Gaeltacht in the city? Yes, there is a Gaeltacht in the city, and it is prospering strongly." (Gaedhealtacht sa chathair? 'Seadh tá Gaedhealtacht sa chathair agus í ag borradh go tréan.) See "Caor," "Gaedhealtacht na Cathrach" (The city Gaeltacht), editorial, *ACS*, 14 November 1914. On the other hand, in a review of Domhnall Ó Murchadha's *Beirt Ghaedhilgeoirí 'na gComhnaidhe 'sa Chathair*, Seosamh Laoide wrote: "There is no Irish-speaking 'colony,' properly so called, in any of our cities, as one finds a French or Italian colony in London, say." See Laoide, "The Gaedhilgeoir in the City," *ACS*, 1 August 1915.

142. P. 26. "Nuair a bhím ar céilidhe, nó ar cuairdidheacht, chois na teineadh, nó i mbuidhin Gaedhilge ar bith, cheapaim go mbíonn Críost i n-aice linn. Nuair a bhím ins na bailtibh móra i rith an lae ní mar sin a bhíos an sgéal."

143. P. 44. "Ba thruagh leo gan an t-Oireachtas a bheith ann i gcómhnuidhe díreach mar bhí cathair na Teamhrach agus aoibhneas na Teamhrach ann ó thús deire na bliadhna i n-allód. Nárbh aoibhinn do Ghaedheala an lae indiu bheith i n-ann teacht ó'n dtuaith chomh minic agus a b'áil leo agus an t-Oireachtas fhághail i mBaile Átha Cliath faoi lántseol rompa!" See also the rhapsodic picture of Dublin in Oireachtas week in Mícheál Breathnach's "Ó 'Chathair an Phréacháin Mhóir' go Baile Átha Cliath" (From "The City of the Big Crow" to Dublin), *ACS*, 27 March 1909. The piece was originally submitted

words applied to a Gaeltacht man in another story, "he contrived to win much pleasure from city life, without indulging in its dissipations."[144] While his fiancée works to help the poor of Dublin, Caoimhghín faces the equally daunting task of assisting the intellectually and spiritually deprived: "There are people in Dublin who in some ways are poorer than the poor. . . . There is no thought or consciousness or spiritual longing in them."[145] Indeed, late in the novel Ó Cearnaigh confronts nativist ideology head-on when a priest friend urges him to return home to the Gaeltacht: "The new literature of Ireland will come from the country. The towns we have are decayed, spoiled. Neither the spirit of Christ nor the spirit of Cú Chulainn is in them. Go back to farming, Caoimhghín, and the stuff of poetry and the stuff of literature will be in your heart every day. Yes, and something far better will be in you— you'll feel the Kingdom of Heaven in you."[146] Unlike virtually all of the urban exiles we have previously encountered, Caoimhghín has the means to follow this advice. Moreover, as an orthodox Gael he accepts the fundamental truth of the priest's condemnation of urban life and wants to go home. The vocation he has come to realize through the course of the novel, however, calls him to stay in Dublin, striving to awaken his fellow citizens from what James Joyce at precisely this time but from an entirely different perspective called their paralysis: "You're right about the towns. They are decayed and spoiled. But no. There is a soul in everyone living in them. The unfortunate thing is that the 'ordinary people' are in control. We must be patient and do our best every day that we live to awaken the 'true person' hidden in every city dweller."[147]

In his serialized 1915–16 novel *An Bhóinn agus an Bhóchna* (The

144. This bilingual story, "Manus O'Gallagher / Maghnus Ó Gallchobhair" deals only briefly with Dublin, for the protagonist emigrates to South Africa for health reasons, fights with the Irish Brigade on the side of the Boers, and eventually returns to marry and live in Ireland. See "Maghnus Ó Gallchobhair," *WF*, 14 March 1908. The English here is from the original. "D'éirigh leis greaca spóirt a bhaint as imtheachtaibh na cathrach, maille leis an gcathughadh is an gcontabhairt a sheachaint."

145. P. 42. "Tá daoine i mBaile Átha Cliath agus ar shlighthibh táid níos boichte 'ná na boicht. . . . Níl smaoineadh, ná cómh-mhothughadh, ná dúil anama ionta."

146. P. 78. "Tiocfaidh nua-litridheacht na h-Éireann ó'n dtuaith. Na bailte móra atá againn tá siad feochta, loitighthe. Níl spiorad Chríost ná spiorad Chúchulainn ionta. Fill ar an bhfeilmeoireacht, a Chaoimhghín, agus béidh ádhbhar fhilidheachta agus ádhbhar litridheachta i do chroidhe gach lá. 'Seadh, agus béidh rud atá i bhfad níos fearr ionat— béidh Ríoghacht Neimhe le mothughadh ionat."

147. P. 79. "Tá an fhírinne agat mar gheall ar na bailte móra. Tá siad feochta, loitighthe. Acht níl. Tá anam i ngach duine atá 'na chomhnuidhe ionta. 'Sé an donas é go bhfuil na 'gnáth-dhaoine' i n-uachdar. Ní fuláir dúinn bheith foighdeach agus ár ndithchill do dhéanamh gach lá dá maireann sinn chun an 'fíor-dhuine' atá fá cheilt i ngach cathruightheoir a mhúsgailt."

Boyne and the sea), Ryan in effect rewrote *Caoimhghín Ó Cearnaigh*, inverting the narrative and thematic conclusions.[148] Again his romantic protagonists are urban Gaels who meet at league headquarters in Parnell Square. Ruairí Ó Duibhir is an intellectual traveling language teacher in Meath, where the proximity of the megalithic tumulus at Newgrange has inspired him to esoteric studies. Like Ó Cearnaigh, Ruairí is a farmer's son who after lonely struggles has made the city his own. His odd blend of activism and the occult enables him to share Ó Cearnaigh's vision of a spiritual Gaelic Dublin, to imagine, at least during league functions, "that there was a link between the Tara of the ancients and present-day Dublin" (go raibh ceangal idir Teamhair na sean agus Baile Átha Cliath an lae inniu).[149] Nonetheless, he still feels drawn to his family's "patch of land" (paisde talmhan) and "the simple neighborly life" (saoghal simplí na gcomharsan), although he simultaneously realizes the harshness of that life and its intellectual constrictions: "He admitted that he felt a great longing for life in the country—in a way. But it was small in comparison with the fascination he felt for the literary life, for the ebb and flow of ideas. And to live on that remote patch of land—that would be like exile from the intellectual life."[150]

Créde Ní Chonghaile, the Dublin-born and university-educated daughter of a philosopher, is scornful of such logic, seeing only sterility beneath the superficial ferment that so captivates Ruairí: "Dublin is far worse than a moor. . . . It's a wasteland. There is beauty in a real moor."[151] A disciple of Feargus Ó Ruanaidhe (a thinly disguised AE figure), she seems at one point willing to wish the entire city right out of corporeal existence. As they wait at Nelson's Pillar for the last tram, she tells Ruairí: "I am delighted to think that the same ugly Pillar—and Dublin itself—are transitory, impermanent: that they have no connection with 'the eternal world.'"[152] Instead, she wills herself out of bodily

---

148. Earlier versions of two sections of the novel had been published in *ACS* as "An Múinteoir Taisdil, Bhergilius, agus an Sagairtín" (The travelling teacher, Virgil, and the little priest") and "Brugh na Bóinne agus an Domhan Thoir" (Newgrange and the Eastern world) on 2 and 23 November 1912 respectively. In these drafts the romantic plot at the heart of the later novel seems absent.

149. ("Cara na nUghdar"), *ACS*, 25 September 1915.

150. *ACS*, 1 January 1916. "D'admhaigh sé go raibh dúil mhór aige i saoghal fá'n dtuaith—ar shlighe. Acht ba bheag í i gcó-mheas leis an dúil a bhí aige i saoghal liteardha, i dtaoideacha smaointe. Agus comhnuidhe ar an bpaisde talmhan iargcúlta—budh hionann é agus deoraidheacht ón saoghal intleachtach."

151. *ACS*, 25 December 1915. "Tá Baile Átha Cliath i bhfad níos measa 'ná riasc. . . . Is fásach é. Bíonn áilneacht i bhfíor-riasc."

152. *ACS*, 2 October 1915. "Is breagh liom a cheapadh go bhfuil an Cholamhain ghránda chéadna—agus Baile Átha Cliath féin—go haimseardha, neamh-bhuan: nach bhfuil baint aca leis 'an domhan síorruidhe.' "

existence, as Ryan, with a startling evasion of any convincing resolution to this philosophical lovers' quarrel, has her literally sail off into the sunset while attending a Gaelic League summer college. Ruairí is neither shocked nor devastated by her deliberate abandonment of this world—what she calls the "dream" (taibhreadh) of her life in Dublin—but rather is inspired to emulation of a sort. As the novel closes, he has retired to a small island off the west coast where they can continue their relationship on a properly spiritual plain: "I am near her already—nearer to her than if we were in the Boyne Valley or in Killiney—and as I work the land and as I fulfill my mind and my soul I will be with her in a more wonderful and more spiritual way."[153] When a friend confronts him with precisely those arguments with which Caoimhghín Ó Cearnaigh justified his commitment to urban activism, Ruairí dismisses his own previous intellectual and social enthusiasms and claims that, in mystical union with Créde on his island retreat, he can perform far more profound service for "the great Ireland, the true Ireland" (an mhór-Éire, an fhíor-Éire).[154]

As we have seen, in their other initiatives the pioneers of Gaelic prose were never long without followers and comrades, and such was again the case with regard to the development of urban fiction in Irish. For once, however, the Oireachtas played a minor role. Thus although the 1917 competition for a collection of short stories on city life would seem to have been ideally timed to build on the example of *Deoraidheacht*, *Eoghan Paor*, and Ryan's two novels, it attracted absolutely no entrants whatsoever,[155] and a similar competition the following year only a pair, of which the judges said that "neither of these two stories has much to do with any city in Ireland."[156] Urban stories were, however, being written—most notably those of Ó Conaire already dis-

---

153. *ACS*, 15 January 1916. "Bím i n-aice léi cheana féin—níos goire di 'ná ar bheith i nGleann na Bóinne nó ar Chill Inghean Léinín dúinn—agus do réir mar shaothróchad an talamh agus mar chuirfead mo mheanma agus m'anam chun críche béad i n-éineacht léi ar shlighe níos iongantaighe agus níos spriodálta."

154. *ACS*, 15 January 1916.

155. See "Toradh na gComórtas" (The results of the competitions), *ACS*, 18 August 1917.

156. "Oireachtas a 1918 / Na Comórtaisí Liteardha / Breatha na Moltóirí" (The 1918 Oireachtas / The literary competitions / The decisions of the judges), *FL*, 19 October 1918. "Is beag baint atá ag ceachtar de'n dhá scéal le héanchathair in Éirinn." Similarly, the London League's generous prize at the 1918 Oireachtas for a "novel dealing with Irish life and thought, and culminating in the events of Easter Week, 1916" also went unclaimed, although it perhaps inspired a work like Ó Grianna's *Mo Dhá Róisín*. See "London League Prizes for 1918," *ACS*, 11 August 1917; and Ó Súilleabháin, *Conradh na Gaeilge i Londain*, 195.

cussed—and what they lacked in number they made up for in variety. One of Seán Ó Faoláin's first published stories was a grim and ironic tale of urban poverty that appeared in the journal of Cork's St. Finbar branch of the league, apparently in 1917.[157] Set in Cork City, it deals with an unemployed and homeless coal porter who reads George Moore and the *Revue des Deux Mondes*. Seeking shelter in the room of a "demi-mondaine," he wanders through a seedy house and comes to the room of an old woman sitting peacefully in a chair with her rosary beads. Moving closer he sees that she is dead, and "he then looked around, and slowly and stiffly sat down and began to warm his hands at the fire, laughing softly to himself. . . . Didn't he have the luck" (8).[158] Another major figure of the future brought his acquired Irish to his urban background at this time. Micheál Mac Liammóir's 1920 story "An Tuirse / Lá Brothallach sa Chathair" (Weariness / A hot day in the city) tells of the ennui of the well-off young Nóra de Búrca despite her cigarettes, French novels, and Chopin sonatas. At first thinking it too hot to go to Grafton Street, she decides to do so after breaking off with her imaginary boyfriend, and "a half-hour later she was drinking coffee in the 'Cairo' with her friend Margaret Carroll, discussing with her the shallowness, the foolishness, and the spitefulness of men."[159] The doings of some of those young men were chronicled in this same year in Séamus Ó Ceallaigh's "Beirt do Chuaidh i gCumann" (Two who fell in love), a story about a group of medical students living in the Dublin suburb of Drumcondra and their misadventures with a dog. Although the city is not particularly important in the story, Ó Ceallaigh deals unself-consciously in Irish with issues of social class and educational background.[160] In 1921, León Ó Broin, whose early enthusiasm for the work of Ó Conaire has already been noted, published two urban stories, neither important. The first, "Cúrsaí Grádha: Seanchas agus Aoitheó" (The course of love: Conversation and the fever point), is a

157. Seán Ó Faoláin, "Teach" (A house), *An Grianán: Páipéar Cinn Bhliadhna do Ghaedhealaibh Chorcaighe, Craobh Naoimh Fionn-Bharra i gCorcaigh* (The sunny chamber: An annual journal for Cork Gaels, St. Finbar's branch in Cork) [1917]: 6–8. There is only this one volume of *An Grianán* in the National Library of Ireland, whose catalogue lists it as "c. 1917," a date confirmed by internal evidence. Ó Faoláin was only seventeen, but he had already published pieces in English and knew Irish well by this time.

158. "Annsan do thug sé feuchaint mór-timcheall air agus go mall righin, do shuidh sé síos agus do thosnuigh sé ar a lámhaibh do ghóradh ag an dteine, agus é ag gáirídhe i gcogar leis féin. . . . Nach air a bhí an t-ádh . . . "

159. *Misneach*, 21 August 1920. "Leath-uair ina dhiaidh sin bhí sí ag ól caifé sa 'gCairo' i dteannta a caraid Maighréad Ní Chearbhaill agus ag cur síos léi ar mhí-dhoimhneas, ar amadántacht, is ar nimhneacht na bhfear."

160. *Branar* 1, no. 5 (February 1920): 207–17.

harmless tale of Gaelic Leaguers in love in an unnamed city that is obviously Dublin.[161] The second, "Árus na nGábhadh" (The house of perils) is a story of the Black and Tan War dealing with a group of IRA men holding a beseiged Dublin suburban house, their escape from it to refuge in another house, and the main character's meeting with the ghost of his grandfather, who had fought in 1798. In the end, the whole adventure turns out to have been a dream.[162]

In Seán Ua Ceallaigh's amusing 1917 story "An Ceithearnach is a Chéile" (The Kerne and his wife), a boorish countryman and his spouse arrive dirty and with no luggage at the most fashionable hotel in Dublin, take the most expensive room after an elevator ride that terrifies the wife, order an enormous meal after asking for a Gaelic menu in place of the French one they can't read, and in general behave in an outlandish manner, scandalizing the quality (an Galántas), but always paying without question and tipping lavishly before departing into legendary status on an ass cart.[163] Most Gaelic writers on urban themes must have shared the couple's sense of being somewhat at sea in exotic surroundings, but few had their unflappable self-possession. Many may have sensed that even in the creative works we have been discussing, the language itself could seem to act as a barrier, isolating writers like Ó Conaire, "Conán Maol," and particularly Ryan from the urban existence that they themselves were actually living. In this sense both these authors and their colleagues intimidated into silence on urban themes were the first victims of what the contemporary Gaelic novelist Diarmaid Ó Súilleabháin has called "the schizophrenic state of the Gaelic novelist" (staid scitsifréineach an úrscéalaí Ghaeilge), a condition brought on by trying to write in Irish of a life lived in English.[164] With considerable nerve these literary trailblazers may have proved that Irish could deal with city life, but they had by no means established that it could do so naturally or comfortably. That challenge was to be taken up most actively by three writers, all of whom were to have long careers and two of whom were to dedicate themselves to stretching the capabilities of the Irish language.

Some of Piaras Béaslaí's diverse literary output from our period is concerned with urban life, although of the original plays he wrote be-

161. *Banba* 1, no. 1 (May 1921): 41–44.
162. *Banba* 1, no. 3 (July 1921): 217–23. Ó Broin wrote a series of essays on Dublin in 1919 and 1920 in which he praised the neighborliness, courage, and patriotism of its citizens. See "Baile Átha Cliath," *Misneach*, 19 December 1919; 10, 24 January 1920.
163. *Irish Weekly Independent*, 10 March 1917.
164. "*An Uain Bheo*: Focal ón Údar" (*An Uain Bheo*: A word from the author), *IMN* (1972): 67.

fore 1921 all have country settings with the exception of the historical drama *Coramac na Cuile*, and it was not until later, in works like *Blúire Páipéir* (A piece of paper) (1937) and *An Fear Fógraidheachta* (The advertising man) (1938) that he put the urban middle class on the Gaelic stage. Of his short stories, "Tír na nÓg i bPort Láirge" (Tír na nÓg in Waterford) (1917) and "Fleadh na Réaltann" (The festival of the stars) (1918) have urban settings, but both are more concerned with journeys of the imagination than with depictions of everyday life in Waterford or Dublin. The same could be also said of his best-known urban story, the fanciful "Tram an Taidhrimh" (The dream tram) (1925), in which an unassuming Dublin clerk boards the Rathmines tram and ends up in a harem in Teheran.[165]

Béaslaí's only novel, *Astronár*, would seem to fall only barely within the time frame of this chapter, for it was serialized in the *Weekly Freeman* beginning in March 1921 and not published as a book until 1928. However, in his preface to that book, Béaslaí informs us that he began the novel as early as 1899 and had it finished by 1912.[166] Since he also states that he left that 1912 work virtually unrevised apart from minor linguistic changes, it may properly be regarded as appropriate to our discussion. The novel's subject and theme explain Béaslaí's insistence on dating its evolution with such precision. *Astronár* recounts the attempt of the eponymous protagonist to liberate "Amora," his fictional eastern European homeland, from the foreign oppression of "Kratónia." No Irish reader taking up the work in 1921 or 1928 could avoid reading it as an allegory of the Irish struggle or even as a roman à clef giving Béaslaí's impressions of his revolutionary comrades. Such a reading was, however, explicitly ruled out by the author in 1921 on grounds of the novel's true date of composition: "I wrote this novel nine years ago, when no one had any idea of the extraordinary events that were to happen in Ireland thereafter. That is no small confirmation that it is no allegory, and that it does not refer to contemporary affairs."[167]

---

165. His stories are collected in *Earc agus Áine agus Scéalta Eile.*

166. "Rémh-Rádh" (Preface) to *Astronár* (Baile Átha Cliath: Muinntir C.S. Ó Fallamhain, Teo., i gcomhair le hOifig an tSoláthair, 1928), iii. He also refers to the novel in one of his contributions to the *SF* debate on urban literature in Irish. See "Language and Literature," *SF*, 30 March 1912.

167. "Rémh-Rádh," iii. "Naoi mbliadhna ó shin iseadh chumas an t-úrsgeul so, nuair ná raibh éan choinne ag éinne leis na heuchta do thuit amach i nÉirinn na dhiaidh sin. Ní beag son de dheimhniú ná fuil éan fhabhal-sgeul ann, ná éan tagairt do chúrsaí na haimsire seo." Béaslaí himself saw the novel primarily as a *Bildungsroman*, "a picture of the mind of a young man becoming acquainted with a world at variance with his opinions and education" (peictiúir . . . de mheón fir óig agus é ag cur aithne ar saoghal atá bunoscionn le na

Nevertheless, if *Astronár* is not a retropective assessment of the recent past, it offers a fascinating and often prescient insight into the internal ideological and tactical debates affecting the advanced nationalist movement in the decade before the Easter Rising.[168] For example, the Amoran exiles in the city of "Chrysopolis" are split into various feuding factions, among them the "Republicans" (Repobaileacánaigh), the "Royalists" (Rioghánaigh), the "Moderates" (Fuarthéhe, literally "Lukewarms"), and the "Reactionaries" (Iarghluaiseánaigh) (79–80).[169] Particulary heated are disagreements between old-guard physical-force nationalists and younger new-world-order socialists with their belief that "tribal hatred is an old superstition. It is nothing but a barbaric remnant of ancient times. Its time is past." To the traditionalists, such views are both heretical and irrelevant: "I don't know what 'tribal hatred' or 'new ways' or 'the freedom of the human race' means. I do know that I have seen things done by the Kratonians in Amora that would drive a person mad" (102).[170] Once revolutionary action is decided on, there is intense debate concerning timing and strategy between those stressing the need for meticulous preparation and those who dismiss such counsel as timid and defeatist, and who want to take an immediate stand even if it be only a symbolic blood sacrifice. Astronár speaks for the radicals in words and images strikingly reminiscent of those of Pearse in "The Fool" (1915): "I am about to risk death. These other men will stay out of danger in this foreign city, talking and planning and procrastinating. If I fail, I will pay for it; they will say

---

thuairmí is lena theagasc). In the novel Astronár is as unlucky in love as he is in politics. Nevertheless, while he is compelled to face the real world he never compromises with it, so that, as Béaslaí comments, "the question is left unsettled as to which of them, himself or the 'sensible' people, is more correct; but it is clear that neither of them is entirely right." (Fágtar an cheist gan réidhteach ciaca aga féin nó ag lucht na "céille" a bhí an chuid ba mhó den cheart; ach is follus ná raibh iomlán an chirt ag ceachtar díobh.) See "Rémh-Rádh," iii–iv.

168. Tracing a development over time in Béaslaí's views on heroism, Pádraig Ó Siadhail finds his chronology "a slight problem" (fadhb bheag) and expresses his "suspicion" (amhras) about Béaslaí's claim to have left his 1912 (and earlier) original largely unchanged in the later published versions. See Ó Siadhail, "Gaiscigh, Gaigí agus Guamóga: Téama an Laochais i Scríbhinní Cruthaitheacha Phiarais Bhéaslaí" (Heroes, fops, and pretty girls: The theme of heroism in the creative writings of Piaras Béaslaí), *IMN* (1990): 137–54.

169. All citations here will be from the book version of the novel.

170. The young argue "sean-phiseóg iseadh fuath na dtreabh . . . níl ann ach iarsma barbardha ón sean-aimsir. Tá a ré caithte." The traditionalists' answer is "Níl a fhios agam cad do chialluigheann 'fuath na dtreabh' ná 'slighthe nuadha' ná 'saoirse an chine dhaona.' . . . Tá fhios agam go bhfeaca nithe á dheunamh age sna Kratóniaigh i nAmora do chuirfadh duine as a mheabhair."

'Poor Astronár was out of his mind,' and they will go on plotting their conspiracy. . . . They are incapable of making a mad leap into the darkness—and we must make that leap if we want to free Amora."[171] In the end, Astronár's plan to seize the principal buildings, including "the Castle," in the Amoran capital of Liparon foreshadows the strategy for Easter 1916, although the utter failure of the attempt is more like that that befell Emmet's insurrection: "The only result of our effort was a bit of fighting in the streets of the city and the ineffectual attack we made on the Kratonian fort. Around a dozen of our men were killed and forty of them wounded and the vast majority were prisoners of the Kratonians."[172]

Not surprisingly, most of Astronár's political plotting and organizing takes place in an urban setting, a shabby Amoran ethnic ghetto in the "Olbian" city of Chrysopolis. Astronár himself is, however, a country boy from the mountainous coastal region of Klydóna, and it is through the eyes of this uprooted rural narrator that the urban Béaslaí depicts the cities in the novel. On the whole, Astronár simply takes for granted the diversity and freedom that make possible his political agitation, as he does the various cultural and social activities, plays, operas, and dances, of which he on rare occasions avails.[173] His is not, however, a familiarity based on any sense of belonging; urban life always remains alien to Astronár:

> I often went that way, past the fort with the big guns and along the twisting uneven path up to Ailéní's Tower, with my heart tired of the life of the city, of the injustice and the oppression that go with it. I often stood on the top of the hill looking back at a world that did not agree with me before I headed toward the woods to reach a world suited to me. I would make a

171. P. 139. "Táimse chun dul i gcontabhairt an bháis. Fanfaidh na fir eile seo slán ó bhaoghal san chathair iasachta so, ag caint is ag tionnsgnamh is ag cur nithe ar cáirde. Má theipeann orm, is mise dhíolfaidh as; deurfaid siad 'As a mheabhair a bhí Astronár bocht,' agus leanfaid siad leó ag beartú a gcomh-cheilge. . . . Níl ionnta léim bhuile a thabhairt san doircheacht—agus caithfimíd an léim sin a thabhairt má's mian linn Amora a shaoradh."

172. See 174 and 199. "Ní raibh de thoradh ar ár saothar ach roint troda i sráideannaibh na cathrach agus an ionnsuidhe gan éifeacht a dheineamair ar an nDún Kratóniach. Bhí tuairim dosaon dár bhfearaibh marbh agus dathad aca leóinte agus a bhformhór mór na bpríosúnachaibh ag na Kratóniacha."

173. He does not, however, avail himself of the services of the brothel discreetly mentioned in the novel, "Halla Circé go raibh droch-cháil air" (Circe's hall of ill-repute). See *Astronár*, 129.

path for myself through the woods, for I did not like the common road(95).[174]

Even as a young man in the capital of his native country, Astronár suffers from a textbook case of urban alienation: "I looked at the lights in the houses of the city, I heard the music and the laughter of the people far from me, and a kind of sorrow and loneliness came over me. I felt that I was a person apart, that I did not understand the world and that the world did not understand me. At last I headed toward the very heart of the city, not knowing where I would go or what I would do (17).[175] And all cities remain for him the "enemy" (97), places where falsehood of all kinds is supreme (36) and where a meaningful spiritual life is all but impossible: "The person who lives amongst the crowds, controlled by the taboos and the prohibitions—laws, customs, manners, popular opinions, the influence of the company of his friends, the need for luxuries ruling his life—he gets many things as a result; but isn't it better to lose the great world and to save your own soul!"[176] Soulless indeed are Béaslaí's city dwellers in the novel, people who are almost without exception depicted as superficial, materialistic, snobbish, and cowardly. (See, for example, 62, 66–67, 152, 155.)

Introducing his first novel, Castar na Daoine ar a Chéile 'sní Chastar na Cnuic nó na Sléibhte (People meet, but the hills and mountains don't), serialized in the Irish Weekly and Ulster Examiner in 1915, Séamus Ó Grianna wrote: "In looking through the different Irish books recently published, it occurred to me that little attempt was being made to describe modern life in Irish—that the language was solely devoted to describing Finn McCool and other myths that had very little interest

---

174. "Ba mhinic dom ag gabháil na slighe sin, thar Dún na ngunaí mór, ar an gcosán casta achrannach suas go dtí Túr Ailéní, agus mo chroidhe go tuirseach de shaoghal na cathrach, den eugcóir agus den daorbhruid do bhain leis. Ba mhinic dom im sheasamh ar mhullach an chnuic, ag feuchaint siar ar an saoghal nár réidhtigh liom, sar a dtabharfainn aghaidh ar an gcoill chun saoghal oireamhnach do bhaint amach dom féin. Do dheininn amach cosán dom fhéin tríd an gcoill, mar níor thaitn an gnáth-bhóthar liom."

175. Béaslaí, Astronár, 17. "D'fheuchas ar na soillse i dtighthe na cathrach, d'éisteas le ceól agus gáirí na ndaoine i bhfad uaim, agus tháinig sadhas bróin agus uaignis orm. Mhothuigheas go rabhas im aonarán, nár thuigeas an saoghal agus nár thuig an saoghal mé. Fé dheireadh thugas aghaidh ar cheartlár na cathrach, agus gan fhios agam cá ngeobhainn ná cad do dheunfainn." See also 63, 86, 96.

176. P. 98. "An té mhaireann imeasg na sluaighte fé smacht na ngeas is na gcol—dlighthe, nósa, beusa, tuairmí an phobuil, rian caidrimh a chompánach, gádh le soghlaistí ag riaradh a shaoghail—faghann sé a lán nithe dá bhárr; ach nach feárr an domhan mór do chailleamhaint ach t'anam féin do shlánú!"

for the ordinary Irish reader, and that if Irish is to become a popular language it must become a vehicle of modern thought."[177] Although the heroine of this love story full of implausible coincidences is a Howth woman and her fiancé a medical student at University College, Dublin,[178] and although both spend time in New York, where he runs a hospital and she is a nurse, the novel gives us little sense of either city. It does, however, provide several opportunities for the language to serve as "a vehicle of modern thought." First of all, the main characters are well-educated, middle-class people able to afford and be comfortable with trans-Atlantic travel (although that comfort is diminished by their decision to take the *Titanic!*) Second, some of the topics they consider would startle the native speakers of An tAthair Peadar or "An Seabhac." For example, the heroine Caitlín Nic Shuibhne has read "Carl Marks," and at one point she and her mother discuss his ideas, with Caitlín saying that while she doesn't agree with "everything that gentleman said," she also rejects uncritical opposition to his views, for "it is my opinion that the truth lies somewhere in the middle between Marx and those who oppose him."[179] Third, the novel deals with issues of real contemporary relevance, as the hero Séamus Ó Domhnaill and Caitlín attend a recruiting rally in the Rotunda and are convinced to offer their services to the imperial forces after hearing a speech arguing that the Irish must prove they merit the Home Rule promised them: "'England's difficulty is Ireland's opportunity.' That is true this time as well, but not in the original sense of the saying. This is the time for Ireland to show England what we can do, and that we are worthy of having good laws given to us."[180] But what is in some ways most interesting about the novel from our perspective is Ó Grianna's willingness to satirize

177. Quoted by Nollaig Mac Congáil, "Úrscéal Dearmadta le Máire" (A forgotten novel by "Máire"), in *Scríbhneoirí Thír Chonaill* (Donegal writers) (Baile Átha Cliath: Foilseacháin Náisiúnta, Teoranta, 1983), 123. The quote originally appeared in the *Irish Weekly and Ulster Examiner* for 24 July 1915. I would like to thank Dr. Mac Congáil not only for drawing my attention to this novel but also for generously providing me with a full typescript of it, from which all citations here will be taken. The irony of Ó Grianna's championing this cause will be evident in Chapter 8.

178. The male protagonist seems to come from the Gaeltacht, but his home place is never specifically identified. The heroine's parents are said to be Irish speakers.

179. *Irish Weekly and Ulster Examiner*, 4 September 1915. "Acht 'sé mo bharamhail go bhfuil an ceart i náit éiginteacht i lár báire eadar Marks agus an dream atá i n-éadan."

180. *Irish Weekly and Ulster Examiner*, 4 December 1915. "'Trioblóid na Sasana, sin áimear na hÉirinn.' Tá sin fíor an iarraidh seo fosta, acht ní sa' chéad chéill a bhí leis an chaint. Seo am na hÉireann le taisbeáint de Shasana goidé a thig linn a dhéanamh, agus gur fiú sinn dligheadh maith a thabhairt dúinn."

motifs from Gaelic rural fiction, as when the story's jokester, Colm Ó
Baoighill, fantasizes about the life the three friends will have when they
return to Ireland: "A black clay pipe for us men, and we sending smoke
to the rafters; a cake of oat bread on the hearthstone; the woman of the
house carding wool, and the old man talking a while about faction
fighting and another while about the wee people."[181]

The difference between Ó Grianna's first and second novels illustrates
memorably what Easter 1916 meant for nationalist Ireland. *Mo Dhá
Róisín* (My two Rosaleens) (1920) is a tale of insurrection and heroic
sacrifice that follows the growing political awareness of Labhras Ó
Baoighill, a young native speaker from the Donegal Rosses, and his
seemingly hopeless love for the other Róisín in his life, a Dublin Gaelic
Leaguer and fervid patriot named Róise Ní Chearbhail. With Róise's
help, Labhras is able to get some education as well as a teaching post
with the league in Dublin. On the whole, the capital plays little active
role in the story, although we do find perfunctory condemnations of
urban artificiality in contrast to the authentic beauty of the world Labhras left behind: "Rain does not become the town as it does the country.
It suits the fields and the trees and the flowers. It is beautiful when it
falls as a bright white foam in the waterfall of the river. It is nice as a
trimming of snow on the hills on a winter's evening, or as shining
drops on the grass on a summer's morning. But it turns the city into
wretched muck. That's the way some of God's whole work fits together.[182]

Labhras himself is pushed to paranoia by his feeling of alienation:
"Labhras found the ways of the city baffling at first. He struggled with
everything, and he thought that everyone was watching him—that
that's all there was on their minds, watching to see what he would do
or say" (42).[183] Moreover, in a significant shift from most of his predecessors, Ó Grianna provided his protagonist no safe halfway house.

---

181. *Irish Weekly and Ulster Examiner*, 30 October 1915. "Píopa dubh cailce ag gach fear
againn, agus sinne ag cur toite go dtí na creathaighibh; bonnóg aráin choirce ar leic an
teallaigh; bean a' toighe ag cardáil, agus an sean duine tamall ag cainnt ar throid
bhataidhe, 'gus tamall eile ar na daoinibh beaga." See also his humorous vision of the
country wedding of Séamus and Caitlín in the installment for 13 November 1915.

182. *Mo Dhá Róisín* (Dún Dealgan: Preas Dhún Dealgan, n.d.), 44. "Ní thig fearthainn
don bhaile-mhór mar thig sí don tír. Foireann sí do na cuibhrinn agus do na crannaibh
agus do na blátha. Tá sí áluinn nuair atá sí ag tuitim anuas 'na cúbhar gheal bhán i n-eas
na h-abhann. Tá sí deas mar bhearradh sneachta ar na cnuic tráthnóna Gheimhridh, nó 'na
deóra loinnireacha ar an fhéar maidin Shamhraidh. Ach ghní sí claib bhocht don bhaile
mhór. Sin an dóigh a bhfuil cuid oibre Dé uilig ag cur le céile."

183. "Tháinig dóigheanna na cathrach achrannach chuig Labhras ar tús. Bhí sé i
n-aimhréidhtighe in gach rud, agus dar leis go rabh gach duine ag coimead air— gur sin
uile a rabh ar a n-intinn, ag breathnú goidé ghníodh sé nó deireadh sé."

Many of the Dublin Gaeilgeoirí of this novel are boorish snobs for whom the language is an irrelevant hobby or a pretext for summer holidays in the country:

> At this time the reputation and fame of the Green Branch had spread through Ireland on account of the work they were doing for the Irish language. And without a lie, they had earned a good share of that reputation. But as good as was their reputation, and as hard as was their work, they still were not so advanced that they could not make fun of young Labhras now and again. The Gaeltacht was good enough to visit in the summer. The native speaker was good enough for a visit or a night's entertainment, but in Dublin, it was hard not to laugh at him. The poor awkward bumpkin, why wasn't he clever enough to speak English like everyone else? (43)[184]

Forced to adapt to his new life, Labhras changes in many ways. For example, he becomes quite a dapper dresser, begins to speak what his father contemptuously dismisses as "Dublin Irish" (Gaedhilg Bhaile-Átha-Cliath), and looks down his nose at the poverty and even the customs of his native place (see 64, 74–75). It is, therefore, little surprise that the people of that place feel he has been corrupted by the capital: "A change, and a heavy one, had come over him. He was another man altogether, with even his Irish perceived as somewhat alien. He had brought many new things with him from the city— Roman Type, Simple Spelling, and many other things that we could make no sense of in Ceann-dubhrann" (75).[185] In one way, however, Ó Grianna clearly feels Labhras has changed for the better, as his experience with the intellectual tumult of urban life permits him a political sophistication far beyond that possible to the Gaeltacht dweller who never left

184. This passage follows immediately upon the one just cited. "Ins an am seo, bhí cliú agus cáil na Craoibhe Glaise ar fud na h-Éireann as an obair a bhí siad á dhéanamh ar son na Gaedhilge. Agus gan bhréig, thabhuigh sí giota mór don chliú chéadna. Ach maith is mar bhí a gcliú, agus cruaidh is mar bhí a gcuid oibre, ní rabh siad fhad 'un tosaigh go fóill is nach dtiocfadh leobhtha corr thamall magaidh a dhéanamh ar Labhras Óg. Bhí an Ghaedhealtacht maith go leór le teacht ar cuairt ann ins an t-Samhradh. Bhí an cainnteóir dúthchais maith go leór le tamall cuartaidheachta nó áirneáil a dhéanamh aige, ach i mBaile-Átha-Cliath, ba dheacair gan gáire a dhéanamh faoi. An úthairt bhocht aimlighe, cad chuige nach mbíonn sé géar-chúiseach agus Béarla labhairt mar dhuine eile?"

185. Ó Grianna himself had no use whatsoever for the linguistic innovations mentioned here. "Ach tháinig áthrach, agus ceann trom, air féin fosta. Bhí sé 'n fhear eile ar fad, nó gan fiú a chuid Gaedhilge nach rabh le h-aithne cineál coimhlightheach. Bhi cuid mhór de rudaí úra leis as an chathair—Cló Rómánach, Leitriú Simplidhe agus mórán eile nach rabh ciall againn dó i gCeann-dubhrann."

home. Thus the motives that lead to his heroic death in the fighting of Easter Week 1916 are incomprehensible to his former neighbors, who seem to espouse a fatalistic defeatism: "It was a tragedy for the poor boy the first day he ever went up to Dublin. There was never any sense at all in the idea that the English army could be beaten" (97).[186] Nonetheless, while Ó Grianna makes plain both that Labhras is a national hero and that he owes the commitment that motivated that heroism to his time in Dublin, the overall treatment of the city in this novel is an ambiguous and uneasy blend of ideologies, nativist and nationalist.

Appropriately enough, the first Gaelic writer to break with the restrictive stereotypes and to treat urban life with confidence from the inside was, at least indirectly, a protégé of Pádraic Ó Conaire. In 1917 Ó Conaire had proposed the establishment of a Gaelic book club to be called "An Ridireacht Liteartha" (the Literary Knighthood).[187] Obviously, the Irish people had more immediately pressing concerns on their minds at this time, and the project limped along for three years before finally expiring in 1920, at which time its literary catalogue consisted of one 59-page book, Liam Ó Rinn's Cad Ba Dhóbair Dó agus Sgeulta Eile (What nearly happened to him and other stories).[188] However disappointed some subscribers may have been with the return on their investment, this slim booklet may well have at least partially justified the high hopes that went into the creation of An Ridireacht Liteartha; in the words of Béaslaí, it gave them a book "you could read

---

186. "Agus ba taismeach a d'éirigh don bhuachaill sin an chéad lá ariamh a chuaidh sé go Baile-Átha-Cliath. Ní rabh ciall ar an dómhan ar scor a' bith le n-a shílstin go bhfuighfidhe buaidh ar arm na Sasana."

187. See, for example, Ó Conaire, "Ridireacht Nuadh: An bhFuil Míle Duine le Fagháil?" (A new knighthood: Are there a thousand people to be found?); "Cumann Nuadh Liteartha: Bhfuil Míle Léightheoirí le Fagháil?" (A new literary club: Are there a thousand readers to be found?); or "An Litridheacht Nuadh. Brostuighidh, A Ridirí" (The new literature: Hurry up, knights), in Aistí Uí Chonaire, 82–83, 84–85, 89–90. These essays originally appeared in ACS on 24 February and 3 and 17 March 1917 respectively. See also Gearóid Denvir's discussion of An Ridireacht Liteartha in "Aguisín II" (Appendix II), in Aistí Uí Chonaire, 271–79.

188. (Baile Átha Cliath: Sealy, Bryers & Walker, 1920). See C. B. Mac an tSaoi, "Gaeilgeoir Cathrach" (An urban Irish speaker), Agus 5, no. 11 (November 1965): 8–9; and Béaslaí's "Réamhrádh" (Preface) to Ó Rinn's essay collection So Súd (This and that) (Baile Átha Cliath: Oifig an tSoláthair, 1953), vii–xii. Seán Mac Réamoinn has written that Mo Chara Stiofán, Ó Rinn's book on Stephen McKenna, had a more profound effect on him at the time of its publication in 1939 than did Idir Shúgradh agus Dáiríre, Máirtín Ó Cadhain's first story collection that appeared in the same year. See Mac Réamoinn, "Branar le Cur" (Fallow land to be planted), Comhar 45, no. 10 (October 1986): 14.

. . . just as you would read a book in English, without thinking about the fact that what you were reading was in Irish.[189]

Dublin-born and -bred, Ó Rinn took a fine and perceptive pleasure in his native place, and many of his characters share his fascination with both the beauties and quirks of the city: "He stopped on O'Connell Bridge and looked around at the streets and at the Liffey, and the sight gladdened him. All the lights were lit in the streets and on the ships, and it seemed to him that the sky was one great blaze, and there was a great stillness."[190] Moreover, for his people, ordinary Dubliners and not Gaeltacht exiles or committed Gaelic Leaguers, the city is a comfortable and secure place in which they can structure their lives around urban routines as stable as those available to country folk. For example, one dapper young city gentleman delights in the familiar sights on a favorite walk over Butt Bridge: "He liked to look at the water and at the boats and at the many other things that are to be seen there on a summer Sunday morning with the sun high in the sky."[191]

Nowhere is Ó Rinn's originality in the treatment of urban themes more evident than in the very first story of the collection, where we find what at first glance seems a stereotypical Gaelic picture of big-city alienation:

There was neither star nor moon to be seen in the sky. He was lonely, troubled, and in despair. It seemed to him when he saw the sky dark and black above him that God himself was against him. He met no one he knew, and that made him more lonely and despairing. The people he saw walking past him weren't people at all, he thought, but shadows—no—spirits. . . . It

189. ("An Ciarruidheach Malluighthe"), "'An Ridireacht' / Gearr-Sgeulaidhe Nua" ("The Ridireacht" / A new writer of short stories), *Irish Weekly Independent*, 6 November 1920. "D'fheudfá na sgeulta so léigheamh díreach mar a léighfá leabhar Beurla gan cuimhneamh air gur Gaedhilg a bhí á léigheamh agat."

190. "An Caillichín Gránna" (The ugly little hag), in *Cad Ba Dhóbair Dó*, 24. "Do stad sé ar Dhroichead Uí Chonaill agus dféach sé mórthimpeall ar na sráideana agus ar an Life agus chuir an radharc áthas air. Bhí na soillse go léir ag lasadh ins na sráideana agus ar na loingeas, agus aon lasair mhór amháin ab ea an spéir, dar leis, agus bhí ciúnas mór ann."

191. "Níl mar a Síltar Bítar" (Things are not as they seem), in *Cad Ba Dhóbair Dó*, 57–58. The story first appeared under the pseudonym "An Connachtach Cantalach" in *FL* for 14 December 1918. "Ba mhaith leis bheith ag féachaint ar an uisce agus ar na báid agus ar a lán eile rudaí deasa a bhíon le feiscint ansan ar maidin Dé Domhnaig sa tsamhradh agus an ghrian go hárd ar an spéir." In his lyrical tribute to his native city in a later essay, Ó Rinn wrote of the Liffey's nightime beauty: "I take delight in standing on Butt Bridge to look at the lovely reflections of the lights in the water of the river." (Is aoibhinn liom seasamh ar dhroichead Butt ag féachaint ar scáileanna gleoite na soillse in uisce na habhann.) See Ó Rinn, "Baile Átha Cliath," in *So Súd*, 51.

seemed to him that he himself was only a spirit of the same sort, a troubled, tormented spirit, weary of the world, sick of itself and everything alive—no—of everything dead, since the world was, it seemed to him, a dead world.[192]

Ó Rinn does not, however, put these tormentedly self-obsessed thoughts into the soul of a tormented protagonist like Ó Conaire's Mícheál Ó Maoláin or Ryan's Caoimhghín Ó Cearnaigh. Rather, they flit incongruously through the superficial mind of a recently jilted young man whose brief flirtation with the grand gesture of suicide is ended when he remembers a pretty and apparently available redhead.[193] In this short and unassuming comic episode Ó Rinn cleverly and no doubt consciously subverted one of the calcified conventions of modern Gaelic literature, and while he hardly put an end to the one-dimensional and stereotypical presentation of urban life in Irish, he at least offered a challenging alternative and made clear that in future Gaelic writers would have to earn their alienation.

A central theme throughout this book has been that while many important answers may have eluded the pioneers of the Gaelic literary movement in the first decades of this century, they did ask most of the right questions. Nowhere was this more true than with regard to their treatment of urban themes. They faced the challenge of creating a new terminology for a new environment, they explored the reactions of rural Irish speakers to a bafflingly different worldview, and perhaps most important they, particularly in the person of Liam Ó Rinn, attempted to show that city writers who had learned the language could deal authentically in Irish with the life they knew best. The fact that neither they nor anyone since has found entirely adequate solutions to these central problems in no way invalidates the contribution of writers like Ó Conaire, Ó Séaghdha, Ryan, Béaslaí, or Ó Rinn.[194] Furthermore,

---

192. "Cad Ba Dhóbair Dó?" in *Cad Ba Dhóbair Dó,* 5–6. "Ní raibh réalt ná gealach le feiscint ar an spéir. Bhí uaigneas air, agus buairt, agus éadóchas. Dar leis, nuair a chonnaic sé an spéir go dubh dorcha os a chionn, bhí Dia féin ina choinnibh. Níor casadh leis éinne ab aithnid dó. Chuir san tuille uaignis agus tuille éadóchais air. Na daoine chonnaic sé ag siúl thairis, níor dhaoine iad in aon chor, dar leis, ach scáileana, ní hea ach sprideana. . . . Ní raibh ann féin, dar leis, ach sprid den tsórt san, sprid bhuartha chráitte, cortha den tsaoghal, bréan de féin agus de gach ní beo—ní hea ach de gach ní marbh, mar ní raibh sa tsaoghal, dar leis, ach saoghal marbh."

193. "Cad Ba Dhóbair Dó?" 8.

194. Doubts do most certainly persist. We have already noted Diarmaid Ó Súilleabháin's sense of "the schizophrenic state of the Gaelic novelist" in an English-speaking Ireland. One such novelist, Pádraig Ua Maoileoin, has written: "If I had any courage I myself would be writing about the life of Dublin because that's what I understand best."

this ongoing tension between an endangered rural language and a still alien though ever more pervasive urban value system has generated and continues to generate some of the most aesthetically and intellectually challenging creative efforts in modern Irish. Writers like Ó Ríordáin, Ó Direáin, Ó Cadhain, Ó hUid, Ó Néill, Ó Tuairisc, Ó Súilleabháin, and most recently Mac Annaidh, to name but a few, the direct descendants of "Beirt Ghaedhilgeoirí 'na gComhnaidhe 'sa Chathair," are still striving to realize the bold optimism of "Fear na Cathrach": "Urban life is not antagonistic to the spirit of any language."[195]

<hr>

(Dá mbeadh aon mhisneach agamsa is ag scríobh ar shaol Bhaile Átha Cliath a bheinn féin mar is é is fearr a thuigim.) See "Scríbhneoirí Chorca Dhuibhne" (Corca Dhuibhne writers), in Ár Leithéidí Arís (Our like again) (Baile Átha Cliath: Clódhanna Teoranta, 1978), 58. Characteristically, Máirtín Ó Cadhain did summon up just such courage: "Some of us have long been saying that there is no special difficulty or artificiality about depicting the town. Of course you must want to do it and you must have command of the place, command of your craft, and command of the Irish language." (Is fada cuid againn ag rá nach bhfuil aon deacracht ná mínádúrthacht ar leith faoi chur síos a dhéanamh ar an mbaile mór. Caithfidh, dar ndóigh, fonn a dhéanta a bheith ort, thú taithithe ar an áit, taithithe ar do cheird agus taithithe ar an nGaeilge.) See Ó Cadhain, "Úrscéalaíocht" (The writing of novels), Irish Times, 12 January 1955, quoted by Gearóid Denvir in Cadhan Aonair: Saothar Liteartha Mháirtín Uí Chadhain (Lone bird: The literary work of Máirtín Ó Cadhain) (Baile Átha Cliath: An Clóchomhar, 1987), 97. The poet Máirtín Ó Direáin was less confident than Ó Cadhain. See his "An File Gaeilge is Saol na Cathrach" (The Gaelic poet and urban life), in Feamainn Bealtaine (May seaweed) (Baile Átha Cliath: An Clóchomhar, 1971), 86–88. The views of the poet Seán Ó Ríordáin, whose themes and language struck some critics and readers as exotic, can be found in "Teangacha Príobháideacha" (Private languages), Scríobh 4 (1979): 13–22, esp. 21–22. For a discussion of the approaches to the challenge adopted by various writers in the first decades of the Revival, see Ní Dhonnchadha, An Gearrscéal sa Ghaeilge, 211–324. For a discussion of more practical aspects of the difficulties involved in adapting the language to city concerns, see Aingeal de Brúch, "An Ghaeilge agus an Chathair" (The Irish language and the city), Crane Bag 5, no. 2 (1981): 12–17.

195. "Fear na Cathrach," "Gaedhilg na Cathrach," FL, 16 July 1898. "Ní chuireann beatha na cathrach i n-aghaidh spioraide aon teangadh."

8

Literature in Limbo

Gaelic Prose from Easter 1916 to the Anglo-Irish Treaty of 1921

"Where have all the writers gone after our twenty-five years?" asked Risteárd Ó Foghludha in the *Irish Rosary* for October 1919.[1] The question must have been rhetorical as its answer was not far to seek. Even more than most aspects of Irish life the Gaelic movement had been changed utterly by Easter 1916, the disruptive impact of which was given graphic expression on the masthead of the first issue of *An Claidheamh Soluis* to appear after the Rising, an issue datelined 29 April 6, 13, 20, and 27 May and dominated by political and military news. Henceforth the energies previously radiated through a spectrum of enterprises, social, intellectual, cultural, and literary, would be focused ever more narrowly and intensely on the "National Question."

Political involvement was not, of course, anything new for the Revival. Most notably the battle for Irish as a required subject at all levels of the educational process had always been a political campaign in every

---

1. "An Cúinne Gaedhilge" (The Gaelic corner), *Irish Rosary* 23, no. 10 (October 1919): 760. "Cá bhfuil na scríbhneóirí go léir tar éis ár gcúig bhliadhna fichead?"

sense of the term, requiring not only the organization of individual sympathisizers, but also the mobilization of public bodies like county councils, and negotiation with the Roman Catholic hierarchy and agencies of the imperial bureaucracy alike. On a more literally militant note, it was in *An Claidheamh Soluis* in November 1913 that Mac Néill published "The North Began" and so set in motion the process that led to the birth of the Irish Volunteers. Yet somehow Douglas Hyde as league president managed for years to maneuver through the partisan maze and find a viable modus vivendi between the personal nationalist and even separatist aspirations of many league menbers and his own and the organization's explicit commitment to a "nonpolitical" public stance. His ultimate failure and resignation from office when the league officially endorsed the principle of "a free Irish nation" as a policy goal at the Dundalk Oireachtas of 1915 only serves to underscore how long he had held the line in what in retrospect can only seem a doomed cause. Indeed, his own wonderment at what he had accomplished and for how long can be read between the lines of a December 1915 letter to Lady Gregory: "I am no longer President of the Gaelic League. I kept them together for 22 years, but the war was too much for me."[2]

Hyde was not the only major revivalist troubled by the growing influence on the language and cultural movement of advanced and eventually physical-force republicanism. Literary figures as diverse as An tAthair Peadar, Henebry, Tomás Ua Concheanainn, and Laoide were to remain aloof from the patriotic fervor of younger colleagues like Pearse, Béaslaí, and Thomas Ashe. Motives here were no doubt individual and complex, but concern about the very identity and mission of the Revival must have had an important influence. In hindsight we can see a real decline in creative innovation, effort, and achievement after the first years of this century, a decline that to a considerable extent coincided with the end of Pearse's inspirational and hortatory tenure as regular and full-time editor of *An Claidheamh Soluis*. Not surprisingly, contemporaries engaged in the many crusades of that time were slower to register this incipient literary stagnation; by 1913, however, the more perceptive were concerned, with Seán Ó Caomhánaigh putting the point bluntly: "There is no doubt but that the literary side of the movement is being greatly neglected."[3] In the following year, one "BLFSN" devoted his *An Claidheamh Soluis* editorial to the subject of "Leabhair"

2. Letter to Lady Gregory, 21 December 1915, Fionán Mac Coluim Papers, National Library of Ireland, MS. 22,957.
3. "Nidhthe Gaedhealach" (Gaelic matters), *SF*, 4 January 1913. "Níl aon amhras ná go bhfuil faillighe mhór dá thabhairt i dtaobh na litiridheachta den nGluaiseacht."

(Books), pondering the reason for their paucity and assigning blame as he saw fit: "It's not the committees but the writers who are negligent. Almost all of them have come to a full stop. Apart from An tAthair Peadar, the world would be unaware that there have been any Gaelic writers in Ireland for the past year. . . . For the past year our writers have been at a stop that it is difficult to understand. What has caused it?"[4]

His question was to be asked with greater frequency, urgency, and cause in the years after the Rising. Even a glance through the pages of the league's weekly organ under its various post-Rising titles—*An Claidheamh Soluis, Fáinne an Lae,* and *Misneach*—shows that while literary issues were still discussed, on occasion at length and in some depth, and while individual works of interest and merit were published, the quantity of original prose fell off dramatically, so that several weeks could pass with no new work whatsoever appearing amid the columns of news and political commentary. Needless to say, the situation with regard to books was even more dire. A striking number of "reviews" in the post-Rising press were in effect appreciations of older titles, sometimes, but by no means exclusively, on the occasion of their reissue. For example, the 18 June 1921 issue of *Misneach* dicusses Ó Conaire's *An Chéad Chloch* and Mac Fhionnlaoich's *Conchubhar Mac Neasa* (both from 1914).[5]

Almost as abundant as new stories and books were explanations, excuses, and accusations for their scarcity, which, however different in focus and / or target, agreed on one basic fact: "Most of the people involved with the Irish language are blind, or half-blind, with regard to the books that already exist, and cold and indifferent about providing any more."[6] *An Claidheamh Soluis* offered a dispassionate analysis of the problem in a 1917 editorial comment: "Irish books were bought on principle by the early Gaelic Leaguers, and as these enthusiasts have a fairly large collection they don't buy largely now. More recent students are content with their text books, and don't look for nor expect to find pleasant or suitable reading in Irish. This is not good for them nor for

---

4. *ACS*, 18 July 1914. "Ní h-iad na coistí ach na sgríobhnóirí atá faillightheach. Tá stad tagaithe ionnta go léir beagnach. Ach an t-Athair Peadar amháin, ní h-eol do'n saoghal go bhfuil scríobhnóir Gaedhilge i nÉirinn le bliadhain. . . . Tá stad éigin gur deacair a thuisgint tagaithe i n-ár lucht sgríobhnóireachta le bliadhain. Cad fé ndeara é?"
5. See the "Imeasg na Leabhar" (Among the books) column.
6. "Leabhra Gaedhilge / Bun-Chloch na hOibre go Léir" (Gaelic books / The foundation stone of all the work), editorial, *Misneach*, 1 January 1921. "Tá an chuid is mó de mhuintir na Gaedhilge dall, nú leath-dall ar na leabhra atá ann cheana féin, agus fuar faillitheach i dtaobh a thuille a sholáthar."

the publication of Irish."[7] But such objectivity was not possible for Piaras Béaslaí in a January 1920 *Misneach* editorial response to a letter from Séamus Ó Dubhghaill concerning the financial failure of his *Muinntear na Tuatha*.[8] Ó Dubhghaill had written: "There is no demand for reading in Irish that costs a shilling or more unless it is on some curriculum. If books were bought, books would be available." Béaslaí agreed: "That is the truth. There is no demand for a shilling's worth of reading in Irish, of no matter what kind. We have, it is to be feared, no respect for books or learning despite the reputation for scholarship we like to claim for ourselves as a nation."[9] Béaslaí took the offensive again with another sweeping indictment nine months later: "A considerable obstacle to the publication of Irish books—since the Gaelic League abdicated its plain duty in the matter—has been the ignorance, timidity, and, I fear, sometimes positive dishonesty of publishers." No such timidity deterred Béaslaí himself from facing the consequences of such derelictions: "As the result of inquiries I have ascertained that there are at least 150 good writers of Irish in Ireland who have published either books or contributions to periodicals. As their work was entirely gratuitous, met with scant recognition, and was done in the spare time of busy lives, it is not surprising that their output in general was not very considerable nor very important."[10]

---

7. "Aonach na Leabhar" (The book fair), *ACS*, 27 January 1917.

8. Béaslaí had just escaped from prison in England when *FL* became *Misneach* in November 1919. For that reason the first editor of *Misneach* was Colm Ó Murchadha, who returned the editorship to Béaslaí soon after the latter's return to Dublin. Lacking specific dates for this transfer, we cannot be absolutely certain that editorials from late 1919 and early 1920 are not the work of Ó Murchadha, a man who was a friend of Béaslaí and shared many of his progressive attitudes to literature.

9. "An Leabhar" (The book), editorial, *Misneach*, 16 January 1920. Ó Dubhghaill had written: "Níl éileamh ar luach sgillinge de leabhar, ná os a chionn, mura bhfuil sé ar Chlár Léighinn. Dá mbeadh ceannach ar leabhraibh do bheadh na leabhair le fagháil." Béaslaí commented: "Siní an fhírinne, níl éileamh ar luach sgillinge de leabhar Ghaedhilge is cuma cén saghas é. Níl aon toradh againn ar leabhra ná ar léigheann is baoghalach d'ainneoin an ainm sgoláireachta is maith linn a thabhairt orainn féin mar náisiún."

10. "Gaelic Critic's Work / Need for Favourable Atmosphere for Literary Propaganda," *Misneach*, 2 October 1920. The following week, Béaslaí, writing as "An Ciarruidheach Malluighthe," again criticized the publishers, but he also indicted his fellow Gaels for their failure to buy books and for their nitpicking criticism of those books they did buy. See "Leabhair Nua / Tuille ag Teacht" (New books / More coming), *Misneach*, 9 October 1920. In January of the following year, one publisher, Maunsel and Roberts, wrote to *Misneach* to explain the problems involved with marketing Gaelic books, most notably the abysmal sales figures. See "Foillsiú Leabhar / Taobh an Fhoillseora den Sgeul" (Publishing books / The publisher's side of the story), *Misneach*, 15 January 1921. Incidentally, it was in part the league's 1915 decision to sharply curtail its publishing

One writer whose work was both considerable and important shared Béaslaí's frustration and anger, and agreed on the whole with his analysis of the factors shaping the situation. Writing in 1920, Pádraic Ó Conaire complained that "after all that has been done for the Irish language for eighteen years, there is less interest in literature today than at any time throughout that period."[11] Several of Ó Conaire's most important contributions to this debate, essays like "Páistí Scoile: Bhfuil Siad ag Milleadh Nualitridheact na Gaedhilge?" (1917), "Lucht Leabhar agus Lucht Peann: Cén Donas Atá Ortha" (1920), and "Sgríobhnóirí agus a gCuid Oibre. An Easba Misnigh Atá Orra?" (1920), have already been discussed in previous chapters, as have his efforts to stimulate creative activity and reading through the book club An Ridireacht Liteartha. Worth additional emphasis here is the seriousness with which he viewed the situation and the fearlessness with which he took to task those he saw responsible, from the lukewarm revivalist unwilling to buy new books,[12] to Sinn Féin politicians offering hypocritical support for Irish in English,[13] to lazy or timid writers,[14] to the Gaelic League's "half-blind old men who are still in charge of the work if one can say that they are at work when no work is being done by them."[15] It was toward such pusillanimous league officials for whom the elementary and secondary school textbook had become the highest, if not the sole, standard of literary accomplishment that Ó Conaire's rage was most bitterly directed: "The league has done another great harm to the Gaelic writer and to the language itself. They lacked the courage or the bold-

---

activities to which he had devoted so many years of his life that caused Seosamh Laoide to withdraw from active involvement in the Revival. See Breathnach and Ní Mhurchú, *Beathaisnéis a hAon*, 36.

11. "Lucht Leabhar agus Lucht Peann: Cé'n Donas Ata Ortha?" in *Aistí Uí Chonaire*, 162. "Thar éis a bhfuil déanta ar son na Gaedhilge le ocht mbliadna déag, is lugha an tsuim cuirtear san litridheacht indiu ná cuireadh aon tráth i gcaitheamh an achair sin." This essay originally appeared in *Old Ireland*, 21 February 1920.

12. See Ó Conaire, "Lucht Leabhar agus Lucht Peann," 162.

13. See Ó Conaire, "Cáirde nach Cáirde: Sinn Féin agus an Teanga" (Friends who are not friends: Sinn Féin and the language), in *Aistí Uí Chonaire*, 169. This essay originally appeared in *Old Ireland*, 3 April 1920.

14. See Ó Conaire, "Sgríobhnóirí agus a gCuid Oibre: An Easba Misnigh Atá Orra?" in *Aistí Uí Chonaire*, 165.

15. Ó Conaire, "Lucht Leabhar agus Lucht Peann," 163. Ó Conaire blasted "na seanóirí leathchaochta seo atá i mbun na h-oibre fós má's féidir le duine a rádh go bhfuilid i mbun oibre agus gan aon obair ar siubhal aca." Commenting specifically on this essay, Béaslaí accepted Ó Conaire's assertion that Gaelic literature was "well behind" (go mór chun deiridh), but placed the blame squarely on the Gaelic writers and readers. See "Pádraic Ó Conaire agus Ceist na Leabhar / 'Seanóirí Leath-Chaochta'" (Pádraic Ó Conaire and the question of the books / "Half-Blind Old Men"), *Misneach*, 13 March 1920.

ness to publish anything but what would satisfy that nun of whom I spoke and those like her, and as a result the interest people had in Gaelic writing withered by degrees."[16] While he was overstating his case here—the league had after all published most of his own work—he was dead on target concerning the source of the problem. Nor was he alone in his opinion. Gaelic intellectuals like Mac Néill[17] and Béaslaí among others knew full well that the movement's own extraordinary success in introducing Irish into the classroom throughout our period had made education an obsession for many leaguers and politically active revivalists, who came to see the schools as the final if not in fact the exclusive battleground for the survival and spread of the language. One may, for example, note the apparently automatic link in the title of an 18 September 1920 front-page leader in *Misneach*: "The Work Before Us / Truly National Education / The Book Question" (An Obair Atá Romhainn / Oideachas Fíor-Náisiúnta / Ceist na Leabhar). In such a climate Ó Conaire's dread "tyranny of the school child" could only extend its stultifying dominion, as indeed it did after the foundation of the Free State ministry of education (ironically under the direction of Mac Néill).[18]

But to return to Ó Foghludha's question with which we began: if a few good men and women had accomplished so much sound literary work in the early years of the Revival, where were the talented few a quarter-century on when so much seems to have been going wrong? Many were dead—Breathnach, Father O' Hickey, and Henebry of natural causes; Pearse, MacDonagh, and Ceannt by firing squad; Thomas Ashe of forced feeding. Others, as a 1919 *Irish Rosary* correspondent stressed in an essay on the 1918 Oireachtas, were fully involved in the struggle for independence: "There is little to boast of with regard to the entries in the literary competitions, that is the written work, on account of the turmoil in the world today and the fact that some of our best writers are at present in prison or on the run."[19] Examples are abundant. Seán Ua Ceallaigh was a member and pro tem speaker of the first Dáil

16. Ó Conaire, "Sgríobhnóirí agus a gCuid Oibre," in *Aistí Uí Chonaire*, 166. Tá dí-oghbháil mhór eile déanta ag an gConnradh ar an sgríobhnóir Gaedhilge agus ar an teangain féin: ní raibh sé de mhisneach ná de dhánacht ionnta aon cheo chur faoi chló acht rudaí shásóchadh an bhean riaghalta sin ar ar labhair mé agus a leithéid agus ar an ádhbhar sin, chuaidh an tsuim bhí ag daoine i sgríobhnóireacht Ghaedhilge i laghad de réir a chéile."

17. See, for example, Tierney, *Eoin Mac Néill*, 38–39.

18. See Brown, *Ireland*, 40–43.

19. "Oireachtus, Éigse, etc." (Oireachtas, learning, etc.), *Irish Rosary* 22, no. 9 (September 1918): 698. "Níor mhaoidhte in éanchor feabhus na n-aistí insna comórtasaí lit-eardha, .i. an obair phinn, de dheasca an chorruidhe atá ar shaoghal an lae indiu, agus roinnt de sna scríbhneoirí is fearr atá againn do bheith fé ghlas nó ar gor fé láthair."

Éireann (the republican parliament), while "Pádraig na Léime" served as a judge in the underground revolutionary courts. Among Gaelic leaders who paid the price for such engagement in prison terms and / or life on the run were Mac Néill, Mhag Ruaidhrí, Blythe, Ó Rinn, Peadar Ó hAnnracháin,[20] and Béaslaí, whose tenure as editor of *Misneach* was punctuated by periods of incarceration. On a less stirring note, as has been indicated, several major figures like Hyde, Ua Concheanainn, and Laoide were unable to commit themselves fully to a movement whose goals and objects seemed to have shifted so rapidly and radically. Of course noninvolvement wasn't always an option either, as is evident from Risteárd Ó Foghludha's complaint in his introductory note to *Gaethe Gréine* II (Rays of sunshine II), the anthology of winning entries from the 1920 Oireachtas: "The enemy snatched some of the other prizewinning essays from the office."[21] The office of *An Lóchrann*, which had relocated to Cork City in 1916, fared even worse, being burned by the Black and Tans during the War of Independence.[22] It was, then, a difficult time and a different movement, one whose original cultural and literary agenda was to a considerable extent suspended for the duration. For most activists, this was, however, simply a fact of life. Thus in his report to the 1921 Ard-Fheis of the league, Pilib Ó Bhaldraithe, an organizer in Mayo whose own papers had been seized by British forces, wrote: "There were only four people along with myself at the largest meeting I held: the disturbed situation was the cause— and in addition the fact that the people who used to help me were too busy, some of them at least, doing great and important work, some of them on the run and all being pursued in the same way."[23]

Literary work did nonetheless continue throughout this period, although over and over one gets the sense of sitting in on the reinvention

20. Blythe and Ó hAnnracháin have left us the most detailed accounts of their tribulations at this time, Blythe in *Gaeil Á Múscailt* (Gaels awakening) (Baile Átha Cliath: Sáirséal agus Dill, 1973); Ó hAnnracháin in the two volumes of *Mar Mhaireas É* (As I lived it) (Baile Átha Cliath: Oifig an tSoláthair, 1953 and 1955).

21. "Oireachtas 1920," *Gaethe Gréine II: Oireachtas 1920* (Baile Átha Cliath: Connradh na Gaedhilge, n.d.), 5. "Roinnt aistí eile dár bhuaidh duais do sciob an namhaid leis as an oifig iad."

22. See Breathnach and Ní Mhurchú, *Beathaisnéis a Dó*, 145.

23. Quoted by Donncha Ó Súilleabháin in *Na Timirí i Ré Tosaigh an Chonartha, 1893–1927* (The organizers in the beginning period of the league, 1893–1927) (Baile Átha Cliath: Conradh na Gaeilge, 1990), 81. "An cruinniú ba mhó dá raibh agam ní raibh i láthair ach ceathrar agus mé féin; an saol corrach ba chiontach leis—agus ag cur leis sin na daoine a chabhródh liom, bhí siad róghnóthach cuid acu agus obair mhór thábhachtach dá dhéanamh acu, cuid eile ar a gcoimeád agus an tóir chéanna ar chuile cheann acu." The spelling here is the standard spelling as found in Ó Súilleabháin, not that of Ó Bhaldraithe's original report.

of the wheel, as old debates were resurrected, old positions retrenched, and old arguments rehashed in terms virtually indistinguishable from those of a decade or more before. It often seems, in Yogi Berra's phrase, to be "déjà vu all over again" with regard to issues like the literary uses of Irish history, myth, and saga; relations with Anglo-Irish contemporaries; the need for a Gaelic drama; and the potential value of translation. On the other hand, while the central ideological divide that is the principal subject of this study—that between nativism and progressivism—not surprisingly remained unresolved, there were definite shifts in both focus and emphasis, as well as some provocative new thinking.

Moreover, closure had come to at least one old isssue. Writing in the Donegal journal *An Crann* (The tree) in 1917, An tAthair Peadar was still fighting his favorite foe: "I often ask myself: who is doing the most harm [to the language]? And after some thought I have become convinced that no group of people has done more to weaken the Irish language than the people who refuse to put it down in books just as it is in the mouths of the old speakers. That man with the pen sitting in his chair and looking up into the sky in the expectation that he will see 'Classical Irish' up there somewhere, he is the one who is killing the Irish language."[24] He needn't have worried. Any such writer was much more likely to be lonely than lethal. With the deaths of O'Neill Russell (1908) and Henebry (1916), Father O'Reilly's withdrawal from the fray, and the simple fact that virtually every single modern writer was almost as dedicated to *cainnt na ndaoine* as Ua Laoghaire himself, "Classical Irish" was dead as a credible literary option.

Meanwhile, the battle continued unabated on other fronts, but there was a noticeable change in relative emphasis with regard to two central tenets of nativist orthodoxy: the link between the Irish language and a specifically Irish version of Roman Catholicism and that between the language and everything conveyed or implied by the word *Gaelachas*. In the post-Rising period, explicit identifications of the language with the faith were much less frequent, although such an identification does implicitly underlie a great deal of the writing in two contemporary Catho-

24. "Gaedhluinn 'Uasal'" ("Noble" Irish), *An Crann*, no. 4 (Feast of St. Adhamhnán 1917): 3. "Bímse gha fhiafraighe díom féin go minic, cé h-iad is mó a dheinean de'n díobháil, agus tar éis mo mhachtnaimh bíon sé buailte isteach am aigne nach bhfuil aon aicme daoíne is mó atá tar éis na Gaedhilge do lagú 'ná an mhuintir gur lag leo í chur síos i leabhraibh díreach mar atá sí i mbéalaibh na seanchainteóirí. An fear úd an chleite atá n-a shuidhe n-a chathaoír agus é ag feuchaint suas sa spéir ag brath air go bhfeicfadh sé 'Classical Irish' lastuas i n-áit éigin, siné atá ag marbhú na Gaedhluinne."

lic Gaelic periodicals, *Timthiridh Chroidhe Neamhtha Íosa*, in whose inaugural edition in 1911 there commenced serialization of An tAthair Peadar's "Eagla Dé" (The fear of God), a tract built on the theme of the language as protective barrier for the faith; and *An Síoladóir*, the journal of Cumann na Sagart nGaedhealach (the Organization of Gaelic Priests), first published in June 1920.

It was, then, in the post-Rising period that *Gaelachas* was elevated to the logically preeminent position in the nativist creed it was to hold for years. The most vigorous voice defining, defending, and advancing the nativist vision of *Gaelachas* throughout this period and into the first decades of independence was Séamus Ó Grianna, whose notion of "Art Gaedhealach" was noted in passing in Chapter 2. Developing Ua Laoghaire's and Henebry's concept of native speech as the principal key to the native wordview, Ó Grianna would move well beyond the linguistic claims of *cainnt na ndaoine* to establish it as a psychological, spiritual, and ultimately ideological touchstone. He began with an aggressive championing of Gaeltacht Irish against "the Irish of the books" (Gaedhilc na leabharthach) in *Fáinne an Lae* in January 1919, in the process kicking off a heated debate in which he gave as good as he got.[25] Over the next two years his ideas coalesced, so that his February 1921 *Misneach* essay on "Aistriú / Na Smaointe agus Ní hIad na Focail" (Translation / The thoughts and not the words) offered an epitomized philosophy of *Gaelachas*: "A large percentage of the people who are learning Irish still don't understand that there is a difference between the soul of an Englishman and the soul of a Gael—that the Englishman is deceitful, full of faults, scoundrelly, and false; and the Gael is straightforward, honest, and innocent. . . . The psychology of the Gael must be understood before his language can be understood and used properly."[26] Such an understanding and the proper use of the language it would make possible would form the basis for "Art Gaedhealach."

In another major essay in *Misneach* the same month, Ó Grianna ac-

25. "Ins an Ghaedhealtacht / Sgeuluidheacht" (In the Gaeltacht / Storytelling), *FL*, 11 January 1919. For a sampling of the controversy, see Mícheál Mac Giolla Coda, "Sceimhle ar Mháire" (Panic on Máire), *FL*, 18 January 1919; or "Seaghán," " 'Searbhfhoghantaí' / Na Gaedhilgeoirí" ("Servants" / The Irish speakers), *FL*, 1 February 1919.

26. "Aistriú / Na Smaointe agus Ní hIad na Focail," *Misneach*, 19 February 1921. "Cuid mhór de na daoinibh atá ag foghluim na Gaedhilge, ní thuigeann siad go bhfuil difir eadar anam an tSasanaigh agus ceann an Ghaedhil—go bhfuil an Sasanach béalachtach, lochtach, bíothmhanta, bréagach, agus an Gaedheal díreach, ionraice, soineanta. . . . Caithfear Psychology an Ghaedhil a thuigbheáil sul ar féidir a theangaidh a thuigbheáil agus a chur in úsáid mar is ceart."

knowledged that Irish was not fully in touch with modern life and needed to come "up to date" (suas chun dáta), an admission that, as we have seen, he had already made in his introductory remarks to his first novel *Castar na Daoine ar a Chéile 'sní Castar na Cnuic nó na Sléibhte*. But by 1921 he probably wished to leave this apprentice effort in obscurity for ideological as well as for political and artistic reasons, as he now argued that any such evolution of Gaelic literature must follow strictly native lines: "The Gaelic storytellers had an art of their own. They had a national way of telling a story. That art grew out of the life and out of the faith of the people. Our own life is not like that of England or France. Nor is our perception, our mind, our faith, or our outlook the same. For that reason it would be proper for us to preserve the art of the old storytelling as long as possible, and at the same time to fashion new words for the things that exist now that did not in their time." In this piece Ó Grianna was careful to ground his conservatism in a commonsense caution concerning disjunctive innovations for which the language, its traditional literature, and its native speakers were unprepared: "It is my opinion that the form of the traditional story should be kept alive and a Gaelic art spun out of it. We are told that this would hold Gaelic literature back, that it was asleep altogether for 300 years and should make up the deficit with a rush that would bring it up with the other languages. But it would seem to me dangerous to set it galloping with sleep still in its eyes. Perhaps it would fall into a bog-hole in its haste."[27] But elsewhere he could be less restrained, as in a May 1921 essay on "Cainnt na nDaoine / Shakespeare vs. an Duine Iargúlta" (The speech of the people / Shakespeare vs. the person from a remote place), in which he pronounced the competition a virtual draw if the countryman were a native Irish speaker, the sort of person whose speech in itself would be literature according to Ó Grianna's definition of litera-

27. "Art na hAimsire Seo / A Nós Féin ag an nGaedhilg" (The art of this time / Irish has its own way), *Misneach*, 26 February 1921. "Bhí art daobhtha féin ag seanchuidhthibh Gaedhilge. Bhí dóigh Náisiúnta aca leis an sgéal innse. D'fhás an t-art sin amach as saoghal agus as creideamh na ndaoine. Ní hionann ár saoghal féin agus ceann na Sasana nó na Fraince. Ní hionann ár mbreathnughadh, ár n-intinn, ár gcreideamh, nó ár leagan amach. Ar an ádhbhar sin ba chóir dúinn art na sean-sgéaluidheachta a choinneáil fad agus b'fhéidir é, agus ins an am chéadna focla úra a chumadh fá choinne na rudaí atá ann anois agus nach rabh ann an uair sin. . . . Do réir mo bharamhla-sa, ba cheart cruth an seansgéil a choinneáil beo, agus art Gaedhlach a shníomh amach as. Deirtear linn go gcoinneochadh seo ar gcúl litridheacht na Gaedhilge. Go rabh sí 'na codladh ar feadh thrí chéad bliadhain agus gur cheart díthe a breis a thabhairt isteach anois le rúideóig a d'fhágfadh i bhfus ag na teangthachaibh eile í. Ach shílfinn go bhfuil sé contabhairteach a cur ar chosaibh anáirde agus an codladh in a súilibh. B'fhéidir gur síos in súmaire a thuitfeadh sí leis an deifre."

ture as "the speech that reveals God neatly" (an chanamhaint a ghníos Dé a léiriú go deismeir).[28] The nativism espoused by Ó Grianna was not left unchallenged. Pádraic Ó Conaire continued to promote an equally aggressive literary progressivism in his periodical contributions throughout the post-Rising period, writing, for example, in February 1920:

> I beseech you, writers, to be bold and courageous, without timidity or fear in face of life, to reveal the truth you know, no matter how that truth offends certain people. You, writers, the teachers and leaders of the people, look at the life that is clear to everyone, look at the life that is not clear to the vast majority, and explain it to us. If you do that, writers, if you express yourselves without timidity or fear in face of the powers that love the half-darkness and the half-truths and the broad easy road, as sure as there is a sun in the sky, you will be listened to and your life will bear fruit.[29]

Even more important than his essays and exhortations was his creative example, as is evident from a review of his *Béal an Uaignis* by "Glugar" in April 1921. Having traced the possible influence on Ó Conaire of Ambrose Bierce, the Russians, Thoreau, Synge, and George Borrow, "Glugar" drew the moral: "I hope I am right in that opinion, for it is high time for Gaelic writers to understand that there are excellences worthy of emulation in the literature of other languages."[30] Incidentally, as must be obvious, "Glugar" was him / herself a committed and even belligerent progressive on this point, willing to take on even Ó Grianna, as he did in his review of *Gaethe Gréine I*: "The back of the hand has here been given to 'Gaelicism' or traditionalism, or whatever else

28. *Misneach*, 21 May 1921. Of this definition, Ó Grianna stated, "That is what literature is when all is said." (Sin litridheacht nuair atá deireadh ráidhte.)

29. "Sgríobhnóirí agus a gCuid Oibre," in *Aistí Uí Chonaire*, 167. "Impighim orraibh, a sgríobhnóirí, bheith dána misneamhail gan sgáth gan eagla roimh an saoghal, acht an fhírinne is eól díbh a nochtadh cuma cé'n olc chuirfeas an fhírinne sin ar dhaoine áithride; sibh-se, a sgríobhnóirí, oidí agus treóraidhthe an phobuil, féachaidh ar an saoghal is soiléir do chách, féachaidh ar an saoghal diamhair nach léir do'n choitchiantacht, agus mínighidh dúinn é; má dhéanann sibh é sin, a sgríbhnóirí, má chuireann sibh sibh-féin i gcéill gan sgáth gan eagla orraibh roimh na comhachtaibh gur áil leó an leathdhorchadas agus an leathfhírinne agus an bóthar leathan réidh, chomh cinnte is tá grian ar an spéir éisteóchar libh agus beidh toradh ar bhur saoghal."

30. "Coillte agus Bóithre: Leabhar Nua ó Phádraic Ó Conaire" (Woods and roads: A new book from Pádraic Ó Conaire), *Misneach*, 2 April 1921. "Tá suil agam go bhfuil an ceart agam sa tuairim sin mar is lán-mhithid do sgríbhneoirí na Gaedhilge a thuisgint go bhfuil maitheasaí gur fiú aithris a dhéanamh ortha i leitríocht theangthach eile."

we want to call it, and we find ourselves in another world altogether, a world bigger and broader than the usual world of Gaelic literature."[31]

But by far the most prolific proponent of Gaelic literary progressivism was Piaras Béaslaí, who somehow found time to think about literature while also serving as a member of the Dáil, as director of publicity for the underground government, as editor of both the Volunteer paper *An t-Óglach* (The volunteer) and of the league organ *Fáinne an Lae / Misneach* from the summer of 1917, and as a prisoner in Ireland and England. Béaslaí's ideas were developed both in occasional critical essays like "Sgríobhadh na Gaedhilge" (Gaelic writing), "Meastachán" (Evaluation), "Léirmheas" (Criticism), and " 'Riaghalacha' agus Léirmheas Litríochta" ("Rules" and the criticism of literature);[32] and in his contributions to specific debates, in particular those with Ó Grianna from 1919 to 1921. For example, in May 1919, he lambasted those like Ó Grianna who demanded from Gaelic literature nothing but reflections of "Gaelic thought" (smaoineamh Gaedhlach) and "the Gaelic mind" (an aigne Ghaedhlach), and asked, "How could any literature progress when the majority of its writers held such a view?"[33]

In a January 1921 editorial on "An Aigne Ghaedhlach / An bhFuil a Leithéid Ann?" (The Gaelic mind / Is there such a thing?), he ridiculed this nativist icon: "But 'the Gaelic mind' is the mystery beyond all mysteries. That mind is so mysterious, so difficult to understand, that only a few chosen people are able to comprehend it or to read it." Then, perhaps motivated by a bit of wishful thinking, he concluded: "One does not hear as much of that talk now, but even if one does not, its effects are felt. The self-absorption is still afoot, although not to so great an extent as it used to be."[34] Within weeks, Ó Grianna was, of course, back in the field with his most thoughtful contribution to this

31. "Idir Olc agus Maith / Duais-Aistí Oireachtais 1919" (Both bad and good / The prize essays of the 1919 Oireachtas), *Misneach*, 23 April 1921.

32. "Sgríobhadh na Gaedhilge," *FL*, 12 January 1918; "Meastachán," *FL*, 19 January 1918; "Léirmheas," *FL*, 9 February 1918; and " 'Riaghalacha' agus Léirmheas Litríochta," *FL*, 17 August 1918. For the sort of response his ideas provoked, see Colm Ó Murchadha ("Taube"), "Leitiríocht" (Literature), *FL*, 2 February 1918.

33. "Lucht na bPeann / An Cumann Scríbhneoirí" (The writers / The writers' club), *FL*, 31 May 1919. "Cionnus fhéadfadh éinteanga a dul chun cinn agus a leithéid de thuairim ag furmhór na scríbhneoirí?"

34. "An Aigne Ghaedhlach / An bhFuil a Leithéid Ann?," *Misneach*, 8 January 1921; see note 8. "Ach an mhistéir thar mistéirí dob í an 'aigne Ghaedhlach' í. Tá an aigne sin chomh diamhair, chomh deacair sin a thuigsint nách féidir ach do bheagán de dhaoine tógtha dul amach uirthe ná í léigheamh. . . . Ní cloistear an chaint sin á dhéanamh chomh minic anois, ach mura gcloistear féin braithtear a hiarsmaí. Tá an leithreachas ar siubhal fós, bíodh is ná fuil chomh mór anois agus a bhíodh."

controversy, and Béaslaí's response paid tribute to the importance of the issue and the sincerity of Ó Grianna's passion while rejecting out of hand his conclusions:

> The essay is worth reading with care for it raises a major question, a question that will have to be settled before another step can be taken on the road to saving and restoring the Irish language. The question is, which of the two worlds now existing in Ireland is more important, which of them is stronger and more worthy of attention in the work of the language? There are two worlds in Ireland at present, the old world and the new world, the world of the Gaeltacht and the world to be found in the rest of Ireland. . . . The question is, then, whether we should save, if possible, and restore to the rest of the country the old world of the Gaeltacht and all that goes with it, or should take the new world as it is and try to Gaelicize it.

For Béaslaí there was really no choice: "For better or worse, contemporary art is the only art contemporary people take interest in."[35]

One writer who had no reservations whatsoever about the virtues of contemporary art in all of its potentially disturbing manifestations was the youthful Micheál Mac Liammóir, who, in one of his very first literary essays in Irish, preached the cause of art for art's sake. In "An tSaoirse / Sglábhuíocht Aigne in Éirinn" (Freedom / Intellectual slavery in Ireland) in *Misneach* for 18 December 1920, Mac Liammóir proclaimed: "I wish to speak here about freedom of literature and of art, and what I have to say is that they should be free, entirely free, as free from the laws of the Church and the State as the Irish nation should be free from the foolish control of England. They must be given the same freedom in Ireland as they are given in France." He then proceeded to isolate the problem as "fear of expressing one thing or another because 'it isn't Gaelic' " (faitchíos . . . seo nó siúd a chur in iúl ar an ábhar

35. "An Dá Shaol / An Seana-Nós agus an Nós Nua" (The two worlds / The old way and the new way), *Misneach*, 26 February 1921. "Is fiú do dhuine an aiste a léigheamh go cúramach mar taraigíon sí ceist mhór anuas, ceist a caithfar a réiteach sara raghfar puinn slí eile ar bhóthar na Gaedhilge do shábháil is d'aithbheochaint. Is í an cheist í ná cé'ca saol den dá shaol atá i nÉirinn is mó tábhacht, cé'ca is treise agus is mó is fiú cuimhneamh air in obair na teangan. Tá dhá shaol in Éirinn i láthair na huaire, an seana-shaol agus an saol nua, saol na Gaeltachta agus an saol atá sa chuid eile d-Éirinn. . . . Is í an cheist í, mar sin, an ceart dúinn seana-shaol na Gaeltachta agus a mbainean leis a shábháil, má's féidir é, agus a thabhairt thar nais sa chuid eile den tír, nú an saol nua atá ann a thógaint mar atá sé agus bheith ad iaraidh é ghaedhlú. . . . Pé'ca olc maith an ní é, is é art an lae iniu an t-aon art amháin go bhfaghan muintir an lae iniu blas air."

'nach bhfuil sé Gaedhealach'), and challenged his fellow Gaelic artists and thinkers in deliberately provocative terms: "The intellectual freedom of Ireland is in our own hands. England cannot take it from us. She cannot make slaves of us. But we can make slaves of ourselves."[36]

If any agreed with him, they kept silent, although Béaslaí's editorial three weeks later was the previously cited attack on the mysteries of "the Gaelic mind." Opposition was louder and came from both of the nation's major religious traditions. A Capuchin priest wrote *Misneach* to lay down the law to Mac Liammóir: "That damned expression 'art for art's sake' should never be heard in Ireland. The law of God does not give unrestricted freedom to the artist."[37] The Protestant revivalist Ernest Joynt ("An Buachaillín Buidhe") took on the young iconoclast at greater length in "Saoirse Aigne / Ní Daoirse É, ach Spadántacht" (Intellectual freedom / It's not bondage, but sloth): "Without being 'Puritans' we must give heed to the teaching of the Church and to the practice of Christianity, even in matters of literature and learning. If a Gaelic culture is in store for us, it would be unfortunate were it not to be pure."[38] Mac Liammóir did not, however, yield an inch, responding with a vigorous and courageous defense that opened by quoting Wilde that "no artist has ethical sympathies," and went on to offer Yeats and Synge as examples of misjudged and mistreated writers.[39] Mac Liammóir's appetite for controversy was apparently unsated; later in the same year he was sharply critical of both An tAthair Peadar's qualifications to translate *Don Quixote* and the result of his efforts: "Yes, An tAthair Peadar tells a new story, creates a new book from the bones of an old book. And I don't find that very artistic—indeed, it's not alto-

36. "Is mian liom labhairt annseo faoi shaoirse na Litríochta agus na hEaladhna, agus séard deirim, go mba chóir dóibh bheith saor, saor ar fad, chó saor ó dhlithe na hEaglaise agus an Stáit is ba cheart do náisiún na hÉireann bheith saor ó smacht díchéillí Shasana. Caithfear saoirse thabhairt dóibh in Éirinn fé mar tugtar dóibh sa bhFrainc. . . . Tá saoirse inntleachtach na hÉireann idir lámhaibh againn féin. Ní thig le Sasana í bhaint dínn. Ní thig léi sglábhuithe dhéanamh dínn. Ach tig linn-ne sglábhuithe dhéanamh dínn féin."

37. "Sagart Capúisíneach," "Saoirse Aigne / Tuairm Shagairt ar an Sgeul" (Intellectual freedom: A priest's opinion of the matter), letter, *Misneach*, 29 January 1921. "An focal damanta úd 'an ealadha ar son na healadhna féin' níor chóir go n-aireochfaí in Éirinn go brách é. Ní thugan dlighe Dé cead a chos d'fhear ealadhna."

38. *Misneach*, 8 January 1921. "Gan bheith 'nár 'bpiúratánaigh' caithfimid aire thabhairt do theagosc na hEaglaise agus do chleachtaibh na Críostaidheachta i gcúrsaíbh litridheachta agus léighinn féin. Má's rud é go bhfuil cultúr Ghaedhealach i ndán dúinn ba olc an scéal gan í bheith go glan." Joynt offered the fleshy delights of Rubens as an example of art unchecked by moral considerations.

39. "Saoirse na hEaladhna / Cad is Págántacht?" (Artistic freedom / What is paganism?), *Misneach*, 5 February 1921.

gether ethical—when one remembers that the old book in question is *Don Quixote.*"[40] On a more pedestrian but practical level, individual progressives continued the task of educating their fellow Gaels about literary and cultural developments in the wider world. Some familiar names and concerns recur in this period. For example, leaving aside translation for the moment, we find Ó Conaire continuing proselytism for the writers of emergent nationalities, Ó Lochlainn and Béaslaí writing of the Danish theater,[41] and Máire Ní Chinnéide discussing the work of René Bazin (as she had been urged to do by critics concerned about her interest in the suspect Anatole France in 1910!)[42] New voices directed the attention of their colleagues to writers as diverse as Blasco Ibánez,[43] Thoreau,[44] and Bierce.[45] That the Oireachtas encouraged this interest is evident from *Gaethe Gréine I* and *II*, the published volumes of prizewinning essays from the 1919 and 1920 competitions. Among topics discussed in these pieces were "La Pléiade," the writings of Alfred de Musset, and the philosophies of Plato, Descartes, and Kant.[46] Curiously enough, another previous focus of progressive concern, the cinema, seems to have been largely ignored in the post-Rising period, with the only major essays on the subject "Rory of the Hill's" "The Gaelic League and the Cinema" in 1919, and Micheál de Paor's "Comhachta an Chinema" (The powers of the cinema) in 1921. While "Rory" did challenge his fellow revivalists by asserting that the Gaelicization of the cinema was "above all others, primarily . . . the work of the Gaelic League," in effect he did little more than echo Seán Ó Caomhánaigh in his desire "to see a great modern science converted from being an engine of An-

---

40. "Don Quijote de la Mancha," *Misneach*, 12 November 1921. "Seadh, innsighean an t-Athair Peadar sgéal nua, cruthuigheann sé leabhar nua as cnámha shean-leabhair. Agus ní dó liom go bhfuil sé sin an-ealadhanta, go deimhin, níl sé ar fad dea'bhéasach, nuair chuimhnighthear gurab é 'Don Quijote' an sean-leabhar atá i gceist."

41. See Béaslaí, "Ludwig Holberg / Athair Litríochta na nDanar" (Ludwig Holberg / The father of Danish literature), *Irish Weekly Independent*, 10 July 1920; and Ó Lochlainn, "The Danish Theatre," *Banba* 2, no. 1 (November 1921): 16–21.

42. Máire Ní Chinnéide, "René Bazin agus Saoghal na Tuaithe" (René Bazin and country life), *Branar* 1, no. 5 (February 1920): 186–90.

43. See Mac Liammóir, "An tSaoirse," *Misneach*, 18 December 1920.

44. See "Feadhach," "Díthreabhach Coille" (A hermit of the woods), *FL*, 23 August 1919.

45. See "Glugar," "Coillte agus Bóithre," *Misneach*, 2 April 1921.

46. Daniel Corkery wrote on "La Pléiade" and Lil Nic Dhonnchadha on Musset in 1919; Seaghán Ua Cúagáin wrote on Kant in the same year; An Bráthair Benedict, O.D.C., on Descartes; and Micheál Ó Murchadha on Plato in 1920.

glicisation into a powerful Gaelic battering ram."[47] Perhaps more revealing of the temper of the times is the fact that Micheál de Paor said
nothing whatsoever about the linguistic medium of this new technology in his discussion of its possible moral hazards and educational and
propaganda potential.[48]

Folk material and stories rooted in country life continued to make up
a significant percentage of the Gaelic prose written in the post-Rising
period, constituting a particularly important element in the Munster
journal An Lóchrann, the Donegal journal An Crann (first published December 1916) and the Connacht journal An Stoc (first published December 1917), a fact that distressed more than a few critics. For example,
writing of the projected Oireachtas competitions for 1919, Béaslaí editorialized in Fáinne an Lae: "For too long those involved with the Irish
language have clung to tales and fireside conversations. Tales and fireside conversations are good things, but there are more important things,
things with which the Irish language has not dealt thus far."[49] More
extreme was the editorial policy of Branar, which in its inaugural number for April 1919 acknowledged the academic and cultural value of
folklore while excluding it from its own pages: "What we have proposed is a monthly magazine in which there will be essays discussing
the following topics: literature, art, history, politics, religion, agriculture, manufactures, current events, etc.; short stories, translations from
foreign languages and some poetry. Only three things are prohibited:
scholarly work, propaganda, and folktales, since they have their own
place." Lest there be any misunderstanding on this point, the editorial
continued: "If we want the language to live, we must adapt it to life as
it is now, and that can best be done through writing . . . without
timidity or fear in face of foreign words or new ways to say things, so
that we will not forever be dependent on Fenian folktales and little rural
anecdotes for reading matter."[50]

47. "Rory of the Hill," "The Gaelic League and the Cinema," An Saoghal Gaedhealach,
the Irish World and Industrial Advocate, 13 September 1919.

48. "Comhachta an Chinema," Misneach, 27 August 1921.

49. "Clár an Oireachtais" (The program of the Oireachtas), editorial, FL, 9 November
1918. "Is rófhada do lucht na Gaedhilge ag claoi le sceultaibh agus le comhrádh cois teine.
Is maith iad na sceulta, is maith é an comhrádh cois teine, ach tá nithe níos tábhachtaighe
ná son ann, nithe ná raibh éan bhaint ag an nGaedhilg leó go dtí so." Despite Béaslaí's
reservations the folktale remained a favored genre at the Oireachtas. See, for example, the
collection of prizewinning folk stories for children from the 1920 Oireachtas published as
Scéalta Triúir (Stories from three people), ed. Risteárd Ó Foghludha (Baile Átha Cliath:
Connradh na Gaedhilge, n.d.)

50. "Tosach na hOibre" (The beginning of the work), editorial, Branar 1, no. 1 (April
1919): 3. Colm Ó Murchadha was the editor. "'Sé rud atá curtha romhainn ná

While the contents of the three provincial journals noted above were in general comparable, the most substantial and long-lived of them, *An Lóchrann*, printed the largest amount of genuine and diverse folk material, from "An Seabhac's" "Sean-Fhocail na Muimhneach" (The proverbs of Munster) to regular contributions from "the Islandman," Tomás Ó Criomhthain, to individual stories and miscellaneous lore from other writers like Fionán Mac Coluim. Significantly, however, even the editor, "An Seabhac" himself, was beginning to have reservations about the generative potential of such material. For example, calling for the collection and publication of folklore in October 1916, he seemed to concede that while traditional matter must and could be preserved, the ethos and worldview of which it was the expression was doomed, and its future cultural contribution would thus be antiquarian and passive: "Someone will say that it is not worthwhile to save those stories from death, that their time has passed. Their time has not passed. It is the traditional storyteller whose time has passed, but print has now replaced the storyteller in the world, and it has more of an audience than the storyteller ever had. . . . The rest of the traditional lore of Munster will die unless we write it down within the next five or six years from the small handful of storytellers still alive."[51] The success of his appeal seems, however, to have created new problems for "An Seabhac" and his journal, prompting him to define more precisely his vision of the new Gaelic literature:

> With regard to writing, there is one thing we would like to make clear. I have a great pile of manuscripts of Fenian tales, of stories of magic horses and giants, etc., as well as of old folk songs, enough with which to fill *An Lóchrann* with nothing else

míosachán, nú irisleabhar míosamhail, 'na mbeidh aistí ag cur síos ar na neithe seo: leitríocht, ealadhain, stair, polaitíocht, creideamh, curadóireacht, déantúisí, cúrsaí an tsaoghail, etc.; sgéalta gearra; aistriúchán ó theangthacha iasachta agus beagán filíochta. Níl ach aon trí neithe amháin coisgithe—sgoláireacht, propaganda, agus seana-sgéaluíocht, mar tá a n-áit féin dóibh sin. . . . Má's maith linn an teanga a mhaireachtaint, ní mór dúinn í 'chur in oireamhaint don saoghal atá anois ann, agus is trí sgríbhneóireacht is mó a déanfar san . . . gan sgáth ná eagla bheith againn roim fhocail iasachta ná roim shlighthe nua chum rudaí a rádh, i dtreo is ná beam go deo i dtaoibh le sean-sgéalta Fiannaigheachta, agus le heachtraí beaga tuatha mar léightheóireacht."

51. "Seanchaidheacht na Mumhan" (The traditional lore of Munster), editorial, *An Lóchrann*, October 1916, 8. "Déarfaidh duine nach fiú na scéalta san a shaoradh ó'n mbás—go bhfuil a ré caithte. Níl a ré caithte. Sé an sean-scéalaidhe go bhfuil a ré caithte, ach tá an cló i n-ionad an scéalaidhe anois sa tsaoghal agus is mó de lucht éistighthe atá aige sin ná mar bhí ag an scéalaidhe riamh. . . . Bás iseadh gheobhaidh an chuid eile de sheanchaidheacht na Mumhan mara scríbhimíd-ne é taobh istigh de chúig nó sé bliadhantaibh ó'n mbeagán beag scéalaidhthe atá fós 'na mbeathaidh."

for five or six years. I do not, however, wish to put more than a very small amount of any of that kind of thing in this paper. That is not what people prefer to read, but rather something original—especially stories having some connection with life as it is now. Few people, however, put themselves to the trouble of composing anything new and it is hard for me to find suitable material at all times.[52]

As in the earlier period, it is, in absence of specific attribution of sources, often difficult to distinguish genuine folktales from "original" stories patterned closely on them, and there is a significant amount of such ambiguous work in *An Lóchrann* and its two provincial counterparts. But tales of this kind were by no means what "An Seabhac" had in mind when he called for "stories woven from the Irish language in which one finds the mind of the Gael" (scéalta 'á bhfighe as Gaedhilg agus aigne Gaedheal ionnta istigh).[53] Nor was he engaging in the ineffable Gaelic exclusivism of Ó Grianna. Rather, he offered as a practical model at this very time his own *Jimín Mháire Thaidhg*, a novel that while it was, as we have seen, a disappointment after the sharp and even cynical realism of *An Baile Seo 'Gainne* was nonetheless a humorous, credible, and not altogether idealized picture of life in the contemporary Kerry Gaeltacht.[54] Another veteran ruralist publishing in *An Lóchrann* at this time was "Gruagach an Tobair," whose most notable work in the post-Rising period was *An Sgóraidheacht* (Neighborly visiting) (1919). Co-authored with Fionán Mac Coluim, the book was a compendium of anecdotes, proverbs, superstitions, and customs presented in the form of conversational skits.[55] The Gaeltacht of "An Gruagach" and Mac Coluim was, however, unlike that of "An Seabhac" already somewhat of a museum piece, a fact noted by "C. Ó M."

52. "Ar gCúram Féin" (Our own business), editorial, *An Lóchrann*, February 1920, 4. "I dtaobh scríbhneoireachta tá rud ba mhaith linn a chur i dtuiscint. Tá ualach mór de MS. sean-scéalta fiannaidheachta agam, de scéalta púcaí agus fathach etc., agus tá chomh maith agam sean-amhráin na ndaoine oiread is ná mbeadh i gcló go ceann cúig mblian agus 'An Lóchrann' ar fad d'fhágaint fúthu: ní mian liom ámhthach ach fíor-bheagán d'aon tsaghas aca a chur sa pháipéar so. Ní h-iad is fearr le daoine a léigheamh ach rud éigin nua-dhéanta—go mór mór scéalta go mbeadh baint aca leis an saoghal atá anois ann. Is beag duine ámhthach a chuireann de dhuagh air féin aon rud nua a cheapadh agus is deacair dom abhar oiriúnach d'fhaghbháil i gcomhnaidhe."

53. "Ar gCúram Féin," *An Lóchrann*, February 1920, 4.

54. See, for example, the reviews by Peadar Ó hAnnracháin and Máire Ní Chinnéide in *Misneach* for 26 November and 3 December 1921 respectively. Ní Chinnéide regarded *Jimín* as primarily a book for young readers.

55. Baile Átha Cliath: Brún agus Ó Nóláin, Teor., n.d.

(probably Colm Ó Murchadha) in his review in *Branar*: "The old Gael-tacht is departing this world . . . and a new Gaeltacht is rising up in its place, but that is another Gaeltacht, a different Gaeltacht altogether. The old Gaeltacht and the mind connected with it will go when the present generation dies. . . . For that reason, the more of the old Gaelic (or perhaps the 'traditional,' since the two are often the same) remnants are collected and published, the better the last spark of the old Gaeltacht of Ireland will be saved."[56]

If Gaeltacht life was so rapidly changing, there seems to have been little awareness of that fact in the rural tales of the post-Rising period. Schoolroom stories for some reason become less popular—they were to return in abundance in the Gaelic autobiographies of the thirties and forties—and with emigration prohibited for the duration of the World War, stories dealing with that social problem,[57] as well as stories in which returned emigrants or Irish-Americans play central roles,[58] pre-dictably become less important. But other thematic patterns traced in Chapter 2 persist, especially the consistent idealization of the Irish-speaking peasantry and their ability to outwit and trivialize British offi-cialdom. Thus we find, among copious examples, "Bó na Baintrighe agus na Síothmhaoir" (The widow's cow and the policemen) by "Cnoc Eala;"[59] "Gliocas / An t-Iascaire 's an Sergeant: Sgeul Grinn ó Chi-araighe" (Cleverness / The fisherman and the sergeant: A humorous story from Kerry) by "Ciarraidheach Macánta;"[60] "An Chéad Eachtra de Chuid an Chonstábla de Búrca" (The first adventure of Constable

---

56. "Léirmheas" (Review), *Branar* 1, no. 4 (September 1919): 168. "Tá an tseana-Ghaedhealtacht san ag imtheacht as an saol . . . agus Gaedhealtacht nua ag eirghe suas 'na hinead, ach Gaedhealtacht eile, Gaedhealtacht dheifiriúil léi ar fad. Imeóidh an tseana-Ghaedhealtacht agus an aigne a ghabhan léi nuair a caillfar an dream atá anois suas. . . . Dá bhrí sin dá mhéid do na sean-iarsmaí Gaedhleacha (nó sean-aimseartha béidir mar is ionan le chéile go minic iad) a baileófar agus a cuirfar i gcló iseadh is fearr a sábhálfar an spré dheirineach do sheana-Ghaedhealtachta na hÉireann." This critic went on to stress that such preserved folk material would provide a storehouse from which later, more sophisticated Gaelic authors could draw.

57. The issue was obviously not absent from the fiction of the period. See, for example, Eoin Ó Searcaigh's "Nuair Thiocfas Fad ar an Lá" (When the days lengthen), *An Crann*, no. 4 (Feast of St. Adhamhnán 1917): 7–10.

58. In "An Ponncán Greanamhar" (The quare Yankee) by "Gruagach an Tobair," the stereotype is suggested, but the Yank turns out to be "a perceptive and sensible Gael" (fear gunta ciallmhar Gaedhealach). See "An Ponncán Greanamhar," *An Lóchrann* No-vember–December 1917.

59. "Cnoc Eala," "Bó na Baintrighe agus na Síothmhaoir," *FL*, 12 October 1918.

60. "Ciarraidheach Macánta," "Gliocas / An t-Iascaire 's an Sergeant / Sgeul Grinn ó Chiarraighe," *Misneach*, 27 March 1920.

Burke") by Seaghán Mac Maoláin;[61] and "Beachúil" (a name) by Pádraig Ághas.[62] An interesting variant on the theme is provided by Séamus Ua Creag in his "Na Buicíní" (The cads), a poitín-brewing story in which the authority figure is the hero, saving the life of a young boy the cowardly moonshiners have imprisoned in a barrel.[63]

For those eager for more sophisticated and challenging literary sustenance, Irish history continued to offer promise. Unfortunately, it was a promise little realized. Discussions of the creative potential of historical themes for fiction and drama tend merely to recycle the thinking of a decade and more before, as does the 1919 review of Mac Néill's *Phases of Irish History* by "C. Ó M.," in which he analyzes the failure of previous scholars of early Ireland: "It is, however, easy to understand what kept them blind. They didn't know Irish, and therefore they were reliant on the foreigners' version of the story."[64] In like manner, Tadhg Ó Donnchadha's complaint of 1917 could just as well have been made in 1907: "History is one of the finest scholarly subjects and there is no other subject more appropriate for the Irish language movement. We have turned our backs on it for a long time, and it is our guiding star if we understood our own affairs and the work we have taken in hand."[65] "Conán Maol's" assessment of the situation two years later seems equally stale: "There are too many people who don't like to read the history of this country, and it's no wonder considering the manner in which it is written. It doesn't suit this country in English dress; it hasn't the same flavor as it would in Irish."[66] "Conán" had, of course, been

61. Seaghán Mac Maoláin, "An Chéad Eachtra de Chuid an Chonstábla de Búrca," *An Crann*, no. 3 (1917): 2–3.

62. Pádraig Ághas ("Tadhg Caoch"), "Beachúil," in *Scéalta Andeas, Oireachtas 1920* (Stories from the South, Oireachtas 1920), ed. Risteárd Ó Foghludha (Baile Átha Cliath: Connradh na Gaedhilge, n.d.), 137–45.

63. Séamus Ua Creag, "Na Buicíní," *An Crann*, no. 4 (The Feast of St. Adhamhnán 1917): 1–3.

64. C. Ó M. "Stair, Nua agus Sean" (History, modern and ancient), *FL*, 13 September 1919. "Is furaiste a thuisgint, ámhthach, cad a chimeád dall iad. Ní raibh an Ghaedhilg acu agus dá bhrígh sin bhíodar i dtaoibh le hinnsint na nGall ar an sgéal." Curiously, and this does represent a change from earlier attitudes, while C. Ó M. stresses Mac Néill's knowledge of Irish, he says nothing of the book's itself being in English. For other comments on Mac Néill's historical work at this time, see "Literary Notes," *An Saoghal Gaedhealach*, 14 September 1918.

65. "Cúrsaí an tSaoghail," *ACS*, 8 September 1917. "Tá an stair ar cheann de na hadhbharaibh léighinn is fearr agus níl aon adhbhar eile is fearr a fheileans do ghluaiseacht na Gaedhilge ná í. Tá cúl ghá thabhairt dí againn le fada agus badh í ár réalt eolais í dá dtuigimís ár sgéal féin agus an obair a ghabhamar de láimh." He called for, among other things, translation of the work of Alice Stopford Green.

66. "Trácht ar Stair" (A discussion of history), *Branar* 1, no. 1 (April 1919): 47. "Tá an

one of the pioneers of historical writing in Irish, and, like Seán Ua Ceallaigh and William P. Ryan, he continued his work after the Rising.[67] Of this trio Ryan was by far the most prolific and original, lecturing the London Gaels in 1917,[68] and publishing a series of essays on early Irish social and cultural history in *Misneach* in 1920. Among the titles in this series were "Na Draoithe / A Réimeas agus a dTeagasg" (The druids / Their time and their teaching"), "Rúindiamhra na Sean / Draoíochas agus Críostuíocht" (The mysteries of the ancients / Druidism and Christianity), and "Aspalacht agus Éigse / Épopée Phádraig Naofa" (Apostlehood and learning / The epic of St. Patrick).[69]

Despite the turbulence of the times, the Oireachtas continued to encourage the creative use of history through its prizes. Of particular interest is the 1919 competition for "a novel about ordinary life in Ireland before Easter 1916, with the end of the story having some connection with that clash" (úrscéal ar ghnáthshaoghal in Éirinn roimh Cháisc 1916, agus baint a bheith ag deire an scéil leis an mbualadh sin).[70] While this specific competition drew but a single entry and awarded no prize, the spirit that motivated it was very much in tune with the times. Recent history at any rate was adequately covered in the period, for there was a spate of fictional treatments of Easter Week. By far the most substantial and impressive were, of course, the stories in Ó Conaire's *Seacht mBuaidh an Éirghe-Amach* and Ó Grianna's novel *Mo Dhá Róisín*. But we also find "Gailitia na Cásca: Seachtain na Troda" (The Gailitia of Easter: The week of the fighting) by "An Fáinneach Fáin;"[71] "Bríd" by "Muircheartach Mór;"[72] "An Chréacht / Bás an Óglaigh" (The Wound / The Volunteer's death) by Micheál Mac Liammóir;[73] "An Sas-

---

iomad daoine ann nách maith leo stair na tíre seo a léigh' agus ní hiongna é toisg an chuma ina sgríobhthar í. Ní oireamhnuighean sí an tír seo i gcrot Béarla, níl an blas céadna uirthi agus bheadh i nGaedhilg." See also "P.S.," "The Language Movement: Occasional Reflections," *An Saoghal Gaedhealach*, 14 September 1918.

67. See "Conán Maol," "Na Flemandaigh" (The Flemings), *FL*, 8–15 March 1919; Ua Ceallaigh, "Cath Inse Subhlóid" (The battle of Inis Subhlóid), *Irish Weekly Independent*, Christmas 1917; or Ua Ceallaigh, "Na Draoithe" (The druids), *Gaethe Gréine I*, 28–42.

68. See "London Gaels and History," *ACS*, 31 March 1917.

69. These essays appeared in *Misneach* on 22 May, 5 and 19 June respectively.

70. "Oireachtas 1919 / Na Comórtasaí Liteardha / Tuairimí na mBreitheamhan" (Oireachtas 1919 / The literary competitions / The opinions of the judges), *Misneach*, 22 November 1919.

71. *FL*, 30 November 1918.

72. *FL*, 29 March 1919. This story actually deals with the subsequent adventures of a wounded Easter veteran who is torpedoed on his way to South Africa, imprisoned by Germans in Cameroon, and finally able to escape home to Ireland.

73. *Misneach*, 31 July 1920.

anach Sásta / Seachtain na Cásca, 1916" (The satisfied Englishman / Easter Week, 1916) by Peadar Mac Fhionnlaoich;[74] and "A Chéad Ghrádh" (His first love) by Seán Ó Conchubhair.[75] Predictably, heroic self-sacrifice was the keynote of virtually all of these works.

In June 1919, Béaslaí urged Gaelic playwrights to seek inspiration in early Irish history, for "there is marvelous dramatic material in the history of the ancient Irish, but little use is made of that material." Among specific topics he suggested were the stories of Gormfhlaith and Niall Glúndubh, of Colm Cille, of Diarmuid Mac Murrough, and of Silken Thomas Fitzgerald.[76] No one seems to have been listening, for the only two historical plays of the 1916–21 period were an unpublished work on Brian Bóroimhe submitted to the 1917 Oireachtas by "Mac Liaigh,"[77] and the 1919 Daniel Corkery and Séamas Ó hAodha collaboration *An Clochar* (*The Convent*), a one-acter for girls set in the Viking era. Stories dealing with medieval Irish life were also rare, and none attempted to re-create the period with any fidelity. Instead we get reworked folktales or stories from the early literature like "Bronntanas an Rí / Sgéal ó'n Sean t-Saoghail" (The king's gift / A story from the ancient world) and others by Micheál Ó Colmáin in *Banba* in 1921;[78] Bríd Ní Shíthchearn's "Murchadh Mac Briain";[79] Gearóid Ó Murchadha's "An Phaidir Gheal" (The bright prayer), a tale about St. Mochuada's curing of a pestilence in the reign of King Guaire;[80] and Pádraic Ó Domhnalláin's "Ceoltóir Uachtar Ard / Dílseacht Chuilm Ruairí Mhóir" (The musician of Oughterard / The loyalty of Colm Ruairí Mhóir), a tale modeled on a story by Archbishop Fénelon.[81]

Nor is there much of anything else. The most ambitious work was probably Muiris Ó Catháin's "Dún an Óir: Eachtra Shibéal de la Russo" (Dún an Óir: The adventure of Sybil de la Russo), a story set in the Dingle Peninsula in 1579 and telling of the Spanish heroine's love

---

74. *Misneach*, 18 December 1920.

75. *Branar* 1, no. 4 (September 1919): 158–63.

76. "'Bord na Taidhse' / Obair le Déanamh" ("The theatrical board" / Work to be done), *FL*, 7 June 1919. "Is iongantach a bhfuil d'adhbhar drámaidheachta i stair na seana-Ghaedheal, acht is beag úsáid atá bainte as an adhbhar son."

77. See "Oireachtas a 1917 / An Roinn Liteardha" (Oireachtas 1917 / The literary division), *ACS*, 15 September 1917.

78. "Bronntanas an Rí / Sgéal ó'n Sean t-Saoghal," *Banba* 2, no. 1 (November 1921): 50–53; and "Domhnall Cam," *Banba* 2, no. 2 (December 1921): 92–94.

79. *An Stoc* 3, no. 1 (September–October 1920): 1–2. Ní Shíthchearn tells us she wrote this story down from the narration of Pádraig Ó Caodháin.

80. *An Reult: Irisleabhar na h-Ollscoile* (The Star: The magazine of the university [UCD]) 1, no. 1 (November 1920): 20–26.

81. *Misneach*, 6 August 1921.

for an Irish sea captain in league with Spain, the death of her father in the slaughter at Smerwick Harbor, and her marriage and subsequent return home, whence her husband continues his work for his own native land.[82] For the Cromwellian period, there are a folkish "Cromaill" by Siubhán Ní Sheaain [sic],[83] and Séamus Ó hAodha's more substantial "Cluain Geal Meala" (Fair Clonmel), recounting the battle for that town, the heroic Irish defense and ultimate defeat as the result of plague and lack of ammunition, and the escape of the fighting men under the leadership of the protagonist, Aodh Dubh Ó Néill.[84] There was also an apparently unpublished 1919 Oireachtas novel dealing with the events of 1647.[85] The Williamite period inspired only one rapparee tale, "Díoghaltas Dhomhnaill Bhacaigh / Aithnighean an Fhuil a Chéile" (The revenge of Domhnall Bacach / Blood is thicker than water) by Tomás Ó hAodha.[86] And surprisingly, for the '98 Rising we seem to have but a single play, and even that a translation of an Anglo-Irish drama for the 1917 Oireachtas.[87] The Fenian Rising was the subject of the long 1920 Oireachtas Prize-winning story "Fínín Shléibhe Calláin" (The Fenian of Sliabh Calláin) by Pádraig Ághas, a story interesting for its harsh view of the Fenian leader James Stephens and its depiction of a fair amount of violence, but typical in its sense of the Rising's anticlimax, its account of the perilous escape to America, and its assertion of an unbroken Fenian tradition of resistance to British rule.[88] With so few original works it is impossible to say anything about thematic continuity or development at this time.

The older native literature attracted even less attention than native history in the post-Rising period, and again there is a wearisome familiarity to what little discussion of the topic there was. For example, in July 1919 Risteárd Ó Foghludha renewed an old attack on an old foe for an old reason: "The important people who are in charge of the Royal Irish Academy have their faces turned to distant lands; they have no interest whatsoever in what happens to anything concerning the place

82. *Misneach*, 3 September 1921.

83. *An Lóchrann*, November 1916, 8.

84. *Branar* 2, no. 1 (August 1920): 6–13.

85. "Oireachtas 1919 / Na Comórtasaí Liteardha / Tuairimí na mBreitheamhan," *Misneach*, 29 November 1919. The author was Seán Tóibín.

86. *Misneach*, 30 July 1921.

87. See "Oireachtas a 1917 / An Roinn Liteardha," *ACS*, 15 September 1917. A winning essay by Pádraig Ághas from the 1920 Oireachtas dealt with "Óglaigh na Bliadhna 1782" (The Volunteers of 1782). See *Gaethe Gréine II*, 31–42.

88. Pádraig Ághas (An Giolla Deacair), "Fínín Shléibhe Calláin," in *Scéalta Andeas*, 71–134.

they themselves live."[89] More positive, but no fresher, was "An Seabhac's" 1917 praise of the work of the Irish Texts Society,[90] or his 1919
criticism of his fellow Gaels for their failure to support it.[91]

The only Gaelic intellectuals in this period writing at any length or
with any regularity in the Irish language on the early literature were
William P. Ryan and Cormac Ó Cadhlaigh. Ryan included among his
1920 *Misneach* essays on early history other pieces like "Éireannaigh
agus Greugaigh / Finnsgeuluíocht an Dá Threabh" (The Irish and the
Greeks / The fabulous literature of the two peoples), "Naoimh agus
Laochra / Dá Shruth Léighinn" (Saints and heroes / Two currents of
learning), and "An Fionn-Saga/Troid is Tuairimí Saoithe" (The Fionn
saga / Controversy and the opinions of sages).[92] He also offered an
overview of Celtic scholarship in "Éigse na Linne Seo / Saoithe 'nar
Measg" (Contemporary learning / Sages in our midst).[93] In 1921 Ó
Cadhlaigh's essays on the Fionn Mac Cumhaill cycle were a regular
feature in *Misneach* under such titles as "An Fhiann / Dualgaisí agus Co-
inghiollacha na Laochra" (The Fian band / Duties and qualifications of
the warriors) and "Clanna Mórna agus Baoisgne / Mac-ghníomhartha
Fhinn" (The clans of Mórna and Baoisgne / The boyhood deeds of
Fionn).[94] Of modernizations or genuine creative adaptations of the early
literature there are really none, just folktales of Fionn like Aíne Bhreathnach's "Cumhall,"[95] Seán Mac Parthaláin's "Oisín i nDiaidh na Féinne"
(Oisín after the Fianna),[96] Pádraig Ó Súileabháin's "Bás Dhiarmada"

---

89. "An Cúinne Gaedhilge," *Irish Rosary* 23, no. 7 (July 1919): 503. "Na daoine móra
atá i gceannas insan R.I.A., tá a n-aighthe ar chríochaibh in imigéin: is cuma leó insa
donas cad imtheoghaidh ar éanrud a bhaineann leis an ndútha ina bhfuil comhnuidhe
ortha féin."

90. "Cumann na dTéx" (The Texts Society), *An Lóchrann*, June 1917, 7.

91. "Cumann na Scríbheann Gaedhilge" (The Irish Texts Society), *An Lóchrann*, April
1919, 4. "An Seabhac" was here returning to a grievance to which he had first given voice
in a 17 January 1914 *ACS* editorial on "Droch-Cháil agus Deagh-Cháil" (Bad reputation
and good reputation).

92. These essays appeared in *Misneach* for 1 May, 20 June, and 7 August respectively.

93. William P. Ryan, "Éigse na Linne Seo / Saoithe 'nar Measg," *Misneach*, 28 August
1920.

94. These essays appeared in *Misneach* for 2 and 9 July 1921 respectively. Pádraig Ó
Modhráin won a 1920 Oireachtas Prize with a substantial essay on "An Fhiann" (The Fian
band). See *Gaethe Gréine II*, 7–28. Seosamh Laoide also edited a major collection of Ossianic verse as *Fian-Laoithe* (Fenian poems) in 1917.

95. *An Stoc* 2, no. 2 (July–August 1918): 2. She attributed the story to the oral narration
of Pádraig Ó Catháin.

96. This story commenced serialization in *An Stoc* in March 1920 and was attributed to
the oral narration of Máirtín Bhachan.

(The death of Diarmaid),[97] and Seán Ó Muircheartaigh's "Oisín na Féinne" (Oisín of the Fianna);[98] or much rarer traditional material based on the Ulster Cycle like Áine Bhreathnach's "Sgéal Conlaoich" (The story of Conlaoch) or "Cúchulainn agus an Garbh" (Cú Chulainn and the Rough One).[99]

Less attention was also paid in the post-Rising period to the Anglo-Irish writers, although there was persistent envy at their wider readership and suspicion of their motives and commitments. For example, in July 1917 Tadhg Ó Donnchadha rejected their claim to be "the most authoritative Irish writers to be found" (na sgríbhneoirí Éireannacha is ughdarásaigh dá bhfuil le fághail), impugned their sincerity (cneastacht), and questioned their right to be considered "friends of the Irish language" (cairde do'n Ghaedhilg):

> They don't respect the Irish language. If they did respect and love it, they wouldn't be ignorant of the Irish language. They are clever people, renowned people with abundant literary talents, but they don't find it worth their while to learn or to speak Irish. They reject Irish outright, and their rejection brings our language into disrepute. What would the foreigner who reads their books say except that Irish is worthless since the writers did not think it worthwhile to speak it or to write it.[100]

Liam Ó Rinn was even harsher three months later, arguing that those writing and trying to restore the Irish language were of necessity "enemies of the English language and of those cultivating the English language" ('nár namhadaibh ag an mBeurla agus ag lucht an Bheurla do shaothrú). Of Irish writers of English, Ó Rinn proclaimed: "I think that all that matters to them is winning fame for themselves. If that were not the case, they would learn Irish and cast away English. I do not understand how it is possible for anyone to have any great love for Ireland if he gives assistance to the English language in gaining a firmer grip on the people of Ireland, and there is no better way to do that than

---

97. *An Lóchrann*, May 1919, 2–3.

98. *An Lóchrann*, November 1920, 5.

99. These two pieces appeared in *An Stoc* in April and June 1919 respectively.

100. "Cúrsaí an tSaoghail," *ACS*, 21 July 1917. "Is amhlaidh nach bhfuil meas aca ar an nGaedhilg. Dá mbeadh meas aca uirthi agus grádh aca di ní bheidís gan Gaedhilg. Daoine cliste atá ionnta, daoine clúitiúla agus buadha litridheachta go leor aca, ach ní fiú leobhtha an Ghaedhilg d'fhoghluim nó do labhairt. Diúltuigheann siad glan do'n Ghaedhilg agus tarraingeann a ndiúltú droch-mheas ar ár dteangain. Céard déarfadh an coigcríoch a léigheann a leabhra ach nach fiú tada an Ghaedhilg nuair nár bhfiú leis na scríbhneoirí í a labhairt nó a sgríobhadh."

to lure and deceive the people of Ireland with a quasi–Gaelic literature."[101]
To be fair, there could also be magnanimity and more. Thus while in
February 1917 *An Claidheamh Soluis* insisted that "the day of the Irish
language will come yet" (tiocfaidh lá na Gaedhilge go fóill), it could
also advocate the development of a bilingual literary criticism of modern Irish writing in both languages: "We would like for William P.
Ryan or Stephen MacKenna to write a review of the two modern literatures (in Irish and in English) that have been created over the past
twenty years."[102] Of course, to some extent such a critical rapproche-
ment had already been initiated the previous year with the posthumous
publication of Thomas MacDonagh's *Literature in Ireland* and its discussion in *An Claidheamh Soluis* by Ryan.[103] P. S. Ua hÉigeartaigh ("Sarsfield") was, as usual bolder, writing in the essay "The Boom in Irish
Literature": "Purists may object to the description of books in English
as Irish literature, but I do not see what other description can fairly be
applied to the present output. It certainly cannot be called English literature, though I suppose a case might be made out for calling it Anglo-
Irish." But even Ua hÉigeartaigh espoused the orthodox line, continuing:

> It voices and it represents a period of transition, a period when
> literature in Ireland, written though it be in English, is instinct
> with Irish feelings, Irish turns of speech and thought; when,
> though it is written in the English language, its imagination is in
> the Irish–Ireland movement, and its face and its heart turned to-
> wards the rising sun of the Irish language. The men and women
> who to-day are writing Irish literature in English know perfectly
> well that they represent a transition period, that in the days to
> come when Irish literature shall be written wholly in Irish the

---

101. "An Bhainrioghain Cheart! [The proper queen!] / 'The Future of English Literature Looks Towards the Liffey,'" *ACS*, 10 November 1917. Ó Rinn was quoting Shane
Leslie in his title. "Sílim gur cuma leo gach aon rud ach árdchlú do thuilleamh dóibh féin.
Dá mbeadh an sceul ar a mhalairt de chuma aca dfoghlumóidís an Ghaedhilg agus do
chaithidís uatha an Beurla. Ní thuigim gur féidir d'éinne aon ghrádh mhór a bheith aige
dÉirinn má thugann sé congnamh don Bheurla chun greim níos daingne dfháil ar mhuintir na hÉireann agus níl aon tslighe is fearr chuige sin ná muintir na hÉireann do
mhealladh agus do bhreugadh le leitríocht leath-Ghaedhlach."
102. "Cúrsaí an tSaoghail," *ACS*, 17 February 1917. "Ba mhaith linn go sgríobhfadh
Liam P. Ó Riain nó Stiophán Mac Énna léirmheas ar an dá nua-litridheacht (i nGaedhilg
agus i mBéarla) a cumadh le fiche bliain anuas."
103. See William P. Ryan, "Tomás Mac Donnchadha," *ACS*, 3 and 10 June 1916.

work of most of them will be forgotten save in literary histories
and maybe in anthologies.[104]

In passing it is also worth noting that when in 1920 Pádraic Ó Conaire
lamented the emigration of "our writers" (ár sgríobhnóirí) he added the
explanatory parenthesis "both Gaelic and Anglo-Irish" (idir Ghaedhil
agus Ghall-Ghaedhil).[105]
In general the old anger and hostility toward individual writers does
seem to have waned. For example, little is said about Yeats, nothing at
all, again, about Joyce, and only the dead Synge was still capable of
stirring strong emotions in some, as when Seán Tóibín ("Lugh Mac
Céin") wrote in 1921: "There is the occasional person today who
praises the work of Synge highly but who would condemn the work of
Lever. It is difficult to understand how anyone who would praise that
'Playboy' by Synge would not praise 'Harry Lorrequer' as well." For
Tóibín the prime criterion for rejecting Synge had not changed since
1902: "Synge did not understand the people of Aran or any other Gaelic
people."[106] Yet, as we have seen, after his death even Synge could be
praised in a Gaelic gathering, as he was when Seán Ó Faoláin addressed
the Cork branch of Cumann an Fháinne in May 1919. In the audience
was Daniel Corkery, which may explain why the report of the meeting
records that "needless to say there was a vigorous debate over the critical discussion of that dramatic work."[107] Corkery himself was, by the
way, the Irish writer of English most respected by the Gaels in this
period,[108] perhaps due more to his wholehearted commitment to the

104. *An Saoghal Gaedhealach*, 7 September 1918. The following week Ua hÉigeartaigh
drew the attention of fellow Gaels to their much-maligned countryman George Bernard
Shaw in "The Secret of Bernard Shaw," *An Saoghal Gaedhealach*, 14 September 1918.
105. "Clódhanna / Brostaighidh a Lucht na bPeann!" in *Iriseoireacht Uí Chonaire*, 92. Ó
Conaire himself had co-authored a play in English, *The Cherry Bird*, with the Canadian
Katherine Hughes, who copyrighted the work in the United States in 1915. See Pádraig
Ó Siadhail, "Ó Emerald go hÉirinn (Spleáchadh ar Bheatha is ar Shaothar Katherine
Hughes, 1876–1925)" (From Emerald to Ireland (A look at the life and work of Katherine
Hughes, 1876–1925)," *IMN* (1991): 19–21, 37.
106. "An 'Playboy' / Fear ón Oileán agus Synge," *Misneach*, 30 April 1921. "Tá
foth-dhuine indiu a mholan gnó Synge go h-árd ach cháinfadh sé sin saothar Lebher.
Aonne a mholan an 'Playboy' úd le Synge ní fuiris a thuigsint canathaobh ná molfadh sé
'Harry Lorrequer' leis. . . . Níor thuig Synge muintir Árainne, 'ná aon mhuintir
Ghaedhlach eile."
107. "Cumann an Fháinne," *FL*, 17 May 1919. "Ní gádh a rádh gur bhríoghmhar an
díospóireacht a deineadh ar chunntas léirmheasa a bhain leis an ndrámuidheacht san."
108. See, for example, the review by "S. Ó M." of his *Threshold of Quiet* and that by
Béaslaí of his *Ó Failbhe Mór* (both English and translation) in *FL* for 2 February 1918 and
31 May 1919 respectively.

cause and to his active literary bilingualism than to the undeniable quality of his work in English. In this regard the Gaelic treatment of Corkery recalls that accorded MacManus and O'Higgins, or better Colum and Stephens, in previous years.

Yet if most literary Gaels were saying little about their Anglo-Irish counterparts, some were allowing those counterparts to address the nation in the national language. There was a marked increase in translation of Anglo-Irish works, a development Seán Ó Faoláin felt should be aggressively pursued, in particular with regard to drama:

> It is of great importance that the Gaelic dramatic convention should be very similar to the original one which was the offspring of the Abbey ideals. Perhaps the easiest way to compass this end would be the production in Irish of say Synge's "Deirdre" or "The Playboy," or "Riders to the Sea"; some of Yeats's short semi-historical pieces—"On Baile's Strand," "The Green Helmet," "The King's Threshold," or "The Hourglass," coupled with the entirely Gaelic peasant-plays of Padraic Colum or Edward Martyn. . . . All these dramas are racy of the soil, they are born of the soul of Ireland and her story, and each one in its poetical expression or its lesson is something that wells up from a true poet-patriot's heart.[109]

Others agreed, though some of the works chosen, and their translators, are rather surprising. For example, "Gruagach an Tobair" provided Gaelic versions of a story by William Gwynn (born in Cork in 1793);[110] as well as of scenes from The Rivals, The School for Scandal, and a recitation piece by Richard Brinsley Sheridan;[111] and a scene from Oliver Goldsmith's She Stoops to Conquer,[112] all of the Sheridan and Goldsmith pieces appearing, again surprisingly, in An Lóchrann. Another of Goldsmith's works, his essay on the harper Turlough O'Carolan, was put into Irish by "Aodh Áigh."[113]

Other sources of translation were more predictable: Standish J. O'Grady's The Bog of the Stars translated as "Móin na Réaltan" by Seán

109. "The Coming of the Gaelic Drama," An Saoghal Gaedhealach, 18 January 1919.

110. "Cathair na nDeamhan" (The city of the demons), Branar 1, no. 1 (April 1919): 50–56.

111. These excerpts were published in An Lóchrann for November 1918, July 1919, and May 1919 respectively.

112. "Mar Oiltear" (As reared), An Lóchrann, October 1918, 6.

113. "An Cearbhallánach / Bard Deireannach na hÉireann" (Carolan / The last Irish bard), Misneach, 21 August 1920.

Tóibín and an excerpt from the same work by Béaslaí;[114] a short story by Alice Deasey in the Irish of "B. an D.";[115] T. C. Murray's play *Spring*, a translation that won a share of the first prize at the 1918 Oireachtas for Séamus Mac Cormaic;[116] and Seán Tóibín's *Fear na nAmhrán* (Pearse's *The Singer*), a winner at the 1920 festival.[117] Rather startlingly, given his just noted opinion of Synge, Tóibín won another 1920 Oireachtas prize with *An Mhuir* (The sea), his version of *Riders to the Sea*, another translation of which had been pronounced unsuccessful by Oireachtas judges two years before.[118] Once again Corkery's work in English drew particular attention from his Gaelic colleagues, and two of his plays were translated: *Clan Falvey (Ó Failbhe Mór)* by Seán Tóibín in 1918, and *The Yellow Bittern (An Bunán Buidhe)* by Liam Mac Eoghain and Pádraig Ó Domhnaill in 1919.[119] Béaslaí had the highest commendation for the former, both original and translation, stating that he would never have known it had been written first in English.[120]

If Ó Faoláin's bold scheme or the existence of these translations of dramatic works gives the impression that the Gaelic theater was thriving or even holding its own, that impression is altogether misleading. Scripts were indeed becoming available, but in almost every other area theater in Irish was in serious regression as the new acting companies that had arisen in Dublin in the years just prior to the Rising were

114. Seán Tóibín, "Móin na Réaltan," in *Scéilíní Anall, Oireachtas 1920* (Short stories from abroad, Oireachtas 1920), ed. Risteárd Ó Foghludha (Baile Átha Cliath: Connradh na Gaedhilge, n.d.), 48–55; and Piaras Béaslaí, "'Historia Hiberniae' / Pilib Ó Súilliováin Beura," *Irish Weekly Independent*, 22 May 1920.

115. "B. an D.," "An Breallaire Liath" (The grey boor), *An Stoc* 1, no. 7 (September–October 1918): 2.

116. See "An tOireachtas / Na hIomuíochta Liteardha" (The Oireachtas / The literary competitions), *FL*, 28 September 1918.

117. In *Cluichíní ón Iasacht, Oireachtas 1920* (Short plays from abroad, Oireachtas 1920), ed. Risteárd Ó Foghludha (Baile Átha Cliath: Connradh na Gaedhilge, n.d.), 29–73.

118. For Tóibín's translation, see *An Mhuir*, in *Cluichíní ó'n Iasacht*, 5–27. For the unsuccessful version, see Béaslaí, "Amharclann Ghaelach / Nach Mithid a Bunú?" (A Gaelic theater / Isn't it time to found it?), *FL*, 5 October 1918.

119. The first was published in *An Lóchrann* commencing in December 1918; the latter in *FL*, 2 August 1919.

120. "'Bord na Taidhse' / Cúrsaí Drámaidheachta / 'Ó Failbhe Mór'") ("The theatrical board" / Theatrical matters / Ó Failbhe Mór), *FL*, 31 May 1919. Béaslaí's standards were not low, and he had little use for many of the Gaelic plays in print at the time: "The main thing that held back the work of every troupe of actors was the lack of suitable plays. However many plays have been composed over the past twenty years, few have been suitable for production." (Isé an rud is mó a bhí ag cur cosc le hobair gach gasra cluicheoirí ná easba drámanna oireamhnach. Dá mhéid drámanna do ceapadh i nGaedhilg le fiche bliadhain anuas, is beag ceann atá oireamhnach i gcóir a léirithe.) See "Amharcla Ghaedhlach" (Gaelic theater), *FL*, 23 November 1918.

overwhelmed by political and military developments. Béaslaí, himself the single most important figure in Gaelic drama at this time, surveyed the situation in 1918: "We were progressing well when Easter Week came and Na hAisteoirí were scattered, for there was not a single man amongst them that did not have some connection with the work of that week."[121] Two years later *Misneach* reported that there had been no Gaelic plays produced in Dublin for two years, and commented that "most likely the troubled times are the cause, but whatever is responsible it has been a great step back and a great detriment to the work for the Irish language."[122] It was a step back more than a decade, for once again a few individual league branches, most notably the Central and Keating branches, were, under the coordination of the Oireachtas, providing the only stages for Gaelic theater in the capital.

So marginal did drama become, particularly in the provinces, that some writers were prompted to spell out, in terms unchanged from the very turn of the century, the reasons why the genre should be developed and promoted. Thus in May 1920 the Tralee journal *An Sgéal Nua* (The news) editorialized: "There is nothing we need more than clever actors or mimics who would perform humorous plays in Irish on stages. They would be a great help in making Irish a living language again in those places where it is withering or has withered."[123] But even Béaslaí could accept that, given the dire state of Gaelic theater in the post-Rising period, it would be necessary to go back—way back—to the basics. Conceding that "some of the Irish-language people were in too great a haste in theatrical matters, thinking they could walk before they had mastered crawling," Béaslaí argued: "In the first place, if we want good plays, we must see to it that there is a good audience in existence to understand them. For that reason it is best to begin with simple little plays, comic plays, in order to lure the public to take inter-

121. "Amharclann Ghaelach / Nach Mithid a Bunú?," *FL*, 5 October 1918. "Bhíomair ag treabhadh chun cinn go maith nuair a tháinig Seachtain na Cásca, agus d'imthigh scaipeadh ar na hAisteoirí, mar ní raibh éan bhuachaill ortha ná go raibh baint aige le hobair na Seachtaine sin."
122. "Drámaí Gaedhilge / Spreagadh Nuadh i nÁth Cliath" (Gaelic dramas / New life in Dublin), *Misneach*, 8 May 1920. "An saoghal buadhartha fé ndeara é, is dócha, ach pé nídh é ba chúis leis, ba mhór an chéim síos agus ba mhór an cheataighe d'obair na Gaedhilge é." Plans for acting companies in branches were discussed by Béaslaí in "Drámaí Gaedhilge / A dTairbhe don Ghluaiseacht" (Gaelic dramas / Their benefit to the movement), 11 September 1920.
123. "Eadrainn Féin" (Amongst ourselves), *An Sgéal Nua*, no. 2 (May 1920): 1. "Níl aon ní is mó a teasdabháil uainn ná aisteoirí clisde nó mimí a imreoch' cluithchí grinn tré Ghaeluinn ar stáidsí. Ba mhaith an cabhair iad chun teanga bheó a dhéanamh den nGaeluinn arís ins na háiteanaibh n-a bhfuil sí a feó nó feóchta."

est in Gaelic drama."[124] Ambitions had lowered since Na hAisteoirí trod the Abbey stage.

Among the sources of suitable plays Béaslaí suggested, and a source he himself tapped, was the translation of foreign works. Nor did he limit his call to the translation of plays alone. Writing in 1920 in the context of his debate with Ó Grianna, he argued: "It is true that some of the blood of English, of the blood of French, of the blood of German, must be brought into the drained veins of the old Irish language. The sooner this is done the better. If we want to make Irish a living language for all the people of Ireland, noble and humble, learned and unlearned, we will have to be constantly translating. We cannot rely on 'the Gaelic mind.' There are many thoughts that never occurred to the Gaelic mind."[125] The following year he returned to the question, asserting that "whatever kind of translation it is, the Irish language is better for it. That must be admitted. Gaelic literature is too constricted within itself, too insular—it must be broadened." He even went so far as to call translation "the most significant element in modern Gaelic literature" (an chuid is mó le rá de nua-leitríocht na Gaedhilge).[126] And he was by no means alone in this opinion; translation into Irish was the one area of literary activity in which there was significant expansion in the post-Rising period, making clear that, whatever its faults, the later translation policy of An Gúm was following rather than setting a cultural trend.

Needless to say, there was considerable debate on the issue although

124. "'Bord na Taidhse' / Obair le Déanamh," *FL*, 7 June 1919. Béaslaí conceded, "bhí fuadar róárd fé chuid de lucht na Gaedhilge i gcúrsaíbh drámaidheachta. Do mheasadar siubhal sara rabhadar istigh ar an lámhancán." He also wrote: "Ar an gcéad dul síos, má theastuigheann drámanna foghanta uainn, ní mór dúinn féachaint chuige go mbeidh pobul foghanta ann chun iad do thuigsint. Dá bhrígh sin is feárr tosnughadh le drámannaí beaga simplidhe, drámanna grinn, d'fhonn an pobul do mhealladh chun spéis a chur i ndrámaidheacht Ghaedhilge." Béaslaí also had his eye very much on the entertainment needs of native speakers in the Gaeltacht. See "Amharclann Ghaelach," *FL*, 5 October 1918.

125. "'Glaine na Teangan' / Leithleachas ná Caitliceacht?" ("The purity of the language" / Idiosyncrasy or universality?), *Irish Weekly Independent*, 16 October 1920. "Is fíor gur gá cuid d'fhuil an Bheurla agus d'fhuil na Fraincise agus d'fhuil na Gearmáinise do thabhairt isteach i bhféithibh tráighte na sean-Ghaedhilge. Dá luathacht a dheunfar son iseadh is feárr. Má's mian linn beo-theanga a dheunamh den Ghaedhilg do mhuinntir na hÉireann go léir idir uasal agus íseal, idir lucht léighinn agus lucht gan léighinn, caithfam bheith ag síor-aistriúchán. Ní féidir dúinn bheith ar dtaobh leis an 'aigne Ghaedhealach.' Tá a lán smaointe nár rith riamh chun an aigne Gaedhealaigh."

126. "Aistriúchán / Saol Nua i Leitríocht na Gaedhilge" (Translation / A new world in Gaelic literature), editorial, *Misneach*, 19 February 1921; see note 8. "Ach pé saghas é an t-aistriúchán is fearrde an Ghaedhilg é. Caithfar an méid sin d'admháil. Tá leitríocht na Gaedhilge ró-chumhang innte féin, ró-oileánach, ní fuláir í d'fhairsingiú."

arguments on both sides showed little real development over those of the first decade of the century. Assessing the situation in 1921, one of the pioneers of that decade, "Conall Cearnach," wrote: "I said to myself that we began writing Irish too soon when we did not do what every other nation in the same predicament as ourselves did—that is when we did not first translate the literary gems of the world and then begin ourselves."[127] "Ros Fáilghe" agreed, though his literary ambitions were humbler: "If we want to compose a new literature, we should, as a start, put the great books of the world into Irish, especially the simple books of fabulous stories, for it is from them that every other literature in existence today has grown. It's no good for us to be trying to put the 'Classics' into Irish, for Irish itself is not sufficiently cultivated for that. Childhood comes first and adulthood afterwards."[128]

One "Coimhead" followed the logic of this argument into more controversial territory in a lengthy and well-reasoned 1917 essay in *An Claidheamh Soluis*. Discussing the complexities and challenges of successful translation, "Coimhead" pronounced such work more difficult than original composition, and continued: "Good translation is of more benefit to a language like Irish (a language that was, after all, dying twenty years ago) than is original composition, just as medicinal food and drink are of more benefit to a sick person than everyday food."[129]

In an essay supporting Ó Conaire's An Ridireacht Liteartha, Ernest

127. "An Madra Muscailte / 'Conall Cearnach' as a Chodladh" (The dog awakened / "Conall Cearnach" out of his sleep), *Misneach*, 18 June 1921. "Dubhairt mé liom féin gur thosuigh muid ró-luath ag scríobhadh na Gaedhilge, nuair nach ndeárnamar an rud do rinne gach náisiún eile bhí sa chás chéadna linne—'sé sin nuair nach ndeárnamar seoda liteardha an tsaoil a aistriú i dtosach, agus annsin tosú féin."

128. "Finnsceuluíocht / Litríocht Ar Sean" (Fabulous stories / The literature of our ancestors), *FL*, 3 August 1918. "Má's maith linn litridheacht nua do chumadh ba cheart dúinn, mar thosnú, Gaedhilg do chur ar leabhraibh móra an domhain, go mór mór na leabhra simplidhe finnsceulacha, mar is uatha soin d'fhás gach aon litridheacht atá ann indiu. Ní haon mhaitheas dúinn bheith ag iarraidh Gaidhilg do chur ar na 'Classics' fós, mar níl an Ghaedhilg féin saothruighthe a dóithin chuige sin. Tagann an leanbhaidheacht ar dtúis agus an fhearamhlacht na dhiaidh." Yet in a September 1920 letter to *Misneach*, "Ros Fáilghe" could also ask "Why don't Gaelic writers set about Gaelicizing the great books of the world? It is likely that there is no small nation in Europe as badly off as are we with regard to books." (Cad 'na thaobh nach luigheann sgríbhneoirí na Gaeilge isteach chun leabhra móra an domhan do Ghaelú? Is dócha nach bhfuil aon náisiún beag san Eoraip chó holc linne i dtaobh leabhar.) See "Ros Fáilghe," letter, *Misneach*, 25 September 1920.

129. "Aistriughchán" (Translation), *ACS*, 29 December 1917. "Déanann aistriughchán foghanta níos mó maitheasa do theangain mar an nGaedhilg (teanga féach, a bhí i riocht báis fiche bliadhain ó shoin) ná bun-chumadóireacht, díreach mar a dhéanann deoch-leighis agus biadh leighis níos mó maitheasa do dhuine bhreoidhte ná deoch agus biadh laetheamhail."

Blythe focused on the importance of translation in providing worthwhile reading matter for the new audience being created by league classes and the schools, particularly in the Gaeltacht: "An abundance of good books could be gotten if it were agreed to translate books from other languages. . . . And I think it far better to produce a translation of a famous book than to throw newly composed rubbish to the people. And another thing, translation is an enterprise that is needed, for young people in the Gaeltacht who want to read would like to read the famous books of the world, and it isn't right that they should have to turn to English before they can do that."[130]

More aesthetic considerations motivated Micheál Mac Liammóir in his negative response to a proposal to translate contemporary Gaelic works into English:

> I think it would be a great thing to leave everything written in Irish as it is, and to publish translations from the other languages of the world—translations from English (in particular from the writings of our own Irish authors who write in the language of the English), from Spanish, from German, from French, etc. Translations are to be found in every living language except Irish, many of them. Translation, putting the best literary efforts into Irish, would, then, be a greater benefit to Irish than would putting the few new works we have in the tongue of the Gael into English.[131]

On the other hand, for some like P. S. Ua hÉigeartaigh translation was at best a harmless exercise and at worst a dissipation of creative

130. "An Ridireacht Nuadh / Deacracht na hOibre" (The new Knighthood / The difficulty of the work), *ACS*, 24 March 1917. "Mar sin féin féadfaidhe reidhse leabhar maith d'fhaghail dá nglactaí le leabhra d'aistrigheadh ó theangthachaibh eile. . . . Agus is dóigh liom-sa gur fearr go mór aistriú maith ar leabhar clúmhail do chur amach ná drabhaoil nua-cheapaithe do chaitheamh chun na ndaoine. Rud eile de, obair 'seadh an t-aistriú go bhfuil gádh léi; óir daoine óga sa Ghaedhealtacht go mbeadh fonn léightheoireachta ortha theastóchadh uatha leabhra clúmhla an domhain do léigheamh, agus níor cheart go mbeadh ortha iompódh chum an Bhéarla sara dtiocfadh leo san do dhéanamh."

131. Micheál Mac Uaimmhóir [sic], "Aistriúchán agus Litridheacht" (Translation and literature), letter, *ACS*, 10 November 1917. "Sílim go mbadh mhór an rud gach a sgríobhtar i nGaedhilg a d'fhágaint mar atá, agus aistriughadh ó theangachaibh eile an domhain do chur fá chló—aistriughadh ó'n mBéarla, (ó sgríbhinnibh ár n-ughdar Éireannacha féin a sgríobhann i dteangain na Sasanach go h-áirighthte), ó'n Spáinnis, ó'n Almáinnis, ó'n bhFrainncis, etc. Bíonn aistriughadh le faghail i ngach aon teanga bheo acht an Ghaedhilg—mórán díobh. Badh mhó an tairbhe do'n Ghaedhilg aistriughadh mar sin— Gaedhilg do chur ar na hiarrachtaí litridheachta is fearr—ná an Béarla do chur ar an méid beag nuadhéanta dá bhfuil againn i dteangain na nGaedheal."

energies better applied to original work.[132] And for those of nativist bent the danger ran far deeper. Their concerns were given most forceful expression by Ó Grianna, who cautioned that indiscriminate translation could do serious harm to "the Gaelic mind." Answering those who argued that translation was the quickest way to introduce modern ideas and themes into Gaelic literature, Ó Grianna stormed: "Of course, if all they want is something modern, and if there is no such thing as the Gaelic mind, why don't they just turn to the language they have right at hand and that is as modern and up-to-date as they desire—that is English?"[133] Ó Grianna was not opposed to translation per se. He simply demanded such imposing qualifications from would-be translators that few—one of them himself—could meet them: "In my opinion no one at all should undertake translation except for the native speaker of Irish who has also mastered the language from which he would be translating."[134]

He was, however, fighting a losing cause, opposed even by his fellow Gaeltacht native "An Seabhac," who opened the pages of *An Lóchrann* to translation on the grounds that "when original composition is but rarely to be found, I must be satisfied with the next best thing— translation from other languages."[135] Other editors obviously agreed, and translations of all sorts from writers both Gaeltacht and Galltacht were a regular feature of Gaelic periodicals at this time. Once again the

132. "Ceist na hAistriúcháin" (The question of translation), *ACS*, 8 December 1917.

133. "'Suas Chun Dáta' / Beul na hUaighe agus Beul na Truaighe" ("Up to date" / The grave mouth and the poor mouth), *Misneach*, 7 May 1921. "Ar ndóighe, mura bhfuil a dhíth ortha ach rud 'moderanta,' agus má tá nach bhfuil aigneadh Gaedhealach ann ar chor ar bith cad chuige nach dtugann siad aghaidh ar an teangaidh ata i gcúl an dorais aca agus atá chomh moderanta agus chomh fada suas chun dáta agus is mian leo—mar tá an Béarla." The immediate source of Ó Grianna's anger here was a piece by Aodh de Blácam, in which he agreed with Ó Grianna about the importance of writers immersing themselves in "Gaelachas," but also stressed that they should read widely in foreign literatures and should translate, since "it is not possible for a storyteller to compose modern stories without this knowledge" (chan féidir scéalta moderna chumadh gan an t-eolas seo ag an scéalaidhe). See de Blácam, "Ceard an Scríbhneóra / Cionnas Í Fhoghluim" (The writer's craft / How to learn it), *Misneach*, 26 March 1921.

134. "Aistriú / Na Smaointe agus Ní hIad na Focail," *Misneach*, 19 February 1921. "Do réir mo bharamhla-sa níor chóir do dhaoinibh ar bith aistriú a dhéanamh ach an té a mbeadh an Ghaedhilc aige ó dhúthchas agus an teangaidh a rabh sé ag aistriú aisti le na cois."

135. "Ar gCúram Féin," *An Lóchrann*, February 1920, 4. "Nuair ná bíonn an ceapadóireacht nua le fagháil ach go gann caithim a bheith sásta leis an gcéim is giorra dhó—aistriú ó theanganaibh eile." "An Seabhac" continued: "We aren't all that fond of that sort of thing either, but it is far better than folktales." (Ní ró mhaith a thaithnigheann an saghas san, leis, linn ach gur fearr go mór é ná na sean-scéalta.)

range of languages and literatures involved was rather narrow. Material from England continued for the most part to be excluded, in part on the sensible grounds laid down by "Ros Fáilghe," who asked why Gaelic writers should waste their time providing works "that any Gael could read in the original if he wanted to" (gur féidir le gach aon Gael iad do léigheamh sa mbunús, má's maith leis é).[136] When Seán Ó Ciarghusa ("Cloch Labhrais") issued a tongue-in-cheek call in *Misneach* for immediate and abundant translation from English, Béaslaí felt compelled to insert the following editorial note: "We think it probable that 'Cloch Labhrais' is joking, but we fear that there are people who won't get the joke."[137] And when Ó Ciarghusa wrote another piece illustrated with absurdly literal translations of English verse, Béaslaí again added a note: "An enormous amount of the kind of 'poetry' that 'Cloch Labhrais' praises is sent to us for this paper."[138] On the other hand, the wisdom of translating Shakespeare was seriously debated in 1917, largely as the result of Seán Tóibín's exercise in putting a scene from *The Merchant of Venice* into Irish in *An Lóchrann*.[139] Of other Anglophone literatures, writing from Scotland, in particular the work of Neil Munro, continued to be of some interest,[140] and there also seems to have been a greater

136. "Sgríobh na Gaedhilge / Aistriú agus Bunús" (Gaelic writing: Translation and originality), *Misneach*, 9 October 1920.

137. See Seán Ó Ciarghusa, "Aistriuchán / An Ghaedhilg Seo Chugainn / Seoda Snasta" (Translation / The Irish of the future / Polished gems"), *Misneach*, 7 February 1920. Béaslaí wrote: "Is dóich linn gur ag magadh atá 'Cloch Labhrais,' ach is baoghlach go bhfuil daoine ann ná tuigfidh an magadh."

138. See Seán Ó Ciarghusa, "Aistriuchán / Filidheacht i nGaedhilg / Cionnus Í Sgríobhadh" (Translation / Poetry in Irish / How to write it), *Misneach*, 6 March 1920. "Cuirtear uathbhás Éireann den tsadhas son 'filidheachta' a mholann 'Cloch Labhrais' ag triall orainn i gcóir an pháipéir seo."

139. "Portia gona Leannánaibh" (Portia with her lovers), *An Lóchrann*, October 1917. At this same time Feargus Ó Nualláin announced that he was at work on a Gaelic *Hamlet*, a project that drew support from "P. Ó G." and opposition from "Dubhán Alla" and Ernest Joynt. See Ó Nualláin, "Amluid i nGaedhilg" (Hamlet in Irish), *ACS*, 17 November 1917; P. Ó G., "Gaedhilg ar Séicspír" (Shakespeare in Irish), *ACS*, 15 December 1917; "Dubhán Alla," "Séicspír i nGaedhilg" (Shakespeare in Irish), *ACS*, 24 November 1917; and Joynt, "Smaointe Nuadha—Béarla Leitre—'Séicspír'" (New thoughts—English spelling—"Shakespeare"), *ACS*, 8 December 1917. Ó Nualláin noted that he had shown his work to Micheál Mhag Ruaidhrí.

140. See Seán Tóibín, "'Liom-sa an Gleann So': 'Red Hand' by Neil Munro. Iar n-a Thiontó go Gaedhilg le Cead a Ughdair" ("This Glen is Mine": "Red Hand" by Neil Munro. Translated into Irish with the permission of its author), *An Lóchrann*, August 1918, 1–2; Tóibín, "Firín Rinn na bhFrancach / Eachtra ó Ghaeltacht na hAlban" ("The Sea Fairy of French Foreland" / An adventure from the Scottish Gaeltacht), *Misneach*, 30 July 1921; and Tóibín, "An 'Sergeant' Mór" ("The Fell Sergeant") and "Murcha Dubh" ("Black Murdo"), in *Scéilíní Anall*, 41–47; 56–75.

appreciation of American literature as a distinct entity. Thus we find
translations or adaptations of three pieces by Twain,[141] of two fables by
Mrs. Stetson,[142] and of stories by Jack London,[143] O. Henry,[144] and
Edgar Allan Poe.[145] Moreover, the Stetson pieces and the London story
were identified as having been originally written in "American" (Pon-
cáinis).

Of the Continental literatures French remained the most popular
source of translation, with the preference continuing to be for the odd
play or the work of noncontroversial figures like Daudet,[146] Maupas-
sant,[147] and Bazin.[148] The most substantial rendering from the French in
the period was Liam Ó Rinn's *Leabhar na Polainne* (The book of Poland), a translation of the French text of Adam Mickiewicz's *Le Livre de
la nation polonaise et des pèlerins polonais.* Along with Ó Rinn other

141. See "Gruagach an Tobair," "Mark Twain agus na Fiacha Dubha" (Mark Twain
and the carrion crows), *An Lóchrann*, February 1919, 1; "Fánaidhe," "Seanduine
Gruamdha / Gan Gol gan Gáire" (A morose old man / Without weeping without laughing), *Misneach*, 8 May 1920; and Béaslaí, "Gaduíocht i dTeampoll / Poncánach i gCrua-
Chás (blúire de 'A Tramp Abroad')" (Theft in a church: A Yankee in a tight situation [a
fragment from *A Tramp Abroad*]), *Irish Weekly Independent*, 19 February 1921.
142. "Ciarraidheach," "Dhá Fabhail-Sgeul" (Two fables), *Misneach*, 11 September 1920.
143. Seán Mac Gabhann, "An Smeara Leighis: Blodh den 'Lost Face' le Jack London,
Americánach é sin" (The healing ointment: An excerpt from *The Lost Face* by the American Jack London), *An Lóchrann*, July 1920, 2.
144. Seán Tóibín, "An Feallaire ná Feallfadh" ("A Double-Dyed Deceiver"), *Misneach*,
12 March 1921.
145. Risteárd Ó Foghludha, "Rí-Rá na Pláighe Fola" ("The Masque of the Red
Death"), in *Scéilíní Anall*, 34–40. Interestingly, in 1902 one "M. O'D" had claimed Poe as
"a famous Irish-American writer." See "Edgar Allan Poe and the Irish Question," *UI*, 18
October 1902.
146. See, for example, Seán Ua Conchubhair, "Léigear Bherlin" ("Le Siège de Berlin"),
FL, 5 April 1919; Mícheál Ó Súilleabháin, "Sagart Parróiste Cille Mártain" ("Le Curé de
Cucugnan"), *An Lóchrann*, March 1920; Risteárd Ó Foghludha, "Tusach Oibre" ("Instal-
lation"), *Misneach*, 18 December 1920; Ó Foghludha, "Rún Cornille Muilteoir" ("Le Secret de Maître Cornille"), *Irish Weekly Independent* (Christmas 1920); Ó Foghludha, "An
Ceacht Deiridh / 'Vive la France!'" ("La Dernière Classe"), *Misneach*, 5 February 1921; Ó
Foghludha, "Minnseach Sheaguin" ("La Chèvre de M. Seguin"), *Irish Weekly Independent*,
24 September 1921; León Ó Broin, "Blanquette," *Banba* 1, no. 5 (September 1921); and
Eibhlín Ní Airtnéide, "An Spídheadóir Óg" ("L'Enfant espion"), *Banba* 2, no. 2 (Decem-
ber 1921).
147. See, for example, Riobárd Ó Brolacháin, "Ag Imirt Chleas" ("Une Ruse"), *Mis-
neach*, 1 May 1920; Ó Brolacháin, "An Bacach / B'Iongna le Cach É" ("Le Vagabond"),
Misneach, 8 May 1920; and Sinéad Ní Chíosáin, "Ag Marcaidheacht" ("À Cheval"),
Branar 2, no. 1 (August 1920): 18–24.
148. See, for example, Mícheál Mac Connraoi, "An Ceathramhadh Fear Déirce" ("Le
Quatrième pauvre"), *FL*, 3 August 1918; and Cormac Ó Cadhlaigh, "Bosga na Leitreach"
("La Boîte aux lettres"), *An Síoladóir* 2, no. 3 (December 1921): 126–31.

prominent revivalists who translated from the French were Máire Ní Chinnéide, León Ó Broin, Cormac Ó Cadhlaigh, Diarmuid Ó Foghludha ("Feargus Finnbhéil"), Risteárd Ó Foghludha, the most prolific among them, and "Ros Fáilghe." From the German, there was again just the odd contribution: an occasional story,[149] excerpts from Heine's *Harzreise*,[150] the synopsis of a play whose author is not identified,[151] and "An Gheilt" (The lunatic) by Paul Heyse, the title story of Colm Ó Murchadha's 1919 book *An Gheilt agus Scéal Eile*.[152] From Italian there was very little, although An tAthair Risteard Pléimeann's "Saighdiúir ag Comhrádh le Dia" (A soldier conversing with God), his serialized translation of the reflections of an Italian soldier killed in the First World War, ran for more than a year in *An Síoladóir* in 1920–21.[153] Two of the great Russians who so inspired Gaelic progressives were also brought into Irish at this time, with Riobárd Ó Brolacháin translating a Chekhov story and "An Seabhac" and Séan Tóibín works by Tolstoy.[154] Whatever Ó Brolacháin's or Tóibín's linguistic backgrounds, "An Seabhac" did not know Russian. Of the Scandinavians, Hans Christian Andersen was frequently translated, although with the exception of "Ros Fáilghe" we should perhaps again assume that those doing the work were reliant on English versions rather than on the Danish originals.[155]

149. See Seán Ua Conchubhair, "Sgéal Dhá Linn" (A story of two times), *Branar* 1, no. 5 (February 1920): 170–74 (the author of the original was not identified); Lil Nic Dhonnchadha, "Gasperl agus Annerl / Eachtraí i dTír an Leabhair" (Gasperl and Annerl / Adventures in bookland), *Misneach*, 31 July 1920 (the original was by Josef Von Eichendorff); Donnchadh Ó Loingsigh, "An Dá Bhóthar" ("The Two Roads" by Richter), *An Síoladóir* 1, no. 5 (July 1921): 42–43.

150. See anonymous, "Goettingen / Tuairisc na Catharach" ("Göttingen / An account of the city), *Misneach*, 24 April 1920; and Béaslaí, "Dr. Archer / Taidhse gan Creideamh" (Dr. Archer / A phantom without faith), *Irish Weekly Independent*, 12 February 1921.

151. Seán Mac Gabhann, "Ceanndánacht" (Stubbornness), *An Lóchrann*, June 1920, 2–3. The original author was not identified.

152. "An Gheilt," in *An Gheilt agus Scéal Eile* (Cill Áirne: Cualacht Bhréanainn, 1919). The other story was Prosper Mérimée's "Tamango." It should also be noted that Risteárd Ó Foghludha translated two of Mérimée's stories in *Scéilíní Anall*.

153. *An Síoladóir* 1, no. 1 (June 1920)—2, no. 2 (Autumn 1921). Colm Ó Murchadha ("Taube") also translated an Italian story by an unidentified author as "Coga na Naomh" (The war of the saints) in *Branar* 2, no. 1 (August 1920): 47–54. Ó Murchadha made plain in a note that he was working from the original language.

154. Riobárd Ó Brolacháin, "An Fiabhras Breac / Sgeul ón Rúisis" (Typhoid fever / A story from the Russian), *Misneach*, 24 April 1920; "An Seabhac," "Cúiteamh an Diabhail Bhig" (The little devil's reward), *An Lóchrann*, June 1919, 1–2; and Seán Tóibín, "Sebhastopol le Linn an Léigir" (Sebastopol during the siege), *Misneach*, 26 February 1921.

155. See "Gráinne na Buaile," "An Seilmide agus an Rosóg" (The snail and the rose-bush), *FL*, 4 January 1919; "Ros Fáilghe," "An Bheirt Leanán / Neamh-mbuaine

On the other hand, Áine Bhreathnach made clear that she was working from the Old Norse in "Bás Bhalair" (The death of Balor) and "Eachtra Thoir" (Thor's adventure) in *An Stoc* in 1917 and 1918.[156]
The only Celtic society that inspired sustained interest at this time was that of Scotland.[157] Again, one could imagine the calendar had been turned back as writer after writer dwelt on the identity of Gaelic culture on both sides of the North Channel. Béaslaí, for example, entitled a 1919 *Fáinne an Lae* editorial "The Two Dialects" (An Dá Chanamhaint), writing: "It is a great pity how few people in Ireland understand that it is the same language that is spoken by the Gaels of Ireland and the Gaels of Scotland."[158] Liam Ó Rinn went further, echoing the Erskine–Pearse plea for "reciprocity" in a lengthy essay "Gaedhil na hÉireann agus Gaedhil na hAlban" (The Gaels of Ireland and the Gaels of Scotland):

> I fear the Gaels of Ireland have no interest in the Gaelic nor in the Gaels of Scotland. It is great pity, for if they had interest in the Gaelic or the Gaels of Scotland it would not be long until there grew from that interest a bond of friendship between the two countries, and both of them would be the better for that friendship in matters concerning the Gaelic language and in political matters. The people of Ireland and the people of Scotland are the offspring of a single race, and the Gaelic of Ireland and the Gaelic of Scotland are variants of a single language.[159]

grádha" ("Koerestefolkene"), *FL*, 26 April 1919; Riobárd Ó Brolacháin, "Suaimhneas Meoin / Siubhlóid san Roilig" (Peace of mind / A walk in the graveyard), *Misneach*, 22 May 1920; "Seáinín," "An Cleite Beag Bán / Eachtra na Circe" (The little white feather / The adventure of the hen), *Misneach*, 3 July 1920; and Béaslaí, "'Lom na Fírinne' / Eachtra an Chleite" ("The bare truth" / The adventure of the feather), *Irish Weekly Independent*, 12 June 1920; "An Mucuidhe / 'Deire leis an Scléip'" (The pig-keeper / "An end to the merriment"), *Irish Weekly Independent*, 26 June 1920; "Ráis na nAinmhithe / Bronnadh na nDuaiseanna" (The race of the animals / The awarding of the prizes), *Irish Weekly Independent*, 22 January 1921.
156. "Bás Bhalair," *An Stoc* 1, no. 1 (December 1917): 3; and "Eachtra Thoir," *An Stoc* 1, no. 6 (July–August 1918): 2.
157. Far less attention was paid to Wales. See "The Welsh Example," editorial, *ACS*, 22 September 1917; and "Saothar na mBreathnach / Filidheacht Nua sa Bhreatnais" (The work of the Welsh / New poetry in Welsh), *Misneach*, 12 March 1921.
158. *FL*, 22 February 1919. "Is mór an truagh a luighead daoine i nÉirinn a thuigeann gurab í an teanga cheudna atá dá labhairt ag Gaedhealaibh na hÉireann agus ag Gaedhealaibh na hAlban."
159. *ACS*, 1 September 1917. "Is eagail liom ná cuirid Gaedhil Éireann puinn suime i nGaedhilg ná i nGaedhlaibh na hAlban. Is mór an truagh é, mar, dá mbeadh suim aca i nGaedhilg agus i nGaedhlaibh na hAlban níor bhfada go dtiocfadh as an suim sin caradas

Interest in other Celtic cultures was so low that it seems to have been indifference more than anything else that made it possible for official Irish representatives to attend without controversy Pan-Celtic gatherings at Birkenhead and on the Isle of Man in 1917 and 1921 respectively. Moreover, according to Peadar Mac Fhionnlaoich, the league had intended to have representatives of all the Celtic nations present for discussion of common issues at the 1919 Oireachtas, an idea of which Mac Fhionnlaoich himself approved but which fell through for unspecified reasons.[160] In his report on his visit to Birkenhead in 1917, Father Paul Walsh stated that both himself and his colleague Liam Ó Briain had been impressed by what they saw, and in particular by the Welsh, of whom he stated in terms virtually identical to those of Mac Fhionnlaoich from 1899: "Wales is already an example to every other Celtic nation, but I would say that these men will perform some feat in the revival of their language that will stir the Irish and the Scots and the Bretons and the Manx to follow them and to emulate them."[161] Ó Briain was similarly taken with the Eisteddfod, encouraging every Gael to see it, for then "he will understand the long road we must still travel in Ireland" (tuigfidh sé cad é an bóthar fada atá le cur dínn againn fós i nÉirinn).[162] In 1921 the league saw the Pan-Celtic Congress on Man important enough to send Hyde and Agnes O'Farrelly as envoys, although the gathering did draw a scornful editorial comment from Béaslaí in *Misneach* for using English as its working language and excluding all discussion of politics.[163]

There was no way the discussion or practice of politics could be excluded from any Irish movement after 1916, and this insistent intrusion of political imperatives into Gaelic cultural deliberations is epitomized

---

do cheangal idir an dá thír agus b'fhearra de dhóibh araon an caradas san i gcúrsaí na Gaedhilge féin agus i gcúrsaí poilitíochta. Sliocht aon chine is adh muintir na hÉireann agus muintir na hAlban agus is ó aon teangain amháin Gaedhilg na hÉireann agus Gaedhilg na hAlban." Ó Rinn could, however, be critical of corruptions and Anglicisms in Scots Gaelic. See his review of the new Scottish periodical *An Rósarnach* in *ACS*, 25 August 1917.

160. "Na Cinidheacha Ceilteacha" (The Celtic races), *Guth na Bliadhna* 16, no. 4 (Winter 1919): 340. Mac Fhionnlaoich himself didn't think much could have developed from such an initiative beyond social and cultural exchanges.

161. Pól Breathnach, "An Chomhdháil Cheilteach i mBirkenhead" (The Celtic Congress at Birkenhead), *Guth na Bliadhna* 14, no. 4 (Winter 1917): 415. "Tá an Bhreatain n'a sompla cheana féin do gach náisiún Ceilteach eile, ach déarfainn go ndéanfaidh na fearaibh seo gníomh éigin i n-aithbheóchaint a dteangan a ghríosfaidh Éireannaigh agus Albannaigh agus muintir na Briotáine agus muintir Innis Mhanann chum iad do leanmhaint agus aithris do dhéanamh orra."

162. "An Chomhdháil Cheilteach," *ACS*, 15 September 1917.

163. "Ceilteachas," editorial, *Misneach*, 2 July 1921.

by the events of the evening of 6 December 1921. That year marked the
600th anniversary of the death of Dante, an occasion that inspired the
odd Gaelic essay,[164] but that was to be celebrated most impressively by a
scholarly colloquium under the auspices of the Dáil's Ministry of Fine
Arts at Dublin's Mansion House on the evening in question. With
Éamonn de Valera in the chair, Máire Ní Chinnéide, Tomás Ó Máille,
and Piaras Béaslaí, among others, were to deliver lectures, Béaslaí's on
"the question of the language in Italy in the time of Dante compared
with the question of the Irish language in Ireland at present" (ceist na
teangan san Iodáil le linn Dante i gcompráid le ceist na Gaedhilge in
Éirinn fé láthair), including a comparison of Dante's meters with those
of Old Irish poetry.[165] As he arrived for the evening, de Valera was met
by Cathal Brugha and Austin Stack with preliminary news of the Anglo-Irish Treaty signed in London early that morning and soon to drive
both the Dáil and the nation into dispute and ultimately civil war. As he
presided at the meeting, Gaelic and Tuscan metrics must have been the
furthest things from his mind.

Writing in *Guth na Bliadhna* in the summer of 1919, Mac Fhionnlaoich had asserted: "Everyone knows that if the Dáil takes control of
the country—and everyone knows that there is at least a chance that it
will—the Irish language will be restored to preeminence in every part
of the country. . . . If Dáil Éireann succeeds in getting full freedom or
even partial freedom for the country, it is not long until we will have
the Irish language on its feet again.[166] Most if not all Gaelic activists
shared his faith, and in late 1921 its realization must have seemed to
many at hand, with a free Ireland theirs to make Gaelic as well.[167] But
after the evening of 6 December neither the members of the Dáil nor the
people they represented were to have time for cultural or bookish pur-
suits. The four glorious decades of the Gaelic Revival were at an end.

164. See Pádraig Eric Mac Fhinn, "Dante," *An Sioladoir* 2, no. 2 (Autumn 1921): 55–57;
and Pádraic Ó Domhnalláin, "Dante Alighieri / Saighdiúir agus Sgoth-Fhile" (Dante
Alighieri / Soldier and master poet), *Misneach*, 8 October 1921.

165. See "Ireland and Dante," *WF*, 3 December 1921; and "Dante," *Misneach*, 17 December 1921.

166. "Dáil Eireann agus an Ghaedhilg" (Dáil Eireann and the Irish language), *Guth na
Bliadhna* 16, no. 2 (Summer 1919): 170. "Tuigeann gach uile dhuine má thig an Dáil i
gceannas na tíre, agus tuigeann gach uile dhuine go bhfuil ar a laghad cunndar (seans) ann
go dtiocfaidh, go gcuirfear an Ghaedhilg in árd-réim i ngach áird sa tír. . . . Má éirgheann
le Dáil Éireann lán-tsaoirse nó fiú leath-shaoirse d'fhághail do'n tír, ní fada go mbeidh an
Ghaedhilg ar a bonnaibh againn arís."

167. For the high ideals and ambivalent achievements of the First Dáil, see Nollaig Ó
Gadhra, *An Chéad Dáil Éireann (1919–1921) agus an Ghaeilge* (The first Dáil Éireann,
1919–1921, and the Irish language) (Baile Átha Cliath: Coiscéim, 1989).

Selected Bibliography

I. Primary Sources

Manuscripts and Personal Papers (all in the National Library of Ireland with the exception of the material from the Pearse Museum)

Patrick Dinneen Papers
J. J. Doyle (Séamus Ó Dubhghaill) Papers
Fionán Mac Coluim Papers
Eoin Mac Néill Papers
Patrick Pearse Papers
Pearse Collection, including books from Pearse's personal library, in the Pearse Museum, Sgoil Éanna, Rathfarnham.
Peadar Ua Laoghaire Papers

Periodicals

All Ireland Review
Árd na h-Éireann: An Irish Ireland Magazine
Banba (1901–6)
Banba (1921)
An Barr Buadh
Bean na hÉireann
Branar
Catholic Bulletin and Book Review
An Claidheamh Soluis
An Connachtach
An Crann
An Craobh Ruadh: Irisleabhar Chonnartha na Gaedhilge ghá Chur Amach ag Muin-ntir na h-Árd-Sgoile, Béal Feirste
Éire go Bragh: A Monthly Bi-lingual Magazine for the Preservation and Promotion of the Language, Industries, Music, Art, and Literature of Ireland
An t-Éireannach (London)
An t-Európach
Fáinne an Lae (1898–1900; 1918–20)
Fianna
Freeman's Journal

An Gaodhal (Brooklyn)
Glór na Ly: Páipéar Nóchda a n-ay an Ví
An Grianán: Páipéar Cinn Bhliadhna do Ghaedhealaibh Chorcaighe, Craobh Naoimh
    Fionn-Bharra i gCorcaigh
Guth na Bliadhna (Glasgow)
Guth na nGaedheal (London)
Inis Fáil: A Magazine for the Irish in London
Irish Freedom
Irish Nation and Peasant and Irish Peasant
Irish Review
Irish Rosary: A Monthly Magazine Conducted by the Dominican Fathers
Irish Weekly Independent
Irisleabhar Mhuighe Nuadhat
Irisleabhar na Gaedhilge
Journal of the Ivernian Society
An Leabharlann
The Leader
Loch Léin
An Lóchrann
An Macaomh
Misneach
An Muimhneach Óg: Irisleabhar Míosamhail chun Cabrughadh leis an Dream atá
    d'Iaraidh Éire Dhéanamh Gaedhealach
Ná Bac Leis
National Student
New Ireland Review
The Republic
An Reult: Irisleabhar na h-Ollscoile
St. Stephen's: A Record of University Life
An Saoghal Gaedhealach, the Irish World and Industrial Advocate
Saothar na h-Éireann (London)
An Sgéal Nua
An Sgiath / The Shield
Shan Van Vocht
Sinn Féin
An Síoladóir
An Sléibhteánach / The Mountaineer: Irisleabhar Choláiste Chnuic Mhellerí
An Stoc
Uladh: A Literary and Critical Magazine
United Irishman
Weekly Freeman, National Press and Irish Agriculturist

Books, Pamphlets, and Articles

Béaslaí, Piaras. Astronár. Baile Átha Cliath: Oifig an tSoláthair, 1928.
———. Earc agus Áine agus Scéalta Eile. Baile Átha Cliath: Oifig an tSoláthair, 1946.
———. "Merriman's Secret: An Interpretation." In Brian Merriman, Cúirt an
    Mheadhon Oidhche, edited by Risteárd Ó Foghludha. Dublin: Hodges and
    Figgis, 1912.

————. *Eachtra Pheadair Schlemihl*. Baile Átha Cliath: Muintir na Leabhar Gaedhilge, 1909.

Borthwick, Norma, trans. *Leabhairín na Leanbh: Roinnt Sgéilíní a Tógadh a' Sgéaltaibh H. C. Andersen*. Baile Átha Cliath: Muintir na Leabhar Gaedhilge, 1913.

Breathnach, Mícheál. *Cnoc na nGabha*. Baile Átha Cliath: Connradh na Gaedhilge, 1906.

————. *Sgríbhinní Mhíchíl Bhreathnaigh, maille le n-a Bheathaidh*. Edited by Tomás Mac Domhnaill. Baile Átha Cliath: M. H. Mac Guill agus a Mhac, 1913.

————. *Stair na hÉireann*. Edited by Seosamh Laoide. 3 parts. Baile Átha Cliath: Connradh na Gaedhilge, 1909–11.

Butler, Mary. *Blátha Bealtaine*. Translated by Tomás Ua Concheanainn. Baile Átha Cliath: Connradh na Gaedhilge, 1902.

Cluichíní ó'n Iasacht, Oireachtas 1920. Edited by Risteárd Ó Foghludha. Baile Átha Cliath: Connradh na Gaedhilge, n.d.

Colum, Mary. *Life and the Dream*. Garden City, N.Y.: Doubleday, 1947.

Colum, Padraic. *An Talamh: Dráma Trí Ghníomh*. Translated by Tadhg Ó Donnchadha. Dublin: Maunsel and Company, 1906.

Cuimhní na bPiarsach. Cuid a 3. Baile Átha Cliath: Coiste Cuimhneacháin na bPiarsach, n.d.

Davis, Thomas. *Prose Writings of Thomas Davis. Edited with an Introduction by T. W. Rolleston*. London: Walter Scott, n.d.

de Blaghd, Earnán. *Gaeil á Múscailt*. Baile Átha Cliath: Sáirséal agus Dill, 1973.

————. *Slán le hUltaibh*. Baile Átha Cliath: Sáirséal agus Dill, 1971.

————. *Trasna na Bóinne*. Baile Átha Cliath: Sáirséal agus Dill, 1957.

Degidon, N. F. *Seosamh Ó Callanáin*. Translated by D. Ó C. Baile Átha Cliath: Oifig "An Teachtaire Éireannaigh," 1908.

De Vere, Aubrey. *The Foray of Queen Maeve and Other Legends of Ireland's Heroic Age*. London: Kegan Paul, Trench, 1882.

Dinneen, Patrick. *Aistí ar Litridheacht Ghréigise agus Laidne*. Baile Átha Cliath: Muinntir C.S. Ó Fallamhain, Teo. i gComhar le hOifig an tSoláthair, 1929.

————. *Cormac Ua Conaill*. Baile Átha Cliath: Connradh na Gaedhilge, 1901.

————. *Creideamh agus Gorta: Tráighidheacht Bhaineas le hAimsir an Droch-Shaoghail, 1847*. Dublin: E. Ponsonby, 1901.

————. *Duan an Nodlag / A Christmas Carol in Prose le Séarlas Dicens, aistrighthe ó'n mBéarla mBunadhasach leis an Athar Pádraig Ua Duinnín*. Baile Átha Cliath: M. H. Gill agus a Mhac, 1903.

————. *Faoistin Naomh-Phádraig i Laidin, i nGaedhilg, agus i mBéarla*. Baile Átha Cliath: M. H. Gill agus a Mhac, 1906.

————. *Foclóir Gaedhilge agus Béarla / An Irish-English Dictionary*. Dublin: Irish Texts Society, 1904.

————. "Irish Love of Learning." In *The Glories of Ireland*, edited by Joseph Dunn and P. J. Lennox. Washington: Phoenix, 1914, 38–43.

————. *Lectures on the Irish Language Movement*. Dublin: M. H. Gill and Son, 1904.

————. *Muinntear Chiarraidhe roimh an Droch-Shaoghal*. Baile Átha Cliath: M. H. Gill agus a Mhac, 1905.

————. *Native History in National Schools*. Dublin: M. H. Gill and Son, 1905.

————. "Poll an Phíobaire," *Irish People*, 5 May 1906.
————. *Prós Gaedhealach / Irish Prose.* Dublin: Society for the Preservation of the Irish Language, 1902.
————. *An Tobar Draoidheachta.* Baile Átha Cliath: Connradh na Gaedhilge, 1902.
————. *Séamus Ó Dubhghaill, "Conán Maol," and "Gruagach an Tobair."* *Scoil Gaedhealach.* Baile Átha Cliath: Connradh na Gaedhilge, 1903.
Eglinton, John. *Anglo-Irish Essays.* New York: John Lane, 1918.
Éigse Suadh is Seanchaidh: Sliocht do Shein-Leabhraibh an Chuid is Mó don Méid-se, idir Prós agus Filidheacht. Baile Átha Cliath: Muintir Ghoill, [1909?].
Eoghan Ruadh Ua Néill, nó Ar Son Tíre agus Chreidimh: Dráma Stardha ag Baint le Cogadh 1641, do Cumadh agus do Céad-Léirigheadh i gColáisde Phádraig i Maigh Nuadhadh. Beirt Mhac Léighinn d'Ullmhuigh agus do Chuir i n-eagar do Chonnradh Chuilm Naomhtha. Baile Átha Cliath: M. H. Gill agus a Mhac, 1907.
Fahy, Francis. *The Irish Language Movement.* London: Gaelic League of London, n.d.
Fay, Frank J. *Towards a National Theatre: The Dramatic Criticism of Frank J. Fay.* Edited by Robert Hogan. Dublin: Dolmen Press, 1970.
Fay, W. G., and Catherine Carswell. *The Fays of the Abbey Theatre: An Auto-biographical Record.* New York: Harcourt, Brace, 1935.
Ferguson, Sir Samuel. *Congal: A Poem in Four Books.* Dublin: Edward Ponsonby, 1872.
Flannery, Thomas (Tomás Ó Flannghaile). *For the Tongue of the Gael: A Selection of Essays Literary and Historical.* 2d. ed. Dublin: Sealy, Bryers, and Walker, 1907.
Fournier, E. E., and R. B. White. *Eachtra Laoghaire Mhic Criomhthainn go Maigh Meall.* Dublin: M. H. Gill and Son [1907].
"An Gae Bolga." A Talk about Irish Literature. Dublin: M. H. Gill and Son, 1907.
Gaethe Gréine I: Aistidhe Duais Oireachtais 1919. Baile Átha Cliath: Connradh na Gaedhilge, n.d.
Gaethe Gréine II: Oireachtas 1920. Baile Átha Claith: Connradh na Gaedhilge, n.d.
Gregory, Lady. *Cuchulain of Muirthemne: The Story of the Men of the Red Branch of Ulster Arrranged and Put into English by Lady Gregory with a Preface by W. B. Yeats.* Gerrards Cross: Colin Smythe, 1970.
————. *Gods and Fighting Men.* Toronto: Macmillan, 1976.
————, ed. *Ideals in Ireland.* London: Unicorn, 1901.
————. *Seventy Years: Being an Autobiography of Lady Gregory.* Edited by Colin Smythe. Gerrards Cross: Colin Smythte, 1974.
Gwynn, Denis. "Patrick Pearse." *Dublin Review* 172 (March 1923): 92–105.
Hamilton, John. *An Roilleán Draoidheachta.* Translated by Pádraic Ó Máille. Dublin: Maunsel and Company, 1908.
Henebry, Father Richard. *Scríbhne Risteird de hIndeberg .i. Sagart dona Déisibh.* Edited by Seán Ó Cuirrín. Baile Átha Cliath: Brún agus Nualáin, n.d.
Holloway, Joseph. *Joseph Holloway's Abbey Theatre: A Selection from His Unpublished Journal "Impressions of a Dublin Playgoer."* Edited by Robert Hogan and Michael J. O'Neill. Carbondale: University of Southern Illinois Press, 1967.

Hull, Eleanor, ed. *The Cuchullin Saga in Irish Literature: Being a Collection of Stories relating to the Hero Cuchullin, Translated from the Irish by Various Scholars.* London: David Nutt, 1898.

Hyde, Douglas. *Casadh an tSúgáin, Dráma Aon-Ghnímh: An Chéad Chluiche Gaedhilge do Léirigheadh i nAmharclainn.* Baile Átha Cliath: Oifig Dhíolta Foillseacháin Rialtais, 1940.

——. *An Cleamhnas: Dráma.* Baile Átha Cliath: An Cló-Chumann, n.d.

——. *Leabhar Sgeulaidheachta.* Dublin: M. H. Gill and Son, 1889.

——. *Maistín an Bhéarla: Dráma Éin-Ghnímh.* Baile Átha Cliath: Oifig Díolta Foilseacháin Rialtais, 1934.

——. *Mise agus an Conradh.* Baile Átha Cliath: Oifig an tSoláthair, 1937.

——. *An Naomh ar Iarraidh.* Corcaigh: Oifig "An Lóchrainn," 1918.

——. "The Necessity for De-Anglicizing Ireland." In *1000 Years of Irish Prose: The Literary Revival,* edited by Vivian Mercier and David H. Greene. New York: Grosset and Dunlap, 1961, 78–89.

——. "A Plea for the Irish Language." *Dublin University Review* (August 1886): 666–76.

——. *Pleusgadh na Bulgóide; or the Bursting of the Bubble.* Baile Átha Cliath: Gill agus a Mhac, n.d.

——. *An Pósadh.* Baile Átha Cliath: Gill agus a Mhac, n.d.

——. *Righ Séamus.* Dublin: M. H. Gill and Son, n.d.

——. *An Tincéar agus an tSidheóg.* Dublin: M. H. Gill and Son, n.d.

——. *Úbhla de'n Chraoibh.* Dublin: M. H. Gill and Son, 1900.

Imtheachta an Oireachtais / Full Report of the Proceedings at the Oireachtas or Irish Literary Festival Held in the Round Room, Rotunda, Dublin, on May 17th, 1897. Including the Prize Pieces, Now Published for the First Time. Dublin: The Gaelic League, 1897.

Imtheachta an Oireachtais, 1898 / The Proceedings of the Second Oireachtas Held in Dublin on Tuesday, 24 May 1898, including the Prize Essays, Stories and Poems, edited, the Prose Pieces by Norma Borthwick, the Poems by Tadhg Ó Donnchadha. Dublin: Gaelic League, 1899.

Imtheachta an Oireachtais 1899. Dublin: Gaelic League, 1899.

Imtheachta an Oireachtais 1900. Baile Átha Cliath: Connradh na Gaedhilge, 1902.

Imtheachta an Oireachtais 1901. Vol. 1. Edited by Tadhg Ó Donnchadha. Baile Átha Cliath: Connradh na Gaedhilge, 1903.

The Irish Language in Intermediate Education. Dublin: Gaelic League, n.d.

Joyce, James. *A Portrait of the Artist as a Young Man.* New York: Viking, 1964.

——. *Ulysses.* New York: Vintage, 1961.

Joyce, P. W., *Old Celtic Romances.* London: David Nutt, 1894.

Kavanagh, Patrick F., O.S.F., *Ireland's Defence—Her Language.* Dublin: Gaelic League [1902?].

Kinsella, Thomas, trans. *The Táin.* London: Oxford University Press, 1969.

Laoide, Seosamh, ed. *Brisleach Mhór Mhaighe Muirtheimhne.* Baile Átha Cliath: Clódhanna, Teo., 1915.

——, ed. *Cruach Chonaill.* Baile Átha Cliath: Connradh na Gaedhilge, 1909.

——, ed. *Dearg-Ruathar Chonaill Chearnaigh: Sgéal Rudhraigheachta.* Baile Átha Cliath: Connradh na Gaedhilge, 1907.

——, ed. *Éan an Cheoil Bhinn.* Baile Átha Cliath: Connradh na Gaedhilge, 1908.

——, ed. *An tÉinín Órdha.* Baile Átha Cliath: Connradh na Gaedhilge, 1910.

————, ed. *Fionn agus Lorcán*. Baile Átha Cliath: Connradh na Gaedhilge, 1903.

————, ed. *Madra na nOcht gCos*. Baile Átha Cliath: Connradh na Gaedhilge, 1907.

————, ed. *Measgán Músgraighe: Cnuasach Beag Sgéalaidheachta*. Baile Átha Cliath: Connradh na Gaedhilge, 1907.

————, ed. *Sgéal Cúchulainn ag Cuan Carn*. Baile Átha Cliath: Connradh na Gaedhilge, 1906.

————, ed. *Tonn Tóime: Tiomargadh Sean-Phisreog, Sean-Róchán, Sean-Sgéal, Sean-Cheist, Sean-Naitheann, Sean-Fhocal, agus Sean-Rádh ó Chiarraighe Luachra*. Baile Átha Cliath: Clódhanna, Teo., 1915.

Leabhar Úrnaighthe. Translated by "Sagart Riaghalta." Baile Átha Cliath: Comhlucht na Fírinne Catoilce, 1904.

Mac A' Bhaird, Seaghán, trans. *Na h-Epistlí agus na Soisgéil do na Domhnaighibh agus Laethibh Saoire ar na d-Tarraingt go Gaedhilc (agus an Sacs-Bheurla ós a coinne)*. Baile Átha Cliath: Brún agus Ó Nualláin, 1904.

Mac an Bháird, Séamus. *Troid Bhaile an Droichid*. Baile Átha Cliath: Connradh na Gaedhilge, 1907.

Mac Aodha, Pádraig. *Fiacha Mac Aodha Ua Broin*. Baile Átha Cliath: Séamus Ó Dubhthaigh agus a Chomh., Teo., 1908.

Mac Domhnaill, Tomás. *Áine agus Caoimhghín: Dráma Éin-Ghníomha*. Baile Átha Cliath: Connradh na Gaedhilge, 1910.

MacDonagh, Thomas. *Literature in Ireland: Studies Irish and Anglo-Irish*. Dublin: Talbot Press, 1916.

Mac Éinrigh, Seaghán P. *Udhacht an Stiocaire*. Baile Átha Cliath: An Cló-Chumann, n.d.

Mac Fhionnlaoich, Peadar. *Ciall na Sean-Ráidhte*. Baile Átha Cliath: Ó Cathail agus a Bhuidhin, 1920.

————. *Conchubhar Mac Neasa: Stair-Sheanchas na Craobhruaidhe*. Baile Átha Cliath: Clódhanna, Teo., 1914.

————. *Eachtra Aodha Ruaidh Uí Dhomhnaill*. Baile Átha Cliath: M. H. Gill agus a Mhac, 1911.

————. *Miondrámanna*. Baile Átha Cliath: Connradh na Gaedhilge, 1902.

————. *Tá na Francaigh ar an Muir*. Dublin: M. H. Gill and Son, n.d.

Mac Gríogóir, Aodhmaín. *Fréamhacha na h-Éireann*. Baile Átha Cliath: Maunsel, 1906.

Mac Grianna, Seosamh. *Pádraic Ó Conaire agus Aistí Eile*. Baile Átha Cliath: Oifig an tSoláthair, 1969.

MacKenna, Stephen. *Journals and Letters of Stephen MacKenna*. Edited by E. R. Dodds. London: Constable, 1936.

————. *Memories of the Dead*. Dublin: Powell, n.d.

MacManus, Seamus. *An Fear Cruadh-Chroidheach / The Hard-Hearted Man*. Translated by Tomás Ua Concheanainn. Dublin: M. H. Gill and Son, 1905.

————. *Liúdaidhe Óg na Leargadh Móire*. Translated by Seán Ua Ceallaigh. Dublin: M. H. Gill and Son, 1906.

————. *An Pleidhseam: Trí Sgéalta Draoidheachta ó Thírchonaill*. Translated by Peadar Mac Fhionnlaoich. Dublin: An Cló-Chumann, 1903.

Mac Meanman, Seaghán. *Sgéalta Goiride Geimhridh*. Dún Dealgan: Preas Dhún Dealgan, 1915.

Mac Néill, Eoin. "When Does Irish History Begin?" *New Ireland Review* 25 (March 1906): 1–18.

————. "Why and How the Irish Language Is To Be Preserved." *Irish Ecclesiastical Review*, 3d ser., 12 (1891): 1099–1108.

Martyn, Edward. *Ireland's Battle for Her Language*. Dublin: Gaelic League [1900?].

Mhag Ruaidhrí, Micheál. *Beatha Aodha Uí Néill*. Baile Átha Cliath: Connradh na Gaedhilge, n.d.

————. *An Fiaclóir*. Dublin: Patrick O'Brien, n.d.

————. *Lúb na Caillighe agus Sgéalta Eile*. Baile Átha Cliath: Connradh na Gaedhilge, 1913.

————. *Triúr Clainne na Bard Scolóige: Sean-Sgéal ó Thír Amhalgadha*. Baile Átha Cliath: Connradh na Gaedhilge, 1914.

Mil na mBeach. Baile Átha Cliath: Muinntir Dollard, n.d.

Mitchell, John. *Irisleabhar Príosúin Sheáin Mhistéil, nó Chúig Bhliadhna i bPríosúnaibh na Breataine*. 2 vols. Translated by Eoghan Ó Neachtain. Baile Átha Cliath: M. H. Mac Goill agus a Mhac, 1910–11.

Moore, George. *Hail and Farewell!* 2 vols. New York: Appleton, 1925.

————. *An tÚr-Ghort*. Translated by Pádraig Ó Súilleabháin. Dublin: Sealy, Bryers and Walker [1902].

Moran, D. P. *The Philosophy of Irish Ireland*. Dublin: James Duffy, 1905.

Morris, Henry. *Donnbó agus Rígh-Sgéalta Eile*. Derry: Messrs. O'Breslin, 1909.

————. *Greann na Gaedhilge*. 7 parts. Baile Átha Cliath: Connradh na Gaedhilge, 1902–7.

————. *Maighdean an tSolais agus Sgéalta Eile*. Dundalk: Dundalgan, 1913.

Murphy, Thomas A., C.SS.R. *The Literature Crusade in Ireland*. Limerick: Munster Printing Works, 1912.

Ní Chinnéide, Máire. *An Dúthchas: Dráma Éin-Ghníomha*. Baile Átha Cliath: Connradh na Gaedhilge, 1908.

Ní Chléirigh, Meadhbh, ed. *Eachtra na gCuradh* (Leabhair ó Láimhsgríbhnibh I). Baile Átha Cliath: Oifig an tSoláthair, 1941.

Nic Philibín, Maighréad, ed. *Na Caisidigh agus a gCuid Filidheachta*. Baile Átha Cliath: Oifig an tSoláthair, 1938.

Nic Shiubhlaigh, Máire. *The Splendid Years: Recollections of Máire Nic Shiubhlaigh as Told to Edward Kenny*. Dublin: James Duffy, 1955.

Ní Dhúnlaing, Searloit. *An Tobar Naomhtha: Dráma Beag chun na Leanbh i gCóir Lae Fhéile Phádraig*. Baile Átha Cliath: M. H. Mac Guill agus a Mhac, 1915.

Ní Shíthe, Máire, and Eilís Ní Mhurchadha. *Beart Nótaí: Dráma Dhá Ghníomh*. Baile Átha Cliath: Cuideachta Bhanba, 1904.

Ó Beirne, Séamus. *Obair!: A Bilingual Play in Four Scenes*. Baile Átha Cliath: M. H. Gill and Son, 1909.

————. *An Dochtúir*. Baile Átha Cliath: M. H. Gill agus a Mhac, 1909.

Ó Braonáin, Cathaoir. *Béarla Sacsan agus an Creideamh i nÉirinn*. Baile Átha Cliath: M. H. Mac Guill agus a Mhac, 1913.

O'Brien, William. *Toradh na Gaedhilge ar Aitheasc agus ar Ghréithribh na nGaedheal*. Translated by Tadhg Ó Murchadha. Baile Átha Cliath: Connradh na Gaedhilge, 1905.

Ó Broin, León. "Pádraic Ó Conaire." *Capuchin Annual* (1934): 254–60.

Ó Bruadair, Dáibhidh. *Duanaire Dháibhidh Uí Bhruadair / The Poems of David Ó Bruadair*. 3 vols. Edited by Rev. John C. Mac Erlean. London: Irish Texts Society, 1910–7.

Ó Cadhla, Seán. *Eachtra Fhinn Mhic Cumhaill le Seachrán na Sál gCam.* Edited by Seosamh Laoide. Baile Átha Cliath: Connradh na Gaedhilge, 1906.

Ó Caomhánaigh, Seán. *Éist le Dubh Dorcha: Cnuasacht d'Aistí.* Edited by Tadhg Ó Dúshláine. Maigh Nuad: An Sagart, 1991.

————, ed. *Sailm Dháibhidh dréir Láimhscríbhinne Bunaidhe Liam Bheidil, Easbog.* Dublin: Hanna and Neale, 1912.

O'Casey, Sean. *Drums under the Windows.* New York: Macmillan. 1960.

————. *Feathers from the Green Crow: Sean O'Casey, 1905–1925.* Edited by Robert Hogan. London: Macmillan, 1963.

————. *The Letters of Sean O'Casey.* Vol. 1. Edited by David Krause. New York: Macmillan, 1975.

Ó Ceallaigh, Tomás. *Airgead na Croise Caoile / The Money of the Slender Cross.* Dublin: M. H. Gill and Son, 1903.

————. *An tAthair Tomás Ó Ceallaigh agus a Shaothar,* edited by An tAthair Tomás S. Ó Láimhín. Gaillimh: Complacht Foillsighthe an Iarthair, Tóránta, 1943.

————. *Deirdre.* Baile Átha Cliath: Connradh na Gaedhilge, 1909.

————. *Eithne, nó Éan an Cheoil Bhinn.* Dublin: M. H. Gill and Son, 1909.

————. *An Fóghmhar.* Baile Átha Cliath: M. H. Gill agus a Mhac, 1908.

Ó Ceithearnaigh, Séamus, ed. *Siabhradh Mhic na Mío-Chomhairle* (Leabhair ó Láimhsgríbhnibh 19). Baile Átha Cliath: Oifig an tSoláthair, 1955.

Ó Cléirigh, Seosamh, trans. *Sáimhín Sógh.* Baile Átha Cliath: Clódhanna, Teo., 1915.

Ó Conaire, Pádraic. *Aistí Phádraic Uí Chonaire.* Edited by Gearóid Denvir. Indreabhán: Cló Chois Fharraige, 1978.

————. *Bairbre Rua agus Drámaí Eile.* Edited by Pádraig Ó Siadhail. Béal an Daingin: Cló Iar-Chonnachta, 1989.

————. *Béal an Uaignis.* Baile Átha Cliath: Mártan Lester, 1921.

————. *An Chéad Chloch.* Edited by Pádraigín Riggs. Baile Átha Cliath: Cló Mercier, 1978.

————. *An Crann Géagach: Aistí agus Scéilíní.* Baile Átha Cliath: Cló na gCoinneal, 1919.

————. *Cubhar na dTonn: Cnuasacht Aistí.* Baile Átha Cliath: Comhlucht Oideachais na hÉireann, n.d.

————. *Deoraidheacht.* Baile Átha Cliath: Cló Talbot, 1973.

————. *Fearfeasa Mac Feasa.* Baile Átha Cliath: Cló-Lucht an Tálbóidigh i Comhar le hOifig an tSoláthair, 1930.

————. *Iriseoireacht Uí Chonaire.* Edited by An tSr. Eibhlín Ní Chionnaith. Béal an Daingin: Cló Iar-Chonnachta, 1989.

————. *Nóra Mharcuis Bhig agus Sgéalta Eile.* Baile Átha Cliath: Connradh na Gaedhilge, 1909.

————. *Seacht mBuaidh an Éirghe-Amach.* Baile Átha Cliath: Sáirséal agus Dill, 1967.

————. *Seoigheach an Ghleanna.* Baile Átha Cliath: An Press Náisiúnta, n.d.

————. *Sgéalta an tSáirsint Rua.* Baile Átha Cliath: An Press Náisiúnta, n.d.

————. *An Sgoláire Bocht agus Sgéalta Eile.* Baile Átha Cliath: Connradh na Gaedhilge, 1913.

————. *Síol Éabha: Sgéalta ó Láimh Phádraic Uí Chonaire.* Baile Átha Cliath: Comhlucht Oideachais na hÉireann, n.d.

Ó Cróinín, Donncha, ed., *Seanchas Amhlaoibh Í Luínse*. Baile Átha Cliath: Comhairle Bhéaloideas Éireann, 1980.

Ó Donnchadha, Tadhg. *Guth ón mBreatain / Llais o Gymru*. Baile Átha Cliath: M. H. Gill agus a Mhac, 1912.

Ó Dubhda, Peadar. *Ar Lorg an tSeanchaidhe*. Dún Dealgan: Preas Dhún Dealgan, 1915.

Ó Dubhghaill, Séamus. *Cathair Conroí agus Sgéalta Eile*. Baile Átha Cliath: Connradh na Gaedhilge, 1907.

——. *Cléibhín Móna*. Baile Átha Cliath: M. H. Guill agus a Mhac, 1907.

——. *Muinntear na Tuatha*. Baile Átha Cliath: M. H. Mac Gill agus a Mhac, 1910.

——. *Prátaí Mhichíl Thaidhg*. Baile Átha Cliath: M. H. Mac Guill agus a Mhac, 1904.

——. *Tadhg Gabha*. Baile Átha Cliath: Connradh na Gaedhilge, 1901.

Ó Duirinne, Séamus. *Ar Son Baile agus Tíre: Dráma Cheithre Ghníomha*. Baile Átha Cliath: Connradh na Gaedhilge, 1905.

O'Farrelly, Agnes. *An Cneamhaire*. Baile Átha Cliath: An Cló-Chumann agus M. H. Gill agus a Mhac, n.d.

——. *Grádh agus Crádh: Úirsgéilín*. Baile Átha Cliath: Connradh na Gaedhilge, 1905.

——, ed. *Leabhar an Athar Eoghan / The O'Growney Memorial Volume*. Dublin: M. H. Gill and Son, 1904.

——. *The Reign of Humbug*. Dublin: Gaelic League, 1901.

Ó Foghludha, Diarmuid. *Finnsgéalta na hAraibe: Cuid I*. Baile Átha Cliath: Connradh na Gaedhilge, 1908.

Ó Foghludha, Risteárd. *Saoghal-Ré Sheathrúin Céitinn: Sagart is Dochtúir san Diadhacht, Staruidhe, File, Ughdar, ↄc.* Baile Átha Cliath: Muinntir an Ghoill, 1908.

Ó Gaora, Colm. *Mise*. Eagrán nua. Baile Átha Cliath: Oifig an tSoláthair, 1969.

O'Grady, Standish James. *The Coming of Cuchulain*. London: Methuen, 1894.

——. *History of Ireland*. 2 vols. London: Sampson, Low, Searle, Marston, and Rivington, 1878–80.

Ó Grianna, Séamus. *Castar na Daoine ar a Chéile 'sní Castar na Cnuic nó na Sléibhte, Irish Weekly and Ulster Examiner* 24 July–18 December 1915.

——. *An Draoidín*. Baile Átha Cliath: Oifig an tSoláthair, 1959.

——. *Feara Fáil*. Dún Dealgan: Cló-Lucht "an Scrúduightheoir," 1933.

——. *Mo Dhá Róisín*. Dún Dealgan: Preas Dhún Dealgan, n.d.

——. *Saoghal Corrach*. Baile Átha Cliath: Cló Mercier, 1981.

Ó hAnnracháin, Peadar. *Fé Bhrat an Chonnartha*. Baile Átha Cliath: Oifig an tSoláthair, 1944.

——. *Mar Mhaireas É*. 2 vols. Baile Átha Cliath: Oifig an tSoláthair, 1953–55.

Ó hAodha, Tomás. *An Gioblachán: Finnsgéal Nuadh-Dhéanta*. Baile Átha Cliath: Connradh na Gaedhilge, 1903.

——. *An Scrabhadóir: Úir-chluiche i dTrí Beartaibh*. Baile Átha Cliath: Clódhanna, Teo., 1909.

——. *Seabhac na Ceathramhan Caoile: Dráma Cheithre Ghníomh*. Baile Átha Cliath: Connradh na Gaedhilge, 1906.

——. *Seaghán na Scuab: Dráma Trí Gníomh*. Baile Átha Cliath: Connradh na Gaedhilge, 1904.

506   Selected Bibliography

Ó Labhradha, Alphonsus. *An tSnaidhm: Dráma Trí nGníomh.* Baile Atha Cliath: Clódhanna, Teo., 1910.
Ó Laoghaire, Diarmuid. *Cogar Mogar.* Baile Átha Cliath: Muintir na Leabhar Gaedhilge, 1909.
Ó Laoghaire, Pádruig. *Sgeuluidheacht Chúige Mumhan.* Baile Átha Cliath: Pádraig Ó Briain, 1895.
Ó Lochlainn, Gearóid. *Ealaín na hAmharclainne.* Baile Átha Cliath: Clódhanna, Teo., 1966.
Ó Lughnaidh, An tAthair Clement. *Na hEpistile agus na Soisgéula do réir na n-Domhnach agus na Saoire tríd an mBliadhain secundum Missale Romanum.* Áth Cliath: Sealy, Bryers agus Walcer, 1902.
Ó Máille, Micheál. *Diarmuid Donn.* Edited by Tomás Ó Máille. Baile Átha Cliath: Oifig an tSoláthair, 1943.
———. *Eochaidh Mac Ríogh 'n-Éirinn.* Baile Átha Cliath: Connradh na Gaedhilge, 1904.
———. *Naoi nGábhadh an Ghiolla Dhuibh.* Edited by Tomás Ó Máille. Baile Átha Cliath: Comhlucht Oideachais na hÉireann, 1922.
Ó Muimhneacháin, Seán. *Procadóir na nDeachmhadh.* N.p., 1907.
Ó Murchadha, Colm. *An Gheilt agus Scéal Eile.* Cill Áirne: Cualacht Bhréanainn, 1919.
Ó Murchadha, Domhnall. *Beirt Ghaedhilgeoirí 'na gComhnaidhe 'sa Chathair.* Edited by Seosamh Laoide. Baile Átha Cliath: Clódhanna, Teo., 1915.
Ó Murchadha, S. E., ed. and trans. *Tiomna Nuadh Ár dTighearna agus Ár Slánaightheóra Íosa Críost ar n-a Tarraing go Fírinneach as Gréigis go Gaoidheilg le h-Uilliam Ó Domhnaill ar n-a glanadh as ar n-a leasughadh go nuadh le Séamas É. Ó Murchadha.* Baile Átha Cliath: Hodges, Figgis agus a gCuideachta, 1910.
Ó Murchadha, Tadhg, trans. *Eachtra Robinson Crúsó: Cuid I.* Baile Átha Cliath: Clódhanna, Teo., 1909.
Ó Neachtain, Eoghan, ed. *Céadtach Mac Fhinn as Éirinn.* Baile Átha Cliath: Connradh na Gaedhilge, 1907.
———. *Dubhaltach Mac Firbisigh.* Baile Átha Cliath: Connradh na Gaedhilge, 1902.
———. *Stair-Cheachta.* 2 parts. Baile Átha Cliath: Connradh na Gaedhilge, 1905–7.
———. *Tochmarc Fhearbhlaidhe.* Baile Átha Cliath: M. H. Mac an Ghoill agus a Mhac, 1912.
Ó Neachtain, Seaghán. *Stair Éamuinn Uí Chléirigh.* Edited by Eoghan Ó Neachtain. Baile Átha Cliath: M. H. Mac an Ghuill agus a Mhac, 1918.
O'Rahilly, Cecile, ed. and trans. *Táin Bó Cúalnge from the Book of Leinster.* Dublin: Dublin Institute for Advanced Studies, 1967.
———, ed. and trans. *Tóruigheacht Gruaidhe Griansholus.* London: Irish Texts Society, 1924.
Ó Rathaille, Aodhagán. *Dánta Aodhagáin Uí Rathaille / The Poems of Egan O'Rahilly.* Edited and translated by Patrick S. Dinneen. London: Irish Texts Society, 1900.
O'Reilly, John M. *Curadh Glas an Eolais.* Baile Átha Cliath: Muintir na Leabhar Gaedhilge, 1905.
———. *The Native Speaker Examined Home: Two Stalking Fallacies Anatomized.* Dublin: Sealy, Bryers and Walker, 1909.

Selected Bibliography 507

———. *The Threatening Metempsychosis of a Nation.* Dublin: Gaelic League [1901].
———. *The Trusty Vehicle of the Faith of the Gael.* Dublin: Gaelic League, 1902.
Ó Rinn, Liam. *Cad Ba Dhóbair Dó agus Sgeulta Eile.* Baile Átha Cliath: Sealy,
  Bryers agus Walker, 1920.
———. *Mo Chara Stiofán.* Baile Átha Cliath: Oifig an tSoláthair, 1939.
———. *So Súd.* Baile Átha Cliath: Oifig an tSoláthair, 1953.
Ó Séaghdha, Pádraig ("Conán Maol"). *An Buaiceas.* Edited by Seosamh Laoide.
  Baile Átha Cliath: Connradh na Gaedhilge, 1903.
———. *Éire: Léigheachta ar Stair na hÉireann.* Baile Átha Cliath: Clódhanna,
  Teo., 1924.
———. *Eoghan Paor.* Baile Átha Cliath: M. H. Gill agus a Mhac [1911].
———. *Mac Fínghín Dubh.* Dublin: Irish Book, 1903.
———. *Seaghán an Díomais: Blúirín as Stair na h-Éireann.* Dublin: Irish Book,
  1901.
Ó Séaghdha, Pádraig ("Gruagach an Tobair"). *Annála na Tuatha.* Baile Átha
  Cliath, Connradh na Gaedhilge, 1905–7.
———. *An Sgoraidheacht.* Edited by Ó Séaghdha and Fionán Mac Coluim. Baile
  Átha Cliath: Brún agus Ó Nóláin, n.d.
Ó Séaghdha, Pádraig ("Pádraig na Léime"). *Mac Cárthaigh Mór: Dráma Éin-
  Ghníomha.* Baile Átha Cliath: Connradh na Gaedhilge, 1908.
———. *Oighreacht Róisín: Dráma Éin-Ghníomha Dhá-Theangach.* Baile Átha
  Cliath: Clódhanna, Teo., 1910.
Ó Searcaigh, Séamus, ed. *Cú na gCleas agus Sgéalta Eile.* Dundalk: Dundalgan,
  1922.
Ó Siochfhradha, Pádraig. *An Baile Seo 'Gainne.* Baile Átha Cliath: Connradh na
  Gaedhilge, n.d.
———. *Cath Fionntrágha.* Baile Átha Cliath: Clódhanna, Teo., 1911.
———. *An Ceithearnach Caoilriabhaigh.* Baile Átha Cliath: Clódhanna, Teo.,
  1910.
———. *Eachtra Thaidhg Mhic Céin.* Baile Átha Cliath: Clódhanna, Teo., 1914.
———. *Jimín Mháire Thaidhg.* Baile Átha Cliath: Maunsel agus Roberts, 1922.
———. *Seáinín, nó Eachtra Mic Mírialta.* Baile Átha Cliath: Maunsel agus Rob-
  erts, 1922.
Ó Tuathail, Domhnall, ed. *Tóraidheacht na bhFíreun ar Lorg Chríosda. Sagart
  Éigin i n-aice le Dúnphádraig a d'Aistrigh 1762.* Baile Átha Cliath: M. H.
  Gill agus a Mhac, 1915.
Partridge, Felix. *An t-Athrughadh Mór.* Dublin: M. H. Gill and Son, 1906.
Pearse, Patrick. *Bodach an Chóta Lachtna.* Baile Átha Cliath: Connradh na Gaed-
  hilge, 1906.
———. *Bruidhean Chaorthainn: Sgéal Fiannaidheachta.* Baile Átha Cliath: Clód-
  hanna, Teo., 1912.
———. *Collected Works of Patrick Pearse.* 5 vols. Dublin: Phoenix, n.d.
———. "The Fianna of Fionn." *Fianna Handbook.* Dublin: Central Council of
  Na Fianna Éireann, n.d.
———. *The Home Life of Pádraig Pearse, as Told by Himself, His Family and
  Friends.* Edited by Mary Brigid Pearse. Dublin: Mercier, 1979.
———. *Íosagán agus Sgéalta Eile.* Baile Átha Cliath: Connradh na Gaedhilge,
  1907.
———. *The Letters of P. H. Pearse.* Edited by Séamas Ó Buachalla. Gerrards
  Cross: Colin Smythe, 1980.

508   Selected Bibliography

————. *The Literary Writings of Patrick Pearse*. Edited by Séamus Ó Buachalla. Dublin: Mercier, 1979.
————. "Litridheacht Nua-Dhéanta." *St. Stephen's: A Record of University Life* 1, no. 1 (June 1901): 8–10.
————. *An Mháthair agus Sgéalta Eile*. Dundalk: William Tempest, The Dundalgan Press, 1918.
————. *Ó Pheann an Phiarsaigh*. Baile Átha Cliath: Comhlucht Oideachais na hÉireann, n.d.
————. *Poll an Phíobaire*. Baile Átha Cliath: Connradh na Gaedhilge, 1906.
————. *Na Scríbhinní Liteartha le Pádraig Mac Piarais*. Edited by Séamas Ó Buachalla. Baile Átha Cliath: Cló Mercier, 1979.
————. *A Significant Irish Educationalist: The Educational Writings of P. H. Pearse*. Edited by Séamas Ó Buachalla. Dublin: Mercier, 1980.
————. *Three Lectures on Gaelic Topics*. Dublin: M. H. Gill and Son, 1898.
Phelan, Michael J., S.J. "A Gaelicised or a Socialised Ireland—Which?" *Catholic Bulletin and Book Review* 3, no. 11 (November 1913): 769–74.
Pléimeann, Donnchadh, trans. *Eachtra na nArgonátach*. Baile Átha Cliath: Connradh na Gaedhilge, 1904.
Rooney, William. *The Prose Writings of William Rooney*. Dublin: M. H. Gill and Son, 1909.
Russell, George (AE). *The Living Torch*. Edited by Monk Gibbon. London: Macmillan, 1937.
Ryan, Desmond. *The Man Called Pearse*. Dublin: Maunsel, 1919.
————. *Remembering Sion: A Chronicle of Storm and Quiet*. London: Arthur Barker. 1934.
Ryan, William P. *An Bhóinn agus an Bhóchna*. ACS, 11 September 1915–15 January 1916.
————. *Caoimhghín Ó Cearnaigh: Sgéal Úrnua*. Baile Átha Cliath: Clódhanna, Teo., 1913.
————. *Lessons from Modern Language Movements*. Dublin: Gaelic League, 1902.
————. *Plays for the People*. Dublin: M. H. Gill and Son, 1904.
————. *The Pope's Green Island*. Boston: Small, Maynard, n.d.
Sgéal Ruaidhrí Uí Mhordha / Autobiography of the Ruairí O'More Branch of the Gaelic League, Portarlington. Dublin: An Cló-Chumann, 1906.
Scéalta Andeas, Oireachtas 1920. Edited by Risteárd Ó Foghludha. Baile Átha Cliath: Connradh na Gaedhilge, n.d.
Scéalta Triúir, Oireachtas 1919. Edited by Risteárd Ó Foghludha. Baile Átha Cliath: Connradh na Gaedhilge, n.d.
Scéilíní Anall, Oireachtas 1920. Edited by Risteárd Ó Foghludha. Baile Átha Cliath: Connradh na Gaedhilge, n.d.
Sheehan, Rev. Michael. *Árthrach an Óir*. Dublin: M. H. Gill and Son, 1910.
————. *Cnó Coilleadh Craobhaighe: The Irish of the People*. Dublin: M. H. Gill and Son, 1907.
————. *Cnuasacht Trágha: From the Foreshore*. Dublin: M. H. Gill and Son, 1908.
————. *Gabha na Coille*. Dublin: M. H. Gill and Son, 1915.
————. *Gile na mBláth*. Dublin: M. H. Gill and Son, 1912.
Synge, John Millington. *Collected Works*. 4 vols. Edited by Robin Skelton, Alan Price, and Ann Saddlemyer. London: Oxford University Press, 1962–68.

An Teagasg Críostaighe Gearr. Baile Átha Cliath: M. H. Gill agus a Mhac, 1899.

Triúr Comhdhalta do Chuallacht Chuilm Cille. *Gadaidhe Géar na Geamh-Oidhche, i n-a bhfuilid suim mhór d'eachtraibh agus d'imtheachtaibh Fhinn agus na Féinne go foir-leathan agus do sgéaltaibh eile nach iad.* Baile Átha Cliath: Muinntir Dollard, 1915.

Ua Ceallaigh, Seán. *Cú Roí.* Baile Átha Cliath: Muinntear Ghuill, n.d.

———. *Saothar Ár Sean i gCéin: Gearr Thuairisc ar Obair na Sean-Ghaedheal ar fuid na hEorpa.* Baile Átha Cliath: Cumann Bhuan-Choimeádta na Gaedhilge, 1904.

Ua Cearbhiúil, Eoin, trans. *Rubaiiat Ro Chan Omar Caiiam.* Chicago: Press of J. J. Collins' Sons, [1908].

Ua Concheannain, Tomás. *Mac-Ghníomhartha Bhriain.* Baile Átha Cliath: Connradh na Gaedhilge, 1905.

Ua Laoghaire, An tAthair Peadar. *Aesop a Tháinig go hÉirinn.* Edited by An Dochtúir Domhnall Ó Mathghamhna. Baile Átha Cliath: Brún agus Ó Nualláin, n.d.

———. *Aodh Ruadh.* 2 parts. Edited by "Conall Cearnach." Baile Átha Cliath: Brún agus Ó Nualláin, 1929.

———. *Ár nDóithin Araon.* Baile Átha Cliath: Brún agus Ó Nóláin, n.d.

———. *Bás Dhalláin* and *Tadhg Saor.* Dublin: Irish Book, 1900.

———. *An Bealach Buidhe: Dráma.* Baile Átha Cliath: Muintir na Leabhar Gaedhilge, 1906.

———. *Bricriu, nó "Is Fearr an t-Imreas 'ná an t-Uaigneas."* Edited by "Conall Cearnach." Baile Átha Cliath: Brún agus Ó Nualláin, n.d.

———. *Cath Ruis na Rí for Bóinn.* Baile Átha Cliath: Brún agus Ó Nóláin, n.d.

———. *An Cleasaidhe.* Baile Átha Cliath: Longman, Brún agus Ó Nualláin, n.d.

———. *Comhairle Ár Leasa.* Baile Átha Cliath: Brún agus Ó Nóláin, n.d.

———. *An Craos-Deamhan.* Baile Átha Cliath: Brún agus Ó Nualláin, n.d.

———. *Don Cíochóté.* Translated by Ua Laoghaire. Edited by "Conall Cearnach." Baile Átha Cliath: Brún agus Ó Nóláin, 1922.

———. *Eisirt.* Baile Átha Cliath: Muintir na Leabhar Gaedhilge, 1909.

———. *Guaire.* 2 parts. Edited by "Conall Cearnach." Baile Átha Cliath: Brún agus Ó Nualláin, n.d.

———. *The Irish Language and Irish Intermediate Education IX.* Dublin: Gaelic League, 1900.

———. *Irish Prose Composition.* Dublin: Muintir na Leabhar Gaedhilge, 1902.

———. *Lughaidh Mac Con.* Baile Átha Cliath: Brún agus Ó Nualláin, n.d.

———. *Méibh. Irish Industrial Journal,* 7 May–25 June 1910.

———. *Mo Sgéal Féin.* Baile Átha Cliath: Brún agus Ó Nualláin, n.d.

———. *Niamh.* Baile Átha Cliath: Muintir na Leabhar Gaedhilge, 1907.

———. *Séadna.* Edited by Liam Mac Mathúna. Baile Átha Cliath: Carbad, 1987.

———. *Sgothbhualadh.* Baile Átha Cliath: Brún agus Ó Nualláin, n.d.

———. *Sliabh na mBan bhFionn agus Cúán Fithise.* Baile Átha Cliath: Muintir na Leabhar Gaedhilge, 1914.

———. *An Soísgéal as Leabhar an Aifrinn.* Dublin: Irish Book, 1902.

———. *An Sprid.* Dublin: Irish Book, 1902.

———. *Táin Bó Cuailnge 'na Dhráma.* Baile Átha Cliath: Muintir na Leabhar Gaedhilge, 1915.

510 Selected Bibliography

Ua Ruaidhrí, Seaghán. *Bliadhain na bhFranncach*. Baile Átha Cliath: Connradh na Gaedhilge, 1907.
Ua Tuathail, Lorcán. *An Deoraidhe: Dráma i n-Aghaidh Imtheachda thar Sáile*. Baile Átha Cliath: Connradh na Gaedhilge, 1906.
Ua Tuathail, Seaghán and Seosamh Laoide, eds. *Teacht agus Imtheacht an Ghiolla Dheacair agus Tóruigheacht Chonáin agus a Chuideachta*. Baile Átha Cliath: Connradh na Gaedhilge, 1905.
Williams, N. J. A., ed. *Eachtra Áodh Mhic Goireachtaidh. Éigse* 13, no. 3 (Spring 1965): 111–42.
———. *Pairlement Chloinne Tomáis*. Dublin: Dublin Institute for Advanced Studies, 1981.
Yeats, William Butler. *Caitlín Ní Uallacháin: Dráma Náisiúnta*. Translated by An tAthair Tomás Ó Ceallaigh. Dublin: M. H. Gill and Son, 1905.
———. *Uncollected Prose*. Vol. 2. Edited by John P. Frayne and Colton Johnson. London: Macmillan, 1975.

II. Secondary Sources

Adams, Michael. *Censorship: The Irish Experience*. University: University of Alabama Press, 1968.
Bairéad, Ciarán. "Seosamh Laoide." *Béaloideas* 15, nos. 1–2 (June–December 1945): 127–40.
Bhaba, Homi K., ed. *Nation and Narration*. London: Routledge, 1990.
Boland, Eavan. "Aspects of Pearse." *Dublin Magazine* 5, no. 1 (Spring 1966): 46–55.
Boyce, D. George. *Nationalism in Ireland*. Baltimore: Johns Hopkins University Press, 1982.
Breathnach, Diarmuid, and Máire Ní Mhurchú. *1882–1982: Beathaisnéis a hAon*. Baile Átha Cliath: An Clóchomhar, 1986.
———. *1882–1982: Beathaisnéis a Dó*. Baile Átha Cliath: An Clóchomhar, 1990.
Breatnach, Pádraig A. "*Séadna*: Saothar Ealaíne." *Studia Hibernica* 9 (1969): 109–24.
Brown, Terence. *Ireland: A Social and Cultural History, 1922 to the Present*. Ithaca: Cornell University Press, 1985.
Bruford, Alan. *Gaelic Folktales and Medieval Romances*. Dublin: Folklore of Ireland Society, 1969.
Cairns, David, and Shaun Richards. *Writing Ireland: Colonialism, Nationalism and Culture*. Manchester: Manchester University Press, 1988.
"Coilin." *Patrick Pearse: A Sketch of His Life*. Dublin: Curtis, n.d.
Corkery, Daniel. *The Hidden Ireland: A Study of Gaelic Munster in the Eighteenth Century*. Dublin: M. H. Gill and Son, 1925.
———. *What's This About the Gaelic League?* Dublin: Gaelic League, 1942.
de Bhaldraithe, Tomás, ed. *Pádraic Ó Conaire: Clocha ar a Charn*. Baile Átha Cliath: An Clóchomhar, 1982.
de Blácam, Aodh. *Gaelic Literature Surveyed*. Dublin: Talbot, 1929.
de Brúch, Aingeal. "An Ghaeilge agus an Chathair." *Crane Bag* 5, no. 2 (1981): 12–17.

de Fréine, Seán. *The Great Silence*. Dublin: Foilseacháin Náisiúnta Teoranta, 1965.

Hayes, Richard J. *Manuscript Sources for the History of Irish Civilisation*. 11 vols., Boston: G. K. Hall, 1965.

Hayes, Richard J. (Risteárd de Hae), and Brighid Ní Dhonnchadha. *Clár Litridheacht na Nua-Ghaedhilge, 1850–1936*. 3 vols. Baile Átha Cliath: Oifig an tSoláthair, 1938–40.

Denvir, Gearóid, ed. *Pádraic Ó Conaire: Léachtaí Cuimhneacháin*. Indreabhán: Cló Chonamara, 1983.

Edwards, Ruth Dudley. *Patrick Pearse: The Triumph of Failure*. London: Victor Gollancz, 1977.

Ellmann, Richard. *James Joyce*. New York: Oxford University Press, 1965.

Énrí Ó Muirgheasa (1874–1945). Baile Átha Cliath: Foilseacháin Náisiúnta Teoranta, n.d.

Farson, Negley. *The Way of the Transgressor*. London: Victor Gollancz, 1935.

Feeney, William J. *Drama in Hardwicke Street: A History of the Irish Theatre Company*. Rutherford, N.J.: Fairleigh Dickinson University Press, 1984.

Fitzgerald, Garret. "Estimates for Baronies of Minimum Level of Irish-Speaking amongst Successive Decenniel Cohorts: 1771–1781 to 1861–1871." *Proceedings of the Royal Irish Academy* 84.C.3 (1984).

Flynn, Joyce. "The Route to the *Táin*: James Stephens' Preparation for His Unfinished Epic." *Proceedings of the Harvard Celtic Colloquium* 1 (1981): 125–44.

Foster, John Wilson. *Fictions of the Irish Literary Revival: A Changeling Art*. Syracuse: Syracuse University Press, 1987.

Garvin, Tom. "Priests and Patriots: Irish Separatism and Fear of the Modern 1890–1914." *Irish Historical Studies* 25, no. 97 (May 1986): 67–81.

Greene, David. *Writing in Irish Today*. Dublin: Cultural Relations Committee of Ireland, 1972.

Gwynn, Dennis. *Edward Martyn and the Irish Revival*. London: Jonathan Cape, 1930.

Hindley, Reg. *The Death of the Irish Language: A Qualified Obituary*. London: Routledge, 1990.

Hobsbawm, Eric, and Terence Ranger, eds. *The Invention of Tradition*. Cambridge: Cambridge University Press, 1984.

———. *Nations and Nationalism since 1780: Programme, Myth, Reality*. Cambridge: Cambridge University Press, 1990.

Hogan, Robert, ed. *The Macmillan Dictionary of Irish Literature*. London: Macmillan, 1979.

Hogan, Robert, et al. *The Modern Irish Drama: A Documentary History*. 5 vols. Dublin: Dolmen, 1975–84.

Hutchinson, John. *The Dynamics of Cultural Nationalism: The Gaelic Revival and the Creation of the Irish Nation State*. London: Allen and Unwin, 1987.

Kelleher, John V. "Matthew Arnold and the Celtic Revival." In *Perspectives in Criticism*, edited by Harry Levin. Cambridge: Harvard University Press, 1950, 197–221.

———. "The *Táin* and the Annals." *Ériu* 22 (1971): 107–27.

Kiberd, Declan. "John Millington Synge agus Athbheochan na Gaeilge." *Scríobh* 4 (1979): 221–33.

———. "Seán Ó Ríordáin: File Angla-Éireannach." In *An Duine is Dual: Aistí ar Sheán Ó Ríordáin*, edited by Eoghan Ó hAnluain. Baile Átha Cliath: An Clóchomhar, 1980.

———. *Synge and the Irish Language*. London: Macmillan, 1979.

Kilroy, James. *The Playboy Riots*. Dublin: Dolmen, 1971.

Lee, Joseph J. *Ireland, 1912–1985: Politics and Society*. Cambridge: Cambridge University Press, 1989.

———. *The Modernisation of Irish Society, 1848–1918*. Dublin: Gill and Macmillan, 1973.

Le Roux, Louis. *Patrick H. Pearse*. Translated by Desmond Ryan. Dublin: Talbot, 1932.

Loftus, Richard J. *Nationalism in Anglo-Irish Poetry*. Madison: University of Wisconsin Press, 1964.

Mac an tSaoi, C. B. "Gaeilgeoir Cathrach." *Agus* 5, no. 11 (November 1965): 8–9.

Mac an tSaoir, Flann. "Pádraig Mac Piarais." *Comhar* 20, no. 11 (November 1960)–21, no. 1 (January 1961).

Mac Aonghusa, Criostóir. "Pádraic Ó Conaire." *Comhar* 15, no. 12 (December 1956): 21–24.

Mac Congáil, Nollaig. *Máire—Clár Saothair*. Baile Átha Cliath: Coiscéim, 1990.

———. *Scríbhneoirí Thír Chonaill*. Baile Átha Cliath: Foilseacháin Náisiúnta Teoranta, 1983.

Mac Fhinn, An Monsignór Pádraig Eric. *An tAthair Mícheál P. Ó hIceadha*. Baile Átha Cliath: Sáirséal agus Dill, 1974.

Mac Mathúna, Seán, and Risteard Mac Gabhann. *Conradh na Gaeilge agus an tOideachas Aosach: Staidéar ar Theagasc na Gaeilge don Phobal Aosach i Ranganna Chonradh na Gaeilge i dTosach a Ré*. Indreabhán: Cló Chois Fharraige, 1981.

Mac Niocláis, Máirtín. *Seán Ó Ruadháin: Saol agus Saothar*. Baile Átha Cliath: An Clóchomhar, 1991.

Mac Réamoinn, Seán. "Branar le Cur." *Comhar* 45, no. 10 (October 1986): 10–15.

"Maol Muire" (Sister Mary Vincent). *An tAthair Peadar Ó Laoghaire agus a Shaothar*. Baile Átha Cliath: Brún agus Ó Nualláin, 1939.

Marcus, Phillip L. *Yeats and the Beginnings of the Irish Renaissance*. Ithaca: Cornell University Press, 1970.

Martin, F. X., and F. J. Byrne, eds. *The Scholar Revolutionary: Eoin Mac Néill, 1867–1945, and the Making of the New Ireland*. New York: Barnes and Noble, 1973.

Murphy, Brian. "Father Peter Yorke's 'Turning of the Tide' (1899): The Strictly Cultural Nationalism of the Early Gaelic League." *Éire/Ireland* 23, no. 1 (Spring 1988): 35–44.

Nic Eoin, Máirín. *An Litríocht Réigiúnach*. Baile Átha Cliath: An Clóchomhar, 1982.

Ní Cheannain, Áine, ed. *Leon an Iarthair: Aistí ar Sheán Mac Héil*. Baile Átha Cliath: An Clóchomhar, 1983.

Ní Chionnaith, An tSr. Eibhlín. "An Rómánsachas i Scríbhneoireacht Uí Chonaire." *An tUltach* 68, nos. 3 and 4 (March and April 1991).

Ní Chnáimhín, Áine. *Pádraic Ó Conaire*. Baile Átha Cliath: Oifig an tSoláthair, 1947.

Ní Dhonnchadha, Aisling. "*Caoimhín Ó Cearnaigh*: Úrscéal de Chuid na hAth-bheochana." In *An tÚrscéal sa Ghaeilge, Léachtaí Cholm Cille* 21 (1991): 154–74.

———. *An Gearrscéal sa Ghaeilge, 1898–1940.* Baile Átha Cliath: An Clóch-omhar, 1981.

Ní Mhuiríosa, Máirín. *Réamhchonraitheoirí: Nótaí ar Chuid de na Daoine a Bhí Gníomhach i nGluaiseacht na Gaeilge idir 1876 agus 1893.* Baile Átha Cliath: Clódhanna, Teo., 1968.

Ó Braonáin, Cathaoir. "Poets of the Insurrection: Patrick H. Pearse." *Studies* 5 (September 1916): 339–50.

O'Brien, Frank. *Filíocht Ghaeilge na Linne Seo.* Baile Átha Cliath: An Clóch-omhar, 1968.

Ó Broin, Tomás. "*Deoraíocht*: Réamhchainteanna agus Iarbhreitheanna." *Feasta* 29, no. 5 (May 1976): 5–7, 22.

———. *Saoirse Anama Uí Chonaire: Compánach d'Úrscéal Fiontrach "Deoraíocht."* Gaillimh: Officina Typographica, 1984.

Ó Buachalla, Breandán. "An tAthair Peadar is Mac Conglinne." *Comhar* 29, no. 12 (December 1970): 6–9.

———. *I mBéal Feirste Cois Cuain.* Baile Átha Cliath: An Clóchomhar, 1968.

Ó Buachalla, Séamas. *Pádraig Mac Piarais agus Éire lena Linn.* Baile Átha Cliath: Cló Mercier, 1979.

Ó Cadhain, Máirtín. "Conradh na Gaeilge agus an Litríocht." In *The Gaelic League Idea*, edited by Seán Ó Tuama, 52–62.

———. "Irish Prose in the Twentieth Century." In *Literature in Celtic Countries.* Cardiff: University of Wales Press, 1971.

———. *Ó Cadhain i bhFeasta.* Edited by Seán Ó Laighin. Baile Átha Cliath: Clódhanna, Teo., 1990.

———. *Páipéir Bhána agus Páipéir Bhreaca.* Baile Átha Cliath: An Clóchomhar, 1969.

———. "Réamhradh" to Saunders Lewis, *Bás nó Beatha?* Translated by Máirtín Ó Cadhain. Baile Átha Cliath: Sáirséal agus Dill, 1963.

———. "Úrscéalaíocht," *Irish Times*, 12 January 1955.

O'Callaghan, Margaret. "Language, Nationality and Cultural Identity in the Irish Free State 1922–27: the *Irish Statesman* and the *Catholic Bulletin* Re-Appraised." *Irish Historical Studies* 24, no. 94 (November 1984): 226–45.

Ó Ceallaigh, Seán. *Eoghan Ó Gramhnaigh: Beathaisnéis.* Baile Átha Cliath: Oifig an tSoláthair, 1968.

Ó Cearra, Aodh, and Séamas Céitinn. *Peadar Ó Dubhda: A Shaol agus a Shao-thar.* Baile Átha Cliath: An Clóchomhar, 1981.

Ó Conaire, Breandán. *Myles na Gaeilge: Lámhleabhar ar Shaothar Gaeilge Bhriain Ó Nualláin.* Baile Átha Cliath: An Clóchomhar, 1986.

Ó Conchúir, Breandán. *Scríobhaithe Chorcaí, 1700–1850.* Baile Átha Cliath: An Clóchomhar, 1982.

Ó Conluain, Proinsias and Donncha Ó Céileachair. *An Duinníneach: An tAthair Pádraig Ó Duinnín: A Shaol, a Shaothar, agus an Ré inar Mhair Sé.* Baile Átha Cliath: Sáirséal agus Dill, 1958.

Ó Croiligh, Pádraig. "Go nGoilleann an Bhróg: Samhlaíocht Phádraig Uí Chonaire." *Irisleabhar Mhá Nuad* (1968): 59–70.

———. "Ní Cúng le Duine an Saol: Sracfhéachaint ar 'Neill' Uí Chonaire." *Irisleabhar Mhá Nuad* (1970): 85–93.

514   Selected Bibliography

Ó Cuív, Shan. "Materials for a Bibliography of the Very Reverend Peter Canon O'Leary, 1839–1920." Supplement to *Celtica* 2, no. 2 (1954).

Ó Direáin, Máirtín. "An File Gaeilge is Saol na Cathrach." In his *Feamainn Bealtaine*. Baile Átha Cliath: An Clóchomhar, 1971, 86–88.

Ó Droighneáin, Muiris. *Taighde i gComhair Stair Litridheachta na Nua-Ghaedhilge ó 1882 Anuas*. Baile Átha Cliath: Oifig Díolta Foillseacháin Rialtais, 1936.

Ó Dúshláine, Tadhg. "Scéal Úirscéil: *Fánaí*, Seán Óg Ó Caomhánaigh, 1927." In *Litríocht na Gaeltachta, Léachtaí Cholm Cille* 19 (1989): 93–128.

Ó Fiannachta, Pádraig. "Ag Cogarnaíl le Cara: An tAthair Peadar mar a Nochtann Litreacha Áirithe dá Chuid Dúinn É." *Irisleabhar Mhá Nuad* (1991): 105–20.

———. "Litríocht an Lae (1800–1850)." In his *Léas ar Ár Litríocht*. Má Nuad: An Sagart, 1974, 102–16.

———. "Scéalta an tSeabhaic." In *Ár Scéalaíocht, Léachtaí Cholm Cille* 14 (1983): 106–20.

O'Flynn, Criostóir. *A Man Called Pearse: A Play in Three Acts*. Dublin: Foilseacháin Náisiúnta Teoranta, 1980.

Ó Gadhra, Nollaig. *An Chéad Dáil Éireann (1919–1921) agus an Ghaeilge*. Baile Átha Cliath: Coiscéim, 1989.

Ó Glaisne, Risteárd. *Ceannródaithe: Scríbhneoirí na Nua-Ré*. Baile Átha Cliath: Foilseacháin Náisiúnta Teoranta, 1974.

Ó hÁinle, Cathal. *Promhadh Pinn*. Má Nuad: An Sagart, 1978.

Ó hAnluain, Eoghan. "Baile Átha Cliath i Nua-Litríocht na Gaeilge." *Scríobh* 4 (1979): 25–46.

Ó hAodha, Séamus. *Pádraic Mac Piarais, Sgéaluidhe / Patrick H. Pearse, Storyteller*. Dublin: Talbot, n.d.

O'Leary, Philip. "Castles of Gold: America and Americans in the Fiction of Séamus Ó Grianna." *Éire / Ireland* 21, no. 2 (Summer 1986): 70–84.

———. "'Children of the Same Mother': Gaelic Relations with the Other Celtic Revival Movements, 1882–1916." *Proceedings of the Harvard Celtic Colloquium* 6 (1986): 101–30.

Ó Liatháin, Donnchadh. *Tomás Ó Flannghaile: Scoláire agus File*. Baile Átha Cliath: Oifig an tSoláthair, n.d.

Ó Maoldomhnaigh, Bernard. "Anam ar Strae: Staidéar ar *Deoraíocht*." *Irisleabhar Mhá Nuad* (1971): 97–107.

Ó Maolmhuaidh, Proinsias. *Uilleog de Búrca: Athair na hAthbheochana*. Baile Átha Cliath: Foilseacháin Náisiúnta Teoranta, 1981.

"Ó'n bhFear Eagair." *Béaloideas* 1, no. 1 (June 1927): 3–4.

Ó Nualláin, Brian ("Myles na gCopaleen"). *An Béal Bocht*. Baile Átha Cliath: An Press Náisiúnta, 1941.

Ó Ríordáin, Seán. "Teangacha Príobháideacha." *Scríobh* 4 (1979): 13–22.

Ó Searcaigh, Séamus. *Pádraig Mac Piarais*. Baile Átha Cliath: Oifig an tSoláthair, n.d.

Ó Siadhail, Pádraig. "Gaiscigh, Gaigí agus Guamóga: Téama an Laochais i Scríbhinní Cruthaitheachta Phiarais Bhéaslaí," *Irisleabhar Mhá Nuad* (1990): 137–54.

———. "Ó Emerald go hÉirinn (Spléachadh ar Bheatha is ar Shaothar Katherine Hughes, 1876–1925)." *Irisleabhar Mhá Nuad* (1991): 13–39.

Ó Siochfhradha, Pádraig. "Notes on Some of Jeremiah Curtin's Storytellers." In *Folk-Tales Collected by Jeremiah Curtin (1835–1906)*, edited by Séamus

Ó Duilearga. Supplement to *Béaloideas* 12, nos. 1–2 (June–December 1942): 153–66.

Ó Súilleabháin, Diarmaid. *"An Uain Bheo:* Focal ón Údar." *Irisleabhar Mhá Nuad* (1972): 65–69.

Ó Súilleabháin, Donncha. *Cath na Gaeilge sa Chóras Oideachais, 1893–1911.* Baile Átha Cliath: Conradh na Gaelige, 1988.

———. *Conradh na Gaeilge i Londain, 1894–1917.* Baile Átha Cliath: Conradh na Gaeilge, 1989.

———. *An Piarsach agus Conradh na Gaeilge.* Baile Átha Cliath: Clódhanna, Teo., 1981.

———. *Scéal an Oireachtais, 1897–1924.* Baile Átha Cliath: An Clóchomhar, 1984.

———. *Na Timirí i Ré Tosaigh an Chonartha, 1893–1927.* Baile Átha Cliath: Conradh na Gaeilge, 1990.

———. "Tús agus Fás Dramaíochta i nGaeilge." *Ardán* (1971–73).

Ó Súilleabháin, Seán. "Pádraig Ó Laoghaire." *Béaloideas* 3, no. 5 (December 1932): 409–12.

Ó Tuama, Seán. *"Cré na Cille* agus *Séadna." Comhar* 14, no. 2 (February 1955): 7–8, 29.

———, ed. *The Gaelic League Idea.* Cork: Mercier, 1972.

———. "Úrscéalta agus Faisnéisí Beatha na Gaeilge: Na Buaicphointí." *Scríobh* 5 (1981): 148–60.

Ó Tuathaigh, M. A. G. "An Chléir Chaitliceach, an Léann Dúchais agus an Cultúr i nÉirinn, c. 1750–1850." In *Léann na Cléire, Léachtaí Cholm Cille* 16 (1986): 110–39.

Pender, Seamus, ed. *Féilscríbhinn Tórna.* Corcaigh: Cló Ollscoile Chorcaí, 1947.

Porter, Raymond. "Language and Literature in Revival Ireland: The Views of P. H. Pearse." In *Modern Irish Literature: Essays in Honor of William York Tindall,* edited by Raymond Porter and James Brophy. New York: Iona College Press, 1973, 46–57.

———. *P. H. Pearse.* New York: Twayne, 1973.

Ryan, Desmond, *The Sword of Light, from the Four Masters to Douglas Hyde, 1636–1938.* London: Arthur Barker, 1939.

Said, Edward. *Nationalism, Colonialism and Literature: Yeats and Decolonization* (Field Day Pamphlet 15). Derry: Field Day Theatre Company, 1988.

"The School of Irish Learning." *Scéala Scoil an Léinn Cheiltigh / Newsletter of the School of Celtic Studies,* no. 3 (November 1989): 30–36.

Shaw, Francis A., S.J. "The Canon of Irish History—A Challenge." *Studies* 61 (Summer 1972): 113–53.

Thompson, William Irwin. *The Imagination of an Insurrection, Dublin, Easter 1916: A Study of an Ideological Movement.* New York: Harper and Row, 1972.

Tierney, Michael. *Eoin Mac Néill, Scholar and Man of Action, 1867–1945.* Oxford: Clarendon Press, 1980.

Titley, Alan. "Litríocht na Gaeilge, Litríocht an Bhéarla, agus Irish Literature." *Scríobh* 5 (1981): 116–39.

———. "Mála an Éithigh." In *An tÚrscéal sa Ghaeilge, Léachtaí Cholm Cille* 21 (1991): 184–206.

———. *An tÚrscéal Gaeilge.* Baile Átha Cliath: An Clóchomhar, 1991.

Ua Ceallaigh, Seán. *Cathal Brugha*. Baile Átha Cliath: M. H. Mac an Ghoill agus a Mhac, 1942.

Ua Maoileoin, Pádraig. "Scríbhneoirí Chorca Dhuibhne." In his *Ár Leithéidí Arís: Cnuasach de Shaothar Ilchineálach*. Baile Átha Cliath: Clódhanna, Teo., 1978, 46–60.

Uí Fhlannagáin, Fionnuala. *Mícheál Ó Lócháin agus An Gaodhal*. Baile Átha Cliath: An Clóchomhar, 1990.

Williams, J. E. Caerwyn, and Máirín Ní Mhuiríosa. *Traidisiún Liteartha na nGael*. Baile Átha Cliath: An Clóchomhar, 1979.

Index

Printed in the United States
204408BV00001B/275/A

973103

Printed in Great Britain by
Amazon.co.uk, Ltd.,
Marston Gate.